Enforcement Mechanisms of the Racial Equality Directive and Minority Protection

“So whatever you wish that others would do to you, do also to them [...].”

Matthew 7:12

ENFORCEMENT MECHANISMS OF THE RACIAL EQUALITY DIRECTIVE AND MINORITY PROTECTION

by

Mónika Ambrus

eleven
international publishing

Published, sold and distributed by Eleven International Publishing
P.O. Box 85576
2508 CG The Hague, The Netherlands
Tel.: +31 70 3307033
Fax: +31 70 3307030
info@elevenpub.com
www.elevenpub.com

Sold and distributed in USA and Canada
International Specialized Book Services
920 NE 58th Avenue, Suite 300
Portland, OR 97213-3786, USA
Tel.: +1 800 944 6190 (toll-free)
Fax: +1 503 280 8832
orders@isbs.com
www.isbs.com

Printed on acid-free paper.

ISBN: 978-90-77596-94-4

Printed in The Netherlands

Preface

This book is a revised and updated version of my doctoral thesis which I defended on March 18, 2010 at the Erasmus University Rotterdam. In addition to providing a solid theoretical basis concerning the enforcement mechanisms of the Racial Equality Directive, this book also aims at serving as a handbook for each practioner and supporting their everyday work in the interpretation and application of the national equal treatment legislation.

Similarly to interpreting and applying law, writing a book is also a very complex activity. If we were asked to describe the picture we have in mind about writing a book, I believe that many of us would imagine the following. The process of writing a book is similar to climbing an arduous mountain: a tiring and heavy activity, which is impossible to accomplish alone. Achieving the top of the mountain is a special moment: at this point one forgets about all the heaviness and difficulties experienced during the journey, and looks around with a rapturous feeling in his/her heart. The view from here is very inspiring, in particular looking back to the path one has taken and seeing the people standing at different points who have helped me achieve the mountaintop. I am glad that I can owe gratitude to many for their assistance and support.

First of all, I cannot be grateful enough for the constant support of my supervisor, Professor Dr. Kristin Henrard. Thank you very much for your subtle guidance, critical remarks, straight-forwardness, openness towards new ideas, trust, encouragement and our inspiring discussions. I especially value our friendship that has evolved and deepened over the years.

I would also like to thank my promoter, Professor Dr. Roel de Lange for giving me freedom in conducting my research and for his critical and constructive comments on my chapters. I equally appreciate the support of my previous promoter, Professor Dr. Douwe Jan Elzinga in my first years. I am also indebted to my ex-promoter, Professor Dr. Gábor Kardos for his guidance during my research in Hungary. I am also thankful to the colleagues both in Rotterdam and Groningen.

I also owe gratitude to all the national experts (scholars, judges, advocates, NGOs), who were ready to find some time for us and share their view during our country visits. These discussions helped us have a better understanding of the situation in the particular countries.

I would like to express my greatest thanks to my colleague in this project, but primarily friend, Marjolein Busstra, for her inspiring and enduring friendship. Working on this book would have been much more difficult without your support and love throughout the years. I also felt the support of my other friends over the years.

Finally, I would like to thank my mother and father for their endless and unconditional love and support. Also, without the unwavering love and encouragement of my fiancé, Benedek, this work could not have been materialised.

Rotterdam, 21 April 2010

Table of Contents

List of Acronyms and Abbreviations

ABET	Advisory Body on Equal Treatment, Hungary
ADA	Anti-Discrimination Act, Belgium
AET	Authority on Equal Treatment, Hungary
ARA	Anti-Racism Act, Belgium
CEOOR	Centre for Equal Opportunities and Opposition to Racism, Belgium
ECA	Employment Contract Act, Estonia
ECHR	European Convention on Human Rights
ECJ	European Court of Justice
ECtHR	European Court of Human Rights
EETA	Equal Treatment Act, Estonia
ETC	Equal Treatment Commission, The Netherlands
FD	Framework Directive
GEA	Gender Equality Act, Estonia
GEC	Gender Equality Commissioner, Estonia
GETA	General Equal Treatment Act, The Netherlands
HETA	Equal Treatment Act, Hungary
LC	Legal Chancellor, Estonia
LCA	Legal Chancellor Act, Estonia
RED	Racial Equality Directive

Table of Cases

European and Global Jurisprudence

European Court of Justice and Court of First Instance

Judgment of 15 October 1969 in Case 15/62, *Württembergische Milchverwertung-Südmilch v. Salvatore Ugliola*, [1969] ECR 363.

Judgment of 27 October 1971 in Case 6/71, *Rheinmühlen Düsseldorf v. Einfuhr- und Vorratsstelle für Getreide und Futtermittel*, [1974] ECR 33.

Judgment of 7 June 1972 in Case 20/71, *Luisa Sabbatini, née Bertoni, v. European Parliament*, [1972] ECR 345.

Judgment of 12 February 1974 in Case 152/73, *Giovanni Maria Sotgiu v. Deutsche Bundespost*, [1974] ECR 153.

Judgment of 8 April 1976 in Case 43/75, *Defrenne v. Societe Anonyme Belge de navigation aerienne Sabena*, [1976] ECR 455.

Judgment of 16 December 1976 in Case 33/76, *Rewe-Zentralfinanz eG et Rewe Zentral AG v. Landwirtschaftskammer für das Saarland*, [1976] ECR 1898.

Judgment of 19 December 1976 in Case 45/76, *Comet v. Produktschap voor Siergewassen*, [1976] ECR 2043.

Judgment of 31 March 1981 in Case 96/80, J.P. *Jenkins v. Kingsgate (Clothing Productions) Ltd.*, [1981] ECR 911.

Judgment of 9 November 1983 in Case 199/82, *State Finance Administration v. SPA San Giorgio*, [1983] ECR 3595.

Judgment of 10 April 1984 in Case 14/83, *Von Colson and Kamann v. Land Nordrhein-Westfalen*, [1984] ECR 1891.

Judgment of 13 May 1986 in Case 170/84, *Bilka-Kaufhaus GmbH v. Karin Weber von Hartz*, [1986] ECR 1607.

Judgment of 15 May 1986 in Case 222/84, *Johnston v. Chief Constable of the Royal Ulster Constabulary*, [1987] ECR 1651.

Judgment of 10 October 1987 in Case C-222/86, *Unectef v. Georges Heylens and others*, [1987] ECR 4097.

Judgment of 25 October 1988 in Case 312/86, *Commission of the European Communities v. French Republic*, [1988] ECR 6315.

Judgment of 21 September 1989 in Case 68/88, *Commission of the European Communities v. Hellenic Republic*, [1989] ECR I-2965.

Judgment of 17 October 1989 in Case C-109/88, *Handels- og Kontorfunktionærernes Forbund I Danmark v. Dansk Arbejdsgiverforening, acting on behalf of Danfoss*, [1989] ECR 3199.
Judgment of 13 December 1989 in Case C-102/88, *Ruzius-Wilbrink v. Bestuur van de bedrijfsvereniging voor Overheidsdiensten*, [1989] ECR 4311.
Judgment of 27 June 1990 in Case C-33/89, *Kowalska v. Freie und Hansestadt Hamburg*, [1990] ECR 1-2591.
Judgment of 8 November 1990 in Case C-177/88, *Dekker v. Stichting Vormingscentrum voor Jong Volwassenen*, [1990] ECR 1-3941.
Judgment of 31 March 1991 in Case C-377/89, *Norah Cotter and Ann McDermott v. Minister for Social Welfare and Attorney General*, [1987] ECR 1453.
Judgment of 11 July 1991 in Case C-31/90, *Johnson v. Chief Adjudication Officer*, [1991] ECR 1-3723.
Judgment of 25 July 1991 in Case C-208/90, *Theresa Emmott v. Minister for Social Welfare and the Attorney General*, [1991] ECR 1-4269.
Judgment of 2 August 1993 in Case C-271/91, *Marshall v. Southampton and South-West Hampshire Area Health Authority*, [1986] ECR 723.
Judgment of 27 October 1993 in Case C-127/92, *Dr. Pamela Mary Enderby v. Frenchay Health Authority and Secretary of State for Health*, [1993] ECR I-5535.
Judgment of 27 October 1993 in Case C-338/91, *Steenhorst-Neerings v. Bestuur van de Bedrijfsvereniging voor Detailhandel Ambachten en Huisvrouwen*, [1993] ECR I-5475.
Judgment of 9 November 1993 in Case C-132/92, *Birds Eye Walls Ltd. v. Friedel M. Roberts*, [1993] ECR I-5579.
Judgment of 1 June 1994 in Case C-136/92, P, *Commission v. Augusto Brazzelli Lualdi and others*, [1994] ECR I-1981.
Judgment of 15 December 1994 in Joined Cases C-399/92, C-409/92, C-425/92, C-34/93, C-50/93 and C-78/93, *Stadt Lengerich v. Angelika Helmig and Waltraud Schmidt v. Deutsche Angestellten-Krankenkase and others*, [1994] ECR I-05727.
Judgment of 17 October 1995 in Case C-450/93, *Eckhard Kalanke v. Freie und Hansestadt Bremen*, [1995] ECR 1-3051.
Judgment of 14 December 1995 in Case C-312/93, *Peterbroeck, Van Campenhout and Cie SCS v. Belgium*, [1995] ECR 1-4599.
Judgment of 23 May 1996 in Case C-237/94, *John O'Flynn v. Adjudication Officer*, [1996] ECR I-2617.
Judgment of 22 April 1997 in Case C-180/95, *Nils Draehmpaehl v. Urunia Immobilienservice OHG*, [1997] ECR 1-2195.
Judgment of 17 September 1997 in Case C-54/96, *Dorsch Consult Ingenieurgesellschaft mbH v. Bundesbaugesellschaft Berlin mbH*, [1997] ECR I-4961.
Judgment of 11 December 1997 in Case C-246/96, *Magorrian and Cunningham v. Eastern Health and Social Services Board and Department of Health and Social Services*, [1997] ECR I-7153.
Judgment of 17 June 1998 in Case C-243/95, *Kathleen Hill and Ann Stapleton v. The Revenue Commissioners and the Department of Finance*, [1998] ECR 1-3739.

Judgment of 22 September 1998 in Case C-185/97, *Coote v. Granada Hospitality Ltd*, [1998] ECR I-5199.
Judgment of 1 December 1998 in Case C-326/96, *Levez v. T.H. Jennings (Harlow Pools) Ltd.*, [1998] ECR 1-7835.
Judgment of 21 January 1999 in Case C-63/01, *Samuel Sidney Evans v. Secretary of State for the Environment and Transport and the Regions and the Motor Insurer's Bureau*, [2003] ECR I-4447.
Judgment of 9 February 1999 in Case C-167/97, *Regina v. Secretary of State for Employment, ex parte Nicole Seymour-Smith and Laura Perez*, [1999] ECR I-623.
Judgment of 22 June 1999 in Case C-412/97, *ED Srl v. Italo Fenocchio*, [1999] ECR 1-3845.
Judgment of 6 April 2000 in Case C-226, *Birgitte Jørgensen v. Foreningen af Speciallæger and Sygesikringens Forhandlingsudvalg g*, [2000] ECR I-02447.
Judgment of 16 May 2000 in Case C-78/98, *Shirley Preston and Others v. Wolverhampton Healthcare NHS Trust and Others and Dorothy Fletcher and Others v. Midland Bank plc.*, [2000] ECR I-03201.
Judgment of 6 July 2000 in Case C-407/98, *Katarina Abrahamsson and Leif Anderson v. Elisabet Fogelqvist*, [2000] ECR I-05539.
Judgment of 30 November 2000 in Case C-195/98, *Österreichischer Gewerkschaftsbund, Gewerkschaft öffentlicher Dienst v. Republik Österreich*, [2000] ECR I-10497.
Judgment of 26 June 2001 in Case C-381/99, *Susanna Brunnhofer v. Bank der Österreichischen Postsparkasse AG*, [2001] ECR I-04961.
Judgment of 18 October 2001 in Case T-333/99, *X v. European Central Bank*, 2001 ECR II-03021.
Judgment of 3 May 2002 in Case T-177/01, *Jégo-Quéré et Cie SA v. Commission*, [2002] ECR II-2365.
Judgment of 9 September 2003 in Case C-25/02, *Katharina Rinke v. Ärztekammer Hamburg*, [2003] ECR I-08349.
Judgment of 16 March 2004 in Case T-11/03, *Elizabeth Afari v. European Central Bank*, [2004] ECR II-00267.
Judgment of 18 March 2004 in Case T-204/01, *Lindorfer v. Council of the European Union*, [2007] ECR I-6467.
Judgment of 8 June 2004 in Case C-220/02, *Österreichischer Gewerkschaftsbund, Gewerkschaft der Privatangetstellten v. Wirtschaftskammer Österreich*, [2004] ECR I-05907.
Judgment of 30 September 2004 in Case C-319/03, *Briheche v. Ministre de l'Intérieur/ Ministre de l'Éducation and Ministre de la Justice*, [2004] ECR I-8807.
Judgment of 12 October 2004 in Case C-313/02, *Nicole Wippel v. Peek & Cloppenburg GmbH & Co. KG.*, [2004] ECR I-09483.
Judgment of 3 October 2006 in Case C-17/05, *B.F. Cadman v. Health & Safety Executive*, [2006] ECR I-09583.
Judgment of 21 June 2007 in Joined Cases C-231/06, C-232/06, C-233/06, *Office national des pensions v. Emilienne Jonkman and Hélène Vercheval and Noëlle Permesaen v. Office national des pensions*, [2007] ECR I-05149.

Judgment of 11 October 2007 in Case C-460/06, *Nadine Paquay v. Société d'architectes Hoet + Minne SPRL.*, [2007] ECR I-08511.
Judgment of 10 July 2008 in Case C-54/07, *Centrum voor gelijkheid van kansen en racismebestrijding v. Firma Feryn N.V.*, [2008] ECR I-05187.
Judgment of 17 July 2008 in Case C-303/06, *S. Coleman v. Attridge Law and Steve Law*, [2008] ECR I-05603.

European Commission and Court of Human Rights
Airey v. Ireland, ECHR (1979) Series A, No. 32, No. 6289/73, 9 October 1979.
Ashingdane v. the United Kingdom, ECHR (1985) Series A, No. 93, No. 8225/78, 28 May 1985.
D.H. and Others v. the Czech Republic, ECHR (2006) No. 57325/00, 7 February 2006.
D.H. and Others v. the Czech Republic, ECHR (2007) No. 57325/00, 13 November 2007.
Golder v. the United Kingdom, ECHR (1975) Series A, No. 18, No. 4451/70, 21 February 1975
Hoogendijk v. the Netherlands, ECHR (2005) No. 58641/00, 6 January 2005
Nachova and Others v. Bulgaria, ECHR (2005) Nos. 43577/98 and 43579/98, 6 July 2005.
Procola v. Luxembourg, ECHR (1995) No. 27/1994/474/555, 31 August 1995.
Sampanis and Others v. Greece, ECHR (2008) No. 32526/05, 5 June 2008.
Stubbings and Others v. United Kingdom, ECHR (1996) Nos. 22083/93 and 22095/93, 22 October 1996.
Timishev v. Russia, ECHR (2001) Nos. 55762/00 and 55974/00, 13 December 2005.
Zarb Adami v. Malta, ECHR (2006) No. 17209/02, 20 June 2006.

Other Jurisdictions
Advisory Opinion regarding Minority Schools in Albania (*Greece v. Albania*), 6 April 1935, 1935 PCIJ (Ser. A/B) No. 64.
Allen v. Wright, 468 U.S. 737 (SC 1984)
Aziz v. Trinity Street Taxis Ltd & Others, IRLR 204 (CA 1988)
Bracebridge Engineering Ltd. v. Darby, IRLR 3 (EAT 1989)
British Telecommunications Plc v. Williams, IRLR 668 (EAT 1997)
Brotherhood of Teamsters v. United States, 431 U.S. 324 (SC 1977)
Canniffe v. East Riding of Yorkshire Council, IRLR 555 (EAT 2000)
Chief Constable of West Yorkshire Police v. Khan, IRLR 830 (HL 2001)
Commissioners of Inland Revenue and others v. Morgan, IRLR 776 (EAT 2002)
Davis v. Mansard, 597 F.Supp 334 (N.D. Ind. 1984)
Dresdner Kleinwort Wasserstein Ltd v. Adebayo, IRLR 514 (EAT 2005)
Driskell v. Peninsula Business Services & Others, IRLR 151 (EAT 2000)
European Roma Rights Center v. Greece, ECSR (2005) No. 15/2003, 7 February 2005
Evers v. Dwyer, 358 U.S. 202 (SC 1958)
Case Concerning the Factory at Chorzów (*Germany v. Poland*), 26 July 1927, 1928 PCIJ (Ser. A.) No. 17.
Ferida Selimović and others v. the Republika Srpska, 7 March 2003, The Human Rights Chamber for Bosnia and Herzegovina, No. CH/01/8365.

Floyd-Mayers v. American Cab Co, 732 F.Supp. 243 (D.D.C. 1990)
Frothingham v. Mellon, 262 U.S. 447 (SC 1923)
Igen Ltd and Others v. Wong and Others, IRLR 258 (CA 2005)
In re Winship, 397 U.S. 358 (SC 1970)
Kirby v. Manpower Services Commission, ICR 420 (EAT 1980)
Lubicon Lake Band v. Canada, UNHRC (1990) No. 167/1984, 26 March 1990
Lujan v. Defenders of Wildlife, 504 U.S. 555 (SC 1992)
MacDonald v. Advocate General for Scotland, Pearce v. Governing Body of Mayfield Secondary School, IRLR 512 (HL 2003)
Mandla v. Lee, IRLR 209 (HL 1983)
Mayagna (Sumo) Awas Tingni Community v. Nicaragua, 31 August 2001, 2001 Inter-Am. Ct. H.R. (Ser. C) No. 79.
McDonnell Douglas Corp. v. Green, 411 U.S. 792 (SC 1973)
Moonsar v. Fiveways Express Transport Ltd, IRLR 9 (EAT 2005)
Morse v. Future Reality Ltd, unreported, ET 54571/95 (ET 1996)
Mukong v. Cameroon, UNHRC (1994) No. 458/1991, Decision 21 July 1994
Oyarce v. Cheshire County Council, ICR 1693 (EAT 2007)
Panesar v. Nestlé Co Ltd, IRLR 60 (EAT 1980)
Pierson v. Ray, 386 U.S. 574 (SC 1967)
R. (on the application of European Roma Rights Centre) v. Immigration Officer at Prague Airport, IRLR 115 (HL 2005)
R. v. Birmingham City Council ex parte Equal Opportunities Commission, IRLR 96 (HC 1988)
Reed & Bull Information Systems v. Stedman, IRLR 299 (EAT 1999)
Ribitsch v. Austria, 4 December 1995, UNHRC, No. 18896/91.
Rogers v. EEOC, 406 U.S. 957 (SC 1972)
Serco Ltd t/a Education Bradford & Ors v. Mr R Quarshie, EAT/0466/05/SM (EAT 2006)
Shammoon v. Chief Constable of the RUC, IRLR 285 (HL 2003)
Showboat Entertainment Centre Ltd v. Owens, IRLR 7 (EAT 1984)
Sidhu v. Aerospace Composite Technology Ltd, IRLR 602 (CA 2000)
Singh v. British Rail Engineering, ICR 22 (EAT 1986)
Smith v. Gardner Merchant Ltd, IRLR 510 (EAT 1998)
Stewart v. Cleveland Guest, IRLR 440 (EAT 1994)
St Helens MBC v. Derbyshire and others, IRLR 540 (HL 2007)
Weathersfield Ltd v. Sargent, IRLR 94 (CA 1999)
West Midlands Passenger Transport Executive v. Singh, IRLR 186 (CA 1988)

National Jurisprudence: Countries under Review

Belgium
Brussels Correctional Court, 6 March 2003
Liège Court of Appeal, 11 March 1988
Gent Court of Cassation, 30 November 2005
Mechelen Labour Court, summary-like proceedings, 16 March 2006

Ghent District Court, no. 03/4440/A, 31 December 2003
Antwerp Court of Appeal, 8 January 2004
Brussels Correctional Court, 31 March 2004
Brussels Correctional Court, 20 October 2004
Arbitration Court, 157-2004, 6 October 2004
Antwerp Correctional Court, 7 December 2004
Brussels Commercial Court, 8 July 2005
Vindevoghel v. Flightcare Belgium, Brussels Labour Court, 6 February 2006
CGKR v. Feryn, Brussels Court of Labour, 24 January 2007
T.S.T v. F.W.A.G, Tongeren Labour Court, 6 March 2007
CGKR and C. Murat v. D. Yves and E-L/ BVBA, Ghent Labour Court, 26 March 2007
L.H. v. S.A. de droit public La Poste, Brussels Labour Court, 25 April 2007
Constitutional Court, 17-2009, 12 February 2009

Estonia
Constitutional Judgment 3-4-1-2-02, 3 April 2002
Constitutional Judgment 3-4-1-1-02, 6 March 2002
Constitutional Judgment 3-4-1-7-03, 21 January 2004
Constitutional Judgment 3-4-1-33-05, 20 March 2006

Hungary
EBH/337/24/2005
EBH/17/40/2006
EBH/22/2006
EBH/58/2006
EBH/69/2006
EBH/181/2006
EBH/141/2006
EBH/450/2006
EBH/553/2006
EBH/611/2006
EBH/142/3/2007
EBH/14/7/2007
EBH/641/11/2007
EBH/56/13/2007
EBH/866/19/2007
EBH/44/14/2007
EBH/1/26/2007
EBH/346/31/2007
EBH/310/33/2007
EBH/86/2007
EBH/271/2007
EBH/418/2007
EBH/516/2007
EBH/671/2007
EBH/700/2007

EBH/704/2007
EBH/588/5/2008
EBH/72/7/2008
EBH/1/37/2008
EBH/54/2008
EBH/81/2008
EBH/94/2008
EBH/108/2008
EBH/170/2008
EBH/231/2008
EBH/240/2008
EBH/476/2008
EBH/511/2008
BH 2004. 255
Constitutional Court, 1/1994, 7 January 1994
Constitutional Court, 35/1994, 24 June 1994
Constitutional Court 14/1995, 13 March 1995
Constitutional Court, 45/2000, 8 December 2000
Metropolitan Labour Court, 10.M.4297/2000/12, 9 October 2001 (F. Katalin)
Metropolitan Court, 49. Mf. 630.368/2001/2, 15 February 2002 (F. Katalin)
Supreme Court, Pvf. IV. 20 822/2001/4 (BH2003. 150), 3 April 2002
Salgótarján Labour Court, 3.M. 170/2003/16, 9 February 2004 (P. Mariann first instance)
Supreme Court, Mfv.I.10.720/2003/3, 11 February 2004 (F. Katalin)
Nógrád County Court, Mf.20.293/2004/4, 8 June 2004 (P. Mariann second instance)
Metropolitan Court, 19.P.21.788/2004/10, 8 October 2004 (Karoli case)
Pest County Labour Court, I.M. 471/2004/3, 13 October 2004 (Cs. Gyula first instance)
Pest County Court, 8.Mf.28.024/2004/3, 11 May 2005 (Cs. Gyula second instance)
Supreme Court PFv. IV.20.687/2005/5, 8 June 2005 (Karoli case)
Szabolcs-Szatmár-Bereg County Court, 1.P. 21.752/2004/26, 13 June 2005 (R. Ágnes first instance)
Debrecen Court of Appeal, PF.II. 20.513/2005/4, 28 October 2005 (R. Ágnes second instance)
Borsod-Abaúj-Zemplén County Court, 13.P.21.660/2005/16, 2 November 2005 (Miskolc first instance)
Miskolc City Court, 6.M.16/2005/17, 28 November 2005 (MÁV-outsourcing first instance)
Metropolitan Labour Court, 29.M.5804/2005/18, 2 May 2006 (R. Norbert)
Metropolitan Court, 20.K.33.285/2005/10, 15 May 2006 (Kenderes local government)
Debrecen Court of Appeal, Pf.I.20.683/2005/7, 9 June 2006 (Miskolc second instance)
Metropolitan Court, 19.P.630.545/2005/8, 7 September 2006.
Miskolc Labour Court, 6.M.1364/2006/4, 14 November 2006 (MÁV-outsourcing first instance)
Metropolitan Court, 55.Mf.635.873/2006/3, 13 April 2007 (R. Norbert)
Metropolitan Court, 8.K.31.635/2006, 26 April 2007 (T. Csaba)

Hajdú-Bihar County Court, 6.P. 20.341/2006/50, 2 May 2007 (Hajdúhadház first instance)
Borsod-Abaúj-Zemplén County Court, 1.Mf.20392/2007/3, 12 June 2007 (MÁV-outsourcing second instance)
Supreme Court, Kfv.IV.37.450/2006/5, 11 July 2007 (Kenderes local government)
Pécs Labour Court, 3.M.615/2006/16, 13 September 2007 (B. István)
Debrecen Court of Appeal, Pf.I.20.361/2007/8, 13 December 2007 (Hajdúhadház second instance)
Baranya County Court, 1.Mf.21.418/2007/3, 20 December 2007
Metropolitan Court, 8.K.33.150/2007/14, 26 May 2008
Supreme Court, Pfv.IV.20.936/2008/4, 19 November 2008 (Hajdúhadház third instance)

The Netherlands
1997-45 ETC
1997-62 ETC
1997-65 ETC
1997-133 ETC
1998-39 ETC
2000-57 ETC
2002-161 ETC
2003-03 ETC
2003-05 ETC
2003-18 ETC
2003-48 ETC
2003-76 ETC
2003-91 ETC
2003-92 ETC
2003-119 ETC
2003-134 ETC
2003-138 ETC
2003-151 ETC
2003-153 ETC
2004-12 ETC
2004-13 ETC
2004-49 ETC
2004-143 ETC
2004-160 ETC
2005-68 ETC
2005-112 ETC
2005-119 ETC
2005-167 ETC
2005-195 ETC
2006-5 ETC
2006-20 ETC
2006-34 ETC

2006-55 ETC
2006-71 ETC
2006-124 ETC
2006-148 ETC
2006-166 ETC
2006-177 ETC
2006-180 ETC
2006-202 ETC
2006-219 ETC
2006-222 ETC
2006-256 ETC
2007-11 ETC
2007-30 ETC
2007-49 ETC
2007-57 ETC
2007-68 ETC
2007-91 ETC
2007-132 ETC
2007-154 ETC
2007-156 ETC
2007-157 ETC
2007-179 ETC
2007-183 ETC
2007-193 ETC
2008-12 ETC
2008-31 ETC
2008-122 ETC
Leeuwarden Appelate Court, LJN AA1048, 4 August 1999
Central Appeal Council, LJN AO3751, 16 February 2004
Utrecht District Court, LJN AP0146, 27 May 2004
Utrecht District Court, LJN AU6168, 15 November 2005
The Hague District Court, LJN AY5005, 26 July 2006
Amsterdam District Court, LJN AZ8045, 31 Januari 2007
Amsterdam District Court, LJN BA6917, 24 May 2007
Amsterdam Appelate Court, LJN BD8720, 29 May 2008
Kaya/Binderen, High Council, NJ 1983, 687, 10 December 1982
Amsterdam Court of Appeal, summary proceedings, 13 January 2000
Cantonal Judge, LJN BH 5158, 5 November 2008

Chapter 1

Introduction

1.1. Setting the Scene: Enforcing the Protection against Racial Discrimination and Enhancing Minority Protection

The need for and the importance of an adequate system of minority protection seems generally acknowledged for ensuring and maintaining a peaceful society and guaranteeing that the special needs of the members of minorities in this society are taken care of.[1] In this respect it is rather remarkable that the European Union[2] does not have an explicit minority protection framework,

[1] "Violent inter-ethnic conflicts of the past decade, indeed the last century, have demonstrated the danger of extreme nationalism. National minorities have frequently suffered in these conflicts. The lessons of the past have underlined the necessity of respect for the rights of persons belonging to national minorities freely to express, preserve and develop their cultural, linguistic or religious identity free of any attempts at assimilation. While maintaining their identity, a minority should be integrated in harmony with others within a State as part of society at large. This is fundamental to international peace, security and prosperity." Sovereignty, responsibilility, and national minorities: statement by Rolf Ekéus, OSCE High Commissioner on National Minorities, The Hague, 26 October 2001.

A similar argumentation can also be found in the Advisory Opinion of the Permanent Court of International Justice regarding Minority Schools in Albana in which case the Court laid down that the aim of a minority protection is to "[s]ecure for certain elements incorporated in a State, the population of which differs from them in race, language or religion, the possibility of living peaceably alongside that population and co-operating amicably with it, while at the same time preserving the characteristics which distinguish them from the majority, and satisfying the ensuing special needs." *Advisory Opinion regarding Minority Schools in Albania (Greece vs. Albania),* 6 April 1935, 1935 PCIJ (Ser. A/B) No. 64, para. 17. See also inter alia Henrard (2000), at 9-10; Kardos (2007), at 8-35.

[2] Although there are important differences between the meanings of the terms 'European Union' and 'European Communities', these are not relevant from the perspective of this book. Accordingly, they will be used as synonyms throughout this book.

especially in the light of its steadily expanding competences.[3] It has been argued that the Union "has never developed a self-conscious minority protection policy or adopted a legal instrument expressly aimed at protecting minority rights."[4] Considering the absence of a clear framework for minority protection, Council Directive 2000/43 on the principle of equal treatment between persons irrespective of racial or ethnic origin (Racial Equality Directive, RED)[5] was very much welcomed as a significant contribution to the creation of an architecture for minority protection.[6]

On the basis of Article 13 TEC the EU Council of Ministers adopted the Racial Equality Directive on 29 June 2000. The purpose of this Directive is "to lay down a framework of combating discrimination on the grounds of racial or ethnic origin, with a view to putting into effect in the Member States the principle of equal treatment."[7] Even though the Directive does not talk about minorities as such, the protection against discrimination on the basis of racial or ethnic origin is apparently important for racial and ethnic groups, and thus also racial and ethnic minorities.[8]

Although there is no generally accepted definition of minorities, some common elements of this concept can still be identified. An agreement can be found on the requirements of numerical minority and non-dominant position, stable ethnic, religious or linguistic features which distinguish them from the majority, and the wish to preserve their separate identity.[9] A problematic aspect of this definition, and arguably, one of the main reasons why no uniform definition has yet been adopted, is related to the criterion of nationality. However, the above stipulated broad definition will be applied in this book, as a certain international trend can be identified away from the nationality requirement towards the acceptance of so-called 'new' minorities.[10] Accordingly, persons with a distinctive racial or ethnic origin whose protection from discrimination is the aim of the RED can often be regarded as falling under the concept of minorities.[11]

---

3 See inter alia Toggenburg (2002), at 241-244; De Witte (2000).

4 De Witte & Horváth (2008), at 365. See also Henrard (2002), at 357.

5 Council Directive 2000/43/EC of 29 June 2000 implementing the principle of equal treatment between persons irrespective of racial or ethnic origin.

6 See inter alia Toggenburg (2002), at 231-244; Henrard (2004), at 41.

7 Art. 1 RED.

8 See inter alia Henrard (2007a), at 22-23; Busstra (2010); Thornberry & Estebanez (2004), at 93 and 95.

9 Henrard (2007a), at 12. For a detailed analysis see Henrard (2000), at 30-48.

10 See inter alia Henrard (2000), at 41-42; Henrard (2003); Meijknecht (2001), at 83; Thornberry (1980), at 448.

11 Also the term 'national minorities' can be used synonymously with 'ethnic, religious and linguistic minorities' as they all seem to be included in the above definition. For a detailed elaboration on this aspect see Henrard (2000), at 53-55.

1.1.1. Two Pillars of Minority Protection

It is generally acknowledged and accepted that an adequate protection of minorities is built upon two pillars: the prohibition of discrimination in combination with individual human rights on the one hand, and minority-specific standards that aim at protecting and promoting the distinctive identities of minorities on the other.[12] Although with respect to the prohibition of discrimination or the right to equal treatment several concepts have been identified and studied, a stable and steady line of interpretation can still be explored on their core meaning. This is the continuum from formal to substantive equality the theoretical foundation of which can be traced back to Aristotle.[13] He explained that likes should be treated alike, and unlikes differently to the extent of their differences. The first part of this definition is identified as describing the concept of formal equality, while the second part is referred to as laying down the foundations of the concept of substantive equality.

As can be seen in this description, the concept of substantive equality can be used to buttress claims of minorities in relation to their special needs, interests and wishes. In this way a link can be established between substantive equality and the right to identity of minorities: the foundational principles – or essential goals – of minority protection. Although the right to identity is a rather vague concept, in terms of minority protection it can be interpreted as referring to the distinctive minority characteristics, such as language, culture and religion. A very important aspect of the minority phenomenon related to the right to identity is its intrinsic group dimension. Hence, the more the legal mechanisms for minority protection do justice to this group dimension, the more beneficial it is for minority protection purposes.

The mentioned goals (substantive equality and the right to identity) also determine the relative importance of the second pillar, as the more these goals can be achieved through the interpretation of the right to non-discrimination (and general human rights), the less minority-specific instruments are necessary.[14] However, as yet it does not seem that such a broad interpretation

---

[12] See Henrard (2000); Henrard (2002), at 370-372; Henrard (2004); Henrard (2006); Henrard (2007a).

[13] "So what is just requires at least four terms: the persons for whom it is just are two, and the shares in which its justice consists are two. There will be the same level of equality between persons as between shares, because the shares will be in the same ratio to one another as the persons. For if the persons are not equal, they will not receive equal shares; in fact quarrels and complaints arise either when equals receive unequal shares in an allocation, or unequals receive equal shares." Aristotle (2000), at 86. On this text in terms of equality law see inter alia Gerards (2005a), at 9-10; Tobler (2005a), at 19-22.

[14] As Henrard argued "certain interpretations of non-discrimination [...] could accommodate/ allow or even impose a duty to adopt special minority measures, and hence would go a long way in providing minority protection." Henrard (2007a), at 15.

is given to the right located in the first pillar. Accordingly, this also means that minority-specific instruments guaranteeing the preservation and promotion of their distinct identity cannot be dispensed with.[15]

1.1.2. Enforcement of the Right to Equal Treatment and Minority Protection

The focus of this book is on the first pillar of minority protection: the prohibition of discrimination. The central research angle therefore concerns the question to what extent the right to non-discrimination, as enshrined in the RED, enhances minority protection. Primarily, the concepts of discrimination and the possibilities for the adoption of positive action measures are analysed in terms of achieving substantive equality.[16] However, measures concerning the enforcement of the right to equality are also important in order to achieve substantive equality and/or appropriately consider the right to identity. Indeed, the way in which the right to equal treatment is enforced can have far-reaching consequences for minority protection in terms of the possible contributions of the first pillar.

Although enforcement provisions are often considered purely technical in nature and somewhat inferior to substantive rights, rights and remedies are in fact closely intertwined. Without remedies, rights are mere symbolic expressions, clearly captured in the principle 'ubi ius, ibi remedium'; namely where there is a right there must be a remedy.[17] The close connection between rights and remedies "lies in the fact that a right must necessarily give rise to a remedy which allows the right to be enforced through [...] judicial process."[18]

The term 'remedy' in this expression is, however, 'capable of slippage'[19] as it has been and can be vested with several meanings. The term in its strict sense is generally interpreted as the right to redress, while in its broad meaning it also includes the procedures leading to and resulting in redress and some related safeguards.[20] For the sake of terminological clarity, the term 'enforcement' is used when it concerns remedy in its broad sense, and the term

15 For *a contrario* argumentations see inter alia O'Brien (1984), at 21; Raïkka (1996); Rodley (1995), at 64.

16 See inter alia Nielsen (2009), at 46; Barnard & Hepple (2000); McInerney (2003); Henrard (2007a).

17 On the relationship between rights and remedies see inter alia Wolcher (2001), at 549-586; Van Gerven (2000), at 522-525.

18 Van Gerven (2000), at 525.

19 Harlow (2000), at 73.

20 In the words of Shelton "[t]he word 'remedies' contains two separate concepts, the first being procedural and the second substantive. In the first sense, remedies are the processes by which arguable claims of human rights violations are heard and decided, whether by courts, administrative agencies, or other competent bodies. The second notion of remedies refers to the outcome of the proceedings, the relief afforded the successful claimant." Shelton (2005), at 7.

'remedies' (or sanctions) is applied when the right to redress (remedies stricto sensu) is in question. Hence, 'enforcement' includes both procedural rules and their safeguards and redress (remedies stricto sensu).

In EU law the situation of enforcing substantive provisions is somewhat complicated as the EC Treaty does not lay down a general scheme for enforcement of EC law.[21] Nevertheless, the ECJ has recognised the fact that without enforcement rights remain pure symbolic expressions ('ubi ius, ibi remedium'), and has played a leading role in developing some requirements concerning the enforcement of the rights established by Community law. In this respect, the Court relied on the principle of effectiveness to make the rights effective in practice through effective enforcement.[22]

---

21 Craig & De Búrca (2003), at 230.

22 The principle of effectiveness is a dynamic one that has to be interpreted in the light of the circumstances, and is open to justification. This principle has undergone a series of developments in the sphere of enforcement. (See inter alia Tridimas (1999), at 276-312; Lewis (1996); Craig & De Búrca (2003), at 230-256; Jacobs (1997), at 25 and 29). It has been argued by several authors that a development from a minimalist approach pertaining to the procedural rules of the particular national system to a more intrusive regime can be explored. Having laid down the mere requirement of effectiveness in the *Rheinmühlen Düsseldorf v. Einfuhr- und Vorratsstelle für Getreide und Futtermittel* case, (Judgment of 27 October 1971 in *Case 6/71, Rheinmühlen Düsseldorf v. Einfuhr- und Vorratsstelle für Getreide und Futtermittel*, [1974] ECR 33) the Court elaborated the criterion of virtual impossibility without linking it to the requirement of effectiveness in the *Rewe-Zentralfinanz eG et Rewe Zentral AG v. Landwirtschaftskammer für das Saarland* (Judgment of 16 December 1976 in *Case 33/76, Rewe-Zentralfinanz eG et Rewe Zentral AG v. Landwirtschaftskammer für das Saarland*, [1976] ECR 1898), *Comet v. Produktschap voor Siergewassen* (Judgment of 19 December 1976 in *Case 45/76, Comet v. Produktschap voor Siergewassen*, [1976] ECR 2043), *Johnston v. Chief Constable of the Royal Ulster Constabulary* (Judgment of 15 May 1986 in *Case 222/84, Johnston v. Chief Constable of the Royal Ulster Constabulary*, [1987] ECR 1651), *Emmott v. Minister for Social Welfare en Attorney General* (Judgment of 25 July 1991 in *Case C-208/90, Theresa Emmott v. Minister for Social Welfare and the Attorney General*, [1991] ECR 1-4269), *Steenhorst-Neerings v. Bestuur van de Bedrijfsvereniging voor Detailhandel* (Judgment of 27 October 1993 in *Case C-338/91, Steenhorst-Neerings v. Bestuur van de Bedrijfsvereniging voor Detailhandel Ambachten en Huisvrouwen*, [1993] ECR I-5475) and *Johnson v. Chief Adjudication Officer* cases (Judgment of 11 July 1991 in *Case C-31/90, Johnson v. Chief Adjudication Officer*, [1991] ECR 1-3723). In the *Peterbroeck, Van Campenhout & Cie SCS v. Belgium* case (Judgment of 14 December 1995 in *Case C-312/93, Peterbroeck, Van Campenhout and Cie SCS v. Belgium*, [1995] ECR 1-4599) the Court complemented this criterion with a more far-reaching requirement: the procedural arrangement in the Member State cannot make the exercise of the particular EC right excessively difficult. It was only in the *Levez v. Jennings (Harlow Pools)* case (Judgment of 1 December 1998 in *Case C-326/96, Levez v. T.H. Jennings (Harlow Pools) Ltd.*, [1998] ECR 1-7835) that the criteria of virtual impossibility and excessive difficulty were linked to the principle of effectiveness.

A somewhat different line of development can be observed with respect to remedies, the other aspect of enforcement related matters. The requirement of effectiveness in this respect has not explicitly been linked to the above-mentioned two criteria, but was complemented with two additional requirements, namely proportionality and dissuasiveness.

The principle of effectiveness derives from the duty imposed on Member States "to take all appropriate measures […] to ensure fulfilment of the obligations arising out of this Treaty or resulting from action taken by the institutions of the Community."[23] Several elements of enforcement matters have been affected or even established by this principle, among which the right to access to justice,[24] the prohibition against victimisation,[25] the allocation of the burden of proof[26] and sanctions[27] – though most of them have remained relatively vague. Based on this principle the following basic requirement has been set up: the enforcement rules cannot make the exercise of the right in hand virtually impossible or excessively difficult.[28] This requirement also implies that the effectiveness of an enforcement measure can only be examined and established with regard to the right at stake as it is related to the exercise of this particular right.

From the perspective of enforcement, the Racial Equality Directive is a very interesting piece of legislation. Not only does it lay down substantive provisions concerning the right to equal treatment, but it also contains several provisions with respect to enforcement-related matters. The most important

[23] Art. 10 (ex-Art. 5) EC. The article lays down the following: "Member States shall take all appropriate measures, whether general or particular, to ensure fulfillment of the obligations arising out of this Treaty or resulting from action taken by the institutions of the Community. They shall facilitate the achievement of the Community's tasks. They shall abstain from any measure which could jeopardize the attainment of the objectives of this Treaty." See inter alia Schermers & Waelbroeck (2001), at 201-201; Craig & De Búrca (2003), at 252; Tridimas (1999), at 418.

[24] See inter alia *Case 222/84, Johnston v. Chief Constable of the Royal Ulster Constabulary*, para. 18.

[25] See Judgment of 22 September 1998 in *Case C-185/97, Coote v. Granada Hospitality Ltd*, [1998] ECR I-5199, para. 24.

[26] See inter alia Judgment of 27 October 1993 in *Case C-127/92, Dr. Pamela Mary Enderby v. Frenchay Health Authority and Secretary of State for Health*, [1993] ECR I-5535; Judgment of 17 October 1989 in *Case C-109/88, Handels- og Kontorfunktionærernes Forbund I Danmark v. Dansk Arbejdsgiverforening, acting on behalf of Danfoss*, [1989] ECR 3199; Judgment of 10 July 2008 in *Case C-54/07, Centrum voor gelijkheid van kansen en racismebestrijding v. Firma Feryn NV.*, [2008] ECR I-05187.

[27] See inter alia Judgment of 10 April 1984 in *Case 14/83, Von Colson and Kamann v. Land Nordrhein-Westfalen,* [1984] ECR 1891; Judgment of 22 April 1997 in *Case C-180/95, Nils Draehmpaehl v. Urunia Immobilienservice OHG*, [1997] ECR 1-2195; Judgment of 21 September 1989 in *Case 68/88, Commission of the European Communities v. Hellenic Republic*, [1989] ECR I-2965.

[28] *Case 33/76, Rewe-Zentralfinanz eG et Rewe Zentral AG v. Landwirtschaftskammer für das Saarland*, para. 5; *Case 45/76, Comet v. Produktschap voor Siergewassen*, para. 16; *Case C-326/96, Levez v. T.H. Jennings (Harlow Pools) Ltd.*, para. 42; Judgment of 16 May 2000 in *Case C-78/98, Shirley Preston and Others v. Wolverhampton Healthcare NHS Trust and Others and Dorothy Fletcher and Others v. Midland Bank plc.*, [2000] ECR I-03201, para. 68.

of these are the rules concerning the allocation of the burden of proof, access to justice, legal standing, victimisation, sanctions and the establishment of specialised bodies.[29] Indeed, these provisions are the subjects of this book.

These provisions also show that a comprehensive approach to enforcement is employed by the RED which was quite unique in the legal order of the European Union at the time of its adoption.[30] Concerning the enforcement provisions of the RED it has been argued that one of its strongest features is "its willingness to engage directly with the problems of enforcement,"[31] and it "has been praised for its attention to tools for practical implementation."[32] The Preamble of the Directive also explicitly stipulates that "[p]ersons who have been subject to discrimination based on racial and ethnic origin should have adequate means of legal protection."[33]

Admittedly, the text of the enforcement provisions in the RED mainly follow the wording of ECJ's case law (concerning the interpretation of directives pertaining to the prohibition of gender discrimination or directives unrelated to equal treatment),[34] which also means that several of the enforcement articles are vaguely formulated. More specifically, with respect to most of the enforcement matters the drafters of the Directive have not adapted the general requirements set in the case law to the particular right in question, namely the right to equal treatment as enshrined in the RED.

The Racial Equality Directive aims to put into effect the principle of equal treatment on the grounds of racial or ethnic origin in relation to the areas of employment, social protection and advantages, education and access to and supply of goods and services. Achieving equal treatment on the grounds of racial or ethnic origin is the first pillar of an adequate system of minority protection. Accordingly, the effectiveness of the enforcement provisions has to be examined in the light of the exercise of the right to non-discrimination on the grounds of racial or ethnic origin. Departing from the two pillars of minority protection and their underlying principles, effective enforcement of

---

29 "[A] comprehensive enforcement approach is very broad indeed. It addresses not only procedural aspects and the substance of remedies (relief and redress for the victims of discrimination) but also broader issues such as victimisation, compliance, mainstreaming and positive action, as well as other innovative measures such as corrective taxation." Tobler (2005b), at 5.

30 In this respect a conflict can, arguably, be discovered between adopting rules in the field of enforcement and national procedural autonomy. This is nicely captured by Prechal according to whom "[t]he actual application and enforcement of Community law is, as a rule, dependent upon the legal systems of the Member States, the national courts accomplish this important task within the framework of national procedures." Prechal (1997), at 3.

31 Bell (2002c), at 183.

32 Bell (2004b), at 226.

33 Recital (19) RED.

34 The only exceptions in this respect are the obligation to give legal standing to organisations stipulated in Article 7(2) RED and the requirement to establish national specialised bodies in Article 13 RED.

the right to equality arguably includes two main requirements. First of all, the enforcement provision in question has to be adapted to the substantive concepts of the RED aiming at substantive equality in order not to render the enforcement of the right to equal treatment virtually impossible or excessively difficult. Secondly, from a minority protection perspective it is of significance in terms of the effective enforcement of the right to equal treatment that the group aspect inherent in the concept of substantive equality and the right to identity of minority groups be considered, and thus the enforcement mechanisms take this aspect into account. The examination of the above-mentioned enforcement provisions of the RED and their implementation in the countries under review will be carried out in the light of these requirements concerning effectiveness.

1.2. Purpose of the Research and Research Questions

1.2.1. Purpose of the Research

The present research forms part of a broader project sponsored by the Dutch Council for Scientific Research (NWO).[35] The aim of this broader project was to study the possible implications of the Racial Equality Directive for minority protection both at the level of European Union and the Member States. Not only earlier, but also recent conflicts have pointed to the significance of and the vital need for an effective system of minority protection that appropriately takes the minority considerations into account when integrating minorities into the society. As indicated supra, the first pillar of creating a peaceful society is combating racial discrimination, which has implicitly also been acknowledged by the relatively swift adoption of the RED as a reaction to the Austrian crisis with its radical right wing, xenophobic party.[36]

Although the RED has been given ample attention not only in the academic world,[37] but also in practice, no deep and solid analysis has been carried out as yet into its implications for minority protection. Moreover, as hinted at

[35] The project was carried out under the supervision of Henrard, and with the participation of Busstra and the author of this book. The research of Busstra focuses on the substantive provisions of the RED and their implementation in the same Member States and their implications for minority protection. See Busstra (2010).

[36] See inter alia Toggenburg (2002), at 232; Happold (2000).

[37] See inter alia Howard (2004); Howard (2005); Howard (2008); Bell (2008); Finlay (2003); Bell (2001a); Bell (2002a); Bell (2002b); Bell (2002c); Bell (2004a); Bell & Waddington (2003); Jones (2003); Masselot (2004); Brennan (2004); O'Hare (2001); Waddington (2003); Waddington & Bell (2001); McInerney (2000); McInerney (2002); McInerney (2003); Brown (2002); Thüsing (2003); Schiek (2002); Guild (2000); De Schutter (2005a); Toggenburg (2002); Flynn (1999); Barry (2003); Niessen (2003); Higgins (2003); Tyson (2001); Tyson (2004); Caruso (2003); Fredman (2001b); Hepple (2004); Meenan (2007).

supra, as with enforcement-related matters of discrimination law in general, the enforcement provisions of the RED in particular have not extensively been examined either. This also means that no specific study has yet been carried out analysing the enforcement-related articles of the RED from the angle of their potentials for enhancing minority protection.

Notwithstanding the fact that all enforcement provisions of the Directive are important for making the enforcement of equality law effective, not all of them are dealt with in this book. This book studies the following enforcement-related provisions of the RED: Article 8 on the allocation of the burden of proof, Article 7 on access to justice and legal standing, Article 9 on the prohibition of victimisation, Article 15 on sanctions and Article 13 on the establishment of specialised bodies. The enumeration of these articles shows that the research project is rather broad: each of these articles could be or have been the subject of an independent book. Accordingly, due to feasibility and space constraints, the remaining enforcement articles of the RED, more specificially the provisions on dissemination of information, social dialogue, dialogue with non-governmental organisations and compliance, will not be scrutinised. Also, their less legal nature makes it reasonable not to include them in this book.

As the focus of this book is the enforcement of the right to equal treatment, no specific considerations will be made with respect to standard setting and the personal and material scope of the RED.[38]

The international and European documents addressing the right to equal treatment/non-discrimination and/or laying down minority-specific rights will also not be presented and analysed for three reasons. Again, the focus of this book is the enforcement of the right to equal treatment on the grounds of racial or ethnic origin, for which reasons it seemed less relevant to analyse the substantive provisions in this respect. Moreover, the academic literature providing a deep insight into these matters is abundant.[39] In addition, the project uses the premises of the research done by Henrard on this topic rendering a thorough overview and analysis of the available international and European mechanisms that are relevant to minority protection unnecessary.

1.2.2. Research Questions

As hinted at above, the aims of this research are interrelated and can principally be broken down in the following two goals: the examination of the possible implications of the enforcement provisions of the RED on minority protection on the one hand; and the analysis of the actual implications of

[38] These matters are the subject of the research carried out by Busstra within the framework of the broader project.

[39] Weller (2007); Thornberry & Estebanez (2004); Weller & Morawa (2004); De Varennes (1996); Thornberry (1991); Weller (2005); Henrard & Dunbar (2008).

the implementation of these provisions in four Member States for minority protection on the other. These two purposes of the research can be captured in four questions that are subsequently addressed in this book.

1) How can the enforcement provisions of the RED be interpreted?
2) What are the possible implications of these enforcement provisions for minority protection? (To what extent do these provisions in theory comply with the requirement of effectiveness as elaborated above?)
3) How have these provisions been implemented in the Member States under review? To what extent does the implementation comply with the RED?
4) What are the actual implications of the implementation of the enforcement provisions for minority protection in the countries under review? (To what extent can these provisions be regarded effective?)

Four countries have been selected for the examination of the implementation of the RED: Belgium, Estonia, Hungary and the Netherlands.[40] The selection of these countries for this comparative research was based on cross-cutting similarities and differences that are relevant in terms of minority protection in order to be able to compare the countries with one another. Undoubtedly, the essential goal of every comparative research is to explore to what extent the approaches of the countries regarding a particular matter are similar and differ from one another, trying to find explanations for these differences, and to draw some conclusions from this. Accordingly, the ultimate purpose of this research is to identify the possible variables and parameters that influence the choice of the particular enforcement mechanisms in relation to the prohibition of racial discrimination and their effect on minority protection.

1.3. Research Method

As explained above, this research has a special focus: to what extent the enforcement provisions of the RED and their implementation can be interpreted and applied in a way that they enhance minority protection. Importantly, the examination of the implementation and application of the enforcement provisions in four countries inherently includes a comparative approach.

[40] For a concise introduction to these countries see below.

1.3.1. Special Angle of the Research: Minority Protection

The research is innovative as far as its special angle (minority protection) and its link with the enforcement provisions of the RED are concerned. The underlying aim is to examine how minority protection can be enhanced through the effective enforcement of the right to non-discrimination on the grounds of racial or ethnic origin. For this reason, the most relevant articles of the RED and the examination of their implementation are set against this aim. In other words, the purpose of the research is not only to describe and analyse these articles in themselves, but also to examine them in the light of the above-mentioned overarching aim.

In order to apply this focus to the research as well as study the sources concerning enforcement-related matters, the examination of substantive matters to some extent was indispensable. In this respect, as hinted at supra, the research mainly relies on the ground works of Henrard in relation to equality and minority protection,[41] and is connected with the research done by Busstra on the substantive provisions of the RED.[42]

1.3.2. Nature of the Research

The nature of the examination of the enforcement matters from this special angle is both theoretical and practice oriented. It is theoretical in terms of setting up a theoretical framework on the basis of the particular enforcement-related provisions of the RED from the perspective of enhancing minority protection against which the implementation of these provisions in the Member States are subsequently set. The research is at the same time practice oriented, as it studies not only the legislative provisions and their theoretical interpretation, but also looks at how they have been and should be applied in practice. Thus, in this respect the classical sources of law are studied: European, international and national legal documents and jurisprudence as well as the relevant secondary literature. In addition, country visits were made during which interviews were conducted with national experts, fact-finders, law-makers, representatives of NGOs and scholars.[43] The research required the studying of different fields of law: the sources were collected from the fields of European, international, constitutional and private law.

---

41 See inter alia Henrard (2000); Henrard (2004); Henrard (2007a); Henrard (2007b); Henrard (2008b).

42 Busstra (2010).

43 For privacy reasons the persons interviewed will not be separately mentioned. The author is grateful to them for their cooperation and positive approach to this project.

1.3.3. Comparative Research

As indicated, the research questions inherently include a functional[44] comparative approach to this topic. A comparative law method[45] is necessary in order to look at the implementation of the RED in the countries under review, explore the similarities and differences in the implementation process and identify the variables and parameters that influenced the choices made for the particular mechanism. Accordingly, the research requires a vertical as well as a horizontal comparative approach.[46] As the implementation is set against a theoretical framework based on the RED, a top-down vertical comparison is necessitated. In addition to examining a particular national system in the light of this framework, the ways in which the four countries have implemented the RED are also compared which, accordingly, includes a horizontal comparison.

Comparative research can be carried out in many different ways as there is no one method of comparative law.[47] In this book the choice has been made for an integrated approach with respect to presenting the analysis of the implementation of these provisions, as opposed to a comparison made on a parallel, separated, country per country basis. In this way the similarities and differences concerning the particular aspects of enforcement can be made more visible; thus, drawing the final conclusions also becomes easier. Naturally, an integrated cross-country comparison is preceded by a thorough analysis of the available mechanisms in each country.

In accordance with the research questions the comparative exercise includes a number of steps.[48] First of all, the hypothesis was formulated that the enforcement provisions of the Racial Equality Directive and their implementation in the countries under review do and can have far-reaching implications for minority protection. For the examination of this effect, in

---

[44] As this comparative research has a particular focus and aim, the reason why it can be regarded functional by nature does not require further elaboration.

The functionalist approach to comparison has dominated the theory and practice of the comparative law method for some time. It emphasises that the comparative law method aims to solve a particular problem. However, this approach has recently been criticised as, for instance, being inherently biased or merely focusing on contemporary matters. "The functional method has become both the mantra and the *bête noire* of comparative law. For its proponents it is the most, perhaps the only fruitful method; to its opponents it represents everything bad about mainstream comparative law." Michaels (2006), at 340. See also Zweigert & Kötz (1998), at 34; Dannemann (2006), at 390; Peters & Schwenke (2000), at 827; Brand (2007), at 417-420.

[45] The literature on the comparative law method is very rich. See inter alia Zweigert & Kötz (1998); Reimann & Zimmermann (2006); De Cruz (1999); Gutteridge (1949).

[46] In this respect the scepticism often pronounced pertaining to either vertical or horizontal comparison as far as the comparability of the legal systems is concerned can reasonably be rebutted as the Directive and the obligation to implement it inherently embrace the comparability of the Member States. See inter alia Dannemann (2006), at 390.

[47] Valcke (2004), at 715.

[48] Compare with Momirov & Naudé Fourie (2009).

a second step a theoretical framework will be drawn up based on the most relevant enforcement-related articles of the Racial Equality Directive, and their possible implications for minority protection will be explored. As a third step, the actual comparison will be carried out against this conceptual model and across the countries. Thus, the vertical as well as the horizontal comparisons are carried out at this stage. In the last step, the comparative performance will result in a synthesis of the ultimate research question, namely the identification of the potential variables and parameters that influence the particular choice of certain mechanisms.

1.3.4. Selection of the Countries under Review

In order to provide a good overview, to be able to draw relevant and well-founded conclusions and to also make the research feasible, four countries were chosen for the case study part. Admittedly, any selection in this respect inherently includes some arbitrariness, and opting for other countries might similarly be supported with reasonable arguments. Nevertheless, convincing reasons can be brought forward for having selected Belgium, Estonia, Hungary and the Netherlands.

The underlying reasons for having chosen these countries are two-fold: comparability of the countries by cross-cutting similarities and differences in terms of the matters relevant from a minority protection perspective on the one hand, and feasibility considerations on the other. As the central legislative document of this research is a Directive of the European Union, it was reasonable to make the very first selection on the basis of an equal number of old and new Member States. From a minority protection perspective two aspects seemed relevant for providing thought-provoking and inspiring insights as far as the comparability of the countries and identifying the possible variables and parameters are concerned: demographic profile and track records pertaining to both minority protection and non-discrimination.

First of all, a comparison can be made on the basis of the demographic profile of these countries. Each country can be regarded as having a diverse population. To start with a very special case, Belgium is a federal country where the division of power is based on its three largest linguistic groups, the Flemings (57.2 %), the Walloons (32.4 %) and the Germans (1.47 %).[49] Accordingly, these groups are the constituent parts of the republic. However,

[49] The federal state of Belgium is composed of four linguistic regions which "indirectly determines the territorial competence of the federated entities of Belgium" (the French-speaking, Dutch-speaking, German-speaking and the bilingual region of Brussels-Capital), three Communities that are mainly competent for educational and for cultural matters (the French Community, the Flemish Community and the German-speaking Community), and three Regions which have "broadly defined competence in the economic area" (the Walloon, the Flemish and the Brussels-Capital Regions). Alen (1992), at 20-21.

Belgium also has to cope with the not insignificant number of immigrants making up approximately 5 % of the population, most of whom are Moroccans and Turks.[50] Also, the situation is Estonia is quite unique as its largest minority group, the Russian-speaking community, totals up to 25.5 % of the whole population.[51] The proportion of the minority population in the other countries is much less. While in Hungary the largest and the most problematic minority group is the Roma (1.9 %),[52] in the Netherlands it is Frisians (4.3 %)[53] that constitute the largest minority group. However, in this latter country it is rather amongst immigrant (Indonesians, Turks, Surinamese, Moroccans, Antillean/Aruban) groups (8-10 %)[54] that the situation can be regarded as problematic from a minority protection perspective. Thus, in terms of demographic profile a clear distinction can be made between Estonia and the other countries as the minority groups problematic from the perspective of equal treatment and minority protection constitute a much smaller segment of the population in Belgium, Hungary and the Netherlands than in Estonia. Also, a comparison can be made between Estonia and Hungary in this respect, as the minority groups concerned are more homogenous than the immigrant groups in Belgium and the Netherlands.

Of these countries, Hungary and the Netherlands have a good reputation in terms of minority protection. Both have ratified the two most important European treaties relevant for minority protection,[55] namely the Framework Convention[56] and the Language Charter.[57] However, in the Netherlands these treaties are not applicable to the immigrant groups.[58] In Hungary the scope of these treaties and the Act on the Rights of National and Ethnic Minorities extends to many minority groups,[59] among which the Roma.[60] Thus, the Hungarian minority protection system provides protection for the group that is

[50] Data retrieved from www.minorityrights.org.

[51] *Id.*

[52] *Id.*

[53] *Id.*

[54] *Id.*

[55] Status of ratification as of 15 May 2009.

[56] Framework Convention for the Protection of National Minorities, 1 February 1995.

[57] European Charter for Regional or Minority Languages, 5 November 1992.

[58] In its declaration to the Framework Convention the Netherlands lays down that "[t]he Kingdom of the Netherlands will apply the Framework Convention to the Frisians."

Similarly, in relation to the Language Charter most of the obligations have been undertaken with respect to those speaking the Frisian language.

[59] 13 minorities are recognised in the Act on National and Ethnic Minorities. Article 61 of the Act on the Rights of National and Ethnic Minorities.

[60] Concerning the Act on the Rights of National and Ethnic Minorities see inter alia Majtényi (2001); Majtényi (2005); Kaltenbach (2001); Majtényi & Pap (2006); Krizsán (2000); Advisory Committee on the Framework Convention for the Protection of National Minorities, Second Opinion on Hungary adopted on 9 December 2004, ACFC/INF/OP/II(2004)003, 14 December 2004, at 9-10; Fourth Report on Hungary, ECRI 2009, at 22-23.

most vulnerable in terms of racial discrimination and accommodating diversity. An important difference in this respect is that Hungary has not been faced with such a large immigration flow as the Netherlands. A parallel situation, however, may occur in the close future as Hungary has a growing immigrant population, dominated by Chinese.[61] This group does not enjoy the protection stemming either from these treaties or the Act on the Rights of National and Ethnic Minorities, as the latter has relatively strict (and somewhat controversial)[62] requirements for acknowledging a group as a national or ethnic minority. Conversely, the Netherlands adopted an anti-discrimination Act as early as 1994,[63] and has a long tradition of enforcing the prohibition of discrimination also on the grounds of racial or ethnic origin, which is not the case in Hungary. It is true that, in Hungary, as well as the Constitutional guarantee on the right to equal treatment,[64] which in practice could only be relied on before the Constitutional Court pertaining to the discriminatory provisions of legislative acts, the Civil Code has enshrined the right not to be discriminated against in its chapter on personal rights.[65] However, this provision was quite similar to that of the Constitution without any clarifications of the different concepts of discrimination, and was therefore difficult to enforce. In actual fact, only a couple of cases have been decided on the basis of this provision,[66] and for this reason it cannot be regarded effective. All in all, it can be seen that as far as the most vulnerable groups in terms of minority protection are concerned, while in Hungary the emphasis was placed on specific minority rights instruments without effective protection against discrimination, in the Netherlands the situation is rather the opposite.

In terms of minority protection Belgium and Estonia are located at the other end of the continuum than Hungary and the Netherlands. Unlike Belgium,[67] Estonia has ratified the Framework Convention, but neither of them have ratified the Language Charter[68] or devised an effective system of minority protection. In Belgium, the federalism, which principally aims to accommodate the linguistic diversity existing in the country and can be regarded in this respect as a form of minority protection, is an on-going process, but does not address the situation concerning immigrants. Although in Estonia an Act aiming to provide some protection for national minorities, the Act on Cultural

61 See inter alia www.minorityrights.org.

62 See inter alia Majtényi (2005), at 110; Majtényi (2001), at 35-36.

63 General Equal Treatment Act. On the relation of this Act to Article 1 of the Constitution stipulating the right to equal treatment see De Lange (2009), at 31.

64 Article 70/A of the Constitution. On this article of the Constitution see for instance Constitutional Court, 35/1994, 24 June 1994; Constitutional Court 14/1995, 13 March 1995; Constitutional Court, 45/2000, 8 December 2000.

65 Articles 75-85 of the Civil Code.

66 See inter alia Farkas, Kádár & Kárpáti (2003), at 121.

67 See also Fourth Report on the Netherlands, ECRI 2009, at 12.

68 Status of ratification as of 15 May 2009.

Autonomy for National Minorities, has been adopted, it has been argued that it can hardly be regarded as effective, partly due to its limited scope.[69] Both the Framework Convention as stipulated in the Estonian declaration and the Act on Cultural Autonomy for National Minorities are to be applied only to citizens of Estonia. In actual fact, one of the most serious problems faced by the Russian-speaking population relates to matters of citizenship.[70] According to the 2006 official data, 7.4 % of the population were citizens of other states and 9 % were residents of undetermined citizenship (thus in fact stateless).[71] Most of these persons belong to the Russian-speaking population. Accordingly, only a part of the Russian-speakers enjoy the protection of the Convention (and the Minority Act).[72] In this respect, however, two important factors should be kept in mind that have influenced the policy of Estonia adopted towards this community: the historical background (occupation by the Soviet Union and the forced immigration of Russian-speakers from the Soviet Union to Estonia and mass deportation of Estonians to the Soviet Union) and the relatively small number of Estonian-speakers (approximately 920,000).[73] The right to equal treatment is stipulated in the Constitutions[74] of both countries which, however, cannot be effectively enforced in individual cases. Importantly, since 1981 certain forms of racial discrimination were prohibited in a separate Act in Belgium. This Act, however, could not be regarded as appropriate in the fight against racial discrimination as only certain forms were prohibited and they were also to be enforced through criminal law. Consequently, before the adoption of the RED in Belgium and Estonia, the most vulnerable persons could enjoy protection neither through anti-discrimination law, nor minority-specific instruments.

[69] See inter alia Thiele (1999), at 11-12; Poleshchuk & Tsilevich (2003), at 289-290; Poleshchuk & Helemäe (2006), at 117; Consideration of Report Submitted by States Parties under Article 9 of the Convention, Concluding Observations of the Committee on the Elimination of Racial Discrimination, CERD/C/EST/CO/7, 22 August 2006, paras. 4 and 9; Advisory Committee on the Framework Convention for the Protection of National Minorities, Second Opinion on Estonia adopted on 24 February 2005, ACFC/INF/OP/II(2005001), 22 July (2005), at 9-14; Mälksoo (2005), at 37-45.

[70] For a detailed discussion of the situation of the Russian-speaking population see inter alia Lauristin & Heidmets (2002); Kirch (1997); Kerikmäe (1997).

[71] Data retrieved from www.minorityrights.org. See also Aasland & Fløtten (2001); Pettai (2001); Lauristin & Heidmets (2002); Kirch (1997).

[72] Indeed, it is mainly the citizenship policy of Estonia that is criticized by international organisations.

[73] Data retrieved from www.minorityrights.org.

[74] Art. 1 of the Dutch Constitution and Article 12 of the Estonian Constitution.

1.4. Scope and Structure

As explained above, the aim of this research is to examine the most important enforcement provisions of the RED and their implementation in the selected countries in the light of the minority protection phenomenon. Each chapter consists of two parts: first a theoretical framework is elaborated in which the particular provision of the RED concerned (or matter related to it) is analysed (research questions 1 and 2); and secondly, the rules and practice of the Member States under review are set against this theoretical framework (research questions 3 and 4).

The structure of the book might have followed either the order of these articles in the RED, or, as the RED is not entirely logical in this respect, the order in which these provisions come up in a procedure. Rather, a combination of these has been applied, with the added consideration that certain matters have been regarded more important in anti-discrimination law than others.

Indeed, the idea to analyse the rules on the allocation of the burden of proof in the first substantive chapter is based on this latter argument. In academic writing on anti-discrimination law matters related to the burden of proof have been given ample attention and Article 8 RED has been considered the most significant enforcement provision,[75] arguably because it is the most closely connected to the substantive provisions of the RED, and the most visible in the argumentation of fact-finders. Accordingly, this introduction will be followed by Chapter 2 which will interpret the rules enshrined in Article 8 RED on the basis of which a proper model of review will be devised, and will subsequently be set against the model of review in the studied countries.

Closely related to the allocation of the burden proof is the question how discrimination can be proven, that is what forms of proof are appropriate and/or sufficient to comply with one's onus of proof. As the concept of discrimination inherently entails comparison, two specific forms of proof seem very appropriate due to the comparative aspect they also include. These two forms, one of which is shortly mentioned in the Preamble of the RED,[76] are statistical data and situation testing. The importance of these forms of proof is also generally acknowledged in academic discussions.[77] For this reason, Chapter 3 will analyse the matters related to these two forms of proof

---

75 See inter alia Schiek, Waddington & Bell (2007), at 237-242; Henrard (2007b), at 136-139; De Prins, Sottiaux & Vrielink (2005), at 112-113; Gijzen (2006), at 73-74; Tobler (2005), at 252-253; Craig (2007), at 138-151.

76 "(15) The appreciation of the facts from which it may be inferred that there has been direct or indirect discrimination is a matter for national judicial or other competent bodies, in accordance with rules of national law and practice. Such rules may provide in particular for indirect discrimination to be established by any means including on the basis of *statistical evidence*" (emphasis added).

77 See inter alia Schiek, Waddington & Bell (2007), at 253-257. & 373-435; De Prins, Sottiaux & Vrielink (2005), at 112-120, Gijzen (2006), at 74-81; De Schutter (2003b).

and devise a proper methodology for their application. Subsequently, it will examine how these forms have been applied in the practice in the Member States under review.

Contrary to the burden of proof provision and the two mentioned forms of proof the topics that will be addressed from Chapter 4 onwards have not gained much attention yet in anti-discrimination law, which underscores the importance of addressing these matters extensively. Chapter 4 will analyse Article 7(1) RED on access to justice, and will subsequently examine the legal system of the studied countries in this respect.

The second paragraph of Article 7 RED will be interpreted in Chapter 5, as the matters related to legal standing also require a detailed elaboration within the framework of discrimination law. Access to justice and legal standing are the sine qua non of each enforcement procedure, as without appropriate procedures and legal standing the violation of the right to equal treatment cannot be taken to a fact-finder leaving the right to equal treatment a pure declaration.

Article 9 RED on the prohibition of victimisation is an important tool to encourage victims to vindicate their right to equal treatment. Chapter 6 will analyse this provision in detail, and devise a model that is the most effective for enforcing the right to equal treatment. The second part of this chapter will subsequently examine how the selected Member States have dealt with this issue.

The last two substantive chapters address Articles 13 RED on national specialised bodies and 15 RED on sanctions, in a different order however than they appear in the Directive. The final step of a legal procedure is the adjudication on sanctions. For this reason, it seemed more logical to discuss Article 15 RED on sanctions before analysing Article 13 RED on national specialised bodies. Accordingly, the focus of Chapter 7 is sanctions in which the requirements set in the RED will be placed in a broader context for the sake of an appropriate analysis of this Article. Admittedly, this article of the RED is the most vaguely formulated among the enforcement provisions, which also makes its analysis more difficult compared to the rest of the provisions. Moreover, due to the broad variety of available sanctions in the countries under review, it is also not an easy task to evaluate the arsenal in terms of Article 15 RED and minority protection. In any event, on the basis of the requirements stipulated for the national sanctions a conceptual model will be elaborated in the theoretical part, against which the national rules and practice will subsequently be set.

As indicated supra, Chapter 8, as the last substantive chapter of this work, will explore Article 13 on national specialised bodies. It seems reasonable to address this article at the end of this book as this provision is considerably different from the other enforcement related provisions of the RED. This is because the requirement for establishing a national specialised body, although closely linked to access to justice, does not aim to define a particular element of the enforcement procedure, but imposes an obligation on the Member States to establish an organisation that provides help in the procedures. Chapter 8 will first analyse what Article 13 RED stipulates, and on the basis of this analysis it will clarify the competences the national bodies have to be vested with and the requirements they have to comply with. An examination will subsequently be made of to what extent the Member States meet the RED requirements in this respect.

Finally, the book ends with the Final Conclusions that will synthesize the findings of the research and will answer the last research question. More specifically, based on the factors that justified the selection of the countries, the variables and parameters that possibly influence the choices made in these countries concerning the particular enforcement mechanism will be identified.

CHAPTER 2

ALLOCATION OF THE BURDEN OF PROOF AND MODEL OF REVIEW IN EQUAL TREATMENT CASES

PART A. THEORETICAL FRAMEWORK

2.1. Introduction

How a claim of discrimination is assessed by the fact-finder depends to a great extent on the rules regulating the allocation of the burden of proof. These rules define who has to prove what and to what extent, on the basis of which a model of review can be set up. The significance of these rules and their application should not be underestimated, since they constitute one of the most important cornerstones of the effective enforcement of anti-discrimination law.[1] As Kokott observed

> [e]xperienced lawyers have long known that many cases are won or lost depending upon which party is better able to convince the court of the existence of facts favourable to it, according to the rules of evidence, rather than upon a dispute about sophisticated questions of interpretation of the law.[2]

Article 8 of the Race Directive, following the model devised by the ECJ in relation to gender discrimination, stipulates a special rule for the allocation of the burden proof in racial discrimination cases. Pursuant to this rule the applicant must first "*establish* [...] *facts from which it may be presumed that there has been direct or indirect discrimination.*" Once the presumption of discrimination has been established, "*it shall be for the respondent to prove that there has been no breach of the principle of equal treatment.*" Contrary to

---

1 See inter alia De Schutter (2003), at 23; Gijzen (2004), at 73; Palmer (2006), at 23; Arnardóttir (2007), at 16.

2 Kokott (1998), at 1.

the general rule in evidence law which states that the applicant has to prove his case, Article 8 RED merely requires the applicant to give rise to a presumption of discrimination. The establishment of the presumption then places the burden of proof on the respondent who has to prove that no discrimination has taken place. Although this rule seems clear enough, several concerns and dilemmas have been raised with respect to the theory and the application of these special rules. These observations clearly show the need for setting up a conceptually proper and at the same time functional model for reviewing discrimination cases.[3]

The first subsection of this chapter will set up a general framework for the model of review and clarify the exact meaning of certain notions that will be used hereafter.[4] Based on this framework, academic writing and case law, a tailor-made and apt model for reviewing discrimination cases will be developed. This model will, finally, be applied to the concepts of harassment and instruction to discriminate.

Article 8 RED stipulates the following:

> Article 8 Burden of Proof
>
> (1) Member States shall take such measures as are necessary, in accordance with their national judicial systems, to ensure that, when persons who consider themselves wronged because the principle of equal treatment has not been applied to them establish, before a court or other competent authority, facts from which it may be presumed that there has been direct or indirect discrimination, it shall be for the respondent to prove that there has been no breach of the principle of equal treatment.
> (2) Paragraph 1 shall not prevent Member States from introducing rules of evidence which are more favourable to plaintiffs.
> (3) Paragraph 1 shall not apply to criminal procedures.
> (4) Paragraphs 1, 2 and 3 shall also apply to any proceedings brought in accordance with Article 7(2).
> (5) Member States need not apply paragraph 1 to proceedings in which it is for the court or competent body to investigate the facts of the case.

[3] In contrast to the substantive approach to the concepts of discrimination the model of review is based on procedural considerations. Specifically, this means that while the substantive approach is addressed from the perspective of the fact-finder, the procedural approach is based on the duties of the parties in relation to the burden of proof. In other words, under the first approach the question is what the fact-finder has to look for, while in the latter case the emphasis is on what the parties have to prove. For this reason there might be some overlaps between the terminologies used from a conceptual and evidentiary perspective, but their meanings might differ. These differences will be duly explained.

[4] On the forms of proof see Chapter 3.

2.2. General Framework for the Model of Review

Prior to the analysis of the relevant provisions of the RED, it is necessary to become acquainted with the relevant concepts and notions in general evidence law that will form the framework for the model of review. In this paragraph the following terms will be briefly analysed: distinction and discrimination, elements of proof, burden of proof and its allocation according to both the general and the special rules. Furthermore, the rationale behind the special rules on the allocation of the burden of proof will also be addressed. Finally, the procedures in which these special rules should and/or can be applied will also be discussed as well as the meaning of the standard of proof and the level of scrutiny in discrimination procedures.

2.2.1. Distinction or Discrimination

There is no general agreement on what the term 'discrimination' exactly means in discrimination law. The concrete question is whether a distinction or differential treatment immediately constitutes discrimination or whether such distinction results in discrimination only when it cannot be justified. Pursuant to the common meaning of these terms a 'distinction' is not necessarily unlawful, while the term 'discrimination' definitely has a negative connotation. For this reason the word 'discrimination' will be used in the meaning of unlawful distinction.[5] Accordingly, there is no discrimination when the distinction is justified.

2.2.2. Constitutive Elements of Proof of a Discrimination Claim

The term 'constitutive elements of proof' describes *what* issues should be proven in a discrimination case. These elements can all be deduced from the definition of discrimination.[6]

---

5 See also Tobler (2005a), at 254; Tobler (2008), at 32. "In contrast, according to an increasing number of academic writers, in the context of indirect discrimination objective justification does not concern justification but rather is an element defining discrimination – meaning that if there is legitimate 'justification', then discrimination simply does not exist. Bamforth describes this as the situation where there is an element preventing a finding of discrimination in the first place." (Tobler (2005a), at 254). Barrett explains on the concept accepted by Schwarze that "[h]e observes that if differentiation between persons or objects is objectively justified, then it cannot be prohibited discrimination, and the question of whether the treatment has in fact been different becomes irrelevant. This approach obviously makes a lack of objective justification a condition precedent to the existence of discrimination – i.e., a question which must be answered before one comes to the question of whether discrimination has occurred." Barrett (2003), at 116-117.

6 See also Bindman (1992), at 50.

Since the aim of this chapter is to set up the general rules for the allocation of the burden of proof applicable to both direct and indirect discrimination cases,[7] the focus will be placed on the common elements of the two concepts; and the relevant differences will be duly specified. In the definitions of direct[8] and indirect[9] discrimination of the Race Directive the following common elements can be identified. There must be (1) a *harm*,[10] that is a less favourable treatment[11] or a particular disadvantage[12] experienced by the applicant(s) (2) on the grounds of or related to his (their) *racial or ethnic origin*.[13] The expressions 'on the grounds of' and 'related to' refer to (3) a *causal relationship* both between the protected ground and the treatment,[14] and between the harm suffered and the challenged treatment, provision, criterion and practice.[15] Admittedly, it is generally the first causal link that is referred to as *the* causal relationship,[16] while as a rule the second form of causality is not addressed at all either by academia or in practice. Although both the terms *'on the grounds of'* and *'related to'* are said to describe the (causal) link between the harm and the protected ground, conceptually they are quite different.[17] In

7 Here it is only direct and indirect discrimination which is referred to in the general model of review. The rules for allocation of the burden of proof, and subsequently the elements of a discrimination claim in cases of harassment and of instruction to discriminate will be discussed below.

8 "[D]irect discrimination shall be taken to occur where one person is treated less favourably than another is, has been or would be treated in a comparable situation on grounds of racial or ethnic origin." Art. 2(2) a) RED.

9 "[I]ndirect discrimination shall be taken to occur where an apparently neutral provision, criterion or practice would put persons of a racial or ethnic origin at a particular disadvantage compared with other persons, unless that provision, criterion or practice is objectively justified by a legitimate aim and the means of achieving that aim are appropriate and necessary." Art. 2(2) b) RED.

10 Hereafter the word harm is used for referring either to less favourable or disparate treatment or to disparate or adverse impact.

11 Art. 2(2) (a) RED, direct discrimination. See inter alia Bindman (1992), at 52.

12 Art. 2(2) (b) RED, indirect discrimination.

13 On the difference between these two formulations, see Busstra (2010).

14 The text of the RED in relation to direct discrimination stipulates that such discrimination occurs when the less favourable treatment happens 'on grounds of racial or ethnic origin'. See inter alia Bindman (1992), at 53-54. For a detailed elaboration concerning the causal link see Busstra (2010).

15 The definition of indirect discrimination in the RED establishes that indirect discrimination occurs when "a [...] provision, criterion or practice would put persons [...] at a particular disadvantage."

16 Gerards (2005a), at 75. Although both causal links are called here causality, since this chapter aims to devise a general model of review, the causal link between the protected ground and the treatment is relevant in relation to direct discrimination, while the (causal) relationship between the harm suffered and the provision, criterion or practice is important in indirect discrimination cases.

17 The definition of indirect discrimination in the RED stipulates that the disparate impact is related to and not founded on the protected ground. See Busstra (2010).

direct discrimination cases the *reason* for the disadvantageous treatment of the victim is his *racial or ethnic origin*. In contrast, in indirect discrimination cases the measure taken is not based on this particular characteristic as it is a neutral measure which 'merely' puts persons of a particular racial or ethnic origin at a disadvantage. Accordingly, in indirect discrimination cases the harm is not based on the racial or ethnic origin of the victim, but 'solely' related to it. In other words, in these cases the reason for taking the particular measure is not (and conceptually cannot be) the protected ground of the victim. Finally, the expressions 'treated *less* favourably than another' and '*compared with* other persons' in the RED suggest that the harm is suffered in relation to someone else (or to others) in a comparable situation. This constitutes (4) the question of *comparison*, *comparator* and *comparability* of the cases.[18] These four elements (harm, protected ground, causal link and comparison) are the constitutive elements of a discrimination claim, and are closely interconnected. In practice it is difficult to separate these elements, which makes the appropriate allocation of the burden of proof even more complicated.

2.2.3. Burden of Proof and the Allocation of the Burden of Proof

In general evidence law two forms of *burden of proof* have been identified: an evidential or subjective burden of proof, also called the *burden of production* and a legal or objective burden of proof, also called the *burden of persuasion*.[19] While the former refers to the "burden of going forward with the evidence by producing evidence,"[20] the latter means the burden of persuading the fact-finder that the allegations made are true.[21] The burden of persuasion is per definition allocated at the beginning of each procedure and remains on the same party during the whole process. On the contrary, the burden of production moves back and forth between the parties because the facts underlying the allegations are generally not established on the basis of the evidence coming only from one party, but they are also refuted, disproved or impaired by the other party.[22] Thus, the importance of this distinction lies in the fact that the

[18] For a detailed elaboration on the question of comparator and comparability see Busstra (2010).

[19] Kokott (1998), at 9-10. See also Bosse (2003), at 12-14; Asser (1998), at 39-40.

[20] Kokott (1998), at 9.

[21] Kokott (1998), at 9. The following definition on the onus of proof given by Erdal in fact defines the burden of persuasion. "The term burden of proof, also known as the onus of proof, refers to the legal obligation on a party to satisfy the fact-finder, to a specified standard of proof, that certain facts are true." Erdal (2001), at 77.

[22] Although scholars in general do not specify which burden of proof they refer to, in fact they discuss the burden of persuasion. Due to the non-specification the two meanings of the burden of proof are often mixed leading to uncertainty concerning the proper allocation of the burden of proof.

party having the burden of persuasion has to make out his case, while the other party only has to make the other's allegations weaker with the help of his burden of production.

In light of the above elaboration, the term '*allocation of the burden of proof*' has two separate meanings. On the one hand, it answers the question who has to face the consequences of the fact-finder's conclusion that the allegations remain unproven.[23] In this sense, the burden of proof pertains to the burden of persuasion. On the other hand, the allocation of the burden of proof might also describe who can or must produce evidence at a particular moment during the process. In this latter meaning it points to the burden of production. Admittedly, regulating the allocation of the burden of production is not important in this respect[24] since, as previously mentioned, it shifts back and forth between the parties during the procedure. Accordingly, the allocation of the burden of proof is hereafter purely meant to describe who bears the burden of persuasion in a concrete case.

2.2.4. Allocation of the Burden of Proof Pursuant to the General Rules of Evidence

Pursuant to the commonly known general rule of evidence '*onus probandi incumbit actori*';[25] the party alleging something is obliged to prove it.[26] On the basis of the general allocation of the burden of proof, accordingly, the burden of persuasion rests with the person who starts a procedure (the claimant) against the other party (the respondent).[27] This also means that it is also the claimant (in civil proceedings) who bears the initial burden of production. When the claimant has complied with his burden of production, this burden shifts to the other party, who has the possibility to submit evidence to support the disproval of the facts provided by the claimant.[28] However, the burden of persuasion stays with the claimant because it is *him* who has to make out his case. The respondent will only try to weaken the claimant's statements and evidence by challenging them through his burden of production.

23 See also Bosse (2003), at 15.

24 Laying down rules for the allocation of the burden of production is only necessary in terms of the specific course of a particular procedure; i.e. when the word is given to the one or the other party.

25 This rule is also referred to as the rule of '*ei incumbit probatie qui dicit, non qui negat*'.

26 See Palmer (2006), at 24; Hidma & Rutgers (2004), at 46-49; Bosse (2003), at 16; Erdal (2001), at 81; Kokott (1998), at 11; Asser (1998), at 40-41.

27 See inter alia Monaghan (2007), at 563.

28 See also Erdal (2001), at 82.

2.2.5. Allocation of the Burden of Proof Pursuant to Article 8 RED

The allocation of the burden of proof as enshrined in Article 8 RED is obviously different from the general distribution of the onus of proof. Pursuant to this article "*when persons who consider themselves wronged because the principle of equal treatment has not been applied to them establish, before a court or other competent authority, facts from which it may be presumed that there has been direct or indirect discrimination, it shall be for the respondent to prove that there has been no breach of the principle of equal treatment.*" On the basis of this definition, a two-phased theoretical model of assessment can be discerned. In the first phase of this model, often called the *prima facie phase*, the applicant has to establish the presumption of discrimination. In the second phase, hereafter called the *refutation phase*, the respondent has to prove that there has been no discrimination. This two-phased model forms the basis for a refined model of review in equal treatment cases.

This special rule and the two-phased model based on it, however, does not explicitly answer the question to what extent this allocation of the burden of proof is different from the general rules. As explained supra, in order to establish how the burden of proof is exactly distributed, and thus to what extent or in which respect its allocation is special, the location of the burden of persuasion has to be detected.[29] It will be argued that the adoption of these special rules would be pointless if the burden of persuasion was not placed on the respondent. Accordingly, the special allocation of the burden of proof means that it is not the applicant (i.e. the person starting the procedure) who bears the burden of persuasion, but instead the burden of persuasion rests with the person who has to disprove the alleged occurrence of discrimination.[30] Strikingly (and thus somewhat confusingly), unlike in procedures with the general allocation of the burden of proof, at the beginning of the discrimination procedure the burdens of production and persuasion do not rest with the same person. The applicant bears the initial burden of production without having the burden of persuasion. Nevertheless, his initial burden of production establishes the respondent's burden of persuasion.[31]

---

[29] See also Haskovec (2006), at 1071; Kokott (1998), at 2.

[30] According to Espín in discrimination cases there is a "change in the direction of proof" could mean that the direction of the burden of persuasion has been changed; i.e. it is not the applicant who settles that someone has committed a violation, but it is the respondent who proves that no violation has taken place. Espín (2005), at 3.

[31] In this context, Espín talks about "the incomplete nature of the evidence". According to him "[a]ll the plaintiff has so far done is to put forward facts from which it may be inferred that there had been a difference in treatment. It is only if the respondent is now not able to furnish evidence of the legality and proportionality of the measure that the presumption turns to evidence that an act of discrimination has indeed occurred." Espín (2005), at 3. See also Bloemeyer (1994), at 44, 88. & 119.

There are at least five arguments supporting this interpretation of the special allocation of the burden of proof. Firstly, from a formal point of view the burden of persuasion does not shift by definition from one person to the other. It is established at the beginning of the procedure and does not shift from one party to the other during the process. Naturally, it is possible to argue that it is exactly the shift of the burden of persuasion from one party to the other that makes the allocation of the burden of proof special. However, this interpretation can be refuted by the second argument, which is that it is a presumption that the applicant has to establish in discrimination cases. Should the applicant bear the burden of persuasion, he would have to prove that there has been discrimination, and raising a presumption would not suffice. Thirdly, as demonstrated supra, if it was only the burden of production which shifted from the applicant to the respondent and the burden of persuasion stayed with the applicant, it would not mean any shift in the burden of proof, since the burden of production always moves back and forth between the parties.[32] As Bindman formulated "[t]he burden on the respondent needs to be more than an *evidential* burden if there is to be a real inducement to avoid discrimination."[33] Fourthly, the Explanatory Memorandum of the Race Directive also stipulates that the *legal* burden of proof should be placed on the respondent.[34] This document explains that

> [n]ormally, the *legal burden of proving* a case rests on the plaintiff. However, obtaining evidence in discrimination cases, where the relevant information is often in the hands of the defendant, can be very problematic. The Commission therefore proposes to shift the burden of proof to the defendant in certain circumstances, as has already been done in the case of sex discrimination.[35]

---

32 For a position according to which it is 'only' the evidential burden of proof which switches to the respondent see for instance Written Comments in the case of *Nachova and others v. Bulgaria*, INTERIGHTS 2005. Retrieved from http://www.justiceinitiative.org/db/resource2/fs/?file_id=15404.

33 Bindman (1992), at 58 (emphasis added).

34 "Normally, the *legal* burden of proving a case rests on the plaintiff. However, obtaining evidence in discrimination cases, where the relevant information is often in the hands of the defendant, can be very problematic. The Commission therefore proposes to shift the burden of proof to the defendant in certain circumstances, as has already been done in the case of sex discrimination" (emphasis added). Proposal for a Council Directive implementing the principle of equal treatment between persons irrespective of racial or ethnic origin, COM(1999) 566 final, 1999/0253, 25 November 1999, at 9.

35 Proposal for a Council Directive implementing the principle of equal treatment between persons irrespective of racial or ethnic origin, COM(1999) 566 final, 1999/0253, 25 November 1999, at 9 (emphasis added). See inter alia the reasoning of the ECJ in the *Enderby* case. "The onus may shift when that is necessary to avoid depriving workers who appear to be the victims of discrimination of any effective means of enforcing the principle of equal pay." Judgment of 27 October 1993 in *Case C-127/92, Dr. Pamela Mary Enderby v. Frenchay Health Authority and Secretary of State for Health*, [1993] ECR I-5535, para. 13.

Finally, a reference can be made to the rationale behind this special allocation of the burden of proof; namely, the applicant in general does not have access to evidence. Thus, in many cases he would not be able to make out his case.[36] In other words, should the burden of persuasion not rest with the respondent, the applicant would not be able to enforce his right to equal treatment. These arguments convincingly show that the special allocation of the burden of proof means that the burden of persuasion rests with the respondent as soon as a presumption of discrimination is established.

It is also important to find an appropriate term describing that the allocation of the burden of proof is somewhat different from the general rules in discrimination cases. In academic writing and case law three terms referring to this special allocation can be pinpointed. These are 'reversal of the burden of proof', 'shift in the burden of proof' and 'sharing the burden of proof'. Neither of these terms, however, properly describes the phenomenon that takes place in the course of proving on the basis of the special rules concerning the allocation of the burden of proof.

Initially,[37] the term '*reversal of the burden of proof*'[38] was used to refer to the special allocation of the burden of proof. However, it has recently been suggested to replace the term 'reversal'[39] because it "connotes that somehow the employer is disadvantaged and required somehow to prove a 'negative fact'."[40] Moreover, it might also point to the fact that the "reversal of the burden of proof would require the employer to prove the conduct was based on objective factors from the start of the lawsuit."[41] In other words, it might indicate that the applicant does not have to submit any evidence, and the respondent has to prove from the very beginning of the procedure that no violation has taken place. As the obscurity of this term can give rise to improper inferences its application is not suggested.

---

36 In Ellis' words, "[t]he real problem from the complainant's point of view is that it is extremely difficult, and sometimes quite impossible, to prove why she was not selected. This is a matter which is peculiarly within the employer's own knowledge, which is why the legal burden of proof should be reversed once a prima facie case has been made out and the employer should then be required to prove to the satisfaction of the tribunal the reason for the relevant decision." Ellis (2005), at 98.

37 For a recent application of this term, see Gijzen (2006), at 74.

38 For the use of this term see inter alia Humblet (2003), at 6.

39 See also Espín (2005), at 2.

40 Palmer (2006), at 26. See also Craig (2007), at 27.

See also the reasoning of the European Parliament on the proposal of the RED according to which "the Commission proposes to share the burden of proof between the plaintiff and defendant. In other words, this is not a complete reversal for the burden of proof. The plaintiff has to prove that there is a case to answer." Report on the proposal for a Council directive on implementing the principle of equal treatment between persons irrespective of racial or ethnic origin, COM(1999) 566 – C5-0067/2000 – 1999/0253(CNS), A5-0136/2000, 16 May 2000, at 37.

41 Luxton (1999), at 373.

At present two terms are generally used for describing the allocation of the burden of proof in discrimination cases. They are the '*shift in the burden of proof*' and the '*sharing of the burden of proof*'. It has been argued that the term 'shift' "accommodates the reality that the facts necessary to prove an explanation of the conduct in question are normally in possession of the employer,"[42] and the term 'sharing' similarly refers to the fact that both parties have certain obligations in the process of providing evidence.[43] However, on the basis of the arguments concerning the allocation of the burden of proof, it can be clearly seen that in fact there is no *shift* in the burden of proof between the parties. The applicant's initial burden of production creates the burden of persuasion of the respondent, but it does not shift from one party to the other during the procedure.[44] Accordingly, the use of the term 'shift' should also be avoided.

As far as the term '*sharing*' is concerned, it raises at least two concerns. On the one hand, in terms of the burden of production there is always a sharing of the burden of proof. On the other hand, as argued above, the burden of persuasion is not shared between the parties at all, but is placed only on the respondent. Thus, on the basis of these conceptual considerations the application of this term is also not desirable.

How then should this allocation of the burden of proof be referred to? Arguably, the term '*special allocation of the burden of proof*' properly describes what actually happens in terms of evidence law. It makes clear that the rules on the distribution of the burden of proof in discrimination cases differ from the general rules. As argued supra, this difference can manifest itself only in placing the burden of persuasion on the respondent.

2.2.6. Rationale behind the Adoption of the Special Rules on the Allocation of the Burden of Proof

In the *Danfoss* case[45] in 1989 it was the first time that the ECJ underscored the importance of a special allocation of the burden of proof in discrimination cases. It declared that "where a system of pay which is totally lacking in

---

42 Palmer (2006), at 26.

43 See also Craig (2007), at 27.

44 In actual fact, a shift can be detected but only compared to other procedures: in procedures other than those related to discrimination the burden of persuasion is on the applicant; the onus shifts to the respondent in the discrimination procedure. Nevertheless, it would be misleading to use the term 'shift' in this meaning as the allocation of the burden of proof is generally understood as referring to the allocation *between the parties* in the same procedure and *not between the different procedures*.

45 Judgment of 17 October 1989 in *Case C-109/88, Handels- og Kontorfunktionærernes Forbund I Danmark v. Dansk Arbejdsgiverforening, acting on behalf of Danfoss*, [1989] ECR 3199.

transparency, it is for the employer to prove that his practice in the matter of wages is not discriminatory, if a female worker establishes, in relation to a relatively large number of employees, that the average pay for women is less than that for men."[46] A similar reasoning was given in the *Enderby* case[47] a couple of years later in which it was argued that "[w]here there is a prima facie case of discrimination, it is for the employer to show that there are objective reasons for the difference in pay."[48] This view of the Court led in 1997 to the codification of this rule in the Burden of Proof Directive.[49] Its provision on the burden of proof has been repeated in the RED and the Framework Directive[50] and in the later directives on equal treatment.[51]

The above-mentioned cases clearly reveal that the general allocation of the burden of proof was considered to cause difficulties for the applicant in discrimination cases,[52]

> particularly in the employment sector where an unequal power relationship between employer and employee exists. The employer tends to be in a considerably stronger position than the employee, principally because much (if not all) of the information about how the allegedly discriminatory decision was arrived at is held by the employer.[53]

If the burden of persuasion was not on the respondent, the applicant would not be able to make out his case, since the evidence is generally in the hands of the respondent.[54] In the words of the ECJ, workers

---

46 *Id.*, para. 11.

47 Judgment of 27 October 1993 in *Case C-127/92, Dr. Pamela Mary Enderby v. Frenchay Health Authority and Secretary of State for Health*, [1993] ECR I-5535.

48 *Id.*, para. 13.

49 Council Directive 97/80/EC of 15 December 1997 on the burden of proof in cases of discrimination based on sex.

50 Council Directive 2000/778/EC of 27 November 2000 establishing a general framework for equal treatment in employment and occupation.

51 Council Directive 2004/113/EC of 13 December 2004 implementing the principle of equal treatment between men and women in the access to and supply of goods and services; Directive 2006/54/EC of the European Parliament and of the Council of 5 July 2006 on the implementation of the principle of equal opportunities and equal treatment of men and women in matters of employment and occupation (the 'Recast Directive'). This latter Directive will replace the Directive on the burden of proof with effect from 15 August 2009.

52 See inter alia Bosse (2003), at 133-134; Luxton (1999), at 358; Asser (1998), at 47.

53 Palmer (2006), at 24. See also Monaghan (2007), at 563-564. & 571; Ellis (2005), at 98. & 110; Latraverse (2005), at 1-2; Luxton (1999), at 358; Leenders (1997), at 7-8; Szyszczak (1997), at 111-112; Written Comments in the case of *Nachova and others v. Bulgaria, supra* note 32, at 7.

54 Ellis (2005), at 98. See also Palmer, who argued that the "[a]pplication of [the general] rule in discrimination cases under civil or employment law would mean that it would be for the claimant to prove discrimination on the balance of probabilities. Failure to so prove would mean that the claimant's case would fail." Palmer (2006), at 24.

> would be deprived of any effective means of enforcing the principle of equal pay before the national courts if the effect of adducing such evidence was not to impose upon the employer the burden of proving that his practice in the matter of wages is not in fact discriminatory.[55]

This at the same time means that the obligation to apply the special allocation of the burden of proof in discrimination cases could also be deduced from the general principle of effective enforcement.[56] According to Kokott "an intimate relationship exists between the *effective* protection of human rights, on the one hand, and adequate material standards as well as the appropriate *allocation of the burden of proof*, on the other."[57] This relationship has also been made clear

---

55 *Case C-127/92, Dr. Pamela Mary Enderby v. Frenchay Health Authority and Secretary of State for Health*, para. 13.

See also the European Court of Human Rights in the *Hoogendijk* case in which it concluded that "[w]here an applicant is able to show, on the basis of undisputed official statistics, the existence of a prima facie indication that a specific rule – although formulated in a neutral manner – in fact affects a clearly higher percentage of women than men, it is for the respondent Government to show that this is the result of objective factors unrelated to any discrimination on grounds of sex. If the onus of demonstrating that a difference in impact for men and women is not in practice discriminatory does not shift to the respondent Government, it will be in practice extremely difficult to prove indirect discrimination." *Hoogendijk v. Netherlands*, ECHR (2005) No. 58641/00, 6 January 2005.

56 The case law, among others, of the European Court of Human Rights on Article 14 clearly shows how important is the appropriate allocation of the burden of proof for the effective enforcement of human rights. As the Interights states in its *amicus curiae* to the *Nachova* case, "[t]here is no doubt that such violence [racist violence against ethnic minorities] breaches the spirit and substance of the Convention, and yet until its recent judgement in *Nachova* this Court had never found a violation of Article 14 in respect of such acts. The problem has been in satisfying the Court in evidentiary terms that such discrimination has actually occurred. These difficulties of proof inevitably have an impact on the effective protection of equality rights" (Written Comments in the case of *Nachova and others v. Bulgaria*, *supra* note 32, at 1. Kokott emphasises that "[l]egal scholars in the United States have demonstrated the mutual dependency between applying adequate rules on the apportionment of the burden of proof, including the adoption of adequate measures of persuasion, and the full enforcement of individual rights" (Kokott (1998), at 57). In the words of Bosse, "[d]e tegemoetkoming in de bewijslast bij discriminatie op grond van het geslacht is gebaseerd op het beginsel van effectieve rechtsbescherming" (Bosse (2003), at 140-141).

The special allocation of the burden of proof is, arguably, also applied in cases other than discrimination. See for instance *Mukong v. Cameroon*, UNHRC (1994) No. 458/1991, Decision 21 July 1994; *Ribitsch v. Austria*, 4 December 1995, UNHRC, No. 18896/91, para. 34. See also Erdal (2001).

57 Kokott (1998), at 1 (emphasis added). See also Written Comments in the case of *Nachova and others v. Bulgaria*, *supra* note 32.

both in the Preamble of the Burden of Proof Directive[58] and in the Preamble of the Race Directive.[59]

Some scholars argue that it was the concept of objective justification in indirect discrimination cases that has lead to the special allocation of the burden of proof.[60] Arguments can even be found in the notion that the general concept of discrimination itself entails this special allocation, so there is no need to regulate it.[61] Although, as elaborated above, the concept of presumption has led to the special allocation of the burden of proof,[62] there are still some defensible elements in both observations. It is true that the special rules on the burden of proof have been developed in cases of indirect discrimination in which the applicant brought up statistical evidence for supporting his case. Fact-finders established on the basis of this statistical evidence that there was a prima facie case of discrimination. However, they could not establish that discrimination occurred as they still had to look at whether the respondent could give a reasonable explanation for the disparate impact the statistics showed.[63] The concept of prima facie case of discrimination has later been extended to the concept of direct discrimination in relation to which these rules should necessarily be adapted.

Importantly, the special allocation of the burden of proof if properly regulated and consistently applied, can encourage victims to turn to a fact-finding organ and pursue their claims.[64] Moreover

[58] Burden of Proof Directive, Recital (17). "Whereas plaintiffs could be deprived of any effective means of enforcing the principle of equal treatment before the national courts if the effect of introducing evidence of an apparent discrimination were not to impose upon the respondent the burden of proving that his practice is not in fact discriminatory."

[59] Race Directive, Recital (21). "The rules on the burden of proof must be adapted when there is a prima facie case of discrimination and, for the principle of equal treatment to be applied effectively, the burden of proof must shift back to the respondent when evidence of such discrimination is brought." See also the Explanatory Memorandum of the Race Directive pursuant to which "[n]ormally, the legal burden of proving a case rests on the plaintiff. However, obtaining evidence in discrimination cases, where the relevant information is often in the hands of the defendant, can be very problematic. The Commission therefore proposes to shift the burden of proof to the defendant in certain circumstances, as has already been done in the case of sex discrimination." Proposal for a Council Directive implementing the principle of equal treatment between persons irrespective of racial or ethnic origin, COM(1999) 566 final, 1999/0253, 25 November 1999, at 9.

[60] Tobler (2005a), at 252.

[61] De Prins, Sottiaux & Vrielink (2005), at 113; De Vos (2004), at 90.

[62] This argument is confirmed by the jurisprudence of the ECtHR in relation to cases of Articles 8-11 in which cases there is a general possibility of objective justification, but the Court does not assess the arguments on the basis of the special application of the burden of proof.

[63] See Shiek and others (2007), at 373.

[64] For other arguments in favour of the proper allocation of the burden of proof see Bosse (2003), at 141; Luxton (1999), at 380.

> [t]his lighter burden may act as a deterrent to those employers currently using or contemplating the use of discriminatory methods by causing them to fear possible repercussions, such as litigation or possible fines.[65]

Thus, a proper and consistent application of the special allocation of the burden of proof can have a preventive effect on the discriminators and can bring more cases to the surface. Through this impact it markedly assists in the effective enforcement of the prohibition of discrimination and hence also contributes to the enhancement of minority protection.

2.2.7. Standard of Proof and Level of Scrutiny

The special allocation of the burden of proof also raises the question what is the standard of proof of the parties in the procedure and how intensively fact-finders have to scrutinize the evidence and explanations of the parties. Justice Harlan defined the standard of proof in the *In Re Winship*[66] case in his concurring opinion as follows:

> a standard of proof represents an attempt to instruct the fact-finder concerning the degree of confidence our society thinks he should have in the correctness of factual conclusions for a particular type of adjudication.[67]

In other words, the term 'standard of proof' refers to the degree to which the allegations have to be proven to be regarded true. The other side of this notion is the 'level of scrutiny' which delineates the intensity with which the fact-finding body examines the facts submitted by the parties. Thus, both notions refer to the same aspect of a case, namely to the *degree of confidence*, but from two different perspectives. While the term 'standard of proof' defines this degree from the perspective of the parties, the term 'level of scrutiny' describes this matter from the angle of the fact-finder.

On the basis of the general allocation of the burden of proof this would mean that it is the applicant who has to reach a certain level of persuasion in order to win his case, while the respondent merely has to refute the applicant's statements. However, the special allocation of the burden of proof makes this question somewhat more complicated since both the applicant and the respondent have to reach a certain degree of probability in order to respectively establish a presumption, and prove that the principle of equal treatment has not been violated. This observation also means that different levels of scrutiny have to be applied by fact-finders with respect to the two parties. Interestingly, in discrimination law, more specifically in and with reference to the case-law of the ECtHR, the term 'standard of proof' is generally used with respect to the applicant's burden of proof, while the terms 'intensity of review' and

---

65 Luxton (1999), at 381.

66 *In re Winship*, 397 U.S. 358 (SC 1970).

67 Kokott (1998), at 25.

'level of scrutiny' are typically employed pertaining to the second phase of the assessment when it is for the respondent to prove that he has observed the principle of equal treatment. At the end of each phase of the model of review the standards of proof of the applicant and the respondent will be analysed separately.

2.2.8. Procedures with the Special Rules on the Burden of Proof

Not only does Article 8 RED lay down special rules for the allocation of the burden of proof, it also stipulates in which procedures these rules must, can and cannot be applied. First of all, Article 8(3) RED explicitly prohibits the application of these rules in criminal procedures. At the same time, the Directive does not lay down such a ban[68] in relation to procedures "in which it is for the court or competent body to investigate the facts of the case."[69] In most cases, such procedures are administrative procedures, and the competent bodies are often the specialised bodies for the promotion of equal treatment. In relation to these procedures the Member States can freely decide whether they apply the special rules on the allocation of the burden of proof. Still, the application of the burden of proof rules in such procedures is possible because subsection (2) of the same article allows the States to introduce rules "which are more favourable to plaintiffs." Finally, pursuant to Article 8(4) the special rules shall also be applied when associations, organisations or other legal entities engage in the procedure.[70]

It is arguably more advantageous to the victim, and therefore more desirable from the perspectives of effective enforcement of the right to equal treatment and minority protection, to apply the special allocation of the burden of proof in as many procedures as possible, naturally with the exception of criminal law procedures. The effective enforcement of the principle of equal treatment might be eroded if these rules are only applied in general civil court proceedings as these might not be the most often used forms of procedures due to their excessive length and costs.

2.3. Model of Review for Direct and Indirect Discrimination

In combination with the special allocation of the burden of proof and the elements that need to be proven a model of reviewing discrimination cases can be set up. As explained supra, from the burden of proof rules, a basic

68 See inter alia Tyson (2004), at 125.

69 Art. 8 (5) RED.

70 "Paragraphs 1, 2 and 3 shall also apply to any proceedings brought in accordance with Article 7(2)." Art. 8(4) RED. See also Tyson (2004), at 125. On the engagement of legal entities in discrimination procedures see Chapter 5.

two-phased model has been deduced. In the first phase the applicant has to establish a prima facie case of discrimination. In the second phase it is for the respondent to prove that no discrimination has taken, is taking or would take place. Notwithstanding the general acceptance of these two phases, there are still many uncertainties concerning this rule. For instance, what kind of test can be adopted in order to establish a prima facie case of discrimination, how can the respondent refute the charge of discrimination, what objective justification exactly means, and so on. In order to eliminate the doubts and uncertainties the purpose of this section is to develop an adequate and conceptually proper model of review which can offer guidance for decision-making in discrimination cases.

This section is divided into two main paragraphs. The first paragraph will discuss the first phase of the model of assessment, which will be followed by an analysis of the respondent's burden of proof in the second paragraph.

2.3.1. First Phase of the Assessment: Burden of Proof of the Applicant

Pursuant to Article 8 RED the applicant shall establish facts from which it may be presumed that there has been discrimination. Stemming from this definition, first of all, a distinction should be made between facts and the presumption of discrimination. A presumption is made on the basis of the facts, but the facts do not constitute a presumption themselves.[71] The presumption comes into existence by drawing inferences from the facts.[72] In other words, the underlying facts from which the presumption of discrimination is shaped have to be proven by the applicant, which is clearly different from proving that he has been discriminated against.

Importantly, the definition of the RED describes the presumption of *discrimination*.[73] In order to devise how the presumption of discrimination can be established it is necessary to go back to the elements of the concept of discrimination. Arguably, the establishment of a presumption of discrimination means that the applicant has to make the causal link both between the harm and the protected ground and between the treatment, provision, criterion, practice and the harm plausible.[74] As far as these causal relationships are

---

[71] See, for instance, the *Feryn* case in which the ECJ stated that "[s]tatements [...] may constitute facts of such a nature as to give rise to a presumption of a discriminatory recruitment policy." Judgment of 10 July 2008 in *Case C-54/07, Centrum voor gelijkheid van kansen en racismebestrijding v. Firma Feryn NV.*, [2008] ECR I-05187, para. 31.

[72] Importantly, in some instances one can, however, find direct evidence as well, which actually proves and not only shows the likeliness that there was discrimination. The conclusion stemming from this evidence is still formulated in terms of presumption. This seems to be a risky approach since it might raise the standard of proof of the applicant.

[73] See also Prechal (2004), at 544.

[74] On first sight it would seem that this proposed model parallels with the test of causality described by Gerards. In her view this test means that the applicant is required to "show that it

concerned, as explained above, a clear distinction has to be made between cases of direct and indirect discrimination. In direct discrimination cases the less favourable treatment is based on the victim's protected ground, while in indirect discrimination cases a particular disadvantage is or can 'merely' be related to a protected ground.[75] This conceptual distinction also means that in indirect discrimination cases showing a disparate impact (particular disadvantage) on a group immediately establishes the causal link between the ground and the harm. Besides this, in direct discrimination cases the link between the harm and the treatment is almost self-evident; while in indirect discrimination cases it is often difficult to find the source of the disparate impact as it is a seemingly neutral provision, criterion or practice.[76] Both links can be made visible with the help of comparison, which is of central importance in the framework of the Aristotelian understanding of equality.[77] Comparison in this respect constitutes a means of evidence. For instance, in the *Jørgensen* case the ECJ stated that national provisions or rules "discriminate indirectly against women where, although worded in neutral terms, they work to the disadvantage of *a much higher* percentage of women *than* men."[78] Manifestly,

is likely that has been suffering a disadvantage by a certain treatment, which would not have happened had he not possessed a specific characteristic" (Gerards (2005a), at 75). In other words, this test puts the emphasis on the link between the harm and the protected ground. She refuses the application of this test because it can only be applied when the list of protected grounds is exhaustive. In terms of racial discrimination it would then mean that it is an appropriate test, since here the protected ground is given. Although she emphasizes that this test can also be applied when it is the effect of a measure that establishes the link with the protected ground, the other causal link, namely the link between the harm and the treatment, provision, criterion or practice, does not get the attention it would deserve. In her view the application of the test of disadvantage would be most appropriate in the first phase of the assessment. Pursuant to this test the applicant should make it plausible that "he has suffered a disadvantage compared to another group through a specific treatment" (Gerards (2005a), at 78). According to her this means that the applicant shows that it is likely that a disadvantage exists. However, her concept of 'disadvantage' is in fact very broad, it includes that there has been a distinction, compared to others through a specific treatment. Thus, her concept of disadvantage is in fact the same as the concept of discrimination. Nevertheless, she clearly excludes the test of comparability from both tests. In other words, in her view it is not for the applicant to prove that his situation is comparable to that of his comparator(s). Keeping in mind the function of comparison as a means of evidence, it can however be observed that her test of disadvantage is in fact not so very different from her test of causality, with the only exception that the test of disadvantage can be applied in this broad meaning to indirect discrimination as well as where the causal link with the protected ground is different. Gerards (2005a), at 57-79.

75 For a detailed elaboration on these concepts see Busstra (2010).

76 Concerning the source of indirect discrimination see also Cunningham (2009).

77 Tobler (2005a), at 43; Monaghan (2007), at 289; Collins (2003), at 32; Fredman (2002), at 96-100; Henrard (2007a), at 13.

78 Judgment of 6 April 2000 in *Case C-226, Birgitte Jørgensen v Foreningen af Speciallæger and Sygesikringens Forhandlingsudvalg g*, [2000] ECR I-02447, para. 29 (emphasis added). A similar argument can be observed in an admissibility decision of the European Court of Human Rights, namely the *Hoogendijk* case from 2005 in which the Court stated that "where

the suffered disadvantage was shown with the help of comparison. Similarly, the comparison made the link visible between the harm and the ground[79] as well as between the harm and the measure.[80]

As a means of evidence, comparison is however not the same as a test of comparability. Pursuant to this test the main question is whether the invoked comparators are in fact in a (non-)comparable situation to the applicant.[81] To prove the comparability of the cases in the first phase of the assessment cannot be regarded conceptually acceptable for several reasons. First of all, it cannot be required from the applicant to prove the comparability of the cases, since it would curtail the essence of the special allocation of the burden of proof: the applicant is hardly in a position to have access to such evidence from which the comparability of the cases could be established. Though implicit, the ECJ also seemed to accept that proving the comparability of the cases

---

an applicant is able to show, on the basis of undisputed official statistics, the existence of a prima facie indication that a specific rule [...] in fact affects a clearly higher percentage of women than men, it is for the respondent Government to show that this is the result of objective factors unrelated to any discrimination on grounds of sex." In Gerards' view this constitutes a disadvantage test. *Hoogendijk v. Netherlands*, ECHR (2005) No. 58641/00, 6 January 2005; Gerards (2005b).

[79] Concerning the protected ground at stake, it has to be remarked that not only the real characteristic of a person, but also the presumed and associated characteristics are protected. See, for instance, the Explanatory Memorandum of the RED which explains that "[t]he principle of equal treatment must apply irrespective of whether the racial or ethnic origin is real or presumed." This can also be shown with the help of comparison. Proposal for a Council Directive implementing the principle of equal treatment between persons irrespective of racial or ethnic origin, COM(1999) 566 final, 1999/0253, 25 November 1999, at 6.

[80] A similar approach seems to be slowly being adopted by the European Court of Human Rights as well. In the *Timishev* case, for instance, the Court accepted that "[o]nce the applicant has shown that there has been a difference in treatment, it is then for the respondent Government to show that the difference in treatment could be justified" (*Timishev v. Russia*, ECHR (2001) Nos. 55762/00 and 55974/00, 13 December 2005, para. 57). This position was applied in the Grand Chamber decision in the *D.H. and Others* case in which the Court accepted that "the relevant statutory provisions [...] had considerably more impact in practice on Roma children than on non-Roma children and resulted in statistically disproportionate numbers of placements of the former in special schools" (*D.H. and Others v. the Czech Republic*, ECHR (2007) No. 57325/00, 13 November 2007, para. 185. See also *Sampanis and others v. Greece*, ECHR (2008) No. 32526/05, 5 June 2008).

[81] See Gerards, who seems to make a distinction between comparison and comparability, when she rejects the application of the comparability test and argues for the application of the disadvantage test. In terms of the latter "[a]ll that is required is that the person affected shows that he has suffered a disadvantage compared to another group through a specific treatment. It is of no further importance whether the other group does or does not find itself in a comparable position." Gerards (2005a), at 78.

Compare this position with the case law in the United Kingdom, most importantly, *Igen Ltd and Others v. Wong and Others*, IRLR 258 (CA 2005); *Dresdner Kleinwort Wasserstein Ltd v. Adebayo*, IRLR 514 (EAT 2005).

cannot be accounted to the applicant. In the much debated *Brunnhofer* case,[82] the Court, arguably mistakenly, refused to apply the special allocation of the burden of proof mainly because, based on the *Danfoss* case, there was no lack of transparency. So the '*normal rules of evidence*' were applied. It accepted that

> [i]t is accordingly for the plaintiff to prove by any form of allowable evidence that the pay she receives from the Bank is less than that of her chosen comparator, and that she does the same work or work of equal value, comparable to that performed by him, so that prima facie she is the victim of discrimination which can be explained only by the difference in sex.[83]

A contrario, one could, accordingly, argue that when the special rules are applied, proving the comparability of the cases cannot be required from the applicant.[84] This approach can also be supported by the rationale behind the special rules and the principle of effectiveness.

It has also been argued that due to its complexity[85] the test of comparability leaves much scope for subjective judicial input, and would mean that a value judgment would have to be made on the acceptability of the distinction as early as in the first phase of the assessment.[86] Arguably, the underlying reason for this very last argument is that a decision on the comparability of the situations is the result and not the point of departure of an examination. In other

---

82 Judgment of 26 June 2001 in *Case C-381/99, Susanna Brunnhofer v. Bank der österreichischen Postsparkasse AG*, [2001] ECR I-04961.

83 *Id.*, para. 58.

84 The approach of the Court to the question of comparability has been regarded problematic and has been criticised by scholars. See inter alia Tobler (2008), at 40; Schiek, Waddington & Bell (2007), at 468.

85 The comparability of the cases cannot be decided in itself, it has to be defined from which perspective the cases are comparable or non-comparable, which means that fact-finders should balance the arguments of both parties as early as in the first phase of the assessment. See inter alia Gerards (2005a), at 57-72; Arnardóttir (2007), at 34; Monaghan (2007), at 158; Tobler (2005a), at 45; De Prins, Sottiaux & Vrielink (2005), at 6 & 90-91; Prechal (2004), at 543-545; Collins (2003), at 32; Arnardóttir (2003), at 84-85; Fredman (2002), at 98.

86 See inter alia Fredman (2002), at 95-100. & 109-111. According to Fredman "[a]t least three problems have been evident in the case-law with regard to the question of comparator. First [...] the need for a norm of comparison, be it male, white or able-bodied, has created powerful conformist pressures. Second, the choice of comparator itself requires a complex value judgment as to which of the myriad differences between any two individuals are relevant and which are irrelevant. The choice of relevant characteristics is often itself determinative of the outcome. Equally problematic, the comparator can be constructed in different ways, leading to entirely different outcomes. Third, there are important situations in which there is simply no appropriate comparator. It was the clear inappropriateness of a comparative approach which finally led courts in different jurisdictions to attempt to formulate a notion of equality which moved beyond the comparative approach." Fredman (2002), at 98. See also Gerards (2005a), at 57-72; Arnardóttir (2007), at 34; Monaghan (2007), at 158; Tobler (2005), at 45; De Prins, Sottiaux & Vrielink (2005), at 6. & 90-91; Prechal (2004), at 543-545; Collins (2003), at 32; Arnardóttir (2003), at 84-85; Fredman (2002), at 98; Craig (2007), at 39-40.

words, cases are comparable in the light of a certain situation, requirement, and so on and comparability does not exist in itself. Accordingly, should the comparability of the cases be proven by the applicant and should the fact-finder aim to establish the comparability of the cases in the first phase of the assessment, a value judgment would already be made on the distinction at this stage.

2.3.1.1. Standard of Proof of the Applicant: Presumption of Discrimination

The special allocation of the burden of proof is inherently connected to the standard of proof of the applicant, and the former determines the latter: it is a presumption of discrimination that the applicant has to establish. Notwithstanding the fact that this requirement is clearly laid down in Article 8 RED, there are still many uncertainties regarding what a presumption actually means. In order to give rise to a presumption, fact-finders have to draw inferences from the facts established by the applicant. In other words the whole concept of presumption requires an active stance from fact-finders. In this context it has been argued that "[e]xperience suggests that courts are particularly reluctant to draw inferences of ethnic discrimination."[87] Also, some factors have been identified by the existence of which fact-finders will not easily accept the existence of a presumption. These are the following: the seriousness of a violation, the gravity of the consequences, and the inherent unlikelihood of an alleged occurrence.

One can easily find examples of racial discrimination cases in which fact-finders did not draw the inference that there was a presumption of discrimination, although they arguably could and should have done so. For instance, in the *Nachova* case the Grand Chamber of the ECtHR first explained that the racially insulting statement of the perpetrator 'is of itself an insufficient basis for concluding that the respondent State is liable for a racist killing',[88] but admitted that "[i]t is true that a number of organisations [...] have expressed concern about the occurrence of such incidents."[89] And they added as a final explanation for rejecting the existence of a presumption of racial discrimination that

> where it is alleged [...] that a violent act was motivated by racial prejudice, such an approach would amount to requiring the respondent Government to prove the absence of a particular subjective attitude on the part of the person concerned.[90]

[87] Craig (2007), at 141.

[88] *Nachova a.o. v. Bulgaria*, ECHR (2005) Nos. 43577/98 and 43579/98, 6 July 2005, para. 153.

[89] *Id.*, para. 155.

[90] *Id.*, para. 157.

Accordingly, it can be clearly seen that partly because of the supposed evidentiary consequences on the respondent, no inference was drawn that there was a presumption of discrimination. Importantly, however, these elements should not play a role in the acceptance of a presumption since this would deflate the concepts of presumption and the special allocation of the burden of proof. One should not hesitate to draw inferences as to the existence of a presumption as soon as there are indications of an alleged occurrence of racial discrimination, since the respondent always has the possibility to refute this presumption.[91]

In order to conclude what the standard of proof of the applicant is, the aim of the special allocation of the burden of proof should also be kept in mind, which is to facilitate the position of the applicant. This is also required by the principle of effectiveness, since in neglecting this requirement the applicant would not be able to enforce his right to equal treatment.

The case law of the ECJ reveals two different approaches to the applicant's standard of proof, depending on the setting of the case. In most cases, a presumption of discrimination has to be shown. For example, the applicant submits statistical data which allow the conclusion that discrimination might have taken place.[92] Thus, when from the facts the suspicion, be it even a very light one, is raised that discrimination may have taken place, the existence of a prima facie case of discrimination should be accepted. This could be called the general or normal standard of proof in discrimination cases.

The other standard of proof devised in the *Danfoss* case by the ECJ[93] concerns cases in which the respondent has not complied with his positive obligations to make his system transparent, systematic and controllable.[94] In such situations the applicant has more difficulties in establishing a prima facie case of discrimination since his access to evidence is more limited than in general. Thus, in such cases the fact-finder should more easily accept the existence of a prima facie case of discrimination, since the applicant simply cannot have access to further evidence.

---

91 Gerards (2005a), at 78-79.

92 See for instance *Case C-127/92, Dr. Pamela Mary Enderby v. Frenchay Health Authority and Secretary of State for Health*; Judgment of 23 May 1996 in *Case C-237/94, John O'Flynn v. Adjudication Officer*, [1996] ECR I-2617.

93 *Case C-109/88, Handels- og Kontorfunktionærernes Forbund I Danmark v. Dansk Arbejdsgiverforening, acting on behalf of Danfoss*.

94 "[W]here an undertaking applies a system of pay which is totally lacking in transparency, it is for the employer to prove that his practice in the matter of wages is not discriminatory, if a female worker establishes, in relation to a relatively large number of employees, that the average pay for women is less than that for men." *Id.*, para. 11.

2.3.2. Second Phase of the Assessment: Burden of Proof of the Respondent

As soon as the applicant gives rise to a presumption as to the existence of discrimination, the burden of persuasion is placed on the respondent. More precisely, this burden of proof is *created* by the establishment of the presumption of discrimination, since it has not existed before in the procedure. The respondent bears the burden of persuading the fact-finder that he has observed the principle of equal treatment.[95] The creation of the burden of persuasion also results in a change in the direction of proof. Instead of examining whether discrimination has taken place, in this phase of the assessment the question is whether the respondent has in fact observed the principle of equal treatment.[96]

The second phase of the assessment is generally referred to as justification, which term is mainly used in relation to indirect discrimination,[97] but can reasonably also be applied when the respondent invokes one of the exception clauses concerning direct discrimination.[98] In this sense justification is interpreted as justification proper, also called objective justification.[99] Coming up with objective justification means that a distinction has been made but this distinction can be "made acceptable as a result of the weighing of conflicting interests, namely of non-discrimination on the one hand and of a concern unrelated to it on the other."[100] This is also described as bringing up 'cross-cutting reasons'[101] which reasons can be "deemed more important than the concern for equality."[102] By examining these reasons the different interests can be properly taken into account and balanced against each other.

Concerning objective justification, two main systems can be distinguished: open and closed systems of justification. In the case of indirect discrimination, the RED applies an open system that theoretically allows any legitimate aim in order to refute that discrimination has taken place. It stipulates that

> [i]ndirect discrimination shall be taken to occur where an apparently neutral provision, criterion or practice would put persons of a racial or ethnic origin at

95 See also Houtzager (2006), at 12.

96 See also Espín (2005), at 3.

97 Monaghan (2007), at 160; Latraverse (2005), at 60; Gill & Monaghan (2003), at 117-12; Bowers & Moran (2002), at 307-312; Gijzen (2006), at 82; Asscher-Vonk (1999), at 39; Luxton (1999), at 381.

98 See inter alia Henrard (2007a,) at 25.

99 See inter alia Tobler (2005a), at 254; Bamforth (1996), at 50; Luxton (1999), at 381; Monaghan (2007), at 160; Gijzen (2006), at 82; Asscher-Vonk (1999), at 39; Luxton (1999), at 381; Latraverse (2005), at 2; Bindman (1992), at 60; Gill & Monaghan (2003), at 117-121; Bowers & Moran (2002), at 307-312; Prechal (2004), at 545.

100 Tobler (2005a), at 69.

101 Leader (1996), at 111.

102 Tobler (2005a), at 254.

> a particular disadvantage compared with other persons, *unless that provision, criterion or practice is objectively justified by a legitimate aim and the means of achieving that aim are appropriate and necessary.*[103]

In other words, the applicant can justify his treatment with a measure which has a legitimate aim with proportional means. On the contrary, with regard to direct discrimination[104] the RED operates closed system of justification (generally referred to as exceptions), as only certain legitimate aims can be accepted as being able to justify the distinction.[105] Nevertheless, the proportionality of the means to achieve the particular aim should be examined, also in the context of a closed system of justification.

However, according to some scholars[106] objective justification (a terminology they use within the framework of indirect discrimination) means that the respondent is able to show the absence of the *causal link* between the harm and the protected ground.[107] Pursuant to this view the respondent's objective justification in the case of indirect discrimination on the grounds of sex means that "it has not been shown that sex was the cause for the disadvantage suffered."[108] Ellis argues that

> if the adverse consequences to one sex can be shown to be attributable to an acceptable and gender-neutral factor, then there is no discrimination. The cause of the adverse impact is something other than sex discrimination.[109]

The position of Ellis is rejected by Tobler using convincing arguments: the requirement of proportionality in the justification test indicates the balancing of interests, so that it refers to justification proper and not to causality; and under Ellis' approach the disparate impact on a group would not be recognised.[110]

---

103 Art. 2 (2) b) RED (emphasis added).

104 Art. 2 (2) a) RED.

105 See Arts. 4 and 5 RED.

106 See for this position in particular Ellis (2005), at 112. See also Tobler (2005a), at 69. & 254; Watson (1995), at 42. & 45; Barnard (1996), at 70; Szyszczak (1996), at 58; Bieback (1997), at 102; Bloemeyer (1994), at 127; Bamforth (1996), at 50.

107 Such reasoning might, arguably, be contributed to the fact that the ECJ stipulated in many cases that "whenever there is evidence of discrimination, it is for the employer to prove that the practice at issue is justified by *objective factors unrelated to any discrimination based on sex*" (emphasis added). See inter alia *Case C-109/88, Handels- og Kontorfunktionærernes Forbund I Danmark v. Dansk Arbejdsgiverforening, acting on behalf of Danfoss*, para. 16. & 22-23; Judgment of 17 June 1998 in *Case C-243/95, Kathleen Hill and Ann Stapleton v. The Revenue Commissioners and the Department of Finance*, [1998] ECR 1-3739, para. 43; Judgment of 3 October 2006 in *Case C-17/05, B. F. Cadman v. Health & Safety Executive*, [2006] ECR I-09583, para. 31.

108 Tobler (2005a), at 254. See also Bamforth (1996), at 50; Lomeyer (1994), at 127.

109 Ellis (1998), at 136. See also Ellis (1994), at 572; Ellis (1997), at 174. For the discussion concerning these arguments see inter alia Tobler (2005a), at 255; De Prins, Sottiaux & Vrielink (2005), at 119-120.

110 Tobler (2005a), at 258.

Tobler's observations can also be complemented by a conceptual argument. By providing an explanation of why the respondent acted in such a way to result in a disparate impact, the respondent does not negate the causal link between the harm and the protected ground. Rather, he provides compelling reasons which he regards as more important than the observation of the principle of equal treatment. Accordingly, the view that justification can be captured by causality language is not convincing for the given reasons.

It has also been observed that the ECJ[111] often uses arguments related to the lack of *comparability* of two particular situations when it examines whether particular treatment can be justified.[112] Conceptually, this use of the term 'justification' is, however, quite confusing and incorrect. Tobler also refuses to accept this approach for two reasons.[113] According to her, from a conceptual point of view the comparability of the cases is rather a prerequisite for equal treatment,[114] so that it cannot be brought up at this stage at all.[115] Secondly, in her view the question of comparability is different from bringing up cross-cutting reasons for the particular treatment. However, the real reason why justification is not the same as examining the lack of comparability is, arguably, somewhat different. Specifically, using comparability in terms of objective justification does not explain from which perspective the cases are comparable or incomparable.[116] By referring to the lack of comparability, the respondent in fact questions the appropriateness of the comparison made by the applicant. However, the lack of comparability is the result of an argumentation; thus, it cannot be the reason itself.[117] This reason is the legitimate aim of the respondent which he tries to achieve with a particular

[111] See inter alia Judgment of 12 February 1974 in *Case 152/73, Giovanni Maria Sotgiu v. Deutsche Bundespost*, [1974] ECR 153; Judgment of 15 October 1969 in *Case 15/62, Württembergische Milchverwertung-Südmilch v. Salvatore Ugliola*, [1969] ECR 363; Judgment of 7 June 1972 in *Case 20/71, Luisa Sabbatini, née Bertoni, v. European Parliament*, [1972] ECR 345. On these cases see also Tobler (2005a), at 73.

[112] Tobler (2005a), at 73; Apollis (1980), at 81; Moon & Allen (2006), at 38. In the context of the European Convention on Human Rights see inter alia Arnardóttir (2003), at 10-38.

[113] Tobler explained that "[t]he term 'justification' does not always refer to 'justification proper' but instead is used in the context of the issue of comparability. This use is confusing because from a conceptual point of view, a finding of comparability is a prerequisite for equal treatment and hence also for a finding of the discrimination resulting from unequal treatment. As such, it differs from the cross-cutting reasons that constitute justification proper and that must be examined only after a prima facie finding of discrimination has been made." Tobler (2005a), at 73.

[114] See also Schiek, Waddington & Bell (2007), at 205-206.

[115] Compare with the first phase of the assessment where it has been explained why the comparability test cannot be regarded appropriate.

[116] See inter alia Barrett (2003), at 114. For arguments pro the comparability test over the assessment against the justification model see, for instance, Blackstone (1969), at 117; Alexy (1985), at 364.

[117] In other words, at the end of the examination of the justification one might conclude that the cases were in fact not comparable as the respondent had good reasons to make the

measure. If his arguments are considered in terms of comparability arguments, fact-finders would miss the examination of the proportionality of the applied means.[118]

From the perspective of the parties comparison merely constitutes a means of evidence[119] which can be called the justificatory use of comparison or justificatory comparison.[120] In the relatively recent *Lindorfer* case,[121] for instance, the Court of First Instance argued in terms of comparability when it established that there was no violation of the principle of equal treatment rather than stipulating that there was a reasonable explanation for the treatment.

> It decided [...] that Ms Lindorfer could not argue that, in that scheme, there is no distinction according to sex as regards officials' contributions, *since* officials who contribute to the Community pension rights by their service in a Community institution are in a *different situation* from those who procure the transfer to the Communities of the actuarial equivalent or redemption value of retirement pension rights which they have acquired in respect of activities before entering the service of the Communities.[122]

As the Grand Chamber of the ECJ itself also observed, "the Court of First Instance did not explain *why* the situations of those two categories of officials *are not comparable*."[123] In the *ÖGB* case the ECJ also looked at the comparability of the cases when it actually examined whether the particular measure was justifiable. The Court had to decide on a distinction made concerning redundancy payment between persons serving with the armed forces and those taking parental leave. It established that

> the suspension of the contract of employment is thus based on particular reasons, more precisely the interests of the worker and family in the case of parental leave and the collective interests of the nation in the case of national service.[124]

Although the Court laid down the perspective from which it established the incomparability of the situations, due to its focus on the question of

---

particular distinction. But one cannot state that the cases were not comparable so that there was a justification.

[118] See inter alia Monaghan (2007), at 159.

[119] However, it can be observed that if justification is accepted, it means that the victim(s) and the comparators were as a matter of fact not in a comparable situation, which is not the same as stating that there is justification because their situations were not comparable.

[120] See Busstra (2010).

[121] Judgment of 18 March 2004 in *Case T-204/01, Lindorfer v. Council of the European Union*, [2007] ECR I-6467.

[122] *Id.*, para. 52 (emphasis added).

[123] *Id.*, para. 53.

[124] Judgment of 8 June 2004 in *Case C-220/02, Österreichischer Gewerkschaftsbund, Gewerkschaft der Privatangetstellten v. Wirtschaftskammer Österreich*, [2004] ECR I-05907, para. 64.

comparability it missed the examination of the proportionality of this reason.[125] Put differently, the question should have been whether the nature of the interests, which thus can be identified as the legitimate aim of the legislators, was a good reason to make this distinction.[126] These cases clearly show that using comparability in terms of justification can result in hiding the real reasons behind the treatment and a shallow examination of the explanation of the respondent. In this way this approach could therefore result in avoiding the application of the proportionality test, which is the essence of the objective justification test.[127]

The clarification of what objective justification means, however, does not give an answer to the question what the second phase of the assessment exactly entails.[128] In answering this question, two considerations seem to be relevant. Firstly, Article 8 RED does not refer to objective justification; it simply stipulates that it is for the respondent to prove that he has observed the principle of equal treatment. This indicates a need to return to the concepts of discrimination and their constitutive elements of proof in order to be able to assess what is meant under the second phase of assessment. Secondly and related to the previous observation, at this phase of the assessment the applicant has already given rise to a presumption of discrimination by showing a possible causal link between the particular elements through the use of comparison. In

125 According to Schiek in the case the Court "introduced a third step into the two-tier test of indirect discrimination, i.e. the question whether the two groups were in a comparable situation." Schiek, Waddington & Bell (2007), at 469.

126 Compare with Judgment of 12 October 2004 in *Case C-313/02*, *Nicole Wippel v Peek & Cloppenburg GmbH & Co. KG.*, [2004] ECR I-09483, paras. 52-62. With respect to this case Schiek argued that it is dogmatically unsound to introduce a comparability test into the indirect discrimination test as it rather belongs to the concept of direct discrimination. However, as explained above, the conclusion of comparability is merely the ultimate result of the justification, it is not the test itself. Accordingly, it cannot more appropriately be applied to one or the other concept. Schiek, Waddington & Bell (2007), at 471.

127 See also the Judgment of 9 November 1993 in *Case C-132/92*, *Birds Eye Walls Ltd. v. Friedel M. Roberts*, [1993] ECR I-5579, paras. 17-20. Compare with the case of *Shamoon v. Chief Constable of the Royal Ulster Constabulary* (Northern Ireland) [2003] ICR 337.

128 Bodrogi and Danka argued that "to rebut prima facie discrimination, respondent may assert 1) that there are no grounds to shift the burden of proof, i.e. that claimant failed to establish a prima facie case, and 2) that there is no discrimination because there were non-discriminatory reasons for the difference in treatment, justifying that difference" (Bodrogi & Danka (2006)). Similarly, De Prins, Sottiaux & Vrielink argue that the respondent, first of all, can rebut the presumption, and should he not succeed in this, he can still provide an objective justification for his treatment (De Prins, Sottiaux & Vrielink (2005), at 115-116). Craig also refers to two steps in the second phase: denying the primary facts presented by the complainant and objective justification. However, as to the first step he argues that four counter-arguments can be provided: the respondent can argue that the complainant did not receive the treatment complained of; the complainant and the comparator are not in comparable situations; the complainant was not treated differently from the comparator; there is no causal link between the treatment and the protected ground (Craig (2007), at 33-36).

other words, the causal relationships are at the level of presumption; they are not yet proven. Accordingly, the respondent should, arguably, be given the possibility to refute this aspect of the case, which clearly cannot be labelled as coming up with compelling reasons. From the perspective of the fact-finder it means that at a certain point of the assessment he has to establish the existence of the causal link.

As explained above, pursuant to the general allocation of the burden of proof the burden of persuasion rests with the party in the interest of whom something has to be proven. In discrimination cases it has been changed so that the respondent bears the burden of persuasion that no discrimination has taken place. Using the terms distinction and discrimination, it can be argued that rebutting causality-related arguments is concerned with the question whether a distinction has been made on the grounds or related to the victim's racial or ethnic origin, while objective justification pertains to the point whether this distinction is lawful; that is whether it constitutes discrimination.

Admittedly, the burden of proving that the distinction made is not unlawful (that is that there was a legitimate aim and the means to achieve this aim was proportionate) would already fall on the respondent on the basis of the general rules, since it is in his interest to prove this aspect.[129] In other words, the special allocation of the burden of proof has in fact implications only regarding the issue whether distinction has been made on the grounds of or related to a particular ground through a particular treatment, provision, criterion or practice. Put differently, it would be in the interest of the applicant to prove that these causal links do exist, but the special allocation of the burden of proof places the burden of persuasion on the respondent, who has to prove that there are no such links. From a conceptual point of view (which is the same as the perspective of the fact-finder) the existence of the causal links has to be accepted on the basis of the presumption of discrimination unless the respondent proves the absence of them. Accordingly, the stage of negation of the causality logically stems from the special allocation of the burden of proof.

The possibility of negating the causal link might be the reason that some scholars argue that the closed system of justification in direct discrimination cases has been broken[130] as they regard the causality argument as an additional ground of justification to the exception clauses. However, as explained above, proving the lack of causality is embedded in the special rules, and it constitutes a step preceding the actual objective justification. Accordingly, the closed system of justification is not broken by the causality argumentation.

The following examples might serve to explain how these two stages of the refutation stand apart from and are related to each other. In the first example, with the help of a situation test, the applicant of Roma origin gives rise to

[129] Compare with the model of review concerning Arts. 8-11 ECHR.

[130] For an analysis of the system of justification for direct discrimination see, inter alia, Tobler (2001); Ellis (2005), at 111-113; Bowers & Moran (2002).

the presumption that he was not allowed to enter a pub because of his ethnic origin. The situation test shows that others not being perceived as Roma could get in without any problems. The burden of persuasion is accordingly placed on the respondent, who argues that the applicants were rejected because they did not have the required membership card. Saying this, the respondent in fact *denies the causal link between the protected ground and the less favourable treatment*. In a similar example, the respondent does not deny that Roma persons were not allowed to enter. He rather argues that with their refusal he wanted to guarantee public security, as Roma persons had caused troubles many times in the past. Accordingly, he *acknowledges the causal relationship* between the protected ground and the treatment, but he argues that he had a *reasonable ground* to do so.

Recalling the elements of discrimination, one might similarly argue that in addition to denying any of the causal links and coming up with a justification the respondent might also argue that the situations of the applicant and the comparator he refers to are not comparable. This argument should, however, not be mixed with interpreting objective justification in terms of comparability. More specifically, the approach based on the elements of the concept of discrimination would interpret proving the incomparability of the cases as a third possibility of providing evidence for the observance of the principle of equal treatment. For instance, Garrone argues that the respondent can escape liability in two ways:

> a) the measure at issue does not lead to inequality because similar situations are treated similarly or different situations are treated differently, without taking into account in any way the prohibited criterion; b) the measure does not lead to discrimination in the strict sense, because it aims at a legitimate objective and is proportionate in that regard.[131]

Thus, he does not accept the negation of causality as a way of escaping liability, but in his view in addition to objective justification the respondent

---

[131] Garrone (1994), at 448. This observation of Garrone is also cited by Tobler (2005a), at 273. Thiery also accepts that, on the one hand, the respondent can refute the comparability aspect and can also objectively justify his treatment, however, he complements this picture with a third element, that is the possibility of refuting the causal link between the protected ground and the suffered harm. As an argument for the comparability refutation, he takes the reasoning of the ECJ in the *Birds Eye Walls Ltd.* case. Arguably, this case can also be taken as a counter-argument to justification in terms of comparability, since here it was also the case that, by using this test, the ECJ avoided the application of the proportionality test. An important positive aspect of this case, however, was that the underlying reason for the non-comparability of the cases was discovered. "Accordingly, although until the age of 60 the financial position of a woman taking early retirement on grounds of ill health is comparable to that of a man in the same situation, neither of them as yet entitled to payment of the State pension, that is no longer the case between the ages of 60 and 65 since that is when women, unlike men, start drawing that pension." *Case C-132/92, Birds Eye Walls Ltd. v. Friedel M. Roberts*, para. 20. See also Thiery (2007), at 758-759; De Prins, Sottiaux & Vrielink (2005), at 119; Tobler (2001), at 125-126.

can also prove the incomparability of the cases. Interestingly, this approach can, arguably, also be discovered in the *Brunnhofer* case, concerning which Advocate-General Geelhoed argued in his Opinion that after the establishment of a presumption of discrimination the question would be 'whether the difference in pay also corresponds to a difference in the work done. If there is a difference in pay, this will in principle have to be reflected in different activities. If *no difference in the activities* can be established, however, the pay ought to be the same, *unless* the employer shows that the difference in pay can be *objectively justified*.'[132] Although the criterion of 'equal pay for equal work' might indicate that a comparability test has to be carried out, it can clearly be compared to the somewhat more abstract requirement 'to treat similars similarly'. Thus, similarly to other equal treatment complaints the comparability of the cases can only be a final conclusion and not the argument itself. In this particular case by negating the comparability of the cases the respondent in fact tried to negate the causal link between the harm (lower pay) and the protected ground (gender). For this reason, the AG should have stated that the respondent's real reason for this treatment had to be examined. In order to deny the causal link the respondent could have relied on comparison as a means of evidence in a causatory manner.[133]

Put briefly, the question whether the situations are comparable is not the cause, but the effect of the distinction. The examination of the comparability of the cases requires a value judgment which cannot be made without knowing from which perspective the comparison should be made. Conclusively, as a means of evidence comparing situations can be used by the respondent both for negating any of the causal links and proving that the distinction can be objectively justified.

In summary, the second phase of the assessment is broader than the possibility of objective justification: the respondent might also negate any of the causal relationships, which is the first stage in the refutation phase. Should the respondent not succeed in the negation of the causality, he might try to come up with compelling reasons in order to justify the distinction.

---

[132] Advocate General Geelhoed in *Case C-381/99, Susanna Brunnhofer v. Bank der österreichischen Postsparkasse AG*, [2001] ECR I-04961, para. 18.

[133] From a conceptual or substantive point of view comparison can be used in two respects. First of all, it can be used to establish that there has been a distinction – irrespective of the question which party has relied on the comparison. Since the existence of a distinction means that the causal links are established (i.e. a distinction has been made on the grounds or related to the protected ground of the victim via a particular treatment, provision, criterion or practice) this comparison can be called causatory use of comparison. Comparison as a means of evidence can also be used in order to objectively justify that the distinction is not unlawful. This comparison can be referred to as the justificatory use of comparison. For a detailed discussion of comparison in these two meanings see Busstra (2010).

2.3.2.1. Stage 1: Negation of Causality

As explained above, two main causal links can be identified in the general concept of discrimination, which differ according to the particular concepts of discrimination. Firstly, there is a causal link between the harm and the protected ground. In direct discrimination cases the harm is based on the protected ground. In other words, the reason for causing a harm is the racial or ethnic origin of the victim. In indirect discrimination cases, however, the harm is 'merely' related to the racial or ethnic origin of the victim(s). In other words, it is the effect of a particular measure on a group that establishes this link. Secondly, there is also a causal link between the harm and the treatment, provision, criterion or practice. In the case of direct discrimination this link is generally quite obvious since the treatment is closely linked to the disadvantage (for instance, not admitting someone to a bar is the treatment which caused the harm). As far as indirect discrimination is concerned, however, this link is far from being so obvious. This means that pertaining to direct discrimination it is the negation of the first causal link that can be reasonably invoked, while in indirect discrimination cases it is rather the second causal relationship that could be realistically challenged. The first causal link in indirect discrimination cases cannot be negated for the reason that the question whether a particular measure has a disparate impact on a group is a question of fact and not of presumption.[134] Similarly, in direct discrimination the link between the treatment and the disadvantage also belongs to the facts and is not concerned with the presumption. These factual questions have to be decided in the first phase of the assessment, when with the help of his burden of production the respondent can disprove the facts alleged by the applicant.

Direct discrimination cases become more and more hidden, so perpetrators often try to negate the causal link between the protected ground and the suffered harm (in open direct discrimination cases this possibility is not useful as the treatment in such cases is explicitly related to the protected ground). No examples can be found in the jurisprudence of the ECJ in this respect, but a couple of examples can be detected in the case law of the European Court of Human Rights, where traces of the negation of causality can, arguably, be discovered in the reasoning of the respondent Government. One of these cases is the *Timishev* case in which

[134] Nevertheless it can also be argued that the negation of the disparate impact is not related to the factual circumstances, but it is a question of causation. Should the respondent provide evidence to the opposite what the statistical evidence submitted by the applicant indicates, he attempts to negate the causal link between the harm and the ground. Conceptually, both positions can be accepted. However, the position that the existence of a disparate impact on a particular group belongs to the facts seem more consistent, and for this reason it will be adopted hereafter.

> [t]he Government rejected the applicant's complaint about discrimination as unsubstantiated because the Russian Constitution did not require citizens to make known their ethnic origin and it was not indicated in a person's identity documents,[135]

thus, in the view of the Government, there was no link between the ethnic origin of the applicant and the challenged treatment. Similarly, the Government of the Czech Republic also tried to negate this causal link in the *D.H.* case.[136] According to the Government "the decisions to place the applicants in special schools were neither arbitrary *nor based on the applicants' ethnic origin* [...]."[137] Nevertheless, it is to be admitted that the ECtHR did not recognise this difference in the argumentation of the respective Governments, and did not carry out different reasoning in its judgments concerning these explanations.

In indirect discrimination cases it is the causal relationship between the suffered harm and the particular provision, criterion or practice that the respondent can negate. In the *Enderby* case, for instance, the national court wished

> to know whether the employer can rely as sufficient justification for the difference in pay upon the fact that the rates of pay of the jobs in question were decided by collective bargaining processes which, although carried out by the same parties, are distinct and which, considered separately, have no discriminatory effect.[138]

In order to escape liability, the respondent tried to rely on the fact that the disparate effect could not be linked back to one single source. In other words, he tried to negate the existence of a causal link between the harm and the provision, criterion or practice. According to the ECJ

> the answer to the [...] question is that the fact that the respective rates of pay of two jobs of equal value, one carried out almost exclusively by women and the other predominantly by men, were arrived at by collective bargaining processes which, although carried out by the same parties, are distinct, and,

[135] *Timishev v. Russia*, ECHR (2001) Nos. 55762/00 and 55974/00, 13 December 2005, para. 52. Similarly, the Government tried to negate the causal link between gender and the obligation of jury service in the *Zarb Adami* case as well. It argued that "the difference in treatment depended on a number of factors. In the first place, jurors were chosen from the part of the population which was active in the economy and in the professions. Moreover, [...] an exemption from jury service might be granted to persons who had to take care of their family. Finally, 'for reasons of cultural orientation', defence lawyers might have had a tendency to challenge female jurors." *Zarb Adami v. Malta*, ECHR (2006) No. 17209/02, 20 June 2006, para. 81.

[136] The respondents and the Court argued in terms of indirect discrimination, however, it might be argued that this was rather concerned with (systematic) direct discrimination.

[137] *D.H. and Others v. the Czech Republic*, ECHR (2006) No. 57325/00, 7 February 2006, para. 34.

[138] *Case C-127/92, Dr. Pamela Mary Enderby v. Frenchay Health Authority and Secretary of State for Health*, para. 20.

> taken separately, have in themselves no discriminatory effect, is not sufficient objective justification for the difference in pay between those two jobs.[139]

Conceptually incorrect, the Court examined the respondent's explanation in terms of objective justification and not as the negation of the causal link. However, the arguments of the respondent and the ECJ clearly show that referring to the lack of a causal link between the bargaining processes and the discriminatory effect is markedly different from coming up with compelling reasons (legitimate aims) for the disparate effect.

The fact that fact-finders are not familiar with the concept of negation of the causality as a stage prior to objective justification might cause difficulties in practice. As the *Enderby* case demonstrated, investigating the existence of this link within the framework of objective justification is obviously inappropriate from a conceptual point of view. Also, fact-finders might examine the existence (and not the mere presumption) of this causal link in the first phase of the assessment, which cannot be considered conceptually correct either. Moreover, this latter approach could lead to a higher burden of proof on the applicant or a lenient scrutiny of the respondent's explanation in this respect. For instance, in the *Nachova* case before the Grand Chamber of the ECtHR,[140] the existence/absence of a causal link between the harm and the protected ground was examined in the first phase of the assessment, and resulted in the rejection of a prima facie case of racial discrimination.[141] In actual fact, the ECtHR required the applicant to *prove* the existence of the causal link; accordingly, it should not have used the language of prima facie case of discrimination. This also shows the need that the negation of causality be addressed prior to and separately from the objective justification.

2.3.2.2. Stage 2: Objective Justification[142]

If the respondent cannot prove the lack of causality, he can still come up with an objective justification,[143] which he can use to explain why the distinction

139 *Id.*, para. 23.

140 *Nachova a.o. v. Bulgaria*, para. 157.

141 The Grand Chamber laid down that "where it is alleged [...] that a violent act was motivated by racial prejudice, such an approach would amount to requiring the respondent Government to prove the absence of a particular subjective attitude on the part of the person concerned. [...] The Grand Chamber does not consider that the alleged failure of the authorities to carry out an effective investigation into the alleged racist motive for the killing should shift the burden of proof to the respondent Government" (*id.*, para. 157). Admittedly, the Grand Chamber was mistaken and inconsistent when it argued that it is the lack of investigation which should shift the burden of proof to the respondent, because previously it referred to the racist intent. Thus, arguably, the respondent's negation of the causal link was already decided at the first phase of the assessment.

142 On objective justification see Busstra (2010).

143 For a detailed elaboration of the objective justification test, see Busstra (2010). See inter

in the given case should not be regarded as discrimination. In other words, at this stage it is already accepted that there is a causal link both between the protected ground and the harm and between the treatment, provision, criterion or practice and the harm. Thus, it is proven that a distinction has been made on the grounds of or related to the victim's racial or ethnic origin. The question is now whether the respondent has a compelling reason for making such a distinction; that is whether this distinction can be regarded as lawful.

As hinted at earlier, the burden of proving that there is an objective explanation for the distinction would fall on the respondent on the basis of the general rules on the allocation of the burden of proof, since it is him who states the existence of a legitimate reason. This can be compared with the application of Articles 8-11 of the ECHR, the second paragraphs of which provide the possibility to justify the particular treatment though without any change in the allocation of the burden of proof. More specifically, within the framework of these articles of the ECHR it is for the applicant to prove that there has been an interference with the rights enshrined in these provisions, but the respondent can prove that these interferences are not unlawful because he had legitimate aims which were proportionate to the means for acting this way. Accordingly, the special allocation of the burden of proof solely entails the first phase of the assessment and the negation of the causality, and does not have any consequences with regard to the objective justification. In any event, the model of review based on these special rules also encompasses the stage of objective justification, which clearly fits the model.

The test of objective justification was elaborated in 1986 in the *Bilka-Kaufhaus* case in which the Commission laid down that

> in order to justify such a pay practice […] the employer must […] put forward *objective* […] *grounds* relating to the management of the undertaking. It is also necessary to ascertain whether the pay practice in question is *necessary and in proportion to the objectives* pursued by the employer.[144]

In other words, the respondent has to prove that he had a legitimate aim for making the contested distinction, and the means to achieve this aim was proportionate. This test has been devised with respect to indirect discrimination cases in which the number of possible legitimate aims the respondent can come up with is quasi unlimited. Pursuant to the RED, however, there are only a couple of aims (exceptions) that are acceptable as justification with respect to direct discrimination.[145]

---

alia Gerards (2005a), at 30-57; Gijzen (2006), at 89; De Prins, Sottiaux & Vrielink (2005), at 7-9; Arnardóttir (2003), at 42-51.

[144] Judgment of 13 May 1986 in *Case 170/84, Bilka-Kaufhaus GmbH v. Karin Weber von Hartz*, [1986] ECR 1607, para. 35 (emphasis added).

[145] On objective justification and the exceptions in case of direct discrimination see Busstra (2010).

2.3.2.3. Standard of Proof of the Respondent: No Violation of the Principle of Equal Treatment

In general, the applicable standard of proof of the respondent is formulated in terms of level of scrutiny.[146] Thus, it seems to be reasonable to address the respondent's standard of proof in terms of scrutiny of review, and then translate the applied scrutiny to his concrete standard of proof. Concerning the practice of the ECJ and the ECtHR, different levels of scrutiny have been identified on the basis of the particular intensity they claim to apply and the realization of this particular intensity in the proportionality test.[147]

Theoretically, three different levels of scrutiny have been identified in human rights law: a lenient, an intermediate and a strict intensity of review.[148] The respondent's standard of proof is subsequently low, intermediate or high. Importantly, these levels have been identified pertaining to the objective justification of the respondentin the application of the proportionality test. Nevertheless, the respondent should also prove that the particular causal relationship does not exist in relation to which a marked level of certainty should also be achieved. Accordingly, the respondent's standard of proof has to be examined with respect to both negating the causal link and providing objective justification.

At least three phenomena can be pinpointed that have relevance for the standard of proof of the respondent. First of all, the respondent has to *prove* that he observed the principle of equal treatment. In terms of the first stage of the refutation phase this means that the fact-finder has to be *convinced* that there is *no causal link* between the particular elements. Importantly, in terms of the special allocation of the burden of proof this means that as long as the fact-finder is not persuaded of the absence of the causal relationship its existence should be accepted. It can be seen that the direction of proof has changed:[149] the question to be answered at this stage is whether there is sufficient evidence supporting the *absence of the causal relationship*. In any event, the respondent's arguments in this context have to be thoroughly examined. Similarly, in terms of objective justification the respondent has to prove and not merely indicate that he had an objective aim the achievement of which was proportionate. Secondly, as a general principle of law, exceptions

---

146 Examples for standard of proof arguments concern cases in which it is argued that in the concrete case very weighty reasons have to be put forward.

147 According to Gerards, "[a] clear variation can be seen in the intensity with which the ECJ judges the permissibility of unequal treatment: in certain cases the ECJ seems to perform a very strict assessment, while in other cases it is satisfied with a very marginal test." Gerards (2005a), at 307.

148 Gerards (2005a), at 81.

149 See also Espín (2005), at 3.

always have to be narrowly interpreted.[150] In terms of the RED this would mean that the respondent's reference to any of the justificatory provisions[151] of the Directive has to be strictly scrutinized. Finally, discrimination on the grounds of one's racial or ethnic origin is generally considered to be a grave violation.[152] This also implies that a strict scrutiny has to be applied with

---

[150] See inter alia Linderfalk (2007), at 286; Henrard (2008c), at 192; Jennings & Watts (1992), at 1279; Merrills (1993), at 77., 114. & 116; Vande Lanotte & Haeck (2005), at 184-185. & 190.

[151] These provisions are the following in the RED: objective justification in indirect discrimination cases, genuine and determining occupational requirement and positive action. Arts. 2(2) b), 4 and 5 respectively.

[152] For instance, the Grand Chamber in the *D.H.* case established that taking into consideration "the fundamental importance of the prohibition of racial discrimination", "the notion of objective and reasonable justification must be interpreted as strictly as possible" (*D.H. and Others v. the Czech Republic*, ECHR (2008) No. 57325/00, 13 November 2007, paras. 204. & 196). It can be clearly seen in this case that the gravity of the violation is also influenced by the *protected ground* at stake.

In the European Union racial discrimination is considered to be one of the biggest enemies of a democratic society. The surprisingly quick adoption of this Directive can also be explained by the fact that such discrimination is regarded as deeply condemnable (see inter alia Ellis (2005), at 29; McCrudden (2003), at 11). Furthermore, the Explanatory Memorandum of the Race Directive states that "[t]he fight against racism is a major concern of the international community and has been at the heart of international cooperation in recent decades. Europe's experiences of wars and conflicts throughout the 20th century – and even at its close – have brought to the fore the dangers of racism and the dramatic attacks on human dignity that have ensued. Yet, at the end of the century, racial discrimination is still not eradicated from everyday life in Europe" (Proposal for a Council Directive implementing the principle of equal treatment between persons irrespective of racial or ethnic origin, COM(1999) 566 final, 1999/0253, 25 November 1999, at 2). Moreover, from the perspective of the European Union, "[d]iscrimination based on racial or ethnic origin may undermine the achievement of the objectives of the EC Treaty, in particular the attainment of a high level of employment and of social protection, the raising of the standard of living and quality of life, economic and social cohesion and solidarity. It may also undermine the objective of developing the European Union as an area of freedom, security and justice" (Preamble (9) RED. See also Ellis (2005), at 29). The importance of the fight against racial discrimination is also underlined by the simple fact that a separate directive has been adopted against racial discrimination on the one hand, and several parliamentary resolutions have been adopted in relation to condemning racial discrimination on the other hand.

Without being exhaustive, the following resolutions can be taken as examples: European Parliament resolution of 15 June 2006 on the increase in racist and homophobic violence in Europe; European Parliament resolution on non-discrimination and equal opportunities for all – a framework strategy, 2005/2191(INI); European Parliament legislative resolution of 13 December 2005 on the proposal for a decision of the European Parliament and the Council on the European Year of Equal Opportunities for All (2007) – Towards a Just Society, COM(2005)0225 – C6-0178/2005 – 2005/0107(COD); European Parliament resolution of 8 June 2006 on the protection of minorities and anti-discrimination policies in an enlarged Europe, 2005/2008(INI); European Parliament resolution of 27 January 2005 on remembrance of the Holocaust, anti-Semitism and racism.

respect to the respondent's explanations.[153] Ergo, irrespective of which stage of the refutation is at stake, the respondent's explanation has to be strictly scrutinized resulting in a high standard of proof on the respondent.[154]

2.3.3. Summary of the Two Phases of the Assessment

First, it is the applicant who has to establish a prima facie case of discrimination. This means that the applicant has to give rise to a presumption that a causal link exist both between the harm and the protected ground, and between the harm and the treatment, provision, criterion or practice. Giving rise to the presumption of discrimination can generally be done by using comparison as a means of evidence.

As soon as a prima facie case of discrimination is established, it is for the respondent to prove that no discrimination took place. Within this framework, he first might want to negate the existence of any of the causal links the presumption of which has been established depending on the concept of discrimination at stake. Should the respondent not argue for the lack of causality, he acknowledges that a distinction has been made. The question is then whether this distinction is lawful. To prove that he acted in accordance with the law the respondent can additionally come up with compelling reasons which should be balanced with the concern for equality. Concerning direct discrimination the RED provides a closed list of possible reasons, while in cases of indirect discrimination the list of legitimate aims is open. In both cases, however, a proportionality test has to be carried out in order to establish whether a balance has been achieved.

2.4. Application of the Model of Review to the Concepts of Harassment and Instruction to Discriminate

2.4.1. General Considerations for Harassment and Instruction to Discriminate

Article 8 of the RED establishes that the burden of proof is on the respondent if the applicant establishes facts "from which it may be presumed that there

It has also been argued that there is a hierarchy of protected grounds, with racial or ethnic origin at the top. See for example Fredman (2001b), at 151; Waddington (2000), at 176; Bell (2000), at 80; Wintermute (2000), at 2-3; Schiek (2000), at 9.

153 See also Hunyor (2004); Tobler (2008), at 43.

154 As the concrete examination of the scrutiny of review the fact-finders apply in the studied countries would require a substantive analysis it will not be addressed in the framework of model of review.

has been *direct or indirect* discrimination."[155] This article, thus, seems to indicate that the special rules on the allocation of the burden of proof are only applicable to cases of direct and indirect discrimination, and do not extend to complaints of harassment and instruction to discriminate.

However, not only does Article 8 RED mention the concepts of direct and indirect discrimination, it also stipulates that the special allocation of the burden of proof is to be applied "when persons [...] consider themselves wronged because the *principle of equal treatment* has not been applied to them".[156] Moreover, the respondent's onus of proof is also related to this principle, since he has to prove that there has been no breach of the *principle of equal treatment*. In addition, the concepts of harassment and instruction to discriminate refer back to the general principle of equal treatment in Article 2 (1), which states that 'the principle of equal treatment shall mean that there shall be no direct or indirect discrimination based on racial or ethnic origin.' Accordingly, it can be argued that since cross-references have been formulated for the principle of equal treatment within the concepts of harassment and instruction to discriminate, and no exclusion clause was inserted in the Race Directive as to the non-applicability of Article 8 in such cases, one could conclude that the special allocation of the burden of proof should also be applied when these concepts are at stake.[157]

2.4.2. Concept of Harassment

2.4.2.1. Definition of Harassment[158]

The RED gives the following definition of harassment.

> Harassment shall be deemed to be discrimination within the meaning of paragraph 1, when an unwanted conduct related to racial or ethnic origin takes place with the purpose or effect of violating the dignity of a person and of creating an intimidating, hostile, degrading, humiliating or offensive environment.[159]

In terms of the elements of a discrimination claim, the definition of harassment can be broken down as follows: a) a conduct; b) a harm; c) causal

155 Art. 8 RED (emphasis added).
156 Art. 8 RED (emphasis added).
157 See also Whittle (2002), at 316-317. Importantly, the Recast Directive lays down the same rule for the allocation of the burden of proof; i.e. no conclusions can be drawn from this Directive as regards the applicability of the burden of proof provision to cases of harassment and instruction to discriminate.
158 See Busstra (2010).
159 Art. 2(2) RED.

relationships[160] can be identified both between the conduct and the specified purpose or effect (harm) and between the conduct and the racial or ethnic origin of the victim; and d) finally, there is no reference to comparators being in a comparable situation.[161] As far as the second causal link is concerned, contrary to the concept of indirect discrimination it is the conduct and not the harm that is related to the protected ground. Nevertheless, the conduct is 'merely' related to the racial or ethnic origin and it is not grounded on it. In harassment cases the existence of this link should be accepted if the conduct has anything to do with this ground.[162]

There have been discussions about whether harassment should be fitted into a discrimination paradigm.[163] In the history of the legal application of the concept of harassment it was first in racial harassment cases that harassment was considered to constitute discrimination and only later was the concept extended to sexual harassment cases too. According to a US court, "[o]ne can readily envision working environments so heavily polluted with discrimination as to destroy completely the emotional and psychological stability of minority group workers."[164] If it is accepted that harassment constitutes discrimination, this might imply that there is a need for a comparator being in a comparable situation. This interpretation has indeed been followed by British courts.[165] In their practice harassment is considered to be a less favourable treatment, and a comparator being in a comparable situation is always required. However, the Race Directive does not seem to subscribe to this interpretation. Even if it regulates the concept in the framework of discrimination and equal treatment, it does not require any comparator being in a comparable situation in its definition of harassment.[166]

2.4.2.2. Application of the Model of Review to Harassment

This subsection will examine how the model of review elaborated for direct and indirect discrimination can be adapted to and applied in harassment cases.

---

160 See inter alia Busstra (2010); Gijzen (2006), at 151; Driessen-Reilly & Driessen (2003), at 497; Moon & Allen (2006), at 25-26.

161 Gijzen (2006), at 149.

162 See also Busstra (2010).

163 See for instance Gijzen (2006), at 140; Friedman & Whitman (2003), at 241-274.

164 *Rogers v. EEOC*, 406 U.S. 957 (SC 1972). Cited by Bacik (2003), at 152.

165 Gijzen (2006), at 149-150. *British Telecommunications Plc v. Williams*, IRLR 668 (EAT 1997); *MacDonald v. Advocate General for Scotland, Pearce v. Governing Body of Mayfield Secondary School*, IRLR 512 (HL 2003).

166 Gijzen (2006), at 149. See also Moon & Allen (2006), at 25. According to them this also implies that "[n]o longer will it be a potential defence to a complaint by a woman of sexist language from her boss that the boss uses sexist language to the male employees." In some cases of harassment, some judges in the UK also seemed to depart from their earlier position. See *Smith v. Gardner Merchant Ltd*, IRLR 510 (EAT 1998); *Sidhu v. Aerospace Composite Technology Ltd*, IRLR 602 (CA 2000).

2.4.2.2.1. First Phase of the Assessment: Presumption of Harassment

Similarly to direct or indirect discrimination, in cases concerning harassment the applicant should not give rise only to one of the elements of the concept, but he should establish the presumption of *harassment* related to the victim's racial or ethnic origin. In other words, the presumption that the double causal relationship does exist has to be given rise to.

Although the definition of harassment, as mentioned above, does not stipulate the need of a comparator being in a comparable situation, it does not mean that the applicant could not make use of comparison as a means of evidence in order to establish a prima facie case of harassment. The comparison, similarly to direct and indirect discrimination, aims at showing the relationship with the racial or ethnic origin of the victim. However, in general the conduct in harassment cases is such as from which the link with the protected ground can be inferred. Although the applicant might use comparison to show this link, relying on comparison is in most cases not necessary since direct evidence is generally available. In other words, similarly to open direct discrimination, it is not a mere presumption that the applicant generally establishes, but he in fact proves that harassment has taken place.

In order to be able to give rise to a presumption of harassment, the conduct has to meet to certain requirements, which are related to the creation of an intimidating, hostile, degrading, humiliating or offensive environment. The practice of the UK courts where several harassment cases have already been decided can reasonably serve as points of departures in this respect. In their practice the following features of the conduct have been crystallised. The subjective judgment of the victim has to be taken into account when determining the extent of the offensiveness of the conduct; even a single incident of a serious nature should amount to harassment;[167] generally harassment occurs when there is a series of alleged incidents;[168] the effect of these incidents should not be considered in isolation;[169] and environmental harassment can also be regarded as harassment.[170] In addition to this, Moon and Allen convincingly argued that "[a]ny unwanted conduct which objectively damages the esteem and respect of the complainant should be enough."[171] Taking into account the severe negative effect such conduct can have on a person or a group of persons, these aspects of the conduct should all be taken into account when examining a harassment case. This also means that harassment cases, in fact, are decided in the first phase of the assessment, since, as will be elaborated hereafter, the respondent can hardly negate any of the causal links and can

167 *Bracebridge Engineering Ltd. v. Darby*, IRLR 3 (EAT 1989).
168 *Reed & Bull Information Systems v. Stedman*, IRLR 299 (EAT 1999).
169 *Driskell v. Peninsula Business Services & Others*, IRLR 151 (EAT 2000).
170 *Stewart v. Cleveland Guest*, IRLR 440 (EAT 1994); *Morse v. Future Reality Ltd*, unreported, ET 54571/95 (ET 1996); *Moonsar v. Fiveways Express Transport Ltd*, IRLR 9 (EAT 2005).
171 Moon & Allen (2006), at 26.

never justify such a severe violation. In other words, whether harassment has taken place depends, to a great extent, on how the requirement of the creation of the hostile, etc. environment and the violation of human dignity is interpreted by national fact-finders.

2.4.2.2.2. Second Phase of the Assessment: Refutation

As soon as the applicant has given rise to a presumption of harassment, it is for the respondent to prove that there has been no harassment related to his racial or ethnic origin.

Stage 1: Negation of Causality
Similarly to the general concept of discrimination, as explained above, there are two causal links in harassment cases too: there is a causal link between the conduct and the harm, and between the conduct and the racial or ethnic origin of the victim. At the first stage of the second phase of the assessment the respondent can provide counter-proof for the existence of these causal links. Arguably, the respondent in negating the relation to the protected ground, the respondent can only escape any liability for harassment if he can provide counter-evidence for the other causal link as well; namely if he proves that the conduct did not have the contested purpose, or it was not the conduct that resulted in that particular effect.

Stage 2: Objective Justification
Similarly to the concept of direct discrimination, the definition of harassment does not itself provide for the possibility of an open system of objective justification. Arguably, no legitimate aims can be put forward that might constitute cross-cutting reasons for conduct violating the dignity of a person and creating an intimidating, hostile, degrading, humiliating or offensive environment. This also means that the enumerated exception grounds that can be invoked for justifying direct discrimination would not apply either because they cannot be considered as constituting acceptable explanations for such conduct.[172]

With respect to the liability of the respondent, a special approach has generally been adopted in the Member States.[173] In the field of employment, where harassment most often occurs, there is no direct or strict liability of the harasser, but it is the employer who might be held vicariously liable for a harassing act of any of his employees. Under such circumstances the employer may have an extra opportunity to escape liability. If he has taken reasonable

172 Busstra (2010).
173 Concerning vicarious liability see inter alia Gijzen (2006), at 152; Busstra (2010).

steps to prevent harassment in the workplace, he will not be held liable.[174] UK courts have relevantly explained in this context that it is insufficient if the employer shows that different complaint procedures were available in the workplace, he also has to take preventive steps in order not to be held vicariously liable.[175] Accordingly, in this specific context, if the employer proves that he acted as a 'good employer', his explanation should be regarded as objective justification, since he comes up with compelling reasons why he cannot be held liable. This means that, with the help of the proportionality test, it has to be examined whether he in fact did everything he could or should have done. Such a strict test would force employers to take effective steps for preventing the occurrence of harassment and/or investigate harassment complaints, and punish the harasser. However, from the perspective of the applicant it would be more desirable if Member States would also allow for the direct responsibility of the harasser in employment related cases.

2.4.3. Concept of Instruction to Discriminate

2.4.3.1. Definition of Instruction to Discriminate[176]

The definition of the Race Directive establishes that "*[a]n instruction to discriminate against persons on grounds of racial or ethnic origin shall be deemed to be discrimination within the meaning of paragraph 1.*" This definition refers back to the concept of direct discrimination[177] when it requires that the instruction be on the grounds of racial or ethnic origin, and not merely related to it. Admittedly, the concept of instruction to discriminate is very rarely invoked and applied since in most cases it can be decided on the basis of the concept of direct discrimination.

This definition can also be interpreted in terms of the elements of the concept: a) the instruction constitutes the challenged treatment; b) the discrimination makes up the harm, and c) there is a causal link between the harm and the instruction and between the harm and the protected ground.

---

174 "[I]f the employer controls the situation in which harassment occurs, but fails to exercise that control so as to prevent the harassment from occurring, he or she will be directly liable for having subjected the employee to harassment. The Court observed that liability in such a situation would arise not from the existence of control, but from the failure to properly exercise that control so as to protect the employee against harassment. To hold otherwise, in the Court's view, would be to confuse vicarious liability, which is strict, with direct liability, which requires a casual link between the act or omission of the employer and the harassment suffered by the employee." Bacik (2003), at 164.

175 *Canniffe v. East Riding of Yorkshire Council*, IRLR 555 (EAT 2000).

176 See Busstra (2010).

177 See Busstra (2010).

This latter causal link is interesting because it is exactly the same link as in direct discrimination cases, although due to the link between the harm and the instruction the instruction is also indirectly linked to the protected ground.

Admittedly, no guidance is given in the Race Directive on what constitutes an instruction from which it could be deduced who can rely on this prohibition against whom. Again, some significant conclusions can be drawn from the practice of UK courts in this respect. Inherently, an instruction presupposes a subordinate relationship. It has been argued that "[i]n essence, this prohibition is intended to prevent organizations such as employers, trade unions and professional bodies from discriminating on any of the 'protected ground' through an intermediary."[178] Accordingly, an instruction can be given by someone who is in a higher hierarchical position than the person instructed.

This observation makes us turn to the other party: who can invoke this provision? Again, on the basis of the case law of the United Kingdom[179] it can be convincingly argued that in theory any person who has been instructed to discriminate can rely on this provision, irrespective of whether they possessed the protected ground. In one case, for instance, an employee was dismissed because he did not follow the instruction to exclude blacks from an amusement arcade.[180] The Tribunal held that the conduct constituted racial discrimination against the applicant even though he was a white person.[181] In addition, it could also be envisaged that persons affected or persons who would be affected by this instruction could also be the victims of instruction to discriminate. In general, they rely most of the time on the concept of direct discrimination but if they can provide certain facts that can support the existence of an instruction they should, arguably, also be able to invoke this provision.

2.4.3.2. Application of the Model of Review to Instruction to Discriminate

2.4.3.2.1. First Phase of the Assessment: Presumption of Instruction to Discriminate

Again, the applicant has to give rise to a presumption of instruction to discriminate on the grounds of racial or ethnic origin; it would not suffice if he only shows the existence of any of the constituent elements. Should the applicant be the person being instructed, it is generally not difficult to give rise to a presumption, since in most cases he has evidence of this instruction.

[178] Whittle (2002), at 316.

[179] *Showboat Entertainment Centre Ltd v. Owens*, IRLR 7 (EAT 1984); *Weathersfield Ltd v. Sargent*, IRLR 94 (CA 1999).

[180] *Showboat Entertainment Centre Ltd v. Owens*.

[181] Under a different jurisdiction, this case might have been brought under the concept of direct discrimination, and the protected ground would have been defined as racial or ethnic origin because of association.

(Arguably, his evidence constitutes even more than a mere presumption.) However, if it is the person affected (or who would be affected) by the instruction, he can, arguably, give rise to a presumption in the same way as in a case of direct discrimination; i.e. by using comparison as a means of evidence.

2.4.3.2.2. Second Phase of the Assessment: Refutation

As soon as the applicant has established a prima facie case, it is for the respondent to prove that the principle of equal treatment has been observed.

Stage 1: Negation of Causality
First, the respondent has the possibility to negate any of the two causal links. He might provide evidence that there is no causal link between the instruction and the harm; in other words that the instruction was not aimed at discrimination. He might also negate the causal link between the harm and the protected ground, which at the same time would mean that he has to prove that his instruction was not aimed at discrimination on the grounds of racial or ethnic origin.

Stage 2: Objective Justification
Because of its strong resemblance to direct discrimination, it can be argued that only those grounds of justification can be applied in case of instruction to discrimination that can be invoked in direct discrimination cases. These grounds are: genuine and determining occupational requirement[182] and positive action.[183]

Part B. Case Studies

2.5. Introduction to the Case Studies

None of the examined countries had laid down any explicit rules on the special allocation of the burden of proof in racial discrimination cases pertaining to all fields falling under the material scope of the RED before the implementation of this Directive. Thus, the impact of the RED is visible in the adoption of the special rules.

The Belgian, Estonian and the Dutch provisions come very close to the wording of the RED, and for this reason also to each other. The most divergent definition for the special allocation of the burden of proof is given in Hungary.

---

182 Art. 4 RED.
183 Art. 5 RED.

In Belgium, it was first the ADA that implemented the burden of proof provisions of the RED (and the FD).[184] It stated that,

> When the victim of discrimination or one of the groups referred to in Article 31 produces before the competent court facts, such as statistical data or field trials, that can give rise to the presumption of direct or indirect discrimination, the burden of proof that there has been no discrimination shall fall on the defendant.[185]

In 2007 the ADA was overruled concerning the grounds of so called race, skin colour, descent, or national or ethnic origin by the amendment of the ARA.[186] This Act was also considered to constitute the implementation of the RED,[187] and this aspect was particularly emphasised in relation to the burden of proof provision.[188] This Act stipulates that,

> [w]hen a person who considers him- or herself a victim of discrimination, the Centre or one of the interest organisations establish before a competent court facts from which it can be presumed that there has been discrimination on one of the protected grounds, it shall be for the respondent to prove that there has been no discrimination.[189]

Since this Act is quite recent no case has yet been decided on the basis of it. As this provision is very similar to the rule in the ADA, the case law based on the ADA definition can also give indications to the possible future application of this rule.[190]

---

[184] De Schutter (2004), at 6.

[185] Art. 19(3) ADA.

[186] For the other protected grounds see the Act of 10 May 2007 to combat certain forms of discrimination and the Act of 10 May 2007 to combat discrimination between women and men.

[187] Wetsontwerp tot wijziging van de wet van 30 juli 1981 tot bestraffing van bepaalde door racisme en xenofobie ingegeven daden, 2720/001, 26 October 2006, at 35.

[188] *Id.*.

[189] Ar. 30(1) ARA.

[190] At the federate level some of the federated organs have also implemented this provision of the RED. The recently adopted Decree of the Flemish Parliament of 10 July 2008 pertaining to a framework for the Flemish policy of equal opportunities and equal treatment, which is aimed at the implementation of, amongst others, the RED, follows the respective text of the ARA. Decree of the Flemish Community of 8 May 2002 pertaining to a balanced participation on the labour market stipulates that "[a]nyone who seems to have an interest, can start a procedure before the competent court for the application of the provisions of this Decree. When such a person establishes before this court facts from which it may be presumed that there has been direct or indirect discrimination, the burden of proof that there has been no breach of the principle of equal treatment falls on the defendant." The same definition has been adopted in Decree of the German Community of 17 May 2004 pertaining to guaranteeing equal treatment on the labour market too. A similar definition can also be found in Decree of the Brussels Capital Region of 22 March 2007 pertaining to the equal treatment of persons in vocational training. Finally, Decree of the Walloon Region of 27 May 2004 pertaining to equal treatment concerning employment and vocational training stipulates that "[w]hen the victim of discrimination or his/her representative establish before the competent court facts, such as

The text of the Anti-Discrimination Act followed and the Anti-Racism Act follows the wording of the RED concerning the two-phased approach, namely it is first for the applicant to give rise to the presumption that there has been (direct or indirect) discrimination, and then the burden of proof falls on the respondent to prove that there has been no discrimination.

There were discussions concerning the naming of this distribution of the onus of proof. Arguments were put forward that this allocation rather concerns a sharing between the parties than a reversal of the burden of proof,[191] since, as argued, the applicant also has obligations under the procedure of proving. It was important to stress this since the introduction of this new rule created strong opposition with the argument that the respondent would be condemned of discrimination without the applicant having to prove anything.[192] Notably, the Arbitration Court did not find this special allocation of the burden of proof unreasonable, stating that such a distribution does not happen automatically, since it is first for the applicant to establish certain facts.[193] Thus, the concept of the special allocation of the burden of proof seems to be accepted.[194]

In Estonia, it was the ECA that first implemented the provision on the allocation of the burden of proof.[195] According to this Act,

> Where an *employee* or a *person applying for employment* finds that the employer has unequally treated him or her on the basis of an attribute specified in Article 10 (3), the employee or person applying for employment shall submit to a labour dispute resolution body or to the Legal Chancellor an application containing the facts in proof of the unequal treatment. If on the basis of the application submitted by an employee or a person applying for employment it may be presumed that direct or indirect unequal treatment has occurred, the employer shall be required, at the requires of the labour dispute resolution body or the Legal Chancellor, to explain the reasons for his or her conduct or decision. The refusal by an employer to give explanations shall be deemed to be equal to acknowledgement of unequal treatment.[196]

statistics or situation testing, from which it may be presumed that there has been direct or indirect discrimination, the burden of proof falls on the defendant to prove that there has been no discrimination." The remaining federated organs did not rule on the special allocation of the burden of proof, which might be attributed to the "hesitation concerning the classification of rules relating to the evidentiary burden"; viz. if these rules are procedural of nature the Regions and Communities are not allowed to regulate them. Since these provisions are very similar to the federal legislation, and the burden of proof arrangement in general is considered to be procedural of nature, hereafter, only the federal legislation and the case law based on it will be analysed.

191 Wetsontwerp tot wijziging ..., *supra* note 187, at 63; Cuypers (2003), at 464; De Prins, Sottiaux & Vrielink (2005), at 546.

192 Wetsontwerp tot wijziging van de wet van 30 juli 1981 tot bestraffing van bepaalde door racisme of xenofobie ingegeven daden, 3-2362/3, 24 April 2007, at 54-56.

193 Arbitration Court, 157-2004, B.83.

194 See also Constitutional Court, 17-2009, 12 February 2009, paras. B.91-B.93.6.

195 Poleschuck (2007), at 55.

196 Art. 144[1](1) ECA (emphasis added).

This provision was overruled by the burden of proof provision of the EETA,[197] which stipulates that,

> (1) A person bringing an action to a court or a labour dispute committee in the claim must bring forward facts from which it can be presumed that there has been discrimination.
> (2) The person, against whom the claim has been submitted, must prove in the proceeding that s/he has not infringed the principle of equal treatment. The refusal to prove is deemed to be equal to acknowledgement of discrimination.[198]

It has been argued in relation to the ECA that its definition does not follow the RED, because an 'explanation' of the respondent might require less than proving.[199] And this seems to be even more striking in the light of the obligation of the applicant, who has to establish facts in order to give rise to a presumption. Since no case law can be found where this rule has been applied, the practical consequences of this wording cannot be seen yet.

Contrary to this provision, the EETA seems to be fully in accordance with the RED as far as its text is concerned.[200] Thus, the two-phased approach is accepted in this Act without further clarification of the different stages. The special allocation of the onus of proof is generally referred to as shifting or sharing the burden of proof.[201]

In the Netherlands, the GETA was amended by the Implementation Act on 21 February 2004 in order to implement, amongst others, the special rules on the allocation of the burden of proof which prior to this date did not exist in the Dutch legislation.[202] According to the provision on the burden of proof

> [i]f a person who considers that he has been wronged through discrimination as referred to in this Act establishes before a court facts from which it may be presumed that discrimination has taken place, it shall be for the respondent to prove that the action in question was not in breach of this Act.[203]

In the Netherlands, the provision on the onus of proof follows the text in the RED almost word by word the only difference being that instead of discrimination it talks about distinction. It has been argued several times that

[197] Art. 27(6) EETA.
[198] Art. 8 EETA.
[199] See also Poleshchuk (2007), at 56; Tavits (2004), at 557. This view was also confirmed in an interview with experts in Estonia.
[200] 262 SE-I, Equal Treatment Act, Draft, Explanatory Memorandum, 08 May 2008.
[201] *Id.*; Poleshchuk (2007), at 56; Tavits (2004), at 557.
[202] Wet van 21 februari 2004 tot wijziging van de Algemene wet gelijke behandeling en enkele andere wetten ter uitvoering van richtlijn nr. 2000/43/EG en richtlijn nr. 2000/78/EG (EG-implementatiewet Awgb). Contrary to the Hungarian provision, it was the amendment of the GETA that implemented the RED and it did not have any provision on the special allocation of the burden of proof before this amendment. Accordingly, it is not necessary to examine the Act before the amendment.
[203] Art. 10 GETA.

the word discrimination does not fit in with the Dutch system.[204] One of these arguments was based on the justifiability of distinction which cannot be held for discrimination. In general, however, it can be concluded that unlawful distinction is used in the same meaning as discrimination.

As mentioned above, although it was the Implementation Act in 2004 which implemented the provision on the special distribution of the burden of proof, the ETC has applied this rule since 1994, and more firmly and consistently since the adoption of the RED in 2000.[205] This is even more remarkable in view of the fact that the ETC is not obliged to apply this provision. Here also, this special distribution of the onus of proof is generally referred to as sharing or shifting the burden of proof.

Last but not least, in Hungary it was the HETA in 2003 that aimed to implement Article 8 RED. This provision has in the meantime been amended as of 1 January 2007, supposedly because the European Commission did not accept these provisions as being in accordance with the RED.[206] In the words of the original version of the HETA:

> (1) In procedures initiated because of a violation of the principle of equal treatment, the injured party or the party entitled to assert claims of public interest *must prove* that
> a) the injured person or group has suffered a disadvantage, and
> b) the injured party or group possesses characteristics defined in Article 8.
> (2) If the case describe in Paragraph (1) has been proven, the other party shall prove that
> a) it has observed or

[204] See inter alia Gerards (2006), at 301-302; Holtmaat (2003); Vrielink (2003b); De Fey, Kellermann & Nieuwbroer (2004), at 151; Waaldijk & Bonini-Baraldi (2004), at 351; Wijziging van de Algemeen wet gelijke behandeling, het Burgerlijk Wetboek, de Wet gelijke behandeling op grond van handicap of chronische ziekte, de Wet gelijke behandeling op grond van leeftijd bij de arbeid en de Wet gelijke behandeling van mannen en vrouwen (aanpassing definities van direct en indirect onderscheid aan richtlijnterminologie), Advies Raad van State en nader rapport, 31 832, No. 4, 2009, at 2-3. & 5.

[205] Gerards (2003), at 78; Wijziging van de Awgb en enkele andere wetten ter uitvoering van richtlijn nummer 2000/43/EG en richtlijn 2000/78/EG (EG-implementatitewet Awgb), Nota naar aanleiding van het verslag, 28 770, Nr. 5, 22 May 2003, at 34; Houtzager & Bochhah (2004), at 272-278; Woltjer (2002), at 16; Rodrigues (2003), at 16; De Fey, Kellermann & Nieuwbroer (2004), at 40-41. & 150-152; Waaldijk & Bonini-Baraldi (2004), at 370.

[206] See the Explanatory Memorandum of the amendment to the HETA, which explains that the amendment aimed to react to the opinion of the European Commission concerning certain provisions on the one hand and to find answers to problems that occurred in practice on the other. Moreover, the European Commission gave a short list of problems that were mentioned in its reasoned opinion for a country that was found not having properly implemented the RED, where in relation to Hungary it mentions the "incorrect definition of the obligation concerning the shift of the burden of proof." 2006. évi CIV. Törvény indokolása az egyenlő bánásmódról és az esélyegyenlőség előmozdításáról szóló 2003. évi CXXV. Törvény módosításáról.

> b) in respect of the relevant relationship was not obliged to observe the principle of equal treatment.[207]

This text has been amended as follows:

> (1) In procedures initiated because of a violation of the principle of equal treatment, the injured party or the party entitled to an actio popularis *must render it probable* that
> a) the injured person or group has suffered a disadvantage, or in the case of an actio popularis, there is a direct danger of such a disadvantage, and
> b) the injured party or group – actually or as assumed by the offending party – possessed any of the characteristics defined in Article 8 at the time of the violation of law.
> (2) If the case described in Paragraph (1) has been rendered probable, the other party shall prove that
> a) *the circumstances rendered probable* by the injured party or by the entity entitled to an actio popularis *did not prevail*, or
> b) he/she/it did observe the principle of equal treatment, or that he/she/it was not obliged to observe the principle of equal treatment in respect of the relevant relationship.[208]

Prior to the HETA, the Labour Code also contained a provision on the special allocation of the burden of proof as an implementation of the Burden of Proof Directive. It laid down that in the case of a debate concerning how the employer had been treated, it was for the respondent to prove that he did not violate the provisions prohibiting the principle of equal treatment. Although this provision was only relied on in a couple of cases, still the burden of proof rules did not have to break entirely new ground.

The Hungarian provision on the burden of proof also divides the procedure of evidence law into two phases. Interestingly, however, in the first phase of the assessment the establishment of a presumption of discrimination is not required. The applicant has to make two elements plausible, and then it is for the respondent to prove that he has observed or was not obliged to observe the principle of equal treatment. At present,[209] this special allocation is, in general,[210] referred to as sharing of the burden of proof.[211]

---

207 Art. 19 HETA before the amendment (emphasis added).

208 Art. 19 HETA (emphasis added).

209 Similarly to the international theoretical developments, in Hungary it can also be observed that earlier it was called the reversal of the burden of proof. Kádár (2001), at 10; BH 2004. 255; Farkas, Kádár & Kárpáti (2003), at 124.

210 At present, one can still observe references to the reversal of the burden of proof. Vékás (2006), at 363; Gyulavári (2007), at 51.

211 Bitskey & Gyulaváry (2004), at 73; Farkas, Kádár & Kárpáti (2006), at 93; Position No. 10.117/1/2006 TT of the Advisory Board of Equal Treatment on the division of the burden of proof, 13 January 2006; Position No. 384/4/2008. (III.28.) TT of the Advisory Board of Equal Treatment on the division of the burden of proof, 28 March 2008.

Admittedly, the idea of the special allocation of the burden of proof was not welcomed by everyone. Counter-arguments, based on autonomy in private law[212] and presumption of innocence in criminal law,[213] were brought up. Currently, however, the concept in general seems to be accepted.

Following this short introduction concerning the relevant regulations in the countries under review, the national procedures, in which the special allocation of the burden of proof has to or can be applied, will be mapped. Thereafter the application of the model of review will be analysed, broken down to the two identified phases and supplemented with the relevant case law in the countries. This examination will be followed by an elaboration on the application of the model of review in cases of harassment and instruction to discriminate in the countries under review.

2.6. Procedures with the Special Allocation of the Burden of Proof

Importantly, all countries allow for the application of rules concerning the special allocation of the burden of proof in civil court procedures. With the exception of Estonia, these special rules are also generally applicable in administrative procedures. These special rules are also to be employed in procedures involving interest organisations. Besides this, with the exception of the Estonian[214] and Belgian[215] ones, the national specialised bodies in Hungary and the Netherlands respectively must and can allocate the burden of proof of the parties in accordance with the special rules.

In Belgium the special allocation of the burden of proof must be applied in all court procedures, with the exception of criminal procedures.[216]

212 Vékás (2006), at 363.

213 Zlinszky (2003), at 136.

214 Art. 8(1) EETA.

215 The national specialised body in Belgium is not a fact-finding body. The CEOOR does not issue either binding or non-binding opinions pertaining to the question whether discrimination has taken place; it 'merely' assists victims in submitting their complaint.

216 Art. 29 ARA. Similar regulation can be found in Art. 14 DFIC1 and in Art. 18 DGC, with an extra exception for cases where more advantageous rules concerning the burden of proof are to be applied. Contradictorily, the DFIC1 does not indicate for whom the burden of proof rules should be more advantageous; and the Dutch version of the DGC stipulates that these rules should be more advantageous to the defendant. This solution in the DGC seems to be a translation mistake, since the French and the German texts refer to the applicant. Furthermore, the DFIC1 has to be interpreted in accordance with the RED; accordingly the rules should be more advantageous to the applicant. Finally, the rule on the special allocation of the burden of proof in the DWR is placed among the civil law provisions, thus, it stipulates that this rule is only applicable in civil procedures.

In Estonia the special rules on the burden of proof are also applicable in the proceedings of courts and labour dispute resolution commissions,[217] but these rules are not applicable in administrative procedures.[218] Prior to the adoption of the EETA in the case of alleged discrimination on the grounds of race it was only possible to start a procedure under labour relations on the basis of the ECA. Pursuant to the ECA, the special rules were to be employed in the procedures of labour dispute resolution bodies (i.e. labour courts and labour resolution commissions) and in the procedures of the Legal Chancellor when it resolved discrimination disputes.[219] As a result of the adoption of the EETA, the Legal Chancellor is no longer obliged to apply the special rules pertaining to the allocation of the burden of proof either in its ombudsman or in conciliation procedures, even though it is mentioned as a body to which parties can turn to for conciliation.[220] Concerning the ombudsman procedure the reason for the lack of obligation of applying the burden of proof arrangement might be that it is the Chancellor himself who investigates the case. In conciliation procedures the aim is to reach an agreement between the parties and not to investigate what has exactly happened.[221] Thus, there is in fact no need for any burden of proof arrangement. Interestingly, however, the Legal Chancellor still seems to apply the special allocation of the burden of proof even in the lack of explicit provisions authorizing him to do so. In a case submitted to him for conciliation, he refused to start the procedure because it 'did not appear' from the application that there might have been discrimination.[222] It seems that the concept of a prima facie discrimination was used as a certain admissibility test. The Act does not extend the applicability of the burden of proof provision to the procedure of the Equal Treatment Commissioner either, most likely because s/he cannot issue binding opinions. This was, however, criticised by the present Gender Equality Commissioner, since she can now rely on this provision in order to make respondents co-operate in her procedure; that is it gives her more authority and power.[223] More specifically, the text of this provision stipulates that the respondent's refusal would be taken as an admission that he has discriminated against the applicant. Arguably, in terms of effective enforcement it would be more advantageous if the burden of proof regulation would be extended to the procedures of the Commissioner as well.

In Hungary, the special allocation of the burden of proof should be applied in many procedures, with the exception of criminal procedures and procedures

217 Art. 8(1) EETA.
218 Art. 8(3) EETA.
219 Ex-Art. 1441 (2) ECA. This article of the ECA has been repealed by the adoption of the EETA. See Art. 27(6) EETA.
220 Art. 23 EETA.
221 See also Poleshchuk (2007).
222 Õiguskantsleri 2006. aasta tegevuse ülevaade, Tallinn 2007, at 393.
223 This view was confirmed in an interview with one of the experts in Estonia.

of minor offences.[224] Accordingly, the special rules should also be applied in all administrative procedures, which is important in the light of the fact that there are several administrative instances proceeding on the basis of administrative law that can also deal with discrimination claims. These special rules should, thus, also be applied by the Authority on Equal Treatment, which is an administrative organ.[225] Moreover, it is explicitly stipulated that this provision can be applied in procedures in which interest groups are involved.[226] This approach is fully in accordance with the RED and the principle of effective enforcement. It has, nevertheless, been argued that it is in fact unnecessary to apply the special allocation of the burden of proof in the procedure of the Authority, since the Authority has to investigate the facts itself.[227] Arguably, the prima facie phase can, however, be regarded as a certain admissibility test on the basis of which the Authority could examine whether it is necessary to start a procedure. The obligation on the respondent in the second phase makes the investigation by the Authority easier, since it is in the interest of the respondent to try to explain why the principle of equal treatment has not been violated in the specific case.

In the Netherlands, the rule on the burden of proof is applicable in civil and administrative procedures. Enforcement of the principle of equal treatment, however, is not typical in administrative procedures. As the ETC does not give binding opinions, it is not obliged to apply these special rules; however, it does, and even before the implementation of the RED did so. In this way it creates good precedent on its application.[228]

2.7. Standard of Proof of the Applicant

With the exception of the legislative provision on the burden of proof in the Hungarian Equal Treatment Act the applicant's standard of proof is the level of presumption in the examined countries. In Hungary, the original text of the Equal Treatment Act laid down that the applicant has to prove the existence of a real or presumed protected ground and a 'disadvantage'. The word *'prove'* in this provision was criticised by the European Commission, and this term was therefore amended to '*showing the likeliness of*'. This means that at present the applicant has to give rise to a presumption of the existence of a real or

224 Art. 19(3) HETA.

225 It will be discussed in Chapter 8 on specialised bodies whether it is necessary for a body having investigative power to apply the special allocation of the burden of proof.

226 Art. 19 HETA.

227 See also Kádár (2006), at 122-123.

228 See inter alia Gerards (2003), at 78; Wijziging van de Awgb ..., *supra* note 187, at 34; Houtzager & Bochhah (2004), at 272-278; Woltjer (2002), at 16; Rodrigues (2003), at 16; De Fey, Kellermann & Nieuwbroer (2004), at 150-152; Waaldijk & Bonini-Baraldi (2004), at 370; Opinion 1997-50 ETC.

presumed protected ground and a harm. In other words, neither the original nor the amended text of the HETA explicitly requires the establishment of a *presumption of discrimination*. In fact both the original provision and the present text merely require that the applicant has to establish to a particular standard of proof the existence of two separate *facts*. Nevertheless, it has been argued that this provision is not contrary to the Directive since it is more favourable to the victims/applicants[229] than Article 8 RED.[230] Although this approach might at first sight further facilitate the applicant's position, neither from a conceptual nor from a practical point of view can the applicant's burden of proof in the HETA be considered appropriate. Conceptually, this approach upsets the whole model of review, since as far as there is no presumption of discrimination the respondent has nothing to refute except for the factual circumstances, but pursuant to the model of review this should take place in the first phase, and not in the second phase of the assessment. Moreover, if in practice the respondent is still required to prove that there has been no discrimination, this obligation might result in a very high burden of proof on him. Contrary to this, the applicant's overly alleviated burden of proof carries the danger that, in the absence of any indications for the occurrence of discrimination, the respondent's arguments will also be easily accepted, resulting in dismissing the applicant's complaint.

However, unlike its literal meaning, this provision could also be interpreted in a way which would conceptually satisfy the RED. Namely, the word 'disadvantage' in the provision could be interpreted as 'discrimination' or 'disadvantageous treatment'. Pursuant to this interpretation, the applicant should show the likeliness of the occurrence of disadvantageous treatment, which is exactly the same as the presumption of discrimination.[231] Remarkably, in its second position paper on the allocation of the burden of proof, the ABET added that the applicant has to assign a comparator in relation to whom he has suffered a harm.[232] Thus this view, albeit implicitly, supports the argument that the applicant in fact needs to establish a presumption of *discrimination* (and not of a harm), since it highlights the importance of comparison[233] which is only relevant for the establishment of discrimination but not for that of the harm.

[229] Pursuant to Art. 8(2) RED "[p]aragraph 1 shall not prevent Member States from introducing rules of evidence which are more favourable to plaintiffs."

[230] Kádár (2006), at 118.

[231] This would also mean that a consistent approach would be followed in terms of the interpretation of 'harm'. At present the Authority's reading of this term shifts from an additional harm to the distinction to accepting the alleged existence of a distinction made.

[232] Position No. 384/4/2008. (III.28.) TT of the Advisory Board of Equal Treatment on the division of the burden of proof, 28 March 2008.

[233] Importantly, an example can be found in which the disadvantage seems to have been interpreted as referring to the presumption of discrimination. For instance, in a case concerning

Notwithstanding this possibility, the Advisory Board to the Authority on Equal Treatment followed the literal interpretation of the Act in its position paper on the allocation of the burden of proof in discrimination cases. It argued that the applicant cannot be required to prove any link between two facts.[234] This approach of the ABET seems to have been formulated as a reaction to the first cases of the AET in which it placed the onus of proving the causal link on the applicant, and did not accept the whole concept of presumption.[235] For instance, in one case the applicant of Roma origin telephoned a potential employer at the House of Equal Chances.[236] Importantly, the applicant had an accent and name typical for a Roma person. The employer informed her that the position concerned had already been filled. Shortly after this conversation, a non-Roma employee of the House also called this employer, and she was told that the position was still available. This was a clear example of covert direct discrimination, the presumption of which has, arguably, been established with the help of situation testing. However, in the view of the Authority no causal link could be found between the Roma origin of the applicant and the false information she was given. In other words, the Authority expected the applicant to carry the burden of persuasion, and it did not accept the concept of presumption.

As a result of the position paper of the Advisory Board the Authority changed its approach to the allocation of the burden of proof, and at present it claims to apply the literal interpretation of the burden of proof provision of the Act. Strikingly, with the amendment of the applicant's burden of proof, no remodelling can be discovered in the application of the rules. In other words, it does not seem that the applicant's burden of proof has been alleviated by amending the requirement of 'proving' to 'showing' the likeliness of those two separate facts. However, in practice it seems that it is generally a presumption of discrimination that needs to be or that is established by the applicants, and not only the existence of two separate facts. For instance, in one case a group of Roma persons were prevented from entering a discotheque while other non-Roma persons were allowed to enter.[237] Although the Authority stated that the applicants showed that they belong to the Roma minority and that they were prevented from entering, as required by the HETA, in fact it was a presumption of discrimination that they established.

the dismissal of Roma cleaners, the Authority established that the disadvantage at stake was the applicants' dismissal on the grounds of their ethnic origin. EBH/346/31/2007.

[234] Position No. 10.117/1/2006 TT of the Advisory Board of Equal Treatment on the division of the burden of proof, 13 January 2006.

[235] See three cases from 2005 on the grounds of ethnic origin (no reference numbers for the cases are given on the website of the Authority from this period). All three cases concerned Roma applicants, and could be classified as hidden direct discrimination. www.egyenlobanasmod.hu.

[236] Case from 2005 (without reference number). www.egyenlobanasmod.hu.

[237] EBH/58/2006.

It seems, however, that neither the concept of presumption nor the wording of the HETA has been uniformly applied by fact-finders. In a couple of cases it can be discovered that rejection of the complaints was based on the fact that the courts were not aware of the concept of presumption and placed a higher standard of proof on the applicant. For instance, in one case an applicant of Roma origin applied for a job, but later in the application process was refused.[238] The applicant explained that he was told on the telephone that the assumption that his Roma origin was the reason of his refusal was close to reality. Nevertheless, the respondent argued that the refusal was based on their halt on openings, which argument was supported with documentary evidence. In the interpretation of the court the applicant did not fulfil his burden of proof because he should have proven that the harm suffered correlated to his ethnic origin.[239] This was clearly a higher standard of proof than a 'mere' presumption.

In Belgium the ADA stipulated, and the ARA stipulates, that it is a presumption of discrimination that has to be established by the applicant in order to place the burden of persuasion on the respondent. However, the concept itself does not seem to be acceptable to everyone.[240] For instance, it has been argued in relation to the elimination method,[241] which has been exemplified as a possible form of proof of discrimination in the ARA, that it constitutes a very low threshold of proof, and according to the Council of State it should not be applied in contexts other than equal pay. Remarkably, this argument has not been uttered in relation to the other acknowledged method of proof in direct discrimination cases, namely the pattern method.[242] It might be concluded that in cases concerned with the elimination method,

[238] Pécs Labour Court, 3.M.615/2006/16, 13 September 2007. See also Fehér Füzet 2007. A Nemzeti és Etnikai Kisebbségi Jogvédő Iroda beszámolója, Másság Alapítvány 2008, at 15-16.

[239] One could argue, though, that in fact the court did apply the concept of presumption of discrimination, it was only their statement in this respect that has not been properly formulated. From this perspective the respondent's argument could be regarded as the negation of causality.

[240] It has been alleged, for instance, that it violates the right to fair trial. Constitutional Court, 19-2009, 12 February 2009.

[241] This method means that, in the case of covert discrimination, in the field of equal pay the applicant should only show that unequal pay is given to those in a comparable situation. Based on the fact that the situations are very similar, all other factors that could have played in the system of pay would be eliminated. Accordingly, this can also be referred to as a 'but for' test. This can, arguably, include both statistics and situation testing; however, it seems that both in the theoretical works and in the *travaux préparatoires* it is only meant to refer to situation testing in the context of direct discrimination. Thiery (2007), at 757-758; Wetsontwerp tot wijziging ..., *supra* note 204, at 75.

[242] Again, it has not been made clear which concrete forms of proof can be deemed to show a certain pattern, but arguably, both statistics and situation testing are able to show systemic discrimination of a certain group. Thiery (2007), at 757.

fact-finders might be reluctant to come to the conclusion from the submitted facts that there is a presumption of discrimination, and in doing so there is a risk to impose a higher standard of proof.

The case law on the ADA on the grounds of racial or ethnic origin seems to indicate that to some extent the hesitation of the Council of State is also shared by some fact-finders. For instance, in a case concerning an application for a job, the applicant was refused because the vacancy was allegedly filled. However, it became clear from another telephone call that the vacancy was still open when the interested person did not have a foreign name and accent.[243] According to the court, in order to apply the special allocation of the burden of proof,[244] the presumptions have to be sufficiently strong and pertinent; otherwise the general rules of proof will be applied. In this particular case it was found that the phone calls in themselves were insufficient to place the burden of proof on the respondent. The level of scrutiny applied by the court was clearly very strict, and the standard of proof was set quite high. The uncertainty surrounding what actually is the applicant's standard of proof in discrimination cases can also be noticed in the *Feryn* case, pertaining to which the court of appeal referred a couple of questions, among which questions related to the allocation of the burden of proof, to the European Court of Justice for preliminary ruling. The court of appeal posed the following questions, relevant from the perspective of the standard of proof,

> [w]hat is to be understood by facts from which it may be presumed that there has been direct or indirect discrimination within the terms of Article 8(1) of the Directive? *How strict* must a national court be in assessing facts which give rise to a presumption of discrimination?[245]

Although the questions seem to have been formulated in terms of the factual circumstances, they are also clearly oriented at the standard of proof which the applicant has to satisfy. In other cases concerning racial or ethnic origin, it is difficult to say which standard of proof was required from the applicant since in those cases either the respondent admitted[246] that he made a distinction on this particular ground or he could not reasonably deny it.[247]

As mentioned, in Estonia, before the adoption of the EETA, special rules for the enforcement of the prohibition of discrimination were laid down in employment relations only in the Employment Contract Act. This Act required

243 Mechelen Labour Court, summary-like proceedings, 16 March 2006.

244 *Id.*, 5.2.2. The terminus used by the court to refer to the special allocation of the burden of proof seems to indicate their stance to the standard of proof. They described this burden of proof rule as 'reversal of the burden of proof'.

245 Reference for a preliminary ruling of 6 February 2007 in *Case C-54/07*, *Centrum voor gelijkheid van kansen en voor racismebestrijding v. NV Firma Feryn*, 2007/C 82/39 (emphasis added).

246 Antwerp Correctional Court, 7 December 2004.

247 *CGKR and C. Murat v. D. Yves and E-L. BVBA*, Gent Labour Court, summary proceedings, no. 176.893, 26 March 2007.

the applicant to submit facts to prove discrimination, which was argued to mean that it was for the applicant to make out his case.[248] However, the second sentence of this provision clarified that the applicant does not need to prove that discrimination happened; he merely had to prove the facts from which it could be presumed that there had been discrimination. Accordingly, this provision was in conformity with the standard set by the RED. Since this provision has never been applied in practice, it cannot be determined how it was interpreted by fact-finders. Nevertheless, the EETA did not copy the phrasing of the ECA, but opted for a wording that closely follows that of Article 8 RED. It stipulates that the applicant should bring forward factual circumstances from which it can be presumed that discrimination has taken place. In the absence of case law, it is, however, difficult to say whether the concept of presumption is accepted in practice or not. The only relevant case so far was decided by the Gender Equality Commissioner on the basis of the GEA, the burden of proof provision of which is similar to that of the EETA. This case concerned unequal treatment in recruitment. Although only a summary of the case is accessible, it seems that the Commissioner does accept the concept of presumption.[249] In this case, a woman argued that she was discriminated against on the grounds of her gender when the job she applied for was given to a male candidate being less qualified than she was. These facts gave rise to a presumption, and the Commissioner called for the respondent to explain this treatment. The Legal Chancellor also seems to accept and apply this concept. In one case, for instance, he seemed to rely on the special allocation of the burden of proof when he refused a request for conciliation procedure.[250] In his view one could not conclude from the facts submitted by the applicant that there *discrimination might have taken place*. Accordingly, he argued in terms of the lack of a presumption of discrimination. In other words, the applicant did not even meet his facilitated standard of proof as he could not establish a prima facie case of discrimination.

In the Netherlands, not only does the relevant provision of the GETA closely follow Article 8 RED, but the concept of presumption is also systematically and consistently applied in the practice. For instance, in one case a woman applied for a position as teacher in an Islamic school.[251] During the application procedure it became clear that the parents of the students would prefer a teacher with an Islamic background, which was discussed with the applicant when she was refused with a reference to her Christian background. These

[248] Art. 144[1] ECA.

[249] A woman with a child applied for a job, but it was given to a man without child. The woman had better qualification also in terms of education and experience. Retrieved from www.svv.ee.

[250] In the yearly report of the Legal Chancellor only a short description is given on the case from which neither the facts nor the approach of the Legal Chancellor can be precisely discerned. Õiguskantsleri 2006. aasta tegevuse ülevaade, Tallinn 2007, at 393.

[251] Opinion 2004-160 ETC. See also inter alia Opinions 2003-76, 2003-119, 2006-124, 2006-219 ETC.

facts were appropriate for the Commission to come to the conclusion that there was a presumption of discrimination on the grounds of religion. It can be seen that the applicant did not have to *prove* that her refusal was based on her religion; it was satisfactory that the presumption of this causal link was established.

As far as the *Danfoss*-formula is concerned, it is only the Equal Treatment Commission in the Netherlands that explicitly refers to and applies this concept. The ETC accepts the existence of a prima facie case of discrimination if the challenged system of the respondent is not transparent, systematic and controllable. For instance, in one case an applicant complained of not being ranked in accordance with his function.[252] The Commission concluded, with reference to the *Danfoss* case, that, due to the fact that the salary system applied by the respondent was not transparent, systematic and controllable, the applicant complied with his standard of proof. In another case the applicants with a certain racial or ethnic group were refused entry to a discotheque, while another group was easily admitted. Importantly, these facts were recounted by the applicants, so it could not be regarded as situation testing. The Commission in this case accepted the existence of a prima facie case of discrimination, arguing that the respondent's system was not transparent, systematic and controllable.[253] Due to the application of the *Danfoss*-formula, a costly situation testing was not necessary.

The Commission has lowered the applicant's standard of proof also if his inability to substantiate his claim with facts is attributable to the non-cooperative attitude of the respondent.[254] Arguably, this kind of reasoning can also be regarded as the application of the *Danfoss*-formula, since in fact it is the respondent's 'system' that is again not transparent. Hence, the ETC takes into consideration both the positive obligations of the respondent, and the weaker position of the applicant in obtaining evidence.

The *Danfoss*-formula has not yet been applied in the three other countries, although some traces of this concept can be discovered in the Estonian Equal Treatment Act. The EETA imposes an additional obligation on the respondent concerning the allocation of the burden of proof. When suspected of having committed discrimination, the respondent is obliged to explain how he treated the person who alleges to have been discriminated against.[255] Pursuant to the Explanatory Memorandum of the EETA, the introduction of this provision was vital

> [s]ince in discrimination cases the victim is generally in a worse position compared to his/her opponent, having above all regard to access to the necessary information for the submission of prima facie application with justified

252 Opinion 2003-151 ETC. See also inter alia Opinions 2003-05, 2003-18, 2003-153 ETC.
253 See also Opinions 2003-151, 2003-18, 2004-49 ETC.
254 Opinions 2003-05, 2003-153 ETC; Rodrigues (2004), at 25-26.
255 Art. 7 EETA.

> suspicion. Therefore, the obligation of the opponent to give explanations needs to be provided for. Otherwise the purpose of the Act to offer protection to the persons suffered from discrimination will not be realized sufficiently, as without the necessary evidence a person cannot appeal to the relevant institutions for the protection of his/her rights.[256]

Here it is clear that this obligation of the respondent is related to the factual circumstances of the case in the first phase and not concerned with the second phase of the assessment as the word 'explanation' might have indicated.[257] From this angle, this provision can be regarded as the legal implementation of the *Danfoss*-formula. In other words, if the applicant cannot provide evidence because of the lack of transparency, it is for the respondent to explain the factual circumstances. However, the question can still be posed: when is someone suspected of discrimination, and what facts have to be submitted by the applicant in order to be able to rely on this provision?

In Belgium, the fact that in discrimination cases even the normal standard of proof of the applicant cannot be regarded as generally accepted indicates that fact-finders, even though the academic literature emphasizes its importance,[258] would not be very keen on accepting an even lower standard.

Finally, in Hungary there has not yet been a case in which the *Danfoss*-formula was at stake. It is therefore difficult to say whether such an argument would be accepted. Departing from the relevant text of the HETA, it seems unlikely that fact-finders would be open to further 'disburdening' the applicant.

As yet, in neither of these countries can any effect of the particular protected ground on the standard of proof of the applicant be spotted. In other words, the establishment of a presumption of discrimination (or the establishment of two separate facts pursuant to the Hungarian approach) is expected from the applicant, irrespective of the characteristic on the ground of or related to which he was allegedly discriminated against.

2.8. First Phase of the Assessment

As explained supra, the concept of presumption seems generally accepted in the countries under review, with the exception of Hungary. In this country the application of this concept does not go smoothly despite the fact that the HETA itself imposes a less onerous standard of proof than the establishment of a presumption. Still, as illustrated, in Hungary it is in fact a presumption of discrimination that is generally established by the applicants and not merely

[256] 262 SE-I, Equal Treatment Act, Draft, Explanatory Memorandum, 8 May 2008.

[257] This view was confirmed in an interview with experts in Estonia.

[258] Thiery (2007), at 758; Wetsontwerp tot wijziging ..., *supra* note 187, at 63.

the existence of two separate facts.[259] The complication seems to be rooted in the application of the concept of presumption to cases where it is the disparate impact on a certain group that should give rise to a presumption. Fact-finders in these cases tend to look for the intent and/or active stance of the respondent to treat the person differently. In other words, the different concepts of discrimination do not seem to be combined with the burden of proof provision. For instance, in the view of the first instance court in the Miskolc segregation case there was no presumption of discrimination because the applicant did not prove that the disadvantage could be attributed to a particular activity of the applicant with the intent to segregate.[260] The same dilemma can be explored in the Hajdúhadház segregation case before the court of appeal.[261] Accordingly, no distinction has been made between direct and indirect discrimination concerning the prima facie case of discrimination, which led to the refusal of the complaint of indirect discrimination. This clearly shows that there are uncertainties concerning how to establish a prima facie case, which test should be applied which hesitations can also be attributed to the problematic wording of the relevant provision of the HETA.

In Belgium, it is generally acknowledged that there are in practice many problems concerning what constitutes a prima facie case of discrimination.[262]

---

259 In terms of the present text of the HETA on the allocation of the burden of proof the requirement to prove/show the likeliness that the victim actually or assumed by the respondent possessed one of (or more) protected characteristic has led to discussions how to prove/show it, see inter alia Bitskey & Gyulavári (2004); Beszámoló a Nemzeti és Etnikai Kisebbségi Jogok Országgyűlési Biztosának tevékenységéről, Nemzeti és Etnikai Kisebbségi Jogok Országgyűlési Biztosa 2005, at 227; A kisebbségi önkormányzatok kézikönyve, Nemzeti és Etnikai Kisebbségi Jogok Országgyűlési Biztosa 2006, at 147. & 161. It was argued that when the protected ground is clearly visible (for this position see inter alia EBH/346/31/2007) the respondent no longer argue that he was not aware of the racial or ethnic origin of the applicant (Position No. 2/2007 (III.23) TT of the Advisory Board of Equal Treatment on segregation in public education, 23 March 2007). It therefore seems that it is mainly the real characteristic that is and would be shown to the fact-finders, or in a couple of cases a ground by association (see inter alia EBH/72/7/2008). Importantly, however, first of all distinction should be made as to which concept of discrimination is at stake. In direct discrimination cases the question is rather what the respondent's perception could have been, and what could have been the assumed characteristic of the applicant. In indirect discrimination cases it is rather the real protected ground of the victims that plays a role, since in these cases the respondent was not aware of the possible negative consequences of its measure on that particular group, and there is accordingly no need to show his perception.

260 Borsod-Abaúj-Zemplén County Court, 13.P.21.660/2005/16, 2 November 2005.

261 Debrecen Court of Appeal, Pf.I.20.361/2007/8, 13 December 2007.

262 Wetsontwerp tot wijziging ..., *supra* note 187, at 142. See also Advies 32.967/2, Raad van State, in: Wetsontwerp tot wijziging van de wet van 30 juli tot bestraffing van bepaalde door racisme of xenofobie ingegeven daden, 3-2362/3, 24 April 2007, at 54; Advies geformuleerd door het Centrum voor gelijkheid van kansen en voor racismebestrijding en goedgekeurd door de Raad van Bestuur op 21 november 2006 inzake Het wetsontwerp ter bestrijding van bepaalde vormen van discriminatie en Het wetsontwerp tot wijziging van de wet van 30 juli

In the legal literature it has been emphasised that for direct discrimination it is the comparability and the causality test[263] which play an important role,[264] while in indirect discrimination cases the test of disadvantage was suggested to be applied.[265] In a couple of cases it seems that it was the causality test that played a decisive role in deciding on the existence of a prima facie case. These cases were concerned with overt direct discrimination, thus, on the basis of the factual circumstances the causal link between the caused harm and the protected ground was clearly visible.[266] Accordingly, the courts did accept that the applicant fulfilled its obligation. Arguably, the applicant established even more than a presumption.[267]

In Estonia, there is no case-law yet on the basis of which it could be examined how the prima facie case of discrimination is established.

Contrary to the Belgian and Hungarian approach, in the Netherlands it seems to be clearly accepted and conceptually consistently applied that the presumption of discrimination in direct discrimination cases means the presumption of a causal relationship between the protected ground and the harm, while this relationship in indirect discrimination cases is established by showing the disparate impact. For instance, in the above-mentioned case concerning the application of a woman for a job as a teacher in an Islamic school, the Commission looked for the presumption of a causal link between her religion and her rejection.[268] Similarly, in a case concerning discrimination on intersectional grounds, the Commission examined whether both grounds at stake did presumably play a role in the suffered disadvantage.[269] In this

1981 tot bestraffing van bepaalde door racisme en xenofobie ingegeven daden, 22 November 2006, at 6; Jaarverslag 2006, CGKR 2007, at 55.

263 According to the *travaux préparatoires* it is mainly the causal link that will lead to problems. Wetsontwerp tot wijziging …, *supra* note 187, at 74.

264 De Prins, Sottiaux & Vrielink (2005), at 469-470; Thiery (2007), at 758-759; De Prins, Sottiaux & Vrielink (2003a), at 267.

265 De Prins, Sottiaux & Vrielink (2005), at 472; Thiery (2007), at 759-760; De Prins, Sottiaux & Vrielink (2003a), at 267.

266 Antwerp Correctional Court, 7 December 2004; *CGKR and C. Murat v. D. Yves and E-L. BVBA*, Gent Labour Court, summary proceedings, no. 176.893, 26 March 2007.

267 For instance in the *Murat* case, which concerned an application of a man of foreign origin for a job offered by the respondents, it was obvious that the applicant was refused because of his origin. In the e-mail in which his application was refused, one of the respondents accidently forwarded a sentence intended for internal communication from which this causal link between the refusal and his origin could be seen. According to the court, on the whole it can be presumed that the applicant was discriminated against on the grounds of national or ethnic origin. In a similar case the respondent explicitly acknowledged that he did not want to rent his apartment to persons of a foreign origin. Here, again, the causal link was established not only at the level of presumption, but it was even proved. In these cases, accordingly, no difficulty has arisen concerning the establishment of a prima facie case. *CGKR and C. Murat v. D. Yves and E-L. BVBA*, Gent Labour Court, summary proceedings, no. 176.893, 26 March 2007.

268 Opinion 2004-160 ETC. See inter alia Opinions 2003-119, 2006-124, 2006-230 ETC.

269 Opinion 2006-256 ETC, 3.21.

case a blind woman of Turkish origin had to take an oral test instead of a test in Braille. A presumption of discrimination was accepted because, compared to other blind persons, her Turkish origin made the test more onerous for her. In another case, the applicant complained that the pre-flights control system at Schiphol Airport puts predominantly persons of a coloured skin at a disadvantage.[270] The respondent follows the advice of this control team without further control, which in fact led to a negative flight advice for those persons. The presumption of discrimination in this case was established by showing the disparate impact on this group.

It seems implicitly accepted in the countries under review that giving rise to a presumption of discrimination can be achieved with the help of comparison, which is a means of evidence, and the burden of proving whether the cases are in fact comparable cannot be placed on the applicant. This can be inferred from the fact that as yet in none of the countries has the applicant been burdened by having to prove the comparability of the cases.

With respect to the Hungarian approach to the first phase of the assessment, it is important to emphasise that the applicants should make use of comparison as a means of evidence in order to be able to win their case.[271] Put differently, they should in fact establish a presumption of discrimination instead of showing the likeliness of the existence of two separate facts. In most cases applicants do make use of comparison as a means of evidence, particularly in cases in which they are supported by an interest organisation. Still, it is important that they are aware of the importance of comparison and its relation to the establishment of a presumption of discrimination.

As explained in the theoretical framework, it is important to make a distinction between facts and the presumption. This aspect of evidence law has raised concerns only in Hungary. It can be seen in a couple of cases that no explicit distinction has been made between these two matters, and commentators generally interpret the presumption of discrimination as if the applicant does not need to prove important circumstances of the case, such as his attendance of a certain place, his application for a job, and so on.[272] The case of F. Katalin[273] was much discussed in this context. In the view of the court the applicant of Roma origin could not prove that she visited the respondent on the given day and that the respondent said that he would not employ a

[270] Opinion 2003-153 ETC. See inter alia Opinions 2003-134, 2007-91, 2007-179 ETC.

[271] See also Position No. 384/4/2008. (III.28.) TT of the Advisory Board of Equal Treatment on the division of the burden of proof, 28 March 2008.

[272] See inter alia Kádár (2006), at 117; Fehér Füzet 2007. A Nemzeti és Etnikai Kisebbségi Jogvédő Iroda beszámolója, Másság Alapítvány 2008, at 17-18.

[273] Metropolitan Labour Court, 10.M.4297/2000./12; Metropolitan Court, 49.Mr.83063B/2001/2; Supreme Court, Mfv.I.10.720/2003/3. See also Metropolitan Labour Court, 29.M.5804/2005/18, 2 May 2006; Metropolitan Court, 55.Mf.635.873/2006/3, 13 April 2007.

Roma girl.[274] This argument of the court was interpreted as not accepting the special allocation of the burden of proof. However, it can be seen that the court was rather concerned with the facts of the case. Nevertheless, the lack of direct evidence does not mean that inferences as to the facts could not have been drawn from circumstantial evidence, much of which was available in this case. In another case the applicant applied for a job but his potential employer refused him, arguing that they were looking for a handsome and good-looking person.[275] Important from the perspective of the applicable protected ground is that the applicant's height and bodyweight were above average, and he had visible signs of his Roma origin. For this reason, the complaint was based on the grounds of his look and Roma origin. The court established that the respondent discriminated against the applicant on the grounds of his looks, but it could not ascertain that the applicant's Roma origin also played a role in his refusal. According to the interest organisation, which represented the victim, the court did not apply the burden of proof provision appropriately and required the applicant to prove the causal link between his Roma origin and his refusal. However, this argument of the organisation does not seem to make a distinction between factual circumstances and the presumption of discrimination either.[276] It can rather be argued that no facts were submitted from which the presumption could have been drawn as to the existence of a presumption of discrimination. Nevertheless, it seems that the fact-finders themselves were not familiar either with the distinction between the facts and the presumption of discrimination as they have not made it explicit.

In Belgium, it seems that the practice implicitly makes a distinction between the facts concerning the circumstances of the cases, and the presumption of discrimination. This was seen in the case of a blind girl who was refused entry to a restaurant with her dog.[277] According to the court, the concrete factual circumstances had not been proven since pure declarations or narratives about the events cannot be taken as facts from which the presumption of

[274] Arguably, if the applicant would have complained of not being employed because of her Roma origin, but not relying on the statements of the employer, a prima facie case of discrimination would have been accepted. (The approach of the Supreme Court seems to put the emphasis to this aspect of the case. This Court argued that in this case it was proven that the employer did not choose the applicant for the position.) In addition, complaining about this aspect, the presumption of discrimination should have also been easily accepted on the basis of the lack of transparency of the solicitation procedure.

[275] Metropolitan Labour Court, 29.M.5804/2005/18, 2 May 2006; Metropolitan Court, 55.MF.635.873/2006/3, 13 April 2007.

[276] Fehér Füzet 2007. A Nemzeti és Etnikai Kisebbségi Jogvédő Iroda beszámolója, Másság Alapítvány 2008, at 17-18. For another case in which the same interest organisation argued in terms of the inappropriate allocation of the burden of proof when the case was arguably concerned with the factual circumstances see Metropolitan Court, 19.P.630.545/2005/8, 7 September 2006; Fehér Füzet 2007. A Nemzeti és Etnikai Kisebbségi Jogvédő Iroda beszámolója, Másság Alapítvány 2008, at 22.

[277] Brussels Commercial Court, 8 July 2005.

discrimination could be drawn.[278] In other words, similarly to the case of F. Katalin in Hungary there was no direct evidence in this case either as to the factual circumstances of the case. The case was not concerned with the presumption of discrimination, but with proving the factual circumstances.

In Estonia in relation to the Gender Equality Act, the text of which is similar to the EETA, it has been argued that

> it will suffice, if the employee *describes* in his or her application why he or she finds that he or she has been discriminated against in employment [...]. Thus, the burden of proof transfers on the employer after the suspicion of discrimination is created.[279]

Arguably, the relevant text of the EETA does, however, not seem to allow such a conclusion. 'Describing' that discrimination has taken place is not only different from establishing facts from which the presumption of discrimination could be concluded, but it does not seem to suffice as a prima facie case of discrimination either. It is yet to be seen whether the interpretation of this provision in terms of making a distinction between facts and the presumption of discrimination will cause difficulties in practice.

Finally, the presumption of discrimination and the facts related to the circumstances of the discrimination are clearly distinguished in the practice of the Dutch Equal Treatment Commission. For instance, a presumption of discrimination was found in a case where the respondent challenged the allegation of the applicant that on a certain day he had said that the reason for withdrawing the contract of the applicant had been her pregnancy. However, from the order of the events it could be seen that this could not be held true. The facts related to the circumstances concern what exactly happened, what could have been said on a given day and how the events took place. The applicant also proved using documents what kind of steps the respondent took before and after becoming aware of the applicant's pregnancy.[280] These are the facts, which can be challenged at the prima facie phase of the assessment. In the view of the Commission and conceptually correctly, if these facts cannot be taken to be true, then the applicant cannot give rise to a presumption.

2.9. Second Phase of the Assessment

As far as the theoretical considerations in and the relevant legislative provisions of the countries under review are concerned, the general view is that the second phase of the assessment refers to objective justification. Only traces generally in the academic discussions can be found that this phase might also include other possibilities than justification proper alone.

278 Compare with the decision of the Arbitration Court, 157-2004, B.83.
279 Muda (2002), at 113 (emphasis added).
280 Opinion 2006-166 ETC, para. 3.8. See also Opinions 2006-148, 2007-183 ETC.

A discussion is going on in Belgium as to what the second phase of the model of assessment exactly means.[281] The general view of fact-finders seems to be that it refers to objective justification. However, other voices can also be heard. For instance, according to De Vos, who believes that there is no need to regulate the burden of proof since it is included in the concept of discrimination,[282] the respondent might on the one hand refute the presumption of discrimination, and on the other hand might give an objective justification to the treatment. By refuting a presumption the respondent can prove that the criteria for giving rise to a presumption are not complied with or can negate the causal link between the protected ground and the suffered harm. In the case of indirect discrimination, in his view, the difference between these two aspects has been diluted. Here, he seems to mix the burden of production with the burden of persuasion, and to interpret objective justification as meaning that there has been discrimination which has, however, been whitewashed by the justification.

Thiery shares his view in terms of the two aspects of the second phase.[283] According to him, in the case of direct discrimination the respondent can on the one hand refute the comparability of the cases, and can on the other hand refute the causal relationship between the protected ground and the harm, though he mixes this latter aspect with objective justification when the case is concerned with indirect discrimination.

According to a third approach to the second phase by De Prins, Sottiaux and Vrielink, the respondent can refute that discrimination took place, or can give an objective justification for his treatment, or can disprove the comparability of the case.[284] It is not quite clear what is meant by the first element, but their approach also seems to rely on the concept that objective justification only makes the established distinction good, but does not eliminate it. Moreover, they also accept that in addition to the objective justification there might be other (though unclear) possibilities in the second phase of the assessment in terms of evidence law.

In Estonia, it has been criticised that on the basis of the ECA, the respondent is only required to *explain* the reasons for his or her conduct or decision, which seems to be more lenient than to justify what has happened.[285] However, read together with Article 102(3) ECA, it can be argued that a fact-finder might have not be easily satisfied with a simple explanation, but the justification of the respondent would also be tested against the proportionality requirement. Due to the lack of case-law, it cannot be examined how this provision was in

281 De Vos (2004), at 90; Thiery (2007), at 758-760.

282 De Vos (2004), at 90-91.

283 Thiery (2007), at 758-760.

284 De Prins, Sottiaux & Vrielink (2005), at 469-472; De Prins, Sottiaux & Vrielink (2003a), at 267.

285 See also Poleshchuk (2007), at 56; Tavits (2004), at 557. This position was also emphasised in an interview with one of the experts in Estonia.

fact applied. Repetition of this formulation was, in any event, avoided both in the GEA and the EETA, which explicitly require the respondent to *prove* that no discrimination has taken place, though it is yet to be seen how this will be applied in practice.

The lack of academic discussions and case law in Estonia mean that only the texts of the ECA and EETA can be relied on for the analysis of the second phase of the assessment. First of all, the ECA indicated that the second phase was to be interpreted as the phase of objective justification. Contrary to this, the Explanatory Memorandum of the EETA argues that as soon as the applicant gives rise to a prima facie discrimination, it is for the respondent to prove 'that s/he has not infringed the principle of equal treatment and that his/her manner of acting has had another acceptable reason, which is not caused by the features' specified in Article 1(1) of the EETA.[286] It is therefore possible to conclude that the second phase of the assessment is interpreted to refer to the possibility of objective justification, which is linked to the causality. This indicates that according to the Estonian legislator if the respondent objectively justifies his treatment, he actually denies the causal link between the protected ground and the harm, and thus, in this sense there is no discrimination.

Given that the Hungarian legislation is very detailed, it has raised very sophisticated and to some extent technical discussions on the second phase of the assessment.[287] Article 19 of the original HETA established that the respondent could prove that he has observed or was not obliged to observe the principle of equal treatment. According to the new formulation, the respondent can also prove that "the circumstances rendered probable by the injured party [...] did not prevail". The Advisory Board to the Authority in its two position papers on the burden of proof also elaborated on the second phase of the assessment.[288] According to the first position paper,[289] the respondent could escape liability by proving that there was no causal link between the two facts that the applicant proved, so the respondent observed the principle of equal treatment.[290] In relation to this, the president of the Authority correctly emphasised that in a case of indirect discrimination, it is not the

[286] 262 SE-I, Equal Treatment Act, Draft, Explanatory Memorandum, 8 May 2008.

[287] See inter alia Iványi (2004); Farkas, Kádár & Kárpáti (2006), at 91-93; Bitskey & Gyulavári (2004); Farkas, Kádár & Kárpáti (2003), at 124-125; Gyulavári (2007), at 51-54.

[288] Position No. 10.117/1/2006 TT of the Advisory Board of Equal Treatment on the division of the burden of proof, 13 January 2006; Position No. 384/4/2008. (III.28.) TT of the Advisory Board of Equal Treatment on the division of the burden of proof, 28 March 2008.

[289] Position No. 10.117/1/2006 TT of the Advisory Board of Equal Treatment on the division of the burden of proof, 13 January 2006.

[290] Based on the original text, the President of the AET further argued that the respondent could prove, in addition to the lack of causality but still within the framework of observing the principle of equal treatment, that in comparison to another person or group being in a comparable situation there was no less favourable treatment. It is not quite clear though what she exactly meant here, supposedly she referred to the lack of harm, which should be decided in the first phase of the assessment. Demeter (2006), at 62.

lack of causality that is relevant, but the respondent can prove that there is no significantly greater disparate impact on one group in comparison to another one.[291] In addition to proving that he observed the principle of equal treatment, the position paper explains that the respondent can also bring forward an objective justification for his treatment/provision/criterion/practice, by which he proves that he was not obliged to observe the principle of equal treatment. This latter observation seems to be based on the concept of formal equality because it regards the second phase as if the principle of equal treatment has already been violated; the respondent can, however, not be held liable. This is problematic in the case of positive action measures aiming at substantive equality. Irrespective of this problematic aspect, the position of the ABET and the president generally seem to be in accordance with the theoretical model concerning the second phase of the assessment.

Somewhat contrary to the above approach, the commentary to the HETA argues that in order to prove that there has been no discrimination the respondent has to prove that the challenged treatment has nothing to do with the protected ground of the applicant.[292] Accordingly, this approach seems to see objective justification as another possibility to disprove the causal link, which means that it blurs the difference between these two aspects. Moreover, this position cannot be applied to cases concerning indirect discrimination.

In its second position paper,[293] the ETAB explained that as a result of the amendment of the HETA in 2007, the respondent can escape liability in three different ways. In addition to the two elements accepted on the basis of the original Act, the respondent can also prove that the circumstances rendered probable do not prevail. Analysing the second phase of the assessment Kádár comes to the conclusion that introducing this new requirement was not necessary, since making the existence of the two elements probable and providing counter-evidence to their existence happens at the same time, namely in the first phase of the assessment.[294] The fact-finder comes to a conclusion as to the probability of the existence of these elements by the balancing the evidence provided by the applicant with the counter-evidence of the respondent. The observation that the introduction of the possibility of counter-evidence was not necessary would therefore seem to be a reasonable one. The main reason for this lies in the fact that this burden of proof concerns the subjective burden of proof (the burden of production) and not the burden of persuasion.[295] Accordingly, the Hungarian legislation here mixes these two

---

291 Demeter (2006), at 62.

292 Farkas, Kádár & Kárpáti (2006), at 89.

293 Position No. 384/4/2008. (III.28.) TT of the Advisory Board of Equal Treatment on the division of the burden of proof, 28 March 2008.

294 Kádár (2006), at 120.

295 This approach can be observed in the famous *McDonnell* case in the US in which the court explained on appeal that "the respondent [the original plaintiff] carried his burden of establishing a prima facie case of racial discrimination and that petitioner [the original respondent]

burdens, which might lead to uncertainties in legal practice. This approach also seems to be based on a view that does not make a distinction between the facts and the presumption itself. As explained, the respondent can in the first phase provide counter-evidence as to the facts, and the refutation of the presumption happens in the second phase.

In the Netherlands, the provision on the burden of proof in the GETA has the same formulation as that of in the RED, thus, it does not specify whether any stages could be distinguished in proving that no breach of the principle of equal treatment has taken place. The second phase of the assessment is generally referred to as objective justification in terms of providing compelling reasons.[296]

The present texts of the equal treatment acts of the studied countries postulate a closed system of justification for direct[297] and an open system of justification for indirect discrimination,[298] an arrangement which entirely satisfies the Race Directive. Before its amendment in 2006, the Hungarian equal treatment legislation also allowed for an open justification for direct discrimination (and segregation). Admittedly, due to the special structure of the Act and the critical burden of proof regulation, there are still uncertainties concerning the exact meaning of the second phase of the assessment.[299]

2.9.1. Stage 1: Negation of Causality

As hinted at supra, with the exception of the Hungarian interpretation of the legislative provision, none of the examined countries explicitly scrutinize the respondent's negation of the causal relationship at a separate stage in the second phase of the assessment. It is generally examined in terms of objective justification which is very inappropriate, both from a conceptual and a practical point of view.

Even though the wording of the HETA lays down and scholars have explained the meaning of this provision, and in a couple of cases even the Authority has also followed this approach, one can still not explore a consistent and appropriate application of the negation of causality in Hungary. Here too, the negation of causality is often mixed with the concept of objective justification. For instance, in a case in which no Roma representative was

successfully rebutted that case. But this does not end the matter. On retrial, respondent [the original plaintiff] must be afforded a fair opportunity to demonstrate that petitioner's assigned reason for refusing to re-employ was a pretext or discriminatory in its application." *McDonnell Douglas Corp. v. Green*, 411 U.S. 792 (SC 1973). On this case see also Parrish (2001); Green (1999).

296 See inter alia Holtmaat (2006b), at 91; Gerards (2003), at 79.

297 Art. 4(8) ARA; Art. 102(2) ECA and Art. 3(2) EETA; Art. 7(3) HETA; Art. 2(4) GETA.

298 Art. 4(7) ARA, Art. 102(3) ECA and Art. 3(4) EETA; Art. 7(2) HETA; Art. 2(1) GETA.

299 On objective justification see Busstra (2010).

elected as a member of a commission for national and ethnic minorities of a local government, the respondent argued that the reason for the non-election of the applicant was attributable to his not being amenable to a compromise. Thus, he negated the causal link between his less favourable treatment and the Roma origin of the applicant. However, the Metropolitan Court did not make any distinction between these two aspects and examined the respondent's arguments in terms of objective justification.[300] It argued that the respondent observed, or was not obliged to observe, the principle of equal treatment. It went on to state that the challenged decisions were objectively justified. Thus, the possibility that the respondent observed the principle of equal treatment is not dealt with separately, and not treated in practice as the possibility to negate the causal relationship, but is examined together with the next possibility, that is that the respondent was not obliged to observe the principle of equal treatment. A similar approach can also be found in a couple of cases of the AET. For instance, in a case concerning an alleged discrimination against Roma candidates for a job, the respondent argued that there were no available places at the time of the applicants' application for a job. Accordingly, he denied that the refusal was based on ethnic origin.[301] However, this argument of the respondent was uncorrectly examined under Article 22(1) HETA, which contains an exception in the case of direct discrimination in the field of employment, and thus constitutes objective justification.

Practice shows that the fact that fact-finders find it difficult to combine the provision on the burden of proof with the justification provisions in the substantive parts of the act, the negation of the causal link is often mixed with justification proper. This proves particularly difficult for direct discrimination on the grounds of racial or ethnic origin due to the closed system of justification even though the burden of proof provision (that the respondent observed the principle of equal treatment) could very well be used to refute the causal relationship. There are cases in which the lack of causal relationship was examined in terms of the special exception clause in the field of employment. In one of the cases the applicant argued that she was dismissed because of her Roma origin.[302] The AET argued that the respondent's measure was based on a legitimate aim and was proportionate; accordingly there was no causal link between the Roma origin of the applicant and her dismissal. Thus, it can be seen that no distinction was made between the causality and the justification test. It might be argued that due to the proportionality test in the justification clause the negation of causality was also thoroughly examined.[303] Nevertheless, this

---

[300] EBH/337/24/2005; Metropolitan Court, 20.K.33.285/2005/10, 15 May 2006; Metropolitan Court, 20.K.33.285/2005/10, 15 May 2006. See also Newsletter of the AET, 2007/5.

[301] EBH/94/2008. See also EBH 72/7/2008.

[302] EBH/476/2008.

[303] The application of the proportionality test would be conceptually be inappropriate when the protected ground was 'merely' one of the grounds of distinction, but not the only ground.

effect does and cannot justify the blurring of these two stages as conceptual obscurity does not encourage a consistent, systematic and correct application of the law.[304]

In addition to the above example, in another case concerning the withdrawal of the managerial position of a pregnant woman, the respondent argued that the reason for withdrawal was not the pregnancy of the applicant, but the fact that someone should fulfil these tasks. The respondent in fact denied the link between the harm and the protected ground. Nevertheless, the AET seemed to have examined this argument in terms of objective justification. More specifically, it laid down that the respondent could not prove that the replacement of the applicant could not have been resolved, which is a clear application of the proportionality test.

This approach can also be observed in the practice of the courts. A court case, for instance, concerned a complaint about the Hungarian Railways that, on transferring some tasks to a private company, also transferred 11 of the 30 employees, who previously fulfilled these tasks, as part of the agreement.[305] Of the 11 employees, 9 were Roma, whereas among the remaining 19 persons no Roma could be found. The court thoroughly examined whether the argument given by the respondent, in which he tried to negate the causality (it was not their Roma origin, but their professional experience and education), could be accepted.[306] Again, the explanation was examined in terms of objective justification, and that is the reason why a proportionality test is applied. As indicated supra, this is a dangerous approach since it could blur the important distinction between the negation of causality and the justification. Accordingly, fact-finders should separate the different arguments of the respondent, they should exactly determine which stage of the second phase they examine, and in the view of this they should give good reasons why the defence of the respondent can or cannot be accepted.

Admittedly, in some cases, the AET explicitly mentions that it first looks at the causal relationship and then examines whether there is objective justification, in doing so making clear the different stages of the examination. It did this in a case concerning a loan of an applicant who was blind, in which the bank posed additional requirements for approval of his loan. The bank did

In such cases the application of the proportionality test at the stage of negation might allow for declaring the distinction lawful. See further Busstra (2010).

[304] Admittedly, even the reference to this exception clause cannot be regarded appropriate in terms of the Directive. See Busstra (2010).

[305] Miskolc City Court, 6.M.16/2005/17, 28 November 2005. See also Borsod-Abaúj-Zemplén County Court, 1.Mf.20392/2007/3, 12 June 2007; Miskolc Labour Court, 6.M.1364/2006/4, 14 November 2006. On these cases see also Fehér Füzet 2005. A Nemzeti és Etnikai Kisebbségi Jogvédő Iroda beszámolója, Másság Alapítvány 2007, at 14. & 40-45; Fehér Füzet 2006. A Nemzeti és Etnikai Kisebbségi Jogvédő Iroda beszámolója, Másság Alapítvány 2007, at 14.

[306] Arguably, the court did not distinguish the two stages in the refutation of the respondent, but it only applied the objective justification test.

not challenge the causality, but came up with arguments in terms of objective justification. The AET still explained that the respondent could not prove the lack of causality and could not reasonably rely on the objective justification.[307] In the light of the above-mentioned cases, it therefore seems that this clear line of examination is only followed by the Authority when the case concerns overt direct discrimination, and there are no doubts concerning the causality.

In Belgium, not only has it theoretically been accepted that in addition to objective justification the respondent can also come up with other refutation, but one might also discover traces of this approach in practice. For instance, in the Murat case the fact-finder seemed to accept that the respondent cannot only provide an objective justification to the challenged treatment, but he can also negate the causal link between the protected ground and the harm. The applicant of foreign origin applied for a position in which he would have dealt with security devices. An e-mail that was accidently sent to the applicant stated that, according to the respondent, security and foreigners cannot be combined. Despite the fact that the refusal of the applicant was clearly linked to his national or ethnic origin, the respondent still tried to negate the causal link between this treatment and the protected ground. He argued on the one hand that he employs persons of a different ethnic background; and on the other hand, he also referred to the labour and legal history of the applicant as a reason for the refusal. Both of these arguments were correctly refused by the court. As to the first argument the court explained that this fact did not mean that the respondent could not have discriminated against the applicant. Concerning the second argument, the court thoroughly examined the facts of the case in order to establish whether this reason of the respondent could be regarded to be true. Taking into consideration the short time that elapsed between the application and the refusal of the applicant, the court found that the respondent could not have been able to obtain any such information about the applicant, thus the respondent could not negate the causal link. Contrary to the other arguments that were also given by the respondent,[308] in relation to these explanations the fact-finder did not apply the terminology of justification, which indicates that this negation was implicitly considered as being different from objective justification, thus constituting a different stage in the refutation of the respondent. In other racial discrimination cases the causal link was so direct that the respondent did not even try to negate this link, so there was no examination of this aspect of the case.[309]

As mentioned above, the theoretical approach to the second phase of the assessment in Estonia is only concerned with objective justification, and no

---

[307] EBH/553/2006.

[308] Clients might discriminate against a security technician who is of foreign origin but the respondent did not prove that the origin of the employee constituted a genuine and determining occupational requirement.

[309] See for instance Antwerp Correctional Court, 7 December 2004.

mention has been made of the possibility of negating the causal link. The case law that can be found in relation to the GEA and the Constitution does not show any indication that the stage of negation would have been or would be acknowledged and/or applied.

Despite the fact that in theoretical discussions in the Netherlands, the negation of causality has not been separately mentioned as a possibility of the respondent to escape liability, the jurisprudence of the ETC still indicates that the Commission implicitly applies this stage of refutation. The examination of the respondent's argument concerning the lack of causality can be identified when the Commission looks at whether the presumption can be refuted (*weerleggen*) by the respondent. Admittedly, this approach is somewhat confusing as the word 'weerleggen' is generally used with respect to the factual circumstances (and not to the inferences drawn from it). However, the ETC lays down that when the respondent's arguments are considered acceptable, there is no presumption anymore. This approach would imply that the existence (and not only the presumption) of the causal link is examined in the first phase of the assessment.

Although from a conceptual perspective this formulation of the Commission is not the most advantageous, in fact, it does examine the respondent's negation of causality somewhat separately from the presumption of discrimination, and the duty to prove the existence of the causal link is not placed on the applicant. This position is also supported by the criticism that was made concerning the scrutiny of the examination of the 'refutation' (*weerleggen*). Namely, it was argued that 'weerleggen' does not comply with the RED as it indicates a less strict approach towards objective justification.[310] In other words, the Commission implicitly makes a distinction between the presumption of discrimination and the negation of causality on the one hand, and between the negation of causality and objective justification on the other. The first distinction was implicitly acknowledged in the criticism as it did not criticise the strictness of the Commission's scrutiny with respect to the presumption of discrimination, but argued that quite lenient scrutiny was applied pertaining to the respondent's explanation. Nevertheless, the criticism cannot be regarded as appropriate with respect to the stage of negation as the Commission strictly scrutinises whether the respondent's explanation was the real reason for the particular treatment. The reason for the critical voice might have been that the criticism itself did not make the distinction between objective justification and negation, and was also looking for a proportionality test at the stage of negation.

An example of the Commission's approach can be found in a case concerning an application for a job by a person of foreign origin.[311] After a thorough

[310] Rodrigues (2004), at 16.

[311] Opinion 2006-180 ETC. See also Opinions 2007-68, 2007-30 ETC; Rodrigues & Van Walsum (2008), at 29 & 32.

examination, the Commission decided that the respondent appropriately refuted the allegations of the applicant because the reason for not inviting the applicant for an interview was not his racial or ethnic origin, but his moderate performance during his internship as a student. According to the Commission by proving this, the respondent refuted the allegations of the applicant, and thus, there are no facts from which the presumption of discrimination could be established. It can be clearly seen that the ETC took the explanation given by the respondent as relating to the factual circumstances, though arguably, the proper approach would have been to first accept the existence of a prima facie case of discrimination and then state that the respondent could disprove the existence of a causal link between the ethnic origin of the applicant and his refusal. The reason for such an approach might be found in the fact that the second phase of the assessment is only considered to include the possibility of objective justification which is, however, not allowed in direct discrimination cases. It should be explicitly acknowledged that there is a separate stage in the second phase of the assessment which is related to the causality. The approach of the Commission cannot be regarded acceptable as the impression is created that the respondent's argument was related to the establishment of a prima facie case of discrimination. However, as this case clearly illustrated, the explanation of the respondent did not disprove the factual circumstances, since the facts were still the same: the applicant had applied for a job and the respondent did not invite him for an interview.

The examination of the negation of the causality with a reference to the lack of presumption is precarious at least from four points of view. First of all, this approach might place a higher burden of proof on the applicant. Secondly, systematically it does not seem to be correct to talk about the non-existence of a presumption when the ETC has already started to examine the refutation of the respondent. Thirdly, the respondent does not disprove any facts in these cases; rather he gives a different interpretation to them. Finally and related to this latter point, this manner of adjudication, similarly to the Hungarian approach, blurs the difference between the burden of persuasion and production. The applicant only has the initial burden of production, during which the respondent also has the burden of production to disprove the facts. However, when it does not relate to the facts anymore, but to the presumption of discrimination, it is the respondent who bears the burden of persuasion that no discrimination has taken place.

2.9.2. Stage 2: Objective Justification

As indicated above, the stage of objective justification is generally identified as the second phase of the model of review, which means that this concept (with the exception of the Netherlands) is often mixed with causality considerations.

Notwithstanding this fact, in the absence of causality-related explanations of the respondent, the concept of objective justification seems to be properly applied.

In Belgium the concept of objective justification is generally accepted in the legal theory. Nevertheless, one cannot in each and every case find an elaborate application of the concept. For instance, in the above-mentioned Murat case,[312] the respondent brought up four different explanations in order to refute the presumption of discrimination. Two of them were related to justification, which the Court also realised, as only these explanations were discussed in terms of justification; that is as coming up with compelling reasons.[313] According to the court, in this case the argument of the respondent that clients might discriminate against a security technician of foreign origin cannot be accepted as objective justification. Moreover, in the view of the court, the respondent did not prove either that the origin of the employee constituted a genuine and determining occupational requirement. Nevertheless, no arguments were given by the court as to which elements of the proportionality test could not prevail. The fact-finder might have considered it obvious that the justification of the respondent could not be accepted, but for the sake of legal certainty and consistency, detailed argumentation is highly desirable. In some cases, however, one can observe a detailed examination of the justification concerning which the elements of the proportionality test are explicitly elaborated.[314]

There is no case-law in Estonia on either the ECA or the GEA, from which it can be concluded how the concept of justification is applied in terms of these special pieces of equal treatment legislations. Importantly, however, the concept of justification is generally applied by the Constitutional Review Chamber of the Supreme Court, which has dealt with many cases concerning Article 12 of the Constitution and applied the different elements of proportionality.[315]

The concept of justification is also used by the Legal Chancellor, which even if it relies on the proportionality test as elaborated by the ECtHR, does not in each and every case apply all the elements of the objective justification test. For instance, in one of his position papers he examined whether on the basis of Article 12 of the Constitution a local government could make it possible for persons with special merits to acquire apartments for considerably lower prices than others. According to the Legal Chancellor,

[312] *CGKR and C. Murat v. D. Yves and E-L. BVBA*, Gent Labour Court, summary proceedings, no. 176.893, 26 March 2007.

[313] The other 'reasons' given by the respondent can be placed in the stage of negation of causality, but the fact-finder did not elaborate on this, it only examined whether these reasons could be accepted.

[314] Tongeren Labour Court, no. N-20070306-6, 6 March 2007.

[315] See for instance Constitutional Judgment 3-4-1-2-02, 3 April 2002; Constitutional Judgment 3-4-1-33-05, 20 March 2006; Constitutional Judgment 3-4-1-7-03, 21 January 2004; Constitutional Judgment 3-4-1-1-02, 6 March 2002.

> taking into consideration the aims and conditions of making use of the apartments, the applicants and the persons treated more favourably should be seen as equal subjects, who should also be treated equally. The merits of these persons cannot be taken as grounds for unequal treatment.[316]

In other words, the special merits of the two persons did not justify the unequal treatment; that is this explanation cannot be accepted as compelling reasons in the light of the principle of equal treatment. To summarise, it seems to be accepted that the respondent can provide justification for his treatment, but it is yet to be seen how it will be applied in practice; whether a case will not be evaluated in terms of causality or comparability when it in fact concerns justification.

As explained above, in many instances justification is blurred with causality in the jurisprudence, and to some extent also in the literature. For instance, in Hungary in the Miskolc segregation case the court of appeal argued that if the respondent could prove that he was not obliged to observe the principle of equal treatment, because his treatment had another objective reason, the causal link between the protected ground and the harm would be broken. This approach therefore relies on the concept of justification as causality. The practical disadvantageous effect of this interpretation might be that it would be more difficult to establish discrimination where the evidence concerns disparate impact since fact-finders look for this causal link, and it might be more difficult for the respondent to refute that there has been discrimination, since fact-finders might want the respondent to prove the lack of causality instead of coming up with evidence that there has been no breach of the principle of equal treatment.

However, in many cases the justification is applied in terms of compelling reasons (either after examination of the existence of the causal relationship or immediately on looking at the justification of the respondent), and a proportionality test is carried out. For instance, in the Hajdúhadház segregation case[317] the court accepted that there was a disparate impact related to the ethnic origin of the segregated children, and examined whether the respondent could come up with an objective justification for his treatment. It established that traditions and financial considerations cannot be taken as reasonable grounds for the treatment.

Nevertheless, the concept of objective justification is not only difficult with respect to its relation to the negation of causality, but also in terms of open versus closed system of justification and the appropriate level of scrutiny. The amendment of the HETA made the application of the concept of justification even more complicated in both respects.[318] Concerning the latter, there is no clear

[316] Seisukoht võrdse kohtlemise põhimõtte rikkumise kohta, Nr. 7-5/070340/00705874, Õiguskantsler 2007.

[317] Hajdú-Bihar County Court, 6.P. 20.341/2006/50, 2 May 2007.

[318] See also Busstra (2010).

guideline as to what is considered to be a fundamental right for which stricter scrutiny (necessity/proportionality test) is applicable, and in which case the applicant's right is a non-fundamental one in relation to which a reasonability/arbitrariness test have to be carried out. An example can be found in which the applicant's right at stake was his human dignity, which was considered to be a fundamental right and so the necessity/proportionality test was applied.[319] An example to the contrary can also be found, when with reference to the violation of the human dignity of the victim and the relevant jurisprudence of the Constitutional Court the test of reasonability/arbitrariness was enforced.[320] This latter case concerned the policy or practice of a pub in which Roma customers had to pay double the price paid by others. The argument of the respondent was that they had to pay more because they were not in possession of a VIP card. (Again, as can be seen, the explanation of the respondent was not concerned with objective justification, rather he denied the causal link with the applicants' ethnic origin.) The Authority argued that this treatment was amenable to violate the human dignity of the applicants, and explained that the criteria for access to this card were arbitrary, and not reasonable.[321] The fact that it is not clear in this case whether the arguments of the respondent were examined in terms of justification or causation makes this case remarkable, because of the closed system of justification for direct discrimination.[322] In other words, where there is a lack of explicit elaboration the formulation of the decision of the Authority might create the impression that there also exists an open justification for direct discrimination. Notwithstanding this obscurity, given that the defence of the respondent concerned the negation of causality, it is very important that a thorough investigation was carried out in this respect.

In the Netherlands, justification in terms of coming up with compelling reasons and carrying out a detailed proportionality test is generally accepted and applied both in theory and in the legal practice. The ETC consistently follows both the concept of justification in terms of compelling reasons and the division between closed and open systems of justification, and examines all the elements of the proportionality test.[323] As far as this latter aspect is concerned,

319 EBH/1/37/2008.

320 EBH/72/7/2008. It is not obvious on the basis of the arguments in the decision whether this test was considered to be the more lenient test among the justification possibilities or whether it was an additional test. If it was the more lenient justification test that was applied, no arguments can be found either concerning what the concrete non-fundamental right at stake was. It should also be added that the respondent as a matter of fact tried to negate the causal link. Thus, it might also be that this test was applied within this framework.

321 This approach might be explained by the wording of the cited Constitutional Court judgment which, however, referred to non-fundamental rights, that can be latched on to the protection against discrimination via the concept of human dignity. The Authority did not even look at which right can be at stake in this case, but immediately used the concept of human dignity.

322 Nevertheless, the Authority did not define the type of discrimination at stake.

323 Opinions 2003-153, 2004-143, 2003-134, 2007-193, 2003-76 ETC.

the ETC has been criticised that in order to be able to apply the open system of justification, in a couple of cases it classified a case of direct discrimination as indirect discrimination.[324] Moreover, as yet in two direct discrimination cases it also considered the breaking of the closed system of justification on the basis of the principle of reasonableness and fairness.[325] In the first case, it came to the conclusion that not applying an open system of justification would lead to unacceptable consequences, so it examined the justification of the respondent, and decided that the free of charge and cheaper vaccination of homosexuals against Hepatitis A and B respectively cannot be considered unlawful since this group has a bigger chance of infection.[326] The second case in which this question came up again concerned vaccination against Hepatitis, but this time cheaper vaccinations for Turkish and Moroccan children. Here, according to the Commission, the application of the closed system did not lead to unacceptable consequences.[327] These cases also show that the Commission tries to apply the concept of justification in the proper sense without mixing it with either comparability or causality considerations.

Importantly, when a case is concerned with the vicarious liability of an employer, his argument that he appropriately investigated the complaint of the victim of discrimination is examined in terms of objective justification by the ETC. In terms of the allocation of the burden of proof, this approach therefore grants sufficient protection for employees in such cases.[328] For instance, in one case[329] in which the applicant complained that the respondent employer did not guarantee a discrimination-free working environment, the Commission did not consider the handling of the applicant's complaint as being thorough and careful, thus, the employer was held liable.

2.10. Application of the Model of Review Concerning Harassment and Instruction to Discriminate

With the partial exception of Belgium, it seems that the special rules on the burden of proof are also self-evidently applicable to the concepts of harassment and instruction to discriminate.

In Belgium, scholars could not agree whether on the basis of the ADA the special allocation of the burden of proof can also be applied in cases of harassment and instruction to discriminate. The ambiguity was caused by the wording of Article 19(3) ADA which stipulated that the applicant had to

[324] Loenen (2006), at 827-828. See for instance Opinion 2007-179 ETC.
[325] Concerning Opinion 2006-20 ETC see Loenen (2006); Gerards (2007).
[326] Opinion 2006-20 ETC.
[327] Opinion 2006-55 ETC.
[328] Opinions 2003-76, 2006-71 ETC.
[329] Opinion 2006-71 ETC.

give rise to a presumption of *direct and/or indirect discrimination*, similarly to the formulation in the RED.[330] At the same time, according to Articles 6 and 7 respectively, harassment and giving instruction to discriminate were considered as particular forms of discrimination.[331] Contrary to the RED, there was, however, no general provision in this Act declaring that the principle of equal treatment would mean the prohibition of discrimination.[332] This would have meant that if it is accepted that harassment and instruction to discriminate could not be regarded as special forms of direct or indirect discrimination, these provisions could not even have been relied on in general because the material scope of the Act also talked only about direct and indirect discrimination.[333] Since no case was decided on the basis of the ADA in relation to harassment or instruction to discriminate, it cannot be examined how the burden of proof provision was applied in practice. Contrary to this approach, the burden of proof rule in the ARA stipulates that the applicant has to give rise to a presumption of discrimination without mentioning any specific forms of it. Although this Act does not classify harassment and instruction to discriminate as special forms of discrimination, Article 3 ARA declares that the aim of this Act is to create a general framework for combating discrimination. It is therefore possible to conclude that harassment and instruction to discriminate also constitute a special form of discrimination. Consequently, the rules on the special allocation of the burden of proof can be applied in such cases as well.[334] Given the lack of jurisprudence in this field, it is yet to be seen how the burden of proof regulation and the model of review will be applied in the future concerning harassment and instruction to discriminate.

Contrary to this, and similarly to the ARA in Belgium, the burden of proof provision in the Estonian EETA does not specify to which form of discrimination it has to be applied, it simply refers to discrimination.[335] Read together with Article 3 EETA,[336] which lays down the different forms of discrimination, it cannot but be concluded that the special allocation of the burden of proof must be applied in cases of harassment and instruction

[330] Fouber (2004), at 1213. Interestingly, De Prins, Sottiaux & Vrielink argue that this problem could be eliminated by interpreting the ADA in accordance with the RED and the FD which, as mentioned above, has the same text as the ADA had. De Prins, Sottiaux & Vrielink (2005), at 546-547.

[331] See also De Schutter (2007), at 43-44.

[332] Art. 1 ADA referred to the Constitution, which might nevertheless be taken as such a provision.

[333] Art. 2(4) ADA.

[334] For some scholars it is not even questionable whether this provision can be applied to the concepts of harassment and instruction to discrimination. See Rorive & Van der Plancke (2008), at 425.

[335] On the previous regulations in the ECA see Poleshchuk (2007), at 21-22.

[336] Art. 3 EETA is entitled 'The principle of equal treatment and discrimination', and its first section establishes that "[t]he principle of equal treatment means that there is no discrimination based on a feature named in Article 1(1) of this Act."

to discriminate as well. It is however yet to be seen whether this Draft will be adopted and how this provision will be applied in practice. As yet, all harassment cases have been decided on the basis of the GEA by the Gender Equality Commissioner. She has established in two cases that the respondent's treatment constituted harassment,[337] but since these cases are not available, it cannot be analysed whether and how the special allocation of the burden of proof was applied in these cases.

The text of the Hungarian HETA does not seem to give rise to any problematic interpretation regarding whether the provisions on the burden of proof can or have to be applied to cases concerning harassment and instruction to discriminate. Article 19 HETA refers to the observance of the principle of equal treatment, and according to Article 7(1) HETA the principle of equal treatment is violated, amongst others, by direct and indirect discrimination, harassment and giving instruction to perpetrate these.[338]

In the Netherlands, the burden of proof provision should be applied in the case of any alleged discrimination (distinction). Both instruction to discriminate[339] and harassment[340] are qualified as constituting distinction.[341] Accordingly, no uncertainty seems to arise regarding whether the burden of proof provision has to be applied in cases of harassment and instruction to discriminate.[342]

In Hungary and the Netherlands some elaborations have also been made on the concept of harassment in terms of the model of review, and in this respect some conclusions can also be drawn from the couple of harassment cases that have come before fact-finders.

In Hungary, concerning the prima facie phase of harassment, it has been argued that problems might arise in practice regarding what should be meant under disadvantage in such cases.[343] As a matter of fact, in such cases the suffered disadvantage should be taken to be the violation of dignity and the creating,

337 This position was confirmed in an interview with one of the experts in Estonia.

338 See also Kádár (2007), at 27; Demeter (2006), at 59.

339 Art. 1(1) a) GETA.

340 Art. 1a(1) GETA.

341 See also Wijziging van de Awgb en enkele andere wetten ter uitvoering van richlijn nr 2000/43/EG en richtlijn 2000/78/EG (EG-Implementatiewet Awgb), Nota naar aanleiding van het verslag, 28 770, Nr. 5, 22 May 2003, at 18-19; Implementatie van richtlijnen inzake gelijke behandeling, Brief van de Staatssecretaris van Sociale Zaken en Werkgelegenheid, 28 187, Nr. 2, 4 April 2002, at 4; Commentaar van de CGB inzake implementatie van de gemeenschappelijke bepalingen van de EC-Kaderrichtlijn en de EC-anti-rassen-discriminatierichtlijn, CGB-advies/2001/03, 30 May 2001, at 5; Implementatie van richtlijnen inzake gelijke behandeling, Brief van de Staatssecretaris van Sociale Zaken en Werkgelegenheid, 28 187, Nr. 1, 18 December 2001, at 8.

342 See also Gerards (2006), at 307.

343 Bitskey & Gyulavári (2004). A similar argument was given in relation to the segregation provision of the HETA concerning which the separation of the children itself constitutes the disadvantage. Gyulavári (2007), at 47.

or the danger of creating an 'intimidating, hostile, degrading, humiliating or offensive environment'. As far as the possible justification of harassment is concerned, the Commentary on the HETA argues that harassment might be objectively justified, depending on the circumstances of the case; however, it immediately adds that in the case of very serious violations no justification seems to be acceptable.[344] Contrary to the first observation it was argued in the theoretical framework that no explanations can be foreseen which could constitute any compelling reason for such a serious violation.

The Equal Treatment Authority had a couple of cases concerning harassment,[345] but it does not explicitly make use of the burden of proof provision in each and every case, and it is in these cases difficult to see how they in fact applied the model of review. In one case, for instance, in which Article 19 HETA on the burden of proof was explicitly applied,[346] the applicant argued that the respondent harassed him when he obliged him to visit a doctor, which was not required from other employees. According to the Authority, the applicant proved that he had a protected ground (health status) and that he suffered a disadvantage (having to visit a doctor). Because the Act required the establishment of these two separate elements (and not the establishment of the presumption of harassment), the burden of proof was placed the respondent to prove that there had been no breach of the principle of equal treatment. Arguably, the Authority applied the burden of proof provision in the same manner as it has done in direct discrimination cases, and considered the conduct as a disadvantage. The explanation of the respondent was placed within the framework of objective justification, and it was accepted that the respondent had a reasonable ground (namely that there was a contradiction in the different doctoral opinions given about the health condition of the applicant) to ask the applicant to make an extra visit to a doctor. In this case, it can be seen again that in the interpretation of the AET, proving/showing a disadvantage means an additional requirement to the degrading, etc. environment. Arguably, if the burden of proof provision were to be read together with the applicable concept of discrimination, such an interpretation of the word 'harm/disadvantage' could be avoided, and the presumption of harassment could be established. Moreover, if the presumption of harassment were to be required, the case might have been decided in the first phase of the assessment by arguing that in fact no degrading, etc. environment had been created. In any event, this explanation of the respondent should not have been decided in terms of justification since it was not concerned with a compelling reason that would justify the violation of human dignity and the creation of a degrading, humiliating, etc. environment. This decision creates the impression

[344] Farkas, Kádár & Kárpáti (2006), at 65.

[345] EBH/81/2008, EBH/54/2008, EBH/671/2007, EBH/704/2007, EBH/86/2007, EBH/69/2006, EBH/22/2006, EBH/450/2006, EBH/611/2006.

[346] EBH/450/2006.

that harassment can be justified, which is clearly not in accordance with the theoretical observations.[347] Strikingly, in another harassment case the AET regarded the violation of human dignity and the creation of a hostile, etc. environment to constitute the disadvantage.[348] In this case, the explanation of the respondent could not be accepted as constituting objective and reasonable justification.

In summary, these cases show that in the Hungarian context harassment does not seem to constitute a serious violation, and the burden of proof is quickly placed on the respondent who can openly justify his treatment, similarly to the concept of indirect discrimination. The application of the concept of harassment by the AET seems somewhat arbitrary as no examination is carried out into the question whether and to what extent the elements of the concept of harassment can be found. As argued supra, the alleged difficulty with the applicant's burden of proof could be solved by interpreting the term 'disadvantage' in harmony with the concept of discrimination at stake.

Concerning the vicarious liability of the employer, an example can be found in which the respondent could not escape liability by proving that an appropriate procedure was introduced for the investigation of the alleged harassment in the workplace.[349] Admittedly, on the basis of the arguments of the AET, it can even be concluded that this defence of the respondent was not even taken into consideration as a possible justification.[350] Thus, it seems that in the view of the Authority, employers would always be held liable when it is proved that their employees have harassed any of their colleagues. This position does not motivate employers to make any efforts to investigate discrimination complaints, which cannot be regarded as a desired approach.

Somewhat contrary to the Hungarian approach, harassment in the Dutch context is deemed to be a qualified and grave form of discrimination that can never be justified.[351] It was observed in the context of direct and indirect

347 In another case, the applicant alleged that he was harassed because of his political opinion. From the material available it cannot be clearly seen whether the evidence provided by the respondent was considered in the second phase of the assessment, but from the wording of the decision, namely that it was reasonable and justified what the respondent did, it seems that a similar approach was followed in this case as well. EBH/86/2007.

348 EBH/866/19/2007.

349 See for instance EBH/516/2007.

350 The applicants complained not only of harassment, but also of direct discrimination by their dismissal, and these two complaints were not clearly separated from each other in the decision. Concerning the refutation of the respondent, the AET argued that "the respondent in the present procedure can escape liability, if he proves that the differential treatment on the grounds of racial or ethnic origin does not purport to be discrimination, since by the nature of the particular occupational activities concerned or of the context in which they are carried out, this characteristic constitutes a genuine and determining occupational requirement provided that the objective is legitimate and the requirement is proportionate."

351 Art. 1a(4) GETA. See also Wijziging van de Awgb en enkele andere wetten ter uitvoering van richlijn nr 2000/43/EG en richtlijn 2000/78/EG (EG-Implementatiewet Awgb), Nota naar aanleiding van het verslag, 28 770, Nr. 5, 22 May 2003, at 19.

discrimination that the ETC examines the existence or lack of causal relationship, that is, arguably, the only possible refutation of the respondent in harassment cases, under the concept of presumption. This fact seems to indicate in relation to harassment, that every case of harassment would be decided in the prima facie phase. Although this seems to be a strict and/or conceptually incorrect approach, it is obvious that in such cases the lack of causal relationship between the conduct and the violation of human dignity and the creation of a threatening, hostile, offensive, humiliating or degrading environment can only be invoked in exceptional circumstances for the general presence of a direct link between these elements. This approach would be similar to an overt direct discrimination case, which in principle is also decided in the first phase of the assessment as the causal link between the elements is clear, and no justification is possible. Accordingly, this is also in accordance with the model of review, if the standard of proof of the applicant remains the level of presumption.

In practice, the ETC follows the Explanatory Memorandum of the GETA concerning harassment.[352] Namely, it considers harassment as a very grave form of violation, which also means that it does not easily accept the argument of the applicant.[353] For instance, the ETC established that a couple of remarks in relation to the origin of the applicant, who felt offended by and complained about these remarks, are not sufficient to give rise to a presumption of harassment.[354] Nevertheless, these facts can give rise to the presumption of direct discrimination (distinction).[355]

In another case, the applicant complained of harassment on the one hand and of discriminatory treatment during the investigation of a complaint commission on the other.[356] The ETC regarded both complaints to be well-founded, though without arguing in terms of the existence of a presumption of harassment, unlike it did in the aforementioned case. Concerning harassment the ETC found that the way the respondent tried to reintegrate the applicant was not appropriate, and created a threatening, hostile, offensive, humiliating or degrading environment.[357] As supposed, this latter complaint was decided in the first phase of the assessment. However, a clear distinction should be made between justification concerning harassment and justification in the case of vicarious liability of the respondent. While harassment as such can never be justified as no compelling reason can be imagined that would justify committing such a violation, the respondent can provide a justification as to why he should not be held liable. For instance, he can prove that he properly investigated the case, or did his best to prevent the occurrence of harassment.

352 Art. 1a(4) GETA. See also Wijziging van de Awgb, *id.*, at 19.
353 See for instance Opinions 2005-167, 2007-11 ETC.
354 Opinion 2005-167 ETC, para. 6.7.
355 Opinion 2005-167 ETC, paras. 6.8-6.13.
356 Opinion 2007-11 ETC.
357 Opinion 2007-11 ETC, para. 3.15.

In this particular case, it was the vicarious liability of the respondent that was at stake, which should have been investigated in terms of objective justification in order to be able to carry out a proportionality test.

2.11. Conclusions

In light of the extreme difficulties faced by victims of racial discrimination in providing (direct) evidence of discrimination when they attempt to vindicate their right to equal treatment before a fact-finding body, it is essential that the victim's procedural position be facilitated by imposing less heavy an onus on the applicant in proving his case of discrimination than he would generally be burdened with. Moreover, these rules should also be extended to as many procedures as possible (with the exception of criminal proceedings). These special rules concerning the allocation of the burden of proof contribute to the effective enforcement of the prohibition of discrimination in several respects: not only is the procedural position of the victims facilitated, but this approach also lowers the threshold for filing lawsuits. Accordingly, the special allocation of the burden of proof is conducive to enhancing minority protection through ensuring effective enforcement of the prohibition of discrimination.

Taking into account the above considerations relating to the victim's difficulties in providing evidence, Article 8 RED requires Member States to adopt special rules for the allocation of the burden of proof. On the basis of these rules a two-phased model of reviewing discrimination cases has been set up. First of all, it is for the applicant to establish that there is a presumption of discrimination. As soon as a prima facie case of discrimination is ascertained, the burden of proof is placed on the respondent who has to prove that in fact no discrimination has occurred.

One of the most complicated and from the perspective of the victim, most crucial aspects pertaining to the special allocation of the burden of proof concerns the presumption of discrimination as there are many uncertainties about what this exactly includes. The presumption of discrimination means that in addition to proving the factual circumstances of the case the applicant also has to show that there might be a causal relationship between his protected ground and the harm suffered on the one hand, and between the particular treatment, provision, criterion or practice and the harm on the other hand. The case studies show how important it is to have a clear understanding of what this concept means. In fact, in the countries under review this concept is far from clear either in theory or in practice. Only in the Netherlands can a systematic and consistent application of this construction be found. The opposite extreme of the clear application of the prima facie case of discrimination is the Hungarian approach, for which it is the legal regulation that is mostly to blame. Instead of requiring that the applicant give rise to a presumption of discrimination, the HETA stipulates that the applicant has to give rise to a presumption of two separate 'facts', namely the existence of the harm and the protected ground. There are many problems with this regulation. First of all, these rules seem to have been modelled for the concept of direct discrimination and therefore are very difficult to apply to the other concepts of discrimination. Secondly, the rules do not mention the presumption of discrimination, and for this reason applicants are not required to show that there might be a link between the elements. Although it seems that these rules are even more favourable to the victims, neither conceptually nor from a practical point of view can this approach be regarded as appropriate. In fact, the conceptual inappropriateness of this regulation (and the unfamiliarity with the concept of presumption) have resulted in the inconsistent application of the model of review, and have many times led fact-finders to impose either a higher burden of proof on the applicant or a less strict scrutiny pertaining to the explanations of the respondent. This therefore confirms the importance of the appropriate allocation of the burden of proof.

The Estonian and Belgian approaches can be located somewhere between these two ends of the continuum. Although the Estonian approach clearly follows the text of the RED in this respect, there is as yet no case law on its application. However, due to the lack of experience in anti-discrimination law, it is to be expected that its application will not be very smooth. Similarly, in Belgium the wording of the equal treatment legislation talks about a presumption of discrimination. However, in practice this standard of proof has not always been accepted by fact-finders, especially when the case concerned covert direct discrimination and the evidence was a form of situation testing.

As soon as the presumption of discrimination has been established, the burden of proof is placed on the respondent who has to prove that there has been no discrimination. The second phase of the assessment includes two stages. First of all, the respondent can negate the causal links which is primarily relevant in the case of direct discrimination. In the second stage he can come up with an objective justification, acknowledging that there has been a distinction on the grounds of or related to the racial or ethnic origin of the victim and giving a reasonable explanation for the measure applied.

The first stage is not explicitly acknowledged either by the ECJ or in the countries under review. In fact, the negation of causality is often mixed with either objective justification or, even more inappropriately, the presumption of discrimination. When the particular legislation operates with a closed system of justification, examining the negation of causality is simply regarded as impossible as this stage is not explicitly enshrined in the legislation and the fact-finders are unfamiliar with this concept. This approach often has repercussions on the first phase of the assessment since fact-finders are reluctant to base their ultimate decision on a presumption of discrimination. In Hungary, applicants have been required in a couple of cases to *prove* the existence of the causal link (thus in fact to prove discrimination), which can be attributed to the uncertainty concerning the stage of negation and when the fact-finder can directly establish whether the causal link is to be found or not. The approach in Hungary is even more striking since the Equal Treatment Act itself seems to refer to the possibility of negation as a stage prior to objective justification. Nevertheless, it has been found difficult in practice to make a distinction between these two stages and to appropriately combine them with the special justification clauses. Only in cases where the existence of a causal link was explicitly acknowledged has the Authority established that this relationship has not been negated, and in other cases it was mixed with objective justification.

The Dutch Equal Treatment Commission has been creative in its approach to this matter due to the closed system of justification for direct discrimination in the Equal Treatment Act. They accepted the existence of a presumption, but still in the same phase examined whether this presumption is rebutted (which is different from being justified). Although the Commission seems to apply the negation of causality in the right way, as it is not clearly explained what this rebuttal in fact means, and as it is linked to the first phase of the assessment, the false impression is created that either the respondent's explanation is leniently scrutinized or the applicant bears a more onerous burden in terms of evidence law.

Whether the creativity of the Dutch Commission will be followed in Estonia is yet to be seen. The wording of the burden of proof provision is almost identical also in this respect to the text of the RED, but there is as yet no case law on its application. Somewhat differently, in Belgium there is some evidence that the negation of causality is somewhat separately examined from the objective justification, but as yet it does not seem that the fact-finders have consciously done so. This carries the danger that conceptually incorrectly the negation of causality will be mixed with objective justification.

Pursuant to the RED Member States are not obliged to introduce these rules in those procedures where it is for the fact-finders to investigate the case. Nevertheless, the countries under review have extended the application of these rules to almost all non-criminal procedures. Most importantly, these rules are generally applied in those procedures that are specifically created for the enforcement of the right to non-discrimination. The fact that these rules are widely used obviously encourages victims to enforce their right.

The above elaborations convincingly point to the fact that the appropriate allocation of the burden of proof and the proper application of the model of review based on this are an important requirement for the effective protection of the right to equal treatment and therefore, for the enhancement of minority protection.

Chapter 3

Forms of Proof in Equal Treatment Cases

Part A. Theoretical Framework

3.1. Introduction

Direct evidence of discrimination is rarely found. This is the reason why the applicant should merely give rise to a presumption of discrimination instead of having to prove that discrimination has taken place. As the Aristotelian concept of equality inherently includes comparison, both giving rise to a presumption of discrimination and proving that no discrimination has happened can be accomplished by using comparison as a means of evidence. Comparison as evidence immediately assigns the forms of proof that could effectively be used in discrimination cases. Accordingly, those forms of proof are particularly appropriate in discrimination cases which can make the comparison visible. In this respect two forms of proof stand out: statistics and situation testing. Naturally, this does not, however, mean that no other forms of proof could be applied, or would be effective, but these two forms deserve special attention due to the fact that, in contrast with other possible forms of proof, they inherently entail comparison. The importance of these two special forms of proof is also acknowledged in the academic literature.[1] Strikingly, the case law both at European level and at the level of the Member States clearly shows that the application and acceptance of these forms of proof is far from being consistent, systematic and unconditional. This subsection, therefore, aims at elaborating a theoretical framework for the application of statistics and situation testing as forms of proof in discrimination cases.

1 See inter alia Schiek, Waddington & Bell (2007), at 253-257. & 373-435; De Prins, Sottiaux & Vrielink (2005), at 112-120; Gijzen (2006), at 74-81; De Schutter (2003b).

Two separate sections will be devoted to these two forms of proof the structures of which will be similar. First of all, a short explanation will be given concerning the relationship between the particular form of proof and the concept of discrimination. This will be followed by a concise history of its application. Next, the methodology of the form of proof at stake will be elaborated by providing a comprehensive analysis of the relevant problematic points. Each paragraph will be closed addressing the sensitive matters encompassing the specific form of proof.

3.2. Statistics

3.2.1. Proving with Statistics

The use of statistical data makes it possible to compare the situation of different groups.[2] Due to its inherent group focus statistics constitute an appropriate form of evidence in cases of indirect discrimination,[3] which is also emphasised in the RED.[4] Moreover, statistics can also constitute evidence in cases of systemic discrimination[5] where, similarly to indirect discrimination, it is the effect of a practice on a group that is the subject of the complaint.[6]
A discussion has been going on regarding whether indirect discrimination can be proven by statistics alone, or whether such data should rather be seen as optional, but not obligatory, evidence of a disparate impact. In this respect two separate but related arguments can be brought up in support of the position that statistics should merely be seen as a possible form of proof. First of all, it has been argued that the RED (and the FD) by acknowledging potential discrimination as a form of discrimination "mark a departure from the statistical evidence approach to indirect discrimination adopted by the Burden of Proof Directive."[7] While the Burden of Proof Directive required that a neutral provision, criterion or practice "*disadvantages a substantially higher proportion* of the members of one sex", the RED stipulates that indirect

---

2 See also Schiek, Waddington & Bell (2007), at 399.

3 See inter alia Tobler (2005a), at 291; Schiek, Waddington & Bell (2007), at 397.

4 "Preamble (15) [...] Such rules may provide in particular for indirect discrimination to be established by any means *including on the basis of statistical evidence*" (emphasis added).

5 On systemic discrimination see inter alia Craig (2007).

6 There are critics according to which statistics are not an appropriate means of evidence to establish the causal link in indirect discrimination cases. Arguably, this position would require the same causal link for indirect discrimination as in the case of direct discrimination, and does not accept that it is the disparate impact that establishes this link in the case of indirect discrimination. For this position see for instance Szente (2006).

7 Gijzen (2006), at 71. See also Tobler (2005a), at 226-228. & 291; Prechal (2004), at 542; McCrudden (2003), at 30; Finlay (2003), at 143; O'Hare (2001), at 147. & 291; Fredman (2001b), at 162; Barnard (2001), at 970.

discrimination occurs when such measures "*would put* persons of a racial or ethnic origin *at a particular disadvantage*."[8] Originally, it was statistical evidence that helped to develop the concept of indirect discrimination which has led to the adoption of the definition in the Burden of Proof Directive.[9] Later this definition with its requirement of submitting concrete data and actual disadvantage was, however, regarded as working to the detriment of this concept, since statistical data is not always available.[10] This evaluation process has resulted in the new definition of indirect discrimination in the RED (and FD), in which the expression of 'would put at a particular disadvantage' indicates that statistical evidence is not a prerequisite for showing a prima facie case of discrimination.

Secondly, the Preamble of the RED also seems to indicate that statistical data is simply one possible form of proof.[11] Recital (15) RED stipulates that national rules concerning the appreciation of the facts "may provide in particular for indirect discrimination to be established *by any means* including on the basis of statistical evidence."[12] In other words, the emphasis seems to be placed on the fact that statistics can be accepted as an appropriate means of evidence as well as means. On the contrary, departing from the same recital it has been argued that

> it depends on national procedural law rather than on EC law whether an instance of prima facie indirect discrimination [is not only possible but] *must* be proven on the basis of statistical data.[13]

In addition to the above explanation on the recital, it can also be argued that even though the Member States retain their procedural autonomy, the procedural rules cannot infringe the principle of effective enforcement. In other words, the procedural rules cannot make the enforcement of the principle of equal treatment virtually impossible or excessively difficult. In terms of statistics it would mean that the enforcement of the principle of equal treatment would be extensively limited if statistical data was required in each and every case,

---

8 Art, 2 (2) b) RED (emphasis added). See also Busstra (2010).

9 See also Schiek, Waddington & Bell (2007), at 373.

10 See also *id.*, at 398-399.

11 See also *id.*, at 423; Tobler (2008), at 43.

12 Recital (15) RED (emphasis added).

13 Gijzen (2006), at 75 (emphasis added). Compare this position with the argument of De Schutter who stated in relation to the RED that "[t]he Council decided [...] to leave it to the Member States to decide whether or not they should provide for the possibility for the victim of discrimination to rely on statistics to establish a presumption of indirect discrimination." De Schutter (2006), at 16; De Schutter (2005b), at 15.

keeping in mind the serious lack of such data;[14] or, on the contrary, if statistics were not accepted as evidence.[15]

3.2.2. A Concise History of the Application of Statistics as Evidence

It was first in the United States that statistical evidence in discrimination cases beat a path to the courtrooms. In *International Brotherhood of Teamsters v. United States* the Court stated that "cases make it unmistakably clear that '[s]tatistical analyses have served and will continue to serve an important role' in cases in which the existence of discrimination is a disputed issue."[16]

The European Court of Justice[17] also accepted statistics early on as potential forms of proof in indirect discrimination cases.[18] The Court, for example, stated in the *Rinke* case[19] that

[14] The Commission, for instance, in relation to sex discrimination explained that "in the field of sex discrimination, the European Court of Justice has required statistical evidence to prove indirect discrimination. However, adequate statistics are not always available." Proposal for a Council Directive implementing the principle of equal treatment between persons irrespective of racial or ethnic origin, COM(1999) 566 final, 1999/0253, 25 November 1999, at 8.

[15] The ECJ in the Judgment of 9 November 1983 in *Case 199/82, State Finance Administration v. SPA San Giorgio*, [1983] ECR 3595 held exactly in relation to the forms of proof that "any requirement of proof which has the effect of making it virtually impossible or excessively difficult to secure the repayment of charges levied contrary to Community law would be incompatible with Community law. That is so particularly in the case of [...] special limitations concerning the form of the evidence to be adduced, such as the exclusion of any kind of evidence other than documentary evidence." In relation to this Goldston also argued that "[t]he Convention could provide useful clarity to governments, courts and potential litigants by mandating a similar rule and by specifying that all forms of evidence consistent with national legislation and rules, including but not limited to statistics, may be used to prove discrimination." Goldston (2005), at 7. See also De Schutter (2006), at 14-16.

[16] *Brotherhood of Teamsters v. United States*, 431 U.S. 324 (SC 1977).

[17] Strikingly, the European Court of Human Rights was more reluctant to draw inference from statistical evidence that there might have been discrimination. For a long time it emphasised that "statistics are not by themselves sufficient to disclose a practice which could be classified as discriminatory." (*Hoogendijk v. Netherlands*, ECHR (2005) No. 58641/00, 6 January 2005). Only in very recent cases can an improvement be discovered in this context. See inter alia *D.H. and Others v. the Czech Republic*, ECHR (2006) No. 57325/00, 7 February 2006. For an overview of the development in the jurisprudence of the ECtHR in this respect see Henrard (2008a).

[18] See for example Judgment of 9 February 1999 in *Case C-167/97, Regina v. Secretary of State for Employment, ex parte Nicole Seymour-Smith and Laura Perez*, [1999] ECR I-623, paras. 60-61; Judgment of 27 October 1993 in *Case C-127/92, Dr. Pamela Mary Enderby v. Frenchay Health Authority and Secretary of State for Health*, [1993] ECR I-5535, para. 19; Judgment of 13 May 1986 in *Case 170/84, Bilka-Kaufhaus GmbH v. Karin Weber von Hartz*, [1986] ECR 1607, para. 29; Judgment of 17 October 1989 in *Case C-109/88, Handels- og Kontorfunktionærernes Forbund I Danmark v. Dansk Arbejdsgiverforening, acting on behalf of Danfoss*, [1989] ECR 3199, para. 16.

[19] Judgment of 9 September 2003 in *Case C-25/02, Katharina Rinke v. Ärztekammer Hamburg*, [2003] ECR I-08349.

> [i]t is clear from the *statistical data* referred to by the Advocate General [...] that the percentage of women working part-time is much higher than that of men working on a part-time basis.[20]

3.2.3. Methodology of Proving with Statistics

3.2.3.1. Comparison

On the basis of statistical data it is possible to compare the composition of two groups, the so called '*reference group*' with the '*selected group*'.[21]

> Within each of these groups the individuals must be divided into two categories, A and B, corresponding to the dominant or majority category and the traditionally disadvantaged or minority category. The distinction between the two categories will be based on criteria such as sex, race or ethnic origin etc. The ratio of category A to category B represents the proportion of the members of each category within the reference group, while the ratio of category A* to category B* will represent the proportions within the selected group.[22]

One has to examine how A:B relates to A*:B*; accordingly, the comparison becomes a relative, and not an absolute one.[23] For instance, in the *Enderby* case the selected group was the group of speech therapists, and the reference group was the group of pharmacists. The ECJ accepted that

> if the pay of speech therapists is significantly lower than that of pharmacists and if the former are almost exclusively women while the latter are predominantly men, there is a prima facie case of discrimination.[24]

Accordingly the proportion of men (A) and women (B) working as pharmacists was compared with that (A* and B*) of speech therapists.[25]

3.2.3.2. Disparate impact[26]

As already hinted at supra, the definition of indirect discrimination in the RED stipulates that indirect discrimination occurs when persons of a racial or ethnic origin would be put at a *particular disadvantage*. Somewhat differently,

20 *Id.*, para. 35 (emphasis added).
21 For a refinement of selected group see pool of comparators below.
22 De Schutter (2003b), at 27.
23 See inter alia Tobler (2005a), at 232; Schiek, Waddington & Bell (2007), at 407.
24 *Case C-127/92, Dr. Pamela Mary Enderby v. Frenchay Health Authority and Secretary of State for Health*, para. 16.
25 Importantly, in many other cases the ECJ is less explicit on the reference group. See for instance Judgment of 23 May 1996 in *Case C-237/94, John O'Flynn v. Adjudication Officer*, [1996] ECR I-2617.
26 For a detailed elaboration from the perspective of the concept of indirect discrimination, see Busstra (2010).

the Burden of Proof Directive laid down that indirect discrimination is at stake when a measure *disadvantages a substantially higher proportion* of members of one sex. The two definitions seem to indicate a different approach concerning what they mean by a disadvantage.[27] While the Burden of Proof Directive describes the disparate impact in terms of the number or proportion of the persons affected, the RED seems to indicate a reference to the gravity of the disadvantage. However, the case law of the ECJ, in particular the *O'Flynn* and the *Rinke* cases, makes it clear that the term 'particular disadvantage' does not only refer to the gravity of the disadvantage, but can also relate to the number or proportion of the persons affected, or rather the number of those affected establishes the gravity of the disadvantage. According to the ECJ

> [i]t is clear from the statistical data that *the percentage of women working part-time is much higher* than that of men working on a part-time basis. [...] Thus, such a requirement does in fact *place women at a particular disadvantage* as compared with men.[28]

The question is now what is meant by a *'particular'* disadvantage, what is the threshold that has to be achieved in order to accept that there is *prima facie* discrimination. It is generally accepted that the case law of the ECJ lacks clarity in this respect, since no relative or absolute numbers have been hinted at by the ECJ.[29] The ECJ uses different formulas concerning the disparate impact: "*far greater number* of women than men"[30] are affected; "*almost exclusively* women, while the latter are *predominantly* men";[31] "places *many more* women than men at disadvantage";[32] "*considerably smaller percentage* of women than men is able to satisfy the condition of two years employment";[33] "*lesser but persistent and relatively constant disparity over a long period*";[34] "*much lower proportion* of women than of men work full time";[35] "they affect

[27] See also Tobler (2005a), at 225-234; Schiek, Waddington & Bell (2007), at 414-419.

[28] *Case C-25/02, Katharina Rinke v. Ärztekammer Hamburg*, para. 35 (emphasis added).

[29] See inter alia De Schutter (2003a), at 27; Barnard & Hepple (1999), at 399 & 403; Ellis (1998), at 118; Drijber & Prechal (1997), at 139; Schiek, Waddington & Bell (2007), at 414. Tobler has even argued that "it may simply be impossible to establish a specific threshold which acts as a means to convincingly rule out other approaches." Tobler (2005a), at 227.

[30] *Case 170/84, Bilka-Kaufhaus GmbH v. Karin Weber von Hartz*, para. 24. See also Gijzen (2006), at 76.

[31] *Case C-127/92, Dr. Pamela Mary Enderby v. Frenchay Health Authority and Secretary of State for Health*, para. 16.

[32] Judgment of 15 December 1994 in *Joined Cases C-399/92, C-409/92, C-425/92, C-34/93, C-50/93 and C-78/93, Stadt Lengerich v. Angelika Helmig and Waltraud Schmidt v. Deutsche Angestellten-Krankenkase and others*, [1994] ECR I-05727, para. 17.

[33] *Case C-167/97, Regina v. Secretary of State for Employment, ex parte Nicole Seymour-Smith and Laura Perez*, para. 60. See also Judgment of 31 March 1981 in *Case 96/80, J.P. Jenkins v. Kingsgate (Clothing Productions) Ltd.*, [1981] ECR 911, para. 13.

[34] *Case C-167/97, Regina v. Secretary of State for Employment, ex parte Nicole Seymour-Smith and Laura Perez*, para. 61.

[35] *Case 170/84, Bilka-Kaufhaus GmbH v. Karin Weber von Hartz*, para. 29.

considerably more women than men";[36] the measure is liable to "affect a *substantially higher proportion* of migrant workers" which seems to be the same in the Court's wording to being intrinsically liable "to *affect* migrant workers *more* than national workers and if there is a consequent risk that it will place the former at a *particular disadvantage*."[37] Thus, it can be seen that the disparate impact is generally related to the number or proportion of the persons affected, irrespective of the fact whether the argument was based on statistical data or other qualitative arguments.

In order to eliminate uncertainties in this respect, a convincing argument seems to be that, as soon as a *statistically significant* difference (over a period of time) can be seen in the proportions, fact-finders should not hesitate to place the burden of persuasion on the respondent. The respondent still has the possibility to objectively justify the particular measure within the framework of which the fact-finder can balance the different interests.[38] All in all, in order to ensure effective enforcement (and achieve substantive equality) the threshold should not be set high.

3.2.3.3. Pool of Comparators

One of the most important methodological matters concerning statistics is the appropriate assessment of the selected groups; that is the pool of comparators.[39] The determination of the pool of comparators arguably comprises two aspects: what is the basis of comparison and at which level the comparison takes place. Concerning the first aspect the ECJ seems to make a comparison between those who can and those who cannot comply with a certain requirement.[40] For instance, the Court in the *Seymour-Smith* case accepted that

> the best approach to the comparison of statistics is to consider, on the one hand, the respective proportions of men [...] *able to satisfy* the requirement of two years' employment under the disputed rule and of those *unable to do so*, and, on the other, to compare those proportions as regards women [...].[41]

In the *Helmig* case the reference group was the group of full-time workers and the selected group (pool of comparators) was the group of part-time workers. In the *Enderby* case the Court compared the proportion of men and women in

---

36 *Joined Cases C-399/92, C-409/92, C-425/92, C-34/93, C-50/93 and C-78/93, Stadt Lengerich v. Angelika Helmig and Waltraud Schmidt v. Deutsche Angestellten-Krankenkase and others*, para. 23.

37 *Case C-237/94, John O'Flynn v. Adjudication Officer*, para. 20. On this aspect see inter alia O'Hare (2001), at 147; Bell (2002c), at 34; Barnard & Hepple (1999), at 406; Vick (2001), at 9.

38 See also Gerards (2005a), at 78-79.

39 See also Makkonen (2007b), at 36; Schiek, Waddington & Bell (2007), at 401-414; Gijzen (2006), at 76; Busstra (2010).

40 See also Schiek, Waddington & Bell (2007), at 409.

41 *Case C-167/97, Regina v. Secretary of State for Employment, ex parte Nicole Seymour-Smith and Laura Perez*, para. 59 (emphasis added).

the group of speech therapists with the proportion of men and women in the group of pharmacists.[42] Admittedly, it is not always clear in the case law of the Court what the actual reference group is. In the *O'Flynn* case, for instance, the Court only stated that one should compare migrant workers with national workers.[43] In this case the reference group included those who work and have funerals in the UK, and the group of persons who work but do not arrange funerals in the UK constituted the selected group. Also, the proportion of migrant workers was compared to the proportion of non-migrant workers in these groups. It can also be seen that the pool of comparators does not include the reference group (the group that suffered disadvantage).[44] On the basis of the case law, it can be concluded that the condition of satisfying/not satisfying a certain requirement seems to be a feasible criterion for selecting the two groups that are compared.

Importantly, in many cases there are no concrete statistics concerning the composition of either the reference or the selected group or both, so often common knowledge or qualitative arguments need to be relied on. This could also be observed in the *O'Flynn* case, where it seemed to be part of the general knowledge that in the UK more migrant workers arrange the funerals of their relatives abroad than non-migrant workers. Relying on common knowledge can be classified as statistical-like evidence, since its application and methodology as far as the comparison is concerned are similar to that of statistical evidence.

As to the level of comparison or the source of the statistics to be obtained, depending on the particular complaint different levels of comparison can be discovered in the case law of the ECJ.[45] In the mentioned *O'Flynn* case the comparison was made at national level (workforce), while in the *Bilka-Kaufhaus* case it was made at company level. Concerning the level of comparison Makkonnen distinguished internal and external statistics.[46] The former means statistics obtained at the level of a company (or a department/ departments of a company), while the latter refers to statistics obtained at the level of society (or a subgroup/subgroups of the society, for instance a certain

[42] On the pool of comparators in the *Enderby* case see inter alia Cunningham (2009), at 213-214.

[43] *Case C-237/94*, *John O'Flynn v. Adjudication Officer*, paras. 20-21. See also the cases of *Panesar v. Nestlé Co Ltd*, IRLR 60 (EAT 1980); *Mandla v. Lee*, IRLR 209 (HL 1983) and *Singh v. British Rail Engineering*, ICR 22 (EAT 1986) in the UK. In these cases it was commonly known that in the first case the prohibiting beards would disparately affect Pakistani persons, and in the two latter cases it concerned persons wearing turbans, which would disparately affect Sikhs.

[44] On the contrary, Schiek, Waddington and Bell argue that it is problematic that not the proportion of those having the protected ground at stake in the disadvantaged group is compared to the proportion of these persons in the whole group (thus including the disadvantaged group as well). Schiek, Waddington & Bell (2007), at 414.

[45] See also *id.*, at 406.

[46] Makkonen (2007b), at 33-35.

geographical area). Applying these terms to the above cases, in the *O'Flynn* case the quantitative evidence (common knowledge) was external, and in the *Bilka-Kaufhaus* it was internal.

Notably, there are cases where only internal statistics are considered sufficient. In other cases external statistics can make up appropriate evidence. There might also be instances where a combination of the two is required. How can the level of comparison be determined? From the above cited cases, it can be seen that when the complaint referred to a national regulation, the comparison was made at national level, thus external statistical-like evidence was used. When the case concerned the staff policy of a department store, the comparison was made at company level. At least two conclusions can be drawn from these observations. Firstly, the level of comparison should be dependent on the respondent, since he can be held liable only for those actions that fall under his responsibility. Accordingly, if the respondent represents a company, internal statistics should be used. However, if the complaint concerns a national policy or legislation, external statistics should be relied on. Secondly, both internal and external statistics can be further categorised, and different gradations can be made, such as statistics only in relation to a certain policy field, or concerning a concrete department of a company, and so on. This angle, arguably, should be determined by the first aspect concerning the pool of comparators; that is who can comply with or satisfy the disputed measure.

3.2.3.4. Nature of Statistics

In some cases, the ECJ has set up certain requirements concerning the quality or nature of the statistical data. In the *Enderby* case, for instance, the ECJ laid down that statistics have to "cover enough individuals," and they must not illustrate "purely fortuitous or short-term phenomena."[47] This stance was confirmed in the subsequent *Seymour-Smith* case.[48] Setting up such conditions aims to prevent someone being held liable on the basis of insignificant, irrelevant or atypical statistics. These requirements do not seem to be unreasonable because their purpose is to impede holding someone liable for situations arising from a statistical margin of error.[49]

Importantly, as mentioned in relation to the *O'Flynn* case, not only statistics but also common knowledge can be relied on where a comparison is made as

---

[47] *Case C-127/92, Dr. Pamela Mary Enderby v. Frenchay Health Authority and Secretary of State for Health*, para. 17. See also Gijzen (2006), at 82.

[48] *Case C-167/97, Regina v. Secretary of State for Employment, ex parte Nicole Seymour-Smith and Laura Perez*, paras. 60-61.

[49] See also Browne (1999), at 412.

to the ethnic composition of two groups.[50] Similarly, surveys and monitoring can also be used as evidence in such cases. The requirements set up for the quality of statistics should therefore also be applied to these.

3.2.3.5. Field of Application[51]

It is commonly known that statistical evidence can be used to show the broader effect of a measure.[52] Accordingly, it is an appropriate means to give rise to a presumption of indirect discrimination (or to prove that there has been no indirect discrimination)[53] since, as argued, "[t]he cognitive tools used to capture indirect discrimination [...] are statistical."[54] That is to say a comparison based on the method of proving with statistics or statistical-like evidence is inherently embedded in the disparate impact approach. Moreover, on the basis of statistics one can also establish a pattern of disparate treatment, thus, it can be applied in cases in which the applicant complains of systemic direct discrimination.[55] For instance, in the *West Midland Transport v. Singh* case the Court of Appeal in the UK stated that

---

50 On common knowledge see also Tobler (2005a), at 228; Wyatt & Dashwood (2000), at 403; Barnard & Hepple (1999), at 406; Vick warns of the potential danger of extended reliance on common knowledge, namely that tribunals might rely on common sense to an undesired extent. Vick (2001), at 9.

51 On difficulties that may derive from statistical evidence concerning certain protected grounds see Makkonen (2007a), at 30-31; Makkonen (2007b), at 75-78; Tobler (2005a), at 233-234; Cahn (2004); Petrova (2004); Bell & Waddington (2003), at 363; Meenan (2003), at 13; Whittle (2002), at 309; Bell (2001b), at 660; De Schutter (2001), at 105.

52 See also De Schutter (2003b), at 23. A comparative study even argued that indirect discrimination can only be established with the help of statistics, which does not exclude the acceptance of, for example, common knowledge. However, in relation to indirect discrimination, the common knowledge argument is also based on proportions. According to this study, "[t]he indirect discrimination concept and the related action schemes are intrinsically linked to statistics by their logic and objective. The definition of indirect discrimination is based on quantitative concepts: significant effects and comparisons between groups. The cognitive tools used to capture indirect discrimination, which is the reasoning on which legal and political developments are based, are statistical" (Simon (2004), at 82). Fredman, by referring to Barnard and Hepple, argues that statistics are not the only way of proving indirect discrimination. "Barnard and Hepple argue that there is no need to substitute this individualistic view of indirect discrimination in order to avoid statistical tangles. Instead, the recent willingness of UK courts and tribunals to interpret the notion of 'considerably smaller' without elaborate statistical evidence, taking account of social facts, demonstrates that it is possible to retain a group dimension and side-step statistical difficulties" (Fredman (2001b), at 162).

53 On the concept of indirect discrimination see Busstra (2010). See inter alia Tobler (2005a); Finlay (2003); Loenen (1999).

54 Simon (2004), at 82.

55 Bindman (1992), at 61. See also *West Midlands Passenger Transport Executive v. Singh*, IRLR 186 (CA 1988). The Court of Appeal in this case established that "[s]tatistical evidence may establish a discernible pattern in the treatment of a particular group [...]."

> [i]f there is evidence of a *high percentage rate* of failure to achieve promotion at particular levels by members of a particular racial group, this may indicate that the real reason for refusal is a *conscious or unconscious racial attitude* which involves *stereotyped assumptions* about members of that group.[56]

Thus, in the Court's view the applicant could give rise to a presumption of discrimination on the basis of statistical data.

As hinted at supra, statistical evidence is also used by respondents to prove there has been no discrimination. Such evidence is also used when direct discrimination against a concrete individual is at stake, and respondents use statistics to prove that they do not have racial prejudices. In other words, they want to show that they do not practice discrimination in general, thus, they could not have discriminated in the concrete case either.[57] However, not being racist does not exclude that the respondent in a concrete case discriminated against a particular individual on the ground of race. It has been observed that "statistics produced by the respondent, showing e.g. a balanced workforce, should not suffice – at least not alone – to rebut a case made by the complainant."[58] When a complaint concerns an individual case, the refutation of the respondent should be concerned with that particular event. Nevertheless, when the applicant argues that there is systemic direct discrimination against a group having a certain racial or ethnic origin, as in the above-mentioned *West Midland Transport v. Singh* case, the respondent's statistical arguments should also be accepted.[59]

Statistics could also constitute appropriate evidence in cases of intersectional discrimination[60] if the available data were broken down on the basis of the different characteristics. This is the case, for instance, when the applicant can show a disparate impact on women of a certain racial or ethnic origin. However, due to a general lack of data on racial or ethnic origin, it is difficult to establish intersectional discrimination one of the grounds of which is race.

In principle, statistics can be applied in all areas falling under the material scope of the Race Directive. Statistics might also prove the existence of discriminatory practices or disparate impact in recruitment, as well as in promotion or in supplying goods and services, and so on. Nevertheless, statistical evidence can most often be found in complaints related to employment or education. The reason for the dominance of these fields might be found in the fact that it is more difficult to collect data with respect to the other fields.

---

56 See also Craig (2007), at 140 (emphasis added).
57 See also Makkonen (2007b), at 31-32.
58 Makkonen (2007b), at 31-32.
59 See also Hunyor (2004), at 546-547.
60 On intersectional discrimination see inter alia Makkonen (2000); Nielsen (2009).

Statistical evidence as a form of proof can also contribute to the effective enforcement of the principle of equal treatment in its broader sense. Namely, it can serve as evidence of discrimination beyond complaints of discrimination before fact-finders. Statistics can be expedient or even inevitable in cases related to the policy of combating discrimination,[61] in particular, when positive action measures are involved.[62] Such measures have a double role in the sense that they can be applied either in anti-discrimination procedures or be concerned with general policy questions.[63] In the first case, statistics are useful to the respondent because he can justify the distinction made with the help of statistics, pointing to the disparities which were intended to be eliminated through the positive action measures. Concerning the second aspect, statistics can help recognize the need for positive action and show the necessity of introducing such measures.[64] Moreover, statistics play an important role in monitoring compliance,[65] assessing the effectiveness of the existing laws, giving guidance to future policy, raising awareness, helping specialised bodies conduct independent surveys and so on.[66] In this context, ECRI Policy Recommendation No. 4 stresses 'that statistical data on racist and discriminatory acts and on the situation of minority groups in all fields of life are vital for the identification of problems and the formulation of policies.'[67] The UN treaty bodies do also ask for information broken down by the particular grounds.[68]

61 Makkonen (2007a), at 21.

62 Makkonen (2007b), 19. & 41.

63 See also Ringelheim (2006), at 16-17.

64 In relation to positive action on the grounds of race or ethnic origin Barton has observed that "[e]thnic monitoring also plays a key role in the development of equal opportunities policies and practices. It has provided powerful evidence that has significantly influenced government policy and practice in a number of areas." Barton (2004). See also Farkas (2004a); Makkonen (2007b), at 5.

65 See also Art. 11(1) RED.

66 See Makkonen (2007b), at 19; Makkonen (2007a), at 21-24; Barton (2004).

67 ECRI General Policy Recommendation No. 4: National Surveys on the Experience and Perception of Discrimination and Racism from the Point of View of Potential Victims, CRI(98) 30, 6 March 1998.

68 See inter alia Consolidated guidelines for state reports, Human Rights Committee, CCPR/66/GUI/Rev.2, 26 February 2001, para. C.6; UN CERD Committee, General Recommendation IV, HRI/GEN/1/Rev.7, 12 May 2004; General recommendation XXVII on discrimination against Roma, HRI/GEN/1/Rev.7, 12 May 2004; Advisory Committee on the Framework Convention for the Protection of National Minorities, Outline for reports to be submitted pursuant to Article 25 paragraph 1 of the Framework Convention for the protection of national minorities, 30 September 1998. In general see Makkonen (2007b), at 21-23.

3.2.4. Sensitive Matters

3.2.4.1. Dehumanisation of the Procedure

Several sensitive questions can be identified in relation to statistics.[69] One of the arguments often raised against the use of statistics is the 'dehumanisation' of the procedure, namely that mathematics will take over the throne of human considerations[70] and statistics will give rise "to some rather technical case law and a lot of practical problems."[71] However, it has never been required that a case be decided purely on the basis of numbers and percentages. This is also the reason why no clear general threshold of a disparate impact can be established. Statistics can give good indications as to the existence of a certain disparity in a certain area in a certain context, but the relevant circumstances always have to be taken into consideration.

3.2.4.2. Definition, Classification and Identification

In addition to the methodological uncertainties surrounding the application of statistical data in discrimination procedures, there are methodological difficulties in relation to collecting data on racial or ethnic origin.[72] First of all, it is not simple to define what racial or ethnic origin means (definition); it is also difficult to determine how particular groups can be recognised as having a certain racial or ethnic origin (group classification); and finally, it is not an easy task to specify how an individual can be considered to belong to a certain racial or ethnic group (individual identification).[73]

3.2.4.3. Lack of Data

Arguably, the main problem with statistics is not the difficulties it raises in terms of methodological questions in relation to the application of statistics in discrimination procedures, or those concerning data collection, but the serious lack of statistical data.[74] Accordingly, one cannot but agree with

---

69 See also Makkonen (2007b), 6. & 49-82.

70 Humblet (2003), at 9. See also Browne (1999), at 411. & 423.

71 Prechal (2004), at 542.

72 See also Reuter, Makkonen & Oosi (2004), at 20-27; Petrova (2004); Ringelheim (2006), at 31-41.

73 These questions in fact belong to the substantive considerations. On the ground of racial or ethnic origin see Busstra (2010).

74 See also Makkonen (2007b), at 6. & 40; Cahn (2004); Goldson (2001); ERRC, The Glass Box. Exclusion of Roma from employment (2007), at 52. The Preamble of the Recast Directive itself directs the attention to the importance of the availability of statistical data even on the grounds of gender, when it states that "[f]or the sake of a better understanding of the different treatment of men and women in matters of employment and occupation, comparable statistics

the observation of Farkas that "[a]t present, viewing statistics as the main proof of indirect discrimination would indeed be counter-productive in race discrimination cases because of the wide-spread absence of such data."[75] The lack of data and the problems caused by this are also highlighted by the ECRI Policy Recommendation No. 1 which requires the Member States of the Council of Europe "to collect [...] where and when appropriate, data which will assist in assessing and evaluating the situation and experiences of groups which are particularly vulnerable to racism, xenophobia, anti-Semitism and intolerance."[76] The Advisory Committee on the Framework Convention for the Protection of National Minorities also pays attention to the availability of statistical data. This Committee has observed that the lack or inappropriateness of statistical data can "seriously hamper the ability of the state to target, implement and monitor measures to ensure the full and effective equality of persons belonging to national minorities."[77] Remarkably, an interesting approach to statistical data can be found at international level. Not 'merely' its supervisory body, but the UN Convention on the Rights of Persons with Disabilities[78] itself recognises the need for statistics in order to provide a sound basis for policy-making, and it makes the collection of data obligatory for the States Parties.[79]

It could be argued that Member States have a positive obligation to ensure that data are collected and available. Should states not comply with this

disaggregated by sex should continue to be developed, analysed and made available at the appropriate levels." Preamble (37) Recast Directive.

75 Farkas (2004a).

76 ECRI General Policy Recommendation No. 1: Combating Racism, Xenophobia, Anti-Semitism and Intolerance, CRI (96) 43 rev., 4 October 1996.

77 Advisory Committee on the Framework Convention for the Protection of National Minorities. Opinion on Slovakia. ACFC/INF/OP/I (2001)001, adopted September 22, 2000, para. 21; Opinion on Czech Republic. ACFC/INF/OP/I (2002)002, adopted on April 6, 2001, para. 28; Opinion on Poland. ACFC/INF/OP/I (2004)005, adopted on November 27, 2003, para. 27. See also Hollo (2006), at 24.

78 The Convention on the Rights of Persons with Disabilities and its Optional Protocol, adopted on 13 December 2006 and entered into force on 3 May 2008.

79 "Article 31 1. States Parties undertake to collect appropriate information including statistical and research data to enable them to formulate and implement policies to give effect to the present Convention. The process of collecting and maintaining this information shall:

a) Comply with legally established safeguards, including legislation on data protection, to ensure confidentiality and respect for the privacy of persons with disabilities;

b) Comply with internationally accepted norms to protect human rights and fundamental freedoms and ethical principles in the collection and use of statistics.

2. The information collected in accordance with this article shall be disaggregated, as appropriate, and used to help assess the implementation of States Parties' obligations under the present Convention and to identify and address the barriers faced by persons with disabilities in exercising their rights.

3. States Parties shall assume responsibility for the dissemination of these statistics and ensure their accessibility to persons with disabilities and others."

obligation, they might be in breach of the principle of effective enforcement, since the lack of statistics could make the enforcement of the right to equal treatment virtually impossible or excessively difficult.[80] In other words, the lack of statistical data should not frustrate the applicant's choice of the particular form of proof he wants to apply. The European Committee of Social Rights stated in a case where the respondent Government was not able to provide any data on the size of the Roma community in Greece that

> when the collection and storage of personal data is prevented for such reasons [constitutional obstacles – MA], but it is also generally acknowledged that a particular group is or could be discriminated against, the authorities have the responsibility for finding alternative means of assessing the extent of the problem and progress towards resolving it that are not subject to such constitutional restrictions.[81]

In other words, Member States have to ensure that data are available which then could be freely used by the applicant and/or the respondent.[82]

3.2.4.4. Data Protection and Privacy

The reason for this remarkable lack of such data[83] might be linked to fears and experiences of data abuse.[84] However, if one looks at the different data

[80] Petrova also argues for a duty to collect data. Petrova (2004). See also Ringelheim (2006), at 12-14; De Schutter & Ringelheim (2008), at 378; O'Cinnéide (2003), at 29-30; Hepple, Coussey & Choudhury (2000), at 63.

[81] *European Roma Rights Center v. Greece*, ECSR (2005) No. 15/2003, 7 February 2005, para. 27.

[82] See also Makkonen (2007a), at 23. Makkonen also observes that "[t]he governments themselves have on several occasions recognised the need to compile such statistics." Makkonen (2007a), at 21. See inter alia the following documents: Copenhagen Declaration on Social Development and Programme of Action of the world Summit for Social Development, A/CONF.166/9, 19 April 1995; Durban Declaration of Plan of Action; Vienna Declaration and Programme of Action, A/CONF.157/23, 12 July 1993; World Programme of Action concerning Disabled Persons, General Assembly, A/RES/37/52, 3 December 1982; Standard Rules on the Equalization of Opportunities for Persons with Disabilities, Annex to the General Assembly, A/RES/48/96, 20 December 1993.

[83] Gijzen argues that "[t]he relaxation of the insistence by EC law of proving indirect discrimination by way of statistics can be explained by reference to the underlying values of different grounds of discrimination. The nature of the discrimination ground 'sex' brings with it that the collection of statistical data on, for example, the participation of women and men in paid labour is a rather insensitive and routine exercise in the Member States. In contrast, some Member States prohibit the collection of statistical data in relation to 'race' and 'ethnicity', either for privacy related reasons, or by reference to the argument that the collection of such statistics is a racist exercise in se." Gijzen (2006), at 71. See also Tyson (2001), at 203. However, the Preamble of the Recast Directive does not seem to support her argument. Preamble (37) calls for further collection of data in relation to gender as well.

[84] De Schutter describes it as a 'paradox': "processing 'sensitive' data is subject to specific restrictions because these data are based on characteristics which, in principle, have no

protection and privacy regulations,[85] it can generally be concluded that the requirements set on the collection and processing of sensitive data are feasible, and they provide appropriate safeguards against the abuse of sensitive data.[86] When the data are rendered anonymous, it is no longer personal data. It can therefore be processed without further restrictions and Member States should not argue in terms of strict rules in this respect. Rules to minimise the threat of abuse of personal data are concerned with unanonymised data, the relevance of which for statistical data as evidence is minimum. In relation to this the EU Data Protection Directive,[87] which has or should have already been implemented in all Member States, contains a general prohibition of processing sensitive data. There are two main exceptions from this prohibition: sensitive data can only be processed with the consent of the person concerned or without his consent if necessary for legal claims or otherwise provided for under national law.[88] Thus, the privacy of the person whose sensitive data are at stake seems to be appropriately protected, and ample scope is given to collect and process sensitive data. Accordingly, states should not be afraid of

relevance in decisions made about an individual and, consequently, processing the data may run the risk of discriminatory practices. But on the other hand, if a victim of discrimination wishes to support his/her legal action with statistical evidence which will establish a prima facie case of discrimination (thereby obliging the defendant to demonstrate that s/he did not commit the alleged discriminatory act), this sort of sensitive data will have to be processed." (De Schutter (2003b), at 28). Contrary to de Schutter, it can be argued that actually no paradox can be found in the fact that certain rules have to be observed during the data processing. The processing of sensitive data is not prohibited, but certain strict rules have to be observed (De Schutter (2003b), at 28. See also De Schutter & Ringelheim (2008), at 363-364. & 376; Gijzen (2006), at 78; Petrova (2004)). By agreeing with de Schutter, Gijzen explains that "[t]his paradox has been recognized by the legislative definitions of indirect discrimination in the RD and EFD" (Gijzen (2006), at 78). Here, she refers to the fact that these Directives use the phrase 'would put' in the definition concerned, accordingly, because there is no need for actual disparate impact, no statistics are required, which means that no processing of sensitive data will be involved. This possibility, however, does not cover all the cases of indirect discrimination, accordingly, one cannot solve the 'paradox' by the liability test on the one hand; on the other hand, since no paradox can actually be discovered, no problems have to be solved concerning the processing of sensitive data.

[85] For example, ICCPR, ECHR as general rules, and the Convention for the Protection of Individuals with regard to Automatic Processing of Personal Data from 1981, European Parliament and Council Directive 95/46/EC of 24 October 1995 on the protection of individuals with regard to the processing of processing of personal data, and on the free movement of such data, as special regulations.

[86] See also Makkonen (2007b), at 14 & 52-64; Makkonen (2007a), at 41-45; De Schutter & Ringelheim (2008), at 372-377.

[87] Directive 95/46/EC of the European Parliament and of the Council of 24 October 1995 on the protection of individuals with regard to the processing of personal data and on the free movement of such data. See also Ringelheim (2006), at 23-31.

[88] See also Makkonen (2007b), at 62.

collecting and processing anonymous sensitive data in a fair and legal way,[89] which is not only in the interest of victims and perpetrators, but also essential for the states themselves in terms of discovering the problematic fields where appropriate actions need to be taken.[90]

3.3. Situation Testing

3.3.1. Proving with Situation Testing

Situation testing is a control in a real life situation over different causal variables that might influence the behaviour of the respondent.[91] Situation testing is often described as a kind of role play: testers are actors pretending to be in a real situation.[92] In a situation testing concerning racial discrimination a comparison is made between two groups being comparable to each other to the greatest extent possible but for their visible or perceivable racial or ethnic origin.[93] The aim of such testing, that *per definitionem* entails comparison, is to make visible that the respondent's behaviour is influenced by and based on the protected ground of the applicant. Accordingly, this method is capable of giving rise to the presumption that direct discrimination has taken place, covert or otherwise.[94] Importantly, situation testing aims to show that the racial or ethnic origin of the applicant could be the cause of the differential treatment. Thus, contrary to the general application of statistics, it is not concerned with demonstrating the effect of a (neutral) measure.

Unlike statistical evidence, the RED does not mention situation testing as a possible form of proof. Accordingly, the dilemma whether such a form is mandatory or optional does not arise in this context. The question is rather whether situation testing can and will be accepted by the Member States, which can naturally also depend on the interpretation of the ECJ in this respect.

89 Preamble (28) of the Directive 95/46/EC. "Whereas any processing of personal data must be lawful and fair to the individuals concerned; whereas, in particular, the data must be adequate, relevant and not excessive in relation to the purposes for which they are processed; whereas such purposes must be explicit and legitimate and must be determined at the time of collection of the data; whereas the purposes of processing further to collection shall not be incompatible with the purposes as they were originally specified."

90 It has been argued that "[c]ertain States fear that, by improving the monitoring of the impact on these groups of their laws and policies, they would be recognizing the existence of such groups and open the way to the vindication of 'special rights' of minorities." De Schutter (2005b), at 15. See also Hollo (2006), at 25.

91 See also Makkonen (2007b), at 46.

92 See inter alia Rorive (2006), at 33. However, such testing cannot always be regarded as 'pretend', since these persons are in real life discriminated against and can, as a response, turn to an enforcement body to get justice.

93 See inter alia De Schutter (2003b), at 32; Rorive (2006), at 36.

94 See inter alia Rorive (2006), at 33; De Schutter (2003b), at 32.

First of all, the fact that Article 8 RED does not specify which facts should be established by the applicant indicates that any evidence obtained legally can and should be accepted. Secondly, in terms of the principle of effectiveness and keeping in mind how difficult it is to prove/show that discrimination has happened, it can be argued that Member States should not hesitate to accept this form of proof.

3.3.2. A Concise History of Situation Testing

In Europe, the date of birth of situation testing in discrimination cases was in the 1970s in the United Kingdom before the Commission for Racial Equality[95] in racial discrimination cases. This type of evidence crossed the ocean from the United States, where it was adopted somewhat earlier, namely at the beginning of the 1960s.[96] Later on, "[i]t was also at the heart of a huge study of ethnic discrimination in recruitment co-ordinated by the International Labour Organisation in the 1990s."[97] Nowadays, situation testing seems to be a generally accepted and applied form of proving covert direct discrimination.[98]

3.3.3. Methodology of Proving with Situation Testing

3.3.3.1. Comparison

The aim of situation testing is, in principle, to compare two situations and to draw inferences from the comparison as to the existence of a less favourable treatment on the grounds of racial or ethnic origin. More precisely, the result of testing is to indicate that there could be a causal relationship between the treatment and the perceived racial or ethnic origin of the alleged victim of discrimination. Besides giving rise to the presumption of direct discrimination, situation testing can also reveal a practice from which the existence of systemic discrimination might be inferred, if the testing extends to a certain period of time and is repeated with some frequency.[99]

---

95 Rorive (2006), at 33. According to Craig it was in 1967, to be more precise. Craig (2007), at 18.

96 See for example *McDonnell Douglas Corp. v. Green*, 411 U.S. 792 (SC 1973). See also Fitsum (2000a), at 76.

97 Rorive (2006), at 33. See also De Schutter (2003b), at 33; Bovenkerk (1992); Craig (2007), at 19; Fitsum (2000a), at 75; Rorive (2009), at 42-43.

98 See inter alia Rorive (2009), at 42.

99 As Makkonen observed "[s]ituation testing is a particularly valuable tool also because it can be used to expose well-concealed forms of discrimination. Results of testing experiments are also often very generalizable, i.e. one can draw conclusions on the basis of such experiments about the actual levels of discrimination in society." Makkonen (2007b), at 47.

Similarly to statistical evidence, in situation testing two groups are generally distinguished; these are the so called selected and reference (control) groups. The group including persons with a visible or recognisable protected racial or ethnic origin is called the 'selected group' and the other group comprising persons without the particular racial or ethnic origin is the 'reference' or 'control group'. However, in addition to these groups there is also a group embracing the original victims, that is the 'victim group'.

The victim group plays an important role in direct discrimination cases in relation to which two situations can be distinguished. In the first situation there is an original victim group, the treatment against which is controlled in a testing with the participation of a selected and a reference group. Thus, in such cases the selected group is different from the victim group; and it would be methodologically incorrect for the selected group to be made up from the victim group, since in this case it would not be possible to eliminate factors other than racial or ethnic origin. In the second situation, however, the victim group itself can be regarded as the selected group, and the treatment of this group is compared to that of the reference group. In this latter testing, the testers have to ensure that variables are applied that could neutralise the circumstances, so that the link with the racial or ethnic origin becomes visible.

With respect to systematic discrimination the situation is somewhat different, since in such cases there is generally no original victim group in the claim: there are only testers controlling the behaviour of the alleged perpetrator. What complicates testing in this context is that it has to be carried out at an aggregate level, which implies that a couple of selected and reference groups have to be involved in the project.

At the end of the testing the treatment of the 'victim group'/'selected group' and the 'control group' is compared. If the previous group is treated less favourably than the control group, it can be presumed that the treatment was on the grounds of the ethnic origin of the members of this group. An example par excellence of situation testing is the case when Roma persons (the victim group) are excluded from a certain service (in a restaurant, discotheque, pub etc.). Two groups are fielded, one of them comprising persons of Roma origin (selected group) and the other persons of non-Roma origin (reference group). Both groups try to make use of the service shortly after each other. By comparing the treatment of the selected group and the victim group with the treatment of the reference group one could draw the inference as to the existence of a presumption of discrimination.

3.3.3.2. Situation Testing as Evidence

The results of situation testing can be used as evidence in two ways. On the one hand, testers might be and generally are required to complete a questionnaire at the end of the testing.[100] In this case, it is the questionnaire that serves as evidence, in fact documentary evidence. On the other hand, testers might be heard as witnesses by the fact-finder. Of course, even if a questionnaire has been submitted to the fact-finder, it can still hear the testers as witnesses.[101]

3.3.3.3. Neutralising Variables: Similarity of the Groups and Timing of Testing

It is generally emphasised that the situation in which this 'role play' takes place has to be well organised and controlled, in order to 'neutralise variables that could falsify the analysis.'[102] In practice this means that the groups have to be similar to each other to the greatest extent possible, and that special attention should be devoted to the timing of the testing (which could arguably also form part of the similarity argument).

As far as the similarity is concerned, first of all the selected group has to be similar to the victim group; that is the persons in the previous group have to have the same racial or ethnic origin, they have to wear similar clothes, the size and the composition of the group should also be very similar and so on. Secondly, the selected group and the reference group also have to be similar to each other to the highest possible degree, except for their protected ground.[103]

Concerning the timing of the testing, it is generally argued that testing should take place as soon as possible after the alleged discrimination, and the tester groups should also follow each other 'at closely spaced intervals'.[104] The appropriate timing of the testing depends to a great extent on the existence of an original victim group in addition to the selected group. If there is a separate victim group a certain, but definitely not long, period of time might elapse between the original discrimination and the situation testing carried out by the selected and the control groups. However, if the selected group unites the victim group, the testing by the selected group should be quickly followed by the control group; otherwise the testing would not be able to eliminate the circumstances other than the protected ground.

There can be situations in which the shortest possible time between the original discrimination and the first testing means one hour, a half day, or at a maximum one day.[105] However, there might also be cases when a longer term

---

100 See also Fitsum (2000b).

101 See also Fitsum (2000b).

102 Rorive (2006), at 35. See also Iványi & Muhi (2004).

103 See inter alia Rorive (2006), at 36; De Schutter (2003a), at 33; Rorive (2009), at 51; Bodrogi (2003), at 7.

104 See inter alia Fitsum (2000b); Bodrogi (2003), at 7.

105 In this context one might think of testing in the so called disco-cases, in which persons from a certain racial group are not allowed to enter into a discotheque. In such cases, the testing should take place on the same evening; otherwise the inferences seem to be more difficult to draw as to the existence of discrimination on the given night.

is also appropriate, depending also on the nature of the policy area. In not paying enough attention to the timing of testing, applicants run the risk that fact-finders might find the causal link between the protected ground and the treatment too remote.

3.3.3.4. Field of Application

Although situation testing is mostly used to give rise to a presumption of discrimination, it can also be applied for negating the causal link. In other words, a situation testing can also be carried out or used in the interest of the respondent. When the testing is carried out for proving the lack of causality it should happen before the respondent is informed about the starting of a lawsuit against him. For instance, a recording of a testing may have been made by an independent organisation. Situation testing is not only suited to giving rise to the presumption that (covert) direct discrimination has taken place, but it can also be used as evidence for systemic discrimination.[106] As Craig observed, "the outcomes for the two test partners [at an aggregate level – M.A.] are compared, and any systemic or statistically significant exclusion of the ethnic minority applicant would then be interpreted as discrimination."[107] In a particular case in the United States statistical disparity could be proven with the help of such an aggregate level of testing in transportation among white and black people.[108]

As shown above, situation testing can be applied only when the protected ground markedly stands out and can be compared with other persons. In cases of intersectional discrimination it is difficult to find appropriate comparators, so also testers. Accordingly, situation testing can be relied on only in very few and particular instances when intersectional grounds are at stake.

Importantly, testing is generally carried out by civil organisations being involved in legal representation or by specialised bodies, since, as explained above, strict methodological requirements are set up for such testing in order to be able to serve as evidence for an alleged discrimination. However, this does not mean that methodologically correct testing carried out by private parties would not be accepted as evidence. Importantly, however, the probative value of a testing carried out by a specialised body is generally the strongest.

Concerning the field of application in terms of the material scope of the RED, practice shows that situation testing can be used in employment, education and access to goods and services. However, it can be observed that due to the lack of appropriate testers[109] in relationships that are already established,

---

106 Since it means the unfolding of a certain pattern against a group, because of the group aspect it is generally considered to be indirect discrimination. See also De Schutter (2003b), at 33-34.

107 Craig (2007), at 18.

108 *Floyd-Mayers v. American Cab Co*, 732 F.Supp. 243 (D.D.C. 1990); Fitsum (2000a), at 77-78.

109 As Makkonen observes, "[i]t is difficult to see how the method could be used to reveal

testing can only be applied in access to employment and access to education, and naturally, as the examples show, access to goods and services.[110] More concretely, based on the jurisprudence in which situation testing was brought up as evidence, it can be said that it has mainly relevance in the field of the employment, catering and entertaining trades.[111]

Finally, not only can testing serve as evidence before a fact-finding organ, but similarly to statistical data it can also contribute to raising awareness, guiding or influencing future policies aimed at combating discrimination, which, though indirectly, still contribute to the effective enforcement of rights and obligations.[112]

3.3.4. Sensitive Matters

3.3.4.1. Provocation and Deception

The application of situation testing as a means of evidence has been criticised of amounting to provocation, and thus, the fairness of the obtained evidence is contested.[113] However, it can be argued that testing, when it is properly executed, cannot be regarded as provocation, since it is simply a control on the approach of the alleged perpetrator. The lack of provocation is also ensured by the utter similarity of the groups.[114]

While provocation is concerned with the object of testing, namely discrimination, the argument of deception, the other objection to testing, relates to the subject of testing, that is the respondent. Based on moral considerations, it has been argued that it should not be allowed that, for the sake of proving a case, the respondent is deceived. Some, however, plead that by virtue of the insincerity of the market itself the consumer might also lie to the liar.[115] Bok complements this not entirely convincing argument by explaining that the justification for lying to the liar is based on the fact that the object of testing (discrimination) is harmful.

---

wage gaps or unequal treatment with respect to promotion, as the examination of these issues would require the conclusion of an employment contract, and is therefore beyond the limits of an experiment." Makkonen (2007b), at 47.

110 See also Humblet (2003), at 9; Iványi & Muhi (2004); Rorive (2009), at 47-48.

111 Makkonen (2007b), at 46.

112 See also Makkonen (2007b), at 47; Bovenkerk (1992).

113 Interestingly, such an objection cannot be found in relation to testing concerning consumer protection and tax control.

114 Compare with De Schutter (2003b), at 35.

115 See inter alia Bok (1978), at 123-133; Riach & Rich (2004), at 462.

> [E]ntrepreneurs in labour and housing markets (in particular) are regularly engaged in deceptive activity, and when this involves discrimination on sexual, racial, religious grounds it does great harm to the social fabric.[116]

The deception argument in relation to testing might also be countered by the argument that the members of the selected group might also start a discrimination procedure against the perpetrator; since they do not pretend their racial or ethnic origin, and similarly to the victim they also experience discrimination.

3.3.4.2. Concerns of Privacy

Situation testing has also been blamed for interfering with privacy.[117] One could argue, however, that protection of privacy is "not a legitimate expectation where public and commercial acts, in the form of advertising vacancies, are involved, and where there is public regulation proscribing discriminatory activities."[118] Thus, there will be no interference with the private life of an individual, if situation testing takes place under controlled circumstances and attention is paid to not obtaining more information than is required for the discrimination case.[119] Arguably, the inconvenience caused to the subject of the examination is outweighed by the importance of information obtained in this way.[120]

3.3.4.3. Avoiding Strategies

In relation to the danger of the widespread application of testing, De Schutter warns that potential discriminators will become more aware of the possibility of such testing and will try to avoid discriminating when they suppose that situation testing is taking place, but will continue discriminating when they do not find any suspicious traces of such testing.[121] There might be such a danger, but this also implies that the number of instances of discrimination will decrease. In actual fact, this is one of the aims of such testing.[122]

---

[116] Riach & Rich (2004), at 462.
[117] See inter alia Rorive (2009), at 47-48.
[118] Riach & Rich (2004), at 459.
[119] See also De Schutter (2003b), at 35.
[120] See also Edley who argues in utilitarian terms that "[w]e can easily justify the use of testers in utilitarian terms reasoning that the moral costs of deception are outweighed by the great benefit of developing a clearer understanding of the social disease." Edley (1993), at 1-49. See also Riach & Rich (2004), at 459-460.
[121] See also De Schutter (2003b), at 34. According to him "[t]he weakness of the situational test method is found in the avoidance strategies to which it will give rise, as long as the tests are generalist."
[122] This method is similarly applied in consumer protection cases where it also aims to avoid abuse by making the goods and service providers aware of the fact that a control could take place at any moment. Accordingly, the danger of being controlled has a preventive effect.

3.3.4.4. Testers as Victims of Discrimination

As hinted at supra, testers themselves could feel discriminated against. Thus, the question is raised whether they too could start a procedure against the perpetrator or whether they can only be taken into account as being 'part' of an evidence. As early as 1982, the Supreme Court of the U.S. has accepted that testers can be claimants in discrimination cases.[123] It is desirable that this approach be generally adopted, since, for testers denied a service on the grounds of their racial or ethnic origin, their right to equal treatment is no less violated than that of the original victim.[124]

PART B. CASE STUDIES

3.4. Statistics

Only in Belgium can explicit reference be found in the equal treatment acts to statistics as possible forms of proof. Here, proof using statistics has never been considered a difficult or sensitive question. It has been generally emphasised that facts that can lead to the presumption of discrimination can be of any kind.[125] Importantly, it was first the ADA implementing the RED (and FD) in which statistics together with situation testing were mentioned as examples of methods to be used to give rise to the presumption of discrimination. This clearly shows the effect of the RED in this respect. The amended ARA also gives examples of the facts that can be to establish a prima facie case of discrimination, among which explicit reference has been made to statistical data.[126]

Unlike the Belgian Act, none of the equal treatment legislations of the other countries include any reference to statistical evidence as a possible means of evidence for establishing a prima facie case of discrimination. Accordingly, the effect of the RED and the case law of the ECJ cannot be determined at the level of legislation. In Estonia, only a short reference can be found to the possible application of statistics in the explanatory memorandum of the Equal Treatment Act. Here, it has been explained that indirect discrimination can mainly be shown with the help of statistical data or sociological surveys

[123] Iványi & Muhi (2004). Some relevant cases are *Evers v. Dwyer*, 358 U.S. 202 (SC 1958); *Pierson v. Ray*, 386 U.S. 574 (SC 1967); *Davis v. Mansard*, 597 F.Supp 334 (N.D. Ind. 1984).

[124] For a partly different position see Bodrogi (2003), at 11. & 15.

[125] Wetsontwerp tot wijziging van de wet van 30 juli 1981 tot bestraffing van bepaalde door racisme en xenofobie ingegeven daden, 2720/009, 19 March 2007, at 26.

[126] *Id.*, at 78.

broken down on the basis of the protected ground.[127] Neither in Hungary nor in the Netherlands have any hints been given in the explanatory memoranda regarding any possible forms of proof. In Hungary the principle of free evaluation of evidence is applicable in civil and administrative procedures, which indicates that statistical evidence will presumably be accepted.[128] In the Netherlands statistics have been accepted for a long time as appropriate and adequate forms of proof in discrimination cases, both in order to give rise to a presumption of discrimination and to refute the alleged discrimination.[129]

3.4.1. Disparate Impact

The extent to which a certain group has to be affected by the particular measure can only be addressed concerning Hungary and the Netherlands where there is relevant case law in this respect. In Belgium, matters encompassing statistical evidence have only been addressed in theory. It has been argued that in this respect, based on the jurisprudence of the ECJ, the discrepancy in relation to the average has to be sufficiently significant[130] or the persons have to be put at a particular disadvantage.[131] Whether this approach will also be followed by the Belgian fact-finders is yet to be seen.

Statistical or statistical-like evidence has already been used in a couple of cases in Hungary: for instance, in an employment case and in cases concerning segregation in education. In the employment case, 9 out of the 11 outsourced employees of the respondent employer were of Roma origin. In one of the segregation cases, the Miskolc case, the court of first instance established that

> it is common knowledge that a *large number* of Roma children currently attend and have attended in the past the schools in question. The law does not define what a 'large number' amounts to.[132]

In the other segregation case, the Hajdúhadház case the applicant proved that in three schools maintained by the first respondent the proportions of Roma children were the following: 28 % in the main building and 86 % and 96 % in the other buildings. These proportions concerning the schools maintained by the second respondent were the following: 22 % in the main building and 100-100 % in the two other buildings. In the wording of the Supreme Court

[127] Poleshchuk (2007), at 18; Draft Equal Treatment Act, 1101 SE, Explanatory Memorandum, at 4.

[128] Article 50(4)-(6) Administrative Procedure Act.

[129] *Kaya/Binderen*, High Council, NJ 1983, 6810, December 1982, 7; Amsterdam Court of Appeal, summary proceedings, 13 January 2000. See also Opinion 2007-91 ETC.

[130] Vrielink (2003a), at 240; De Prins, Sottiaux & Vrielink (2003b), para. 131.

[131] Thiery (2007), at 761.

[132] Borsod-Abaúj-Zemplén County Court, 13.P.21.660/2005/16, 2 November 2005 (emphasis added). See also the judgment of the court of appeal Debrecen Court of Appeal, Pf.I.20.683/2005/7, 9 June 2006. On this case see Farkas (2005).

this meant that Roma children were educated either entirely or to a significant extent separately.[133] Accordingly, the 'particular disadvantage' has been considered to refer to the number or proportion of those affected by a certain measure: 9 persons out of the 11 outsourced employees were of Roma origin, a *large number* of Roma children visited the schools under dispute, and in one of the schools *a significant proportion of* and in the other school *all* Roma children were affected by the particular measure.[134]

Even though the Dutch definition of indirect discrimination does not include the requirement 'disparate impact', the ETC still applies this test, following the ECJ in this respect. And similarly to the Hungarian approach, this test is interpreted by the ETC in terms of the number or proportion of persons affected by a certain measure, and not as referring to the seriousness of a disadvantage. For instance, a caravan dweller wished to take out an insurance policy on his home contents, but was refused. The Commission established that declining a request for contents insurance for a caravan affects in particular caravan dwellers belonging to this ethnic group. The ETC in most of the cases accepts the presumption of discrimination, if *in particular*,[135] *predominantly*[136] or *to a disproportionate extent more*[137] persons belonging to a certain racial or ethnic group are affected by a certain measure. Also a *considerable*[138] difference in ethnic composition of certain districts can also give rise to a presumption. Importantly, not only pure statistics, but also common knowledge is accepted both by the ETC and courts for establishing the composition of a certain group.[139]

In earlier cases,[140] which were heavily criticised,[141] the ETC required a disadvantage factor of 1.5 in order to accept a presumption of discrimination. This factor meant that persons from a certain group be affected 1.5 times more than those not belonging to this group. In two cases this test was rigidly applied. One of the cases was dismissed since this factor only reached 1.3.[142] Since 2004 the ETC has, however, not used this standard anymore.[143] This is a welcome decision as cases are rarely so clear-cut and this approach would have led to the dehumanization of the process.

[133] Supreme Court, Pfv.IV.20.936/2008/4, 19 November 2008. See also the judgment of the first and second instance courts. Hajdú-Bihar County Court, 6.P. 20.341/2006/50, 2 May 2007; Debrecen Court of Appeal, Pf.I.20.361/2007/8, 13 December 2007.

[134] See also EBH/700/2007 and EBH/337/24/2005.

[135] See inter alia Opinion 2006-5 ETC.

[136] See inter alia Opinions 2005-68 and 2007-109 ETC.

[137] See inter alia Opinion 2008-12 ETC.

[138] See inter alia Opinion 2007-91 ETC.

[139] See inter alia Central Court of Appeal, 23 January 2003, 96/10513 AW; Opinion 2008-12 ETC.

[140] See Opinions 1997-45 and 2002-161 ETC.

[141] Gerards (2003), at 83; Waaldijk & Hendriks (2000), at 49-50.

[142] Opinions 1997-45 and 2002-161 ETC.

[143] Holtmaat (2007), at 27.

In a couple of more recent cases concerning the pay system the ETC has started to elaborate and to apply other, allegedly complicated, methods of calculation.[144] In this context a 'computer tool is being developed (Equal Pay Quickscan) to help the Commission and others to gain insight into the staffing and pay structures of organisations.'[145]

3.4.2. Pool of Comparators

Although it is only in Hungary and the Netherlands that the application of statistical evidence can be found in practice, the regulation in the Belgian Anti-Racism Act does also contain some indications with respect to the pool of comparators.

As hinted at supra, the Belgian ARA concretely mentions statistics as possible forms of evidence of indirect discrimination, and makes a distinction between general and elementary statistics. According to the Act, general statistics and common knowledge can describe the situation in which the victim of discrimination is situated; and elementary statistics can show a less favourable treatment. In the *travaux préparatoires* it has been made clear that general statistics concern external statistics; that is statistics at macro level. On the contrary, elementary statistics relate to the concrete situation of the group which the victim belongs to. These statistics could be described as internal statistics, or statistics at micro level.[146] Although this is an important distinction in terms of the pool of comparators, it is yet to be seen whether it will be clear in practice when internal or external statistics should be used. Remarkably, though in the context of the ADA, the legal literature acknowledges the significance of this distinction when it is argued that statistics have to pertain to the respondent or the organisation of the respondent. In other words, the pool of comparators should be determined in relation to the respondent.[147]

Both the Hungarian and the Dutch approach seem to make the comparison in an appropriate way. The case law in Hungary shows that the reference group includes those unable to comply with the particular requirement, while the 'victim' group is made up of those who satisfy the requirement. For instance, in the previously mentioned employment racial discrimination case, 11 persons were outsourced and 19 stayed with the same employer, and the composition of those two groups was compared. More specifically, 11 persons 'complied' with the criterion, and 19 did not meet the requirement. The composition of

[144] See Holtmaat (2007), at 27-28; Opinions 2003-91 and 2003-92 ETC.

[145] Commentary of the Netherlands' Equal Treatment Commission on the fifteenth and sixteenth Periodic Report of the Kingdom of the Netherlands on the implementation of the Convention on the Elimination of all forms of Racial Discrimination (CERD/C/452/Add.3), CGB-advies/2004/02, 26 February 2004, at 3.

[146] Thiery (2007), at 760; Wetsontwerp tot wijziging …, *supra* note 125, at 80.

[147] De Boeck (2003), at 437-438; Vrielink (2003a), at 240.

these two groups was compared. In the Miskolc segregation case, the ethnic composition of those attending one of the schools was compared with the ethnic composition of the students at the other school. However, it is yet to be seen whether this line will be followed in later cases too.

In the Netherlands, the ETC also seems to follow the approach of the ECJ in this respect: comparing the composition of those who can with those who cannot comply with a particular requirement. For instance, in a couple of cases it compared the proportion of dwellers among those not living in caravans with their proportion among those living in caravans.[148] Similarly, in a case concerning a complaint of indirect discrimination on the grounds of gender, the Commission compared the gender composition of those working part-time with those working full-time. In this case, the importance of comparing the composition of the reference group with the selected group became obvious because the number of female part-time workers was the same as of men. The Commission stated that of 26 female employees, 13 worked part-time and 13 full-time, while of the 124 male employees, 13 worked part-time and 111 full-time. Finally, in another case a sport school generally prohibited the wearing of headscarves with the exception of medical or other reasons. Here the Commission established that it is a fact of common knowledge that a higher proportion of Muslim women would be affected by a neutral rule.[149] In this case, one should not compare the religious affiliation of those wearing headscarves with that of those not wearing it. Rather, one should examine the religious commitment of those wearing headscarves for medical reason and the rest. This case clearly showed that it is often only the result of a comparison that is pronounced, without explicit reference to the ground of comparison and the selected and reference groups.

It also seems that in the view of the Commission the reference group has to be as small as possible,[150] which clearly safeguards that the respondent would not be held responsible for those acts that are not within his reach.[151] For instance, in one case a pension insurance company requested that the Commission examine whether its policy, in which an explicit difference was made based on age, was in accordance with the GETA.[152] In this case the reference group was taken at national level since the company offered its product throughout the country. However, in another case concerning pre-flight controls, the reference group was taken from the passengers of a specific flight, namely the Amsterdam-Curacao flight,[153] since the respondent was only responsible for this flight.

---

[148] See inter alia Opinions 2006-5 and 2007-109 ETC.

[149] Opinion 2008-12 ETC.

[150] Gerards (2003), at 81; Dierx & Siegers (1990), at 358. See for instance Opinion 2000-57 ETC.

[151] See inter alia Opinions 2006-177 and 2003-153 ETC.

[152] Opinion 2006-177 ETC.

[153] Opinion 2003-153 ETC.

3.4.3. Nature of Statistics

While in the Netherlands no specific requirements have been set up concerning the nature of statistics, in Belgium and Hungary some theoretical and practical criteria can be found.

In Belgium in relation to the nature of statistics it has been emphasised in theory that, stemming from the jurisprudence of the ECJ, statistics have to be sufficiently clear and significant,[154] reliable, essentially important,[155] precise and in agreement with each other.[156] Due to the lack of relevant case law,[157] it is yet to be seen in practice whether the particular disadvantage will refer to the proportion or number of those affected.

In Hungary, some conclusions can be drawn from the segregation cases in this respect. In these cases, relatively high requirements were set regarding the quality of the data, which means that it would be costly for the applicants to appropriately substantiate their case. In one of the segregation cases, the Hajdúhadház case, not only did the court examine the professional skills of the *ad hoc* expert, but it also specified the methodology for collecting and processing the data.[158] The court finally accepted that

> [i]t can be established on the basis of the expert opinion, the statement of the expert preparing it and the testimony of the representatives of the Minority Self-Government participating in the preparation of the expert opinion that the proportions laid down in the expert opinion concerning ethnic minority pupils truly specify the proportion of persons who are actually of Roma ethnicity or are considered to be of Roma ethnicity by the Roma community with sufficient certainty and with a maximum of 1% default. The expert opinion does not infringe any data protection regulations concerning anonymity.[159]

---

[154] See inter alia De Boeck (2003), at 437; Wetsontwerp tot wijziging ..., *supra* note 125, at 191.

[155] De Prins, Sottiaux & Vrielink (2003b), para. 131.

[156] Advies 32.967/2, Raad van State, in: Wetsontwerp tot wijziging van de wet van 30 juli tot bestraffing van bepaalde door racisme of xenofobie ingegeven daden, 3-2362/3, 24 April 2007, at 8-9.

[157] Holtmaat (2007), at 38.

[158] "[I.]e. given that it is required for the preparation of the expert opinion, the appointed forensic expert is to involve a sociologist expert in his work and for the preparation of the expert opinion involve the Roma Minority Self-government of Hajdúhadház, which is to disclose the data, information and opinions required by the forensic expert to prepare his opinion; the expert is to have an on-site inspection in the educational institutions concerned, in all of the buildings and all of the classes concerned, obtain the required and available data and information from the heads of the educational institutions and the Roma minority Self-government of Hajdúhadház; in case figures are uncertain, the expert is to determine the lowest figure that provides an answer at a certain level as well as the limits within which the uncertainty exists, while considering pupils of Roma ethnicity or considered by others to be of Roma ethnicity when establishing the proportions." Hajdú-Bihar County Court, 6.P. 20.341/2006/50, 2 May 2007.

[159] Hajdú-Bihar County Court, 6.P. 20.341/2006/50, 2 May 2007.

Nevertheless, common knowledge alone was not accepted, which is even more striking in the light of the fact that both the Civil Procedure Act and the Administrative Procedure Act explicitly mention common knowledge as appropriate means of evidence, which needs no further proof.[160] Setting up such strict requirements does not seem to be in harmony with the jurisprudence of the ECJ in this respect.

3.4.4. Field of Application

The Member States under review are generally of the view that statistical data can serve as evidence in indirect discrimination cases. An implicit exception from this view can be found in the Belgian anti-discrimination legislation.

The amended ARA gives examples of the facts which can be used to establish a prima facie case of discrimination.[161] Pursuant to Article 30(3) ARA general and elementary statistics can give rise to the presumption of indirect discrimination. Moreover, Article 30(2) ARA exemplifies facts which can establish prima facie direct discrimination; including the 'pattern method'. The aim of this method is to establish a certain pattern which could serve as evidence of direct discrimination. Although it has not been specified any further how this method could be used and what form it should take, it can be presumed that it could best be done with the help of situation testing, an explicit mention of which the legislators wanted to avoid.[162] Arguably, however, a pattern can also be determined based on statistical data: statistical data can also show how often a particular form of discrimination occurs and in this way alleged systemic[163] direct discrimination can be substantiated with statistical evidence.

In Estonia, as indicated supra, only a short reference can be found to statistical data and that is indeed within the framework of indirect discrimination: the explanatory memorandum of the EETA has explained that indirect discrimination can mainly be shown with the help of statistical data or sociological surveys, broken down on the basis of the protected ground.[164]

---

[160] Arts. 163(3) Civil Code and 50(3) Administrative Procedure Act.

[161] Wetsontwerp tot wijziging ..., *supra* note 125, at 78.

[162] *Id.*, at 78-79.

[163] Situation testing can, arguably, give rise to the presumption of discrimination both at individual and at group level; i.e. the pattern in this context can refer to patterns of a narrower and a broader scale. Contrary to this, statistics as such focus on the effect on groups; consequently, they constitute appropriate evidence in case of systematic direct discrimination.

[164] Poleshchuk (2007), at 18; Draft Equal Treatment Act, 1101 SE, Explanatory Memorandum, at 4.

In Hungary, statistical or statistical-like data has been relied on in cases of segregation[165] and direct[166] and indirect[167] discrimination.

Similarly, in the Netherlands statistics are regarded as being capable of constituting evidence, mainly in cases identified as indirect discrimination,[168] a couple of which, however, should rather be seen as systemic direct discrimination.[169]

In terms of the material field, in Hungary the cases in which statistics were relied on were related to education and employment, while in the Netherlands they were concerned with employment, social protection and providing goods and services. This indicates that in fact statistics can be used in all spheres of life.

In general it seems that statistical data in support of the respondent's refutation can also be used in each country under review (with the exception of Estonia where as yet no case law can be found in this respect). There are, however, difficulties with respect to its proper application since in a couple of cases statistical arguments have been accepted by fact-finders in cases concerned with individual discrimination.

In Belgium, in a case from 2006 the respondent submitted its staff register from which it could be seen that more than 30 % of the employees were immigrants or foreigners. On the basis of this, the court came to the conclusion that in the individual case there was no presumption of discrimination.[170] Importantly, this is a typical case in which statistics brought up by the respondent could not have been taken into account since the applicant complained of discrimination in an individual case, and the data of the respondent was only able to show that he does not discriminate on a systemic basis. It is nevertheless remarkable that it was not a problem for the respondent to provide data.

In Hungary, there are also cases in which the respondent also relied on statistics in order to refute the alleged discrimination against an individual. In one of these cases the respondent's argument that he does employ Roma persons was incorrectly accepted by a court.[171] In other cases, however, the

[165] See for instance the Hajdúhadház segregation cases. Hajdú-Bihar County Court, 6.P. 20.341/2006/50, 2 May 2007; Debrecen Court of Appeal, Pf.I.20.361/2007/8, 13 December 2007; Supreme Court, Pfv.IV.20.936/2008/4, 19 November 2008.

[166] See for instance Borsod-Abaúj-Zemplén County Court, 1.Mf.20392/2007/3, 12 June 2007; Miskolc Labour Court, 6.M.1364/2006/4, 14 November 2006; Miskolc City Court, 6.M.16/2005/17, 28 November 2005.

[167] See for instance EBH/337/24/2005.

[168] See inter alia Opinion 2007-91 ETC.

[169] See inter alia Opinion 2003-153 ETC.

[170] Mechelen Labour Court, summary-like proceedings, 16 March 2006, para. 4.

[171] Metropolitan Labour Court, 10.M.4297/2000/12, 9 October 2001. See also the judgments of the court of appeal and the Supreme Court in the same case Metropolitan Court, 49. Mf. 630.368/2001/2, 15 February 2002; Supreme Court, Mfv.I.10.720/2003/3, 11 February 2004.

AET explicitly emphasised that the facts that Roma persons are employed or can visit a discotheque cannot refute the presumption of discrimination in an individual case.[172]

In the Netherlands, concerning statistics provided by the respondent, a case of age discrimination can be mentioned. In this case the respondent stated that the age restriction for referees aimed to avoid such situations where there is no available referee because of the longer time that is needed for persons above a certain age to recover from injuries. This defence, however, has not been accepted since, to the court, the defendant did not submit any *statistical* or medical evidence in support of his statements.[173] First of all, this shows that respondents are also able to support their arguments using statistical data. Secondly, in this case statistical data brought up by the respondent would have served as appropriate evidence since the applicant did not complain of individual discrimination. Based on the facts that the Commission's approach to direct and indirect discrimination can be generally regarded as conceptually proper, and that the use of statistics is clearly linked to the concepts of discrimination, it can be concluded that statistical evidence will be used appropriately by the ETC in this respect.

3.4.5. Sensitive Matters

This concerns the theoretical observation that it is the general lack of available statistical data that constitutes the most problematic aspect of the possibility of substantiating a claim and/or refutation with statistical evidence.

In Belgium, it has been emphasised that the lack of data considered attributable to the strict data protection rules[174] would definitely limit the application of statistics, particularly in private relationships.[175]

Similarly, in Estonia the strict rules on data protection have also been blamed for making it "rather difficult for employees or clients to get any statistical evidence to prove cases of indirect discrimination."[176] Admittedly, however, the most vulnerable group in this context is the Russian-speaking minority, the identification of whom does not seem to be difficult even under the data protection rules, since on the basis of their mother tongue they can quite easily be recognised and registered.

172 See for instance EBH/72/7/2008.

173 Amsterdam Court of Appeal, summary proceedings, 13 January 2000, para. 4.16.

174 Act on the Protection of the Right to Private Life with Respect to the Processing of Personal Data, 18 March 1992. See also Holtmaat (2007), at 39-41.

175 Kusters (2003), at 565; Holtmaat (2007), at 39.

176 Poleshchuk (2007), at 19; Personal Data Protection Act, RT I 2003, 26, 158.

In Hungary the segregation cases clearly show the difficulties stemming from the lack of data due to the strict data and privacy protection rules.[177] Importantly, in case of the employment discrimination, when all the Roma persons were outsourced, no problems have arisen in this respect. This could arguably be attributed to the fact that it only concerned a small group of persons.[178] However, in the segregation cases statistical evidence was required at an aggregate level. Here, an attempt was made to avoid the data protection and privacy related questions by relying on surveys made by *ad hoc* experts and common knowledge.[179] In the Miskolc segregation case, for instance, the court established that

> it is *common knowledge* that a large number of Roma children currently attend and have attended in the past the schools in question. The law does not define what a 'large number' amounts to. [...] In the opinion of the county court, the sociological studies submitted by the plaintiff are adequate evidence.[180]

Remarkably, there is a quasi contradiction in this statement, since the court accepts that it is a common knowledge that many Roma children attend the schools under dispute, yet it still explains that sociological surveys can provide adequate evidence in this context. Be it a real or a quasi contradiction, the impression is nevertheless created that there is a need to substantiate a claim with exact data, since relying merely on common knowledge does not seem to meet the requirements of fact-finders. The present Hungarian law on data protection allows for the handling of data on racial and ethnic origin only with the consent of the person concerned. It has, nevertheless, been argued that it "shall under no circumstances be taken to mean that data on the perceived ethnic origin of individuals cannot be handled."[181] The perceived ethnic origin in indirect discrimination cases, in which it is mainly the real protected ground of the victims that counts, can be taken as adequate evidence as far as belonging to the Roma minority is concerned, since this usually manifests itself as particular physical characteristics. Moreover, as soon as data is made anonymous no issue should arise as to the collection, processing and storing of sensitive data. In addition, the Data Protection Act does not exclude the processing of personal data for scientific and statistical purposes.[182]

---

177 See inter alia Advisory Committee on the Framework Convention for the Protection of National Minorities, Second Opinion on Hungary adopted on 9 December 2004, ACFC/INF/OP/II(2004)003, 14 December 2004, at 5. & 10-11.

178 9 Roma persons out of 30 involved employers.

179 See inter alia Kádár (2007), at 23; Farkas (2004a); Farkas (2003).

180 Borsod-Abaúj-Zemplén County Court, 13.P.21.660/2005/16, 2 November 2005 (emphasis added). See also the judgment of the court of appeal Debrecen Court of Appeal, Pf.I.20.683/2005/7, 9 June 2006. On this case see Farkas (2005).

181 Farkas (2004a).

182 Kádár (2007), at 23.

In the Netherlands too there are strict rules on data and privacy protection,[183] and the only explicit exception from the general prohibition of processing and storing sensitive data is related to positive action measures.[184] Nevertheless, identification does not seem to be a problem,[185] since the minorities living there can generally be identified by their place of birth and the origin of their parents.[186] As yet no case can be found in which the lack of statistical data would have resulted in the refusal of the applicant's claim. This fact can arguably be explained by the general acceptance of statistical-like evidence (mainly common knowledge).

3.5. Situation Testing

Contrary to statistical data, the RED itself does not mention situation testing as a possible form of proof, which at the same time means that the effect of the RED in this respect is much more difficult to explore. The influence of the Directive can be indirectly discovered in the fact that the concepts and the assessment of discrimination are publicly addressed and discussed, encouraging fact-finders to draw inferences from such evidence. With the exception of Belgium, situation testing seems to be generally accepted and is able to give rise to a presumption of discrimination.

---

183 Interestingly, in 1998 an Act was adopted in order to obtain data on the ethnic composition of the workforce, which required employers to register the ethnic origin of their employees 'with a view to measure progress in implementing the principle of equal treatment and equal occupation opportunities' (Commentary of the Netherlands' Equal Treatment Commission on the fifteenth and sixteenth Periodic Report of the Kingdom of the Netherlands on the implementation of the Convention on the Elimination of all forms of Racial Discrimination (CERD/C/452/Add.3), CGB-advies/2004/02, 26 February 2004, at 3.). The Act was in force until 31 December 2003. The ETC argued that this Act helped them evaluate the ethnic composition of the different groups, and therefore did not have to face a lack of data on ethnic origin (see inter alia Commentary of the Netherlands' Equal Treatment Commission on the fifteenth and sixteenth Periodic Report of the Kingdom of the Netherlands on the implementation of the Convention on the Elimination of all forms of Racial Discrimination (CERD/C/452/Add.3), CGB-advies/2004/02, 26 February 2004, at 3). "Although the effectiveness of this Act was disputed, the Commission holds the opinion that in the absence of an alternative policy instrument to measure and combat the under-representation of racial and ethnic minorities in the labour market, the Government could have considered to preserve the Act until a better alternative was available" (Commentary of the Netherlands' Equal Treatment Commission on the fifteenth and sixteenth Periodic Report of the Kingdom of the Netherlands on the implementation of the Convention on the Elimination of all forms of Racial Discrimination (CERD/C/452/Add.3), CGB-advies/2004/02, 26 February 2004, at 3). In other words, the Commission acknowledges that under certain circumstances it might be difficult for the applicant to substantiate his claim with appropriate evidence.

184 Holtmaat (2007), at 28.

185 See also Davidović & Walsum (2009), at 30.

186 Holtmaat (2007), at 29.

Long discussions long discussions have been devoted in Belgium to the acceptability and fairness of providing proof using situation testing,[187] which in a couple of cases resulted in the reluctance of fact-finders to accept testing as evidence of a prima facie case of discrimination.

Strikingly, in Estonia no mention can be found of this form of proof in the *travaux préparatoires* of any of the drafts. As with statistics, Poleshchuk argues that the absence of any reference to testing can rather be linked to a lack of awareness of this method, rather than a reluctance to consider such evidence as admissible.[188]

At present, situation testing in Hungary seems to be a generally acknowledged and applied form of proof in discrimination cases, especially before the AET.[189] However, the road leading to this general acceptance was not smooth.[190] It was an NGO that started proving direct discrimination with the help of situation testing. In the beginning courts were, however, somewhat reluctant to draw conclusions from the result of the testing.

Testing in the Netherlands was a generally accepted form of proof in discrimination cases even before the adoption and the implementation of the RED.[191] The very first cases in which situation testing has been used go back to the 1980s.[192] Most importantly, not only courts but also the ETC accepts such evidence.

3.5.1. Situation Testing as Evidence

Although some problems have occurred in the application of situation testing, it is mainly in Belgium where fact-finders refuse to draw conclusions from this proof. In Belgium these discussions started with the adoption of the first general anti-discrimination act which explicitly referred to situation testing as a possible form of proof. The very first concern was related to the text of the ADA, stipulating that a Royal Decree would lay down the detailed rules concerning situation testing,[193] the lack of which, however, made courts refuse such evidence.[194] In one of these cases, where even a bailiff was present, the fact-finder refused to accept the results of situation testing as evidence, arguing

---

187 Cuypers (2003), at 464.

188 Holtmaat (2007), at 17.

189 See for instance EBH/180/2006, EBH/58/2006.

190 Kádár (2007), at 17; Iványi & Muhi (2004).

191 See inter alia Arbeidsmarktbeleid etnische minderheden, 2000-2003, at 7; Holtmaat (2007), at 22-24; Asscher-Vonk & Groenendijk (1999), at 225.

192 Holtmaat (2007), at 23.

193 Art. 19 (4) ADA.

194 Gent Labour Court, summary proceedings, 31 December 2003; Mechelen Labour Court, summary-like proceedings, 16 March 2006; Wetsontwerp tot wijziging …, *supra* note 125, at 71.

that the rules regulating the execution of testing were not yet accepted.[195] This position was changed by the court of appeal by classifying the submitted evidence not as testing but as 'recording' by the bailiff.[196]

Admittedly, the text of the ADA concerning the need of such regulation was not clear-cut: it could be interpreted either way. However, the underlying aim, to explicitly mention situation testing, was to help fact-finders decide on acceptable forms of proof. Moreover, it is ultimately for fact-finders to decide on the admissibility of the concrete evidence.[197] Accordingly, it could be argued that the heralded decree would have elaborated only on some methodological questions related to the desirable execution of testing.[198] Thus fact-finders cannot reasonably reject such proof by referring to the absence of a Decree.[199]

The other problematic area, in relation to which, however, the ADA seemed to be clearer, concerned the presence of a bailiff. In a case, where testing took place through telephone calls, the fact-finder refused to accept the result as evidence, arguing that a bailiff was not present.[200] The text of the ADA stipulated that such a test *could* be carried out by a bailiff. Thus, it seemed to be a facultative possibility, a position also taken by scholars.

In any event, the amended ARA tried to avoid these dilemmas and does not explicitly mention situation testing as a possible form of proof in discrimination cases or stipulate that any further rules will be layed down in a Royal Decree.[201] In the new ARA two 'facts' have been brought up as examples that can possibly serve as evidence in direct discrimination cases: these are the already-mentioned pattern method and the 'method of elimination'.[202] Concerning the first method, the applicant establishes facts from which a certain pattern of unfavourable treatment related to persons with a certain protected characteristics can be deduced. With the help of the second method the applicant shows that no such distinction would have been made but for the applicant's protected ground. Thus it eliminates all other possible grounds (this is why this method can also be described as the 'but for' test). Not only has the legislator left unspecified how such facts can be established, but the

195 Gent Labour Court, summary proceedings, 31 December 2003, para. 4.1.

196 Gent Court of Cassation, 30 November 2005, para. 4.3.

197 De Prins, Sottiaux & Vrielink (2003b), para. 128; Wetsontwerp tot wijziging …, *supra* note 125, at 71.

198 See for instance Wetsontwerp tot wijziging …, *supra* note 125, at 71.

199 Admittedly, the hesitation whether this form of proof is acceptable even in the lack of the Royal Decree can be linked to the discussion that such proof might make up provocation. See below concerning sensitive matters.

200 Mechelen Labour Court, summary-like proceedings, 16 March 2006, para. 5.2.2.

201 Remarkably, the Act was blamed for not explicitly referring to this test, since this indicated to the critics that it was then not accepted at all. Er komen geen praktijktests, *Het Belang van Limburg*, 19 January 2007.

202 See also above.

enumeration of the different methods is also exemplative, which indicate that the application of situation testing is not limited in any way. Importantly, the result of situation testing seems to be appropriate both to establish facts from which a certain pattern can be deduced, and to eliminate the non-relevant aspects of the distinction.

On the basis of the previous ARA, thus in criminal cases, situation testing arranged by the applicant himself was clearly accepted as appropriate evidence, from which one might draw the striking conclusion that stricter requirements were set for situation testing in civil discrimination cases than in criminal cases.[203] Arguably, it was, however, not only the obscurity of the ADA that led to a general refusal by fact-finders, but also the fact that such evidence can only constitute indirect proof, which requires an active stance from the fact-finder, and which seemed to be too low a level of proof for such a serious violation. Remarkably, as mentioned supra, in relation to the elimination method it was also argued that it does not reach the required standard of proof.[204] Thus, it is yet to be seen whether the ARA would engender change in the acceptance and admissibility of situation testing.

In principle, any forms of proof can be used as evidence in civil procedures in Estonia, thus, courts cannot reasonably refuse the result of situation testing which has been executed in a methodologically correct way. Still, it remains unanswered whether situation testing will be regarded as sufficient evidence to give rise to a presumption of discrimination.

In Hungary, shortly after its establishment, the AET was also reluctant to accept that the result of situation testing could give rise to a presumption. This reluctance was arguably mainly related to its unfamiliarity with the concepts of covert direct discrimination, presumption of discrimination and special allocation of the burden of proof. In one case, for instance, an applicant with a Roma name and accent called an employer who was looking for a new employee.[205] The telephone call was made from the office of the House of Chances in her town, thus, an officer of the House could overhear what she was saying. The applicant (victim) was told that the vacancy had already been filled. Shortly after, the officer of the House (reference person),[206] who was not of Roma origin, also called this employer and she was told that the vacancy was still open. The AET, however, argued that the result of situation testing does not show that the Roma origin of the applicant was the cause of her rejection. This rejection can arguably be linked to the unfamiliarity with the concept of presumption.

203 Brussels Correctional Tribunal, 31 March 2004.
204 See section on the standard of proof of the applicant. See also Thiery (2007), at 757-758.
205 www.egyenlobanasmod.hu, cases from 2005 (without reference number).
206 No selected person was involved in this case.

In later cases, however, no such difficulties have occurred.[207] For instance, a very similar case also concerned a job advertisement for which the applicant applied by telephone call. He called from an office of the local government and an officer could also hear a part of his conversation. Following this call, an NGO conducted a situation testing in which two persons called the employer, one of them seemed to be Roma with a typical Roma name and the other one a non-Roma person. This testing was clearly accepted as evidence, however, the reason for this cannot, arguably be related either to the participation of the NGO in the testing procedure, or to the fact that this testing was methodologically more correct or professional. Arguably, it was rather the position paper of the ABET in which it was argued that the applicant does not have to prove or show the causality that made the Authority revise its stance.[208] Nevertheless, the execution of situation testing in this case clearly followed the methodological rules. While in the previous case no selected group was involved, here in addition to the original victim, and in order to control whether the distinction made was in fact related to his protected ground, a selected and a reference person were also involved in the procedure.

In any event, it seems that in the practice of the AET no strict requirements are set up in relation to situation testing for which at least three reasons can be found. Firstly, the AET has to investigate the case itself, therefore it does not rely only on the arguments and evidence submitted by the parties. Secondly, the Authority can also carry out situation testing. Thirdly, pursuant to the HETA the applicant is not required to show a possible causal link which the situation testing as a matter of fact aims to do.

Keeping in mind the burden of provision in the HETA and the above mentioned position paper of the Advisory Board it is surprising that Article 13 of the Government Decree on the Authority stipulates that the AET can conduct situation testing 'in order to check compliance with the requirement of equal treatment.' Pursuant to this article "[t]he results of such testing may be used as evidence in proceedings launched due to the breach of equal treatment."[209] This regulation in fact acknowledges that at some point the causal link between the different elements should be shown. On the basis of this mandate, the AET has already carried out such testing in several cases.[210] Since such testing was already conducted prior to the position paper of the

[207] See for instance EBH/180/2006 and EBH/58/2006.

[208] This can be clearly seen in the arguments of the AET, namely that the respondent could not give any reasonable justification for such treatment or prove the lack of causal relationship between the Roma origin of the applicant and the disputed treatment. See EBH/180/2006.

[209] Art. 13(2) GDAET.

[210] See for instance EBH/310/33/2007; a case related to disability in 2005 (without reference number).

ABET, it can be concluded that the main reason for refusing the applicant's complaint was not related to a reluctance of accepting situation testing as a form of proof.[211]

Finally, in the Netherlands situation testing has been relied on for a long time. In the very first cases in which situation testing was used before the ETC, testing was carried out by interest organisations, and only later have both the reliance on and the acceptance of this evidence become more widespread.[212] In one case, situation testing was used to show the allegedly discriminatory entrance policy of a discotheque.[213] In this respect the same complaint was submitted to the Commission twice. The first complaint was refused arguably due to the methodologically incorrect testing which could not give rise to a presumption of discrimination.[214] The same interest organisation engaged in the procedure carried out another testing keeping in mind the instructions and considerations given by the Commission. In the first case the problem was that the control group did not even try to enter the discotheque after the selected group had been refused the reason given that they needed a membership card. For this reason, in the view of the Commission the testing was not executed in a methodologically correct way. To be concrete, the testing could not reveal that the membership card was not the real reason for their refusal. The second time, however, the interest organisation carried out a proper and methodologically correct testing during which the control group also tried to enter the discotheque in more or less the same way as the selected group.

Importantly, testing not carried out by interest organisations, but by the victims themselves, was also accepted as appropriate evidence.[215] Similarly to Hungary, testing has also been approved when executed by telephone.[216]

3.5.2. Neutralising Variables: Similarity of the Groups and Timing of Testing

The neutralising variables have been addressed only in Hungary and the Netherlands. The methodological requirement that both groups have to be similar to each other to the greatest extent possible has been clearly, though implicitly accepted in both countries. It has also been acknowledged that the inappropriate timing of the testing could lead to a situation in which the irrelevant factors cannot be eliminated.

---

211 A case from 2005 related to disability (without reference number).

212 Compare for instance the following cases: Opinions 1997-62, 1997-133, 1998-39, 2004-13, 2006-180 and 2007-156 ETC.

213 Opinion 1997-133 ETC.

214 Opinion 1997-62 ETC.

215 See inter alia Opinions 2004-13 and 2007-156 ETC.

216 See inter alia EBH/180/2006.

In Hungary, the Governmental Decree on the Authority lays down how situation testing has to be carried out.

> During such testing, the Authority involves other persons that are different regarding their position, characteristics or attributes (characteristics) defined in Article 8 of the Act on Equal Treatment, but are otherwise *similar* and puts them into an *identical situation* regarding the conduct, measures, condition, omission, instruction or practice (disposition) of the person drawn under the procedure, and examines the disposition of the person drawn under the procedure regarding compliance with the obligation of equal treatment.[217]

Concerning the timing of testing in Hungary, in one case, for instance, the applicants explained that they were denied entrance to a disco twice one month having elapsed between the two occasions. Concerning both cases they argued that they were discriminated against on the grounds of their Roma origin. Following their second refusal, a reference group was able to enter on the same evening without any difficulties. The court of appeal did not accept that the applicants' refusal was on the ground of their Roma origin. The respondent argued that on the first occasion they were drunk, and their second refusal was based on their behaviour on the first occasion. This explanation by the respondent was accepted by the court, the reasoning of which could be interpreted that the testing of the second instance could not prove that their refusal on the first occasion was on the ground of their ethnic origin. It has been explained in relation to this argument that

> [t]he problem with this approach was that in the interpretation of numerous judges, the result of testing performed this way may not be taken into consideration as evidence, because only the original, individual violation may be the subject matter of the lawsuit, and the testing is so distantly related to this subject matter that no conclusions can retrospectively be drawn from the result of the testing with regard to the original violation.[218]

Arguably, the problems of interpretation, in addition to the lenient scrutiny of the respondent's explanation, were caused by the incorrect application of situation testing. More specifically, the testing was methodologically incorrect, since the alleged discrimination on the first occasion was not shortly followed with the testing of a control group. Moreover, the victim group in the second case was the same as the victim group in the first case. Moreover, the testing of the control group was not capable of eliminating the irrelevant factors. Arguably, a selected group should have been drawn into the testing in the second case.

In the Netherlands, the Commission laid down that the selected and the reference groups in a testing have to be similar to each other to the greatest extent possible, for example in terms of age, appearance, and behaviour.[219] In

217 Art. 13 (1) GDAET (emphasis added).
218 Kádár (2007), at 17; Farkas, Kádár & Kárpáti (2006), at 80.
219 Opinion 1997-133 ETC.

the above-mentioned case concerning the requirement of a membership card for entering a disco, the ETC explicitly emphasised some relevant elements of similarity. It specified that in the particular case neither of the members of the group had previously visited the place, and neither of them had membership cards. This could lead to the conclusion that the membership requirement could not be the real reason for their refusal. In another case, the applicant complained of discrimination on renting a hall for a family party, the applicant being of Turkish origin. In this case, an anti-discrimination bureau acted as representative and accomplished three situation testings.[220] In the view of the Commission the result of these testings could not, however, give rise to a presumption of discrimination. According to the ETC the treatment of the selected and reference groups in the first two instances did not differ to a great extent. Moreover, during the third testing even if there was a difference, no further conclusions could be drawn from this as to the reason for this differential treatment, due to the elapse of time between the enquiry of the selected and the reference group. In other words, the Commission, correctly, did not regard the result of testing as such which could eliminate all the other possible grounds or reasons for the differential treatment.

In cases concerning the entrance policy of a discotheque the Commission also emphasised that it is desirable that testing take place within the shortest possible time.[221] In these cases, the treatment of the victim group was compared with that of the reference group without the involvement of a selected group. Remarkably, it was also partly due to the timing of testing that the situation testing could not eliminate the other possible reasons for the differential treatment in the above mentioned case concerning the renting of a hall for a family party to a Turkish person.[222] In relation to this case, three separate testings were accomplished, and in the third instance the selected group was told that none of the four dates they were enquiring about were available, while the reference group was informed on the next day that two of these dates were free. In the view of the Commission and in line with the theoretical elaborations, due to the particular character of renting halls, namely that the reservations can change in a very short period of time, no prima facie case of discrimination on the grounds of racial origin could be established.

3.5.3. Field of Application

Testing as evidence for a prima facie case of discrimination has been used in cases of direct discrimination both in Hungary and the Netherlands. In the latter, in the case of the renting of a hall for a family party, as mentioned, the

220 Opinion 1998-39 ETC.
221 See for instance Opinions 1997-62 and 1997-133 ETC.
222 Opinion 1998-39 ETC.

anti-discrimination bureau carried out three situation testings, which could be interpreted as aiming to show a particular pattern. In other words, this testing could have given rise to a presumption of systematic discrimination as well, even though the aim of the interest organisation was to make out a prima facie case of discrimination in relation to the situation of the Turkish applicant.[223]

Situation testing has been relied on in cases in the fields of providing goods and services and employment. More specifically, in Hungary situation testing has so far been used in cases concerning application procedures and entrance into discotheques. Importantly, the AET has also conducted situation testing not only for the sake of establishing a prima facie case of (direct) discrimination, but also for controlling whether the respondent observes the Authority's decision, and to determine the most effective sanction.[224]

In the Netherlands the result of testing was taken as appropriate evidence in relation to job application procedures[225] and access to services, such as entrance policies in discotheques,[226] membership in fitness clubs[227] and renting rooms for social gatherings.[228]

Remarkably, along with the *Danfoss*-formula, a lighter form of situation testing has also been accepted by the ETC as appropriate evidence which could give rise to presumption.[229] In one case, a group of Turkish persons tried to enter a bar. While they were refused, non-immigrant persons were let in without any difficulties. According to the Commission, the fact that the entrance system of the defendant was not transparent, systematic and controllable, and could allow arbitrary treatment, taken together with the refusal towards the applicant, gave rise to a presumption of discrimination. Notably, in this case neither the selected nor the reference group included 'testers' in the sense of role playing or creating an artificial situation, still the main elements of testing were present, and together with the transparency requirement it could make a presumption.

3.5.4. Sensitive Matters

The application of situation testing has raised a couple of concerns in the countries under review (with the exception of Estonia): mainly concerns of provocation and privacy were called upon.

In Belgium, the refusal to accept situation testing as constituting a form of evidence of discrimination and to adopt a Royal Decree on the methodology

223 See for instance Opinion 1998-39 ETC.
224 EBH/58/2006.
225 See for instance Opinion 2006-180 ETC.
226 See for instance Opinion 2004-13 ETC.
227 See for instance Opinion 2007-156 ETC.
228 See for instance Opinion 1998-39 ETC.
229 Opinion 2004-13 ETC.

of executing the testing can, to a great extent, be linked to the concerns that testing constitutes provocation and/or violation of privacy.[230] This argument is remarkable, as the application of situation testing even in criminal cases can be traced back to the 1980s,[231] and as mentioned supra, it is ultimately for the judge to decide whether situation testing has been properly carried out, and so whether provocation was at stake.

In the Netherlands, privacy concerns were brought up concerning the use of the results of situation testing. For instance, in a case in which a video was made of the testing, the Commission stipulated that consideration of this tape as evidence does not violate anyone's right to privacy.[232] Thus, it can be seen that the Commission decides on the applicability on testing as evidence in accordance with the law. The same can be stated with respect to the argument of provocation, and for this reason this question has not triggered any specific discussion in the context of discrimination law.[233]

As yet it has not come up in practice that members of the selected group also wish to submit a complaint of discrimination. Accordingly, it cannot be answered with certainty whether their complaints would be regarded as admissible. However, the fact, that both in Hungary and the Netherlands not only testing in its strict sense, but also testing made by the applicant and his friends[234] was accepted as giving rise to a presumption of discrimination, indicates that the complaint made by testers might not be refused by the fact-finders.

3.6. Conclusions

As discrimination inherently includes comparison, it is essential that the evidence submitted by the applicant either be comparative in nature or entail comparative elements.[235] Comparison is present in the nature of two important forms of proof: statistical evidence and situation testing. For the effective enforcement of the right to equal treatment and thus enhancing minority protection, it is essential that these forms are accepted by fact-

230 Cuypers (2003), at 464-465; De Prins (2007).

231 Liège Court of Appeal, 11 March 1988; De Prins, Sottiaux & Vrielink (2005), at 357-358; Rorive (2009), at 58.

232 Opinion 1997-65 ETC, para. 5.4.

233 Some reluctance concerning its application can only be discovered in criminal cases. See also Holtmaat (2007), at 22-23.

234 See inter alia EBH/58/2006; Opinions 2007-156 and 2004-13 ETC.

235 As elaborated in the theoretical framework, the respondent can of course also make use of these forms of proof, but they are more relevant to the establishment of a prima facie case of discrimination.

finders as appropriate and sufficient proof for establishing a presumption of discrimination. Moreover, it is also important that the rules relating to their methodology are not stricter than conceptually necessary.

With the help of these particular forms of proof the applicant can give rise to the presumption that the particular causal relationships do exist. Statistical evidence can show both the disparate impact on the group with the particular racial or ethnic origin and the potential link between this impact and the challenged provision, criterion or practice. Similarly, situation testing can demonstrate that there is a supposed relationship between the particular treatment and the harm suffered as well as between the protected ground and the harm. In this way testing eliminates the other possible factors that could be the causes of the particular harm.

Although several potential problems can be and have been identified concerning the application of statistical evidence, it seems that the lack of data and the strict data protection rules (or the overly cautious application of these rules) make fact-finders set strict requirements for the quality of statistical evidence. In Hungary, segregation cases have shown that applicants cannot rely on common knowledge concerning the composition of the classes of the schools concerned and that, due to the lack of data (that can actually be attributed to the data protection rules), they have to invite sociologists as experts to prepare surveys, on the basis of which the concrete proportions of pupils can be ascertained. The time and cost involved in such a procedure means that this statistical evidence approach makes litigation less effective. Moreover, victims of discrimination, who generally come from the most vulnerable segment of society, are hardly in a position to initiate these kinds of procedures if such ponderous conditions are applied. It is therefore highly desirable, for the effective enforcement of the right to non-discrimination, that Member States collect or make arrangements for the collection of data which could then also be made accessible to those who may want to use them in a lawsuit. In the other countries no racial discrimination cases can be found yet in which statistical evidence (in its strict sense) was relied on.

Notwithstanding the fact that the application of statistical proof has in theory been regarded as more problematic, the case studies indicate that it is rather the acceptance and correct application of situation testing that raises concerns. This unease with situation testing might be assigned to the lack of application by the ECJ, the absence of reference in the RED to this particular form of proof and/or the unfamiliarity with the concept of presumption in direct discrimination cases. In Belgium, it is still not clear whether this form of proof will be accepted by fact-finders. In Estonia, given that, unlike statistical evidence, no reference has been made to this particular form of proof, it is yet to be seen whether situation testing will be accepted as an appropriate form of proof that can give rise to a presumption of discrimination. In Hungary, the application of this form of proof did not go smoothly at the beginning, mainly due to the unfamiliarity with the concept of presumption. Although no clear rules have been drawn up concerning the method of situation testing, both in Hungary and in the Netherlands a couple of cases were rejected due to the inappropriateness of the testing. In these cases, the testing was carried out in a methodologically inaccurate manner since the neutralising variables were arguably not appropriately considered and taken care of. For this reason the other possible causes of the harm could not be eliminated. Thus, it could not be concluded that the protected ground of the victim/selected group was the reason why they were treated less favourably than the other group. Importantly, however, not only can methodologically correct testing be executed by experts or interest organisations, but such a control performed by the victims themselves can and are also accepted by fact-finders.

In conclusion, the approval and admittance of statistical data and situation testing as appropriate forms of proof clearly contribute to facilitating the victim's procedural position, and encourage them to vindicate their right. This clearly enhances the effectiveness of enforcing the right to equal treatment, the first pillar of minority protection.

Chapter 4

Access to Justice

Part A. Theoretical Framework

As explained above, the Race Directive stands out amongst the different directives by virtue of its detailed provisions on enforcement. Its chapter on enforcement begins with Article 7 on the defence of rights. This article can be divided into two parts: access to justice and legal standing. The present chapter focuses on the right to access to justice.

4.1. Introduction

When one's right to equal treatment is violated, access to justice is of great importance to the victim, since without a legal mechanism for their enforcement, substantive rights would remain mere declarative provisions. For this reason, the right to access to justice is one of the most important fundamental rights in general, the ponderousness of which has also been acknowledged in EC law.[1] Concerning the application of the RED the EP resolution also "[e]mphasises that laws are effective only when citizens [...] have easy access to the courts."[2] As the Preamble of the RED is very succinct

---

1 See inter alia Tridimas (1999), at 279; Szyszczak (1997), at 107. The ECJ has emphasised its importance, for instance, in the *Johnston* case. It argued that "[t]he requirement of judicial control stipulated by that Article [Art. 6 ETD] reflects a general principle of law which underlies the constitutional traditions common to the Member States. This principle is also laid down in Articles 6 and 13 of the European Convention for the Protection of Human Rights and Fundamental Freedoms of 4 November 1950." Judgment of 15 May 1986 in *Case 222/84, Johnston v. Chief Constable of the Royal Ulster Constabulary*, [1987] ECR 1651, para. 18.

2 European Parliament resolution of 27 September 2007 on the application of Council Directive 2000/43/EC of 29 June 2000 implementing the principle of equal treatment between persons irrespective of racial or ethnic origin, 2007/2094(INI), para. 20.

concerning the aim of the provision on access to justice, the Preamble of the Recast Directive,[3] Article 17(1) of which contains a very similar rule,[4] can be called upon. Pursuant to its Recital (29) "[t]he provision of adequate judicial or administrative procedures for the enforcement of the obligations imposed by this Directive is *essential* to the effective implementation of the principle of equal treatment."[5]

In the theoretical part of this chapter, a detailed analysis of Article 7(1) RED will first of all be given. More specifically, it will be examined what should be understood by the terms judicial and/or administrative procedures; what conciliation procedures mean; a possible interpretation of the phrase 'enforcement of obligation' will be provided; and it will also be discussed what the expression 'even after the relationship has ended' implies and what kind of time-limits can be applied. The theoretical part will be closed with mapping further requirements that are not explicitly enshrined in Article 7, but could be set on the basis of the legislative proposal.

Article 7 RED lays down the following:

> Article 7 Defence of Rights
>
> (1) Member States shall ensure that judicial and/or administrative procedures, including where they deem it appropriate conciliation procedures, for the enforcement of obligations under this Directive are available to all persons who consider themselves wronged by failure to apply the principle of equal treatment to them, even after the relationship in which the discrimination is alleged to have occurred has ended.
> (2) Member States shall ensure that associations, organisations or other legal entities, which have, in accordance with the criteria laid down by their national law, a legitimate interest in ensuring that the provisions of this Directive are complied with, may engage, either on behalf or in support of the complainant, with his or her approval, in any judicial and/or administrative procedure provided for the enforcement of obligations under this Directive.
> (3) Paragraphs 1 and 2 are without prejudice to national rules relating to time limits for bringing actions as regards the principle of equality of treatment.

---

3 Directive 2006/54/EC of the European Parliament and of the Council of 5 July 2006 on the implementation of the principle of equal opportunities and equal treatment of men and women in matters of employment and occupation (Recast Directive).

4 "Member States shall ensure that, after possible recourse to other competent authorities including where they deem it appropriate conciliation procedures, judicial procedures for the enforcement of obligations under this Directive are available to all persons who consider themselves wronged by failure to apply the principle of equal treatment to them, even after the relationship in which the discrimination is alleged to have occurred has ended."

5 Recital (29) Recast Directive.

4.2. Types of Procedures

4.2.1. Judicial and/or Administrative Procedures

Article 7(1) RED stipulates that judicial and/or administrative procedures should be available for victims. The wording of the provision in relation to these procedures raises at least three questions. Firstly, what the meanings of judicial and administrative procedures are and what the difference is between these two types of procedures. The second question is closely related to the first one: whether a judicial procedure in terms of the RED is a civil or a criminal procedure or whether it covers both. Thirdly, how should one interpret the conjunctions in this expression: do we need both procedures (and what is their relative importance) or would just one of them suffice?

4.2.1.1. Judicial versus Administrative Procedures: Meaning

The wording of Article 7(1) RED[6] signals a significant shift from similar provisions in earlier equal treatment directives.[7] The first directive laying down the right to access to justice in the context of anti-discrimination law was Council Directive 75/117/EEC on equal pay. Article 2 of this Directive required ensuring the availability of a judicial procedure "after possible recourse to other competent authorities."[8] This has been repeated in subsequent Directives concerning the equal treatment of men and women.[9] It was the

6 This position has been followed in other Directives as well. Council Directive 2000/78/EC of 27 November 2000 establishing a general framework for equal treatment in employment and occupation; Directive 2002/73/EC of the European Parliament and of the Council of 23 September 2002 amending Council Directive 76/207/EEC on the implementation of the principle of equal treatment for men and women as regards access to employment, vocational training and promotion, and working conditions; Council Directive 2004/113/EC of 13 December 2004 implementing the principle of equal treatment between men and women in the access to and supply of goods and services; Directive 2006/54/EC.

7 Similar wording can be found in the ECRI model legislation. ECRI General Policy Recommendation No 7 on national Legislation to Combat Racism and Racial Discrimination, 13 December 2002, CRI (2003) 8, para. 10.

8 Council Directive 75/117/EEC Art. 2. "Member States shall introduce into their national legal systems such measures as are necessary to enable all employees who consider themselves wronged by failure to apply the principle of equal pay to pursue their claims by judicial process after possible recourse to other competent authorities."

9 Council Directive 76/207/EEC of 9 February 1976 on the implementation of the principle of equal treatment for men and women as regards access to employment, vocational training and promotion, and working conditions; Council Directive 79/7/EEC of 19 December 1978 on the progressive implementation of the principle of equal treatment for men and women in matters of social security; Council Directive 91/533/EEC of 14 October 1991 on an employer's obligation to inform employees of the conditions applicable to the contract or employment relationship; Council Directive 92/85/EEC of 19 October 1992 on the introduction of measures

RED which for the first time explicitly mentioned administrative procedures as possible forms of access to justice.[10]

Several differences and similarities can be found between a judicial and an administrative procedure. First of all, judicial procedures are always linked to courts or tribunals, while this is not the case with administrative procedures, which can be related to either courts/tribunals or administrative organs. Arguably, those administrative procedures in which courts/tribunals proceed can be categorised as judicial procedures, thus, hereafter the term 'administrative procedures' will be used for procedures in which administrative bodies take the decisions. The differences between these two types of procedures can be hightlighted with the help of the definition of courts/tribunals given by the ECJ in the context of Article 234 (ex Article 177) EC. In the interpretation of the ECJ, the following elements are relevant in defining whether a body can be identified as a court/tribunal (hereafter court). Such an organ is established on a statutory basis as a permanent body, it has mandatory jurisdiction, it applies legal rules and its proceedings are adversarial. Besides this, judicial bodies have to be independent and impartial.[11] An organ proceeding in an administrative procedure is generally also established on a statutory basis as a permanent body, has mandatory jurisdiction, and applies legal rules. However, the procedure of an administrative organ is, generally speaking, rather more investigatory than adversarial. Also, such a body is closely linked to the administration, thus cannot generally be regarded as being independent and impartial.

---

to encourage improvements in the safety and health at work of pregnant workers and workers who have recently given birth or are breastfeeding (tenth individual Directive within the meaning of Art. 16 (1) of Directive 89/381/EEC). In a different context see Council Directive 98/49/EC of 29 June 1998 on safeguarding the supplementary pension rights of employed and self-employed persons moving within the Community; Council Directive 2001/23/EC of 12 March 2001 on the approximation of the laws of the Member States relating to the safeguarding of employees' rights in the event of transfers of undertakings, businesses or parts of undertakings or businesses.

10 It is to be noted that Article 6 of the Equal Treatment Directive (ETD) has now been amended by Directive 2002/73/EC "to ensure coherence between secondary legislation on identical issues." Proposal for a Directive of the European Parliament and of the Council amending Council Directive 76/207/EEC on the implementation of the principle of equal treatment for men and women as regards access to employment, vocational training and promotion, and working conditions, COM(2000) 334 final – COD 2000/0142, 7 June 2000, paras. 8. & 32. See also Moon (2004), at 2-3.

11 See inter alia Craig & De Búrca (2003), at 436-439; Judgment of 17 September 1997 in *Case C-54/96, Dorsch Consult Ingenieurgesellschaft mbH v. Bundesbaugesellschaft Berlin mbH*, [1997] ECR I-4961, para. 23; Judgment of 6 July 2000 in *Case C-407/98, Katarina Abrahamsson and Leif Anderson v. Elisabet Fogelqvist*, [2000] ECR I-05539, para. 29; Judgment of 30 November 2000 in *Case C-195/98, Österreichischer Gewerkschaftsbund, Gewerkschaft öffentlicher Dienst v. Republik Österreich*, [2000] ECR I-10497, para. 24.

4.2.1.2. Judicial Procedure: Civil or Criminal?

A judicial procedure can be either a civil or a criminal law procedure.[12] Concerning equal treatment legislation "[n]ational legal traditions vary greatly [...], from states that focus on civil law remedies, to those that have placed the accent on criminal law sanctions."[13]

Arguably, the RED principally focuses on civil law procedures, but it also envisages enforcing the right to equal treatment through criminal law.[14] The Directive contains two explicit references to criminal law. Firstly, Article 8 RED stipulates that the burden of proof provision is not to be applied in criminal law procedures. Secondly, the term 'sanction' in Article 15 RED also indicates that it could include criminal law sanctions.[15] However, the fact that one of the most important aspects of effective enforcement in discrimination cases, the special allocation of the burden of proof, has to be applied in civil law cases implies that the RED in fact prefers and concentrates on civil law enforcement.[16] Similarly, Article 15 RED on sanctions mentions compensation as an appropriate form of remedy, which in principle does not amount to penal redress. Moreover, the concepts of direct and indirect discrimination, contrary to criminal law definitions, do not include any reference to the intent of the perpetrator.[17] Finally, criminal law regulations are to be adopted within the framework of the third pillar, while the RED is a first pillar directive. Indeed, the recent Framework Decision which requires the Member States to criminalise certain aspects of discrimination law has been adopted in the third pillar.[18] Accordingly, it can be concluded that the legislators of the RED have kept a principally civil law framework in mind when they referred to judicial procedures.[19]

---

12 On the meaning of judicial procedures in the context of the RED see also Moon (2004), at 2-3; Tyson (2004), at 124; Bell (2004b), at 224.

13 Bell (2004b), at 224.

14 See also Tyson (2004), at 124.

15 This position is also strengthened by the requirement of 'dissuasiveness' concerning the quality of sanctions. On this aspect see Ch. 7 on sanctions.

16 Art. 8 RED.

17 See also Tyson (2004), at 124.

18 Yet the Proposal for a Council Framework Decision on combating racism and xenophobia lays down that "[a]dequate criminal law measures also form an important tool for combating racism and xenophobia." Proposal for a Council Framework Decision on combating racism and xenophobia, COM(2001) 664 final – 2001/0270 (CS), 28 November 2001. See also its final text Council Framework Decision 2008/913/JHA of 28 November 2008 on combating certain forms and expressions of racism and xenophobia by means of criminal law.

19 Moon, for instance, argued that "[i]n order to be truly effective, both as a norm for societal behaviour, and as a readily accessible and enforceable remedy, both civil and criminal procedures, should co-exist and complement one another." Moon (2004), at 3. See also Bell (2004b), at 224.

4.2.1.3. Judicial AND/OR Administrative Procedures: Is One of Them Appropriate?

At first sight the disjunctive conjunction 'or' may convey the impression that either judicial or administrative procedures in themselves are appropriate for ensuring effective enforcement. Interestingly, during the negotiations the introduction of administrative procedures into the RED as a possible type of procedure "provoked some discussion as to whether administrative procedures really provided sufficient protection."[20] The Commission's argument was that these provisions proved to be effective in certain Member States.[21] Ergo the criterion of effectiveness justified the mentioning of administrative procedures.[22]

It can, however, be argued that a purely administrative system of enforcement would not be in harmony with the principle of effectiveness.[23] It is highly probable that the enforceability of obligations would be in danger if only administrative procedures were provided for because, amongst others, administrative bodies cannot proceed in each and every case. Also, contrary to judicial organs, these bodies cannot in general be regarded as impartial and independent. Moreover, in terms of sanctions, a system of purely administrative remedies might not be accepted as being effective, proportionate and dissuasive, since, unlike judicial organs administrative bodies normally do not aim to compensate the victim.[24] Finally, it can be argued that discrimination is such a grave violation of human rights that it would require the authority of a judicial organ to be available in all cases – at least as a last resort.[25]

The plea for judicial procedure[26] can be supported with arguments from the *travaux préparatoires* of the RED and other Directives,[27] and similarly

[20] Tyson (2004), at 123.
[21] Moon (2004), at 2.
[22] Tyson (2004), at 123.
[23] See also Higgins (2003), at 396-397. Koukoulis-Spiliotopoulos (2005), at 363.
[24] On appropriate remedies see Ch. 7 on sanctions.
[25] Arguably, this argument can be also deduced from Heylens case in which the ECJ stated that "since free access to employment is a fundamental right [...] the existence of a remedy of a judicial nature [...] is essential [...]." Judgment of 10 October 1987 in *Case C-222/86, Unectef v. Georges Heylens and others*, [1987] ECR 4097, para. 14. On the argument see also Brown (2002), at 218; Toggenburg (2002), at 239-240. Compare with the CESCR's General Comment on 'The domestic application of the Covenant' from 1998, which laid down that "the Committee considers that, in many cases, the other 'means' used could be rendered ineffective if they are not reinforced or complemented by judicial measures." CESCR, General Comment Nr. 9, The domestic application of the Covenant, E/C.12/1998/24, 3 December 1998, para. 3. On this Comment see McCrudden (2001), at 280-281.
[26] See also Tobler (2005b), at 33.
[27] See also Art. 4(4) of the proposal of the Starting Line which lays down that "Member States shall ensure that: a) their legal systems provide appropriate and effective measures whereby all persons who consider themselves to have been wronged by failure to apply to them the principle of equal treatment as set out in this Directive may have recourse to a judicial remedy,

with the case law of the European Court of Justice.[28] According to the Draft Legislative Resolution of the RED "[i]n the first place, there must always be the possibility of seeking redress through the courts. This right must not be impaired by the existence of alternative procedures."[29] In other words, the aim of the legislators was definitely not to give priority to administrative procedures. This position can also be deduced from the case law of the ECJ. For instance in the *Heylens* case[30] concerning free access to employment on the basis of Article 48 EEC Treaty the Court stated that

> since free access to employment is a fundamental right which the Treaty confers individually on each worker in the Community, the existence of a *remedy of a judicial nature* against any decision of a national authority refusing the benefit of that right is essential in order to secure for the individual effective protection for his right.[31]

This can be interpreted as meaning that in case of fundamental rights there should always be a possibility for judicial enforcement, at least after the administrative procedures.[32] Similarly, in the *Jégo-Quéré & Cie SA v. Commission of the European Communities*[33] case

> the CFI accentuated that *access to the courts* is one of the essential elements of a community based on the rule of law, and that such access is guaranteed in the legal order based on the EC Treaty.[34]

The argument of Advocate General Alber concerning the need for judicial procedures even after a quicker and more cost-effective insurance procedure can *mutatis mutandis* be applied to administrative procedures. In his view

> [*e*]*ven if* the procedure under the Agreement might have been *quicker* and *more cost-effective than* compulsory insurance proceedings before *ordinary courts*, this still does *not* amount to sufficient *justification for depriving* injured parties of effective legal protection in the form of a determination of the facts by an *ordinary court*.[35]

---

in accordance with the most effective national procedures, after possible recourse to other competent authorities where appropriate." On the Starting Line proposal see Chopin & Niessen (2001).

28 *Case C-222/86, Unectef v. Georges Heylens and others*.

29 Report on the proposal for a Council directive on implementing the principle of equal treatment between persons irrespective of racial or ethnic origin, COM(1999) 566 – C5-0067/2000 – 1999/0253(CNS), A5-0136/2000, 16 May 2000, at 37.

30 *Case C-222/86, Unectef v. Georges Heylens and others*.

31 *Id.*, para. 14 (emphasis added).

32 See also Rombouts, Sardaro & Vandeginste (2006), at 360; Higgins (2003), at 397; Toggenburg (2002), at 239-240.

33 Judgment of 3 May 2002 in *Case T-177/01, Jégo-Quéré et Cie SA v. Commission*, [2002] ECR II-2365.

34 Bårdsen (2007), at 102 (emphasis added).

35 Advocate General Alber in *Case C-63/01, Samuel Sidney Evans v. Secretary of State for the Environment and Transport and the Regions and the Motor Insurer's Bureau*, [2003] ECR I-4447, para. 111 (emphasis added). Compare with the relevant case law of the European Court

Finally, it is also worth taking a look at the relevant article of the Recast Directive,[36] the Explanatory Memorandum of which explains that

> the reference to judicial and/or administrative procedures is unfortunately worded in that it tends to create the wrong impression that Member States have a choice between granting access to one or the other or both and could thus restrict judicial review on the grounds of the possibility to launch an administrative complaints procedure.[37]

The concerned article of the Recast Directive was amended in order to avoid any misinterpretations because of the 'unfortunate' wording of Article 7(1) RED. Accordingly, it can be concluded that on the basis of EU law it would not suffice if only administrative organs would be assigned as competent authorities in discrimination complaint procedures.

Conversely, it can also be argued that a system based purely on judicial, as explained mainly civil, procedures cannot be regarded as a fully effective way of fighting discrimination either. These procedures are generally time-consuming and expensive.[38] In the context of debt recovery, which can now be applied by analogy to administrative procedures, Advocate General Cosmas argued that although in the light of national procedural autonomy it is for the Member States to regulate the different procedures,

> this does not negate the *basic need for special simplified procedures* for debt recovery, a need which [...] is in essence connected with conferring complete, effective and timely judicial protection. National legislation can therefore provide for the necessary and appropriate prohibitions or restrictions on

of Human Rights, for instance, with the *Golder v. the United Kingdom*, ECHR (1975) Series A, No. 18, No. 4451/70, 21 February 1975, *Airey v. Ireland*, ECHR (1979) Series A, No. 32, No. 6289/73, 9 October 1979 and *Ashingdane v. the United Kingdom*, ECHR (1985) Series A, No. 93, No. 8225/78, 28 May 1985 cases. On these cases from the perspective of access to justice, see Varjú (2005), at 66.

36 Art. 17 (1) Member States shall ensure that, after possible recourse to other competent authorities including where they deem it appropriate conciliation procedures, judicial procedures for the enforcement of obligations under this Directive are available to all persons who consider themselves wronged by failure to apply the principle of equal treatment to them, even after the relationship in which the discrimination is alleged to have occurred has ended.

37 Amended proposal for a Directive of the European Parliament and of the Council on the implementation of the principle of equal treatment of men and women in matters of employment and occupation (recast version), COM(2005) 0380 final – COD 2004/0084, para. 2.1.25.

38 According to Advocate-General Maduro "one of the problems is that most instances of discrimination will never reach court simply because parties are not informed, or they do not have the means to get information, or to organize themselves to protect their rights. [...] The other problem relates to the length of time of proceedings. [...] In justice time is always of the essence, but particularly in these cases. [...] From the perspective of the court therefore, the interpretation of the procedural rules of access to courts is very important. [...] In addition, from the point of view of the legislator, it is important to define mechanisms and alternative forms of brining cases of discrimination before the courts." Maduro (2005), at 22.

> those procedures by relying on fundamental rights and the abovementioned Community law principles. However, it cannot prohibit such procedures generally or without justification.[39]

The Commission in its concluding report on the application of the RED has also observed that "[i]t is clear from the information provided by NGO's and governments that many victims of discrimination do not proceed to court with their complaints because of *cost*."[40] Accordingly, administrative procedures might be regarded as appropriate ways of enforcement preceding to and complementing civil procedures, because they are generally decided in a short period of time and are free of charge. Creating 'fast-track' procedures have been required by the ECRI model legislation[41] as well, proceeding from the reasoning that

> [t]hese procedures are important in those situations where the immediate consequences of the alleged discriminatory act are particularly serious or even irreparable. Thus, for example, the victims of a discriminatory eviction from a flat should be able to suspend this measure through an interim judicial decision, pending the final judgment of the case.[42]

Generally, administrative procedures are reasonably prompt, accordingly, this can also be a good argument for having administrative procedures in addition to judicial ones.[43]

Importantly, in administrative procedures fact-finders are usually obliged to unravel all relevant circumstances of the case themselves, since they are investigatory bodies. This fact constitutes an additional argument in favour of administrative procedures since in investigatory procedures the burden of proof of the applicant is less cumbersome. Moreover, from the perspective of the victim a preceding administrative procedure can also be a good start for a judicial procedure, since the administrative fact-finding body has already disclosed most of the circumstances of the case.[44] In summary, an administrative procedure can often be a necessary and effective complement to judicial review.

---

[39] Advocate General Cosmas in *Case C-412/97, ED Srl v. Italo Fenocchio*, [1999] ECR 1-3845, paras. 37-38 (emphasis added).

[40] Report from the Commission to the Council and the European Parliament – The application of Directive 2000/43/EC of 29 June 2000 implementing the principle of equal treatment between persons irrespective of racial or ethnic origin, COM(2006) 643 final/2, 15 December 2006, para. 3.1 (emphasis added).

[41] ECRI General Policy Recommendation No 7 on National Legislation to Combat Racism and Racial Discrimination, CRI (2003) 8, 13 December 2002, para. 10.

[42] Explanatory Memorandum to ECRI General Policy Recommendation No 7 on National Legislation to Combat Racism and Racial Discrimination, para. 28.

[43] Certain legal systems, however, do know fast-track judicial procedures, which would imply that here the necessity for administrative procedures are less important, depending, naturally, on the general and concrete circumstances.

[44] See also Kádár (2006), at 122-123.

Consequently, when deciding which procedure should be applied in discrimination cases, Member States are required to observe the general principle of effectiveness. It has been argued that without judicial procedure access to justice can only exceptionally be regarded as effective; administrative procedures might compensate for the disadvantages of judicial procedures, but only as complementary procedures to judicial ones and not as a replacement. Accordingly, the most effective way of ensuring the right to access to court would, in general, be to have judicial as well as administrative procedures.

4.2.2. Conciliation Procedures

Contrary to the original proposal of the RED, the present text of Article 7(1) RED includes a reference to conciliation procedures.[45] It was the European Parliament which proposed the following text:

> Member States are urged to ensure that appropriate conciliation procedures are available. These procedures must not be compulsory and are without prejudice to the complainant's right of recourse to judicial protection as set out in paragraph 7(1).[46]

As a reaction to this proposal, the Commission amended the original draft.[47]

4.2.2.1. What Does 'Conciliation' Mean?

In general, conciliation procedures are regarded as special forms of alternative dispute resolution (ADR), amongst which mediation, negotiation and arbitration can also be found. However, it does not seem logical that the legislators of the RED, instead of attempting to reach *amicus* settlements in general, would have aspired to refer to a special form of alternative dispute resolution. The reason for choosing this terminology can be found neither in the original nor in the amended proposals of the Directive, but recourse to other relevant EU legislation is possible. For instance, the *travaux préparatoires* of the Recast Directive[48] in relation to Article 17(1) can give some guidance on this matter. From the proposals and amendments it becomes clear that there were some discussions on the formulation of the phrase '*conciliation procedures*' in this article. Some proposals aimed to introduce mediation and arbitration in

---

45 See also McCrudden (2001), at 295; McCrudden (1999), at 300.

46 Report on the proposal for a Council Directive on implementing the principle of equal treatment between persons irrespective of racial or ethnic origin, COM(1999)566 – C5-0067/2000 – 1999/0253(CNS), A5-0136/2000 final, 16 May 2000, at 22-23. & 60.

47 Amended proposal for a Council Directive implementing the principle of equal treatment between persons irrespective of racial or ethnic origin, COM(2000) 328 final – 1999/0253 (CNS), 31 May 2000, Article 7(1).

48 Directive 2006/54/EC.

addition to the notion of conciliation procedure "as other forms of amicably settling disputes."[49] The Commission, however, did not find it necessary to add the different forms of alternative dispute settlement because it found that

> no value added is brought about by going into more detail as regards the different types of efforts to find an amicable solution. This would also imply the introduction of an unnecessary discrepancy as compared to other Directives in this field.[50]

Accordingly, it can be argued that instead of striving for a special type of ADR, the purpose of including conciliation procedures in the particular provisions was to emphasise the possibility of, or in certain cases the necessity for, finding amicable settlements. The only reason for not amending the text of this provision of the Recast Directive was to stay in harmony with the other Directives in this field, amongst which the RED. Moreover, it can also be argued, that the Commission did not find it necessary to amend the text because it supposed that this expression does not give rise to any ambiguity.[51]

In conclusion, it can be established that the term 'conciliation' does not refer to one of the special forms of alternative dispute resolutions, rather it means the possibility to have an out-of-court procedure for friendly settlement. The terms 'conciliation' and 'alternative dispute resolution' will be used synonymously from now on.

---

49 Amended proposal for a Directive of the European Parliament and of the Council on the implementation of the principle of equal treatment of men and women in matters of employment and occupation (recast version), COM/2005/0380 final – COD 2004/0084, 25 August 2005, para. 2.1.25, Amendment 61.

50 *Id.*

51 This elaboration can further also be supported, for example, by Article 20(2) of the Framework Directive on electronic communications networks and the related documents. This article makes it possible for national regulatory authorities to decline to resolve a dispute "where other mechanisms, including mediation, exist and would better contribute to resolution of the dispute in a timely manner" before turning to the 'national regulatory authorities' (NRAs). This provision seemingly also takes only one special form of alternative dispute resolution. However, the Commission staff working document in relation to this article states the following: "NRAs may decline to resolve disputes (for a certain time) when there are alternative dispute resolution mechanisms, e.g. mediation that would be more effective in helping to resolve the dispute (Article 20(2) of the Framework Directive)." The working document makes it clear that mediation was only meant as an example, and as a matter of fact, in Article 20(2) it refers to alternative dispute resolution mechanisms. Directive 2002/21/EC of the European Parliament and of the Council of 7 March 2002 on a common regulatory framework for electronic communications networks and services (Framework Directive); Commission staff working document – Annex to the Communication for the Commission to the European Parliament, the Council, the European Economic and Social Committee and the Committee of the Regions – European electronic communications regulation and markets 2006 (12th Report) COM(2007) 155 final, SEC/2007/0403, 29 June 2006.

4.2.2.2. 'When [the Member States] Deem It Appropriate' to Introduce Conciliation Procedures

Pursuant to the RED, Member States shall ensure that conciliation procedures are available when they deem it appropriate. This formulation indicates that Member States are free whether they introduce such procedures.

It is generally accepted that "[c]onciliation can make a positive contribution to resolving a conflict."[52] For some victims, depending naturally on the circumstances of the case, conciliation might be a good way of dealing with their complaint.[53] "Proponents of ADR maintain that ADR methods provide qualitatively better results in a more efficient manner."[54] Several arguments can be given in support of this statement.[55] It is commonly known that an alternative dispute resolution is generally easily accessible, flexible, faster than a judicial proceeding and much cheaper, which is very advantageous from the perspective of victims of discrimination whose aim is to be able to turn to a fact-finding body in the shortest time possible and to get a quick decision on their case.[56] ADR facilitates settlement between parties, which at the same time means that the parties have a more active role than in a judicial procedure, they "escape the stress which, as a rule, accompanies legal proceedings, and they have better possibilities to preserve good relations."[57] This is an important aspect in discrimination cases since the chance is greater that the eventual prejudices can be abolished with the help of an ADR procedure. Moreover, the

[52] Report on the proposal for a Council Directive on implementing the principle of equal treatment between persons irrespective of racial or ethnic origin, COM(1999) 566 – C5-0067/2000 – 1999/0253(CNS), A5-0136/2000 final, 16 May 2000, at 22-23.

[53] *Id.*, at 60.

[54] Ellis (1996), at 18.

[55] See further Green paper on alternative dispute resolution in civil and commercial law, COM/2002/0196 final, 19 April 2002; Lindell (2007), at 313. The arguments given hereafter are mainly based on these two papers.

[56] See also Cohen (2004), at 22.

Pursuant to the Green paper on payment procedure alternative dispute resolution "would have the advantage that the workload of courts would be reduced as well as costs. There could be substantial savings in legal fees and other litigation expenses and in the time and energy of the parties and judges. Also, a compromise is most likely to be reached faster than a judgment rendered and enforced." Green Paper on a European order for payment procedure and on measures to simplify and speed up small claims litigation, COM/2002/0746 final, 20 December 2002, para. 6.3. See also Communication from the Commission to the European Parliament and the Council – Enhancing the patent system in Europe, COM(2007) 165 final, 3 April 2007, para. 3.4.1; Communication from the Commission to the European Parliament and the Council – Report on the implementation, functioning and effectiveness of the ".eu" TLD, COM(2007) 385 final, 6 July 2007, para. 3.2.3; Proposal for a Directive of the European Parliament and of the Council on the protection of consumers in respect of certain aspects of timeshare, long-term holiday products, resale and exchange, COM/2007/0303 final – COD 2007/0113, 7 June 2007, Recital (14), Art. 10.

[57] Lindell (2007), at 313.

reached agreement is 'tailor-made' and unique. Instead of merely managing it, the aim of such a mechanism is to solve the conflict. Not only the purely legally relevant aspects of a complaint are taken into account in an ADR procedure, but during the negotiations the whole context is considered. Ergo an ADR procedure operates with a broad problem definition, trying to attain social harmony as well. It has a relief function, too, which means that courts can devote their time and energy to cases not capable of being solved through ADR. In summary, ADR can definitely improve general access to justice in everyday life.

ADR procedures do however also have disadvantages.[58] Since the aim of these procedures is to achieve a compromise between the two parties, the agreement is generally not public. Accordingly it does not have a deterrent or educating effect on the society as a whole, which would, arguably, be extremely important in racial discrimination cases. Moreover, in some jurisdictions, an ADR procedure "if unsuccessful, eats up the time within which a formal complaint can be launched."[59] As mentioned above, the outcome in such cases is generally a compromise between the parties, which as a rule does not contribute to raising awareness of the concepts of discrimination and developing the practical application of the relevant legislation. In this respect it has been argued that such "settlements are seen as a way of stopping cases short of resolution, rather than as resolving cases by a quicker method than going to a hearing."[60]

Balancing the advantages and disadvantages of such procedures from the perspectives of effective enforcement in general and facilitating the position of victims of discrimination in particular, it can be concluded that Article 7(1) RED includes an obligation on the Member States to explore under which circumstances it would be useful and effective to introduce these procedures. This duty was acknowledged and accentuated in 1979 in a seminar of the United Nations on Recourse Procedures Available to Victims of Racial Discrimination and Activities to be Undertaken at the Regional Level.[61] Admittedly, it is difficult for the ECJ to enforce this obligation.[62]

---

[58] For a critical approach see for instance Baker (2004).

[59] Opinion of the European Economic and Social Committee on the Proposal for a Directive of the European Parliament and of the Council amending Council Directives 89/665/EEC and 92/13/EEC with regard to improving the effectiveness of review procedures concerning the award of public contracts, COM(2006) 095 final/2 – COD 2006/0066, 18 January 2007, para. 4.5.4.

[60] McCrudden (1999), at 300.

[61] McCrudden (2001), at 275. McCrudden cites one of the conclusions of the Seminar in this respect pursuant to which states "should follow or at least consider the example of conciliation procedures in minor cases or racial discrimination, or in the most common cases."

[62] Arguably, when no quick, easily accessible and cost-effectives are created, the ECJ might conclude that the respondent state did not comply with its duty to give ample attention to this possibility.

Similarly to administrative procedures, it is, however, insufficient if only ADR procedures are available. The EP resolution on the application of the RED also made this explicit when it stipulated that "alternative dispute resolution procedures should not pre-empt access to the courts."[63] Importantly, participation in such procedures should not be made obligatory for the victim or the alleged perpetrator.[64]

4.2.2.3. 'Including' Conciliation Procedures: The Relationship between Administrative and Conciliation Procedures

The expression 'judicial and/or administrative procedures, *including* [...] conciliation procedures' might indicate that conciliation procedures are regarded as a special form of administrative procedures. Indeed, the Committee on Employment and Social Affairs of the EP argued that ADR procedures, in fact, fall under the term 'administrative procedures', but it is important to mention them separately for the sake of clarity.[65] However, these procedures are generally not regulated by administrative law provisions. While administrative procedures are conducted by administrative bodies, a conciliation procedure is usually carried out by bodies independent of the administration of the state. In terms of the Recast Directive,[66] a conciliation procedure as well as an administrative procedure can precede a judicial procedure. Accordingly, the term 'including' might be interpreted as referring to any possibility of

[63] European Parliament resolution of 27 September 2007 on the application of Council Directive 2000/43/EC of 29 June 2000 implementing the principle of equal treatment between persons irrespective of racial or ethnic origin, 2007/2094(INI), Z. See also the Report on the proposal for a Council Directive on implementing the principle of equal treatment between persons irrespective of racial or ethnic origin , COM(1999) 566 – C5-0067/2000 – 1999/0253(CNS), A5-0136/2000 final, 16 May 2000, at 22-23, which explained that "[t]he decision to have recourse to a conciliation procedure must not mean that recourse to a judicial remedy is ruled out thereafter."

See also the Art. 4(4) f) of the proposal of the Starting Line, according to which "Member States shall ensure that: f) appropriate conciliation procedures are made available which are capable of resolving difficulties between various individuals; such conciliation procedures shall not be mandatory; this shall be without prejudice to the right of the complainant to have recourse to judicial remedies [...]." On this proposal see Chopin & Niessen (2001).

[64] See inter alia Report on the proposal for a Council Directive on implementing the principle of equal treatment between persons irrespective of racial or ethnic origin, COM(1999)566 – C5-0067/2000 – 1999/0253(CNS), A5-0136/2000 final, 16 May 2000, at 22.

[65] *Id.*, at 60.

[66] Art. 17 (1) of the Recast Directive stipulates that "Member States shall ensure that, *after possible recourse to other competent authorities* including where they deem it appropriate conciliation procedures, judicial procedures for the enforcement of obligations under this Directive are available to all persons who consider themselves wronged by failure to apply the principle of equal treatment to them, even after the relationship in which the discrimination is alleged to have occurred has ended" (emphasis added).

recourse to a competent body (be it a conciliation procedure falling under administrative procedural law or any other law) after which it is still possible to turn to a judicial organ.

In conclusion, the word 'including' does not seem to mean that conciliation proceedings are qualified as administrative procedures; rather it refers to a procedure which could precede judicial enforcement.

4.2.3. 'Enforcement of Obligations under this Directive': The Material Scope of Enforcement

The expression 'enforcement of obligations under this Directive' can arguably be described as referring to the material scope of the enforcement provisions. At the same time this expression also designates the boundaries of the Member States' national procedural autonomy with regard to providing access to courts. More specifically, a procedure can be regarded as effective when it is capable of ensuring the enforcement of obligations projected in the RED.[67]

As far as the obligations arising from the RED are concerned, first of all a distinction should be made between the obligations of private persons and those of public authorities/state. In general, private persons have negative obligations: they have to refrain from violating the right of others to equal treatment. Thus, in terms of Article 7(1) RED there has to be an enforcement procedure when private persons do not comply with their obligation.

Similarly to private persons, states are also not allowed to breach the prohibition of discrimination. In addition, states also have to ensure the realisation of the principle of equal treatment, which can be translated in terms of positive obligations. Moreover, states also need to ensure that in the case of a violation by either private persons or public entities, effective enforcement mechanisms are available.

To conclude, access to justice has to be guaranteed when the substantive provisions of the RED are violated both by private and public entities and when the state does not create mechanisms for the enforcement of the substantive provisions.

4.3. Timing of Procedures

Two timing-related questions can be posed in the context of access to justice. Firstly how can the requirement of Article 7(3) RED which lays down that these procedures are 'without prejudice to national rules relating to time

[67] See also Tyson (2004), at 123. The requirement of enforceability has also been crystallised in the case-law of the European Court of Human Rights. See inter alia Jacobs & White (2006), at 174.

limits for bringing actions as regards the principle of equality of treatment' be interpreted? Secondly, what does it mean under the RED that judicial and/or administrative procedures have to be available, even after the relationship in which the discrimination is alleged to have occurred has ended?

4.3.1. Time Limits

According to the RED, the right to access to justice is "without prejudice to national rules relating to time limits for bringing actions as regards the principle of equality of treatment."[68] Strikingly, this provision can be found neither in the original, nor in the amended proposal of the RED. It has been introduced only in the very last phase of the negotiation process.[69] An observer to the negotiations explained that "Member States [...] wished to clarify that national time limit within which cases must be submitted to the court or other body would not be affected by the Directive."[70] The underlying reason for this cautiousness might have been the aim to avoid a situation similar to that in the *Emmott* case.[71] In this case the ECJ established that the time-limit set by the given Member State had affected the right to access to justice in such a way that it made its exercise virtually impossible in practice. Hence, this time-limit was not acceptable since it violated the principle of effectiveness.[72] As Tyson illuminated, the Council finally agreed on the adoption of this provision because the Member States cannot in fact avoid "respecting the conditions laid down by the European Court of Justice in Emmott."[73] Similarly, the European Parliament is also aware of the importance of national time limits, since in its resolution on the application of the RED it emphasises that "Member States should undertake independent reviews of the impact of national time limits."[74]

---

68 Art. 7(3) RED

69 This view is supported by the fact that the proposal of the Starting Line did not have any reference to time-limits. Chopin & Niessen (2001), at 43.

70 Tyson (2004), at 124.

71 Judgment of 25 July 1991 in *Case C-208/90, Theresa Emmott v. Minister for Social Welfare and the Attorney General*, [1991] ECR 1-4269.

72 It has been argued that in later cases the Court has deviated from its *Emmott* judgment (*Id.*). However, it can also be argued that in the cases following *Emmott* the ECJ only made clear that "Emmott did not apply to all forms of national procedural rules on time-limits. [...] its ration was not overruled, merely confined to limitation periods whose expiry prior to correct implementation of a directive left the applicant without remedy." Flynn (2000), at 58. See also Jans et al. (2007), at 296-301; Craig (2006), at 800-803.

73 Tyson (2004), at 124.

74 European Parliament resolution of 27 September 2007 on the application of Council Directive 2000/43/EC of 29 June 2000 implementing the principle of equal treatment between persons irrespective of racial or ethnic origin, 2007/2094(INI), para. 17.

In its case law, the Court has established two main conditions concerning the time-limits set up by the Member States.[75] First of all, the time-limit cannot be subject to less favourable conditions than those that apply to similar domestic actions.[76] Secondly, as the general principle has been formulated in the *Emmott* case, the procedural provision cannot affect the right to enforcement itself;[77] that is time-limits cannot make the right to enforcement virtually impossible or excessively difficult.[78]

With reference to ADR procedures, it can be argued that the right to enforcement might be made excessively difficult or even virtually impossible when an out-of-court proceeding does not end the limitation period for turning to a court. In other words, at the end of this procedure the limitation period might be extensively reduced or the right to turn to a court might even be extinguished.[79] Due to the growing popularity of out-of-court proceedings this

---

[75] In principle, very similar restrictions can also be found in the case-law of the European Court of Human Rights. The Court, for example, in the *Stubbings* case accepted that "[i]t must be satisfied that the limitations applied do not restrict or reduce the access left to the individual in such a way or to such an extent that the very essence of the right is impaired. Furthermore, a limitation will not be compatible with Article 6 para. 1 if it does not pursue a legitimate aim and if there is not a reasonable relationship of proportionality between the means employed and the aim sought to be achieved." Accordingly, Member States can have their own time-limits, but they have to be proportionate to the aim served. *Stubbings and others v. United Kingdom*, ECHR (1996) Nos. 22083/93 and 22095/93, 22 October 1996, para. 50. See also Jacobs & White (2006), at 171.

[76] See for example Judgment of 16 December 1976 in *Case 33/76, Rewe-Zentralfinanz eG et Rewe Zentral AG v. Landwirtschaftskammer für das Saarland*, [1976] ECR 1898, para. 5; Judgment of 19 December 1976 in *Case 45/76, Comet v. Produktschap voor Siergewassen*, [1976] ECR 2043, para. 13; Judgment of 11 July 1991 in *Case C-31/90, Johnson v. Chief Adjudication Officer*, [1991] ECR 1-3723, para. 22.

[77] See for example *Case C-208/90, Theresa Emmott v. Minister for Social Welfare and the Attorney General*, para. 19, Judgment of 27 October 1993 in *Case C-338/91, Steenhorst-Neerings v. Bestuur van de Bedrijfsvereniging voor Detailhandel Ambachten en Huisvrouwen*, [1993] ECR I-5475, para. 21. On the relationship between *Emmott* and *Steenhorst-Neerings* see, for example, Flynn (2000), at 58; Szyszczak (1997), at 110.

[78] See for example *Case 33/76, Rewe-Zentralfinanz eG et Rewe Zentral AG v. Landwirtschaftskammer für das Saarland*, para. 5; *Case 45/76, Comet v. Produktschap voor Siergewassen*, para. 16; Judgment of 1 December 1998 in *Case C-326/96, Levez v. T.H. Jennings (Harlow Pools) Ltd.*, [1998] ECR 1-7835, para. 42; Judgment of 16 May 2000 in *Case C-78/98, Shirley Preston and Othes v. Wolverhampton Healthcare NHS Trust and Others and Dorothy Fletcher and Others v. Midland Bank plc.*, [2000] ECR I-03201, para. 68. On the cases of *Emmott*, *Levez* and *Preston* see inter alia Higgins (2003), at 402-404.

[79] See also Opinion of the European Economic and Social Committee on the Proposal for a Directive of the European Parliament and of the Council amending Council Directives 89/665/EEC and 92/113/EEC with regard to improving the effectiveness of review procedures concerning the award of public contracts, COM(2006)195 final/2 – COD 2006/0066, 18 January 2007, para. 4.5.4.

is a highly relevant problem. In reaction to this, the European Commission in its Green paper on alternative dispute resolution in civil and commercial law has suggested that

> [i]n order to promote ADR, it may therefore be necessary to amend the civil procedure rules with regard to limitation periods, whereby the period could be interrupted when ADR procedure begins and subsequently resume when the procedure ends without a settlement having been reached.[80]

It can be argued that this proposal should also be applicable when an agreement is reached, that is not enforceable in legal terms. Thus, Member States should revise their procedural regulations in this respect.

4.3.2. Even After the Relationship Has Ended

The RED stipulates that access to justice has to be available "*even after the relationship in which the discrimination is alleged to have occurred has ended.*" This provision could, arguably, be read as including two different situations.[81] Firstly, it can cover a situation in which the discrimination is suffered during the existence of a relationship, but the applicant brings an action only after the relationship has ended. The other possible interpretation of this provision originates from the *Coote* case of the ECJ.[82] In this case, the respondent refused to provide references as a reaction to legal proceedings brought to enforce compliance with the principle of equal treatment. Accordingly, the applicant was discriminated against after the relationship had ended, but the alleged discrimination could be linked to that relationship.[83] In relation to this latter situation, two sub-versions might also be distinguished. On the one hand, the applicant must be protected in cases in which the challenged act can be considered as either direct or indirect discrimination (or harassment and instruction to discriminate). On the other hand, the protection should, arguably, also extend to situations in which it is victimisation (which, as will be shown, can also be considered as a special form of discrimination)

[80] Green paper on alternative dispute resolution in civil and commercial law, COM(2002) 196 final, 19 April 2002, para. 69.

[81] Brown argued that it is as actually "unclear whether Article 7(1) applies to discrimination occurring after an employment relationship has terminated. […] Article 7(1) appears only to enable victims to complain post-employment about discrimination which occurred during that relationship." Brown (2002), at 218.

[82] Judgment of 22 September 1998 in *Case C-185/97*, *Coote v. Granada Hospitality Ltd*, [1998] ECR I-5199, para. 28; Proposal for a Directive of the European Parliament and of the Council amending Council Directive 76/207/EEC on the implementation of the principle of equal treatment for men and women as regards access to employment, vocational training and promotion, and working conditions, COM(2000) 334 final – COD 2000/0142, 7 June 2006, para. 45.

[83] See also Higgins (2003), at 398-399.

that occurs after the relationship has ended, such as in the above-cited *Coote* case.[84] Accordingly, the protection must be ensured for the applicants "even after the relationship *giving rise to* an alleged breach of the principle of equal treatment has ended."[85]

Although the provision talks about all types of relationships falling under the material scope of the Directive, situations in which the end of relationship is relevant are most usually related to employment by virtue of the nature of discrimination.

4.4. Further Requirements of Article 7(1) RED

A proposal to ensure additional guarantees to the right to access to justice have been formulated but it has remained at this level.[86] The European Parliament proposed a regulation on the legal costs of proceedings.[87] Pursuant to the explanation the purpose of this provision would have been to facilitate "access to legal redress against instances of discrimination."[88] A similar, but more detailed proposal can also be found in the ECRI model legislation. This recommendation proposed that

> [t]he law should guarantee free legal aid and, where necessary, a court-appointed lawyer, for victims who wish to go before the courts as applicants or plaintiffs and who do not have the necessary means to do so. If necessary, an interpreter should be provided free of charge.[89]

All these proposals aimed to make procedures more accessible to the alleged victim of discrimination, either in the form of contributing to the costs of the procedure or by providing legal aid.[90]

---

84 On victimisation see Ch. 6.

85 Recital (32) Recast Directive (emphasis added).

86 See also Bell (2004b), at 226-227.

87 "Member States shall provide support in respect of legal costs in accordance with the most favourable provisions of national law." The proposal of the Starting Line also involved a provision concerning the legal costs. Chopin & Niessen (2001), at 43.

88 Report on the proposal for a Council Directive on implementing the principle of equal treatment between persons irrespective of racial or ethnic origin, COM(1999) 566 – C5-0067/2000 – 1999/0253(CNS), A5-0136/2000 final, 16 May 2000, at 60. See also the proposal of the Starting Line Group.

89 ECRI General Policy Recommendation No 7: National Legislation to Combat Racism and Racial Discrimination, CRI(2003) 8, 13 December 2002, Art. 26.

90 The Report from the Commission on the application of the RED states that "[i]t is clear from the information provided by the NGOs and governments that many victims of discrimination do not proceed to court with their complaints because of the cost." Similarly, the EP resolution on the application of the RED partly attributes the low number of court proceedings to the cost-aspect. Report from the Commission to the Council and the European Parliament – The application of Directive 2000/43/EC of 29 June 2000 implementing the principle of equal treatment between persons irrespective of racial or ethnic origin, COM(2006) 643 final/2,

Although the proposal of the EP has not been adopted, it would be desirable both from the perspective of victims of discrimination and the effective enforcement of the principle of equal treatment that states try to make access to justice substantively equal to everyone. For achieving this contribution to the legal costs would be an effective means.

PART B. CASE STUDIES

4.5. Introduction

As far as the available procedures for discrimination cases are concerned, the most important effect of the RED can be explored in the fact that general anti-discrimination Acts have been passed in Belgium, Estonia and Hungary extending the applicability of general civil law procedures to include discrimination complaints. In the Netherlands the effect of the RED in terms of access to justice is not perceptible because, since the adoption of the GETA, the same procedures have been available for enforcing discrimination complaints.

In Belgium it was first the ADA in 2003 that made the civil law enforcement of a racial discrimination complaint generally available.[91] In 2007 the ADA was repealed and separate anti-discrimination Acts were adopted and/or amended. Until its amendment in 2007 the ARA was only enforceable in criminal law procedures. Since this time most of the complaints on the basis of this Act are decided in civil law procedures.

Similarly, in Estonia it was the EETA that laid down that discrimination complaints are to be enforced in civil law procedures and before labour dispute resolution commissions.[92]

Although the Hungarian Civil Code included a provision on the prohibition of discrimination and thus made claims of discrimination enforceable in civil law procedures, this prohibition did not include detailed rules on the concepts of discrimination and did not contain special enforcement related provision. It was the adoption of the HETA that changed this situation, and effectively extended the applicability of civil law procedures to equal treatment cases.

30 October 2006, para. 3.1; European Parliament resolution of 27 September 2007 on the application of Council Directive 2000/43/EC of 29 June 2000 implementing the principle of equal treatment between persons irrespective of racial or ethnic origin, 2007/2094(INI), AA.

[91] Before the adoption of the ADA the general prohibition of discrimination in the Constitution could be invoked. This provision, however, does not define the different concepts of discrimination, objective justification, and most importantly it does not contain any enforcement related provisions.

[92] Similarly to Belgium, it was generally the prohibition of discrimination in the Constitution that could be invoked before the adoption of the EETA.

In addition to making civil law procedures generally available some special procedures have also been introduced for the enforcement of the principle of equal treatment in the new anti-discrimination codes of the countries under review. The establishment of these procedures can also be attributed to the effect of the RED (and FD) either stemming from Article 7(1) RED or based on this article in combination with Article 13 RED on specialised bodies. In Belgium, the ADA introduced a fast-track civil law procedure, summary-like procedure, in discrimination cases which has been subsequently incorporated in the ARA. In Estonia, first the mandate of the Legal Chancellor was extended by giving him the competence to proceed in conciliation procedures between private parties in addition to his general competence to act as ombudsman. With the adoption of the Gender Equality Act and the EETA a new institution has also been created, the Gender Equality and Equal Treatment Commissioner whose decisions are non-binding. In Hungary, an Authority has been established, which proceeds on the basis of administrative law and the decisions of which are of binding nature. Finally, in the Netherlands it is the Commission's procedure that can be regarded as an alternative to civil law proceedings. However, the effect of the RED is hardly visible in this respect, as the Commission was established six years before the adoption of the RED. This part of this chapter examines the available procedures for enforcing a discrimination claim in the countries under review. In harmony with the theoretical framework, the emphasis is put on determining to what extent judicial procedures are available and are complemented with either administrative or conciliation or other procedures that can make the applicant's access to justice more effective. It will also be explored how the studied Member States comply with the RED and EC law with respect to the timing of the procedures, and whether some additional rules or practices can be found aiming to achieve substantively equal access to justice.

4.6. Types of Procedures

4.6.1. Judicial Procedures

As hinted at above and in accordance with EC law, judicial procedures for the enforcement of the principle of equal treatment are available in each country under review either in the form of civil or criminal procedure. Taking into account the fact that only some aspects of anti-discrimination law are penalised, and that this is not the most often-used way of enforcement, the attention will rather be devoted to civil law procedures.[93]

[93] As this chapter has a different perspective, no distinction is made between legislative and non-legislative provisions that are allegedly discriminatory. For this reason it does not address separately and extensively how to file claims against discriminatory provisions of

In Belgium civil law procedures have generally been available since 2003. Pursuant to Article 16 ARA, applicants can ask for compensation in accordance with the rules of contract or tort law. However, due to the fact that these procedures can generally be regarded as neither cost- nor time-effective, the legislator decided to introduce fast-track civil law procedures.[94] The invention of this procedure is regarded as the most important aspect of the enforcement of anti-discrimination law[95] and most of the complaints are decided in these procedures. This procedure is similar to the summary-like procedure (also called a procedure to cease and desist) introduced by the ADA, the only difference being that the ARA also allows for forfaitair compensation in these proceedings. A summary-like procedure is not entirely the same as a general summary procedure on the basis of the Civil Procedure Code. While certain differences being mainly technical of nature are explicitly acknowledged in the ARA,[96] other differences derive from the special characteristics of anti-discrimination law and its enforcement. Contrary to summary procedures, in a procedure to cease and desist the urgency of the complaint is legally presupposed. In other words, the admissibility of discrimination complaints in summary-like procedures cannot be challenged by lack-of-urgency arguments.[97] In summary-like procedures the complainants can ask the fact-finding judicial organ to "rule on the existence of an act that falls even under

legislative acts. For the control whether legislative acts are in harmony with the principle of equal treatment, somewhat different rules are applicable. Belgium and the Netherlands can be compared in this respect as there is a general prohibition on the control of legislative acts against the constitution by courts. In Belgium, Art. 11(1) ARA excludes any control on the basis of this Act on legislative acts in terms of discrimination. In other words, legislative acts cannot be tested against the ARA by any courts. However, it does not mean – because of the direct effect of directives at least in vertical relations – that courts could not control the conformity of legislative acts with the RED. Relevantly, it was accepted as early as 1971 that, in this context, each judge has to deny the application of an Act that is contrary to international treaties with direct effect (see inter alia Alen (1995), at 271.). Accordingly, and notwithstanding Art. 11 ARA, applicants can initiate proceedings stating that a legislative Act is discriminatory on the grounds of racial or ethnic origin, and courts have to control whether they are in harmony with the RED. Likewise, in the Netherlands judges cannot refrain from testing a legislative act against the RED (see Arts. 94 and 120 of the Constitution. This is naturally not applicable to the ETC which has already denied testing legislative acts due to lack of competence. See for instance Opinion 2008-122 ETC). In Estonia this control is exercised by the Constitutional Chamber of the Supreme Court; that is not by civil court judges. Somewhat similarly, in Hungary when the challenged measure is a legislative act, it is for the Constitutional Court to decide on the constitutionality of the given act or provisions thereof. Art. 70/A of the Constitution stipulates the principle of equal treatment, which constitutes the basis in reviewing the complaint at stake.

94 Art. 18 ARA.

95 Taelman (2004a), at 208.

96 Art. 18 ARA.

97 See inter alia *CGKR and C. Murat v. D. Yves and E-L. BVBA*, Gent Labour Court, summary proceedings, nr. 176.893, 26 March 2007; *CGKR v. Feryn*, Brussels Court of Labour, 24 January 2007.

penal law, whereby the provisions of this act are violated" and to "order the cessation thereof."[98] It has been argued in relation to the ARA that, even if the criteria for ordering the cessation of a deed do not prevail,[99] the applicant has an interest in forfaitair compensation.[100] The interest in a decision to cease is linked to the danger of recurrence of the discriminatory act, since this verdict aims to forbid the unlawful practice and not one particular act. In other words, the lack of interest in such a decision can only be established when the recurrence of the discriminatory act can be objectively ruled out.[101] In racial discrimination cases it is hard to imagine that a particular act could not be repeated and could not occur again. Thus, the recurrence of discrimination cannot be easily foreclosed, an observation that is also supported in practice. For instance, in one of the cases it has been accepted that the fact that the apartment was rented to a third person cannot dispel the applicant's interest, since it cannot be excluded that in the future the apartment would again be available for rent.[102] In another case, neither the fact that the applicant found a job nor the declaration on the website regarding observing the principle of equal treatment could preclude the recurrence of the alleged discrimination.[103] Accordingly, it seems that the different criteria established for submitting complaints in summary-like procedures are not difficult to comply with, therefore making these procedures easily accessible for victims of racial discrimination.

In Estonia procedures can be started on the basis of Article 23 EETA, which stipulates that a complaint of discrimination will be decided either

---

[98] Art. 18(1) ARA. See also Art. 19(1) ADA.

[99] Admittedly, uncertainties could be discovered in the jurisprudence regarding whether the fact that due to the particular circumstances of the case the cessation of the deed could not be enacted is concerned with the admissibility of a case or is related to the substantive aspect of the complaint. For instance in one of the cases the question whether the applicant has an 'interest' in litigation was linked to the feasibility of requiring the cessation of a deed, while in another case the possibility of cessation merely constituted an additional component of the claim and was linked to the substance of the case. Gent Labour Court, no. 03/4440/A, 31 December 2003, para. 1.2; *CGKR and C. Murat v. D. Yves and E-L. BVBA*, nr. 176.893, Gent Labour Court, 26 March 2007, para. 3.

[100] Compare the position of Thiery with the arguments of Closset-Marchal and Van Droogenbroeck in this respect. Thiery (2007), at 768; Closset-Marchal & Van Droogenbroeck (2008), at 374. Compare with the regulation of the ADA in relation to which see inter alia Taelman (2004b), at 508; Swennen, Demuynck & Straetmans (2002), at 1244.

[101] See also Gent Labour Court, no. 03/4440/A, 31 December 2003. Compare with *CGKR and C. Murat v. D. Yves and E-L. BVBA*, nr. 176.893, Gent Labour Court, summary proceedings, 26 March 2007.

[102] Gent Labour Court, no. 03/4440/A, 31 December 2003, para. 1.2.

[103] *CGKR and C. Murat v. D. Yves and E-L. BVBA*, nr. 176.893, Gent Labour Court, summary proceedings, 26 March 2007.

in a civil law procedure[104] or by a labour dispute resolution commission.[105] These commissions are independent and established alongside the Labour Inspectorate.[106] Their decision is binding, and the complaint is regarded as *res judicata*.[107] When a complaint is submitted against a public organ the case is decided by administrative courts. On the basis of the old Employment Contract Act which was meant to partly implement the RED, no racial discrimination complaint has been submitted either to the labour courts or the resolution commissions. No complaint of racial discrimination has been decided yet by administrative courts either. The lack of decisions might indicate that victims of discrimination might be reluctant to rely on general civil law procedures.

In Hungary the general principle of equal treatment is generally enforceable in general civil law procedures on the basis of Articles 75 and 76 of the Civil Code, which stipulate that inherent rights, amongst which the right to equal treatment, are protected by the Civil Code.[108] This general provision on the right to equal treatment is now given substance by the rules of the HETA. In addition to civil courts, applicants can also turn to labour courts with their complaint of discrimination in employment. In this case, Article 5(1) of the Labour Code is invoked, which stipulates that the principle of equal treatment shall be observed in employment related matters. Again, this rule refers back to the HETA. A couple of cases have been decided in judicial procedures since its adoption, mainly with the involvement of interest organisations. It is yet to be seen to what extent these procedures can be regarded effective without the engagement of these organisations.

In the Netherlands the right to equal treatment similarly to the Belgian approach can be enforced through either contract or tort law. Concerning public employment and public services[109] administrative judicial procedural rules have to be followed, which are also located within judicial, and not administrative review. These procedures, like summary procedures presented hereafter, are often relied on. This indicates that these proceedings can be regarded as effective judicial procedures. In addition to the general civil law procedures, summary procedures are also available for applicants complaining

[104] Poleshchuk (2007), at 47. & 53-54.

[105] Art. 4(1) of the Act on Resolution of Individual Labour Conflicts. On these commissions before the adoption of the EETA see Tavits (2004), at 556-557; Poleshchuk (2007), at 52.

[106] Arts. 10 and 11 Act on Resolution of Individual Labour Conflicts.

[107] Art. 4(3) Act on Resolution of Individual Labour Conflicts.

[108] See also Kádár (2007), at 60-65; Beszámoló a Nemzeti és Etnikai Kisebbségi Jogok Országgyűlési Biztosának tevékenységéről Beszámoló a Nemzeti és Etnikai Kisebbségi Jogok Országgyűlési Biztosának tevékenységéről, Nemzeti és Etnikai Kisebbségi Jogok Országgyűlési Biztosa 2006, at 306-310; Indokolás az egyenlő bánásmódról és esélyegyenlőség előmozdításáról szóló törvényjavaslathoz, at 6-7; Gyulavári (2007), 33. & 59-60.

[109] With the exclusion of unilateral acts or decisions of the administration or legislator. See Holtmaat (2007), at 60.

of discrimination when the urgency of a decision is proven.[110] Contrary to the Belgian summary-like procedures, these procedures are generally available for certain civil claims. In other words, they are not specially devised for discrimination cases. "Summary procedures are frequently used by applicants[111] who want to stop discriminatory behaviour, fight dismissal [...] and are effective in this respect."[112] Although in the Netherlands there exists no presumption for the urgency of a discrimination complaint, in practice it seems to be easily accepted when a case should be considered 'urgent'. The urgency of the decision was accepted for instance in a case related to taking maternity leave due to the financial questions concerned,[113] or in a case pertaining to being able to attend the school of choice because of the child's age and interests.[114]

4.6.2. Administrative Procedures

Although administrative procedures for the enforcement of the principle of equal treatment can be found in each country, the equal treatment acts of the countries under review are generally not invoked in these procedures and/ or applicants do not often make use of administrative procedures.[115] In this respect Hungary is a clear exception as a special administrative procedure has been established for the enforcement of the HETA.

---

110 Art. 8:81 General Administrative Act and Article 254. Civil Procedure Act. See also De Fey, Kellermann & Nieuwbroer (2004), at 118-119.

111 See for instance Utrecht District Court, LJN: AU6168, 15 November 2005; Amsterdam District Court, LJN: AZ8045, 31 January 2007; Amsterdam District Court, LJN: BA6917, 24 May 2007; The Hague District Court, LJN: AY5005, 26 July 2006; Utrecht District Court, LJN: AP0146, 27 May 2004.

112 Zwamborn (2002), at 23.

113 Utrecht District Court, LJN: AU6168, 15 November 2005.

114 Amsterdam District Court, LJN: AZ8045, 31 January 2007.

115 In this respect some data are available with regard to Estonia. After a request for information in 2007 from the Legal Centre of Human Rights, the Labour Inspectorate gave a short statistics on the discrimination cases that occurred in 2006. 7 complaints of discrimination were received by the Inspectorate during that year, from which one was repetitive and one was withdrawn. From the remaining 5 cases, discrimination was found to have occurred in 3 cases. Interview with Vadim Poleshchuk on 16 April 2007.

In the Netherlands administrative bodies generally decide discrimination complaints on the basis of the general principle of equality in terms of good administration, and no special administrative body has been appointed for investigating discrimination cases, with the exception of the ETC which is an 'independent administrative organ'. It has been argued that the reason why administrative bodies do not rely on the equal treatment legislation is that the concept of discrimination is quite compound, and the norm in this respect is very abstract, thus no concrete line of conduct can be prescribed for administrative organs. See inter alia Arbeidsmarktbeleid etnische minderheden 2000-2003, Brief van de Staatssecretaris van Sociale Zaken en Werkgelegenheid, 27 223, Nr. 73, 14 October 2005, at 4-5.

In fact, in Hungary the most important channel to enforce one's right to equal treatment is the administrative procedure before the AET.[116] From the perspective of victims the most advantageous procedure is that of the Authority since as an administrative body, it issues binding decisions, it has to decide in a certain period of time, and its proceedings are free of charge. However, when victims of discrimination want to receive compensation for the violation that occurred to them, they should go to civil courts, since the Authority cannot adjudicate on this question.[117] Also, appeal against the decisions has to be submitted with courts, thus there is no administrative appeal procedure.

4.6.3. Conciliation

In order to implement the RED in Estonia legislators have extended the competence of the Legal Chancellor to conciliate between private persons in disputes of discrimination. In the other countries, conciliation procedures are also available in discrimination cases, but their establishment cannot be regarded as a consequence of the obligation to implement the RED.

In 2004 the Estonian Legal Chancellor, as one of the two national specialised bodies for the promotion of equal treatment, was given the task of mediating in discrimination cases, when a person finds that he has been discriminated against by a natural person or a person falling under private law.[118] At that time a complaint of discrimination could only be submitted on the basis of the Constitution or the ECA. Notwithstanding the fact that it can be regarded as a low-threshold body, since 2004 only a couple of complaints have been submitted with the Chancellor. However, none of these cases were effectively conciliated mainly due to the refusal of the respondent to

[116] Besides this there are other administrative bodies too which can proceed in case of an alleged violation of the prohibition of discrimination. In principle, these bodies proceed on the basis of the Administrative Procedure Act and have to apply the HETA. In most of the field of law falling under the material scope of the HETA special legislations have been adopted which in many cases have created separate administrative organs specialised in the given field. These acts establish a link with the HETA by requiring the observation of the principle of equal treatment the *lex specialis* for which is the HETA. Thus, in case of a breach of this principle these specialised administrative bodies have to rely on the Equal Treatment Act to the extent that it provides for special rules both at substantial and procedural level. In terms of enforcement, it means that, for instance, the burden of proof provision of the HETA provides for special rules vis-à-vis the Administrative Procedure Act. Such specialised administrative bodies are created in relation to labour supervision (labour inspectorates), consumer protection (consumer inspectorates), education, and health and social care. See inter alia Kádár (2007), at 59.

[117] The HETA exludes starting parallel procedures by creating the obligation to inform the Authority as soon as a procedure on the basis of the HETA is initiated. Arts. 15(2)-(4) and 15/A(1)-(3) HETA. See also Kádár (2007), at 61.

[118] Art. 142(2) ECA also stipulates that the Legal Chancellor can be approached in discrimination cases concerning employment.

take part in the procedure as these procedures are optional for the parties.[119] For instance, in 2007 five conciliation procedures were initiated before the Chancellor, of which in three cases the respondent refused to co-operate.[120] Thus, this procedure can hardly be regarded as effective in itself or as an effective complement to judicial enforcement.

In Belgium the CEOOR also conducts conciliation in discrimination disputes.[121] Although no data are available on the number of cases and the effectiveness of the conciliation in this respect, at least the procedures are not impeded by the refusal of the respondent.

In Hungary[122] the AET as an administrative organ is authorised to resolve disputes through mediation if the nature of the disagreement allows for such a procedure. The final agreement is included in a decision.[123] However, when no agreement can be reached, the Authority continues its proceedings.[124] Furthermore, this procedure does not deprive the parties of their right to access to justice.[125] Although no concrete statistics are available on the number and long-term effectiveness of the cases mediated by the Authority, it seems to be difficult to accept the AET as an independent and impartial third party due to its being an administrative organ with the competence to impose sanctions.[126] In other words, respondents might take part in the mediation only in order to avoid sanctions, but not for the reason to solve the problem at its roots. This would clearly not ensure the long-term effectiveness of the achieved agreement. Notwithstanding the fact that it is very advantageous that the

119 Õiguskantsleri 2006. aasta tegevuse ülevaade, Tallinn 2007, at 393; Õiguskantsleri 2005. aasta tegevuse ülevaade, Tallinn 2006, at 361; Õiguskantsleri 2004. aasta tegevuse ülevaade, Tallinn 2005, at 205. In 2004 one conciliation procedure was initiated, but the respondent refused to participate in the procedure. In 2005 three applications were received for conciliation of which in one case the respondent was not willing to participate, and the two other cases were refused on other grounds. Finally, in 2006 the Legal Chancellor was approached for conciliation in two cases, which were refused for other reasons than the lack of co-operation. In total, thus, the Chancellor received 11 requests for conciliation, of which five cases could not be launched because of the respondent's refusal to participate. The other reasons were related to issues such as time-limits, anonymous application and so on.

120 The two remaining cases were referred to the Gender Equality Commissioner. Õiguskantsleri 2007. aasta tegevuse ülevaade, Tallinn 2008, at 315-317.

121 Art. 3 Act of 15 February 1993 on the establishment of the Centre. See also Jaarverslag 2006, CGKR 2007, at 8.

122 See also Farkas (2004b).

123 Arts. 64(2) and 76 Administrative Procedure Act. See for instance EBH/54/2008, EBH/17/40/2006.

124 The Act LV of 2002 on Mediation regulates the settling of civil law disputes including personal rights of persons. Admittedly, other administrative bodies having the competence to decide in discrimination cases, such as the labour inspectorate, consumer inspectorate, etc., can also mediate in the disputes brought before them; still it is the AET that deals with discrimination complaints.

125 Art. 36 Mediation Act.

126 See also Kádár (2007), at 61.

Authority tries to mediate between the parties before starting the investigation procedure, a clear separation of powers would, however, be necessary within the Office of the Authority in order to be accepted as a neutral third party.[127]

Finally, in the Netherlands the ETC has recently started mediation with the help of external mediators and has also initiated other alternative forms of dispute resolutions.[128] The ETC applied mediation as an experiment between 2005 and 2006,[129] and since 2007 it structurally added mediation to its scope of activities. Similarly to mediation, in the framework of alternative forms of dispute resolutions the ETC tries to reach an agreement between the parties, however, this does not result in a 'decision', rather it ends up with a withdrawal of the complaint.[130] It is the ETC itself which determines whether the case is suitable for alternative dispute resolution.[131] The Commission has to give careful consideration to its decision whether to hand over the case for mediation or not, because mediated cases will not furnish precedent, thus the standard setting purpose of the ETC will not be accomplished.[132] In this context it has been suggested that cases should not be transmitted to mediation when they concern essential or yet unresolved issues, or when they are of high social importance.[133] The statistics clearly show the success of these alternative forms of resolving disputes.[134] The success of ADRs with the participation of the ETC might also be explained by the fact that, contrary to the Hungarian Authority, the Commission is not an administrative sanctioning body, so that it can easily be regarded as a neutral third party.

---

127 In this respect see Ch. 8 on specialised equality bodies.

128 See Het verschil gemaakt. Evaluatie AWGB en werkzaamheden CGB 1999-2004, CGB 2005, at 92; Jaarverslag 2007, CGB 2008, at 9. & 32-35; Pel (2003), at 109. & 118.

129 Het verschil gemaakt, *supra* note 128, at 92; Jaarverslag 2006, CGB 2007, at 8.

130 For a statistical overview see Jaarverslag 2007, CGB 2008, at 32-35.

131 See inter alia Mediation via de CGB. Retrieved from http://www.cgb.nl/brochure/mediation.

132 Pel (2003), at 109.

133 Pel (2003), at 115 & 118.

134 Jaarverslag 2007, CGB 2008, at 32; Pel (2003), at 118-119; Jaarverslag 2006, CGB 2007, at 8.

4.6.4. Other Procedures

In addition to judicial and administrative procedures in Estonia and the Netherlands special, quasi-judicial procedures[135] are also available for settling discrimination disputes in the form of the procedures of the national specialised bodies.[136]

In addition to the ombudsman procedures in Estonia and the Netherlands victims can also turn to the national specialised bodies for non-binding opinions whether discrimination has taken place.

In Estonia on 1 January 2009 the institution of the Gender Equality and Equal Treatment Commissioner was established.[137] The Commissioner is an independent expert whose procedure is free of charge, and she gives her opinion within two months. The Commissioner has the possibility to create an authority similar to that of the ombudsmen[138] that would make perpetrators follow its opinions. It is yet to be seen to what extent these procedures can be regarded as an effective complement to judicial procedures.

The national specialised body in the Netherlands, the ETC, is considered to be a semi-judicial body rendering non-binding opinions following which

---

135 Importantly, general quasi-judicial procedures (such as ombudsman-procedures) can be found in each country, but these procedures are not specifically established for discrimination cases.

In Belgium the institution of Federal Ombudsman has been established, but victims of discrimination generally use the other channels (http://federaalombudsman.be). The same can be stated with respect to the institution of ombudsman in the Netherlands (http://www.ombudsman.nl).

In Estonia, the power of ombudsman has been given to the Legal Chancellor. Pursuant to Art. 19(1) of the Legal Chancellor Act, everyone can turn to the Chancellor with a claim to control whether a concrete public organ observes the principle of ensuring fundamental rights and freedoms and the rule of sound administration. At the end of the procedure the Chancellor gives his opinion, and makes proposals which are not of legally binding nature (Art. 351 of the Legal Chancellor Act). Nevertheless, the Act itself foresees a mechanism to ensure the compliance with the observations of the Chancellor (Art. 352 of the Legal Chancellor Act). In 2007 the Chancellor had to deal with 54 complaints of discrimination allegedly committed by public bodies (Õiguskantsleri 2007. aasta tegevuse ülevaade, Tallinn 2008, at 317). This number is quite remarkable and surprising in the view of both the unsuccessful conciliation procedures before the Chancellor and the lack of discrimination complaints before courts.

In Hungary the ombuds-procedures are generally known, and for this reason can be regarded as important channels examining discrimination complaints. Although none of the ombudsmen adopt binding decisions, at the end of their investigation they can formulate recommendation to the public body concerned. Since they are generally respected and they can use naming and faming as 'sanction', their recommendations are generally taken seriously. Victims of racial discrimination generally turn to the Parliamentary Commissioner for the Rights of National and Ethnic Minorities (http://www.kisebbsegiombudsman.hu. See also Krizsán (2001)).

136 On the competences and mandates of these bodies see Ch. 8 on national specialised bodies.

137 Arts. 15-22 EETA.

138 See also Õiguskantsleri 2006. aasta tegevuse ülevaade, Tallinn 2007, at 393.

an applicant can still file a claim in a judicial procedure. The ETC has to deliver its opinion within a short period of time, making the procedure much less time-consuming than judicial proceedings. The ETC is an independent and impartial body with aggregated expertise in the field of equal treatment law. In most of the cases applicants turn to the ETC because it is generally seen as a low threshold body.[139] Even though the opinions of the ETC are non-binding on the parties, around 75 % of its opinions are complied with,[140] which might be attributed to its expertise and authority. Accordingly, this procedure can undoubtedly be regarded as an effective fast-track and low threshold complement to judicial procedures.

4.7. Timing of Procedures

4.7.1. Time Limits

As far as time limits are concerned, the countries under review have generally observed the principle of equivalence. In other words, in most of the cases no special time limits are enshrined for discrimination cases, so that the general rules are applicable.

To some extent, the Netherlands constitutes an exception in this regard. Although generally, similarly to the other countries, the principle of equivalence is respected, there are a couple of special rules for discrimination complaints related to the timing of the procedures. First of all, separate time limits are enshrined for the discriminatory or retaliatory termination of an employment relationship. In such cases, the applicant who wishes to contest the lawfulness of the termination must do so within two months after the termination of the employment contract.[141] Arguably, these time limits might be justified by the particularity of the complaint. More specifically, the complaint concerns the termination of an employment relationship in which case it does not seem to be reasonable to allow long term uncertainty, and this is also not practical in terms of available evidence. Moreover, in the case of the termination of a contract employees might also want to act as soon as possible to clarify the situation. Accordingly, this time limit does not seem to be unreasonable.

Secondly, in the procedures before the ETC it is up to the Commission to decide whether the complaint has been launched within a *reasonable time*.[142]

---

139 See also Holtmaat (2007), at 6.6+ & 60; Goldschmidt (2005), at 286.

140 Jaarverslag 2007, CGB 2008, at 7; Mediation via de CGB, *supra* note 131.

141 Art. 8(2) GETA. The two months is the general principle, and he can challenge the lawfulness of the termination even by informing the employer over his disagreement. And pursuant to Art. 8(3) GETA, the employee has 6 months after the day on which the employment contract was terminated to take his case to the court.

142 Art. 14(1) c) GETA. See also Asscher-Vonk & Hendriks (2005), at 170.

As yet the Commission has never declared a complaint inadmissible on the grounds of not having been submitted within a reasonable time. On the contrary, the ETC even accepted claims in relation to which the respondents argued that they had already elapsed on the basis of the Civil Code. In these cases, the Commission argued that establishing that the claim had elapsed is the task of the judge, and not of the Commission; accordingly, the ETC would have to give a decision on the substance. Nevertheless, the fact that the applicant had not taken any action was considered in the elaboration on the substance.[143] Thus, it seems that the time between the occurrence of discrimination and the filing of a complaint does not determine the interest of the applicant in the decision, but it does influence the decision on the substance. The average period of time in which the ETC came to its opinion was nine months both in 2002 and 2003, which seems reasonable. In some special cases the decision is made in speed procedures, in which cases the Commission has to come to a conclusion in eight weeks.[144]

Moreover, the procedure of the ETC does not suspend the time of elapse, which might be related to the non-bindingness of the Commission's opinions. This aspect might be problematic, especially taking into account the average period of time in which the ETC adopts its opinion and the fact that in most cases applicants first turn to the ETC with their complaint. Admittedly, the applicants generally still have enough time to submit their claims in a judicial procedure even after the Commission's procedure. Nevertheless, the Commission should pay particular attention to the time-limits in specific cases in order not to deprive applicants from their right to judicial review. Should there be a possible problem concerning the time of elapse the ETC should inform the applicant of this.

In Belgium, the principle of equivalence is also observed. However, a special aspect of discrimination procedures related to time limits has been explicitly regulated. When a summary-like procedure is started after filing a criminal complaint on the same issue, the criminal court will rule on the claim only after a definitive decision has been handed down in the summary-like procedure. During the suspension period, the lapse of the criminal proceedings is likewise suspended.[145] This latter provision is a significant one, since it guarantees that in the case of a somewhat longer summary-like procedure the criminal complaint will not elapse.

The Estonian EETA does not provide for any special time limits for discrimination cases, accordingly the general rules both in labour and civil law are to be followed. In this respect it deviates from the Gender Equality Act which stipulates that the applicants can file a claim for compensation within one year of when they became aware or should have become aware of

143 Opinion 2008-31 ETC, paras. 3.3. & 3.17; Opinion 2003-3 ETC, paras. 5.2. & 5.12.

144 See also Zoontjens (2006), at 163.

145 Art. 18(4) ARA (Art. 22 ADA).

the alleged discrimination. This limitation was also stipulated in the original proposal of the EETA, but for some reason was withdrawn in a later draft.[146] Importantly, this provision might have been in contradiction with the principle of equivalence, since according to the general rule the time of elapse for compensation is three years.

The general rules are also applicable in the ombudsman procedures of the Legal Chancellor. Importantly, however, separate time limits are enshrined for submitting a request for conciliation in a discrimination dispute. This time limit is four months.[147] This period cannot, arguably, be regarded as unreasonable taking into account the fact that the claim is concerned with reinstating a certain relation, which after a certain period of time seems to be difficult to conciliate. As yet, only one request for conciliation has had to be refused due to the lapse of time in the practice of the Legal Chancellor. The alleged discrimination had taken place eleven months before the applicant turned to the Legal Chancellor.[148] Importantly, in such cases the applicants still have other options, since in the case of a conciliation procedure it is not required that the applicant has already made use of all other legal options to enforce his right to equal treatment. Accordingly, this time limit cannot be considered to limit or reduce the effectiveness of enforcement.

Similarly to Belgium, the general time limits are applicable for discrimination cases in Hungary too. Concerning the relationship between judicial and quasi-judicial procedures, it is important and favourable to the victim that conciliation procedures before the AET suspend the lapse of time.[149]

4.7.2. Even after the Relationship Has Ended

Submitting a complaint of discrimination arising after the relationship to which it can be linked has ended is neither explicitly allowed nor prohibited in the countries under review.[150] The lack of prohibition indicates that national legislations are in accordance with the RED in this respect.

In this regard it is only the Netherlands that constitutes an exception to some extent, since a time limit is imposed for the initiation of such complaints. Pursuant to Articles 8(2) and (3) GETA, complaints of discrimination can be filed within two or six months (depending on the nature of the claim) following the termination of the employment relationship.[151] Nevertheless, within the

146 This position was confirmed in an interview with one of the experts in Estonia.
147 Art. 356 Legal Chancellor Act.
148 Õiguskantsleri 2006. aasta tegevuse ülevaade, Tallinn 2007, at 393.
149 Arts. 32 and 64 Administrative Procedure Act.
150 The application of this requirement with respect to victimisation will be examined in Ch. 6 on victimisation.
151 See for instance Opinion 2004-12 ETC.

enshrined time limit, which, as argued supra, can be regarded as reasonable, applicants are free to submit their complaints. In the substantive provisions no further restriction can be found in this respect.

In Belgium, on the basis of the concepts of discrimination and the material scope of the ARA, it can be argued that the lack of explicit authorisation in this regard will not lead to difficulties in practice. More specifically, the concepts of discrimination cover each type of discrimination that can be related to a relationship, and the material scope of the ARA extends to all aspects of employment in which this issue most often occurs.[152] Thus, it seems that it is the alleged discrimination committed by someone that matters and not whether the relationship in which the discrimination had allegedly occurred has ended.

Similarly, in Estonia the applicable time limits indicate that there is no restriction on filing a complaint even after the relationship in which the discrimination occurred has ended. On the basis of the ECA and LCA claims can be filed within a certain period of time after the date on which they became aware or should have become aware of the violation of their rights. Accordingly, the time limit is not linked to the end of the relationship, rather to the date when the discrimination happened. In this respect no restriction can be found in the EETA either. Moreover, the Commissioner proceeds on the basis of administrative procedure law which has a similar approach to the start of the elapse of time of the ECA and LCA. Accordingly, there seems to be no restriction on filing claims even after the relationship giving rise to discrimination has ended.

In theory, nothing hinders applicants in Hungary either to file a complaint to any of the fact-finding bodies concerning such a situation. The material scope of the HETA covers all fields of life, and relevantly all aspects of employment, which indicates that the scope of the Act does not include any limitation. Moreover, the Civil Procedure Code explicitly enumerates lawsuits that are related to employment, but the action is launched after the employment relationship has ended.[153]

4.8. Further Dispositions

In the countries under review, the procedures or the assistance provided by the national specialised bodies are free of charge. This approach clearly enhances the effectiveness of the enforcement of the right to equal treatment by making the enforcement more accessible to victims.

152 Art. 5(1) ARA.

153 Art. 349(2) a) Civil Procedure Code. See also Kádár (2007), at 65.

In Belgium, the only special rule concerning legal aid for victims of discrimination can be found in the Act establishing the CEOOR.[154] Pursuant to Article 3 of this Act victims can be given either advice or the Centre can start a procedure to enforce their right to equality. In this latter case, not only would victims be assisted in their procedure, but their legal costs would also be significantly reduced.

In Estonia, the procedures of both the labour dispute resolution commissions and the Legal Chancellor are exempt from state fees. Similarly, the procedure before the Commissioner is also free of charge. Accordingly, the accessibility of these bodies is facilitated in this respect as well. Moreover, the Legal Chancellor can also suggest in cases falling under his competence that the applicant be given free legal aid and be exempt from state fees in court procedures.[155] Accordingly, in such cases not only quasi-judicial bodies are made more easily accessible, but access to judicial procedures is also facilitated.

In Hungary, victims of discrimination most often bring cases to the Authority, which can be attributed to the fact that in addition to a reasonably quick delivery of its decision, its procedure is generally also exempt from state fee. Costs might only occur in relation to experts, and so on, whose charges have to be advanced by the respondent.[156] Importantly, under the supervision of the Ministry of Justice, a special service department was established in 2001 to provide legal aid to Roma victims of discrimination and to advance their substantive access to justice.[157]

In the Netherlands, the procedure of the ETC is free of charge which is an important factor in being a low threshold and so an easily accessible body.[158] There have been discussions concerning the introduction of a fixed state fee in order to filter out flippant complaints. However, the ETC argued that a fee would hardly prevent such, whilst endangering the low threshold of the body.[159] It can be added to this argument that the complaints of mere 'busybodies' can already be rejected at the admissibility phase.

---

[154] Art. 3 of Act of 15 February 1993 on the establishment of a Centre for Equal Opportunities and Opposition to Racism. See also Jaarverslag 2006, CGKR 2007; Popelier (2003), at 282-283; Vrielink (2003a), at 223-225; De Prins, Sottiaux & Vrielink (2005), at 403-411; Specialised Bodies to Promote Equality and/or Combat Discrimination, Final Report, European Commission 2002, at 12.

[155] Art. 353 LCA.

[156] Art. 15(8) ETA.

[157] http://www.irm.gov.hu/?katid=174&id=199.

[158] Holtmaat (2007), at 60.

[159] Havinga (2007), at 243.

4.9. Conclusions

Easy access to justice is a prerequisite for an effective enforcement of the right to equal treatment, the first pillar of minority protection. 'Easy access to justice' indicates that an effective enforcement mechanism in this respect includes two aspects: the availability of judicial procedures, and of low-threshold procedures. This means that on the one hand, the higher level protection can be guaranteed by judicial review, the more effective the enforcement becomes; and on the other hand, the lower the threshold for submitting a complaint and vindicating the right to equal treatment, the more properly effective enforcement can be ensured.

Indeed, Article 7(1) RED acknowledges the fact that access to justice is essential for the effective enforcement of the right to equal treatment. It is remarkable that this provision is enshrined in this Directive, as it requires the states to reconsider whether the previously available procedures are really effective as far as the enforcement of complaints of discrimination on the grounds of racial or ethnic origin is concerned. In this respect, the Race Directive above all requires the establishment of judicial procedures which can (and under certain circumstances should) be complemented with administrative or other non-judicial procedures, arguably in order to ensure that victims have access to fast-track procedures for the enforcement of their rights. Given the legislative history and the context of the RED, it can be concluded that the requirement of the establishment of judicial procedures essentially refers to civil law procedures. It seems that the drafters of the RED realised that the widespread use of criminal law enforcement in racial discrimination cases cannot always be regarded as effective from the perspective of the victims. Indeed, in criminal procedures in general, the special interests of the victims of discrimination (thus mostly of minorities) cannot be taken into account, a deficiency which can be compensated by the establishment of civil law procedures. Therefore, the existence of civil law procedures would particularly enhance minority protection. Furthermore, the RED also requires the establishment of low-threshold and fast-track procedures in order to facilitate the procedural position of the victim when attempting to vindicate his right to equal treatment.

In this context, the most important amendments to the national legislation of the countries under review can be explored in the adoption of comprehensive equal treatment legislation which can generally be enforced in civil law procedures. Generally speaking, the existing procedures have not been amended, but their material scope has been extended to the enforcement of the right to equal treatment.

Some additional procedures have also been introduced in the studied countries for ensuring more effective access to justice in terms of establishing low-threshold and fast-track procedures. In Belgium, special procedures have been created within the framework of civil law procedures: summary-like procedures have been established which have also become the most important channel for enforcing complaints of discrimination. These procedures clearly take into account the difficulties a victim of discrimination might face when using the general summary procedures: it is not required that the victim prove the urgency of the case, as it is an irrefutable legal presumption that the urgency (and thus the danger of recurrence) is always present in discrimination cases. This arrangement certainly facilitates the victim's position, and thus contributes to effective access to justice.

In Hungary, the legislator has chosen for a special procedure within administrative law in order to ensure easy access to justice. This procedure has several advantages: it is fast, the Authority on Equal Treatment is a low threshold body, its procedure is free of charge, and the AET is also an investigatory body which further facilitates the victim's procedural position. However, as it is an administrative procedure, the emphasis is placed on punishing the perpetrator rather than redressing the victim. Accordingly, this procedure cannot be regarded as a fully effective alternative to civil law procedures.

Contrary to these procedures, in order to ensure an easily accessible procedure for the enforcement of the right to equal treatment in Estonia and the Netherlands the choice has been made to establish national specialised bodies with the competence to issue non-binding opinions. As the Commissioner in Estonia is a very new institution it is not yet possible to evaluate the effectiveness of its procedure. In the Netherlands, however, the procedure of the Equal Treatment Commission has proved to be quite effective, irrespective of the non-binding nature of its decisions and the fact that it cannot award redress to the victim. Actually, most victims of discrimination first turn to the ETC in order to hear its opinions, and these opinions are followed in 80% of the cases. For this reason, the procedure can be regarded as an effective complement to civil law procedures.

The case studies clearly demonstrate how important it is to have civil law procedures for the enforcement of the right to equal treatment. Moreover, it is also obvious that these procedures in themselves do not suffice due to the time and costs they involve. Practice shows that the existence of fast-track and easily accessible proceedings is essential for the effective enforcement of the right to equal treatment.

Chapter 5

Legal Standing

Part A. Theoretical Framework

In addition to access to justice, Article 7 RED also addresses the question who is entitled to have legal standing in a procedure for the enforcement of the protection against discrimination, which is the subject of this chapter.

5.1. Introduction

A decision on who should be given legal standing in a procedure has far-reaching consequences.[1] Some examples might help to illuminate the essence of *locus standi* and the particular relevance to minorities and minority protection. In the first example, a Roma man applies for a job by sending his curriculum vitae and a photograph to the human resources department of an organisation. He is the only one not to be invited for an interview. In the second example, 20 Romani families are evicted and provided with alternative, but substandard, housing.[2] Finally, in the third case many Roma children are placed in special schools on the basis of the results of intelligence examinations carried out by education experts.

In the first case, an individual has been discriminated against and may want to receive compensation for this treatment from the organisation. However, he might not be in a position either financially or capacity-wise to begin and successfully pursue litigation, so he is in need of assistance. In the second

---

1 As Hare observed in relation to public interest litigation, "[d]ecisions to accord or deny standing to certain individuals or groups may determine not only the extent of the judicial caseload, but also the manner in which legal argument is formulated and hence the type of question which is remitted to the judicial branch of government." Hare (2000), at 301.

2 This case took place in Romania. See Dobrushi (2007).

case, a group of people have suffered from the discriminatory treatment, and they all may want to receive compensation, but they all might also need assistance for the enforcement of their rights. Finally, the third case concerns a practice. Although there are individual victims in this case too, the main aim of the envisaged litigation is not so much to endeavour to obtain compensation for the victims, but rather to change the particular practice. (This does not, however, mean that some individual victims might not want to start individual litigations as well.)

These cases clearly illustrate that the question of legal standing requires a sophisticated approach, in racial discrimination cases too. The problems can be summarised as follows: victims of discrimination do in general need assistance in pursuing their claims; when more victims are to be found and all suffer from the same treatment common litigation would be the most practicable and useful; and finally, in order to change a discriminatory practice special procedures would be useful in which no individualized victims are required. Accordingly, it can be argued that the effective enforcement of the equal treatment legislation would require victim-oriented[3] and broad-based[4] legal standing.

There is no general agreement on what Article 7(2) RED, the provision on legal standing, exactly requires. According to some this provision calls for the introduction of class action procedures,[5] while others regret that the Directive does not envisage either collective enforcement or group justice.[6] It is a general criticism against the RED that while the substantive provisions indicate a broadening in terms of the taking into account the group-aspect of discrimination, the enforcement provisions do not reflect this broadening, and the procedural part of the Directive is still based on the individual justice model.[7] The different arguments and the differing and even conflicting conclusions might be attributed to the fact that the term 'legal standing' has different dimensions.

In order to make clear what the Race Directive precisely requires in terms of legal standing and what would be advantageous in terms of minority protection a theoretical model will be elaborated and applied to the RED. First of all, the term 'legal standing' will be defined. This will be followed by a short discussion on the decision concerning legal standing. More concretely, an examination will be made of what this decision substantively includes, and

3 This means that the different forms of legal standing should accommodate the forms of victim status.

4 Compare with the observation of Hare concerning the Indian processual legislation. Hare (2000), at 302.

5 See Bodrogi (2007), at 25.

6 See inter alia Brown (2002), at 219; Barry (2003), at 421.

7 "[I]n the directive a more collective notion of discrimination which the concept of indirect discrimination reflects is in no way matched by the accompanying procedural mechanisms." Townshend-Smith (2000), at 297.

when such decision is taken. Subsequently, the main components of locus standi will be analysed, and different forms of legal standing will be identified and mapped out based on the combination of the components. The theoretical part of this chapter will end with the examination of the different possible forms of legal standing envisaged by the Directive.

The relevant article of the RED sounds as follows:

> Article 7 Defence of Rights
>
> (2) Member States shall ensure that associations, organisations or other legal entities, which have, in accordance with the criteria laid down by their national law, a legitimate interest in ensuring that the provisions of this Directive are complied with, may engage, either on behalf or in support of the complainant, with his or her approval, in any judicial and/or administrative procedure provided for the enforcement of obligations under this Directive.

5.2. Definition of Legal Standing

Locus standi is generally defined as the capacity of the *applicant* to commence legal proceedings,[8] which is briefly referred to as the right to bring an action. However, the concept of locus standi is arguably broader than purely the applicant's capacity to file a claim. On the one hand, the locus standi is also related to the particular forms of victim status and representation. On the other hand, not only applicants but also the respondents have legal standing in the lawsuit.

Although the legal standing of both the applicant and the respondent is similarly important, here less attention will be devoted to the locus standi of the respondent, since it merely raises a couple of matters that are particular from the perspective of effective enforcement of the principle of equal treatment and minority protection.

5.3. Decision on Legal Standing

A decision on locus standi has at least two aspects. On the one hand, it has a substantive aspect; that is the content of the decision on the admissibility of the complaint. On the other hand, it also includes a procedural question; namely when the decision has to be made. These two aspects will be analysed concerning both the applicant and the respondent.

[8] Hare (2000), at 301.

5.3.1. Decision on the Legal Standing of the Applicant

The substantive decision on the locus standi of the applicant concerns the question whether the applicant is the appropriate person to bring such a procedure; in other words whether the applicant has *sufficient interest* in filing a claim. The sufficient interest test is often formulated in terms of the victim status of the applicant. Concerning the refusal of the applicant's claim it has been argued that

> [a] decision on the merits is evidence that the court considers the challenge unarguable [...]; whereas a decision on locus is that the applicant is not the appropriate person to bring the proceedings, whatever the strength of the grounds of review.[9]

Thus, while a decision on locus standi answers the question whether the case of the applicant is admissible, in the decision on the merits it is established whether there has been discrimination in the specific case, and what kind of sanctions and remedies can be adjudicated.

Arguably, the sufficient interest test can be further divided into two aspects.[10] On the one hand, it concerns the question whether the applicant is *affected* by the challenged measure. On the other hand, it also includes the examination of the seriousness of the injury suffered by the victim, which can be translated into the requirement of '*significancy*' of the interest.[11]

In order to facilitate the access to justice of victims of discrimination and achieve the effective enforcement of the principle of equal treatment the applicant should be regarded as being *affected* as soon as any disadvantage suffered by him can be shown. Concerning the examination of being *'affected'* difficulties might occur in cases in which discrimination takes place by association. When someone is discriminated by association the person should be regarded as belonging to the particular group with which he has been associated and as having suffered the same disadvantage. When a complaint is filed by an interest organisation in *actio popularis* claims the requirement of being affected can be translated in terms of the *legitimate interest* of the organisations formulated in their statute.

The second aspect, the *significancy* of the interest, is more difficult to answer, since it seems to require[12] a more substantive judgment already at the admissibility phase. However, it can be argued that a decision on the

---

9 Hare (2000), at 311.

10 Generally, in the legal literature and practice it is merely the victim status (sufficient interest) that is referred to as the test for legal standing.

11 This second aspect is somewhat more explicitly formulated by the US Supreme Court. On the requirements of standing see *Frothingham v. Mellon*, 262 U.S. 447 (SC 1923); *Allen v. Wright*, 468 U.S. 737 (SC 1984); *Lujan v. Defenders of Wildlife*, 504 U.S. 555 (SC 1992).

12 In fact, the case law of the ECtHR clearly shows in this respect that the Court thoroughly examines the facts submitted by the parties in relation to the complaint and also makes a

legal standing should be based on the statements of the applicant only. In other words, at this phase of the adjudication there is no need to establish whether the facts alleged by the applicant are true or the conclusions drawn from them persuasive. Admittedly, at the moment no general test can be found to determine the significance of a complaint. It therefore depends to a great extent on the fact-finder's appreciation of the facts. The only guarantee in this respect would be that fact-finders provide sound reasoning on this aspect which could serve as a guarantee against arbitrary and eventually value-based decisions. Fact-finders might argue that a complaint is not significant enough if the material harm caused is not substantial. On the contrary, they might also argue that the violation of human dignity, which is mostly at stake in discrimination cases, indicates that the complaint cannot be declared insignificant. In order to avoid the arbitrary application of the admissibility phase, it is suggested that a distinction be made at this stage between direct and indirect discrimination. Concerning direct racial discrimination, it can be argued that, irrespective of the material harm, the complaint is always significant, since racial or ethnic origin can hardly be accepted as relevant grounds for distinction, which means that such treatment clearly violates the victim's human dignity.[13] With respect to indirect discrimination, it can be argued that the significance of the complaint is closely related to the disparate impact. In relation to the substantive aspect of the complaint it has been argued that as soon as a statistically relevant difference can be discovered, the presumption of discrimination should be accepted. Since the significance test is only concerned with the admissibility of the complaint the approach to the disparate impact cannot be stricter than that applied to the examination of the presumption of discrimination. Moreover, similarly to direct discrimination, it should not be examined whether the statistics or the allegations in this respect are in fact true, in this phase they should be regarded as true. It also follows from this elaboration that in the case of the legal standing of organisations no further significance-related requirements should be imposed.

As far as the procedural aspect of the decision is concerned, as indicated above, the locus standi is concerned with the admissibility of the complaint. Accordingly, it should obviously be decided at the beginning of the procedure even before the establishment of a presumption of discrimination. As hinted at supra, the presumption is based on the facts which are already proven, while for the admissibility of the complaint these facts are merely accepted as true.

---

judgment that there has been no violation of the provision at hand. See for instance *Hoogendijk v. the Netherlands*, ECHR (2005) No. 58641/00, 6 January 2005.

[13] See in this respect *Timishev v. Russia*, ECHR (2001) Nos. 55762/00 and 55974/00, 13 December 2005. The same argument can be brought up with respect to harassment.

5.3.1.1. Legitimate Interest of Associations, Organisations and Other Legal Entities

The Directive leaves it to the Member States to define the legitimate interest of these organisations that enables them to engage in legal procedures.[14] The requirement of legitimate interest might also eliminate the fear of the misuse of the organisations' engagement in the procedures. Importantly, the restrictions pertaining to the legitimate interest that the Member States can impose on the organisations can for instance include the requirement of specific legal forms for such entities, the length of existence, the field of operation according to its statute, the field in relation to which they can engage, and so on. Taking into consideration the above elaboration the legitimate interest of organisations should not be concerned with criteria on the significancy of the complaint. Rather, Member States should merely focus on establishing requirements for 'being affected' by the discrimination.

It has been argued that allowing Member States to define the legitimate interest of these organisations gives a broad discretion to national legislation in determining which entities can engage in a procedure, since they might lay down such requirements which exclude certain important organisations.[15] Although the Directive explicitly states that Member States have free rein in defining the legitimate interest, the general principle of effective judicial protection does constitute a limitation on the legislation of the Member States in this respect. This principle means that the exercise of the right at stake cannot be made excessively difficult or virtually impossible by setting up certain criteria pertaining to the legitimate interest of organisations. In this context the question is immediately raised as to what the particular right is.[16] Contrary to the arguments of Higgins, according to whom a difference should be made in this context between the right to be representative and the right to non-discrimination,[17] it should rather be looked at whether the *effective enforcement of the right to non-discrimination* would not be made excessively difficult or virtually impossible.[18] It can be argued that in many instances the victims of discrimination, who often belong to racial or ethnic

[14] See also the rules in the United States concerning such interest. In 1977 the Rules Committee of the Supreme Court introduced new rules in relation to the necessary interest for having locus standi. This new rule required 'sufficient interest', "which could sufficiently embrace all classes of those who might apply and yet permit sufficient flexibility in any particular case to determine whether or not sufficient interest was in fact shown." See further Beloff (2000), at 275.

[15] See inter alia Higgins (2003), at 400; Brown (2002), at 219.

[16] Compare with Higgins' elaboration on this aspect of the principle of effectiveness. Higgins (2003), at 400.

[17] Higgins (2003), at 400.

[18] Importantly, stemming from the general principle of no right without remedy, the right to non-discrimination is also made excessively difficult or virtually impossible if its enforcement is not effective.

minorities, are really in need of the engagement of interest organisations, and their right to effective enforcement would be made unreasonably difficult, if overly restrictive criteria are set for the legal standing of such organisations.

5.3.1.2. 'Associations, Organisations or Other Legal Entities'

The RED stipulates that it is 'associations, organisations or other legal entities' that should be enabled to engage on behalf of the victims in judicial and/or administrative procedures. It was the Commission that proposed the introduction of the phrase 'associations, organisations or other legal entities'; and during the negotiations no amendments were put forward concerning any of these terms. Interestingly, however, the ECRI model legislation has a somewhat different approach. The general recommendation uses a collective noun referring to all entities which are entitled to bring cases; and that is 'organisations'. The model legislation also exemplifies the legal form of such organisations: associations, trade unions and other legal entities.

Taking into consideration that no general definition exists as to what an organisation is, and there is no consistent application of this term, as the ECRI general recommendation also shows, it might, arguably, be concluded that it is meant to include all entities with or without legal personality. Also, arguably in order to be sure to include the broadest possible range of relevant activities, the RED still added the classes 'associations' and 'other legal entities'. The aim does not seem to have been to exclude any entities which might provide helpful to the victim. Admittedly, the underlying aim of the Commission might have been to provide civil society organisations (NGOs, and trade unions with legal standing) in whatever form they might exist. As Tyson, who monitored the negotiation procedure of the RED, explained

> [i]n the Commission's view, the precise status of such an organisation before the court is less important than the access to support from a respected organisation, which greatly influences the ability of a complainant to win a case.[19]

In conclusion, the legal position of an organisation should not impede the legal standing of interest organisations.[20]

5.3.2. Decision on the Legal Standing of the Respondent

In terms of the substantive aspect of admissibility, it also has to be decided whether it is the appropriate respondent against whom the procedure is initiated. This 'appropriateness' can be translated into the question whether the

19 Tyson (2001), at 212.
20 See also Waddington & Bell (2001), at 607.

respondent could be held liable for the alleged violation, if he was somehow involved in the alleged breach. Similarly to the decision on the locus standi of the applicant, this also means the application of the test of being affected.

This decision should also precede the adjudication on the merits, otherwise it would be mixed with the justification and might lead to conceptual inconsistencies. These phases of the adjudication concern different questions. While a decision on the merits establishes that the respondent cannot be held liable because there was no discrimination, a decision on standing settles that the respondent cannot be held responsible because he was not the appropriate person against whom the procedure was initiated.

Article 3 of the RED establishes that the provisions of the Directive 'shall apply to all persons'. Although a literal interpretation indicates that principally all persons can be held liable, it is yet to be seen how broad an interpretation this provision will be given.[21] Nevertheless, no limitation is included in relation to the perpetrator in the enforcement provisions. This indicates that anyone who, on the basis of the concepts of discrimination, is somehow involved in the wrong-doing can be taken as the perpetrator. Accordingly, no further limitations other than those inherently included in the concepts of discrimination are imposed pertaining to the respondent.

There is generally no difficulty when the complaint is concerned with a treatment, provision or criterion, conduct or instruction: the person who committed the treatment, adopted the provision or criterion, conducted or instructed can be taken as the perpetrator. However, when either direct[22] or indirect discrimination concerns a practice it is less clear who is responsible for it: the person applying the practice, the person being in a position to decide on changing the practice, and/or the person supervising the practice, and so on. This question is difficult to answer *in abstracto*, but it has to be kept in mind that a certain involvement in the practice is required on the one hand, and the power to be able to change the given practice also seems to be necessary, on the other. Although in terms of effective protection of and effective remedies for victims of discrimination the procedure should principally be launched against the perpetrator, it is often the person vicariously liable for a certain treatment who will act as respondent in the lawsuit. His 'interest' in the procedure pertaining to his legal standing is, arguably, created by his position of being responsible for ensuring a discrimination-free environment.

---

21 In this respect see Busstra (2010).

22 There are cases when direct discrimination can be seen as a practice. See for example *R. (on the application of European Roma Rights Centre) v. Immigration Officer at Prague Airport*, IRLR 115 (HL 2005) or *Floyd-Mayers v. American Cab Co*, 732 F.Supp. 243 (D.D.C. 1990). For more details see Busstra (2010).

5.4. Forms of Victim Status and Representation

As hinted at supra, two main components of the concept of legal standing can be identified: the victim and his representation. It will be shown and analysed in this paragraph, what forms these components can take.

5.4.1. Forms of Victim Status

As the examples above illustrate different forms of *victim status* can be identified. Taking these examples as points of departure, one can, first of all, distinguish *individual victims,* such as the Roma candidate for the job. In the example of eviction, a group of people was similarly affected by the same decision, and it would be advantageous for them if their cases were decided in one procedure. The group can be called *collective victims*; that is, a 'collective' or community of individual victims. Finally, the segregation case aimed to change a discriminatory practice against a group having a certain racial or ethnic background. Accordingly, the group itself was the victim, which can be referred to as *group victim.* In case of a group victim, contrary to collective victims, no individual victim is and/or can be or needs to be identified, since the complaint is directed at the discrimination that has been committed against the group.[23]

5.4.2. Forms of Representation

Concerning the forms of representation the question to be answered is who can represent the applicant.[24] It is generally known that the applicant can be represented not only by an advocate but also by another individual. If one person is the representative, this is referred to as *individual representation*, be it an advocate or a 'mere' individual.

However, in relation to consumer protection, environmental law and competition law, it has been generally acknowledged, that certain groups should also be given locus standi, since otherwise nobody would vindicate the rights at stake.[25] Similar arguments can be put forward pertaining to discrimination. Advocates, not specialised in discrimination law, are generally not so familiar with this field, and do not have the expertise that an NGO might have. Accordingly, in many cases there is an explicit need for the involvement

[23] Naturally, in proving discrimination the violations against the particular individuals can also be regarded as evidence, but these individuals do not act as applicants in the case.

[24] Obviously, the same question can be posed in relation to the respondent, but his situation gives rise to less difficult concerns.

[25] See inter alia Kombos (2006); Afilalo (1999); Hare (2000).

of organisations with expertise in discrimination law. When it is an organisation and not an individual that represents the 'victim' in discrimination cases, it is referred to as *collective representation*.[26]

Admittedly, there is a general reluctance to provide legal standing to organisations, associations or other legal entities, which might be attributed to the problem how to ensure that the organisation in question adequately represent the victims, that the victims have influence on their case and their misfortune is not only used for the interest of the organisation.[27] However, as will be shown below, these fears can be eliminated by incorporating some guarantees.

5.5. Forms of Legal Standing

Several classifications can be found in relation to the matter of legal standing: McCrudden talks of individual and group enforcement model,[28] Boom distinguishes between class and group actions and public and private enforcement,[29] Koch describes individual and group litigation,[30] others refer to non-individual litigation as class actions, and so on.[31]

Two main forms of legal standing can be identified on the basis of the combination of the forms of victim status and representation: individual litigation/legal standing and collective litigation/legal standing.

5.5.1. Individual Litigation

Individual litigation means that there is an individual victim on behalf of whom a procedure is commenced, as in the first example given above. The victim in this form of litigation can be represented either individually or collectively. More specifically, the victim might be represented by a particular organisation with experience in anti-discrimination law. In this sense the emphasis is on the fact that each individual obtains an individualised remedy, usually in the form of compensation. Individual litigation is very important since it is the most commonly used method to vindicate an individual's rights.

Pursuant to Article 7(1) RED the personal scope of enforcement is limited to those persons "who consider themselves *wronged* by failure to apply the

26 Collective standing is often called as group action or group litigation. The term here is explicitly chosen to refer to the *standing*, and not to the form of *litigation*.

27 See also Koch (2001), at 358.

28 McCrudden (1999); McCrudden (2001); McCrudden (2003).

29 Van Boom & Loos (2007), at 241. & 250.

30 Koch (2001).

31 See inter alia Lindblom (1996), at 15; Hodges (2001); Hensler (2001); Cooper (2001).

principle of equal treatment to them."[32] This criterion can be described as *being affected* by a particular measure or the applicant's *legitimate interest.* This provision is a clear expression of the individual enforcement model: the person having suffered a violation of his right can personally turn to a fact-finding body.

Importantly, the Directive requires that Member States ensure the engagement of 'associations, organisations or other legal entities' in a procedure *on behalf* of the complainant with his consent.[33] This engagement of the named entities first and foremost seems to mean that they can represent victims in the procedure. This interpretation is also confirmed by the communication of the European Commission on the application of the RED.[34]

Allowing the engagement of organisations in procedures is a novel and innovative feature of the Directive. According to Bell, this refers to the recognition that an individual alone may have neither the appropriate expertise in this field nor the adequate financial resources to support his case, not even when represented by an advocate. He argues that this provision supplements individual complaints.[35] Toggenburg in this respect emphasises that giving legal standing to organisations "may demonstrate that European legal perceptions of equality are shifting not only from a formal to a substantive, but also from an individual to a collective nature."[36]

It is an important development especially in the light of the fact that for some Member States acceptance of this provision has caused some difficulties.[37] The hesitation of the states is surprising,[38] since it does not differ very much from a general engagement scheme: the organisation is engaging on behalf of the complainant, there is a need for the approval of the complainant, and it is the complainant who will be remedied. Still, their engagement clearly contributes to the effective enforcement of the principle of equal treatment and clearly provides support to vulnerable groups.

---

32 Art. 7(1) RED.

33 See also Waddington & Bell (2001), at 607.

34 "In most Member States associations are able to help victims or represent them in court [...]." Communication from the Commission to the Council and the European Parliament – The application of Directive 2000/43/EC of 29 June 2000 implementing the principle of equal treatment between persons irrespective of racial or ethnic origin, COM(2006) 643 final, 30 October 2006, para. 3.1.

35 Bell (2004b), at 227.

36 Toggenburg (2002), at 239.

37 See Tyson (2004), at 124.

38 No further explanations can be found in the *travaux préparatoires* on this position of the States.

5.5.1.1. 'Associations, Organisations or Other Legal Entities' versus Equality Bodies

Pursuant to Article 13 RED "Member States shall designate a body or bodies for the promotion of equal treatment of all persons without discrimination on the grounds of racial or ethnic origin." In terms of legal standing the question is raised whether equality bodies could also be given legal standing; that is whether these bodies are included in the phrase 'associations, organisations or other legal entities'.

Generally speaking an equality body can be qualified as falling under the terms 'associations, organisations or other legal entities'. This observation is based on the facts that the underlying idea was to include the broadest possible range of entities existing in any forms;[39] and, like interest organisations, specialised bodies also aim to promote the right to non-discrimination. Moreover, there are also overlaps in the competences of equality bodies and the tasks of these 'associations, organisations and other legal entities'. Pursuant to Article 13(2) RED, one of the competences of these bodies is to provide "independent assistance to victims of discrimination in pursuing their complaints about discrimination."[40] This competence is "without prejudice to the right of victims and of associations, organisations or other legal entities referred to in Article 7(2)."[41] In other words, the assistance that can be provided by specialised bodies is similar to the tasks or part of the tasks of those entities under Article 7(2) RED.[42] Thus, this provision makes clear that the RED does not exclude specialised bodies from being able to engage in procedures on behalf of the victims.

5.5.1.2. In any Judicial and/or Administrative Procedures

Since the phrase 'in any judicial and/or administrative procedure' is the same as that found in Article 7(1) RED the same meaning can be attached to them. Nevertheless, in relation to locus standi the question is also raised whether associations, organisations and other legal entities may engage in the procedure in one way or another before an equality body if this body is a decision-making/fact-finding organ. If the equality body is a decision-making organ, and its procedure can be regarded as being either a judicial or administrative procedure, associations, organisations and other legal entities should be given legal standing – naturally with the consent of the complainant. However, when the procedure of the equality body cannot be classified as

[39] See the observation of Tyson above. Tyson (2001), at 212.

[40] Art. 13(2) RED.

[41] Art. 13(2) RED.

[42] The competence of equality bodies to give assistance will be discussed in more details in Ch. 8.

being any of the above-mentioned, Member States are not obliged to give them legal standing. Nevertheless, in the light of the importance of actio popularis claims and the effective enforcement of the right to equal treatment it would be desirable if associations, organisations or other legal entities could have legal standing before the fact-finding equality body – at least when an actio popularis claim would be appropriate.

5.5.2. Collective Litigation

Notwithstanding the importance of individual litigation, it is generally accepted that individual litigation in itself cannot ensure full protection in pursuing discrimination claims.[43] Victims of discrimination, for instance, are often afraid of the negative consequences of their legal procedure: retaliation in the work place, to mention the most prevalent example. Or, as can be seen in the above examples, individual litigation does not adequately address discrimination against more individuals or against a group – thus, discrimination of a more systemic character. Farkas formulated this limitation in relation to Roma persons as follows:

> [t]he perception of Roma as an impoverished and disenfranchised group, and the identification of discrimination against this group as systemic and institutional, highlights sharply the limitations of an individual justice model that foresees a private individual bringing and pursuing a claim against inherently biased institutions.[44]

The most important limitations inherent in individual enforcement can be solved by collective enforcement.

Collective enforcement means that the interest of more victims is litigated. Again, depending on the forms of victim status and representation two main types of collective enforcement can be distinguished: these are class action litigation and actio popularis claims. In class action litigation all victims are individualised and act as applicants, while in actio popularis claims it is the interest of the group that has been discriminated against that is represented by an interest group without any individualised victim as applicant.

As a matter of fact, in the legal literature the terms and their meanings relating to collective enforcement are blurred: the term ‘class actions’ often includes actio popularis claims, or class actions are called collective enforcement without including actio popularis claims, and sometimes it is not specified which type of claim is understood by the term ‘collective interest litigation’.

---

43 See for instance Higgins (2003), at 399; McCrudden (1999), at 302-303.

44 Farkas (2006), at 27.

5.5.2.1. Class Action

One of the solutions offered to fill in the gaps inherent in individual litigation is allowing class action, the need for which can be illustrated by the second example concerning the eviction of Roma. The fatherland of class actions is the United States, where legal discussion on this issue started as early as in 1938, in relation to relatively small harms.[45] The 'real' introduction of class action procedures however took place in the 1960s and 1970s with the new experience of mass torts. The Preamble to the Class Action Fairness Act of 2005 passed by the United States Congress uncovers the *ratio legis* of class action litigation. Pursuant to this provision

> [c]lass action lawsuits are an important and valuable part of the legal system when they permit the fair and efficient resolution of legitimate claims of numerous parties by allowing the claims to be aggregated into a single action against a defendant that has allegedly caused harm.[46]

On the basis of this description the following main characteristics of a class action can be identified.[47] First of all, there is more than one complainant with similar claims against the same respondent contracted into one common claim. This, at the same time, indicates that the complainants are individualised, and they all give their consent to the proceedings. In class action procedures as in individual litigation, individuals can be represented by an advocate, an individual from the group, or a third party, for example an organisation. In cases in which more individuals have been discriminated against by the same perpetrator, affected by the same criterion, provision, practice or treatment, that is when there is a link between the complainants, such procedures seem to be appropriate. In terms of the different concepts of discrimination, such actions are appropriate either in the case of direct (when it is more systemic of nature) or indirect discrimination.

---

[45] Taruffo (2001), at 409. It is remarkable that "[t]raditionally, class actions were understood to be representative litigation, pursued on behalf of absent parties." Hensler (2001), at 182.

[46] A huge class action claim concerning discrimination against women is pending in the U.S. In this case over two million women are estimated to be part of the lawsuit, where the company Wal-Mart has allegedly discriminated against women in promotions, jobs assignments, training and pay throughout the United States. If one thinks of the examples taken at the beginning, this case can be compared with both the second and the third example. There are individual victims who suffered discrimination and want to get compensation. However, one might ask whether it is really efficient to look at the individual victims and represent them in one case. To decide on two million different individual claims taking into consideration all the individual circumstances in order to establish the appropriate compensation is an enormous task, which might take years. Keeping in mind the third case, it might be argued that it would be preferable to proceed for changing the practice because it would be in the interest of the whole group without the need for identifying them all individually. And this takes us to the actio popularis claims. See http://www.walmartclass.com.

[47] On class action and its relation to mass tort litigation see inter alia Hensler (2001).

The main advantage of such an action is that it costs far less than filing several individual cases. Moreover, in certain cases the individual harm is so small that the complainant alone would not start a procedure,[48] but together with others it is worth doing so. It might create a stronger case if more victims appear with the same case, and submit evidence supporting each other's allegations. Finally, as the many small claims of the individual victims are contracted into one class action complaint, the chance that the individual will be given remedy is also higher.[49] To put it simply, the presence of several applicants in the lawsuit contributes to the effective enforcement of each individual's claim.[50]

However, due to the fact that the victims and their remedies are individualised class action litigation does not much differ from individual litigation in this respect. This also means that, as in individual litigation, the parties in the class action are also individualised so that the occurrence of victimisation cannot be prevented either. In addition, it is quite difficult to 'collect' a significant number of victims in order to be able to launch such a procedure. In general, the application of class actions does not yet seem to be popular in Europe.

Article 7(2) RED does not impose an obligation on the Member States to introduce such procedures in which more victims can be accumulated into one case. Article 7(2) RED merely talks about one complainant who should be allowed to be represented by such an organisation. This obviously refers to one person being allegedly a victim of discrimination. In other words, Member States may allow that more victims form a group to start a procedure and they might be represented by an association, organisation or other legal entity, but the Directive does not impose such an obligation on the states.[51]

---

48 Compare with the sufficient interest test.

49 In the US class action proceedings are accepted and widely used. Interestingly, the European approach in general is completely different to the question of class actions. A general resistance against such proceedings can be observed (Taruffo (2001), at 413). However, Europeans should not close their eyes to change in the world. As a matter of fact, their eyes are half closed (or half open): not accepting the general application of class actions, but "the goal pursued by most of the (few) European legislators when enacting statues in this area is to provide for new regulations, or to change the existing ones, with regard to specific and relatively narrow areas of the legal system" (Taruffo (2001), at 411). Accordingly, it is, for instance, possible to find class action in competition law, or in consumer protection law etc., but not in general. A similar approach can be found in EC law as well, notwithstanding that the general starting point is the national procedural autonomy. Only in relation to certain fields of law has the EU adopted provisions on class actions to make the enforcement of rights effective (see for example Directive 98/27/EC of the European Parliament and of the Council of 19 May 1998 on injunctions for the protection of consumers' interests). As Micklitz observed, "[t]he European law on all sorts of collective actions is rather underdeveloped. The only well settled collective remedy at EC level is the action for injunction." Micklitz (2007), at 33.

50 On the advangates of class action procedures see inter alia Weinstein (2001), at 172; Andrews (2001), at 258; Watson (2001), at 269-271. & 285.

51 A different view is accepted by Bodrogi, according to whom the RED provides "an

As shown above, although class action litigation does not rule out all the disadvantages of individual litigation, under certain circumstances it might be a good complement to it. Looking at from the victim's perspective having a stronger case,[52] having a greater chance to obtain remedy for the individuals making out the 'class', and cost-efficiency can all be regarded as the most advantageous aspects of class action litigation. However, these aspects constitute mere 'efficiency justifications',[53] thus, their lack does not make the right to effective enforcement of non-discrimination excessively difficult or virtually impossible. Accordingly, no obligation to introduce such litigation can be deduced from the general principle of effectiveness either.[54]

5.5.2.2. Actio Popularis

Finally, actio popularis claims aim to represent the interest of a group that has been discriminated against. The procedure is called *actio popularis litigation* as the claim is filed by an organisation acting in the name of public interest[55] that is fighting against racial discrimination. While in a class action one talks of collective victims ('the class'), in an actio popularis claim a *group victim* can be identified. In other words, the members of the group are not individually identified, and the emphasis is on the treatment of or the impact on the group as in the segregation example. In Lacey's words,[56]

> [t]he essence of the action would be seen not so much as an assertion of the existence of widespread individual acts of discrimination against members of the group, but of an unjust disadvantage suffered by the group, the ultimate source of which would not be the subject of technical legal proof.[57]

Hence, these procedures can be regarded highly relevant from the perspective of minorities being often the victims of racial discrimination.

---

opportunity to challenge more institutionalised forms of discrimination by introducing the possibility of actio popularis and class action procedures." This statement is, on the one hand, not supported by further arguments, and on the other hand, it talks only about a possibility and not an obligation. Bodrogi (2007), at 27.

52 Arguably, the harm (violation of human dignity) in racial discrimination cases cannot be regarded so small that it would necessitate class action litigation.

53 Cooper (2001), at 218.

54 As a matter of fact, class action proceedings are often allowed in national legislations because of cost-efficiency reasons. They are generally called joint actions, intervention, consolidation and so on. See inter alia Cooper (2001), at 217; Resnik (1991), at 26.

55 Kombos refers to this public interest as 'ideological claim'. Kombos (2006), at 383.

56 He calls this type of action class action, but he does not differentiate between the different forms of legal standing. On the basis of his analysis, he, as a matter of fact, talks about both class action and actio popularis claims. Accordingly, his ideas are interpreted in conformity with the claim at stake.

57 Lacey (1992), at 114.

This approach solves many problems previously referred to in connection with both the individual enforcement model and class actions. First of all, there is no need in this claim for individually named victims, since the main point is that the group as such has been, is, or would be affected by the given provision, criterion, practice or treatment. Also, actio popularis is the only option to offer the possibility of avoiding retaliation against the members of the group.[58] Moreover, such action provides for "the possibility of touching on discrimination as a patterned structure rather than as individual pathology."[59] Accordingly, in terms of enforcement this is the best way to ensure judicial protection in the case of structural discrimination, in which cases an individual applicant could hardly achieve any structural change. Such a procedure is mostly an appropriate form of enforcing the right to equal treatment in the case of indirect discrimination.[60] At the same time, this possibility widens the access to legal redress: those who would otherwise never be able to enforce their right to equal treatment can also be protected through the protection of the group they belong to. Moreover, the claim is brought by interest organisations which "are often best placed to bring well-informed and well-targeted claims that can resolve the issues, making the most effective use of resources."[61] The only concern that could be raised in this respect is related to the remedies.[62] Since the procedure is initiated in the name of the group it is the group and not the individual members of it that should be provided with a remedy.[63]

Different standpoints have been formulated concerning Article 7(2) RED and actio popularis claims. The general view is that this article cannot be interpreted as either providing for or requiring the possibility of actio popularis claims, since the consent of the victim is required.[64] Nevertheless, voices can also be found according to which the Directive either "*enables* Member States to introduce the institution of actio popularis";[65] or

[58] However, this possibility still does not give one hundred percent protection against retaliation, since the persons who are considered to belong to this group might suffer retaliation because of filing that claim. See also Brown (2002), at 219.

[59] Lacey (1992), at 115. See also Brown (2002), at 219.

[60] Admittedly, complaints of direct discrimination can also be litigated in actio popularis procedures, though this option is rather an exception. When a complaint in an actio popularis procedure concerns direct discrimination, usually it can be categorised as institutional or structural discrimination.

[61] Brown (2002), at 219.

[62] Although it will be discussed later in a separate chapter, some words on remedies/sanctions still seem to be appropriate here.

[63] For this several options might be envisaged, amongst which the most common is to impose a fine on the perpetrator, which should be devoted to positive action measures, or be given to the protecting organisation which could then use it in the interest of the group. Another solution might be that the respondent pays 'compensation' to the interest group. See inter alia Lacey (1992), at 114.

[64] See for instance Higgins (2003), at 399-400; Barry (2003), at 421.

[65] Bodrogi (2007), at 25.

> [a]ccording to a wide and teleological interpretation of this provision which reflects a fundamental principle, above entities *shall also be entitled* to bring in their own name proceedings for the annulment or modification of administrative acts of general applicability and collective agreements, something that already applies in several Member States.[66]

As elaborated above, the main characteristic of such a claim is that there is no need for the approval of the victim since the victims are not individually identified in these actions. The consent of the victim is, however, a clear requirement in Article 7(2) RED. Admittedly, the phrase 'with his or her approval' triggered much discussion during the adoption of the RED. The original text of the Commission included the consent of the complainant, while the legislative proposal of the Parliament emphasised the importance of not having such a requirement. According to the Parliament

> [t]he key point [...] is that organisations should be able to bring a case without the approval of a victim, in particular where the discrimination affects a group of persons and it may not be feasible to obtain the approval of each individual affected. There is often a high threshold to overcome before the victims of discrimination will seek legal protection and fear of victimisation may hold them back from asserting their rights.[67]

In the draft legislative resolution the European Parliament acknowledges the possibility given by the Commission to these organisations to take action on behalf of the victims,[68] but it stated that "it does not alter the fact that the

[66] Koukoulis-Spilitopoulos (2005), at 364 (emphasis added). Although this latter argument was given in the context of the Recast Directive, it does not derogate its argumentative force in relation to the RED since their wording on legal standing is the same.

[67] Report on the proposal for a Council Directive on implementing the principle of equal treatment between persons irrespective of racial or ethnic origin, COM(1999) 566 – C5-0067/2000 – 1999/0253(CNS), A5-0136/2000 final, 16 May 2000, at 38. See also European Parliament resolution of 27 September 2007 on the application of Council Directive 2000/43/EC of 29 June 2000 implementing the principle of equal treatment between persons irrespective of racial or ethnic origin, 2007/2094(INI), AA.

[68] Tyson, when describing the negotiation of the Race Directive, observed that "[s]ome groups in the European Parliament in particular wanted to see this as a provision requiring the possibility of class action, while some Member States were strongly opposed to class actions as they were not foreseen in their own judicial systems. [...] For some Member States, it was even difficult to accept that an organisation or association should act in its own name on behalf of an identified victim, though they could accept that such organisations should be able to support a victim, including by providing them with legal counsel to fight a case. In the Commission's view, the précised status of such an organisation before the court is less important than the access to support from a respected organisation, which greatly influences the ability of a complainant to win a case. In that light, the Commission was content to allow the Member States to define the nature of organisations which should have such rights (i.e. those 'which have, in accordance with the criteria laid down by their national law, a legitimate interest in ensuring the provisions of this Directive are complied with') and to allow Member States to decide whether such organisations should be empowered to act on their own behalf or only in support of a particular complainant." Tyson (2004), at 123-124.

directive does not include the right of collective action – and this is a serious shortcoming."[69] Notwithstanding these concerns the Commission opposed the proposal of the Parliament and inserted its own original text into the amended proposal.[70] Thus, it seems that the Commission[71] wanted to exclude the possibility of actions that could be launched without the consent of the victim.[72]

Remarkably, it was not only the Parliament that wanted to introduce the possibility of actio popularis actions, but the Starting Line proposal can also be interpreted in such a way[73] as it did not require the consent of the victim.[74] The creation of actio popularis procedures was also recommended by the ECRI.[75] According to its model legislation

> [t]he law should provide that organisations such as associations, trade unions and other legal entities which have, according to the criteria laid down by the national law, a legitimate interest in combating racism and racial discrimination, are entitled to bring civil cases, intervene in administrative cases or make civil

---

[69] Report on the proposal for a Council Directive on implementing the principle of equal treatment between persons irrespective of racial or ethnic origin, COM(1999) 566 – C5-0067/2000 – 1999/0253(CNS), A5-0136/2000 final, 16 May 2000, at 43. & 88. "The key point in the last part of the amendment is that organisations should be able to bring a case without the approval of a victim, in particular where the discrimination affects a group of persons and it may not be feasible to obtain the approval of each individual affected." The Parliament further stated that "[t]he importance of the right of collective action has been recognized by the Commission and the Council in the directive on consumer protection. The proposals of the right of collective action in respect of equal treatment of persons or groups of persons regardless of race or ethnic origin are based on this." Report on the proposal for a Council directive on implementing the principle of equal treatment between persons irrespective of racial or ethnic origin, COM(1999) 566 – C5-0067/2000 – 1999/0253(CNS), A5-0136/2000 final, 16 May 2000, at 38.

[70] Amended proposal for a Council Directive implementing the principle of equal treatment between persons irrespective of racial or ethnic origin, 1999/0253 (CNS), 31 May 2000, at 9-10.

[71] Compare with Proposal for a Directive of the European Parliament and of the Council amending Council Directive 76/207/EEC on the implementation of the principle of equal treatment for men and women as regards access to employment, vocational training and promotion, and working conditions, COM(2000) 334 final – COD 2000/0142, 7 June 2000. The EP during the legislation process proposed an amendment to allow for actio popularis claims which was rejected by the European Commission. According to this proposal "[associations, organisations and other legal entities] may [...] bring a collective action [...] on their own initiative and aside from the particular circumstances of an individual case." Recommendation for second reading on the Council common position for adopting a European Parliament and Council directive on amending Council Directive 76/207/EEC, 9848/1/2001 – C5-0387/2001 – COD 2000/0142, A5-0358/2001, 17 October 2001, at 13.

[72] See inter alia Brown (2002), at 219; Waddington & Bell (2001), at 607.

[73] Chopin & Niessen (2001), at 42.

[74] Art. 4(4) of the Starting Line proposal. For more details see Chopin & Niessen (2001), at 43.

[75] See also Hepple, Coussey & Choudhury (2000), at 95-97; Harrington (2001), at 764; Howard (2005), at 480-481.

> complaints, even if a specific victim is not referred to. If a specific victim is referred to, it should be necessary of the victim's consent to be obtained.'[76]

Pursuant to the explanation there is a need for such procedures where a victim is afraid of victimisation or "where it is difficult to identify such a victim or cases which affect an indeterminate number of victims."[77] Finally, the relevant provision of the UN Model Legislation can also be mentioned. It lays down that "[l]egal persons [...] shall also be entitled to enter complaints alleging racial discrimination under this Act, including complaints on behalf (or with the consent) of the victim or the alleged victim."[78] Importantly, this provision of the UN Model Legislation was also referred to in the Explanatory Memorandum of the RED on Article 7(2).[79] Thus, the model legislations and the legislative proposal of the EP acknowledged the need for the introduction of actio popularis claims.

However, not only does the RED give legal standing to organisations, associations or other legal entities *on behalf* of the complainant, but it also prescribes an obligation for the Member States to ensure that these organs can *support* the complainant in a judicial and/or administrative procedure. It is remarkable that the original proposal of the Commission did not include this phrase, it was proposed only later by the Parliament and accepted by the Commission – though without any explanation.[80] Arguably, the mentioning of this possibility gains importance only when support means more than providing someone with legal information, legal assistance, and so on, as no special authorisation is necessary for such activities in a legal procedure and the interest organisation will not become a party to the procedure by providing legal aid.[81] Accordingly, engagement of organisations in support of

[76] ECRI General Policy Recommendation No 7 on national legislation to combat racism and racial discrimination, para. 25.

[77] *Id.*, CRI(2003) 8, 13 December 2002, Explanatory Memorandum, para. 56. See also Bell (2002b), at 397-398. Bell argued that "[...] institutionalised forms of discrimination, which by their nature, are deeply entrenched, may be less susceptible to individual litigation."

[78] Model National Legislation for the Guidance of Governments in the Enactment of Further Legislation Against Racial Discrimination. Third Decade to Combat Racism and Racial Discrimination (1993-2003), at 13.

[79] Proposal for a Council Directive implementing the principle of equal treatment between persons irrespective of racial or ethnic origin, COM(1999)566 final, 1999/0253, 25 November 1999, at 9.

[80] Report on the proposal for a Council Directive on implementing the principle of equal treatment between persons irrespective of racial or ethnic origin, COM(1999)566 – C5-0067/2000 – 1999/0253(CNS), A5-0136/2000 final, 16 May 2000, at 22, 43 & 60. The proposed text was the following: "Member States shall ensure that associations, organisations or other legal entities may be entitled to institute or support any judicial and/or administrative procedure providing for the enforcement of obligations under this Directive."

[81] In Bodrogi's view support means a whole process, and she does not differentiate between the different forms or methods of support. In her words, "the victim of discrimination first contacts a civil society organisation which carries out professional fact-finding and prepares the case

the complainant might arguably refer to the possibility that in addition to the victim they can also act as applicants in order to strengthen the position of the victim and/or emphasise the group dimension of the discrimination. In other words, the organisation is also a complainant to the procedure which is only possible when its claim is related to the interest of a group. In conclusion, Article 7(2) RED might be interpreted as imposing an obligation on the Member States to introduce actio popularis litigation only as a complement to a claim initiated by an individualised victim.

The position that Article 7 RED does not lay down any obligation for the introduction of actio popularis claims without an identified complainant is also confirmed by the ECJ in the first extensive judgment on the RED. It explained in the *Feryn* case that

> the requirements of Article 7 of Directive 2000/43 are, as stated in Article 6 thereof, only *minimum requirements* and the Directive does not preclude Member States from introducing or maintaining provisions which are more favourable to the protection of the principle of equal treatment. Consequently, Article 7 of Directive 2000/43 *does not preclude* Member States from laying down, in their national legislation, the right for association with a legitimate interest in ensuring compliance with that directive, [...], to bring legal or administrative proceedings to enforce the obligations resulting therefrom without acting in the name of a specific complainant or *in the absence of an identifiable complainant.*[82]

Accordingly, it is obvious that contrary to some opinions the RED does not oblige the Member States to establish actio popularis procedures in their classical meaning. Nevertheless, the Court also makes it clear that Article 7(2) RED does not prohibit the introduction of such actions either.

Although Article 7(2) RED does not prescribe the establishment of actio popularis procedures without an identifiable complainant, this might be required by the general principle of effectiveness. As already elaborated above and as can be seen in the example of segregation cases,[83] in certain cases, in particular in relation to indirect and systemic discrimination, the effective enforcement of the right to equal treatment might not be possible without actio popularis claims. Concretely, the right could be made excessively difficult

for litigation. In a second phase the organisation co-operates with an advocate who represents the client before the court and they decide on legal strategy together. The organisation – in the absence of legal standing – is not a party to proceedings and it is only the victim and their representative who stand in front of the legal forum. More specifically, the representation takes place on the basis of powers given directly by the victim to the advocate." Bodrogi (2007), at 25.

[82] Judgment of 10 July 2008 in *Case C-54/07, Centrum voor gelijkheid van kansen en racismebestrijding v. Firma Feryn NV.*, [2008] ECR I-05187, paras. 26-27 (emphasis added).

[83] The importance of the fight against segregation can be found in many documents. See for instance European Parliament resolution of 27 September 2007 on the application of Council Directive 2000/43/EC of 29 June 2000 implementing the principle of equal treatment between persons irrespective of racial or ethnic origin, 2007/2094(INI), 15, 19. & 22; General Recommendation No. 19, The Committee on the Elimination of Racial Discrimination 1995.

or even virtually impossible. Moreover, actio popularis procedures might also be necessary due to the need for protection against victimisation which has also been emphasised throughout the *travaux préparatoires*.[84] Arguably, the most effective way of preventing victimisation seems to be by creating actio popularis procedures since a lack of individualised victims means no one can be victimised. Without actio popularis procedures, victims would be forced to turn individually to fact-finders, and thus, to take the risk of being victimised. In summary, it can be convincingly argued that Member States should introduce actio popularis procedures even without identifiable victims if they want to avoid violating the general principle of effective enforcement.

PART B. CASE STUDIES

5.6. Introduction

The RED had a clear effect on national legislation with respect to legal standing, with the exception of the Netherlands. During the adoption of their equal treatment act the three other countries allowed, though to different extents, for the engagement of interest organisations in the procedures for enforcing the right to equal treatment. Prior to the adoption of these equal treatment legislations interest organisations could not participate in legal procedures in these countries.

This section analyses the legal provisions and the jurisprudence in the countries under review as far as legal standing is concerned. First of all, the decisions on the legal standing of both the applicant and the respondent will be examined. This will be followed by an exploration of the different forms of legal standing. Here, as in the theoretical framework, the emphasis will be on the role of interest organisations in the procedures that aim to enforce the principle of equal treatment. In this regard, a closer look will also be taken on the possible engagement of interest organisations in the procedures before national specialised bodies and this will be discussed within the framework of the particular form of litigation.

5.7. Decision on Legal Standing

In general it can be established that in most cases no problems occur as far as the decision regarding the legal standing of both the applicant and the

[84] Communication from the Commission to the Council and the European Parliament – The application of Directive 2000/43/EC of 29 June 2000 implementing the principle of equal treatment between persons irrespective of racial or ethnic origin, COM(2006) 643 final, 30 October 2006, at 4; European Parliament resolution of 27 September 2007, *supra* note 83, at 17.

respondent is concerned. Still, in some instances or with respect to some rules difficulties do or might arise.

5.7.1. Decision on the Legal Standing of the Applicant

In the absence of special rules for the decision on the locus standi of individual applicants in civil and administrative law procedures the general rules are to be applied in all countries under review. This means that applicants have to have an interest in receiving a decision from fact-finding bodies, which criterion could be translated in terms of *being affected*. Fact-finders do not usually examine in the admissibility phase, at least not separately, the other element of sufficient interest, namely whether this interest is significant enough.[85] This latter approach guarantees that the applicant's claim will not be refused without substantive examination. In this respect the procedure of the Equal Treatment Commission in the Netherlands constitutes an exception to some extent.

The GETA lays down some additional rules for the locus standi of individual applicants before the Equal Treatment Commission. The ETC examines whether the applicant has legal standing on the basis of Article 12(2) taken together with Article 14(1) GETA. Article 12(2) GETA defines who can submit a complaint, and Article 14(1) GETA lays down which cases are inadmissible. It is regarded inadmissible: a) if the claim is manifestly ill-founded; and b) if the interest of the applicant or the gravity of the behaviour is manifestly insufficient.[86]

The statistics provided by the Commission on the number of inadmissible cases do not make a distinction pertaining to which points of Article 14(1) GETA were the basis of the inadmissibility decision. Nevertheless, the overview of the cases of the Commission shows that point a) is applied when applicants do not specify their complaints, the protected ground or the field does not fall under the GETA, or it concerns unilateral governmental

[85] As elaborated in the context of access to justice a special procedure has been established in Belgium for discrimination cases, that is summary-like procedure. It has been argued that on the basis of the ARA no additional criteria have, arguably, been set up for the applicant's interest. Thus, neither the danger of recurrence nor the urgency of the case, which should generally be proven in summary proceedings, has to be established by the applicant since in discrimination cases their existence is presumed. Accordingly, the general procedural rules are applicable for determining the capability of the victim to take action. See Ch. 3 on access to justice. See also Thiery (2007), at 769; De Prins, Sottiaux & Vrielink (2005), at 538-541; Taelman (2004b), at 509.

[86] Also a third criterion is set up in Art. 14(1) GETA. Pursuant to point c) the complaint is also inadmissible if the period of time which has elapsed since the discrimination took place is such that an investigation can no longer be reasonably conducted. This criterion is clearly not concerned with the legal standing of the applicants, but relates to the time limit of starting the procedure. For this reason this requirement is addressed in Ch. 3 on access to justice and time limits.

decisions (in which cases the ETC does not have competence). All the other cases are classified because the applicant did not have any interest or the interest was insignificant.[87] Translating these admissibility requirements to the test elaborated in the theoretical framework, it can be seen that point a) and the first part of point b) (interest of the applicant) can be classified as *being affected* by the challenged measure, while the second part of point b) (gravity of the behaviour) refers to the *significance of the interest* of the applicant.

Concerning the requirement of being affected, for instance, a mother of a schoolgirl was not considered to have interest in a decision when the school accepted a regulation that except for religious reasons no head-covering scarves were allowed. In the view of the Commission it did not appear that the applicant or her daughter had suffered any disadvantage because of this regulation.[88] In several similar cases the ETC has turned the perspective around and argued that an interest organisation would be able to launch a procedure, but the organisations' right to proceed cannot be given to individuals.[89] This approach clearly shows that when the case concerns the locus standi of an individual, he has to be personally affected. When, however, an interest organisation files a claim, it is simply its aim that is examined.[90]

As yet, only in one case did the ETC considered a complaint inadmissible on the ground of not being significant enough. The case concerned a taxi station which offered female-only taxis. The Commission explained that it would not often occur that only female-only taxis were available at the station, and in any case the only disadvantage men would face would be a waiting time of five to ten minutes. These 'harms' were not considered to constitute a significant disadvantage.[91] Clearly, there was a distinction on the ground of gender; however, men were considered not to suffer any serious disadvantage from this treatment.[92] It is an important aspect of the case that it was not the 'vulnerable' group that started a procedure due to the alleged violation of their rights to equal treatment; instead it was the 'majority' group in the name of which the procedure was initiated. This raises the question whether the Commission would have ruled the same way had it been men (thus the non-vulnerable group) for whom separate taxis had been reserved. It seems that the Commission took into account the position of men and women in its

87 In 5 % of the inadmissible cases it was the lack of interest on the basis of which the complaint was declared inadmissible. Jaarverslag 2007, CGB 2008, at 33.

88 Opinion 2006-122 ETC, para. 3.7. See also Opinions 2008-98, 2006-225 ETC.

89 See for instance Opinion 2001-21 ETC.

90 See inter alia Rodrigues (2002), at 91-104.

91 Opinion 2008-102 ETC, paras. 3.13 & 3.16.

92 Admittedly, one of the underlying reasons in declaring the complaint inadmissible was that the policy of the taxi station can be considered as a positive action measure, with the aim of helping those in a more vulnerable position. One can, thus, also wonder whether the Commission would have ruled in the same way was it men for whom separate taxis had been reserved.

admissibility decision, which arguably, should rather have been considered in a substantive decision. On the contrary, if their dominant position had not played a role in the admissibility decision, the significance of the claim would have been decided on the basis of the harm suffered by the distinction. This latter approach to the significance test carries the potential danger that cases, in which the material harm is insignificant but the victim's human dignity has been violated, will not be declared admissible. In other words, in such cases a lot depends on how the harm is identified. Thus, there are more dangers involved in the application of a significance test than the advantage it would carry. All in all, cases like this one should rather be decided in the substantive phase.

As far as the locus standi of interest organisations is concerned the picture is more varied. The legitimate interest which is required for their legal standing has been defined differently by the countries under review.

In this respect the Belgian rules can be regarded as the most restrictive. Articles 31 and 32 ARA[93] lay down that the following organisations may have legal standing in a discrimination claim: the CEOOR, each organisation of public utility with legal personality for at least three years and with the aim to protect human rights or combat discrimination; representative employees' and employers' organisations; certain representative professional organisations; and representative organisations of the self-employed.[94] These rules set up two main requirements for the legal standing of the organisations: legal personality and a certain period of existence. Arguably, these criteria could limit the range of organisations that could initiate proceedings, and for this reason they can be regarded as restrictive. Nevertheless, it has been explained that the purpose of imposing these requirements was to guarantee that only experienced organisations with a stable background would start procedures. Importantly, the required period of existence was originally five years in the ADA. This has been changed in the ARA partly because of the European Commission's dissatisfaction with it.[95] It is accepted in the jurisprudence that the existence of five years (now three years) only refers to the legal status of these organisations. Thus, it is not required that the aim to protect human rights has also existed for this period.[96] One could argue that there are already a

93 For the examination of these criteria see for instance Président du Tribunal du Commerce de Bruxelles, 7 March 2005, para. 1.

94 If there is an individual, identified victim, it is also controlled whether the body acts with the consent of the particular victim. Article 33 ARA. See also *CGKR and C. Murat v. D. Yves and E-L. BVBA*, Gent Labour Court, summary proceedings, no. 176.893, 26 March 2007, para. 3.

95 Closset-Marchal & Van Drooghenbroeck (2008), at 384; Wetsontwerp tot wijziging van de wet van 30 juli 1981 tot bestraffing van bepaalde door racisme en xenofobie ingegeven daden, 2720/001, 26 October 2006, at 35-36; Wetsontwerp tot wijziging van de wet van 30 juli 1981 tot bestraffing van bepaalde door racisme en xenofobie ingegeven daden, 2720/009, 19 March 2007, at 26.

96 See inter alia Closset-Marchal & Van Drooghenbroeck (2008), at 383.

couple of organisations that can initiate such procedures, thus this requirement is not that restrictive. However, important civil society organisations might still be excluded on the basis of these criteria – especially on the grounds of the three years requirement. It can be argued that the requirement of legal personality should already provide sufficient guarantees against any abuse, and the criterion of three years existence is then excessive.

The Estonian legislator has set up two requirements concerning the legitimate interest of the organisations: they have to have legal personality and they have to aim to monitor the observance of the principle of equal treatment.[97] These requirements cannot be regarded as more restrictive than necessary.

In Hungary, in order to be able to engage in procedures, an organisation has to aim to promote equal opportunities for socially disadvantaged groups or to protect human rights. With respect to ethnic or national minorities the minority self-governments can also be regarded as interest bodies and concerning certain aspects related to the employees' circumstances a trade union should also be taken as an interest body.[98]

When the interest organisations want to file a claim of actio popularis further requirements are postulated. Interest organisations are entitled to initiate proceedings in their own name when the protected ground at stake is an essential feature of the individual, and the violation or the danger of the violation affects a larger group of persons that cannot be determined accurately. In terms of locus standi these requirements can, arguably, be interpreted as an obligation to show that the affected interest is significant enough, which in the theoretical elaboration was regarded as undesirable. These requirements, thus, contrary to the Belgian rules in this respect, are not concerned with the legitimate interest of the organisation, but relate to the significance of the interest. In other words, the Hungarian legislators seem to aim to allow for public interest litigation only in momentous cases.

It has been argued that, due to conjunctive criteria, this regulation is quite restrictive.[99] This might be the case in particular with respect to the requirement that the characteristic has to be an inherent one.[100] It seems though that these criteria merely articulate the practice of other countries and aim to ensure that interest organisations act only in cases of serious violations.[101] Nevertheless, it can be argued that the requirement of 'aiming at the protection of the right to equal treatment' would have been satisfactory, and thus, fact-finders could have interpreted it in accordance with the particular circumstances of the case.

97 Arts. 23(2) ECA and 17(1) EETA.
98 Arts. 3 e) and 18.
99 Farkas, Kádár & Kárpáti (2006), at 98.
100 See the Miskolc case in this respect Borsod-Abaúj-Zemplén County Court, 13.P.21.660/2005/16, 2 November 2005; Debrecen Court of Appeal, Pf.I.20.683/2005/7, 9 June 2006.
101 See also Farkas, Kádár & Kárpáti (2006), at 98.

The very first judicial case decided under the HETA is very telling in this regard. The case concerned a general declaration of a denominational university excluding homosexual students from theological education. Importantly, at the time of the lawsuit the danger of violation was not yet included in the HETA, and the defendant tried to use this reasoning against the legal standing of the interest organisation in addition to arguing that sexual orientation is not an essential feature of the individual. The court, however, did not accept these arguments, and came to the conclusion that homosexuality is an inherent feature of one's personality and the danger of an infringement of the right to equal treatment suffices in terms of filing an actio popularis claim.[102] In relation to this latter aspect the court of first instance explained that only an

> interpretation can be appropriate which does not force the court to decide on the merits when examining the locus standi. When an established violation would be the precondition of the locus standi, all further examination in the suit would be meaningless according to the court.[103]

Thus, the court clearly applied the rules of the Act, and did not mix the question of standing with the decision on the merits. From the above reasoning it is also possible to conclude that ethnic or racial origin would be clearly regarded as essential features of the individual. Accordingly, the interest to launch procedures concerning racial discrimination would be considered significant enough. This was indeed the case in the Miskolc[104] and Hajdúhadház[105] segregation cases. In both cases it was accepted that ethnic origin constituted an essential feature of each person, which could also be deduced from the jurisprudence of the Constitutional Court.[106]

Finally, in the Netherlands the locus standi of interest organisations before the Commission as well as in judicial procedures is regulated in the GETA and in the Civil Code. Pursuant to Article 12(2) d) and e) GETA "a *works council* or comparable *employee participation body* which believes that discrimination as referred to in this Act [...] is taking place in the organisation for which it was appointed" or "an *association with full legal powers* or a *foundation* which, in accordance with its constitution or statutes, represents

[102] Metropolitan Court, 19.P.21.788/2004/10, 8 October 2004; Supreme Court PFv. IV.20.687/2005/5, 8 June 2005. See also Kárpáti (2005); Kádár (2007), at 65-66.

[103] Metropolitan Court, *id.*; Supreme Court, *id.*

[104] Borsod-Abaúj-Zemplén County Court, 13.P.21.660/2005/16, 2 November 2005; Debrecen Court of Appeal, Pf.I.20.683/2005/7, 9 June 2006.

[105] Hajdú-Bihar County Court, 6.P. 20.341/2006/50, 2 May 2007; Debrecen Court of Appeal, Pf.I.20.361/2007/8, 13 December 2007; Supreme Court, Pfv.IV.20.936/2008/4, 19 November 2008.

[106] It is remarkable that in the Miskolc, case the disadvantageous social situation of the group of victims was not accepted as an essential feature of the individual, and in this respect the legal standing of the applicant was refused. Borsod-Abaúj-Zemplén County Court, 13.P.21.660/2005/16, 2 November 2005; Debrecen Court of Appeal, Pf.I.20.683/2005/7, 9 June 2006.

the interests of those whose protection is the objective of this Act" can have legal standing in discrimination cases.[107] Accordingly, organisations have to be established in a certain legal form to have legitimate interest. This criterion cannot be regarded as very restrictive since it is not difficult to establish either a foundation or an association. Thus the Dutch system does not unreasonably restrict the legitimate interest of organisations.

5.7.2. Decision on the Legal Standing of the Respondent

There are no special rules on the locus standi of the respondent in the countries under review. Also, with the exception of Belgium no complication has yet taken place in practice concerning the decision on the legal standing of the respondent. A problematic field in this context might be the vicarious liability of the employers, since their locus standi in such cases should always be accepted, and whether they fulfilled their obligations as good employers should be examined in the second phase of the assessment. Again, in general it seems that the examination of the employers' legal standing will not cause problems in this respect either.

Although it seems to be generally acknowledged in Belgium that the decision on the legal standing of the respondent should be taken in the admissibility phase,[108] in a particular case[109] this did not happen. Here the respondents argued that they did not have standing, since they did not personally commit the alleged violation which is a prerequisite in summary-like proceedings (procedure to cease and desist). However, the court held the case admissible since in their view the respondents' argument concerned the merits of the case rather than the admissibility of the claim. Nevertheless, the complaint was refused on the merits that two of the respondents, being the owners of the apartment, did not have any contact with either the agency or the alleged victims, and the third respondent, who in fact decided on whom to rent the apartment to, did not have official authorisation from the owners.[110] However, these arguments are not related to the substance of the case at all; they clearly pertain to the legal standing of the respondents.[111] As mixing admissibility considerations with substance-related arguments has not yet occurred in other discrimination cases, it is likely and also to be hoped that in the future a consistent approach will be applied in this respect.

---

[107] Article 12(2) d)-e) GETA (emphasis added).

[108] Gent Labour Court, summary proceedings, no. 03/4440/A, 31 December 2003.

[109] *Id.*; Gent Court of Appeal, 30 November 2005.

[110] It is, arguably, questionable though whether this was a relevant criterion to refuse the claim on the substance.

[111] Naturally, it is a different question whether the lack of their locus standi was properly established.

In Hungary the decision on the legal standing of the respondent has not yet raised any problems. In the Károli case, for instance, in the admissibility phase it was immediately examined whether the university should be regarded as a religious legal person to the religious activities of which the Act is not applicable.[112] In other words, contrary to the Belgian fact-finder, it was accepted without any hesitation that this argument was related to locus standi considerations and did not concerned the respondent's refutation.

Finally, the same observation can be made with respect to the Netherlands. In the case-law of the Commission a couple of cases can be found in which the person having allegedly discriminated against the applicant could not be taken as respondent *in casu.*[113] Interestingly, however, the inadmissibility argument was linked to the locus standi of the applicant, since a person can only be regarded as an 'interested' person on the basis of Article 12(2) a) GETA when he summons a person who is an addressee of the GETA.[114]

5.8. Forms of Legal Standing

This section will examine to what extent the three main forms of legal standing can be found in the countries under review in discrimination cases, and to what degree these possibilities have been applied.

5.8.1. Individual Litigation

In each country under review the main form of litigation is individual: individuals themselves and/or represented individuals initiate proceedings against the alleged perpetrator. Importantly, each country allows for the engagement of interest organisations on behalf of the applicant as it is required by Article 7(2) RED, but to varying extents. In this respect the Estonian and Hungarian approach have a starting position significantly different from the other two countries. While in the latter countries the legislators seem to have interpreted Article 7(2) RED as giving these organisations the right to pursue claims on behalf of the complainant, but in their own right, in Estonia and Hungary these organisations are given the 'right' to act as representatives of the victim.

Contrary to the Hungarian legislation, in Estonia the possibility that organisations can act as representatives in disputes related to discrimination

[112] Metropolitan Court, 19.P.21.788/2004/10, 8 October 2004; Supreme Court PFv. IV.20.687/2005/5, 8 June 2005.

[113] See for instance Opinions 2006-204, 2006-203, 2007-21, 2008-109 ETC.

[114] "Omdat het handelen van verweerster niet valt onder één van de bepalingen van [...] de AWGB [...], is verzoeker niet ontvankelijk in zijn verzoek om een oordeel tegen verweerster." Opinion 2008-109 ETC, para. 3.6.

is not extended to all procedures. It is only in disputes in the field of labour law (labour courts and labour dispute resolution commissions)[115] and in the conciliation procedure before the Legal Chancellor[116] where victims of discrimination can give authorisation to interest organisations for their representation. To put it differently, outside the field of employment organisations are not allowed to engage in court procedures, which is clearly contrary to the RED.

Although it is an important novelty of the HETA[117] that organisations can be given authorisation for acting as representatives in judicial and administrative procedures, in many cases before the adoption of the Act victims of discrimination were represented by advocates employed by interest organisations.[118] The introduction of this possibility in the HETA, however, further facilitates the position of the victims since now the interest organisation can directly represent the victim. This possibility has already been used in many instances. For example, in one of the cases before the Authority an NGO represented a victim of Roma origin who applied for a job, but was not selected.[119] The NGO carried out situation testing in order to support the complaint that discrimination had taken place on the ground of ethnic origin. Without the support of the civil organisation the applicant's position would have been more difficult since he would not have been able to carry out such convincing testing. Nevertheless, in many instances brought before courts the engagement of an NGO in the procedure does not seem to have any effect on the adjudication. Strikingly, there are also cases in which despite the engagement of an NGO with expertise in the field of anti-discrimination law the court did not interpret the allocation of the burden of proof in accordance with the HETA and the RED.[120]

Notably, not only interest organisations, but the national specialised body, the Authority on Equal Treatment can also represent victims in procedures concerning the violation of the principle of equal treatment even though the AET is an administrative body issuing binding decisions.[121] The fact that it is

---

[115] Art. 31(1) EETA amended the relevant provision (Art. 14(2)) of the Individual Labour Dispute Resolution Act. See also Proposal for a Council Directive implementing the principle of equal treatment between persons irrespective of racial or ethnic origin, COM(1999) 566 final, 1999/0253, 25 November 1999, at 10-11.

[116] This possibility has been introduced as of 1 January 2004. Article 23(2) Legal Chancellor Act. See also Poleshchuk (2007), at 54.

[117] Art. 18 HETA. See also Kádár (2007), at 65.

[118] See the White Booklets (Fehér Füzetek) of NEKI. www.neki.hu.

[119] EBH/180/1/2006. See also EBH/271/26/2007.

[120] See for instance Borsod-Abaúj-Zemplén County Court, 13.P.21.660/2005/16, 2 November 2005.

[121] Although the Act allows for representation by the Authority in all kind of procedures initiated because of the violation of the principle of equal treatment, therefore, also before the Authority, the AET will not file such a complaint. Several reasons can be identified for this, but the two main ones are the impartiality and independence related arguments, and the division

possible for a decision-making specialised body to represent the victims of discrimination is unique amongst the Member States under review. Arguably, this competence of the Authority could not be regarded as a fortunate choice of the legislators, since its independence and impartiality as a decision-making organ might be impaired.[122] This might be one of the reasons why as yet the Authority has not acted as representative in court procedures. Although no precedent can be found yet with regard to the engagement of interest organisations in addition to individualised victims in legal procedures, the provision on actio popularis claims does not seem to exclude this possibility.[123] It is yet to be seen whether this interpretation will be accepted and the engagement of interest organisations in their own name and in support of the complainant will also be allowed in addition to representation.

Unlike in Estonia and Hungary, the equal treatment legislation in Belgium and the Netherlands regulates the interest organisations' engagement in the procedures in their own name. This regulation can be regarded as the implementation of the requirement of the RED to allow for the engagement of interest organisations in procedures '*support of*' the complainant. In Belgium, pursuant to Articles 18(1), 31 and 32 ARA, the CEOOR and other interest organisations can engage in the procedure on behalf of the applicant, but in their own name.[124] This procedural position of the CEOOR and the other interest organisations was first created in Articles 19(1) and 31 ADA as an implementation of Article 7(2) RED, and has subsequently been repeated in the amended ARA. Although in principle the interest organisations engage in the interest of the individual victim, still their presence emphasizes the person's belonging to the particular group on the ground of which he has been discriminated against. By this his claim also gains a group focus. This happened, for instance, in the Murat case in which the CEOOR engaged in the procedure on behalf of the victim but as a second applicant. The victim alleged that he had been discriminated against on the grounds of racial or ethnic origin during recruitment. In addition, the CEOOR also argued that the respondent had a discriminatory recruitment policy in general. Both claims were investigated, and the CEOOR was also given remedy. In this respect the court merely explained that the CEOOR's engagement in the procedure gave an additional dimension to the dispute.[125] Arguably, this 'additional dimension' can be interpreted as an actio popularis claim on the top of individual litigation.

---

of tasks in the Office of the Authority. This will be discussed in further detail in Chapter 8 on specialised bodies.

[122] This aspect of AET's engaging in procedures will be discussed in Ch. 8 on specialised bodies.

[123] Article 20 HETA. This provision will be discussed in further detail below within the framework of actio popularis claims.

[124] See for instance Gent Labour Court, summary proceedings, no. 03/4440/A, 31 December 2003.

[125] *CGKR and C. Murat v. D. Yves and E-L. BVBA*, Gent Labour Court, summary proceedings, no. 176.893, 26 March 2007.

However, from the perspective of the victim the engagement of the CEOOR can also be interpreted as representation by this organisation. Indeed, no additional representative was authorised by the victim; the CEOOR can be regarded as having acted as representative. Thus, it seems that in such cases there is, in fact, no need for separate representation for the interest organisation represents the interests of the victim in addition to its own interests. It can be argued that there might be cases, though, in which the discrimination is clearly directed against a particular individual and in which it would be impossible to prove that the respondent has a general discriminatory policy. Thus, it would seem that in this case the engagement of the organisation would not be permitted due to the lack of interest. This means that, as the organisations cannot act as representatives, in such cases the applicant has to look for an advocate, or the advocate of the organisations has to be the representative. In this respect, the Belgian approach is not in accordance with the RED. However, as soon as a prejudice seems to be present, which is always the case in direct racial discrimination, the engagement of the organisation cannot reasonably be refused, since it aims to protect the group of persons having a certain racial or ethnic origin.

As mentioned supra, in the Netherlands the RED did not have any effect in this respect on the legislation, since the engagement of interest organisations was already established both in civil and administrative procedural law.[126] This engagement of an organisation has been interpreted in terms of taking action on its own right, and not as an authorised representative of the victim, which is contrary to the Directive.

The procedure of the Commission is somewhat different in this respect. First of all, the GETA makes it clear that a request for an opinion may be submitted by "a person who believes that he/she is or will be discriminated against".[127] Although the GETA itself does not mention it, the Commission has explained that the victims can also be *represented* by interest organisations.[128] Nevertheless, in the practice of the ETC it is the employees of these organisations that are authorised to represent the victim rather than the organisation itself.[129] It would therefore be more desirable if the GETA would allow for representation by organisations as well.

Moreover, pursuant to Article 12(2) e) GETA these organisations can also submit complaints in their own name, which are actio popularis claims. Similarly to the Belgian practice, the engagement of an interest organisation in support of the complainant can be interpreted as representation. However, due to the fact that not each case has a more systemic or group related dimension,

[126] Art. 3:305a Civil Code. See also Art. 10(2).
[127] Art. 12(2) a) GETA.
[128] Examples of Good Practices. Specialised Bodies: Equal Treatment Commission. The Netherlands. Retrieved from http://www.coe.int/t/e/human_rights/ecri/1-ecri/3-general_themes/2-examples_of_good_practices/1-Specialised_Bodies/SB_Netherlands.asp#TopOfPage.
[129] See inter alia Opinions 2005-167 and 2007-156 ETC.

the interest organisations cannot be always given legal standing under this particular provision of the GETA. This might be the reason why individual victims are mostly represented by an employee of an interest organisation. One of the few cases, in which an interest organisation also engaged in its own name in addition to the individual victim, concerned an alleged discrimination on the grounds of racial origin and religion with respect to the membership requirements of a sport school, therefore a measure that disparately affects more persons.[130] As in the Murat case in Belgium, the individual victim as applicant I asked the Commission to examine whether discrimination has been committed against her when she applied for a membership. The complaint of the organisation as applicant II was related to the general membership policy of the respondent. The complaints were examined separately by the Commission. Also, the complainant has no legal representative in this case. Nevertheless, as explained with respect to the Belgian approach, this regulation cannot entirely be considered to comply with the requirements of the RED.

5.8.2. Class Action

The possibility of initiating class action procedures is not explicitly regulated in the equal treatment legislations of the countries under review. Importantly, however, some general procedural rules do allow joint cases.[131] As yet no class action procedure has been initiated in any of the countries for the enforcement of the principle of equal treatment.

The need for class action procedures can be identified for instance in the case law of the Dutch ETC, though the number of those cases in which it would have been useful is admittedly not very high. At present the Commission elaborates on the same complaints initiated by different applicants in separate opinions.[132]

5.8.3. Actio Popularis

Although, as argued supra, Article 7(2) RED does not stipulate an obligation to have or to create actio popularis litigation in its classical meaning (thus without the need of identified victim acting as complainant), still all the countries under review provide for the possibility of initiating such actions – arguably mainly because most of them seemed to interpret the RED as

[130] Opinion 2008-12 ETC.

[131] Art. 30 of the Belgian Civil Procedure Code; Art. 207 of the Estonian Civil Procedure Code; Arts. 51-53 of the Hungarian Civil Procedure Code; Art. 29 (6) of the Hungarian Administrative Procedure Act; Art. 217 of the Dutch Civil Procedure Code.

[132] See for instance Opinions 2001-73, 2001-74, 2001-75, 2001-76, 2001-77, 2001-78 ETC.

imposing such an obligation.[133] Nevertheless, the particular regulations vary to some extent, and there are also some uncertainties regarding the application of these rules.

Despite the fact that the case law seems to be clear in this respect, arguments have nevertheless been advanced regarding the lack of actio popularis claims in the Belgian legislation as Article 33 ARA requires the consent of the identified victim. Arguably, however, as also explained in the Explanatory Memorandum, the consent of the victim is required only when he can be identified. "A contrario, no consent is required when it concerns several unidentified persons."[134] Moreover, contrary to the RED, the ARA talks of the consent of the *victim* and not of the *complainant*. Accordingly, it might be accepted that Articles 18, 31 and 32 ARA provide for the possibility of starting actio popularis claims. Thus, interest organisations can also engage in the procedures when there is no identified victim.[135] The importance of the right to actio popularis has also been emphasised in the academic literature.[136] Moreover, according to the Arbitration Court this possibility can be justified by the special character of the dispute in which the organisations can initiate a procedure, and by the experience of these organisations in this field of law.[137] These provisions can be divided into two main possibilities: launching summary-like procedures and other procedures. The former can be initiated by the CEOOR, interest organisations, the public prosecutor and the labour inspectorate (depending on the type of alleged violation at stake).[138] All other procedures can be initiated by the CEOOR and interest organisations.

For instance, in the famed *Feryn* case the legal standing of the CEOOR was not contested despite the lack of specific identified victims; the case was dismissed on conceptual grounds.[139] In another employment case, it was again

[133] This observation is based on the fact that actio popularis claims were introduced in Belgium, Estonia and Hungary during the implementation of the RED (and FD).

[134] Wetsontwerp tot wijziging … 2720/009, *supra* note 95, at 34 & 47. See also Closset-Marchal & Van Drooghenbroeck (2008), at 389.

[135] Similar provisions were stipulated in the ADA.

[136] Cuypers (2003), at 463.

[137] Arbitration Court, 157/2004, 6 October 2004.

[138] Giving legal standing to the public prosecutor and the labour inspectorate was considered to be an important innovation in anti-discrimination law. The Explanatory Memorandum of the ARA explains that giving such procedural rights to the public prosecutor and the labour inspectorate has symbolic value and implements the idea in practice that society as such (represented by the public prosecutor) has an interest in combating discrimination. Wetsontwerp tot wijziging … 2720/001, *supra* note 95, at 36. See inter alia Closset-Marchal & Van Drooghenbroeck (2008), at 396-397.

[139] President of the Brussels Labour Court, 26 June 2006. It is important to emphasise that the case was dismissed on other grounds than the question of legal standing, since the arguments of the intervening countries in the *Feryn* case before the ECJ were actually based on the lack of a possibility for actio popularis claims in the RED. "By order of 26 June 2006, the president of the Brussels Labour Court […] dismissed Centrum voor gelijkheid van kansen en voor

the CEOOR that launched an actio popularis claim, and its legal standing was accepted without any hesitation.[140]

Although in most of the cases the CEOOR launches procedures, examples can also be found in which other interest organisations initiate proceedings without specific identifiable victims. For instance, a consumer association started a procedure against an insurance company that allegedly discriminated on the ground of age.[141]

As mentioned in the context of individual litigation there are also cases in which the interest organisation engages in the procedure in the form of an actio popularis claim with the consent of the individual complainant.

In Estonia the general view is that the Estonian legislator has not created the possibility of actio popularis suits.[142] It is definitely true that in general civil and administrative law procedures interest organisations are not authorised to submit actio popularis claims. However, this is clearly possible in the procedure of the Gender Equality and Equal Treatment Commissioner, and submitting actio popularis claims might also be allowed before the Legal Chancellor. Pursuant to Article 17 EETA

> [t]he commissioner gives an opinion on the occurrence of discrimination to the person submitting the application and upon necessity to a person who has legitimate interest to monitor the compliance with the requirements of equal treatment.

As far as the procedures Legal Chancellor are concerned, again, a distinction should be made between his ombudsman and conciliation procedures. With regard to the former the Act on the Legal Chancellor lays down that the claim needs to concern the protection of the rights of the applicant. It can be argued that an interest body could claim that its rights have been violated by a discriminatory treatment against a group of persons, since the protection of them is one of the aims of the interest body. However, it is yet to be seen whether this interpretation will be taken up.

Concerning conciliation procedures the same Act uses a different formulation pertaining to the legal standing of the applicant. The provision concerned requires that the particular person be discriminated against. Thus, it in fact refers to natural persons, which is also understandable in the light of the aim of conciliation procedures.[143]

---

racismebestrijding's application, stating, in particular, that there was no proof nor was there a presumption that a person had applied for a job and had not been employed as a result of his ethnic origin." *Case C-54/07, Centrum voor gelijkheid van kansen en racismebestrijding v. Firma Feryn NV.*, para. 17.

[140] And this is even more remarkable due to the fact that the testers carrying out the situation testing could have been regarded as individual victims. Mechelen Labour Court, summary-like proceedings, 16 March 2006.

[141] Président du Tribunal Du Commerce De Bruxelles, 7 March 2005.

[142] Poleshchuk (2007), at 55.

[143] Compare with Article 9(2) of the Constitution.

While in Estonia and Belgium the question is whether particular provisions related to legal standing can be interpreted as a possibility for actio popularis claims, in Hungary the relevant provision of the HETA is entirely clear in this respect. During the implementation of the RED (and FD) Hungary has explicitly and consciously chosen for the introduction of actio popularis claims.[144] As already hinted at supra, pursuant to Article 20 HETA, a lawsuit can be initiated before courts by the public prosecutor,[145] the Authority or any social and interest representation organisation, if the principle of equal treatment is violated or there is a direct danger thereof, provided that the alleged violation was based on a characteristic that is an essential feature of the individual, and the infringement affects a larger group of persons the size of which cannot be precisely determined.

It has been explained that actio popularis claims will be effective and useful when the legitimacy of quasi norm provisions, segregation or discriminatory advertisements are at stake.[146] Pertaining to this observation it has been doubted whether the possibility of actio popularis procedures "would significantly contribute to increase the volume of court procedures, as the circle of the described disputes is rather limited."[147] However, as explained in the theoretical framework, without actio popularis claims only individuals could enforce their individual right and the discrimination against the group would remain unaddressed and unremedied.[148] Also, even though the number of actio popularis claims is lower than that of individual claims as they settle an entire practice, thus covering more individuals, with very broad ranging implications, the volume of the case itself would be significantly larger.

With the amendment of the HETA actio popularis claims were extended to the procedure before the Authority.[149] Thus, as of 1 January 2007 interest organisations can also start procedures before the AET, even if there is a lack of identified victims. The very first actio popularis claim before the Authority was submitted by an organisation that aims to help and assist homeless

144 See also Farkas, Kádár & Kárpáti (2006), at 97; Kollonay-Lehoczky (2005), at 488.

145 Giving legal standing to the public prosecutor can be ustified by the public interest that is at stake in such case. See Farkas, Kádár & Kárpáti (2006), at 95.

Before the changing of the regime the public prosecutor had an unlimited right to initiate lawsuits in civil procedures. This situation was changed by a Constitutional Court judgment in 1994 which declared this unlimited right of the prosecutor unconstitutional. For these historical and constitutional reasons legislators are very moderate when it comes to the legal standing of the public prosecutor in civil law cases. See Constitutional Court, 1/1994, 7 January 1994.

146 See Kárpáti (2005), at 106; Gyulavári (2007), at 55; Bitskey & Gyulavári (2004); Farkas, Kádár & Kárpáti (2006), at 99.

147 Bitskey & Gyulavári (2004).

148 This is the case even in the light of the opening of the concept of indirect discrimination towards the group perspective, since generally the group will not be remedied when it is merely an individual who has filed the lawsuit.

149 See also Kádár (2007), at 65; Kárpáti (2006), at 5; Gyulavári (2007), at 55; Kaltenbach et al. (2007), at 74-75.

persons.[150] The legal standing of the interest organisation was accepted in this case without any discussion as to whether the protected ground (in this case it was considered to fall under 'other grounds') is a personal characteristic. This is even more striking in view of the Miskolc segregation case in which the actio popularis claim on the ground of disadvantageous social situation was refused by the court because this ground could not be considered as an essential feature of a person's personality.[151] The Miskolc case thus clearly shows the danger the criteria set up for action popularis claims entail.

In the very first actio popularis case, the Károli case,[152] the court also explicitly elaborated on the question whether the particular ground at stake could be regarded as an inherent characteristic. In this case the admissions policy of a university providing a religious studies course was challenged as being discriminatory against homosexuals.[153] The applicant was an interest organisation protecting the rights of homosexuals, and after a short discussion on whether homosexuality can be regarded as an inherent characteristic, their legal standing was accepted.

An actio popularis claim was also filed in another segregation case, the Hajdúhadház case.[154] Here, as in the Miskolc case, an interest organisation protecting the rights of Roma children filed the lawsuit against the schools and their maintainers that allegedly segregated Roma children. The applicant has supported its allegations with accurate statistical data made based on social surveys conducted by experts, and no victim was individually named. The claim was oriented at showing the discriminatory practice. However, a couple of parents of the Roma children affected by the segregation demanded the NGO discontinue the action. Their declaration might arguably be interpreted as the lack or withdrawal of their consent to start the procedure. Nevertheless, the court explained that this declaration was irrelevant to the legal standing of the applicant because the number and the specific members of this group could not be exactly defined. Furthermore, both the number and the members of the group changed every school year, also making it impossible to individually identify those who were and would be affected. Arguably, what the courts seemed to say is that the procedure does not aim to examine whether particular individuals have been discriminated against. For this reason there is no need

[150] EBH/513/2007. See also EBH/732/2008.

[151] Borsod-Abaúj-Zemplén County Court, 13.P.21.660/2005/16, 2 November 2005. See also the judgment of the court of appeal Debrecen Court of Appeal, Pf.I.20.683/2005/7, 9 June 2006.

[152] Metropolitan Court, 19.P.21.788/2004/10, 8 October 2004; Supreme Court PFv. IV.20.687/2005/5, 8 June 2005.

[153] On the Károli case see Kárpáti (2005).

[154] Hajdú-Bihar County Court, 6.P. 20.341/2006/50, 2 May 2007; Debrecen Court of Appeal, Pf.I.20.361/2007/8, 13 December 2007; Supreme Court, Pfv.IV.20.936/2008/4, 19 November 2008.

for the consent of the victims. This position is quite convincing and to be welcomed also in the light of the fact that the individual victims can still initiate separate actions.

In the Netherlands, as indicated supra, the GETA referring to the Civil Code and the General Administrative Act regulates the possibility of launching actio popularis[155] claims.[156] Within this framework the Equal Treatment Commission is also given the competence to launch actio popularis claims before courts, however, as yet, it has not made use of this possibility.[157] Like most of the provisions of the GETA, the introduction of actio popularis procedures was not influenced by the RED, since it had already been in force before the adoption of the Directive. Filing actio popularis claims before the Commission is possible on the basis of Article 12(2) e) GETA.[158] An actio popularis claim was argued to be "an important vehicle to combat structural forms of discrimination."[159] In this respect, local anti-discrimination bureaus were considered to be "an important channel for bringing racial discrimination cases" before the Commission.[160] In addition to anti-discrimination bureaus trade unions and other employee's associations[161] may also file petitions to the Commission, but their petitions must concern equal treatment within their own company or organisation.[162]

Two complaints of racial discrimination were filed as actio popularis claims before the ETC in 2006, and four in 2007.[163] Examples of actio popularis claims (not only on the ground of racial or ethnic origin) can be found in all fields falling under the material scope of the Act; for example in the fields of housing,[164] goods and services,[165] employment,[166] and education.[167] All

155 On actio popularis claims in the Netherlands in general see Jongbloed (2002); Rodrigues (2002).

156 Art. 12(2) d) & e) GETA, Art. 3:305a Civil Code, and Arts. 1:2 General Administrative Act.

157 See also Holtmaat (2007), at 65. For a detailed elaboration on the competences and mandates of the Equal Treatment Commission see Chapter 8 on national specialised bodies.

158 See also Examples of Good Practices. Specialised Bodies: Equal Treatment Commission. The Netherlands. Retrieved from http://www.coe.int/t/e/human_rights/ecri/1-ecri/3-general_themes/2-examples_of_good_practices/1-Specialised_Bodies/SB_Netherlands.asp#TopOfPage.

159 Dierx & Rodrigues (2003). See also Rodrigues (2004), at 32.

160 Zwamborn (2002), at 10.

161 The special accent of the GETA on the protection of those who are more vulnerable and are at a lower level in the hierarchical relationship can be clearly seen here, since it is only the associations of employees that are armed with the possibility of starting actio popularis claims. For a detailed discussion on this aspect, see Busstra (2010).

162 Art. 12(2) d) GETA. See also Examples of Good Practices, *supra* note 158.

163 Rodrigues & Van Walsum (2008), at 41. See also Holtmaat (2007), at 10.

164 See for instance Opinion 2003-65 ETC. Compare with Opinion 2002-159 ETC in which individual complaints were submitted in the field of housing.

165 See for instance Opinions 2002-68, 2008-102 ETC.

166 See for instance Opinion 2002-22 ETC.

167 See for instance Opinion 2005-25 ETC.

of these cases concerned measures that had a disadvantageous impact on a certain group of persons without individually identifiable victims, which could therefore be categorised as structural discrimination. For instance, in one of the cases the interest organisation complained of the policy of a meeting club according to which only persons with a reasonable level of the Dutch language were allowed to visit the club. As mentioned supra, the ETC is consistent in its approach that general interest litigation can only be given to organisations, and not to individuals.[168]

The complication concerning the consent of an individualised victim has also come up in the Netherlands. In one of the actio popularis claims the Commission did not examine whether the individually identified victims has given their consent to the procedure.[169] In its complaint the interest organisation referred to the specific events that occurred regarding these victims. This approach was highly criticised.[170] Contrary to the Hungarian segregation case, some victims were individually identified and named, and the disadvantage they suffered was used as evidence. Accordingly, their consent should have been obtained.

As indicated supra and similarly to the situation in Belgium, in the jurisprudence it is also possible to find cases, where in addition to individual complainant an interest organisation has also engaged in the procedure in the form of an actio popularis claim concerning the group interest. This was the case, for instance, when a homosexual couple challenged the rules concerning dance competitions, in which only a couple of the opposite sex could participate.[171] Two interest organisations were also joined to the complaint and their claim was also regarded admissible after an examination of whether the requirements of the Civil Code[172] were fulfilled.

5.9. Conclusions

The forms of legal standing restrict the capacity of victims to commence legal proceedings. As discrimination can take various shapes, and thus persons belonging to a racial or ethnic group can become victims of discrimination in different ways, it is essential that the forms of locus standi take these differences into account. Accordingly, effective enforcement of the right to equal treatment can be ensured when the form of locus standi adjusts to the forms of victim status. Such an approach focuses on achieving substantive equality, the first pillar of an adequate system of minority protection.

168 See for instance Opinion 2001-21 ETC, para. 4.3.
169 Opinion 2007-157 ETC.
170 The approach of the ETC was criticised. Rodrigues & Van Walsum (2008), at 35-36.
171 The Hague District Court, LJN: AY5005, 26 July 2006.
172 Art. 3:305a(1) & (2) Civil Code.

Two main forms of legal standing can be distinguished, with the help of which all possible forms of discrimination could be vindicated: individual and collective litigation. The latter can be further divided into class action and actio popularis procedures. While individual litigation is crucial in most cases of direct discrimination, actio popularis claims are indispensable in cases of indirect and systemic discrimination. Regrettably, however, the RED focuses on individual litigation. For this reason, the enforcement of the right to equal treatment becomes less effective. Nevertheless, the RED expands the boundaries of individual litigation to some extent when it requires the Member States to allow the engagement of interest organisations in the enforcement procedures either on behalf of or in support of the victim, with his consent.

Although the RED does not impose the obligation to introduce legal standing without individually identified victims, each country has already introduced actio popularis litigation in addition to individual legal standing. This approach clearly and markedly contributes to the more effective enforcement of the right to non-discrimination, by taking the group aspect of the complaint into account. Of the countries studied, the Hungarian regulation is outstanding, as the relevant provision explicitly aims to enforce structural forms of discrimination when individual litigation would not suffice. This form of litigation has already been applied in cases of segregation, indirect and systemic discrimination where it proved to be essential, as otherwise no enforcement responses could have been given to these violations. By contrast, in Belgium the legal provision does not make it entirely clear whether in addition to allowing for the engagement of interest organisations in individual claims it also includes actio popularis suits without the presence of an individual victim. However, it seems that the position will be taken that procedures initiated by interest organisations alone will also be permitted. In Estonia these actions are only permitted before the two national specialised bodies. As neither of these bodies can issue binding decisions the effective enforcement of the right to equal treatment is not entirely guaranteed. Finally, in the Netherlands actio popularis claims are generally allowed before courts on the basis of the Civil Code, and the Equal Treatment Act also allows the initiation of such procedures before the ETC. Similarly to Hungary, it was in structural discrimination cases that actio popularis complaints were submitted to the ETC.

Interestingly, the concrete requirements of the RED, namely that Member States should allow interest organisations to engage in procedures *on behalf of the victims*, have been interpreted differently by the countries under review. While in Estonia and Hungary these organisations can act as representatives of the victims in individual litigation, in Belgium and the Netherlands the situation is different. In Belgium the legal provision does not make it entirely clear whether the interest organisation can act as a representative of an individual victim when the claim is not concerned with discrimination against a group. Until now, interest organisations have only been involved in cases with a group dimension, and their claim can actually be regarded as an actio popularis claim in addition to individual discrimination. Somewhat differently, in the Netherlands, in a case concerning discrimination against an individual, it is generally an employee of an interest organisation that acts as a representative of the victim, but not the organisation itself. Arguably, the purpose of the RED was in fact to prevent or put an end to a practice which forces organisations to find ways to get involved in the procedure for giving assistance to the victim. Accordingly, the legal rules in these two latter countries do not entirely comply with the requirements of the RED.

Concerning the involvement of interest organisations the RED gives some leeway to the Member States to define which organisations can be given locus standi. The Member States can assess this by setting up requirements in terms of the legitimate interest of these organs. In this respect the most restrictive approach is followed by Belgium, where several requirements are set for these bodies. The other countries are generally satisfied by merely defining the legitimate aim of these organisations.

The case studies demonstrate the importance of and need for the existence of different forms of legal standing and the engagement of interest organisations in the procedures for an effective enforcement of the right to equal treatment. A special form of legal standing, actio popularis claims, would particularly contribute to enhancing minority protection by taking into account the fact that certain forms of discrimination inherently include a group aspect.

Chapter 6

Victimisation

Part A. Theoretical Framework

6.1. Introduction

The definition of victimisation in Article 9 RED defines victimisation as adverse treatment or an adverse consequence on a person because of his involvement in a complaint or procedure that aims to enforce the right to equal treatment on the grounds of racial or ethnic origin.

Prior to Article 9 RED EU law did not know such a general prohibition of victimisation. The ETD did have a rule on victimisation but only concerning the prohibition of dismissal as a reaction to a complaint or procedure in the employment sphere.[1] It was the ECJ that first extended the protection from dismissal to other harms suffered as a reaction to a complaint or procedure in its *Coote* case.[2] It is supposedly this case that formed the basis for the text of Article 9 RED, which therefore differs in this respect from the respective provision in the ETD.

The general aim of this provision is to encourage those who have been victims of discrimination to enforce their rights to equal treatment, since 'victims may be deterred from exercising their right due to the risk of retaliation.'[3] In other words, it is directed at making the enforcement of the right to equal treatment more effective.

---

1 Art. 7 ETD stipulated that "Member States shall take the necessary measures to protect employees against dismissal by the employer as a reaction to a complaint within the undertaking or to any legal proceedings aimed at enforcing compliance with the principle of equal treatment."

2 On a different aspect of the *Coote* case see below and Ch. 4 on the access to justice. Judgment of 22 September 1998 in *Case C-185/97*, *Coote v. Granada Hospitality Ltd*, [1998] ECR I-5199.

3 Proposal for a Council Directive implementing the principle of equal treatment between

After examining the possible readings of the prohibition of victimisation, the constitutive elements of this concept will be mapped and examined. This will be followed by an analysis of the enforcement of the protection against victimisation.

The article concerned stipulates the following:

> Article 9 Victimisation
>
> Member States shall introduce into their national legal systems such measures as are necessary to protect individuals from any adverse treatment or adverse consequence as a reaction to a complaint or to proceedings aimed at enforcing compliance with the principle of equal treatment.

6.2. Possible Interpretations of the Concept of Victimisation

Although Article 9 RED is situated among the enforcement provisions the concept of victimisation is not only concerned with the enforcement of the so-called substantive provisions of the RED, it can be argued that it also has its own substantive meaning that needs to be enforced. Hereafter these two meanings of the concept of victimisation will be analysed.

6.2.1. Victimisation in its Procedural Meaning

The provision on victimisation originates from the aim to provide for effective judicial protection, as the European Court of Justice laid down in its *Coote* case.[4] In this case the Court stated that

> [t]he *principle of effective judicial control* laid down in Article 6 of the Directive would be deprived of an essential part of its effectiveness if the protection which it provides did not cover measures which, as in the main proceedings in this case, an employer might take as a reaction to legal proceedings brought by an employee with the aim of enforcing compliance with the principle of equal treatment.[5]

In other words, the aim of this provision is to eliminate the fear of retaliation.[6] Accordingly, the prohibition of victimisation in its procedural sense means

persons irrespective of racial or ethnic origin, COM(1999) 566 final – 1999/0253 (CNS), 25 November 1999, Art. 9. Schiek, Waddington and Bell (2007) state that the "prohibition of victimisation is [...] crucial in protecting the integrity of anti-discrimination laws." at 603.

4 *Case C-185/97*, *Coote v. Granada Hospitality Ltd.* On the *Coote* case in the context of victimisation see Connolly (2007), at 368. & 372; Parmar (2004), at 151; Waddington (2003), at 43; Connolly (2002), at 170; Dougan (1999), at 665.

5 *Case C-185/97*, *Coote v. Granada Hospitality Ltd*, para. 24 (emphasis added).

6 See again *id.*, para. 24; "*Fear of such measures* [...] might deter workers who consider themselves the victims of discrimination from pursuing their claims by judicial process, and

that this provision contributes to or guarantees the effective enforcement of the principle of equal treatment because it encourages victims to turn to fact-finding bodies.[7]

6.2.2. Victimisation in its Substantive Meaning

Obviously, the prohibition of victimisation can have its desired deterrent effect in its procedural meaning only if it can be enforced, namely if it is given a substantive meaning. The objective of the concept in its substantive meaning is to provide redress when someone has been victimized. The ECJ itself referred to this aspect in the *Coote* case,[8] albeit implicitly, when stated that

> [f]ear of such [retaliatory] measures, *where no legal remedy is available against them*, might deter workers who considered themselves the victims of discrimination from pursuing their claims by judicial process, and would consequently be liable seriously to jeopardize implementation of the aim pursued by the Directive.[9]

Similarly, both the European Parliament's proposal for amendments (Draft Legislative Resolution)[10] and the ECRI Model Legislation[11] emphasised the need for redress in the case of victimisation. The UN Model National Legislation Against Racial Discrimination makes victimisation a downright offence.[12] All in all, the substantive aspect of the victimisation provision has been implicitly highlighted by different bodies.

---

would consequently be liable seriously to jeopardise implementation of the aim pursued by the Directive" (emphasis added).

7 See also Tyson (2004), at 126; Barry (2003), at 417.

8 See also Dougan (1999), at 665. In relation to the *Coote* case he observed that the Court examined "the substantive issue of the scope of protection against victimisation guaranteed by the ETD."

9 *Case C-185/97, Coote v. Granada Hospitality Ltd*, para. 24 (emphasis added).

10 "However, a system of penalties is needed to back up such measures. If these penalties are a sufficient deterrent, this will no doubt contribute to the effective protection which should be afforded to victims." Report on the proposal for a Council directive on implementing the principle of equal treatment between persons irrespective of racial or ethnic origin, COM(1999) 566 – C5-0067/2000 – 1999/0253(CNS), A5-0136/2000, 16 May 2000, at 38.

11 ECRI Model Legislation, para. 57. "In order to be effective, the legal provisions protecting against retaliation should provide for an appropriate and clear sanction. This might include the possibility of an injunction order to stop the retaliatory acts and/or to compensate victims of such acts."

12 Model National Legislation for the Guidance of Governments in the Enactment of Further Legislation Against Racial Discrimination, Third Decade to Combat Racism and Racial Discrimination (1993-2003), para. 44. "It is an offence to threaten a victim or alleged victim of racial discrimination or in any way to obstruct his or her efforts to obtain redress through proceedings brought under this Act in accordance with recourse procedures in force."

6.2.3. Victimisation as a Special Form of Discrimination

Admittedly, Article 9 RED does not define victimisation as a special form of discrimination.[13] Still, it seems that conceptually the substantive meaning of victimisation constitutes a special form of discrimination, which approach would also be desirable from a practical perspective. To be specific, it would be ensured that the special rules on the allocation of the burden of proof also apply to the concept of victimisation.

According to Article 9 RED victimisation occurs when one is (has been or would be) treated adversely or has suffered (suffers or would suffer) an adverse consequence because of a complaint or procedure concerning the violation of the prohibition of discrimination on the grounds of racial or ethnic origin. This formulation clearly resembles the concept of discrimination: it can be seen that the applicant suffers harm (adverse treatment or consequence) on the ground of carrying out an act (complaint or procedure) which enjoys protection under the RED.[14] With respect to this provision the legislative proposal of the EP referred back to the articles on the concepts of discrimination when it gave its justification for the proposed amendment concerning the personal scope of the victimisation provision.[15] This indicates that, in the view of the EP, the concept of victimisation is at least comparable to that of discrimination. This position seems to recur in the EP's resolution on the RED in which it suggests the application of the special allocation of the burden of proof in victimisation cases as well.[16] In other words, the EP clearly uses discrimination arguments in relation to the concept of victimisation. Also, the ECJ seemed to regard victimisation as a possible way of violating the principle of equal treatment. In the already-mentioned *Coote* case[17] the Court applied an enforcement requirement of the ETD that was related to the principle of equal treatment without further hesitation to the victimisation claim.

---

[13] No such reference can be found in the Explanatory Memorandum either.

[14] See also Connolly (2009), at 153-154. & 172-175.

[15] The EP proposed the following amendment to the victimisation provision: "to protect both natural and legal persons and non-formalised groups of persons". This proposal was explained as follows: "[i]t is also necessary to protect groups of persons, for example, those having a particular ethnic origin, from discrimination." Report on the proposal for a Council directive on implementing the principle of equal treatment between persons irrespective of racial or ethnic origin, COM(1999) 566 – C5-0067/2000 – 1999/0253(CNS), A5-0136/2000, 16 May 2000, at 6. & 24.

[16] European Parliament resolution of 27 September 2007 on the application of Council directive 2000/43/EC of 29 June 2000 implementing the principle of equal treatment between persons irrespective of racial or ethnic origin, 2007/2094(INI), H. On the allocation of the burden of proof in cases of victimisation see below.

[17] "As the Court also held, Article 6 of the Directive is an essential factor for attaining the fundamental objective of equal treatment [...], which, as the Court has repeatedly held is one of the fundamental human rights whose observance the Court has a duty to ensure." *Case C-185/97, Coote v. Granada Hospitality Ltd*, para. 23.

In fact, the idea that victimisation can or should be considered a form of discrimination is not new: a couple of examples can be found in different national measures where victimisation is explicitly defined as discrimination. For instance, in the United States not only is victimisation considered to be discrimination, such claims also form a large part of equal treatment cases in labour law: in 2004 around 20 000 retaliation cases were filed with the Equal Opportunity Commission.[18]

The provision on victimisation features a conduct that needs to be protected; that is treating someone adversely on the basis of this conduct is prohibited. For this reason this conduct can be called the protected act. Comparing the concept of victimisation with that of direct discrimination it can be seen that in the latter case fact-finders look for a causal link between the protected ground and the harm, while in victimisation cases this link should be established between the protected act and the suffered harm.[19] Thus, in victimisation cases the protected ground in the original complaint plays a role only in an indirect way: it is the *protected act* that is and needs to be related to the protected ground. Still, the logic of the concept of victimisation can clearly be compared with that of direct discrimination: a clear and direct *causal link* has to be found.[20] This similarity seems to be implicitly acknowledged by the RED which extended an argument used by the ECJ concerning victimisation to the concept of discrimination. More specifically, the ECJ explained in the *Coote* case that persons enjoy protection from victimisation even after the relationship giving rise to discrimination has ended, which provision has been made applicable in the RED to discrimination.[21]

Finally, reading victimisation as a form of discrimination is also desirable from a conceptual and practical point of view because it would ensure the applicability of the special rules concerning the allocation of the burden of proof. Similarly to discrimination cases victims of victimisation do not have easy access to evidence either, which was the underlying reason for elaborating special burden of proof arrangements in discrimination cases. Should the special allocation of the burden of proof not be applicable to victimisation cases, the applicant would in many instances be unable to prove the causal link between the protected act and the suffered harm due to the lack of accessible

18 Greenhouse (2006).

19 See also Connolly (2009).

20 Although the concept of victimisation is somewhat different in the United Kingdom (in the Race Relations Act 1976, in Section 2 victimisation is classified as 'discrimination by way of discrimination'), in this context it is still worth citing Lord Nicholls' words in the *Shammoon v. Chief Constable of the RUC* case, in which he argued that "[p]ersons who exercise their statutory rights are not to be penalised for doing so. Employers and others who *retaliate* in this way are *guilty of discrimination*. The *victimisation provisions adopt substantially the same structure as the direct discrimination provisions*." *Shammoon v. Chief Constable of the RUC*, IRLR 285 (HL 2003), para. 5 (emphasis added).

21 *Case C-185/97, Coote v. Granada Hospitality Ltd*, para. 28.

evidence. In this way the enforcement of the right not to be victimised would be made virtually impossible or excessively difficult, impairing the right to effective enforcement. Hence, following the special rules the applicant should 'merely' establish the presumption of victimisation, and the respondent can prove that no victimisation has taken place.

If it is accepted that victimisation in fact constitutes a special form of discrimination three questions need to be further addressed: (1) what is meant by harm, (2) what are the protected ground and act, and (3) whether justification exists for such a conduct.

6.2.3.1. Adverse Treatment or Adverse Consequence

In the original Equal Treatment Directive the only adverse treatment that enjoyed protection as a reaction to a complaint was dismissal. However, the Court in the *Coote* case looked at the aim of the regulation and broadened the protection on the basis of Article 6 ETD.[22] In the Court's view the respondent 'victimised' the applicant when he had refused "to provide references as a reaction to legal proceedings brought to enforce compliance with the principle of equal treatment within the meaning of the Directive."[23]

Article 9 RED now explicitly establishes protection against any adverse treatment or consequence. It means that any harm which can be related to the complaint or procedure can be regarded as victimisation.[24] Article 9 RED does not specify further the concrete forms adverse treatment and consequence can take. Thus, it can be argued that in accordance with the principle of effective enforcement these terms should be interpreted broadly. In principle, two main forms of adverse treatment/consequence can be distinguished. On the one hand, victimisation can be manifested in, for example, dismissal, change in shift, change in place of work, demotion, not providing a reference, less bonus, and so on. Thus, the harm is to some extent tangible. Contrary to this, the adverse treatment might also take the shape of offending remarks, e-mails, behaviour, and so on, which can be regarded as a less tangible form of harm, similarly to the concept of harassment.[25]

Unlike in the concept of direct discrimination, the wording 'adverse treatment or adverse consequence' in the concept of victimisation does not indicate that the treatment or the consequence should be less favourable than the treatment of or the consequence on someone else. However, the fact, that adverse treatment and consequence are related to a complaint or procedure, makes it clear that those persons having submitted or supported a complaint

[22] See also Waddington (2003), at 43.

[23] *Case C-185/97, Coote v. Granada Hospitality Ltd*, para. 28.

[24] See also Koukoulis-Spilitopoulos (2005), at 364.

[25] For instance in the case of *IRC v. Morgan* in Great-Britain, it was the circulation of a memo which was considered as a harm. *Commissioners of Inland Revenue and others v. Morgan*, IRLR 776 (EAT 2002). See also Monaghan (2007), at 440.

are treated differently from those who have not conducted such an act; that is they are in fact treated less favourably or are exposed to less favourable consequences.[26]

6.2.3.2. Protected Ground and Protected Act

As explained above, in victimisation cases the causal link should be established between the protected act and the harm, and the protected ground comes into the picture in an indirect way through the protected act. It is in fact the protected act that is related to the protected ground and the protected ground is thus indirectly linked to that harm. This would indicate that in fact no special attention should be devoted to the protected ground in the examination of the complaint. However, weighty arguments can be brought up in favour of explicitly identifying the concrete ground.

The question of protected ground is relevant for at least two reasons. First of all, it is important in terms of classifying this conduct in national legislations and adjudications. If a Member State adopted an anti-discrimination legislation with open list of grounds, it might be up to the fact-finder whether he creates a separate ground for the concept of victimisation or brings it under the ground of racial or ethnic origin. However, if the legislation operates with a closed system of grounds, no such choice is available; thus, the question of protected ground becomes highly relevant. Moreover, it seems to be more consistent to bring this violation under the grounds of racial or ethnic origin, since the retaliation is in fact related to these grounds. This is because the prohibition of victimisation when someone has submitted a complaint of discrimination on grounds of racial or ethnic origin aims to protect persons with this ground or associated with that ground. Consequently, not acknowledging racial or ethnic origin as the protected ground in case of victimisation

> may undermine the achievement of the objectives of the EC Treaty, in particular the attainment of a high level of employment and of social protection, the raising of the standard of living and quality of life, economic and social cohesion and solidarity.[27]

In this respect it would also collide with the requirement of the RED that "any direct or indirect discrimination based on racial or ethnic origin as regards the areas covered by this Directive, should be prohibited throughout the Community."[28]

Secondly, the question of protected ground is relevant in terms of defining the level of scrutiny. It has generally been accepted that, as a point of departure, the explanation of the respondent in racial discrimination cases has to be strictly scrutinised. Not referring to this ground might create the danger

26 See also Connolly (2009), at 152-153.
27 Preamble (9) RED.
28 Preamble (13) RED.

of a less intense review. Thus, it is essential that the protected ground in the case of victimisation is also racial or ethnic origin. Arguably, no "adequate judicial protection against victimisation"[29] can be guaranteed if the complaint of victimisation is not appropriately scrutinised.

Concerning cases of victimisation it is also an important to examine what kind of complaints or proceedings can be accepted as underlying reasons (protected act) for a retaliation claim. This aspect raises at least three questions that need to be addressed.

First of all, it has to be examined whether the *intent* to file a complaint or start a procedure is also protected by the victimisation provision of the RED. This possibility is explicitly allowed in English law; however, there is no jurisprudence yet on its application. As already indicated supra, Article 9 lays down that any adverse treatment or consequence *as a reaction to a complaint or to proceedings* is forbidden. Although in the most typical case, for which this provision has arguably been drafted, the complaint has already been filed and the proceedings have already been started, there is nothing in this text that would narrow the claim to one that has already been filed. Accordingly, national legislations might not exclude the intent to file a claim of discrimination from the protection against victimisation.[30]

Secondly, and closely related to the first point, the meaning of the terms *'complaint'* and *'proceedings'* needs to be clarified. The choice of these terms has not been explained in the *travaux préparatoires*, thus, their ordinary meaning seems to be applicable. A complaint generally refers to the reasons for starting a procedure; it describes the cause of action. Proceedings mostly involve a sequence or course of actions, therefore conducting or instituting legal action. Neither the complaint nor the proceedings have to be judicial – the complaint might be submitted to and the proceedings might be initiated before an internal investigatory body of an employer as well as a judicial organ.

Finally, the question is also raised what the RED requires in respect of the occurrence of the adverse treatment and consequence. More concretely, whether the *danger* of the occurrence of such treatment and consequence (potential victimisation) would also be protected as in the case of indirect discrimination,[31] or whether the treatment and consequence must already have taken place at the time of filing a claim of victimisation. The provision on victimisation in the RED stipulates that Member States shall "*protect*

[29] Preamble (20) RED.

[30] Naturally, it is a different question how the link between the intent to file a complaint and the harm can be established.

[31] Compare with the definition of indirect discrimination in Art. 2(2) b) of the RED: "indirect discrimination shall be taken to occur where an apparently neutral provision, criterion or practice *would put* persons of a racial or ethnic origin at a particular disadvantage compared with other persons [...]" (emphasis added). See also Busstra (2010).

individuals from any adverse treatment or adverse consequence."[32] Arguably, the word 'protect' includes preventive action which indicates that the adverse treatment or consequence do not necessarily have to have occurred at the time when the claim of victimisation was filed. Accordingly, the danger of victimisation might suffice for complaining of victimisation, although there might be difficulties in proving it.

6.2.3.3. Justification

If victimisation is considered to be a form of discrimination, one could argue that the respondent can also come up with reasons that could justify treating someone adversely on the grounds of submitting a complaint.[33] Although conceptually the possibility is given to the respondent to justify his conduct, no such measures can possibly be envisaged that could be regarded proportionate in the light of the aim attained.

First of all, there are strong indications that no open justification is possible for victimisation. Similarly to Article 2(2) a) RED on direct discrimination and contrary to Article 2(2) b) RED on indirect discrimination, Article 9 RED itself does not allow for any justification. Like the concept of direct discrimination, the concept of victimisation also protects a phenomenon, which cannot be accepted as a legitimate aim for treating someone adversely. This means that the protected ground in direct discrimination cases and the protected act in victimisation cases can only under very exceptional circumstances operate as an acceptable underlying reason for a less favourable treatment.

Secondly, neither do the two possible justifications of (exceptions for) direct discrimination seem to be applicable to a victimisation complaint. These two exceptions are the genuine and determining occupational requirement[34] and positive action measures.[35] Theoretically, the genuine and determining occupational requirement cannot be applied at all, since this requirement is concerned with the protected ground, and not the protected act. As far as positive action measures are concerned no situation could reasonably be envisaged in which an adverse treatment based on a complaint of discrimination against a vulnerable group on the grounds of their racial or ethnic origin would be necessary in order to prevent or compensate for disadvantages linked to racial or ethnic origin. All in all, it can be concluded that the RED does not allow for any possible justification in victimisation cases.

32 Art. 9 RED (emphasis added).
33 Concerning the justification defence in victimisation cases see also Connelly (2009), at 173. & 175-176.
34 Art. 4 RED.
35 Art. 5 RED.

6.3. Enforcing Protection against Victimisation

The following four examples feature some significant enforcement-related aspects of the concept of victimisation. In the first example, an NGO starts a procedure enforcing the right to non-discrimination against a service-provider. This NGO has been mandated with a specific task by a company. The company, finding out that such a procedure is taking place, decides that it will not prolong the contract with the NGO, although they have already had discussions about their further co-operation. In the second case, an NGO files an actio popularis claim concerning segregation in education. As a reaction to this the school against which the procedure has been started adopts adverse measures against those children in the interest of whom the NGO had taken action. In the third example, a victim of discrimination files a complaint against one of his colleagues to the employer. A friend of this victim supports the applicant as witness in the internal investigation procedure. Soon this witness quits his job for a certain reason, and the employer refuses to provide him with a reference. Finally, a married couple works for the same employer. The wife is discriminated against and she launches a complaint of discrimination with a competent body. As a reaction to this complaint the husband, who did not participate as a witness in the discrimination complaint, is dismissed.

These examples raise several questions including the following: are legal persons protected against retaliatory measures, do the applicants have to be the same in the discrimination and the victimisation procedures, are witnesses covered by Article 9 RED, are relatives or those associated with the applicant protected from retaliation, against whom should this complaint be filed or the proceedings initiated, against whom can the victimisation claim be filed and is there protection after the relationship has ended? The following sub-sections will try to answer these questions addressing the personal and material scope of victimisation, the additional requirements for enforcing the protection against victimisation, and the allocation of the burden of proof in cases of victimisation.

6.3.1. Personal Scope of the Prohibition of Victimisation: Beneficiaries

6.3.1.1. Individuals

The present text of the RED stipulates that *individuals* should be protected from victimisation. Accordingly, legal or other non-natural persons are not included in this provision. This restriction generated some discussions during the adoption of the Directive. The Parliament wished to protect "both natural and legal persons and non-formalised groups of persons,"[36] and proposed to change the word 'individuals' to 'persons'.[37] Although the amended proposal of the Commission followed this proposal,[38] in the final version, as can be seen, only individuals are included. The reasons for this reversal were not reported. The fact that only individuals are protected can create a gap in the effective enforcement of the principle of equal treatment if one thinks of the first example above. Accordingly, even though the RED does not explicitly require this, protection against victimisation is necessary for non-natural persons too.

Article 9 RED also indicates that it aims to protect not only those, who themselves have submitted the underlying discrimination complaint, as they are not the only ones who may suffer retaliation. The definition of victimisation prohibits "any adverse treatment or adverse consequence *as a reaction to a complaint or to proceedings*."[39] Accordingly, when it can be proven that the adverse treatment or consequence is linked to the complaint, it does not matter that the original applicant was someone else.[40] Theoretically speaking, the protection against retaliation extends to the victims of victimisation by way of association via the protected ground of the applicant in the discrimination case.[41] The protection against retaliation should extend to them not only for the reason that it frustrates their right not to be victimised, but they should also be protected from the perspective of the victim of the underlying discrimination complaint. Persons should be protected against any adverse treatment through association since, as Maduro AG explained in the *Coleman* case concerning discrimination through association,

36 Report on the proposal for a Council directive on implementing the principle of equal treatment between persons irrespective of racial or ethnic origin, COM(1999) 566 – C5-0067/2000 – 1999/0253(CNS), A5-0136/2000, 16 May 2000, at 24. The justification given by the EP is somewhat strange because it refers back to the justification given in relation to Art. 2 RED, where a similar amendment was proposed. According to the explanation it is "necessary to protect groups of persons, for example, those having a particular ethnic origin, from discrimination." Arguably, this group aspect is not so relevant in victimisation cases because it is generally one individual who starts a procedure against the respondent.

37 *Id.*, at 24. The following justification was given by the Committee that originally proposed the amendment: "[t]he amendment seeks to ensure that relevant organisations as well as individuals may bring evidence to the independent body." *Id.*, at 83.

38 No justification can be found for this amendment, and more broadly, no documentation can be found concerning this last phase of the legislative process. Interestingly, according to Tyson who observed the negotiation of the RED, "[t]here was no controversy surrounding this provision in the Council, with the only amendment being made to some language versions to make clear that the protections apply not only to victims of discrimination but also to others who may support a complainant by acting as witnesses etc." Tyson (2004), at 126.

39 Art. 9 RED (emphasis added).

40 For this position see also Rombouts, Sardaro & Vandeginste (2006), at 360.

41 On discrimination by association see inter alia Busstra (2010); Waddington (2007).

> [o]ne way of undermining the dignity and autonomy of people who belong to a certain group is to target not them, but third persons who are closely associated with them and not themselves belong to the group.[42]

6.3.1.2. Victims and Those Assisting Them

In addition to broadening the scope of beneficiaries by way of association, Article 9 RED extends protection also to those who have assisted in the complaint or in the proceedings. According to the Explanatory Memorandum of the ECRI Model Legislation,

> [s]uch protection [against victimisation – M.A.] should not only be afforded to the person who initiates proceedings or brings the complaint, but should also be *extended to those who provide evidence, information or other assistance in connection with the court proceedings or the complaint.* Such protection is vital to encourage the victims of racist offences and discrimination to put forward their complaints to the authorities and to encourage witnesses to give evidence.[43]

Since Article 9 RED does not include any restriction in this respect, it seems that in addition to witnesses the protection against retaliation similarly extends to all persons who were somehow involved in the complaint by assisting the applicant.[44]

6.3.2. Personal Scope of the Prohibition of Victimisation: Addressees

As Article 9 RED is silent on the addressees of the concept of victimisation, it seems that all persons falling under the personal scope of the RED can commit victimisation; therefore they can have legal standing as respondents.[45] Generally, victimisation complaints or procedures are filed against a respondent against whom the underlying discrimination claim has also been submitted. However, cases might also occur in which the two respondents are not the same. In the UK this question was explicitly addressed, for instance, in the *Waters v. Commissioner of the Metropolis* case[46] in which a policewoman who had been sexually assaulted by a male colleague whilst off duty, complained that she was victimised at the workplace after having submitted a complaint of discrimination against this colleague. However, the EAT did not share her

---

42 Advocate General Maduro in *Case C-303/06, S. Coleman v. Attridge Law and Steve Law*, [2008] ECR I-05603, para. 12.

43 ECRI Model Legislation, para. 57 (emphasis added). It is remarkable that the proposed article does not seem to suggest such a broad interpretation.

44 See also Capacity Building of Civil Society dealing with Anti-Discrimination. A Training Manual. European Commission (2005), at 11-12; Koukoulis-Spiliotopoulos (2005), at 364; O'Hare (2001), at 150.

45 On the personal scope of the RED see Busstra (2010).

46 *Waters v. Commissioner of the Metropolis,* 1997 ICR 1073; 1997 IRLR 589 CA.

opinion, and considered that the treatment complained of cannot be regarded as a protected act, since the employer could not be held liable for the sexual assault which had not been committed during the course of employment. In other words, according to the EAT a complaint of victimisation can only be submitted against a respondent, who is different from the perpetrator of discrimination, if in one way or another he could be or could have been held liable for the underlying discrimination claim as well. This mainly occurs in employment relations where in the internal complaint the alleged perpetrator is a colleague of the victim, but the employer is in any event responsible for ensuring a discrimination-free environment.

Nevertheless, this position does not seem to be supported by the text of the RED. Article 9 RED merely stipulates that any adverse treatments or consequences made as a reaction to a complaint or procedure of discrimination are forbidden. Accordingly, no limitation is foreseen as to the respondent in the discrimination case. This might indicate that a discrimination procedure against, for example, a service provider might also be the reason for being victimised in the workplace. Admittedly, in such cases it is more difficult to prove a causal link between the protected act and the suffered harm, though the RED does not exclude this possibility.

In addition to this, situations can also be envisaged where it is the colleagues of the original applicant who start harassing him on the ground of his submitting a complaint. At national level, in such cases it is often the employer, and not the perpetrator himself who would be held vicariously liable, similarly to harassment cases. Again, the RED itself does not indicate that it is only the employer that could be held liable for victimisation in the workplace. On the contrary, Article 3(1) RED stipulates that "this Directive should apply to *all persons*".[47] Although it is not entirely clear what 'all persons' in this respect means,[48] it would be desirable if it were possible to launch a complaint or proceedings against the concrete victimiser.[49] To start a procedure against the perpetrator himself is also preferable in terms of appropriate remedies, since there may be no satisfaction if it is not the perpetrator himself who is held liable.[50] However, when national legislation does not allow direct liability, based on vicarious liability[51] the respondent (again, mainly the employer) has a justification ground; namely that he did his best to avoid such a situation or

[47] Art. 3(1) RED (emphasis added).

[48] In this respect see Busstra (2010).

[49] It does not take away the fact that under the national labour law an employer may not be held liable for not guaranteeing a working environment free from victimisation (similarly to harassment cases).

[50] See Ch. 7 on sanctions. The argument can however be made that in order to get appropriate monetary compensation the possibility of vicarious liability can be very important.

[51] On vicarious liability see also Busstra (2010).

to provide appropriate procedures and redress within the framework of the internal complaint procedure.[52] This would be the only justification ground in victimisation cases.

6.3.3. Material Scope of the Prohibition of Victimisation

Article 9 RED does not restrict the material scope of the RED in relation to victimisation. Thus, the prohibition of victimisation extends to all fields falling under the RED. Admittedly, protection against victimisation is mainly relevant in employment relations because this is where the relationship between the parties continues in one way or another following a complaint of alleged discrimination. However, it does not preclude that such protection might also prove to be necessary in other fields within the material scope of the RED.

In general, there is a need for protection against retaliation measures in hierarchical relationships. In other relationships the complainant is not in a dependant position, accordingly, the risk of being deterred from starting a procedure is either absent or very low. As mentioned, underling positions are generally to be found in employment relations. Nevertheless, another pronounced situation where the victim of discrimination might be in a hierarchical position is education. It could, moreover, also be envisaged that such a relationship is present in other fields falling within the scope of the RED, typically when the circle of providers is very narrow and there is a general need for the 'service' of this provider. For instance, a teacher might victimise a student or a company providing water could also retaliate against a customer who launches a discrimination procedure against them.

6.3.4. Some Additional Enforcement Related Issues

As the RED does not stipulate otherwise and the concept of victimisation is vested with substantive meaning, which, as argued, can be read as a form of discrimination, the enforcement provisions of the RED also seem to be applicable to victimisation cases.[53] More precisely, the mechanisms on access to justice, legal standing and remedies are to be applied in victimisation cases as well.[54] These rules do not seem to raise any special issues in terms of the concept of victimisation, with the exception of one particular issue concerning access to justice, that is the application of the requirement 'even after the relationship has ended' in Article 7(1) RED to victimisation cases. According

[52] See Ch. 2 on the model of review.

[53] For the applicability of the burden of proof see also above on victimisation as a special form of discrimination.

[54] See below on model of review in victimisation cases.

to Article 7(1) RED, access to justice should be available to all persons 'even after the relationship in which the discrimination is alleged to have occurred has ended.' This provision found its basis in the case law of the ECJ, more specifically in the *Coote* case, which has also served as the ground for extending the concept of victimisation. The ECJ argued that Member States are required

> to introduce into their national legal systems such measures as are necessary to ensure judicial protection for workers whose employer, after the employment relationship has ended, refuses to provide references as a reaction to legal proceedings brought to enforce compliance with the principle of equal treatment.[55]

Accordingly, in the *Coote* case the Court established that the prohibition of victimisation extends to situations when the retaliatory treatment takes place after the relationship has ended.[56]

In terms of victimisation, this requirement would mean that the protection against victimisation extends to situations where the relationship giving rise to discrimination has ended. Admittedly, however, in most cases it means that the underlying discrimination is committed during the relationship or the discrimination manifests itself in dismissal, and the victimisation happens after the relationship has been ended. Situations in which both discrimination and victimisation take place after the termination of the relationship are relatively rare.[57]

6.3.5. Model of Review Concerning Victimisation

As explained, Article 8 RED is not entirely clear as to which concepts of discrimination the special allocation of the burden of proof can be applied. It has been argued that in addition to direct and indirect discrimination it is also applicable to complaints of harassment and instruction to discriminate because they are also considered a special form of violating the principle of equal treatment. The question is relevantly raised whether this rule also applies to cases of victimisation. As briefly argued above, for the effective enforcement of the right to equal treatment it would be desirable if this was the case.

---

[55] *Case C-185/97*, *Coote v. Granada Hospitality Ltd*, para. 28.

[56] This judgment of the Court has led to extending the protection in similar situations to discrimination as well. Accordingly, persons enjoy protection against discrimination even after the relationship giving rise to *discrimination* has ended.

[57] One can imagine for instance a case in which a Roma person asks for a reference from his previous employer, but he refuses to provide it, which can be deemed to be discrimination on the grounds of his ethnic origin. The Roma person decides to start a procedure against this employer, as a reaction to which he does not let the applicant enter his previous workplace in order to collect his private belongings.

The importance of the special allocation of the burden of proof can be clearly seen in an example from the jurisprudence of the EAT in Great-Britain in which the special rules were not applied. In the *Serco Ltd t/a Education Bradford & Ors v. Mr R Quarshie*[58] case the EAT accepted the tribunal's position that

> we can detect no evidential basis for suggesting that the Respondents were trying to victimise, punish, or take less favourable treatment against Mr Quarshie in any way because of an allegation of racism that he had raised. Accepting that the burden of proof remains on Mr Quarshie to establish his case, we do not think he has done so on this point and decline to draw the inference that management were influenced by a desire to victimise Mr Quarshie.[59]

Had the special rules been applied, the Tribunal might arguably have come to a different conclusion.

The legislative history of the Race Directive shows that the Starting Line proposal suggested the application of the special allocation of the burden of proof in victimisation cases too, since it situated the provision on victimisation among the concepts of discrimination.[60] Notwithstanding this proposal, the *travaux préparatoires* have no explicit reference to the potential application of the special rules to victimisation. It was only in 2007 that the European Parliament paid direct attention to this matter. In its resolution on the application of the RED it laid down that

> the effective implementation of the principle of equality would be helped if the rules on the burden of proof in civil and administrative cases were extended to judicial provisions against victimisation.[61]

This indicates that, in the view of the drafters of the RED, Article 8 RED in its present form does not extend the application of the special allocation of the burden of proof to victimisation cases. This position was also explicitly supported in a victimisation case before the EAT in 2007. In the *L Oyarce v. Cheshire County Council* case the tribunal accepted the view that

> having looked at the provisions of both Section 54A and the Council Directive 2000/43/EC it certainly seems to us that there has been an apparently deliberate attempt to distinguish between discrimination on grounds of race, and victimisation in that the reverse burden applies to the former but not to the latter. We cannot see our way clear to construing them otherwise.[62]

58 *Serco Ltd t/a Education Bradford & Ors v. Mr R Quarshie*, EAT/0466/05/SM (EAT 2006).
59 *Id.*, para. 44, citing the Employment Tribunal.
60 On the Starting Line proposal in this respect see Chopin & Niessen (2001), at 28.
61 European Parliament resolution of 27 September 2007 on the application of Council Directive 2000/43/EC of 29 June 2000 implementing the principle of equal treatment between persons irrespective of racial or ethnic origin, 2007/2094(INI), H.
62 *Oyarce v. Cheshire County Council*, ICR 1693 (EAT 2007), para. 38.

Although not explicitly stipulated, it can still be argued that Article 8(1) RED can also be applied to victimisation complaints. In the previously-mentioned *Coote* case the ECJ applied an enforcement provision which was linked to the principle of equal treatment to a victimisation complaint.[63] Similarly to Article 7(1) RED, Article 6 ETD, on which basis the *Coote* case was decided, required that judicial procedures be available for persons who consider themselves wronged by the failure to apply the principle of equal treatment to them even after the relationship, in which the discrimination is alleged to have occurred, has ended. It can be argued that the fact that victimisation has also been linked to the principle of equal treatment indicates that, similarly to the concepts of harassment and instruction to discriminate, the special rules are also applicable in complaints of victimisation. Moreover, should the protection against victimisation not be effective, victims of discrimination would not try to enforce their complaints of discrimination. Thus, the concept of victimisation can also indirectly be linked to the principle of equal treatment.

Also, in the light of the arguments concerning the concept of victimisation as discrimination and recalling the aim of the victimisation provision, one could argue that the concept of victimisation also concerns the principle of equal treatment; accordingly the special rules should be applicable to victimisation complaints as well. This position can be further supported with the argument that, similarly to discrimination complaints, victims of victimisation also have difficulties in accessing evidence, which was the underlying reason for the introduction of the special rules.[64] Finally, the principle of effective enforcement would also require that the special rules be applicable since the enforcement of the right not to be retaliated against could be made virtually impossible or excessively difficult should the special rules not be applicable to his complaint. All in all, it seems highly desirable, and weighty arguments support the position, that the special rules should be applied to victimisation cases as well.

In terms of evidence law, the special allocation of the burden of proof in victimisation cases would mean that the applicant should only give rise to the presumption that victimisation has taken place. It would then be for the respondent to prove that there was no victimisation.

6.3.5.1. Presumption of Victimisation

The applicant's burden of proof means that first of all he has to establish that there was an underlying claim and that he has been treated adversely. Following

[63] *Case C-185/97*, *Coote v. Granada Hospitality Ltd*, para. 28.

[64] See inter alia Judgment of 27 October 1993 in *Case C-127/92*, *Dr. Pamela Mary Enderby v. Frenchay Health Authority and Secretary of State for Health*, [1993] ECR I-5535. For a detailed discussion on the rationale behind the adoption of special rules see Ch. 2 on the model of review.

this either on the basis of these facts or by submitting some additional evidence the applicant has to show at the level of presumption that there is (or might be) a causal link between the protected act and the harm, which can in most cases be done with the help of comparison.[65] The appropriate comparators in terms of the presumption are those who have not filed a complaint or launched proceedings concerning discrimination on the given protected ground. The comparators can also be hypothetical ones.

The presumption of victimisation means that as soon as any indications can be found that the complaint of discrimination did play any role in adopting the adverse measure, the burden of proof should be placed on the respondent. Thus, similarly to the protected ground in direct discrimination cases, the protected act concerning victimisation does not have to be the only reason for causing that particular harm.

6.3.5.2. Refutation

It has already been argued above that no objective justification can be envisaged for a retaliatory treatment with the exception of the justification concerning vicarious liability. Nevertheless, in accordance with the model of review for discrimination cases the respondent can still prove that the harm was not linked to the protected act (the underlying complaint or procedure); that is he can negate the causal link between these two elements.[66]

In practice, the explanation of the respondent is often too easily accepted. Arguably, this was also the case in the only victimisation case brought on the basis of the RED, before the Court of First Instance.[67] The Court stated in this particular case that

> the applicant was not disciplined for having formally made a complaint or having brought legal proceedings aimed at enforcing the principle of equal treatment, *but for* having directly *called Mr B. a racist* without producing sufficient evidence to support that accusation and for having made unsupported accusations against the management of the European Central Bank.[68]

The respondent thus denied the causal link between the adverse treatment and the proceedings. By negating this, the respondent gave his 'real' reason for disciplining the applicant, namely that she called Mr B. a racist. The Court did not however examine whether this argument of the respondent was the real

[65] The question of comparator has been regarded a very important and highly debated aspect of a victimisation claim in the UK. On the question of comparator see for instance, Connolly (2002); Connolly (2000).

[66] This is contrary to the view of Connolly, according to whom "[t]he only defence to the causative test appears to be where the defendant had no knowledge of the protected act." Connolly (2000), at 309.

[67] Judgment of 16 March 2004 in *Case T-11/03*, *Elizabeth Afari v. European Central Bank*, [2004] ECR II-00267.

[68] *Id.*, para. 174 (emphasis added).

reason and/or a reasonable explanation. This does not however necessarily mean that such a consideration did not implicitly play a role. The finding of the Court might be interpreted as follows: to call someone a racist without providing evidence for this accusation seems to be a serious statement, from which a *'reasonable'* employer might infer the need for disciplining the person alleging this. A similar case occurred in 1980, brought before the Employment Appeal Tribunal in the United Kingdom.[69] In that case the respondent stated that the applicant "had been demoted because he *breached his duty of confidentiality* towards client employers by reporting to the Council for Community Relations racially discriminatory actions taken by them."[70] This explanation was accepted by the Tribunal, but again, no elaboration was given as to why this was a satisfactory explanation. These cases show that to avoid arbitrary decisions first of all a thorough examination of the respondent's explanation is necessary. Fact-finders should also make explicit why certain explanations can be accepted and others cannot.

As in discrimination cases, the respondent can use comparison as a means of evidence in victimisation cases too. The appropriate comparator also raises concerns in this respect, a question that has triggered much discussion in Great-Britain.[71] Here, pursuant to the traditional view the refutation of the respondent has generally been regarded to be the question of comparability instead of applying comparison as a means of evidence in order to substantiate the respondent's argument. For instance, in the *Aziz* case[72] the applicant of Asian origin was dismissed after making secret tape recordings as evidence in his procedure concerning alleged discrimination. The respondent argued that the appropriate comparator in this case should be a person who had also made secret tape recordings. His argument can as a matter of fact be translated as follows. The reason for the dismissal of the applicant was not based on his complaint, but on his making secret tape recordings. In terms of comparison and comparators, his argument means that everybody who made secret tape recordings would have been dismissed. However, this approach was refused by the Court of Appeal arguing that the respondent did not rely on the correct comparator, since the comparison should not include any element of the protected act. And thus, the correct comparison would have been with a non-Asian member of the taxi company who had not made secret tape recordings. Contrary to the general position that the case is concerned with comparability and comparators, the main question is that the real reason for treating the applicant adversely was because he made secret tape recordings. This reason can be shown with the help of comparison. The respondent could make a

[69] The jurisprudence of the Courts in the UK deserves attention because they have the most elaborated concept of victimisation.

[70] *Kirby v. Manpower Services Commission*, ICR 420 (EAT 1980) (emphasis added).

[71] See inter alia Connelly (2000); Connelly (2002); Connelly (2009).

[72] *Aziz v. Trinity Street Taxis Ltd & Others*, IRLR 204 (CA 1988).

comparison with those who are not, have not been or would not be involved in the protected act at all. Thus, the appropriate comparators would have been those who had not started any procedure at all irrespective of the nature of the underlying complaint or procedure.[73]

Although it seems to be a justificatory argument, an explanation of the following type is also concerned with the negation of causality. In the *Khan* case, for instance, the respondent refused to provide the applicant with a reference, and stated that he withheld the reference in order to protect himself from further claims and to preserve his position in the underlying procedure. Lord Nicholls accepted this reasoning and stated that "[e]mployers, acting *reasonably and honestly*, ought to be able to take steps to preserve their position in pending proceedings without laying themselves open to a charge of victimisation."[74] This argument can be translated as follows: the respondent would treat anyone who have started any procedure in the same way, irrespective of the type of procedure. Accordingly, this treatment has nothing to do with the discrimination complaint on the grounds of racial or ethnic origin. At the same time, the respondent does not deny the fact that the applicant was adversely treated as a reaction to a procedure. Thus, he clearly negates the existence of the causal link between the harm and the protected act. Accordingly, similar arguments made by the respondent have to be examined in terms of the negation of causality. It has to be thoroughly scrutinized whether this explanation was the real reason of the respondent.

PART B. CASE STUDIES

6.4. Introduction

A general prohibition of victimisation could be found in none of the countries under review prior to the implementation of the RED. While the Belgian ADA and the Dutch GETA[75] prohibited victimisation only in the sphere of

[73] Comparison in the context of direct discrimination see Busstra (2010).

[74] *Chief Constable of West Yorkshire Police v. Khan*, IRLR 830 (HL 2001), para. 31 (emphasis added). On this case see Connolly (2002). See also *Commissioners of Inland Revenue and others v. Morgan*, IRLR 776 (EAT 2002) and *St Helens MBC v. Derbyshire and others*, IRLR 540 (HL 2007).

[75] On the effect of the RED on the Dutch legislation see inter alia Third Report on the Netherlands, ECRI 2007, at 11; Wijziging van de Awgb en enkele andere wetten ter uitvoering van richtlijn 2000/43/EG en 2000/78/EG (EG-implementatiewet), Memorie van toelichting, 28 770, nr. 3, 2003, at 16; Havinga (2007), at 252.

employment, the Estonian[76] and Hungarian[77] legislation did not know the concept at all. Accordingly, the effect of the RED can be clearly seen on the adoption of a general prohibition of victimisation.

An evaluation will first be made of the concepts of victimisation adopted in the Member States. In this context it will be discovered whether the concepts are more substantive in nature or are rather closer to a procedural approach, how broad an interpretation is given to the 'adverse treatment/consequence', what is the role of the protected ground and how it relates to the protected act, and whether and what kind of justification is possible. This will be followed by an examination of the personal scope of the concept of victimisation both in terms of beneficiaries and addressees. Closely related to this aspect, an exploration will be made of the breadth of the material scope of the concept in the countries. Before closing the case studies with an analysis of the applicable model of review in cases of victimisation, some enforcement-related issues will also be discussed.

6.5. Concept of Victimisation

6.5.1. Substantive versus Procedural Concepts of Victimisation

Not only do the equal treatment legislations of Estonia[78] and Hungary[79] locate the prohibition of victimisation among the substantive provisions, thus vesting it with a clear substantive meaning, but they also explicitly define it as a specific form of discrimination.[80] The formulation in the Estonian[81] and

[76] The original GEA did not include the prohibition of victimisation either. A proposal for amending this Act has been submitted introducing, among others, the concept of victimisation as well. Pursuant to this provision "[a] malicious treatment of a person, and similarly engendering negative consequences to a person because this person has relied on the rights and obligations enshrined in this Act or supported another person in his defending his rights stipulated in this Act."

[77] See inter alia Holtmaat (2007), at 68; Bitskey & Gyulavári (2004).

[78] Art. (6) EETA defines victimisation as follows:

"An action is also considered to be discrimination where a person is treated less favourably than others or he incurs negative consequences on account of his having submitted a complaint on discrimination or supported a person who has submitted such a complaint."

[79] Article 7(1) HETA. Article 10(3) HETA gives the following definition to retaliation:

"A conduct causing, aiming at or threatening with infringement of rights of a person who on account of the violation of the principle of equal treatment has raised an objection, initiated a procedure or assisted in the procedure is considered to be retaliation."

[80] Concerning the substantive meaning of the Hungarian provision see inter alia Demeter (2006), at 66; Position No. 384/3/2008 (II.27) Advisory Board of Equal Treatment on victimisation, 27 February 2008.

[81] Contrary to harassment which is seen as a form of direct discrimination and similarly to instruction to discriminate which has been 'simply' declared to be a form of discrimination, the Estonian Act does not specify which form of discrimination victimisation can take.

Hungarian Acts brings the concept of victimisation very close to the concept of direct discrimination (less favourable or adverse treatment on the ground of filing a complaint).[82]

As opposed to this position and similarly to the RED, the Belgian[83] and the Dutch[84] provisions on victimisation adopt a procedural approach, since the prohibition of victimisation is located in the chapter on enforcement and remedies.[85] This procedural understanding is also confirmed by the facts that victimisation is not considered as a form of discrimination, and the special allocation of the burden of proof is not applicable to them.[86] However, in both countries this strict procedural approach has been softened in different ways. In both equal treatment acts instead of a vague prohibition a clear definition is given of what should be regarded as victimisation. The ARA provides a very detailed regulation in this respect: it clearly defines what the terms 'complaint' and 'procedure' mean, and it arms the concept with special enforcement provisions, including special time limits and special rules on the allocation of the burden of proof. Moreover, concerning remedies it refers to those rules that are applicable to the concept of discrimination, laying down that the amount of forfaitair compensation is increased when the respondent cannot prove that

82 In relation to the Estonian legislation one could further argue that since victimisation can be regarded as a form of discrimination, it can also be brought under the general prohibition of discrimination in the ECA. Admittedly, such a broad interpretation could hardly be expected in the view of the fact that this general prohibition is further specified in the forms of direct and indirect discrimination. And it seems to be even more difficult to bring the prohibition of victimisation under direct discrimination.

83 Contrary to the ADA which only prohibited discrimination in the employment sphere, in the ARA separate articles have been adopted with respect to victimisation in and outside the field of employment and social security. According to Arts. 14(1) and 15(1) ARA:

"When a complaint has been filed by or in the interest of a person on grounds of a violation of this act [...], those against whom the complaint has been filed/employers are not allowed to take adverse measures with respect to the person concerned except for reasons unrelated to the complaint."

84 The Dutch legislation did know the concept of victimisation in equal treatment legislation even before the adoption of the RED: it was laid down in Art. 8 GETA. However, the concept was restricted to the field of employment and to dismissal as a retaliatory measure. This has been extended with the adoption of the Implementation Act that was intended to implement the RED (and FD) into the GETA. This Act introduced a new Art. 8a in addition to the original one. The articles define victimisation as follows:

Article 8 "Termination of the employment relationship by the employer contrary to Article 5, on account of the fact that the employee has invoked Article 5 in or out of court or has assisted in this connection is voidable."

Article 8a "It is prohibited to put persons at a disadvantage on the ground of the fact that they have invoked this Act in or out of court, or have assisted in this connection."

85 The *travaux préparatoires* have put the emphasis on the procedural aspect in the Dutch concept of victimisation. See, inter alia, Wijziging van de Awgb en enkele andere wetten ter uitvoering van richtlijn nr 2000/43/EG en richtlijn nr 2000/78/EG (EG-Implementatiewet Awgb), Nota naar aanleiding van het verslag, 28770, Nr. 5, 22 May 2003, at 35.

86 For the model of review in victimisation cases see below.

an unfavourable or adverse treatment would also have been carried into effect on non-discriminatory grounds (or due to other circumstances).[87] Since this approach is based on arguments related to discrimination, it seems that in this respect victimisation is considered and treated as a form of discrimination.

The substantive approach towards victimisation in the Netherlands is supported by the fact that the ETC also gives an opinion in cases of victimisation, even though it is 'merely' empowered to give an opinion in cases of discrimination (distinction). Moreover, in a couple of cases a victimisation claim was subsidiary to a complaint of discrimination,[88] which also shows their interrelatedness. In summary, the above considerations show that the Belgian and Dutch concepts of victimisation are also vested with substantive meaning. This substantive meaning in Belgium comes very close to the concept of direct discrimination, which will also be illuminated below.[89]

6.5.2. Adverse Treatment or Consequence

Each country under examination has adopted a broad concept of adverse treatment or consequence, and in this respect they are clearly in line with the theoretical elaborations. The Belgian provision talks about *adverse measures*, some typical forms of which are exemplified in relation to employment[90] (such as termination of employment and unilateral alterations of working conditions).[91] The Estonian provision prohibits any *less favourable treatment* or *provoking negative consequences*, which on the one hand makes it very similar to the concept of direct discrimination, and on the other hand can include any possible forms of harm. The Hungarian provision prohibits the *infringement of the rights of persons*. In relation to this formulation it has been argued that not only does it refer to the violation of particular legal provisions,

[87] Art. 14(4) ARA concerning remedies in fields other than employment and social security stipulates that in the case of victimisation the respondent has to pay either forfaitair compensation or compensation based on the suffered harm – according to the choice of the applicant and in accordance with Art. 16(2) ARA. At the same time Art. 16(1) ARA, in relation to which the possible forms of compensations have been elaborated in para. (2), regulates the procedure in which *victims of discrimination* can obtain compensation. Moreover, the amount of compensation is higher when the respondent cannot prove that the challenged less favourable or adverse treatment would also have been carried into effect on *non-discriminatory grounds* or for reasons related to other circumstances.

[88] See for instance Opinion 2005-112 ETC.

[89] In the paragraph below on the model of review the link between victimisation and discrimination becomes more apparent.

[90] Art. 15(2) ARA.

[91] Examples can be found for terminating the employment contract on the ground of submitting a complaint of harassment on the basis of the Harassment Act of 1996. See for instance, *L.H. v. S.A. de droit public La Poste*, Brussels Labour Court, 25 April 2007.

but it also includes all possible harms.[92] This infringement can be carried out both actively and passively,[93] and it can also take the form of harassment.[94] Finally, the GETA stipulates that *putting someone at a disadvantage* on the ground of filing a complaint of discrimination constitutes victimisation. This formulation also indicates that a broad range of harms could fall under this concept.[95] The approach of the Commission clearly shows that, indeed, this expression is interpreted broadly. The following harms have, for instance, been regarded as a 'disadvantage' under Articles 8 and 8a GETA: during a reintegration period the applicant was not given the opportunity to adjust the image her colleagues had of her;[96] the employer did not make any effort to search for a suitable function for the applicant;[97] relocation of the applicant;[98] dismissal;[99] not entering into a new employment contract with the applicant,[100] and so on.[101] In summary, each of the countries either theoretically or in practice accept that not only tangible but also pestering behaviours can constitute adverse treatment or consequence under the concept of victimisation.

As far as potential victimisation is concerned, it is only the Hungarian definition of victimisation (aiming at or threatening with infringements of rights) which explicitly prohibits it. However, a broad reading of the harm might also include any potential violation of the right not to be victimised.[102]

---

92 It has been argued that this expression has to be interpreted broadly, since the violation of human dignity can ultimately be regarded as an infringement. The Commentary further supported this position relying on the formulation of the burden of proof provision which also stipulates the presumption of an infringement of a right, while the concepts of direct and indirect discrimination simply refer to harms. Farkas, Kádár & Kárpáti (2006), at 68; Position No. 384/3/2008 (II.27) Advisory Board of Equal Treatment on victimisation, 27 February 2008.

93 Farkas, Kádár & Kárpáti (2006), at 68; Position No. 384/3/2008 (II.27) Advisory Board of Equal Treatment on Victimisation.

94 Position No. 384/3/2008 (II.27) Advisory Board of Equal Treatment on victimisation, 27 February 2008.

95 See also Implementatie van richtlijnen inzake gelijke behandeling, Brief van de Staatssecretaris van Sociale Zaken en Werkgelegenheid, 28 187, Nr. 1, 18 December 2001, at 6-7.

96 Opinion 2007-11 ETC.

97 Opinion 2006-166 ETC.

98 Opinion 2007-132 ETC.

99 Opinion 2005-195 ETC.

100 Opinion 2003-48 ETC.

101 Moreover, the term 'dismissal' had also been broadly interpreted by the Commission at the time when Art. 8a GETA had not yet been introduced, but Art. 9 RED was applicable. In the view of the Commission there is no essential difference between a dismissal and a rejection of entrance into a new employment contract, thus this latter one could fall under Art. 8, which would also be in line with the requirements of the RED that had to be implemented in the Dutch legislation. This interpretation is important in terms of the possible remedies that can be given in case of victimisation. See for instance Opinion 2003-48 ETC.

102 As yet there is no case law supporting this view, but admittedly potential victimisation is not common form of victimisation.

6.5.3. Protected Ground and Protected Act

Neither of the examined countries mentions in their victimisation provisions the protected ground. This indicates that the causal relationship first and foremost has to be established between the harm and the protected act. Nevertheless, with the exception of Belgium, there are a couple of signs in the legislation and case law of the countries under review that the protected ground does or is supposed to have a certain role in the adjudication, especially in Estonia and Hungary where victimisation is a form of discrimination.

To begin with the mentioned exception, the ARA has established a couple of separate rules for the concept of victimisation, among them the separate burden of proof regulation, which does not necessitate any examination of the protected ground.

Contrary to this in the Netherlands, where victimisation is not regarded as a form of discrimination either, a couple of complaints that could arguably have been identified as victimisation were decided under the concept of discrimination on the ground of the underlying protected ground.[103] In other words, as soon as the complaint is decided in terms of discrimination the protected ground has some relevance.

Stemming from its structure, the EETA includes a couple of indications that the protected ground has to be examined in each and every case. First of all, the Act operates with a closed system of protected grounds, which in itself implies that the applicant will not be able to enforce his right not to be victimised should it not be linked to the protected ground in the underlying complaint. More specifically, pursuant to Article 1(1) EETA the purpose of this piece of legislation is to protect persons from discrimination based on the exhaustively enumerated grounds. Moreover, the first paragraph of Article 3 EETA defining the different concepts of discrimination also links the general prohibition of discrimination to the enumerated protected grounds. Remarkably, identifying the protected ground is also important in terms of the fields concerning which the prohibition of victimisation can be enforced, since the applicable material scope of the Act differs according to the protected ground at stake.[104] On the whole this indicates that fact-finders will have to identify the protected ground, which logically seems to be based on the protected ground in the underlying complaint of discrimination. This approach would then also ensure that victimisation would be appropriately scrutinised. Nevertheless, it is yet to be seen whehter this approach will be followed.

[103] See for instance Opinions 2005-119, 2005-112, 2003-138 ETC.

[104] The material scope of the EETA is broader for racial and ethnic origin than for the other grounds. On the material scope of the Act see Busstra (2010).

The lack of reference to the protected ground in the Hungarian provision on victimisation[105] is troublesome in terms of the burden of proof rules which explicitly require the applicant to show his protected ground. The position paper of the ABET solves this complication by arguing that the burden of proof provision has to be read together with the concept of retaliation, which would then mean that it is the harm and the underlying complaint/procedure that has to be shown, and that there is no need to look for the protected ground.[106] In other words, they emphasise the importance of the protected act against the protected ground. Notwithstanding this approach of the position paper, it is very likely that fact-finders, in particular the Authority, would analyse the protected act in terms of protected ground and would bring it under the so called 'other ground' in the open list of grounds in order to carry out their investigation in accordance with the burden of proof provision.[107] Although no case has yet been brought before the Authority on victimisation, the above approach can be found in a case which should, arguably, have been decided on the basis of the prohibition of victimisation. In this case the applicant stated to have been victim of discrimination because her husband had submitted a discrimination complaint to the AET against their common employer. The Authority investigated the complaint in terms of discrimination on 'other grounds'. From the Authority's reasoning it can be deduced that, in their view, in the case concerned the disagreement between the applicant's husband and the employer was considered to be the protected ground (under the 'other grounds').[108] All in all, in the view of both the ABET and the Authority the protected ground does and should not play any role in a complaint of retaliation. In the light of the theoretical elaboration the approach of the ABET and the Authority might lead to improper level of scrutiny, and might give extended refutation possibilities to the respondent. Moreover, this approach does not make it clear that the application of retaliatory measures is in fact linked to the protected ground in the original complaint. How the protected ground could be taken into account on the basis of the HETA will be discussed in the section on the model of review below.

The protected act seems to be or can be broadly conceived in each of the countries depending naturally on the interpretation of the fact-finding organs. This means that in accordance with the RED both internal and external complaints and procedures will be accepted as protected acts. However, the

[105] Importantly, this is the only form of discrimination which does not refer to the protected grounds enumerated in Art. 8.

[106] Position No. 384/3/2008 (II.27) Advisory Board of Equal Treatment on victimisation, 27 February 2008. Moreover, these documents also emphasise that this provision also aims at the protection of those who themselves do not possess a protected characteristic enumerated in the Act. The allocation of the burden of proof will be discussed below in the section on the model of review.

[107] Art. 8 t) HETA.

[108] EBH/231/2008.

positions of the countries are less clear concerning the question whether the intent to file a complaint should also be protected. Although, none of them stipulate that the intent of filing a claim is also protected, but most of the regulations, with the exception of the Belgian Act, could possibly be interpreted in a way that it would include this aspect of the protected act as well.

With respect to the protected act, the Belgian ARA explicitly and extensively lay down what can and should be accepted as a complaint. The following are regarded as complaints under the ARA: a reasoned complaint submitted by the concerned person with the organisation or institution against which the complaint has been filed (in the field of employment it should be filed at company or department level under which the applicant is employed); a reasoned complaint submitted in the interest of the concerned person by an interest organisation or the Centre (in the field of employment this is submitted by a special inspectorate or the Centre against the company or department); and a legal action initiated by the person concerned or in the interest of the person concerned by an interest organisation or the Centre. Although the interpretation of the protected act is considerably broad, this exhaustive enumeration still restricts to some extent the possible forms of complaints: the intent to submit such a claim is clearly not regarded as a protected act.

The victimisation provisions in the other countries are not so detailed; they merely include a broad reference to the protected act in the definition of victimisation, the interpretation of which will depend to a great extent on the fact-finders. The Estonian EETA simply refers to complaints of discrimination without any specification whether in addition to judicial claims internal complaints are also included; and whether the intent to file a complaint would also be protected.

According to the Hungarian HETA raising an objection and initiating a procedure concerning the violation of the principle of equal treatment are considered to constitute the protected acts. Neither 'objection' nor 'procedure' is however defined in the Act. This indicates that one should rely on the common meaning of these words and give as broad as possible an interpretation to them. Since the Hungarian version uses the word 'objection' instead of complaint, it gives the impression that it refers to complaints having been made internally, while procedures can be interpreted as both internal procedures or proceedings launched before a fact-finding body. Again, it depends on the fact-finders whether such a broad interpretation will be adopted.

The Dutch GETA clearly has a broad approach in this respect since relying on the GETA either in or out of court explicitly enjoys protection. And the Commission has even further extended the scope of 'invoking the GETA' by arguing that the Act has to be broadly interpreted so that it also includes the intent to make a complaint of discrimination.[109]

[109] See for instance Opinion 2006-166 ETC, para. 3.15.

6.5.4. Justification

As argued in the theoretical framework, no possible reasons can be envisaged that would justify the adoption of retaliatory measures, since it would deprive the concept of its importance. From this perspective legislations which do not consider victimisation as a form of discrimination are more advantageous to the victims. In Belgium and the Netherlands, where victimisation is not regulated in terms of discrimination, it is clear that no justification is possible for victimisation,[110] an approach clearly in line with the RED.

However, in Estonia and Hungary where victimisation is considered to be a special form of discrimination, it seems that the respondent is given the possibility to justify the retaliatory treatment. Concerning the EETA it is important to first look at how justification is regulated as far as the other concepts of discrimination are concerned. Contrary to the definition of indirect discrimination, the concept of direct discrimination does not include any general justification clause. This indicates that only the exceptions explicitly taken up in the EETA are applicable to direct discrimination. Similarly, the definition of victimisation does not include any general justification either, thus theoretically the particular exceptions seem to be applicable to this form of discrimination as well. Three of the exception clauses can be applied at this theoretical level: positive action measures,[111] genuine and determining occupational requirement[112] and a broad justification clause.[113] Generally, it does not seem that fact-finders in Estonia would accept either positive action or genuine and determining occupational requirement justifications under this concept because of their obvious inapplicability. However, there is a danger that the third exception might be applied and accepted by the fact-finders. For example, someone has been dismissed due to submitting a complaint of discrimination and the respondent argues that it was in the interest of protecting the rights of others to undisturbed work. Arguably, such a measure can never be proportionate to the aim attained. Yet, it is to be seen how fact-finders will deal with this justification.

The question of justification is considerably complicated in the HETA mainly because the Act is divided into a general and a special part, and it is not entirely clear in what way they relate to one another.[114] Thus, it is not obvious in which cases one can invoke the general objective justification clause and when only the special exemptions are applicable. Nevertheless, the general

---

[110] In the Netherlands, the Commission has explicitly stated that there is no justification in victimisation cases. See for instance Opinion 2006-34 ETC, para. 3.19. (Importantly, this decision was based on an Act other than the GETA, but the victimisation provision in this Act is similar to that in the GETA.)

[111] Art. 6 EETA.

[112] Art. 10 EETA.

[113] Art. 9 EETA.

[114] See Busstra 2010 for a more detailed analysis of justification.

point of departure seems to be based on the facts that retaliation is considered to be a form of discrimination, and Article 7(3) HETA does not exclude the application of the general objective justification to the concept of victimisation. Accordingly, respondents have the possibility, at least theoretically, to rely on either the possibility of objective justification or other special exemption clauses. This approach is also followed by the position paper of the ABET, explaining that not only can the respondent prove the lack of causal link, but he can also make use of the justification grounds.[115] Naturally, it is yet to be seen whether the justifications will be accepted in practice; nonetheless this approach is clearly not in line with the theoretical considerations.

6.6. Personal Scope of the Prohibition of Victimisation

6.6.1. Beneficiaries

Concerning the scope of beneficiaries, the legal provisions on victimisation are quite broad in all of the examined countries, an approach that clearly contributes to the more effective enforcement of the principle of equal treatment.

First of all, the concepts of victimisation talk about 'persons', and therefore do not exclude legal persons.[116] In this respect the national provisions are broader than the definition in the RED itself.[117] Secondly, the protection also covers a certain range of persons having assisted in the underlying claim.[118] Remarkably, in this context the Belgian Act provides protection only for witnesses,[119] an approach that does not entirely agree with the RED.[120] Thirdly,

[115] Position No. 384/3/2008 (II.27) Advisory Board of Equal Treatment on victimisation, 27 February 2008.

[116] With respect to the Hungarian Act see inter alia Farkas, Kádár & Kárpáti (2006), at 68; Position No. 384/3/2008 *id.*

[117] In this respect, the Dutch regulation is interesting, since the personal scope of the GETA does not cover legal persons as beneficiaries. However, the enforcement provisions clearly allows for actio popularis claims by interest organisations. Accordingly, legal persons are limited to those organisations that can and have initiated actio popularis claims in the discrimination complaint. On the Hungarian provision in this respect see inter alia Farkas, Kádár & Kárpáti (2006), at 68; Position No. 384/3/2008 *id.*

[118] The Estonian provision talks about those who have supported the person in the discrimination complaint; and the Hungarian and Dutch regulations protect those who have assisted in the procedure.

[119] The term 'witness' is formally defined in the ARA. Arts. 14(5) and 15(9) ARA.

[120] Importantly, the extension of the protection to those who acted as witnesses in the discrimination complaint was clearly based on the RED. See inter alia Wetsontwerp tot wijziging van de wet van 30 juli 1981 tot bestraffing van bepaalde door racisme en xenofobie ingegeven daden, 2720/001, 26 October 2006, at 54. & 56.

with the exception of the Belgian legislation,[121] the wording of the national provisions indicates that the applicant in the underlying claim has to be the same as in the victimisation claim.[122] Thus, the regulation from the perspective of the scope of beneficiaries does not provide appropriate protection as those on the behalf of whom the complaint has been submitted will not be protected from victimisation.[123] However, accepting the possibility of victimisation by way of association the protection can clearly be extended to those who have not themselves submitted the underlying discrimination complaint and/ or initiated the discrimination procedure.[124] Accordingly, in this way the protection can be extended to situations where the protected act was initiated by interest organisations within the framework of actio popularis claims.[125] In this respect, the explicit protection of those in the interest of whom the complaint has been filed and the possibility of further extending the protection by way of association seem to some extent to rectify the Belgian restriction of protection to witnesses.

6.6.2. Addressees

The main question with respect to the addressees in the context of victimisation is whether the legislations of the examined countries allow that the respondent in the underlying discrimination complaint might be different from the respondent in the victimisation claim. With the partial exception of the

[121] Arts. 14(1) and 15(1) of the ARA explicitly stipulate that the protection extends to those who have filed the complaint or in the interest of whom this has been filed.

[122] On this aspect of the Dutch provision see inter alia Waaldijk & Bonini-Baraldi (2004), at 371.

[123] See also Waaldijk & Bonini-Baraldi (2004), at 371.

[124] In Hungary in a specific case the applicant (A) was dismissed because she was pregnant. She initiated a procedure following which her partner (B), who worked for the same employer, has also been dismissed. As a reaction to this, B launched a victimisation complaint which was not accepted because the respondent could refute the charges. But importantly, the complaint was not regarded as inadmissible on the grounds that the applicants were not the same in the two procedures, and B was not a person assisting the applicant. This approach can be interpreted as B could start a victimisation procedure because he was associated with the protected ground of A. See reference to this case in EBH/511/2008.

[125] Interestingly, in Hungary the position paper written by the Advisory Board argues that this provision also provides protection to those who themselves do not possess any of the protected characteristics of the Act, but have initiated or assisted in a procedure. It seems to be logical that those who have assisted in a procedure do not have to possess any of the protected characteristics since they are protected on the basis of their status of having given assistance. However, those who have initiated but do not possess any of the characteristics laid down in the Act can refer to two situations. First of all, it can refer to discrimination by association. Secondly, it can include actio popularis claims since the organisations initiating the proceedings do not have the protected characteristics themselves, but they can be treated adversely on the grounds of initiating a procedure against discrimination.

Belgian regulation, the legislative provisions of all the countries seem to allow for a broad interpretation concerning the addressees, since they are silent on who can commit victimisation. In Hungary the President of the Authority (in the lack of concrete victimisation cases) has given an example of possible victimisation, from which it can be concluded that the respondents do not necessarily have to be the same in the discrimination and the victimisation complaints.[126] In a concrete case which served as the basis for the victimisation example, the respondent of the discrimination complaint was an entrepreneur who had a contract with an owner of a shopping centre for cleaning services. At the request of the owner, he did not employ Roma persons on the day shift, which treatment was considered to constitute direct discrimination. In the view of Demeter, if the contract with the entrepreneur would have been terminated when, in accordance with the AET's decision, he used Roma persons during the daytime, the owner could be regarded as the respondent in the victimisation case. It is definitely to be welcomed that the Authority seems to be open to cases of victimisation in which the respondent is not the same as in the underlying discrimination case. Nevertheless, the reason for the distinction has to be made clear, since in this case, as it was described by Demeter, the reason for the owner to terminate the contract was not based on the complaint, but was related to the fact that he uses Roma persons during the day. This should be decided under the concept of direct discrimination on the grounds of racial or ethnic origin, and not in terms of victimisation.

Similarly, the Dutch Equal Treatment Commission has also accepted a complaint of victimisation in which the respondents were not the same in the two complaints.[127] In the underlying internal complaint the 'respondent' was one of the managers of the company, while in the victimisation complaint it was the employer of the applicant. The examples make it clear that it is very important to accept a broad interpretation of 'addressees' as not admitting a victimisation case against a respondent different from that in the underlying discrimination claim would limit the scope of protection against victimisation. As far as the Belgian regulation is concerned, pursuant to the two definitions of the prohibition of victimisation it is either the employer (in fields of employment and social security) or the person against whom the discrimination complaint has been filed (in the fields other than employment and social security under the ARA) who can have legal standing as respondent. Concerning this latter case (that is fields other than employment and social security), it is clear that the respondents have to be the same in both complaints, which might raise problems in concrete cases. Nevertheless, as indicated in the theoretical framework, it is difficult to envisage victimisation occurring in fields other than employment. This theoretically problematic aspect of the regulation might therefore not lead to difficulties in practice. Regarding the fields of

126 Demeter (2006), at 66.

127 See for instance Opinion 2007-11 ETC.

employment and social security, it is important that the rule sets a prohibition of victimisation on the employer, since this indicates that in the underlying complaint (which is often an internal procedure) the 'respondent' does not necessarily have to be the employer himself. For instance, the applicant might submit an internal complaint of harassment by a colleague. In this complaint, it is the colleague who would be seen as 'respondent' in the internal procedure. But when the employer victimises the applicant on the ground of his complaint, the procedure can be launched against the employer. Moreover, the legislator extended the prohibition of victimisation to those who give instructions to people or set them to work and are different from the employer.[128] The question, however, rises as to whether the employer can be taken as respondent when it is not he who adopts a retaliatory measure against the applicant. One could imagine situations in which a complaint of discrimination is submitted against a colleague of the employee, and as a reaction to this complaint other colleagues start to harass him. It seems logical that the duty of care of the employer extends to these situations as well; that is he has vicarious liability in this respect as well. In this regard the problem might arise in the filing of a law-suit against the colleagues.[129] In any event, it seems that the Belgian legislation gives legal standing to a respondent in a victimisation claim who is different from that in the underlying discrimination complaint.

6.7. Material Scope of the Prohibition of Victimisation

The material scope of the prohibition of victimisation extends to all fields falling under the equal treatment legislations. In this respect the effect of the RED can be clearly explored in the Belgian ARA[130] and the Dutch GETA. The ADA that preceded the ARA prohibited victimisation only in the field of employment. Similarly, before the amendment of the GETA by the Implementation Act in 2004 only employment-related complaints enjoyed protection. However, as predicted, so far all claims of victimisation have been related to employment.

Such a problem has not occurred in Estonia and Hungary, where victimisation is a form of discrimination. Accordingly, the concept can be enforced in relation to the material scope of the Equal Treatment Acts. Importantly, as discussed above,[131] the Estonian EETA links the applicable material scope to the protected ground at stake[132] and the material scope is limited in cases of

---

[128] Art. 15(10) ARA.

[129] See also Ch. 5 on legal standing; Busstra (2010).

[130] See also Thiery (2007), at 771.

[131] See above concerning the protected ground and protected act.

[132] This approach of the Estonian legislator originates from the will to implement the RED and the FD in one act.

discrimination on grounds other than racial or ethnic origin.[133] This means that it is of the utmost importance in the Estonian context that the protected ground be identified and not ignored.[134]

6.8. Enforcement Related Matters

In Estonia and Hungary where victimisation is considered a special form of discrimination the enforcement provisions elaborated for discrimination complaints are arguably applicable to victimisation cases as well. This is buttressed by the fact that no special enforcement provisions are developed for victimisation complaints.

In the Netherlands, as victimisation is not regulated as a form of discrimination and no special enforcement-related provisions exist either (with the exception of one special remedy-related provision) the general enforcement rules of civil and administrative law are to be applied. Accordingly, the special rules for the allocation of the burden of proof are not applicable either.[135] The only enforcement-related special provision enshrined in the GETA regulates the sanction when victimisation is embodied in dismissal. In such cases the termination of the employment contract can be declared null and void.[136]

As already indicated supra, the Belgian concept of victimisation is supplied with special enforcement-related provisions. These are: special rules with respect to compensation, allocation of the burden of proof and time limits. Concerning all other enforcement matters, the general civil and administrative procedure rules are applicable as victimisation is not defined as a form of discrimination. Articles 14(4) and 15(6) ARA lay down that the applicant of a victimisation complaint should be given forfaitair compensation,[137] the amount

[133] On the material scope of the EETA see Busstra (2010).

[134] Difficulties might arise when the underlying complaint was concerned with intersectional discrimination, concerning which one of the protected grounds was the victim's racial or ethnic origin. In order to be in harmony with the RED in such cases the material scope with respect to racial or ethnic origin should be applicable based on the argument that racial or ethnic origin was one of the grounds that played a role in the discrimination.

[135] For a more detailed elaboration see below on the model of review in victimisation cases.

[136] When victimisation was prohibited only in the form of victimisatory dismissal a discussion was going on as to whether it would be necessary to provide for other special remedies in case of victimisation so that applicants could immediately invoke this provision without having to rely on the concept of unlawful act or abuse of law, or other open norms. See inter alia Veldman (2001), at 327-333.

[137] The regulation of forfaitair compensation has been explained within the framework of the concept of victimisation; that is whether it has a substantive or procedural meaning. As elaborated, Art. 14(4) ARA refers to Art. 16(2) ARA which lays down rules for forfaitair compensation when discrimination has taken place. Strikingly, Art. 15(6) ARA regulating compensation in the fields of employment and social security does not contain any reference to this article.

of which depends on the applicable field of law (i.e. whether the complaint is related to employment and social security or to other fields).[138] The fact that the amount of compensation is the same as in discrimination cases not only enhances the enforcement of victimisation complaints, but also contributes to a more effective enforcement of the right to equal treatment.[139] Separate rules are stipulated in the Act for the allocation of the burden of proof,[140] the application of which seems to be made subject to a time limit of 12 months after submitting a complaint of discrimination. Nevertheless, the similar provision in the Act of 1996 on the well-being of employees in the workplace has been interpreted differently by courts. In a case of alleged victimisation against an employee, the court argued that there are four conjunctive criteria that have to be fulfilled in order to be able to establish that victimisation has taken place.[141] One of these criteria requires that the challenged dismissal, which was at stake in the particular case, happened within the 12 months stipulated in the burden of proof provision. In the court's reading, accordingly, the 12 months period does not relate to the applicability of the special rules on the burden of proof, but it in fact restricts the period of time during which persons are protected against retaliatory measures and can turn to fact-finding bodies. Such a restriction is clearly in contradiction with the principle of equivalence. Pursuant to the last sentences of Articles 15(2) and 15(5) ARA an employee cannot demand re-employment when the adverse measure was taken after the employment relationship had been terminated.[142] Thus, the Act takes it for granted that the protection extends to the period after the termination of the concrete relationship, also with respect to victimisation and fields other than employment and social security. This regulation agrees with the RED.

6.9. Model of Review Concerning Victimisation

Concerning the model of review, a distinction can again be made between the examined countries on the basis of whether they regard victimisation as a form of discrimination, or whether they regulate the concept using the enforcement provisions. Accordingly, in Belgium and the Netherlands, where victimisation is rather considered to be an enforcement provision, the special allocation of the burden of proof enshrined for discrimination cases is not explicitly held to be applicable to complaints of victimisation. However, as will be shown, some openings can be explored in both countries regarding the application of the special rules. These openings also support the position that the concept of

[138] See also Wetsontwerp tot wijziging van de wet van 30 juli 1981 tot bestraffing van bepaalde door racisme en xenofobie ingegeven daden, 2720/001, 26 October 2006, at 55.

[139] Moreover, it also brings the concept of victimisation closer to the concept of discrimination.

[140] Arts. 14(3) and 15(4) ARA.

[141] *L.H. v. S.A. de droit public La Poste*, Brussels Labour Court, 25 April 2007.

[142] Wetsontwerp tot wijziging …, *supra* note 138, at 56.

victimisation is also vested with substantive maning and comes close to that of direct discrimination. On the contrary, in Estonia and Hungary these special rules, and thus the model based on these special rules, are clearly to be applied in victimisation cases. Still, the application of these rules is not without further complications.

As mentioned supra, in Belgium the articles regulating the prohibition of victimisation also include provisions on the allocation of the burden of proof.[143] These separate rules are comparable to the rules on the special allocation of the burden of proof in discrimination cases.[144] Arguably, these special rules only accommodate the special allocation of the burden of proof to the concept of victimisation. Pursuant to Articles 14(3) and 15(4) ARA

> when an adverse measure has been taken within 12 months after submitting the complaint, the burden of proof that the adverse measures have been taken for reasons untinged by the complaint falls on the respondent.

Although this provision does not explicitly lay down that it is a presumption of victimisation that the applicant has to establish, the formulation indicates that as soon as the applicant shows that adverse measures have been taken within 12 months of submitting the complaint, there is a prima facie case of victimisation, and then it is for the respondent to prove that the challenged measure was not retaliatory. Importantly, the Explanatory Memorandum did describe the first part of the above sentence as a 'refutable presumption'.[145] In other words, the existence of an adverse measure in combination with the time limit creates a presumption of victimisation. Thus the applicant does not have to show a possible causal link between the protected ground and the harm because it is legally presumed based on the time limit and the disadvantage.

This favourable arrangement is only applicable within the set time limit (if it is interpreted as being only concerned with the applicability of the burden of proof rules, and not constituting a general time limit for filing a complaint of victimisation). Once this period has lapsed, the general allocation of the burden of proof seems to apply, which means that it would be for the applicant to prove that not only has an adverse measure been taken against him, but this adverse treatment was done for retaliatory reasons. Arguably, however, when retaliation takes place, the person whose right has been violated generally takes steps within a relatively short time. In other words, the 12 month time period seems to be fair for those who really want to launch a procedure. Nevertheless, this time limit might lead to some limitations in practice on the effective enforcement of the right not to be victimised.

Furthermore, in relationships other than those involving employment and social security, the judge before whom the underlying claim (i.e. the claim

143 See also Castermans (2009), at 257.

144 See also Bayart & Bosmans (2008), at 588; Maes (2003), at 175.

145 Wetsontwerp tot wijziging ..., *supra* note 138, at 54. See also Thiery (2007), at 771.

of discrimination) is pending can shorten this period on the request of the respondent. In the *travaux préparatoires* it was explained that this is necessary in view of the fact that these relationships are much more undefined or uncertain than employment relations.[146] This seems to be a reasonable argument, but in order to be able to establish the need for a shortening of this period the judge should definitely take into account all relevant circumstances of the case (including the position of the applicant), and bring a well-reasoned decision on this aspect. This shortening again might under certain circumstances impair the right to effective enforcement, therefore fact-finders should substantially deliberate on its application.

The respondent's burden in a victimisation claim can also be compared with his onus in a discrimination case. After the applicant has given rise to a presumption it is for the respondent to prove (the burden of persuasion is on him) that there has been no victimisation.[147] Notably, the victimisation articles do not include any reference to possible justifications, which in terms of the model of review means that the respondent can only come up with the negation of the causal link as refutation. This position is also confirmed by the formulation of the articles concerned, since, as mentioned supra, they lay down that "the burden of proof that the adverse measures have been taken *for reasons untinged by the complaint* falls on the respondent."[148] On the basis of the above elaborations, it seems that in Belgium the allocation of the burden of proof in victimisation cases comes very close to the special allocation of the burden of proof. For this reason, it can be regarded to be in accordance with the theoretical model of review devised for victimisation cases.

Contrary to this approach, in the Netherlands no separate rules have been adopted for victimisation cases, and the Commission itself has emphasised in a couple of cases and has been consistent in its approach that it is the general allocation of the burden of proof that is applicable to victimisation complaints.[149] This means that it is for the applicant to prove that the harm was linked to the complaint. In other words, not only does the applicant have to show facts from which the presumption of victimisation can be concluded, but he also has to prove that he was involved in a complaint of discrimination and that he was treated adversely for this reason. The case law of the Commission clearly shows that in many instances the applicant failed in his case because he could not prove this causal relationship.[150]

---

146 Wetsontwerp tot wijziging van de wet van 30 juli 1981 tot bestraffing van bepaalde door racisme of xenofobie ingegeven daden, 3-2362/3, 24 April 2007, at 38.

147 If charged with having committed discrimination, the respondent has to prove that there has been no discrimination after the presumption has been established by the applicant.

148 Arts. 14(3) and 15(4) ARA (emphasis added).

149 See for instance Opinions 2006-166, 2006-148, 2005-68 ETC; Cantonal Judge, LJN: BH 5158, 5 November 2008. See also Davidović & Walsum (2009), at 41.

150 See for instance Opinions 2006-124, 2005-195 ETC.

It is, however, remarkable that the Commission has found at least three ways to facilitate the applicant's burden of proof in victimisation cases. First of all, the Commission accepted that invoking the GETA victimisation can be established if a complaint of discrimination was one of the reasons. In other words the complaint does not have to be the only reason for the adverse treatment. Secondly, a couple of examples can also be found in which it seems that the case was concerned with victimisation, yet the complaint was still decided in terms of discrimination with the application of the special allocation of the burden of proof.[151] These cases are interesting from the perspective of the refutation of the respondent and the arguments of the Commission, since they are based on the lack of causal relationship between the harm and the complaint. This causality argument shows that these cases in fact concerned victimisation. They also show how close the concept of victimisation is to direct discrimination, so it does not seem reasonable to apply separate burden of proof rules to this concept in this light either. Finally, in a couple of cases in which the victimisation complaint was submitted together with the discrimination claim, the victimisation arguments seemed to be more easily accepted. It seems that the special allocation of the burden of proof was, in these cases, extended to the victimisation aspect as well.[152] Notwithstanding all these efforts to facilitate the applicant's burden of proof, the Dutch approach cannot be regarded to be in line with the theoretical model. Accordingly, from the perspective of effective enforcement and in the light of the theoretical elaborations the most advantageous approach would be to apply the special rules in victimisation cases as well.

In Estonia the special rules on the allocation of the burden of proof are clearly applicable to complaints of victimisation. Pursuant to these rules the applicant should establish a presumption of victimisation, and it would then be for the respondent to prove that no victimisation has taken place. This approach is fully in accordance with the theoretical considerations. It is, however, yet to be seen whether these rules will be applied to complaints of victimisation, and how they will be adapted to the concept of victimisation.

In Hungary, as hinted at supra, due to the formulation of the rules on the burden of proof it seems a very complicated task for the fact-finders to apply the special allocation arrangement for the concept of victimisation. First of all, it is for the applicant to give rise to the presumption of a disadvantage and that he possessed (or the respondent might have thought that he possessed) one of the protected characteristics enumerated in Article 8 HETA. It is remarkable that in the HETA victimisation is the only form of discrimination which does not refer to the protected grounds of Article 8. Arguably, this allows for two possible interpretations of the burden of proof rules in terms of the concept of victimisation. The first reading is adopted in the position paper of the

151 See for instance Opinions 2005-112, 2005-68, 2003-138 ETC.
152 See for instance Opinions 2006-166, 2006-34 ETC.

ABET. Pursuant to this interpretation the applicant has to show that there was a disadvantage and that there was an underlying claim of discrimination.[153] These arguments of the position paper are based on the fact that the causal link in the case of victimisation should be found between the complaint and the disadvantage; for this reason the protected ground does not have any role at all in such complaints.[154] The second, and conceptually more convincing reading, would be that the applicant refers to the protected ground in the underlying claim and the term 'disadvantage' is interpreted as the presumption of retaliation. Accordingly, the possible causal link between the harm and the complaint can be made visible at this point. This interpretation would also be in line with the application of the burden of proof rules to the other forms of discrimination, since as argued before the applicant should establish a prima facie case of discrimination and not only show the existence of two separate facts.[155] Moreover, it also makes the protected ground visible, which plays an important role in the determination of the intensity of review. However, practice does not seem to follow (or at least not consistently) any of these interpretations. In one of the above-mentioned cases before the AET, the established facts of which indicated that it was concerned with retaliation, the Authority seemed to decide it under the concept of direct discrimination – though it did not specify which concept of discrimination was at stake –, and examined the protected act as a protected ground under the 'other grounds'.[156]

Concerning the respondent's burden of proof, the Act seems to be less ambiguous. As soon as the applicant has complied with his burden of proof, it is for the respondent to prove that there has been no victimisation. As explained earlier, on the basis of the HETA the respondent can prove that the factual circumstances established by the applicant did not prevail, that he observed the principle of equal treatment or that he was not obliged to observe it.[157] It has been argued that the first element is unnecessary since it concerns a burden of production, and the factual circumstances have to be established in the first phase of the assessment. This is similarly true in the present context. The second element refers to the negation of the causal link. In the ABET's view this means that it was not the complaint or procedure or the assistance

[153] Position No. 384/3/2008 (II.27) Advisory Board of Equal Treatment on victimisation, 27 February 2008.

[154] However, if one agrees with the position that the protected ground does not have to play a role in victimisation cases another explanation seems to be more preferable taking into consideration the fact that this causality-based argument cannot be applied to all concepts of discrimination, in particular to indirect discrimination. The reasoning should rather be based on the lack of any reference in the definition of retaliation to the protected grounds in Article 8 HETA, while Art. 19(1) HETA explicitly refers to Article 8 HETA grounds.

[155] See Ch. 2 on the model of review.

[156] EBH/231/2008.

[157] See also the position paper of the Advisory Board. Position No. 384/3/2008 (II.27) Advisory Board of Equal Treatment on victimisation, 27 February 2008.

in the procedure that caused the harm. This means the negation of the causal link between the protected act and the harm. Finally, the respondent also has the possibility of justification, which does not comply with the theoretical observations. It is yet to be seen whether any justification arguments will be accepted by fact-finders. In the already-mentioned case that was decided under the concept of direct discrimination instead of victimisation,[158] the AET explained that the respondent could not prove that the ground of treating the applicant adversely was not related to the disagreement between the applicant's husband and the director of the school. It is not however clear, on the basis of the short summary, whether the respondent's arguments were taken into account as a negation of the causal link or as justification. In any event, it can be seen that the respondent (at least as the first step in the refutation phase) has to prove the lack of the causal link in order to escape liability. In the only case of victimisation decided by a court until now, it was established that there was no retaliation since the respondent refused to extend the applicant's contract on the grounds of economic reasons, and not on the grounds of his partner's complaint of discrimination.[159] Again, it is not clear from the reasoning whether the explanation was considered to be the negation of causality or justification. The fact that economic reasons are explicitly mentioned as possible grounds for the treatment indicates that it was considered to be a justification, though it was in fact the negation of causality. This approach introduces the danger that many explanations of the respondent might be accepted. Moreover, this justification reasoning also inherently involves the refusal of a victimisation complaint if submitting a complaint was not the only, but one of the reasons for treating the applicant adversely. It would accordingly be preferable that fact-finders appropriately applied the model of review and the Act excluded any justification in victimisation cases.

6.10. Conclusions

Similarly to the enforcement of the protection against discrimination, the right not to be victimised can be effectively enforced, if the prohibition of victimisation is adequately addressed and the victim's procedural position is appropriately facilitated. Accordingly, the more substantive a reading is given to the concept of victimisation and the easier it is for the victim to vindicate his claim, the more effective enforcement becomes, which would contribute to enhancing minority protection.

Although Article 9 RED on the prohibition of victimisation is located among the enforcement provisions, the concept is, arguably, much broader than a mere procedural means. The concept of victimisation can be vested

[158] EBH/231/2008.

[159] See reference to this case in EBH/511/2008.

with substantive meaning, based on which it can be interpreted as a particular form of discrimination. This interpretation would ensure the effective enforcement of the prohibition of victimisation. Effective protection against victimisation would definitely encourage victims of racial discrimination to file their complaints of discrimination on the grounds of racial or ethnic origin, and contribute to the effective enforcement of the right to equal treatment. As the RED itself does not regard the concept of victimisation as a form of discrimination, the protection it requires does not seem to be entirely effective. The most important implication of the approach of the RED is that the special rules concerning the allocation of the burden of proof do not seem to be applicable to complaints of victimisation. Accordingly, the victim's procedural position is not facilitated when he attempts to vindicate his right not to be victimised.

In the countries under review two main views can be explored pertaining to the concept of victimisation. While the Belgian and the Dutch legislators follow the approach of the RED and regard victimisation as a provision that aims to improve the enforcement of the right to equal treatment, in Estonia and Hungary victimisation is deemed a special form of discrimination. These two different approaches also influence the enforcement of the violation of the prohibition of victimisation, and thus, that of the right to equal treatment. In those countries where victimisation is merely a procedural regulation, the enforcement of the right to non-discrimination also becomes less effective, as it is more difficult to enforce a complaint concerning a breach of the prohibition of victimisation.

The question of less effective enforcement becomes visible when it comes to burden of proof related matters, as the special allocation of the burden of proof is not applicable to the concept of victimisation in Belgium and the Netherlands. This problematic aspect seems to have been recognised by these countries as they have found several ways to facilitate the applicant's procedural position in these cases, and thus to open the regulation to a more substantial reading. Consequently, it is implicitly acknowledged how important it is to apply the special allocation of the burden of proof to the concept of victimisation as well.

Although in Estonia and Hungary it is clear that the special allocation of the burden of proof is applicable to complaints of victimisation, it is as yet unclear or concerns can be raised, as to how these rules will be applied to the concept of victimisation. More specifically, complications could arise as far as the identification of the causal relationship between the protected act and the harm is concerned and their relationship to the protected ground. In this respect, the potential complication is inherent in the Hungarian regulation of the allocation of the burden of proof, as it requires the applicant to show the protected ground. There is a substantial danger of the conceptually inappropriate application of the burden of proof arrangement, which at the same time endangers the effectiveness of the enforcement of the right to equal treatment.

There is also uncertainty about the possible grounds of justification in those two countries where victimisation is regarded as a special form of discrimination. Notwithstanding the fact that, theoretically, victimisation cannot be justified, neither the burden of proof nor the substantial regulations are very clear in this respect. Such a conceptually obscure arrangement jeopardises effective protection against both victimisation and discrimination.

All in all, while a mere procedural approach to the concept of victimisation puts the enforcement of victimisation complaints at risk, a conceptually ill-defined application of the enforcement provisions in cases of victimisation also endangers the effective enforcement of the right not to be victimised and discriminated against, and thus would not contribute to enhancing minority protection.

Chapter 7

Sanctions

Part A. Theoretical Framework

7.1. Introduction

The general principle of '*ubi ius, ibi remedium*' holds that rights are mere declarations when there are no remedies for their violation. This is similarly true for human rights law in general, and anti-discrimination/equality law in particular. By virtue of including special provisions on remedies and enforcement the Race Directive acknowledges the danger residing in defining important rights without stipulating any redress in the event of their violation.

The theoretical part of this chapter is devoted to the examination of Article 15 on Sanctions in the last chapter of the RED and how it contributes to the effective enforcement of the right to equal treatment and how effective remedies can promote the achievement of substantive equality and enhance minority protection. In this context, first of all, it will be examined what 'sanctions' means or can mean, and what the relationship is between Article 15 RED and Chapter II on Enforcement and Remedies. Following these terminological and systemic clarifications attention will turn to the specific requirements of Article 15 RED: what the terms 'effective', 'proportionate' and 'dissuasive' mean considering the jurisprudence of the ECJ. This elaboration will be followed by a concise analysis of the possible forms of remedies. Stemming from the requirements of effectiveness, proportionality and dissuasiveness some factors will be identified that arguably need to be balanced when adjudicating whether remedies are effective. Finally, positive action measures will be considered as possible remedies since positive action is highly relevant to achieving substantive equality and thus an enhanced level of minority protection.

Article 15 RED on sanctions stipulates the following:

> Article 15 Sanctions
>
> Member States shall lay down the rules on sanctions applicable to infringements of the national provisions adopted pursuant to this Directive and shall take all measures necessary to ensure that they are applied. The sanctions, which may comprise the payment of compensation to the victim, must be effective, proportionate and dissuasive.

7.2. Terminological Clarification

Several terms are used to describe the final stage of an adjudication process; that is when redress is awarded. The redress is often referred to as remedies, sanctions or penalties.

It is a general principle of law that where there is a right there must be a remedy. As explained earlier, the term 'remedy' in this phrase can be interpreted in many ways. Generally the term is regarded to refer to the process leading to redress, namely to remedies in their broad sense. However, "it is a principle of international law, and even a general conception of law, that any breach of an engagement involves an obligation to make reparation."[1] In this context the term 'remedy' concerns the right to redress, and that is remedy in its strict sense. For the sake of terminological clarity, the process and the redress together are called 'enforcement', which is remedy in its broad sense.[2] In this chapter remedy is used in its strict sense as referring to redress, and not including the process leading to the redress.

Zakrzewski defines remedy in its narrow sense as a *court order* "which a party obtains to redress a grievance existing before an action is brought [...] and which are available at trial".[3] This definition will be accepted here as well, since it fits with the division between enforcement and remedies, and can be effectively used in analysing Article 15 of the Race Directive. Nevertheless, a small amendment is necessary in view of the procedural aspects of non-discrimination law. It has been elaborated that several procedures, beyond judicial ones, can be regarded as effective. For instance, conciliation procedures or the quasi-judicial procedures of national specialised bodies can also form part of an effective enforcement system. In order to include all these 'decisions' in the definition of remedies, it is suggested that not only judicial, but quasi-judicial orders, agreements, and so on also be considered as 'orders'. The RED has a separate chapter on Remedies and Enforcement which only concerns remedies in their broad sense; namely, access to justice, legal standing,

1 *Case Concerning the Factory at Chorzów (Germany v. Poland)*, 26 July 1927, 1928 PCIJ (Ser. A.) No. 17. See also Rombouts, Sardaro & Vandeginste (2006), at 362.

2 On this terminological question see also Zakrzewski (2005), at 44-47.

3 Zakrzewski (2005), at 44-45.

burden of proof, prohibition of victimisation, and so on. No provision can be found on the right to redress in this chapter. This is rather striking in the light of the original proposal which clearly indicated that this chapter would deal with

> two main conditions for effective legislation against discrimination: the right of victims to a *personal remedy* against the person or body who has perpetrated the discrimination; and the *existence of an appropriate mechanism* in each Member State to ensure adequate levels of enforcement.[4]

According to Tobler, the lack of a concrete provision on redress can be traced back to the case law of the ECJ, which interpreted the right to judicial review as including the right to redress.[5] Thus, the jurisprudence of the ECJ seems to indicate that no separate provision is required on remedies at all. Still, Article 15 was included in the RED, under the title 'sanctions', and not 'remedies'.[6]

The term 'sanction' is generally linked to criminal law because the word itself is conceptually linked to punishing the perpetrator. On the contrary, the term 'remedy' is associated with civil law as it focuses on the victim or applicant, the violation of whose rights should be remedied. Nevertheless the reference to compensation in this article makes clear that this provision does not only refer to criminal law sanctions, but includes civil law remedies as well.[7] Moreover, 'sanctions' is the term generally used by the ECJ in its case law pertaining to remedial matters under civil law.[8] Remarkably, in the original proposal of the RED this article was entitled as 'Penalties', and contained no reference to compensation. The Parliament's legislative proposal interpreted this provision as regulating only criminal sanctions. The Parliament's argument for amending this provision clearly shows this perception. More specifically, they argued that it was necessary to bring the RED

> into line with the wording of the UN Convention on the Elimination of All Forms of Racial Discrimination; in particular Article 4, and therefore [the Parliament] provides a more explicit description of the offences which would be punishable by law under the Directive.[9]

---

4 Proposal for a Council Directive implementing the principle of equal treatment between persons irrespective of racial or ethnic origin, COM(1999) 566 final – 1999/0253 (CNS), 25 November 1999, at 9 (emphasis added). The same phrasing can be found in the Proposal for a Council Directive establishing a general framework for equal treatment in employment and occupation. This latter document moreover emphasised, citing a report of the Commission that "there remains a number of outstanding problems in the application of Community law: [...] the effectiveness of legal remedies and sanctions [...]." *Id.*, at 12.

5 See for instance Judgment of 10 April 1984 in *Case 14/83*, *Von Colson and Kamann v. Land Nordrhein-Westfalen*, [1984] ECR 1891.

6 See also Tobler (2005a), at 32.

7 See also Tobler (2005a), at 32.

8 See inter alia *Case 14/83*, *Von Colson and Kamann v. Land Nordrhein-Westfalen*.

9 According to the original proposal "Member States shall lay down the rules on penalties applicable to infringements of the national provisions adopted pursuant to this Directive and shall

However, the corresponding part of the Recast Directive does not aspire to harmonise EC law with the CERD or any other conventions with penal provisions even though it is also entitled as 'Penalties' and has similar requirements to that of Article 15 RED.[10]

For the above reasons, it can be concluded that Article 15 RED is concerned with remedies in general, and does not specifically relate to criminal law measures. Tobler argues in this context that

> [i]ndeed, this is the way that they are generally interpreted in academic writing according to which it is here that the right to a general and personal remedy can be found in the Directives.[11]

Accordingly, the term 'sanction' is used to refer to remedies *strictu senso.*

7.3. Effective, Proportionate and Dissuasive

Article 15 RED stipulates that remedies for infringements of the national provisions adopted pursuant to the RED have to be effective, proportionate and dissuasive. These requirements find their origin in the case law on sex

---

take all measures necessary to ensure that they are implemented." The Parliament complemented this provision by stipulating that "[t]his will include prohibiting by legal sanction: incitement or pressure to racial discrimination; any act or practice by a public authority or public institution or racial discrimination against persons, groups of persons or institution. Penalties may include the payment of compensation to victim." Report on the proposal for a Council directive on implementing the principle of equal treatment between persons irrespective of racial or ethnic origin, COM(1999)566 – C5-0067/2000 – 1999/0253(CNS), A5-0136/2000, 16 May 2000, at 29.

Interestingly, however, the original proposal of the Framework Directive in relation to Article 14 on Penalties set out that "[t]his provision does not oblige the Member States to introduce penal sanctions." Proposal for a Council Directive establishing a general framework for equal treatment in employment and occupation, COM(1999)565 final– 1999/0225 (CNS), 25 November 1999, at 14.

[10] Directive 2006/54/EC of the European Parliament and of the Council of 5 July 2006 on the implementation of the principle of equal opportunities and equal treatment of men and women in matters of employment and occupation (the 'Recast Directive'). "Article 18 Compensation and Reparation Member States shall introduce into their national legal systems such measures as are necessary to ensure *real and effective* compensation or reparation as the Member States determine so for the loss and damage sustained by a person injured as a result of discrimination on grounds of sex, in a way which is *dissuasive and proportionate* to the damage suffered. Such compensation or reparation may not be restricted by the fixing of a prior upper limit, except in cases where the employer can prove that the only damage suffered by an applicant as a result of discrimination within the meaning of the Directive is the refusal to take his/her job application into consideration" (emphasis added).

It can be seen that it clearly establishes the same requirements as Art. 15 RED and Art. 25 Recast Directive. The only difference is that it explicitly lays down the prohibition of upper limits on damages, which has been established in the case law.

[11] Tobler (2005a), at 32. See also Toms (2008), at 3.

equality flowing from the general principle of effective judicial protection.[12] It was first in the *Von Colson* case that the Court explicitly laid down these requirements when it stated that sanctions have to

> be such as to guarantee real and effective judicial protection. Moreover it must also have a real deterrent effect on the employer. [...] where a Member State chooses to penalize the breach of the prohibition of discrimination by the award of compensation, that compensation must in any event be adequate in relation to the damage sustained.[13]

It has also been argued that at present there "exists a general Community law requirement that remedies must be effective, proportionate, and dissuasive."[14] Notwithstanding this general requirement, the three criteria have remained relatively vague both in the case law of the Court and in the RED.

In the light of this explanation, it is not surprising that several definitions of these requirements have been suggested by scholars. Cohen, for instance, explained that

> [t]o be effective, remedies and sanctions must achieve the desired outcome; to be proportionate, they must adequately reflect the gravity, nature and extent of the loss and/or harm; and to be dissuasive, sanctions must deter future acts of discrimination.[15]

According to Moore, in order to be effective, a remedy "must redress the harm done according to the objectives of the legislation."[16] Shelton argued that

> [t]he degree of sanction should be proportionate to the gravity of the act deserving of punishment. Deterrence, in contrast, seeks to influence the behaviour of the particular wrongdoer and all others who might be tempted to act in the same way in the future.[17]

In Prechal's view

> [e]ffectiveness could perhaps be understood as producing the desired result: to compel observance of the terms and spirit of Community law. [...] Proportionality [...] refers to the relationship between the nature of the breach and the sanction imposed or remedy granted. Dissuasiveness seems to aim at preventing disobedience to the Community rules.[18]

---

12 See inter alia Tobler (2005b), at 8; Waddington (2003), at 44; Barry (2003), at 415; Higgins (2003), at 407; Bell (2002a), at 25. Concerning the case law of the ECJ see in this respect among others *Case 14/83*, *Von Colson and Kamann v. Land Nordrhein-Westfalen*; Judgment of 22 April 1997 in *Case C-180/95*, *Nils Draehmpaehl v. Urunia Immobilienservice OHG*, [1997] ECR 1-2195; *Commission of the European Communities v. Hellenic Republic,* Case 68/88, 21 September 1989.

13 *Case 14/83*, *Von Colson and Kamann v. Land Nordrhein-Westfalen*, para. 23.

14 Tobler (2005b), at 15.

15 Cohen (2004), at 19; Tobler (2005b), at 10. On deterrence see also Shelton (1999), at 281.

16 Moore (1993), at 538.

17 Shelton (1999), at 281.

18 Prechal (1997), at 9-10.

On the basis of the case law, it has been argued that effectiveness means "real and effective judicial protection", dissuasiveness means "real and deterrent effect on the employer", and proportionality when it concerns compensation means that it "must in any event be adequate in relation to the damage sustained".[19] And on the basis of these and similar definitions Tobler concluded that "[b]eyond such broad definitions it is hardly possible to formulate generally applicable criteria for judging the requirements of effectiveness, proportionality and dissuasiveness."[20] She also added that

> there may be only one general guideline for the determination of the effectiveness, proportionality and dissuasiveness of national remedies for breach of EC discrimination law, namely the duty to determine the remedy in the light of the concrete circumstances of each individual case.[21]

Despite this conclusion, some observations can still be made with respect to each element both in general and on the basis of the ECJ's jurisprudence. First of all, these requirements are conjunctive. This means that the remedies should fulfil all these requirements, it is not appropriate if only one of them is complied with. Still, the idea is not conveyed that only one particular remedy should comply with the criteria. This raises the question whether it is satisfactory if the palette of sanctions complies with these requirements. It can be argued that this is indeed necessary, but not sufficient as the requirements of the RED might still not be observed in individual cases. Accordingly, it is more important that these requirements are complied with in individual cases in which it would be appropriate if the remedies awarded together satisfy these benchmarks. This also means that it might be the case that the palette of available remedies in a particular country fulfils these requirements, they however might not be taken into account in the deliberation process.

The requirement of *effectiveness* of sanctions clearly derives from the *principle of effective judicial protection*, as could also be seen in the *Von Colson* case. This principle can be linked in turn back to the *general principle of effectiveness*, pursuant to which the enforcement of rights cannot be made excessively difficult or virtually impossible. In terms of sanctions this requirement could initially be translated to the requirement of the effective availability of sanctions, in accordance with the jurisprudence of the ECJ. The Court has, for instance, in the *Marshall* case laid down that measures "should be capable of being effectively relied upon by the persons concerned before

19 As Tobler observed, "[a]n examination of the Court's case law regarding the requirements of effectiveness, proportionality and dissuasiveness in relation to national remedies under general EC law gives the impression that the Court does not explain precisely how it arrives at the conclusion that a given remedy is or is not acceptable." Tobler (2005b), at 15.

20 Tobler (2005b), at 10.

21 Tobler (2005b), at 17. & 33.

national courts."[22] These remedies, in accordance inter alia with the *Coote* case, have to achieve the aim of the particular directive.[23] In terms of the RED the purpose to be achieved is to combat discrimination on the grounds of racial and ethnic origin and put into effect the principle of equal treatment. In this respect it has been emphasised in the case law that

> the objective is to arrive at real equality of opportunity and cannot therefore be attained in the absence of *measures appropriate to restore such equality* when it has not been observed.[24]

Thus, sanctions can be regarded as effective only when they are capable of helping the victims to achieve real equality of opportunity. Accordingly, the requirement of effectiveness focuses on the *victim* and the purpose of the victim.[25] With regard to this criterion the ECJ has also specified that achieving this aim has to be done by levelling up.[26] This means that the measures aimed at achieving equality cannot make the situation of the comparator/majority group worse, instead the position of the members of the minority's group should be brought up to the level of the majority's situation. For instance, in the *Defrenne* case[27] the Court clearly stated that as the social progress and the

---

[22] Judgment of 2 August 1993 in *Case C-271/91, Marshall v. Southampton and South-West Hampshire Area Health Authority*, [1986] ECR 723, para. 22.

[23] Judgment of 22 September 1998 in *Case C-185/97, Coote v. Granada Hospitality Ltd*, [1998] ECR I-5199, para. 20.

[24] *Case C-271/91, Marshall v. Southampton and South-West Hampshire Area Health Authority*, para. 24 (emphasis added). See also Judgment of 11 October 2007 in *Case C-460/06, Nadine Paquay v. Société d'architectes Hoet + Minne SPRL.*, [2007] ECR I-08511, para. 45; Judgment of 8 November 1990 in *Case C-177/88, Dekker v. Stichting Vormingscentrum voor Jong Volwassenen*, [1990] ECR 1-3941, para. 8. & 26.

[25] This view seems to have been implicitly formulated by Rombouts, Sardaro and Vandeginse according to whom "a remedy is effective only if it can either prevent the alleged violation or its continuation, or provide adequate redress for any violation that has already occurred." Rombouts, Sardaro & Vandeginste (2006), at 368.

[26] See inter alia Judgment of 21 June 2007 in *Joined Cases C-231/06, C-232/06, C-233/06, Office national des pensions v. Emilienne Jonkman and Hélène Vercheval and Noëlle Permesaen v. Office national des pensions*, [2007] ECR I-05149; Judgment of 13 December 1989 in *Case C-102/88, Ruzius-Wilbrink v. Bestuur van de bedrijfsvereniging voor Overheidsdiensten*, [1989] ECR 4311; Judgment of 27 June 1990 in *Case C-33/89, Kowalska v. Freie und Hansestadt Hamburg*, [1990] ECR 1-2591; Judgment of 31 March 1991 in *Case C-377/89, Norah Cotter and Ann McDermott v. Minister for Social Welfare and Attorney General*, [1987] ECR 1453; Judgment of 11 July 1991 in *Case C-31/90, Johnson v. Chief Adjudication Officer*, [1991] ECR 1-3723; Judgment of 8 April 1976 in *Case 43/75, Defrenne v. Societe Anonyme Belge de navigation aerienne Sabena*, [1976] ECR 455, especially paras. 10 & 15; Judgment of 11 December 1997 in *Case C-246/96, Magorrian and Cunningham v. Eastern Health and Social Services Board and Department of Health and Social Services*, [1997] ECR I-7153.

[27] *Case 43/75, Defrenne v. Societe Anonyme Belge de navigation aerienne Sabena.*

constant improvement of living and working conditions have to be ensured, equality cannot be achieved by not raising the salary of women to the level of the salary of men.

As far as the *proportionality* of a remedy is concerned the ECJ seems to examine in this respect to what extent the remedy redresses the harm suffered by the victim. More specifically, the ECJ has specified that the remedies have to be proportionate to the *damage suffered by the applicant*. For instance, in the *Marshall* case the Court established that

> [w]here financial compensation is the measure adopted in order to achieve the objective [...], it must be adequate, in that it must enable the loss and damage actually sustained as a result of the discriminatory dismissal to be made good in full.[28]

The Court has also added that the requirement of proportionality does not allow for generally setting upper limits on compensation,[29] arguably because it might endanger a full, and thus a proportionate compensation of all the damages suffered. These elements of the requirement of proportionality have been explicitly transplanted into the Recast Directive.[30]

Last but not least the criterion of *dissuasiveness* arguably aims at "preventing disobedience to the Community rules."[31] In other words, it is oriented at the particular and future potential *perpetrators*.[32] It does not, however, mean that the sanctions that could be in harmony with this criterion should be punitive in nature. It is commonly known that the fact that a victim can effectively vindicate his right to equal treatment before fact-finding bodies irrespective of

---

28 *Case C-271/91, Marshall v. Southampton and South-West Hampshire Area Health Authority*, para. 26. See also *Case C-180/95, Nils Draehmpaehl v. Urunia Immobilienservice OHG*, para. 27; *Case C-460/06, Nadine Paquay v. Société d'architectes Hoet + Minne SPRL.*, para. 45.

29 *Case C-180/95, Nils Draehmpaehl v. Urunia Immobilienservice OHG*, para. 35.

30 Art. 18 of the Recast Directive. "Article 18 Compensation and Reparation "Member States shall introduce into their national legal systems such measures as are necessary to ensure real and effective compensation or reparation as the Member States so determine for the loss and damage sustained by a person injured as a result of discrimination on grounds of sex, in a way which is dissuasive and *proportionate to the damage suffered*. Such compensation or reparation may not be restricted by the *fixing of a priori upper limit*, except in cases where the employer can prove that the only damage suffered by an applicant as a result of discrimination within the meaning of the Directive is the refusal to take his/her job application into consideration" (emphasis added).

31 Prechal (1997), at 9-10.

32 In this respect it has, for instance, been argued that the requirement of deterrence and effectiveness might conflict with each other. An example can be that the compensation awarded is proportionate to the damage suffered, but it cannot be regarded to have deterrent effect on the employer. This is called the concept of 'discrimination pays'. However, in these cases the remedy that has been awarded cannot be regarded as being effective either. See inter alia Tobler (2005b), at 10; Shelton (2005), at 22.

the awarded redress has a deterrent effect on potential perpetrators.[33] The fact that not only punitive measures can have a deterrent effect is also confirmed by the ECJ, which has also applied the requirement of dissuasiveness with respect to compensation. AG Van Gerven explained in his opinion on the *Marschall* case[34] that, amongst others, "[*c*]*ompensation* would be adequate if the limit was pitched high enough so that the sanction was not deprived of its 'effective, uniform and *deterrent* nature'."[35] Nevertheless, the language used by the Court in terms of deterrent effect seems to indicate that discrimination (on the grounds of gender and, due to the similar formulation in the RED, obviously on the grounds of racial and ethnic origin) is a grave violation, the redress of which should react to this gravity. In this context Ellis also argued that

> deterrence is not normally regarded as one of the objectives of the civil law. The express mention of deterrence in the context of remedies for sex discrimination seems to underlie what a serious view the ECJ takes of the issue of sex equality.[36]

Accordingly, the question is rather "how much deterrence is required."[37] Arguably, if the requirements of effectiveness and proportionality are complied with, the remedy also has a deterrent effect. In order to guarantee further deterrent effect, the circumstances related to the perpetrator has to be taken into account when adjudicating on the redress.

7.4. Forms of Sanctions

In order to be able to examine whether the sanctions existing in the countries under review comply with these criteria, it is necessary to classify these sanctions. In academic writing several classifications can be found. They are based, for instance, on the type of law, purpose, function, form of the remedy, the effect it has on substantive rights and the level at which they are intended

---

33 According to Lindblom, "[i]t is a matter of an interaction of functions, a cross-fertilization between behaviour modification and conflict resolution." Lindblom (2007), at 292. It has been argued that concerning deterrence research "shows a correlation between the certainty of consequences and the reduction of offences, but little correlation between the severity of punishment and reduced incidence of wrongdoing." Shelton (2005), at 14.

34 Advocate General Van Gerven in *Case C-271/91, Marshall v. Southampton and South-West Hampshire Area Health Authority*, [1986] ECR 723, para. 16.

35 Moore (1993), at 537.

36 Ellis (2005), at 264.

37 Shelton (2005), at 13. According to Lindblom, "[i]t is a matter of an interaction of functions, a cross-fertilization between behaviour modification and conflict resolution." Lindblom (2007), at 292. In McCrudden's view "[t]he sanctions to be provided at the national level must be 'effective, proportionate and dissuasive' but without defining how far the inclusion of 'dissuasion' expands the role of the remedy beyond mere compensation for individuals." McCrudden (2001), at 295. See also Toms (2008), at 9.

to operate, reflecting the different theories of remedies, or relying on the orientation of the remedy, and so on.[38]

Due to the fact that the requirements of the RED on sanctions focus on the aim of the sanction, hereafter a classification that is also based on the purpose of the remedy will be relied on. This classification will make it easier to allocate the requirements of the RED on the palette of sanctions and this makes it possible to evaluate the available sanctions in the countries under review. On the basis of the aims of the sanctions three main forms can be and have been distinguished: reparative, punitive, and preventive.[39] This classification seems useful, as in addition to referring to the aim of the remedy they, to some extent, also determine the form and function of the remedy, and can uniformly be applied to all types of procedures.

According to the ECJ's steady line of jurisprudence concerning the ETD, which was subsequently confirmed in the *Feryn* case in relation to the RED,[40] "the Directive does not impose a specific sanction on the Member States"[41] and "it leaves Member States free to choose between the different solutions suitable for achieving its objective."[42] This indicates that in principle all forms of sanctions can be appropriate that comply with the benchmarks of the RED.

7.4.1. Reparative Sanctions

Arguably, the very first aim of every civil procedure is to give reparation to the victims of discrimination; that is to compensate, in one way or another, for the damage incurred by the victim. Of the different forms of sanctions reparative sanctions are the only ones explicitly and primarily concentrating on the victim and aiming to provide him with redress. As reparative sanctions primarily have a victim focus, and are therefore preferred in discrimination cases. Reparation can be made in two ways: it can take the form of restitution, and when this is not possible or not desired the victim can also be compensated for the damages incurred by him.

---

[38] For a short summary of these classifications, see Tobler (2005b), at 5. On the classification of remedies see inter alia Zakrzweski (2005). He tried to reclassify remedies on the basis of a narrow meaning of the word 'remedies', that is a court order. He excluded all the other possible meanings of remedies from the classification.

[39] See inter alia Shelton (2005); Zakrzewski (2005); Lewis (1996); Rombouts, Sardaro & Vandeginste (2006); Tobler (2005b), at 36; Cane (2002), at 43-44.

[40] Judgment of 10 July 2008 in *Case C-54/07, Centrum voor gelijkheid van kansen en racismebestrijding v. Firma Feryn NV.*, [2008] ECR I-05187, para. 37. "Directive 2000/43 does not [...] prescribe a specific sanction, but leaves Member States free to choose between the different solutions suitable for achieving its objective."

[41] *Case C-180/95, Nils Draehmpaehl v. Urunia Immobilienservice OHG*, para. 24.

[42] *Case 14/83, Von Colson and Kamann v. Land Nordrhein-Westfalen*, para. 18.

7.4.1.1. Restitutionary Sanctions

Restitution sets out to create a situation as if the violation had not happened; namely, to restitute the situation that existed before the violation took place.[43] It has been argued that restitutive measures "simply restate prior substantive rights,"[44] which means that "[t]hey do not require the defendant to do anything that the defendant was not required to do already."[45] In this respect the Permanent Court of International Justice explained that

> reparation must, as far as possible, wipe out all the consequence of the illegal act and re-establish the situation which would, in all probability, have existed if that act had not been committed.[46]

Shelton also argues that "[t]he primary goal of human rights remedies should be rectification or restitution rather than compensation."[47] This has been accepted as the principle of primacy of restitution, which means that restitution should be preferred to other forms of remedies. Moreover, this principle also includes that among the different forms of restitution, those remedies should be preferred that are "most capable of recreating the situation that would have existed."[48]

Restitution can, naturally, take different forms depending on the individual circumstances. For instance, it can embody the return of land to indigenous people. Restitution can, accordingly, provide fact-finders with the opportunity to find creative remedies, and to impose positive obligations on the perpetrators. Thus, restitution can take many forms depending on the needs of the victims. For this reason, and as the above example shows, not only can restitutionary remedies contribute to a more effective enforcement of the right to equal treatment, it can also enhance minority protection by paying attention to the special needs of the particular minority group.

7.4.1.2. Compensatory Sanctions

Nevertheless, restitution may not always be possible, it may not, in all cases, be the most effective remedy, or some additional measures may also be required in order to make a sanction effective. Accordingly, there is a need

43 Zakrzewski describes reparative measures as replicative remedies, since they "simply restate prior substantive rights. They do not require the defendant to do anything that the defendant was not required to do already. Nor do they release the defendant from doing something that the defendant was required to do." Zakrzewski (2005), at 203.

44 Zakrzewski (2005), at 203.

45 Zakrzewski (2005), at 203.

46 *Case Concerning the Factory at Chorzów (Germany v. Poland)*, 26 July 1927, 1928 PCIJ (Ser. A.) No. 17. See also Rombouts, Sardaro & Vandeginste (2006), at 395.

47 Shelton (2005), at 21.

48 Rombouts, Sardaro & Vandeginste (2006), at 395.

for complementary remedies. The most often applied sanction with the aim of recovering the injuries the victim has suffered is compensation,[49] which can also be classified as a form of corrective remedy.[50] It is generally accepted that compensation should include both pecuniary and non-pecuniary damages incurred by the victim, together with interest and attorney's fees.[51]

Monetary compensation is usually awarded, but the damages can also be recovered in natura. The dividing line between this latter modus and restitution is very thin; the distinction can arguably only be made pertaining to the original situation.[52] The distinction can be discovered in the aim of the measure. For instance, in the *Aloeboetoe* case, which concerned the physical attack, abduction and arbitrary killing of a group of unarmed people of the Saramaka tribe, the Inter-American Court ordered the reopening of a school in order to enable the children of the victims "to continue their education until they reach a certain age."[53] This remedy can be regarded as constituting compensation in natura for the children because the aim of the fact-finder was to compensate the harm suffered and not to restitute the original situation. Similarly, the simple establishment that the perpetrator has discriminated against the applicant could also suffice the victim under certain circumstances, and thus, can be interpreted as compensation in natura.[54]

---

49 Zakrzewski describes compensation as transformational remedy since it transforms or modifies "the legal relationship between the claimant and the defendant which existed before trial. A transformative remedy is a legal relation that significantly differs from any legal relation that existed before the court order was made." Zakrzewski (2005), at 203. See also at 168.

50 See inter alia Zakrzewski (2005), at 168; Shelton (2005), at 10. According to Shelton "compensation in the framework of basic rights serves to restore to individuals to the extent possible their capacity to achieve the ends that they personally value. As such, compensation may have an important rehabilitative effect, alleviate suffering, and provide for material needs." Shelton (2005), at 11.

51 See inter alia Tobler (2005b), at 36; Moore (1993), at 539. For the case law of the ECJ see for instance *Case C-271/91, Marshall v. Southampton and South-West Hampshire Area Health Authority*, para. 31; Judgment of 1 June 1994 in *Case C-136/92, P, Commission v. Augusto Brazzelli Lualdi and others*, [1994] ECR I-1981, para. 35. See also the Advocate General Van Gerven in *Case C-271/91, Marshall v. Southampton and South-West Hampshire Area Health Authority*, [1986] ECR 723, para. 18.

52 According to Shelton, "[a]n order for specific conduct does more than eliminate the present unlawful conditions. It denies to the wrongdoer the possibility of paying damages and continuing to do harm. It also obviates the need for victims to have the will and financial ability to initiate repeated litigation for declaratory judgments or damages. It reduces the plaintiff's risk that the remedy will turn out to be ineffective." Shelton (2005), at 45.

53 On this case see Rombouts, Sardaro & Vandeginste (2006), at 407.

54 As Rombouts, Sardaro and Vandeginste argued, "[t]here are cases where damages are not awarded, notwithstanding the finding of violation. It is quite frequent in human rights adjudication [...] that a judgment upholding the applicant's contention on the existence of a wrongful act attributable to the defendant State, is deemed capable of providing some redress and therefore is categorized in itself as a form of reparation for the victim." Rombouts, Sardaro & Vandeginste (2006), at 392-393. See also Toms (2008), at 6.

Compensation in natura has the advantage that fact-finders (naturally, within the limit of law) can order different performances which under certain circumstances can constitute more appropriate compensation than monetary compensation. For instance, similarly to restitution, positive obligations can be imposed on the respondents. Also, when applying the remedy of compensation in natura the special needs of victims and the group aspect of the case can be taken into account. It is somewhat more difficult and quite rarely applied to redress a whole group with monetary compensation, especially when the complaint is filed in an individual enforcement procedure. When the aim is to compensate the whole group, the claim should be enforced through an actio popularis complaint. In the case of individual enforcement, additional remedies should also be found to change the contested discriminatory practice. One could think of, for instance, imposing positive obligations on the respondents, such as anti-discrimination training, mainstreaming, and so on.

7.4.2. Punitive Sanctions

Punitive sanctions, as the name also shows, aim to punish the perpetrator for committing discrimination.[55] As already indicated supra, the primary aim of a discrimination procedure is to achieve substantive equality and compensate the victim. Accordingly, punitive measures should not be the dominant colours on the palette of sanctions; they should merely be applied as complementary measures to the reparative sanctions.

In civil and administrative procedures[56] punitive sanctions can take the form of punitive or exemplary damages and fines.[57] The ECJ itself has also mentioned fines as a possible means of effective redress.[58] Examples for

[55] In Shelton's view, "[r]emedies express opprobrium to the wrongdoer. This is usually incorporated in the application of punishment, sometimes as a vindication of society's interest in retribution, or it can take the form of fines or exemplary or punitive damages. Sanctions express the social conviction that disrespect for the rights of others impairs the wrongdoer's status as a moral claimant." Shelton (2005), at 12.

[56] As argued in Ch. 3 on access to justice the enforcement provisions of the RED are generally concerned with civil and/or administrative law measures, and due to this fact no special considerations will here be given to criminal law sanctions.

[57] Some scholars differentiate between exemplary and punitive damages. The aim of the former is deterrence, while the latter focuses on punishment. In practice, however, it is difficult to make such a clear distinction. Shelton (2005), at 41.

[58] *Case 14/83*, *Von Colson and Kamann v. Land Nordrhein-Westfalen*. The Court laid down that "provisions requiring the employer to offer a post to the candidate discriminated against or giving the candidate adequate financial compensation, backed up where necessary by a system of fines." According to Tobler, "[t]his statement carries the important message that fines, be they of an administrative or of a criminal nature, are merely complementary, rather than being at the forefront of the national enforcement system." Tobler (2005b), at 11. Arguably, however, it could also be interpreted as indicating that the victim should not be forgotten

employing punitive measures can also be found in international adjudication. In the *Mayagna (Sumo) Awas Tingni Community* case,[59] for instance, concerning the violations of the rights of an indigenous community, the Inter-American Court ordered the State, in addition to reparatory measures, to invest a given sum in "works or services of collective interest of the Awas Tingni Community, by common agreement with the Community and under the supervision of the Inter-American Commission."[60] This sum for works and services could be classified as punitive damage since it was imposed in addition to the reparative measures. This case also shows that in some cases punitive measures can come very close to reparative sanctions if the fine is to be devoted to a particular purpose.

In the *Feryn* case the ECJ also seemed to accept that under certain circumstances punitive sanctions can also be regarded appropriate. It established that

> [i]f it appears appropriate to the situation at issue in the main proceedings, those sanctions may [...] include a finding of discrimination by the court or the competent administrative authority in conjunction with an adequate level of publicity [...].[61]

Arguably, a mere punitive sanction can only be considered satisfactory if the perspective of the victim and/or applicant is appropriately taken into consideration. In this concrete case, it seems that the ECJ took this aspect into account. More specifically, the applicant was an interest organisation in an actio popularis claim and not an individual person, which seems to justify the acceptability of a primarily punitive redress instead of compensation for the damages.

7.4.3. Preventive Sanctions

Sanctions can also primarily aim to prevent the future occurrence of a violation. All the above forms of sanctions generally have a dissuasive effect, but this prevention dimension is merely ancilliary. However, there are some particular sanctions that aim primarily to prevent discrimination.[62] This is, for

---

during the enforcement procedure; in other words, when fines are adjudicated, a certain form of compensation is still necessary.

[59] *Mayagna (Sumo) Awas Tingni Community v. Nicaragua*, 31 August 2001, 2001 Inter-Am. Ct. H.R. (Ser. C) No. 79.

[60] See also Rombouts, Sardaro & Vandeginste (2006), at 408.

[61] *Case C-54/07, Centrum voor gelijkheid van kansen en racismebestrijding v. Firma Feryn NV.*, para. 39.

[62] According to Rombouts, Sardaro and Vandegiste "[w]hile it is fair to assume that any remedial measures – and particularly those considered so far – may constitute a positive contribution for ensuring future compliance with human rights, their main aim remains the undoing or the redress of the adverse consequences of the violations found by the supervisory

instance, the case when the court prohibits further discrimination, or orders the publication of the decisions with the primary aim to inform the public.[63] From a minority protection perspective this sanction has a clear group perspective as it aims to prevent the breach of the right to equal treatment of persons with a certain racial or ethnic origin. Again, this sanction in itself can hardly provide appropriate remedy as it concentrates on the perpetrator. Nevertheless, similarly to punitive sanction, they can be regarded as satisfactory if the victim's perspective is appropriately considered.

7.5. Factors Determining the Form and Extent of Remedies

Naturally, the individual circumstances[64] vary from case to case, but among the particular cases some common factors can still be discovered that could give a helping hand in determining the most effective remedy in a specific case.[65] As argued above, it is of the utmost importance that the victim's perspective is taken into account, which is an extremely significant development in racial discrimination cases. Earlier racial discrimination cases were considered to fall under criminal law, which concentrated on the punishment of the perpetrator. Some other factors have also been mentioned which would, for instance, influence the amount of aggravated damages, such as the gravity of the violation or the intent of the wrongdoer.[66]

Departing from the purpose of these criteria in the RED and the problems occurring in theory and practice, the following factors will be distinguished: the nature of the violation, the circumstances related to the victim and the circumstances related to the perpetrator. Taking these factors into account would enable fact-finders to fulfil the requirements of effectiveness, proportionality and dissuasiveness. A couple of these factors are rather obvious, and others are also often taken into account in the adjudication process, however, generally not in a systematic, explicit and consistent way.

In order to appropriately address all forms of discrimination these factors need to be taken into account. In this way not only discrimination against an individual can be effectively remedied, but the group aspect of the violation

body. There are some measures, however, that are not concerned with redress, but only with the prevention of the recurrence of similar violations in the future." Rombouts, Sardaro & Vandeginste (2006), at 409.

63 Naturally, the publication goes hand in hand with a punitive effect by virtue of naming and shaming.

64 Tobler (2005b), at 17.

65 Cohen argued that "[a] number of variables need to be considered when seeking to assess the quality and effectiveness of either existing or proposed remedies and sanctions." Cohen (2004), at 17.

66 On the factors that might influence the quantification of non-pecuniary damages, see inter alia Rombouts, Sardaro & Vandeginste (2006), at 388; Cohen (2004), at 17.

can also be considered. These factors would thus contribute to attaining a group justice model in addition to individual justice which is the main focus of the enforcement provisions of the RED.[67]

7.5.1. Circumstances Related to the Victim

As explained, it is in fact the victim's perspective that must be the guiding principle in determining the form and extent of sanctions.[68] The World Conference on remedies,[69] for instance, "stressed that it is with the most vulnerable that enforcement structures and remedies should be particularly concerned."[70] Similarly, following the *Von Colson* case the ECJ explicitly requires that the redress be tailored to the victim's situation. Thus, there has to be a personal remedy.[71] By taking the victim's perspective and wishes into account, the requirement of effectiveness in Article 15 RED can be ensured.

Three important factors can be distinguished with respect to the victims' circumstances: the nature of the victim, the protected ground of the victim that played a role in the violation, and the own fault or responsibility of the victim.

First of all, a very significant aspect that needs to be taken into consideration is the question *what the nature* of the victim is. This sub-factor would affect the form of remedy. Similarly to legal standing,[72] a distinction can be made between individual, collective and group victims.[73] Evidently, one can talk of an *individual victim* when it is one person who is discriminated against, which mostly happens in direct discrimination cases. A *collective victim* is a group of individual victims. In such cases, the emphasis is on the single individual violations; that is the discrimination is not directed against a group as such, the individual victims merely enforce their right in a single procedure. A *group victim* can be identified when the discrimination is oriented at the group as such. Group victims can be identified in indirect and structural discrimination cases. The World Conference on remedies has also clearly recognised the 'collective or group dimension'[74] of certain forms of discrimination in terms of redress. It has been emphasised that "[e]ffective remedies should be made

[67] See inter alia Waddington (2003), at 51; Higgins (2003), at 399.

[68] See inter alia Rombouts, Sardaro & Vandeginste (2006), at 358; McCrudden (2001), at 300; Tobler (2005b), at 8; Kinsman (2007), at 6.

[69] World Conference against Racism, Racial Discrimination, Xenophobia and Related Intolerance, Declaration, Durban, 31 August – 8 September 2001.

[70] McCrudden (2001), at 300.

[71] Kinsman (2007), at 6; Tobler (2005b), at 8.

[72] See Ch. 5 on legal standing.

[73] See the theory of McCrudden concerning the individual and group justice model. McCrudden (2003), at 23; McCrudden (1999), at 328; McCrudden (2001), at 297.

[74] McCrudden (2001), at 300.

available for the collective as well as the individual rights of indigenous peoples."[75] Rombouts and others argue that

> [s]ince the principal aim of reparation consists in making good the damage to protected interests, it is natural that remedial measures of a collective nature are particularly appropriate in cases of violations of collective rights.[76]

The victim status does often become visible via the particular form of legal standing: the group aspect of the discrimination is generally considered in actio popularis claims. In the first case substantially pertaining to the RED the Court explicitly laid down that

> [i]n a case [...], where there is no direct victim of discrimination but a body empowered to do so by law seeks a finding of discrimination and the imposition of a penalty, the sanctions which Article 15 of Directive 2000/43 requires to be laid down in national law must also be effective, proportionate and dissuasive.[77]

From the perspective of minority protection, remedies for a group victim are very important. In such cases, financial compensation can only exceptionally provide effective remedy.[78] On the one hand, it is difficult to define the amount of compensation; and on the other hand, this compensation is difficult to distribute amongst the whole group. Monetary compensation can often only be regarded as an appropriate remedy when the procedure is initiated by an interest organisation in an actio popularis claim, and the compensation is awarded to this organisation, which devotes this amount in one way or another to support the group concerned. Accordingly, in most cases other reparative measures should be found if the group is to be addressed as a whole. McCrudden, for instance, takes the example of indigenous people whose lands were expropriated. In such cases returning them their lands or providing them with other lands would be the most effective remedy, rather than financial compensation to the group.[79] In the *Lubicon Lake Band v. Canada case*,[80] the Human Rights Committee indicated that an effective remedy may constitute community-building programmes aimed at the whole group.[81] Similarly, in the *Srebrenica* case,[82] which rather concerns collective victims than group

---

75 Cited by McCrudden (2001), at 300.

76 Rombouts, Sardaro & Vandeginste (2006), at 407.

77 *Case C-54/07, Centrum voor gelijkheid van kansen en racismebestrijding v. Firma Feryn NV.*, para. 38.

78 Financial compensation can, for instance, constitute an effective remedy also from a group perspective when the claim is initiated in an actio popularis procedure, and the awarded amount is devoted to achieving equal opportunities for the particular group. On actio popularis claims see Chapter 5 on legal standing.

79 McCrudden (2001), at 256.

80 *Lubicon Lake Band v. Canada*, UNHRC (1990) No. 167/1984, 26 March 1990.

81 On this case see Rombouts, Sardaro & Vandeginste (2006), at 369.

82 *Ferida Selimović and others v. the Republika Srpska*, 7 March 2003, The Human Rights Chamber for Bosnia and Herzegovina, No. CH/01/8365.

victims, there were no individual awards of compensation, rather a lump sum contribution was ordered to be paid to a foundation in order that all family members of the missing persons could benefit from it.

The second aspect related to the victim overlaps with the nature of the violation; that is the *protected ground* of the victim. This sub-factor is particularly important to minorities whose special needs can be considered in this way. Importantly, especially in intersectional discrimination cases, fact-finders should leave it to the victims to define their protected ground that is allegedly in play, since only then can their interest be effectively taken into account.[83]

The final aspect that needs to be considered in this context is the own *fault or own responsibility* of the victim in a given case. In general, this sub-factor defines the extent of the particular sanction rather than the form of it. An example can be found in the *Draehmpaehl* case of the ECJ, in which the Court made a distinction between those who "would not have obtained the position to be filled since the applicant appointed had superior qualifications" and those who "would have obtained the position if there had been no discrimination in the selection process."[84] According to the Court,

> it does not seem unreasonable for a Member State to lay down a statutory presumption that the damage suffered by an applicant belonging to the first category may not exceed a ceiling of three months' salary.[85]

However, it precludes such an upper limit "where that applicant would have obtained the vacant position if the selection process had been carried out without discrimination."[86] Being appropriately qualified belongs to the own responsibility of the applicants influencing the extent of the remedy at stake.

7.5.2. Nature of the Violation

The nature of the violation is an important factor in determining the form and extent of the appropriate remedy. In terms of the requirements of the RED this factor in general aims to fulfil the criterion of proportionality.

This factor can be broken down into at least three sub-factors. These are the form and gravity of the violation, the material scope concerning which the violation has taken place and the protected ground related to which or on the grounds of which the violation happened.

---

83 See also Fredman (2005b), at 16. "Only when minority women are given the opportunity to frame their own position, from the perspective of both gender discrimination and discrimination based on ethnicity, race or religion, will it be possible to address this issue."

84 *Case C-180/95, Nils Draehmpaehl v. Urunia Immobilienservice OHG*, para. 33.

85 *Id.*, para. 35.

86 *Id.*, para. 37.

First of all, the *form and gravity of the violation* have to be considered.[87] This aspect above all refers to the particular right that has been violated in addition to the right to non-discrimination. As Zakrzewski observed, "once a substantive right is recognized as existing then it is the substantive right which drives the remedy."[88] This aspect, in general, describes what kind of violation we are faced with, for instance, whether it is the violation of property rights, or a violation of contract law provisions. The form and extent of a violation can be further narrowed with respect to discrimination. Accordingly, it specifically refers to the form of discrimination, and the way it has been committed. For instance, since direct discrimination is based on prejudice, it can be taken as a more serious form of discrimination than indirect discrimination which actually means the lack of attention to the interests of others. This aspect seems to have also been taken into account in the case of *X v. European Central Bank* where the Court of First Instance, inter alia, had to determine whether the penalty imposed on the applicant due to his harassment of a colleague was disproportionate. The Court in this context stated that "the penalty to be imposed is to be determined on the basis of an overall assessment [...] of all the concrete facts and matters appertaining to the individual case,"[89] and more closely, it looked at "*the number and frequency of the incidents recorded*."[90] Not only is this sub-factor important from the perspective of addressing the harm, but it is also relevant in terms of the other two criteria; that is effectiveness and dissuasiveness. With the help of this sub-factor the harm caused to the whole group can also be taken into account.

The *material scope*[91] in the context of which the violation happened can be taken as the second aspect of the nature of the violation. This aspect is also quasi intuitively taken into account, and refers to the field in relation to which the discrimination has happened: whether it was an employment case, or related to providing services, or concerned education.[92] The ECJ has emphasised, for instance in the *Von Colson* case, that remedies have to be "sufficiently effective to achieve the objective of the directive"[93] that was in the given case to guarantee "the principle of equal treatment [...] as regards

---

87 This aspect is often mentioned in the academic literature, mainly in the context of aggravating circumstances. Cohen refers to this aspect as the circumstances of the violation; Shelton calls it the level of wrongdoing or level of suffering. Cohen (2004), at 17; Shelton (2005), at 36.

88 Zakrzewski (2005), at 58.

89 Judgment of 18 October 2001 in *Case T-333/99*, *X v. European Central Bank*, 2001 ECR II-03021, para. 221.

90 *Id.*, para. 224 (emphasis added).

91 On the material scope of the Directive see Busstra (2010).

92 See also Farkas (2006), at 25.

93 Judgment of 10 April 1984 in *Case 14/83*, *Von Colson and Kamann v. Land Nordrhein-Westfalen*, [1984] ECR 1891, para. 18.

access to employment."[94] More explicitly in the *Marshall* case, the Court took into consideration that the violation concerned a dismissal, so it stipulated that the "situation of equality could not be restored without either reinstating the victim of discrimination or [...] financial compensation."[95] Thus, in this case the suggested remedy was precisely tailored, among other factors, to the field in which the violation took place. This sub-factor mainly has an effect on the particular form of the sanction, and plays much less a role in determining the extent of it.

Finally, and again a rather obvious element, overlapping with the circumstances related to the victim, is the *protected ground*, which does and should play a role in the examination of the harm. This generally does not cause any problem, since it is obviously related to the factual circumstances. With the proper examination of this factor the group aspect of the case can also be considered.

7.5.3. Circumstances Related to the Perpetrator

The criterion of dissuasiveness clearly requires the examination of the circumstances related to the perpetrator. Nevertheless, as explained above, this factor should not be given too much emphasis as the fact that the circumstances related to the victim and the nature of the violation are appropriately taken into consideration has a dissuasive effect in itself. Admittedly, this factor gains more significance when punitive measures are preferred to reparative measures.

This factor can also be broken down into sub-factors: the size and market position of the perpetrator, whether the respondent is a private or public entity, overlapping with the nature of the violation the material scope in relation to which the violation has taken place, and the fault or intent of the perpetrator.

Firstly, the *size and market position* of the perpetrator should be taken into account in order to determine the form and, more importantly, the extent of the sanction. Undoubtedly, a multinational company would not be much deterred by financial compensation; it is more concerned with its good reputation. On the contrary, a small enterprise would be put into a disadvantageous situation if it had to pay a large amount of compensation. Importantly, when the ECJ emphasises that a sanction "must also have a real deterrent effect on the employer,"[96] it seems to refer mainly to the fact that the sanction has to fit the size and market position of the perpetrator.

---

[94] *Case 14/83, Von Colson and Kamann v. Land Nordrhein-Westfalen*, para. 17 (emphasis added).

[95] *Case C-271/91, Marshall v. Southampton and South-West Hampshire Area Health Authority*, para. 25.

[96] *Case 14/83, Von Colson and Kamann v. Land Nordrhein-Westfalen*, para. 23, *Case C-271/91, Marshall v. Southampton and South-West Hampshire Area Health Authority*, para. 24.

Secondly, it should also be taken into account whether the respondent is a *private or public entity*. In the case of a public body, financial compensation might not be dissuasive (enough) as it finances its expenses from the state budget.[97] Such bodies should set an example rather than discriminating, thus, imposing sanctions that involve positive obligations might be more effective in such instances.

The third important aspect that needs to be taken into account in the balancing process of determining the most appropriate remedy overlaps with the nature of the violation. It concerns the field in which the violation took place; that is the *material scope*. Evidently, if the perpetrator is an actor in the field of providing services, it would require a different approach from the case of an educational institution.

Lastly, the *fault* (in addition to the discrimination) *or intent* of the respondent should also be considered. It is generally accepted in discrimination cases and the ECJ also laid down, for instance, in the *Dekker* case that in discrimination cases

> the Directive [of 76/207] does not make liability on the part of the person guilty of discrimination conditional in any way on proof of fault or on the absence of any ground discharging such liability.[98]

It does not mean, however, that the fault of the respondent could not constitute an aggravating circumstance.[99] The House of Lords has, for instance, emphasised that "[t]he intention or motive of the defendant to discrimination, though it *may be relevant so far as remedies are concerned* […], is not a necessary condition of liability."[100] A similar approach can also be discovered in the *Levez* case[101] brought before the ECJ. The employer in this case did not provide the employee with accurate information as to the level of remuneration, so that she could not compare her salary with the remuneration of her male colleague. Later on, however, she discovered the difference in the remuneration in relation to his male predecessor, but due to the lapse of time she could only partially declare her damages. Although in this case the Court had to consider the question whether the national time limit could be applied in this case, the problem was somewhat broader, since it concerned the redress to the victim as well. It was the respondent's fault (in addition to the discrimination) in this case which made it impossible for her to enforce the whole claim for damages. Thus, one might re-formulate the problem as follows: the compensation given to the applicant could not be regarded as

97 See also Shelton (2005), at 14; Wolcher (2001), at 529.

98 *Case C-177/88, Dekker v. Stichting Vormingscentrum voor Jong Volwassenen*, para. 22.

99 See also Shelton (2005), at 14.

100 *R. v. Birmingham City Council ex parte Equal Opportunities Commission*, IRLR 96 (HC 1988) (emphasis added). On this case see inter alia Barmes (2003), at 202.

101 Judgment of 1 December 1998 in *Case C-326/96, Levez v. T.H. Jennings (Harlow Pools) Ltd.*, [1998] ECR 1-7835.

effective, since, among other factors, the respondent's fault was neglected. Accordingly, the Court indicated that a remedy could be deemed appropriate only when the respondent's fault was also taken into account.

In summary, it is important that these factors are deliberately and consistently taken into account when fact-finders decide on the forms and extent of sanctions in particular cases, so that sanctions are effective, proportionate and dissuasive.

7.6. Positive Action as Remedy

Positive action is a very broad concept,[102] which is also described under different names,[103] and has also been subject to different interpretations. The various possible interpretations would all be consistent with the qualification of positive action measures as specific forms of remedies. Article 15 RED does not exclude any forms of remedies from its scope. Furthermore, under certain circumstances the requirement of effectiveness might actually require the adoption of positive action measures in order to guarantee an effective remedy.

A definition will be given below of what should be understood by the term 'positive action measures'. On the basis of the definition three main lines of interpretation of positive action measures will be mapped and explained: positive action as exception, as duty and as remedy. This latter approach will be elaborated in more detail.

7.6.1. Definition of Positive Action

Several definitions have been drafted in relation to positive action, among which one in the RED. Pursuant to Article 5 RED entitled as 'positive action' 'the principle of equal treatment shall not prevent any Member State from maintaining or adopting specific measures to prevent or compensate for disadvantages linked to racial or ethnic origin.' In the different definitions, including the above definition in Article 5 RED, some common characteristics

[102] For a detailed discussion on positive action measures see Busstra (2010). See also O'Cinnéide (2003); O'Cinnéide (2006); De Vos (2007); Boerefijn et al. (2003); Costello (2003); Fredman (2000); Hucker (1999); Jackson (1999); Kovács (2006); Faundez (1994); McCrudden (1986); Mulder (1999); O'Donovan (1985); Pager (2003); Russel & O'Cinnéide (2003); Stratigaki (2005); Tobler (2006); Veldman (1999); Bossuyt (2002); Dhami, Squires & Modood (2006); Putting Equality into Practice What role for positive action? European Commission (2007); Charpentier (1998); Cohn (2003); Kollonay-Lehoczky (2006); Gijzen (2006), at 207-262.

[103] The most common names are: affirmative action, positive discrimination and reverse discrimination. See inter alia De Vos (2007), para. 6.

can be revealed.[104] First of all, a clear *group focus* is and can be identified,[105] and related to that there is an underlying *substantive equality* goal, which goes beyond addressing discrimination at individual level. Thirdly, and not inseparable from the group aspect, it is concerned with broader, *structural, institutional or societal changes*, instead of reacting to individual cases.[106] Finally, positive action measures can be both proactive and retroactive. Traditionally, positive action was adopted as a reaction to past discrimination, and only recently has the concept also opened up to preventive, prophylactic measures.[107] Although the compensatory view of positive action measures might seem to be similar or close to regarding positive action as a form of remedy in a discrimination complaint, they are clearly different in nature. Contrary to remedies in general, a positive action measure as redress for past disadvantage is not adopted as a reaction to a particular discrimination complaint. Nevertheless, understanding positive action as a particular form of remedy in a discrimination complaint is not excluded from the retroactive perception of positive action measures.

7.6.2. Different Approaches to Positive Action

As the above elaboration on positive action hinted at, positive action can be interpreted in different ways. Here three main approaches to positive action measures will be identified: positive action as exception to the principle of equal treatment, positive action as duty, and positive action as remedy. Naturally, this distinction is not watertight; there are several overlaps between the categories, but this classification seems to lead us closer to an understanding of positive action as a potential remedy.

7.6.2.1. Positive Action as an Exception to the Principle of Equal Treatment

In EC law, positive action is mainly regarded as an exception to the principle of equal treatment, even when the inherent relation to substantive equality

[104] For a detailed discussion see Busstra (2010). On the definitions see inter alia De Vos (2007), para. 5; Bossuyt (2002), para. 3; Pitt (1992), at 282; O'Cinnéide (2006), at 354; Costello (2003), at 178; Schiek, Waddington & Bell (2007), at 757-762; Gijzen (2006), at 208-216.

[105] See inter alia Fredman (2002), at 128-129; De Vos (2007), para. 9; Henrard (2007a), at 29; Gijzen (2006), at 211.

[106] See inter alia Costello (2003), at 178; O'Cinnéide (2006), at 354; Brown (2002), at 216.

[107] See inter alia Henrard (2007a), at 29. For instance, in the United States affirmative action measures were originally introduced as policy instruments to compensate black people for past disadvantages. Similarly, the Canadian Supreme Court accepted "affirmative action programmes that remedy proven systemic discrimination, even where such programmes entail remedial quotas or introduce positive discrimination for the previously marginalized group." De Vos (2007), at 64.

is increasingly being acknowledged.[108] Under this approach positive action constitutes objective justification.[109] This means that a member of a majority group starts a discrimination procedure against a respondent who preferred a person from a minority group to him. The respondent argues that his preference was based on a positive action regarding the members of that particular vulnerable group. It is for the fact-finder to examine whether the positive action can be accepted as objective justification for the differential treatment. In this respect "the prohibition of discrimination determines the outer limits of legitimate positive action measures."[110] As indicated supra, the Article 5 RED follows this interpretation; that is that positive action measures can justify a direct distinction, provided they are proportionate.[111] According to the Court such a measure cannot "guarantee [...] absolute and unconditional priority,"[112] and they should be "intended to eliminate or reduce actual instances of inequality which may exist in the reality of social life,"[113] or "remedying existing situation of imbalance,"[114] and cannot "be disproportionate to the aim pursued."[115]

7.6.2.2. Positive Action as a Duty

In theory, positive action measures can also be seen as being a duty.[116] Certain duties can be identified at international level to take action in the interest of vulnerable racial or ethnic groups. In EC equality law some positive duties

[108] See inter alia Costello (2003), at 183-184; Davies & Costello (2006), at 1595; Prechal (2004), at 539; Masselot (2004), at 101; Brown (2002), at 216.

[109] See inter alia Henrard (2007a), at 31; Schiek (2002), at 298.

[110] Henrard (2007a), 29. She further explains that "[i]n terms of the general justification model this would require a legitimate aim and measures which are proportionate to that aim. While the legitimate aim of affirmative action measures seems a given, namely to contribute to the achievement of substantive equality, there is still the additional need for the measures concerned to be proportional. The latter tends to be the most contentious factor, and the situation in terms of EC law is further complicated by the fact that direct differentiations require an explicit legislative basis."

[111] The approach of the ECJ to positive action measures has been criticised to be rather restrictive in the field of EC law on gender equality. See inter alia Henrard (2007a), at 29; Caruso (2003), at 3; Pager (2003), at 37; Costello (2003), at 177-212.

[112] Judgment of 17 October 1995 in *Case C-450/93, Eckhard Kalanke v. Freie und Hansestadt Bremen*, [1995] ECR 1-3051, para. 22.

[113] Judgment of 25 October 1988 in *Case 312/86, Commission of the European Communities v. French Republic*, [1988] ECR 6315, para. 15.

[114] Judgment of 30 September 2004 in *Case C-319/03, Briheche v. Ministre de l'Intérieur/Ministre de l'Éducation and Ministre de la Justice*, [2004] ECR I-8807, para. 31.

[115] Judgment of 6 July 2000 in *Case C-407/98, Katarina Abrahamsson and Leif Anderson v. Elisabet Fogelqvist*, [2000] ECR I-05539, para. 55. See also *Case C-319/03, Briheche v. Ministre de l'Intérieur/Ministre de l'Éducation and Ministre de la Justice*, para. 31.

[116] For a detailed analysis see Busstra (2010).

have been established in relation to indirect discrimination.[117] Nevertheless, the ECJ has not yet identified a duty to adopt positive action measures.[118] Similarly, the RED 'merely' makes it possible for the Member States to adopt such measures, but does not oblige them to do so. This also means that no procedure can be initiated against the liable person to adopt such measures.

In any event, certain obligations can still be deduced from different articles of the RED. First of all, the concept of indirect discrimination can also impose a duty to positive action on the basis of the RED. Such a duty also seems to be present in Articles 10,[119] 11[120] and 12[121] on the dissemination of information, social dialogue and dialogue with non-governmental organisations respectively. Finally, and most importantly from the perspective of sanctions, a duty to positive action could arguably also be detected in Article 15 on sanctions. More specifically, under certain circumstances the requirements of effectiveness, proportionality and dissuasiveness might lead to the adoption of positive action measures as redressing the violation of the victims' right to equal treatment, as will be shown below.

7.6.2.3. Positive Action as a Remedy

As argued above, Article 15 RED can impose a duty to adopt positive action measures as remedy.[122] This interpretation is also possible on the basis of Article 5 RED. As already mentioned above, this article defines positive action

---

117 For a detailed analysis in this regard see Busstra (2010).

118 See inter alia Henrard (2007a), at 31; Holtmaat & Tobler (2005), at 414.

119 Art. 10 RED. "Member States shall take care that the provisions adopted pursuant to this Directive, together with the relevant provisions already in force, are brought to the attention of the persons concerned by all appropriate means throughout their territory."

120 Art. 11 RED. "1. Member States shall, in accordance with national traditions and practice, take adequate measures to promote the social dialogue between the two sides of industry with a view to fostering equal treatment, including through the monitoring of workplace practices, collective agreements, codes of conduct, research or exchange of experiences and good practices. 2. Where consistent with national traditions and practice, Member States shall encourage the two sides of the industry without prejudice to their autonomy to conclude, at the appropriate level, agreements laying down anti-discrimination rules in the fields referred to in Article 3 which fall within the scope of collective bargaining. These agreements shall respect the minimum requirements laid down by this Directive and the relevant national implementing measures."

121 Art. 12 RED. "Member States shall encourage dialogue with appropriate non-governmental organisations which have, in accordance with their national law and practice, a legitimate interest in contributing to the fight against discrimination on grounds of racial and ethnic origin with a view to promoting the principle of equal treatment."

122 Contrary to this position O'Hare, who argued that "[n]one of the measures, however, encourage Member States to make provision for what Barnard terms pro-active remedies, such as a legally binding direction as to future conduct or a programme of affirmative action measures in the event of a finding of discrimination." O'Hare (2001), at 154.

as a measure that prevents or *compensates* for disadvantages.[123] Importantly, the ECRI also suggests that, under certain circumstances, positive action measures should be imposed as sanctions, which could contribute to promoting long term change in an organisation.[124]

The limits of individual enforcement have been emphasised in academic writing and can be discovered in practice. It is argued that individual enforcement is not appropriate to address indirect and structural discrimination. However, as Whittle observed in relation to indirect discrimination,

> whilst a claim of indirect discrimination may have been made by just one individual, the benefits of a successful challenge in this regard [...] would normally apply to all persons sharing the same [...] characteristics and therefore benefit the 'group' as a whole.[125]

This would be the case, if appropriate remedies, for example, positive action measures with their group focus, were awarded. In Craig's words, "[i]n those jurisdictions which permit enforcement orders to change an employment policy or practice found in violation of the prohibition against indirect discrimination, this concept can have far reaching consequences."[126] Also, 'enforcement orders to change an employment policy or practice' can clearly be regarded as positive action measures. Indirect and structural discrimination with their explicit group focus would, arguably, require remedies concentrating on the group. All in all, if broadly interpreted "[t]he provision for positive action evidences [...] a progressive vision of appropriate remedies."[127]

In terms of the classification of sanctions, positive action measures can generally be considered as constituting reparative sanctions, when these sanctions have a group focus. As McInerney also observed, "[t]he provisions of the RED on affirmative action conform with restitutionary and remedial tenets."[128]

In general, fact-finders are limited in the adjudication of the form and extent of remedies, since the possible forms of remedies are generally foreseen in legally binding acts. However, there are possibilities to include positive action measures in these particular forms of sanctions. More specifically, these forms might be broadly interpreted, there might be some open clauses, or the legislator itself might lay down some positive action measures as possible forms of remedy.

From the perspective of achieving substantive equality and/or enhancing minority protection a couple of advantages of the remedial approach to positive action can be identified. First of all, this approach can be a useful

123 See also De Vos (2007), at 28.
124 ECRI General Policy Recommendation Nr. 7. This is analysed by Lam (2004), at 17.
125 Whittle (2002), at 308.
126 Craig (2007), at 87.
127 McInerney (2002), at 77.
128 McInerney (2002), at 77.

complement to an eventually formal approach to equality. More specifically, it can be important when systemic discrimination is enforced by an individual applicant because no actio popularis action is allowed. For instance, an individual of a certain racial or ethnic origin complains that he was discriminated against in an application procedure, and it becomes also clear that this employer discriminates against persons of the same racial or ethnic origin in a systemic way. In such a case in addition to awarding redress to the individual victim, the fact-finding body might also require the employer to arrange anti-discrimination training for the staff, which can be classified as a positive action measure. Also, an *asymmetrical* approach to equal treatment might be more easily adopted when positive action measures are applied as remedies. Moreover, the duty to provide effective remedies can in certain cases lead to a *duty to adopt a positive action measure*. And finally, adopting positive action measures as remedies might also make them *more acceptable* to the broader public since, as it has been observed, there is "something deeply unattractive"[129] about positive action measures as exceptions because they are regarded as "further acts of discrimination."[130] Arguably, a positive action measure as a remedy in a discrimination claim seems more reasonable in the eyes of the majority since it is adopted as a result of a procedure in which the different interests have been clearly balanced, and which measures are adapted to the particular circumstances.

Similarly to the process of assessing effective remedies, the same factors have to be weighed when redress takes the form of positive action. Since positive action measures are not usually welcomed by all members of society, fact-finders should be more cautious and more elaborate when contemplating on positive action measures as remedy. Good reasoning would in any case provide a better understanding of the need for such measures. In addition to these factors, the tenets elaborated by the ECJ in relation to positive action measures should also be taken into consideration, even though these considerations were formulated with regard to positive action as justification.

With respect to balancing the different factors an additional aspect of positive action measures is also raised. A general problem in relation to positive action measures is the group *versus* individual interest.[131] How can the group interest be promoted without violating the individual interest? AG Maduro in the *Briheche* case addressed this issue and accepted that for the sake of general interest there might be individual differential treatment, but these measures are then only apparently discriminatory and cannot be regarded as constituting discrimination.[132]

[129] Ellis (2005), at 309.

[130] Ellis (2005), at 309. See also Cardinale (2007), at 36.

[131] On the group perspective see inter alia Abrams (1998); Beaton & Tougas (2001); Lacey (1992); Lerner (2003).

[132] "The Court assumes that positive discriminatory measures can be accepted only if they are designed, in effect, to prevent discrimination in each individual case by forcing the employer

As a matter of fact, this question arises in a different form if positive action measures are applied as remedies. In this case, the question is to what extent fact-finders should consider the individual victim bringing the case to the court when the scope of the case is more far-reaching. In other words one has to answer the question to what extent the disadvantage suffered by the individual applicant has to be remedied on the top of tackling the more general problem that this individual case demonstrates. It is undoubtedly remedied to some extent when a positive action measure has been ordered, since the individual victim also belongs to that group affected by the positive action measure. However, this would not encourage individual victims to go to a fact-finding body with their claims, which admittedly, until now has proved to be one of the most effective ways of enforcing the principle of equal treatment. Accordingly, contrary to Maduro's argument the individual's interest should *not* be "overridden by concerns of substantive equality between groups"[133] when a positive action measure is imposed as remedy.[134] In other words, the individual victims should also be effectively remedied – if and to the extent that the collective or group remedy cannot be regarded as an effective redress for them.

PART B. CASE STUDIES

7.7. Introduction

Given that it is difficult to find out new forms of sanctions at an abstract level, of the enforcement provisions, the RED has the least effect on sanctions. Arguably, the requirements of Article 15 RED are primarily related to the application of the existing remedies.

New forms of sanctions have not been adopted within the framework of the implementation of the RED either in Estonia or in the Netherlands. The effect of the RED in Estonia can only be perceived at a more general level, in the adoption of a general anti-discrimination code which can be enforced via the general civil procedures. Thus, the remedies in a civil procedure have now been extended to discrimination cases as well.

---

to place women in a similar position to men. Positive discriminatory measures are, in this light, only apparently discriminatory." Advocate General Maduro in *Case C-319/03*, *Briheche v. Ministre de l'Intérieur/Ministre de l'Éducation and Ministre de la Justice*, [2004] ECR I-8807, para. 42.

[133] *Id.*, para. 41. "[M]easures to be proportionate in balancing the benefits of the positive action in promoting equality for women against the costs imposed on other individuals. These requirements appear necessary to prevent equality between individuals from being overridden by concerns of substantive equality between groups." See also Maduro (2005), at 25-26.

[134] See above concerning the circumstances related to the victim.

In Belgium and Hungary some new forms of remedies have been introduced with the national transposition. In Belgium the ARA introduced the institution of forfaitair compensation in discrimination cases as compensation on the basis of the general rules did not prove to be effective, proportionate and dissuasive enough in practice. The Hungarian Equal Treatment Act has created a specialised national body with the competence to issue binding decisions and impose a couple of newly adopted sanctions. The Authority may: (1) order that the situation constituting a violation of law be eliminated, (2) prohibit the further continuation of the conduct constituting a violation of law, (3) order that its decision establishing the violation of law be published, (4) impose a fine, and (5) apply any legal consequence determined in legal acts.[135]

The different forms of sanctions adopted by the countries under review will first be identified. An analysis will be carried out within this framework of whether the particular sanction could result in the adoption of positive action measures. This elaboration will be followed by an examination of whether and to what extent the factors elaborated above are taken into account either in national legislation or by fact-finders. Both aspects will be taken into consideration in an exploration of whether they comply with the requirements of the RED.

7.8. Forms of Sanctions

7.8.1. Reparative Sanctions

7.8.1.1. Restitutionary Sanctions

Although, pursuant to the general rule in civil procedures, the original situation has to be restored as far as possible, as hinted at supra, in discrimination cases *restitution* can be demanded only in a limited number of cases, because of the special features of the relationships in these cases.

Only the Hungarian Civil Code includes explicitly the sanction of restitution in cases of a breach of the right to equal treatment. Pursuant to Article 84(1) d) Civil Code the applicant can demand the cessation of the injurious situation and the restitution of the situation preceding the breach of his right. In addition to explicitly demanding restitution, other particular forms of sanctions can and do in fact result in restitution. These sanctions are the following: *invalidity* of a particular provision and, under certain circumstances, an *order to cease and desist*. Although it is not explicitly acknowledged when the group aspect of the case is taken into account in deliberating on the form of the sanction,

135 Art. 16(1) HETA.

the particular restitutionary remedy can amount to a positive action measure because a positive duty is imposed on the respondent with an effect on a whole group.

Pertaining to employment-related discrimination, all the countries under review have explicitly regulated the sanction of *invalidity* in discrimination cases. The Belgian ARA lays down special rules for victimisation complaints arising in employment relationships. Within this framework, Article 15(5) ARA explicitly stipulates that the applicant can request to be reinstated or to be allowed to pursue his function under the same conditions as formerly. Moreover, in a broader context (that is not only concerning victimisation), Article 16(2) ARA also indicates that under certain circumstances the material damage can be restored by declaring the provisions that are contrary to the ARA null and void.[136] Likewise, the Estonian ECA stipulates that employment contract terms or terms established by unilateral decisions of employers which are less favourable to employees than those prescribed by law, administrative legislation or a collective agreement are invalid.[137] Pursuant to Article 117 ECA, upon the illegal termination of the employment contract by the employer the employee can demand reinstatement to his previous position.[138] Similar provisions are also enshrined in the Hungarian Labour Code: labour agreements that are contrary to laws are null and void,[139] and the employee can also demand reinstatement when the termination of the employment was unlawful.[140] Finally, the Dutch GETA also follows this line: discriminatory dismissals are voidable,[141] and contractual provisions contrary to the GETA are

[136] Art. 13 ARA stipulates that "[p]rovisions of an agreement which run contrary to the provisions of this act and terms and conditions that stipulate that one or more contracting parties are to relinquish in advance rights guaranteed to them by this act, shall be null and void." On the function of invalidity as restitution see also Taelman (2004a), at 205-206.

[137] See Articles 15 and 16 ECA. "Article 15 Employment contract terms which are less favourable to employees than those prescribed by law, administrative legislation or a collective agreement are invalid." "Article 16 Terms established by unilateral decisions of employers which are less favourable to employees than those prescribed by law, administrative legislation, collective agreements or employment contracts are invalid."

[138] See also Art. 144 ECA. "Article 144 (1) In the case of a dispute over the termination of an employment contract on the bases prescribed in clauses 86 6)-8), a labour dispute resolution body has the right to assess the circumstances of the wrongful act of the employee and the purposefulness of termination of the employment contract, and to reinstate the employee in employment."

[139] Pursuant to Art. 8(1) of the Hungarian Labour Code "[a]n agreement interfering with regulations concerning labour relations or other laws is null and void."

[140] Pursuant to Art. 100(1) of the Hungarian Labour Code "[w]hen the court establishes that the employer has unlawfully terminated the employee's contract, on request of the employee he has to be reinstated."

[141] Pursuant to Art. 8 GETA "[t]ermination of an employee's contract by the employer in contravention of Article 5, on the grounds that the employee has invoked Article 5 either at law or otherwise, or has provided assistance in relation to it, such termination shall be invalid."

null and void.[142] Similarly to the Belgian ARA, the invalidity of termination is applicable also to victimisation dismissals on the basis of the GETA.[143] Importantly, Articles 13 ARA and 9 GETA extend the sanction of invalidity to all fields falling under the material scope of the Acts.[144] In other words, this form of restitution can be applied in fields other than employment, though it is generally in employment relations where this sanction is the most appropriate. It is advantageous that all the countries have such special rules for invalidity in discrimination cases, as it clearly shows that restitutionary remedies that have been argued to be preferred in discrimination cases play an important role in complaints of the violation of the right to equal treatment.

In addition to these special rules for employment-related situations, the sanction of invalidity can also be applied on the basis of general civil and administrative law, although here its application in discrimination cases is less common than in the field of employment.

With respect to invalidity and reinstatement, it has been emphasised in each country that[145] their application cannot result in an obligation to enter into a contract with someone.[146] In a specific case based on the ADA, the judge explicitly pronounced that the termination of the employment relationship could not be declared invalid as it would result in a duty of contract.[147] Given the freedom of contract, these private law considerations are understandable. However, one should not forget about the fact that offering goods and services

[142] Pursuant to Art. 9 GETA "[a]ll contractual provisions which conflict with this Act shall be null and void." See inter alia Holtmaat (2007), at 63; Implementatie van richtlijnen gelijke behandeling, Brief van de Staatssecretaris van Sociale Zaken en Werkgelegenheid, 28 187, Nr. 1, 18 December 2001, at 18-19; Dierx & Rodrigues (2003); Gijzen (2004), at 47; Jaarverslag 2006, CGKR 2007, at 59; Asscher-Vonk & Hendriks (2005), at 183-184; Cremers-Hartman (2004), at 162-163; Heringa (1991), at 20-21; From Principle to Practice. Evaluation of Legislation Dealing with Racial and Ethnic Discrimination in certain EU Member States, ENAR 2001, at 34; Gerards & Heringa (2003), at 197-200.

[143] See Art. 8 GETA.

[144] See also Advies inzake de ingebrekestelling van Nederland door de Europese Commissie in verband met het niet correct omzetten van Richtlijn 2000/78/EG, CGB-Advies/2008/02, March 2008, at 5.

[145] Contrary to voidability, invalidity means an absolute and partial invalidity. See Labour Court Tongeren, Case No 199/2005, 6 March 2007.

On invalidity see inter alia Wetsontwerp tot wijziging van de wet van 30 juli 1981 tot bestraffing van bepaalde door racisme en xenofobie ingegeven daden, 2720/001, 26 October 2006, at 40 & 53; Wetsontwerp tot wijziging van de wet van 30 juli tot bestraffing van bepaalde door racisme of xenofobie ingegeven daden, 3-2362/3, 24 April 2007, at 37; Taelman (2004a), at 203-206; Thiery (2007), at 767; De Boeck (2003), at 436, De Prins, Sottiaux & Vrielink (2005), at 535-537; Aanpak discriminatie en racisme, CGKR 2004; Bayart & Bosmans (2008), at 581.

[146] See inter alia Bernauw (2004), at 301; Poleshchuck (2007), at 57; Tavits (2004), at 556; Gerards & Heringa (2003), at 197-200.

[147] *Vindevoghel v. Flightcare Belgium*, Brussels Labour Court, No 70/05, summary-like proceedings, 6 February 2006. See also Bernauw (2004), at 301; Cuypers (2003), at 466.

to the public includes obligations as well, such as observing the principle of equality. To avoid any uncertainty, now the ARA clearly and appropriately stipulates when the freedom of contract can be limited: during and on termination of the employment relationship,[148] but not on the establishment of it.[149]

In Belgium too, it has been stated with respect to the sanction of invalidity that it has to result in levelling up the situation of the victim to that of his comparator.[150] In one particular case[151] the court imposed the sanction of invalidity of the challenged provision of a collective labour agreement which was considered to be discriminatory against mineworkers. This position is clearly in accordance with the requirement of effectiveness, and also makes positive action measures possible.[152]

Under certain circumstances the *cessation of a certain activity* can also result in restitution. This sanction can also be found in civil and administrative procedures in each country, but also some special rules have also been introduced in their equal treatment legislations. In Belgium, special summary-like procedures have been introduced, aiming at the cessation of discrimination.[153] The main enforcement organ of the principle of equal treatment in Hungary, the Authority on Equal Treatment can also order the termination of the unlawful situation,[154] a sanction that has not yet been applied to reinstate the original situation, rather as compensation in natura.[155]

7.8.1.2. Compensatory Sanctions

Compensation can be awarded either in natura or, more often, monetary compensation is given to the applicants in the countries under review.[156] Again, not only compensation in kind, but other forms of sanctions adopted in the countries under review can also lead to compensation in natura; these are *invalidity* of the contested measure and *cessation or termination* of

[148] Art. 15(5) ARA.

[149] See inter alia Bernauw (2004), at 301; De Boeck (2003), at 432; Kusters (2003), at 567; Cuypers (2003), at 466.

[150] See also Bayart & Bosmans (2008), at 582.

[151] *T.S.T v. F.W.A.G,* Tongeren Labour Court, 6 March 2007, C.4, at 31.

[152] See inter alia De Prins, Sottiaux & Vrielink (2005), at 537.

[153] It has been demonstrated in Ch. 4 on access to justice what the summary-like procedures in Belgium mean.

[154] Art. 16(1) a) HETA. For a short discussion whether the Authority could impose positive obligations in addition to this sanction see Farkas & Kárpáti (2004); Farkas, Kádár & Kárpáti (2006), at 84.

[155] See below.

[156] See inter alia De Boeck (2003), at 431; Bernauw (2004), at 301.

discrimination. Similarly to restitution, these measures can also amount to positive action when again the group aspect of the complaint is taken into account.

The *cessation of discrimination* has led to compensation in natura in a couple of civil cases in Hungary. For instance, in the Hajdúhadház desegregation case, adjudicated in an actio popularis procedure, the court obliged the respondent to eliminate the discriminatory situation.[157] This decision amounts to compensation in natura, with a clear group effect on all those belonging to the Roma minority in these schools.[158] The question is to what extent the respondent will aim to level up the situation of the Roma children to that of non-Roma children, as the court did not require it in its judgment.[159] It is highly desirable that fact-finders consider this aspect of the case as well; otherwise equal treatment might be achieved by levelling down the status of the majority group. As long as cessation will result in levelling up, it can be distinctly regarded as a positive action measure.

Likewise, the Hungarian Supreme Court ordered the cessation of the wrongful situation in the case concerning the lack of Roma members in a local government minority committee.[160] The court argued that the fact that no Roma members had been elected violates the Roma minority's right to representation and participation in public life, and was also contrary to the Local Governments Act which laid down that it was reasonable (but not required) to elect minority members of the local government to the minority committee. Importantly, the sanction imposed by the court resulted in levelling up the status of the Roma community to that of the majority. Both here and in the segregation case, we are faced with an unlawful omission, the sanction for which results in imposing positive obligations on the respondents.

As mentioned supra, in the most often applied procedure in equal treatment cases, the procedure of the AET, the cessation of the wrongful situation can also be ordered, though as yet only a couple of cases can be found of its application. In one of the few cases where this was ordered the complaint concerned a system of efficiency evaluation which had a negative effect on those who were frequently on sick leave and mothers who had to stay at home because

---

157 Hajdú-Bihar County Court, 6.P. 20.341/2006/50, 2 May 2007; Debrecen Court of Appeal, Pf.I.20.361/2007/8, 13 December 2007; Supreme Court, Pfv.IV.20.936/2008/4, 19 November 2008.

158 Remarkably, the applicant also complained of the worse conditions in the schools attended mainly by Roma children, which was acknowledged and taken into consideration by the court in establishing the existence of direct discrimination in addition to segregation. However, in imposing the sanction these two aspects of the case were not separately mentioned, they were described as wrongful situation.

159 From a different perspective see also Kádár (2007), at 40.

160 Supreme Court, Kfv.IV.37.450/2006/5, 11 July 2007. On the same case see also EBH/337/24/2005; Metropolitan Court, 20.K.33.285/2005/10, 15 May 2006.

their children were ill.[161] The Authority ordered the cessation of the wrongful situation by amending the practice and the regulation of the evaluation system. Since this sanction led to a change in the applicants' situation, and because the regulation before the introduction of this evaluation system is not known or at least was not invoked in the case, it can be argued that the amendment, at least partly, provided compensation in kind for the applicants. Moreover, this sanction resulted in levelling up the situation of the applicants (and all those affected by this measure). For this reason, the cessation can be regarded as having amounted to a positive action measure. The sanction of cessation of the wrongful situation has not often been applied by the AET, arguably because of the positive obligations this sanction includes.[162] It is strongly suggested that instead of applying punitive sanctions the Authority place more emphasis on this sanction as it can have more far-reaching effects, such as changing a certain practice. Similarly to the Dutch ETC, the AET might also prepare recommendations in its decisions of how to realise equality in the particular case.

Similarly, in the Netherlands the cessation of discrimination in civil procedures has, arguably, led to compensation in natura, for example in a case against an insurance company whose practice was considered discriminatory on the grounds of pregnancy.[163] The case was decided in a summary procedure at the end of which the court ordered the termination of discrimination. In this particular case this sanction resulted in obliging the respondent to pay the as yet unpaid daily allowances of the applicant. At first sight this remedy might be regarded as monetary compensation, but it can be argued that because of the nature of the complaint it in fact constitutes compensation in natura or even restitution of the original situation.

Because of the distinct character of discrimination cases, the most often applied sanction (remedy) in civil law is *monetary* compensation for material and non-material damages. It is also the main rule in civil law in all the examined countries. Notwithstanding the fact that this is a general rule, awarding compensation for non-material damages remains problematical in some cases, especially when material damages are also awarded. The reason for this might be due to the fact that the material harm caused by the discrimination is considered more important than the violation of human dignity, namely the immaterial harm.

Traces of this problem can be found in Belgium. Here, several cases based on the old ARA (that is criminal procedures), can be found in which only one euro was awarded as moral compensation to the CEOOR or the interest

---

[161] EBH/700/2007.

[162] This sanction has been mainly imposed when the complaint was concerned with reasonable accommodation.

[163] Utrecht District Court, LJN: AU6168, 15 November 2005.

organisation,[164] which seems to be far from appropriate. Arguably, the fact that the compensation is given to an interest organisation and not to an individual victim does not make it less necessary to provide an appropriate amount of compensation, since it cannot have a deterrent effect, and cannot be regarded as proportionate either.[165]

Given the lack of case law on discrimination in Estonia, it is difficult to predict what the approach of the fact-finding bodies will be under the EETA.[166] With respect to other fields of law it has, however, been observed that compensation[167] for non-material damage has been very rare and low.[168] "For instance, in 2000 the Civil Law Chamber of the National Court obliged the state to pay compensation for moral damage caused by the unlawful actions of a public official. The damage recognised as being approximately equal to the average monthly salary 'taking into consideration the level of prosperity in society'."[169] Remarkably, however, in one of the few cases of discrimination before the Labour Dispute Resolution Commission the compensation for moral damage caused by harassment was fixed at 10,000 EEK (this amounts to approximately 700 Euros)[170] which, in the Estonian context, cannot be regarded as inadequate at all. It is thus to be awaited what effect the EETA in this respect will have. In any event, pursuant to Article 24(2) EETA, in addition to the material damages caused by the discrimination it is also possible to claim 'a reasonable amount as compensation for the non-material damage caused by the violation.' With this provision, the Act explicitly acknowledges that discrimination in itself results in suffering irrespective of the material disadvantage caused by the discrimination. Again, it is yet to be seen how fact-finders will apply this provision in practice.

Somewhat contrary to the Belgian approach, in Hungary the amount of compensation for immaterial damages in civil cases cannot in general be regarded as low.[171] It ranges from 400 to 2,000 Euros depending on the circumstances of the case. With respect to immaterial damage, the Hungarian Supreme Court explicitly established that compensation for such damage is an appropriate means of compensating the applicant for the discrimination

[164] See inter alia Brussels Correctional Court, 6 March 2003; Brussels Correctional Court, 31 March 2004; Brussel Correctional Court, 20 October 2004; Antwerp Court of Appeal, 8 January 2004.

[165] See inter alia Borghs (2003), at 31; Wetsontwerp tot wijziging …, *supra* note 145, at 27.

[166] For an optimistic view see Muda (2002), at 113.

[167] See inter alia Explanatory Memorandum, Draft Equal Treatment Act, 384 SE; Explanatory Memorandum, Draft Equal Treatment Act, 262 SE.

[168] As observed by Poleshchuck "[u]ntil recently, court judgments regarding the payment of moral compensation were rare in Estonia. There is a degree of consensus in the local legal community that moral compensation is to be paid only in exceptional cases and that this compensation shall not be very large." Poleshchuck (2007), at 58.

[169] Poleshchuck (2007), at 59.

[170] Saaremaa Töövaidluskomisjon. Information letter. 8 February 2007.

[171] See inter alia Farkas, Kádár & Kárpáti (2006), at 92.

suffered.[172] This has been interpreted as indicating that in discrimination cases the applicant always has the right to compensation for immaterial damage, it is merely the amount that should be decided on a case by case basis.[173] This approach therefore clearly acknowledges the fact that discrimination, irrespective of or in addition to the material damage, always causes mental suffering. The focus is therefore on the victim and the harm suffered addressing which is the main purpose of a discrimination complaint. Nevertheless, awarding high immaterial damages also has a punitive effect on the respondent.[174]

Finally, in the Netherlands monetary compensation[175] for immaterial damage varies to a great extent in terms of whether and what amount of compensation is awarded. For instance, 750 Euros compensation was awarded in a case concerning inappropriate complaint treatment;[176] in another case this sum amounted to 5,000 Euros when the respondent did not enforce its affirmative action policy with respect to the victim;[177] and in another case concerning systemic direct discrimination on the grounds of racial or ethnic origin which had resulted in serious mental sufferings the amount of compensation was fixed at 23,000 Euros.[178] In conclusion, in the Netherlands the compensation for immaterial damage caused by discriminatory treatment also seems to be proportionate to the injury caused to the victim.

In accordance with the rulings of the ECJ, none of the countries has imposed any ceiling on the amount of compensation in their civil law regulations, with the sole exception of the Belgian ARA. The ARA introduced the possibility of forfaitair compensation to make the frequently used summary-like procedures more effective.[179] The introduction of this remedy stemmed from the fact that, in practice, the amount of compensation for immaterial damages was unreasonably low (symbolic).[180] Moreover, the summary-like procedures were not regarded as sufficiently effective because applicants could not

[172] Supreme Court, BH 2002.90; Supreme Court, BH 2001.15. See also Pest County Labour Court, I.M. 471/2004/3, 13 October 2004.

[173] Iványi (2005).

[174] See below.

[175] See inter alia Van Der Heijden (2001); Dierx & Rodrigues (2003).

[176] Amsterdam Appelate Court, LJN: BD8720, 29 May 2008.

[177] Leeuwarden Appelate Court, LJN: AA1048, 4 August 1999.

[178] Central Appeal Council, LJN: AO3751, 16 February 2004.

[179] See inter alia Wetsontwerp tot wijziging ..., *supra* note 145, at 25-28; Bayart & Bosmans (2008), 579-580. & 583-585.

[180] Wetsontwerp tot wijziging van de wet van 30 juli 1981 tot bestraffing van bepaalde door racisme of xenfobie ingegeven daden, 3-2362/3, 24 April 2007, at 19; Wetsontwerp tot wijziging ..., *supra* note 145, at 27; Wetsontwerp tot wijziging van de wet van 30 juli 1981 tot bestraffing van bepaalde door racisme en xenofobie ingegeven daden, 2720/009, 19 March 2007, at 140; Castermans (2009), at 249.

demand compensation.[181] Since it is up to the applicant whether he accepts the forfaitair compensation or proves the actual damage, it can be argued that this ceiling is not contrary to the prohibition imposed by the ECJ.[182] Admittedly, the underlying idea behind the adoption of this measure was to harmonise the sanction system in discrimination law with the requirements of the RED (and FD).[183] Interestingly, while in fields other than employment this forfaitair amount means compensation for immaterial damage, with respect to labour relations and supplementary rules for social security this sum aims to compensate for both material and immaterial damage.[184] This distinction might be explained by the special character of employment relations in which the material damage that can be caused is related to the salary of the victim.

Importantly, Article 117(2) ECA in Estonia has contained a ceiling of six months salary in the case of the illegal termination of the employment contract by the employer, which was criticized as being contrary to EU law.[185] With the adoption of the EETA, however, this ceiling has been repealed,[186] and the legislation is now in harmony with EU law in this respect.

7.8.2. Punitive Sanctions

A sanction with a pre-eminently punitive nature, found in almost all the countries[187] is the *publication* of the ultimate decision of the fact-finding body, a measure that can also be interpreted as a sanction of 'naming and shaming'.[188] The possibility of making a decision public as a sanction can

[181] See inter alia Taelman (2004b), at 508; Antwoorden op de vragen van de Commissie over richtlijn 43/2000; Wetsontwerp tot wijziging ..., *supra* note 145, at 27; Wetsontwerp tot wijziging van de wet van 30 juli 1981 tot bestraffing van bepaalde door racisme en xenofobie ingegeven daden, 2720/009, 19 March 2007, at 21; Thiery (2007), at 769.

[182] Article 16(1) ARA stipulates that the applicant can (and has to) choose between the forfaitair amount and the actually suffered damage.

[183] See inter alia Wetsontwerp tot wijziging ..., *supra* note 145, at 27; Wetsontwerp tot wijziging van de wet van 30 juli 1981 tot bestraffing van bepaalde door racisme en xenofobie ingegeven daden, 2720/009, 19 March 2007, at 21; Thiery (2007), at 770.

[184] In employment-related cases this section furthermore lays down that when the material damage suffered as a consequence of discrimination can be recovered through application of the sanction of invalidity on the basis of Article 13 ARA the amount of forfaitair compensation will be decided on the basis of point 1. In fact this regulation allows for additional 'compensation' (invalidity) in addition to the forfaitair amount, a possibility that was explicitly excluded in Article 16(1) ARA. However, this provision cannot be regarded to contradict section (1), since it only allows for compensation via invalidity, which as mentioned above, can be effectively invoked and applied in employment relations.

[185] Poleshchuck (2007), at 58.

[186] Art. 27(5) EETA.

[187] With the exception of Estonia.

[188] 18(3) ARA; 84(1) c) Hungarian Civil Code; 16(1) c) HETA; 3:305a(3), 6:196 Dutch Civil Procedure Code.

also be found in the equal treatment legislation in Belgium, Hungary and the Netherlands. Pursuant to Article 18(3) ARA, in summary-like procedures the judge can suggest that his decision or the summary of it be made public.[189] The publication of the court's decision was, for instance, requested in the Murat case in which the respondent refused a candidate for a position on the grounds of his ethnic origin.[190] Although the primary aim of the court was to educate the public, it still had the side-effect of naming and shaming.

Similarly, pursuant to Article 16(1) c) HETA the AET can make its decision public.[191] The Authority has relied in several instances on this provision and made its decision public.[192] In racial discrimination cases the publication of the decision seems to be the rule, and waiving the disclosure of its findings can be explained only by the special circumstances of the case. This approach also shows that the main aim of the procedure of the AET is to punish the perpetrator and less attention is devoted to repairing the damage suffered by the victim. In one of these cases, for instance, the respondents proposed an agreement with the applicants, namely that in the future they would comply with the principle of equal treatment, and that they would also undertake some positive obligations in this respect.[193] This agreement was, however, refused by one of the applicants. Consequently, the Authority had to impose sanctions, one of which being that it did not order the publication of the decision. The renouncement of this sanction does, arguably, show that because of the respondents' clear willingness to comply with their obligations the Authority did not regard it appropriate to sanction them with naming and shaming.[194] Although the Authority's justification for demanding the publication of its decision does not include any reference to the need for punishing the respondent,[195] still it does undoubtedly have this effect.

Finally, on the basis of the Dutch GETA, publication of its opinion (naming the respondent) is limited to imparting the ETC's opinions to certain entities when it considers it appropriate.[196] Although no data is available on

---

[189] Although the ARA puts the emphasis on the preventive effect of publication, it has been argued in the literature that it does also have punitive effect. See inter alia Taelman (2004a), at 234-235.

[190] *CGKR and C. Murat v. D. Yves and E-L/ BVBA*, Ghent Labour Court, 26 March 2007.

[191] On the punitive character of the publication of the decision see also Szajbély (2005c).

[192] See inter alia EBH/94/2008; EBH/170/2008; EBH/1/26/2007.

[193] EBH/240/2008.

[194] In relation to this it has been argued that the 30 days period during which the decision was made available on their website is quite short in order to be regarded effective. Presumably, as a reaction to this observation, decisions are currently made directly public for six months, and left indirectly accessible for five years on the website of the Authority. See Gyulavári (2007), at 36.

[195] See inter alia EBH/94/2008; EBH/170/2008; www.egyenlobanasmod.hu.

[196] Art. 13 GETA. See inter alia Het verschil gemaakt. Evaluatie AWGB en werkzaamheden CGB 1999-2004, CGB 2005, at 83; Asscher-Vonk & Groenendijk (1999), at 208; Asscher-Vonk & Hendriks (2005), at 193.

this practice, it can still be concluded that conveying its opinions to these particular bodies can and does have punitive effect even though the opinions (with the name of the respondent) are not available to the general public.

The possibility is created to order the publication of the judgment in the civil codes of Hungary and the Netherlands too. Pursuant to Article 84(1) c) of the Hungarian Civil Code, in the case of a violation of personal rights, the applicant can demand that the respondent make a declaration or recompense in another way and, if necessary, that this be made public. Thus, in Hungary, even in civil law a clearly punitive measure can also be imposed on the respondent. Admittedly, in individual litigation this measure is generally not applied without awarding compensation.

In the Dutch Civil Code the publication is restricted to two situations: depending on the circumstances of the case it can be imposed in actio popularis claims and in relation to certain advertisements.[197] Thus, the range of situations in which it can be applied is rather limited. At the same time, it indicates that providing redress to the victim is considered more important than punishing the perpetrator.

On the basis of the national Equal Treatment Acts the Belgian and Hungarian fact-finding bodies can impose *fines*. In this respect the fine in the ARA is special, as it is linked to the order to cease and desist in the summary-like procedure: should the respondent not comply with the order (put an end to discrimination), he is faced with a penalty.[198] In this respect this fine rather aims to ensure compliance by threatening the perpetrator with punishment; in other words it is an auxiliary punitive measure.

In the Netherlands the specialised body in equal treatment cases cannot issue binding decisions and is not given any enforcement power.[199] Still, in order to be able to make thorough investigations and bring well-reasoned opinions it lobbied for enacting the possibility of imposing fines in the case of unwillingness to comply with the obligation to provide information during the Commission's investigation procedure.[200] However, this proposal was quickly opposed by the government, which argued that the available palette of sanctions in discrimination cases was in harmony with the relevant directives.[201] Accordingly, the Commission has no means with which it can

---

197 3:305a(3), 6:196 Civil Procedure Code. See also Gerards & Heringa (2003), at 200-201; Jaspers (2001), at 143.

198 See also Taelman (2004b), at 517-518; Wetsontwerp tot wijziging ..., *supra* note 145, at 58.

199 The introduction of an administrative fine in the field of employment was refused. See inter alia Arbeidsmarktbeleid etnische minderheden 2000-2003, Brief van de Staatssecretaris van Sociale Zaken en Werkgelegenheid, 27 223, Nr. 73, 14 October 2005, at 5.

200 See Commentaar van de CGB inzake implementatie van de gemeenschappelijke bepalingen van de EC-Kaderrichtlijn en de EC-anti-rassen-discriminatierichtlijn, CGB-advies/2001/03, 30 May 2001, at 7.

201 Implementatie van richtlijnen inzake gelijke behandeling, Brief van de Staatssecretaris van Sociale Zaken en Werkgelegenheid, 28 187, Nr. 1, 18 December 2001, at 19.

oblige persons to provide information during its investigations. The lack of punitive measures in this respect could work to the detriment of an effective investigation and so to the effective enforcement of the principle of equal treatment.

Under the HETA the Authority can impose a fine on the perpetrator directly.[202] The amount of the fine can range from 200 to 24,000 Euros. Pursuant to Article 14/A(1) of the Government Decree on the Authority, half of the fine should be devoted to the promotion of equal treatment and achieving equality of opportunities, which can be clearly regarded as a positive action measure. According to the statistics on the cases brought before the AET in 2007, of 29 cases in which a violation was found to have taken place, it imposed fines in 14 instances.[203] In practice, the imposed fines ranged from 1,200 to 12,000 euro.[204] Most importantly the amount of the fines can in principle be regarded as having a clear dissuasive effect since they add up to a more than symbolic sum. The amount of the fine varies widely, depending mainly on the financial situation of the respondent.[205]

The fact that in Hungary the main channel of enforcement of the principle of equal treatment is the Authority, which as an administrative body can and does impose fines, indicates that the emphasis in the Hungarian remedial system is on punitive measures.[206] As explained above, a purely punitive system cannot be regarded appropriate as it neglects the victim's perspective. Importantly, however, the AET has never imposed fines alone; they have always been combined with a reparative-like measure, such as ordering the termination of the discrimination. In this way, the harm caused to the victim can to some extent be redressed. Should the victim not be satisfied with the remedy provided by the AET, he can still initiate a civil procedure with the aim of obtaining compensation.

---

202 See inter alia Kádár (2007), at 71; Farkas & Kárpáti (2004), at 34; Iványi at 2005.

203 Az Egyenlő Bánásmód Hatóság 2008. évi tevékenysége a számok tükrében. Egyenlő Bánásmód Hatóság (2009). Retrieved from http://www.egyenlobanasmod.hu/data/2008tevekenyseg_szamok_tukreben.pdf.

204 See also Kádár (2007), at 71.

205 The imposed fines range from 1,200 to 12,000 Euros. See inter alia EBH/588/5/2008, EBH/108/2008, EBH/94/2008, EBH/72/7/2008, EBH/641/11/2007, EBH/346/31/2007, EBH/310/33/2007, EBH/271/2007, EBH/271/2007, EBH/142/3/2007, EBH/56/13/2007, EBH/44/14/2007, EBH/14/7/2007, EBH/553/2006.

206 In Hungary some administrative supervisory bodies working in a specific field are also empowered to investigate discrimination cases within their competence and to impose fines by breach of the HETA. Because of their lack of expertise it seems that they transpose the complaint to the AET, and the administrative organ concerned takes part in the procedure as expert. Nevertheless, a couple of cases in the field of labour law can be found in which the labour inspectorates have imposed fines, the amount of which was however limited to 400 Euros. Accordingly, in terms of dissuasiveness the procedure by the AET can be regarded more effective.

Interestingly, the Civil Code also lays down a primarily punitive sanction, the *public interest fine*.[207] Pursuant to Article 84(2) of the Civil Code if the compensation that can be awarded is not proportionate to the gravity of the violation the court can impose a public interest fine on the perpetrator. Importantly, the Supreme Court has accepted that a public interest fine can also be imposed when no claim for compensation has been submitted, provided the violation is unreasonably grave, the behaviour leading to the violation is attributable to the respondent and the complaint was enforced in a proper way so that the possibility of awarding compensation could not be excluded.[208] Such a fine can generally be imposed in an actio popularis claim. The punitive character of this measure was clearly visible when the fine was to be paid to the state budget.[209] However, with the amendment of the HETA this provision has been repealed. At present, it is not clear to whom this fine should be paid. It seems that it is for the fact-finder to decide on the addressee of the fine. Presumably, the fact-finders would then award this fine to the interest organisation initiating the procedure. Should this be the case, the punitive character of this measure would be replaced by its compensatory nature. Moreover, this measure could then also amount to a positive action measure as the group aspect is taken into consideration and the interest organisation can (or should) devote the amount concerned to the interest of the protected group. This would be an important development since interest organisations could not until now sue for compensation.

Finally, the amount of *compensation* pertaining to immaterial damage can and does have a punitive impact on the respondent as a side effect. This has been clearly acknowledged in relation to forfaitair compensation in Belgium,[210] but it can, arguably, also be stated with respect to the other countries when they award a high amount of immaterial compensation.

7.8.3. Preventive Sanctions

In fact only a couple of sanctions can be found with an explicit preventive characteristic, which is quite understandable in the view of the preventive side-effect of the other forms of sanctions. The following sanctions can be regarded to primarily aim at preventing future violation: *termination of discrimination*,

207 See inter alia Kádár (2007), at 71.

208 Supreme Court, Pvf. IV. 20 822/2001/4 (BH2003. 150), 3 April 2002. See also Iványi (2005). For a critical approach to this sanction due to its uneven application see Farkas (2003).

209 Ex-Art. 20(2) HETA.

210 See inter alia Advies geformuleerd door het Centrum voor gelijke kansen en racismebestrijding door de Raad van Bestuur op 21 november 2006 inzake Het wetsontwerp ter bestrijding van bepaalde vormen van discriminatie en Het wetsontwerp tot wijziging van de wet van 30 juli 1981 tot bestraffing van bepaalde door racisme en xenofobie ingegeven daden, 22 November 2006, at 4.; Wetsontwerp tot wijziging ..., *supra* note 145, at 28.

publication of the decision of the fact-finding body, the *opinions* of the Estonian Commissioner and the Dutch Equal Treatment Commission, and the protection against *victimisation*.

A preventive sanction that can be found in almost each country[211] under review is the order to *terminate discrimination*. In Belgium the underlying aim of general summary procedures (and thus also of the summary-like procedures in discrimination cases) is to eliminate the wrongful act as soon as possible, and for this reason it is also called the procedure to cease and desist.[212] The termination of discrimination can usually also be imposed as a sanction when there is a risk of recurrence, which has a clear preventive effect.[213] The preventive effect of this measure is primarily directed at the relationship between the applicant and the respondent, but by taking into account the group aspect of the case it could possibly result in a change in practice or policy of the respondent pertaining to all his potential clients, employees, and so on. Should this be the case, the termination of discrimination would clearly amount to a positive action measure. For instance, in the Murat case concerning the refusal of a candidate for a position on the grounds of his racial or ethnic origin, the judge demanded the discontinuation of discrimination not only in relation to the particular applicant, but also with respect to the recruitment policy and procedure of the respondent.[214] Thus, the judgment was clearly directed at preventing future discrimination by the respondent.

A similar provision can also be found in the Estonian EETA, which as yet has not been applied.

Both the Hungarian Civil Code[215] and the HETA[216] stipulate the prohibition of future discrimination as a possible sanction in a discrimination case,[217] which can be regarded as a preventive version of the sanction of termination of discrimination. Interestingly, the original text of the respective provision in the HETA stipulated that the AET can demand the discontinuation of discrimination.[218] In the case law of the Authority, however, these sanctions have been applied in the same way and seem to be interpreted to serve as preventive measures, including 'merely' negative obligations.[219] Contrary to

[211] No similar provision can be found in the Netherlands.

[212] Art. 18 ARA.

[213] See also Taelman (2004b), at 508.

[214] Gent Labour Court, A.R. No. 176.893, 26 March 2007.

[215] Art. 84(1) b) Civil Code.

[216] Art. 16(1) b) HETA.

[217] This sanction should not be mixed with the sanctions under Articles 16(1) a) HETA and 84(1) d) Civil Code regulating the cessation of the discriminatory situation/status. These sanctions have been discussed within the framework of reparative sanctions. See also Farkas (2003).

[218] No explanation can be found on this amendment in the *travaux préparatoires*.

[219] See for instance EBH/588/5/2008; EBH/170/2008; EBH/109/8/2008; EBH/516/2007; EBH/346/31/2007.

the sanction of ordering the termination of the discriminatory situation the sanction of prohibition of future discrimination is relatively often imposed by the AET. When the applicant complains of discrimination through omission this measure could arguably also result in positive duties. In this sense, the difference vanishes between the prohibition of future discrimination and the termination of the discriminatory situation. However, the AET does not seem to be willing to impose positive duties on respondents, which would work to the detriment of effective enforcement as discrimination through omissions can only be terminated by imposing positive duties.

Although in some cases the sanction of *publication* of the decision clearly aims to name and shame, in other cases the purpose is to prevent future violation by raising awareness. As mentioned supra, the judge can order the publication of its decision in a summary-like procedure pursuant to Article 18(3) ARA.[220] Importantly, such a publication is aim-oriented: it can be imposed as a sanction as far as it can contribute to the purpose of the summary-like procedure, that is the termination of discrimination.[221] Again, in the Murat case the court believed that by publishing the judgment it would be made clear to the public that the ADA is a living instrument, which is effectively enforced.[222] In other words, the publication of this judgment was aimed to prevent future violation of the Act by emphasizing the justiciability of its provisions. Similarly, the Hungarian Authority on Equal Treatment has also emphasized in many cases that the publication of its decision is necessary in order to prevent potential perpetrators from violating the principle of equal treatment.[223] Importantly, in most of the racial discrimination cases in which a violation of the principle of equal treatment is found, the Authority orders the publication of its decision.[224] In 2007 of 29 cases, in which a violation has been found, the Authority required the publication of its decision in 15 cases.[225] The publication of the decisions clearly raises awareness and therefore prevents discrimination by potential perpetrators.

Importantly, the competence and mandate of the Estonian and Dutch equal treatment bodies also focus on preventing discrimination rather than repairing

[220] See also De Prins, Sottiaux & Vrielink (2003b), para. 123; Taelman (2004a), at 234-235.

[221] See also De Prins, Sottiaux &Vrienlink (2003b), para. 123.

[222] Gent Labour Court, A.R. no. 176.893, 26 March 2007.

[223] See for instance EBH/94/2008, EBH/72/7/2008, EBH/516/2007, EBH/346/31/2007, EBH/271/2007.

[224] The lack of publication in the few racial discrimination cases can be justified by the special circumstances of the case. In one of these cases, for instance, the respondents offered an agreement to the applicants, namely that in the future they would comply with the principle of equal treatment and would also undertake some positive obligations in this respect. It seems that the Authority EBH/240/2008.

[225] Az Egyenlő Bánásmód Hatóság 2008. évi tevékenysége a számok tükrében. Egyenlő Bánásmód Hatóság (2009). Retrieved from http://www.egyenlobanasmod.hu/data/2008tevekenyseg_szamok_tukreben.pdf.

it or punishing the perpetrator. Neither of the bodies can issue binding decisions and their conclusions are mere *opinions*, the compliance with which is fully dependent on the willingness of the respondents. As the Gender Equality Commissioner, who became the Gender Equality and Equal Treatment Commissioner as of 1 January 2009, is a fairly new institution in Estonia, it is difficult to evaluate to what extent its opinions are and will observed by the perpetrators, or to what extent it will work preventively. By contrast, the Dutch ETC has carried out a survey on the follow-up of its opinions, the result of which showed that in 80% of the cases the respondents do take into account the observations of the Commission and try to comply with those positions. Importantly, the ETC uses a quite broad concept of equality and expects the respondents to comply with their positive obligations as well.[226] Arguably for this reason, it seems that complying with the recommendations and/or opinions of the ETC is realised through the adoption of structural measures,[227] which can and do often take the form of positive action measures. It was also discovered that the recommendations of the Commission are also considered and/or applied even in those instances where the ETC has not found a violation of the principle of equal treatment. Also, the Commission can inform certain instances of its findings which can also operate as a preventive measure.[228]

As mentioned in the chapter on *victimisation*, protection against retaliation encourages victims of discrimination to pursue their claim and thus indirectly aims to prevent potential perpetrators committing discrimination.[229] Protection against victimisation can be found in each country under review.[230] Thus, in this respect, victims of discrimination are invited to pursue their complaints with fact-finders.

[226] See inter alia Het verschil gemaakt. Evaluatie AWGB en werkzaamheden CGB 1999-2004, CGB 2005, at 20.

[227] See inter alia Havinga (2007), at 257; Het verschil gemaakt. *id.*, at 50.

[228] Art. 13(3) GETA. See also Holtmaat (2007), at 63; Het verschil gemaakt. *id.*, at 83.

[229] In the Belgian context see inter alia Wetsontwerp tot wijziging ..., *supra* note 145, at 25-26; Bayart & Bosmans (2008), at 588.

[230] See Ch. 6 on victimisation for a detailed analysis of the law and practice of the four countries in this respect.

7.9. Factors Determining the Form and Extent of Remedies

7.9.1. Circumstances Related to the Victim

7.9.1.1. Nature of the Victim

The jurisprudence in the countries under review demonstrates that in general, the nature of the victim does have significant weight in the adjudication on the appropriate sanctions. In this respect, thus, the victim's perspective is taken into account in this phase of the assessment.

In Belgium, the examination of the victim's perspective can be found in different aspects of the deliberation. For instance, in the Murat case in which in addition to the individual applicant the CEOOR was also involved, not only did the court order the termination of discrimination committed against the individual applicant, but it also required that the discrimination be terminated with respect to other potential candidates.[231] The court explicitly laid down that the engagement of the CEOOR gave the conflict an extra bearing: not only the violation of the subjective right, but also the respect for the provisions of the equal treatment legislation came to the fore. Arguably, without the engagement of the CEOOR in the procedure the court would not have paid attention to the other candidates, would have concentrated only on the breach of the right to equal treatment of Mr C. Murat in access to employment.[232] This also shows the importance of the engagement of interest organisations.

The same approach can also be explored in the Hungarian jurisprudence. In the two segregation claims initiated as actio popularis procedures, no compensation was awarded as no individually identified victim was involved in the complaint.[233] In another case in the field of providing goods and services Roma persons were refused a particular service. Here the court considered the fact that the respondent had concretely discriminated against the particular applicants, but at the same time his treatment also constituted discrimination against others not being engaged in the procedure.[234] For this reason, in addition to awarding compensation to the applicants, it also imposed a public interest fine on the respondent. The victim status was broadly interpreted in

[231] Gent Labour Court, summary proceedings, A.R. no. 176.893, 26 March 2007.

[232] Similarly, in criminal cases, in which compensation has been awarded to the individual victim for immaterial damages, courts have also acknowledged that the NGO's aims have also been violated by the violation of the right to equal treatment, and have awarded a symbolic compensation for immaterial damages. See inter alia Antwerp Court of Appeal, 8 January 2004; Brussels Correctional Court, 31 March 2004.

[233] Borsod-Abaúj-Zemplén County Court, 13.P.21.660/2005/16, 2 November 2005; Debrecen Court of Appeal, Pf.I.20.683/2005/7, 9 June 2006; Hajdú-Bihar County Court, 6.P. 20.341/2006/50, 2 May 2007; Debrecen Court of Appeal, Pf.I.20.361/2007/8, 13 December 2007; Supreme Court, Pfv.IV.20.936/2008/4, 19 November 2008.

[234] Supreme Court, Pvf. IV. 20 822/2001/4 (BH2003. 150), 3 April 2002.

these cases and included the whole group to which the applicants belonged. This approach obviously stretched the ambit of individual litigation to a more group oriented lawsuit.

Finally, in the Netherlands the effect of this factor can to some extent also be discovered in the recommendations of the ETC. For instance, the Commission concluded that a fitness club discriminated against an individual victim on the grounds of her racial or ethnic origin and religion by including discriminatory provisions among the membership criteria. In this case, in addition to this concrete victim, an NGO was also engaged in the procedure before the Commission.[235] Arguably due to the engagement of this interest organisation, the Commission in its recommendation concentrated on the possible effects of the challenged practice on others belonging to the same group. The possible effect of the nature of the victim on the recommendation of the ETC is even more noticeable when compared to a similar case initiated against another fitness club in which no recommendation was made by the ETC.[236] In this case there was only an individual victim complaining of discrimination. Importantly, no specific discriminatory provision was included in the membership requirements; the club 'merely' discriminated against this particular individual. Still, the Commission could have suggested the respondent behave differently in similar situations in the future. Nevertheless, the Commission is usually very pro-active in its approach: it often proposes the adoption of such measures that would prevent future discrimination against persons belonging to the same group as the applicants. In any event, when a group is disparately affected by a certain measure the complaint is generally not made by individual victims, but by organisations promoting equal treatment. Accordingly, consideration of the group effect often goes hand in hand with the consideration of the nature of the victim. In any event, it would be desirable to take the group aspect into account, even in individual litigation.

7.9.1.2. Protected Ground

The protected ground does generally have an effect on the sanctions in each country, again with the exception of Estonia. In most cases, the adjudication on sanctions is rather formulated in terms of the form and gravity of the violation, and not so much linked to the protected ground.

Belgium is an exception in this respect, as the protected ground is explicitly mentioned as a relevant factor in the determination of the sanction. Pursuant to Article 16(2) ARA, the amount of the forfaitair compensation is increased if the respondent cannot prove that the contested measures would also have been taken on non-discriminatory grounds. This provision can be interpreted

[235] Opinion 2008-12 ETC.
[236] Opinion 2007-156 ETC.

as making the violation more serious if the protected ground was the only reason for adopting the particular measure. In awarding compensation for non-material damage, the Hungarian courts take into consideration that discrimination on the grounds of racial or ethnic origin is very degrading to the victims.[237] In the Netherlands, again, the effect of the protected ground is less visible in the recommendations of the ETC, but arguably it still has some influence. For instance, in a case, concerning the housing of caravan dwellers, although the ETC did not find a violation of the GETA, it still made a recommendation that the local authorities should introduce a system through which caravan dwellers could express their special wishes, and on the basis of this system the local authorities could compare the supply and demand in order to adopt appropriate measures.[238] It can be argued that it was partly the special position of these persons that led the Commission to prepare its recommendation, even in the absence of finding a breach. Thus, it seems that by considering the protected ground, even in individual discrimination cases, the group aspect of the complaint is also taken into account. Contrary to the approach of the Commission to the nature of the victim, in this way the boundaries of individual enforcement could be stretched towards a group justice model.

7.9.1.3. Fault or Own Responsibility of the Victim

As yet no case can be found in any of the countries under review in which the fault or own responsibility of the victim could have played a role and/ or would have been considered within the framework of imposing sanctions in discrimination cases.[239] Nor are there any indications in the national legislation for consideration of this aspect in the decision on the sanctions. Thus, it is yet to be seen whether the fault or own responsibility of the victim would decrease the amount of compensation awarded, or whether would have a different effect.

7.9.2. Nature of the Violation

7.9.2.1. Form and Gravity of the Violation

The form and gravity of the violation is a factor that is almost intuitively taken into account in the countries under review in the determination of the sanctions. It seems that within this framework the broader effect on the group

[237] See inter alia Supreme Court, Pvf. IV. 20 822/2001/4 (BH2003. 150), 3 April 2002.
[238] Opinion 2006-222 ETC.
[239] See Castermans (2009), at 245-248.

to which the individual belongs is also considered. This approach is clearly in accordance with the requirement of the RED regarding the proportionality of the sanctions. This factor primarily determines the amount of compensation.

The Belgian, Estonian and Hungarian equal treatment legislation explicitly enumerates this factor as an element that should be considered in determining the amount of compensation. Pursuant to Article 16(2) of the Belgian ARA, the amount of forfaitair compensation is raised when the moral damage is very grave.

Similarly, the EETA lays down that in "determining the amount of compensation, the court or the labour dispute committee will among other things consider *the extent, duration and nature* of the discrimination."[240] As yet, neither of these provisions has been applied in practice. Notwithstanding the lack of practice in this respect, within the framework of general tort law this factor will influence fact-finders. For instance, in a victimisation case in Belgium the amount of compensation seemed to have fixed because of the serious effect retaliation could have on the enforcement of the right to equal treatment.[241]

Pursuant to Article 16(2) HETA, when imposing a particular sanction the Authority has to and does include in its deliberations consequences of the violation, the duration of the wrongful situation and the recurrence of violation.[242] For instance, in a case concerning the application of three Roma persons for a job the fact that the labour market position of Roma persons is very unfavourable played an important role in imposing the specific fine on the respondent.[243] Courts also take this factor into account. For instance, in the case of R. Ágnes a group of Roma persons were refused entry to a discotheque, and in fixing the amount of compensation the court explicitly referred to the fact that this refusal was degrading for them, and was even committed more than once.[244]

Similarly, in a racial direct discrimination case in the Netherlands in quantifying the immaterial damage the court took into account the fact that the discrimination lasted a long time and was committed in a systematic way.[245]

This factor also influences the forms of sanctions. In the Belgian Murat case, for instance, the Court took into consideration the fact that the case was surrounded by great publicity, and for this reason it ordered the publication of the judgment.[246] Likewise, this factor is also taken into account in imposing a

---

240 Art. 24(3) EETA (emphasis added).

241 Brussels Court of Labour, RG No 48.823, 25 April 2007.

242 See also Indokolás az egyenlő bánásmódról és az esélyegyenlőség előmozdításáról szóló törvényjavaslathoz, at 8.

243 EBH/94/2008.

244 Szabolcs-Szatmár-Bereg County Court, 1.P. 21.752/2004/26, 13 June 2005.

245 Central Appeal Council, LJN: AO3751, 16 February 2004, para. 4.2.

246 *CGKR and C. Murat v. D. Yves and E-L. BVBA*, Gent Labour Court, summary proceedings, no. 176.893, 26 March 2007.

public interest fine in Hungarian civil cases. For instance, in the case in which Roma persons were excluded from a pub on the grounds of their Roma origin, public interest fine was imposed on the perpetrators because, in addition to the individual discrimination, they also violated the right to equal treatment of all persons of Roma origin, and the discrimination was committed repeatedly in a public place.[247] Accordingly, the fact-finders stretched the boundaries of individual enforcement towards a more group oriented approach by taking into account the group aspect of the case in awarding remedies.

7.9.2.2. Material Scope

Similarly to the above factor, this aspect of the case also almost automatically influences the fact-finding body's decision on the appropriate sanction, and fosters the proportionality of the sanctions.

In Belgium it is only in an employment-related case that racial discrimination was found to have occurred and sanctions imposed. The form of sanction in this case was clearly related to employment: the court required the reintegration of the applicant whose dismissal was found to be discriminatory.[248]

On the contrary, both in Hungary and in the Netherlands cases have been decided in several fields falling under the material scope of the RED. Although the two main segregation cases in education in Hungary were actio popularis claims, where public interest fines generally seem appropriate, the court did not impose this sanction.[249] It merely ordered the publication of part of the judgment in both cases. In addition, in one of the cases it obliged the respondents to discontinue discrimination, prohibited the committing of future violation and ordered the termination of the discriminatory situation. In contrast, in the field of providing goods and services an example can be found in which a public interest fine was imposed.[250] Thus, it seems that fact-finders in Hungary are willing to impose positive obligations on the respondents in the field of education[251] and adopt punitive measures with respect to goods and services.[252]

As most of the cases in the Netherlands are decided by the Equal Treatment Commissioner, the role of the material scope in the remedies can be explored in its recommendations, in which it generally expects the respondents to take

---

[247] Supreme Court, Pvf. IV. 20 822/2001/4 (BH2003. 150), 3 April 2002.

[248] Brussels Labour Court, No 70/05 summary proceedings, Rep. Nr 06/02456, 6 February 2006.

[249] See also Farkas, Kádár & Kárpáti (2006), at 84.

[250] Supreme Court, Pvf. IV. 20 822/2001/4 (BH2003. 150), 3 April 2002.

[251] It has also been argued that in education preference should be given to conciliation because of the special character of the relationship.

[252] For a plea for making distinction according to the field of law with respect to the available sanctions see inter alia Szajbély (2005c). For a plea for uniform fines irrespective of the material scope see Farkas, Kádár & Kárpáti (2003).

positive measures. It seems that, somewhat similarly to the approach of the Hungarian AET, the ETC is more demanding when discrimination takes place in the field of providing goods and services than in employment related cases. For instance, while the Commission recommended a fitness centre amend its membership requirements in order not to discriminate against persons of a certain religion,[253] in an employment related case it 'simply' suggested an employer explain its reasons for refusal to the candidate who presumed that his refusal was based on his racial or ethnic origin.[254] This difference between the fields might be explained by the fact that employment relations are regulated in detail, while this is not the case with respect to goods and services.

7.9.3. Circumstances Related to the Perpetrator

As indicated in the theoretical framework, the circumstances related to the perpetrator are mainly taken into account when punitive or primarily punitive sanctions are imposed. Accordingly, these circumstances are generally weighed by the application of the following measures: imposing *fines*, and ordering the *publication* of the judgment with the aim of naming and shaming.

7.9.3.1. Size and Market Position

As explained, in Hungary the emphasis in the enforcement of the right to equal treatment is on punitive measures. Most often the Authority imposes fines on the perpetrators. Notwithstanding the fact that the attention should rather be turned to victim-oriented sanctions it is very important in terms of dissuasiveness that the size and market position of the respondent are consistently considered in the fixing of the amount of the fines. In order to be capable of appropriately fixing the amount of the fine the AET even requests the respondent to submit its financial statement.[255] In the lack of such a statement the respondent's financial situation is estimated on the basis of common knowledge.[256]

In the Belgian context, it has been argued that forfaitair compensation can also be regarded as a punitive sanction in addition to its compensatory character. It is remarkable that when awarding forfaitair compensation fact-finders do not have to take into account the size and market position of the respondent. Accordingly, the dissuasive effect of forfaitair compensation might

[253] Opinion 2008-12 ETC.
[254] Opinion 2006-180 ETC.
[255] See inter alia EBH/94/2008, EBH/641/11/2007.
[256] See inter alia EBH/310/33/2007.

differ from one respondent to another depending on their size and market position.[257] This also shows that, in Belgium, the victim's perspective and the caused harm are considered more important than punishing the perpetrator.

As yet, no example can be found where the size and market position played a dominant role in ordering the *publication* of the judgment with the purpose of naming and shaming. Ordering the publication of the judgment is generally related to either awareness-raising or the nature of the violation.

7.9.3.2. Private or Public Entity

Again, though not explicitly, this factor also seems to have influenced the fact-finding organs in a couple of cases as far as ordering or proposing the adoption of positive measures is concerned. Accordingly, the private or public character of the respondent not only has an effect on the punitive measures, but it also influences the reparative sanctions. These cases clearly indicate that appropriately taking into account this factor could also contribute to a more group-oriented enforcement of the principle of the equal treatment, even in individual litigation.

In Hungary, the school desegregation cases[258] can be taken as good examples of the courts obliging the public schools and responsible local authorities to terminate the segregation. Imposing positive obligations seems to be related to the public character of these entities. The Authority has also explicitly emphasised the special role of local authorities in observing and enforcing the right to equal treatment.[259]

In the Netherlands, as with the previous factors, the Commission's recommendation seems to have been implicitly influenced by this factor. It seems that the Commission imposes more far-reaching obligations on public bodies than on private organisations. For instance, even though the Commission did not find a violation of the principle of equal treatment, it required a particular local authority to adopt measures in the field of housing in order to make it possible for caravan dwellers to pronounce their wishes, in the light of which the local authority could possibly adjust its supply to the demand.[260]

---

[257] With respect to social security see inter alia Bernauw (2004), at 301-302; Taelman (2004a), at 771.

[258] Borsod-Abaúj-Zemplén County Court, 13.P.21.660/2005/16, 2 November 2005; Debrecen Court of Appeal, Pf.I.20.683/2005/7, 9 June 2006; Hajdú-Bihar County Court, 6.P. 20.341/2006/50, 2 May 2007; Debrecen Court of Appeal, Pf.I.20.361/2007/8, 13 December 2007; Supreme Court, Pfv.IV.20.936/2008/4, 19 November 2008.

[259] EBH/172/2/2006.

[260] Opinion 2006-222 ETC. See also Opinion 2006-202 ETC.

7.9.3.3. Fault or Intent of the Respondent

Among the factors pertaining to the respondent his fault or intent is the most explicitly present in the adjudication on the form or extent of the sanctions.

Remarkably, the Belgian ARA explicitly stipulates that the amount of the forfaitair compensation will be raised if the respondent cannot prove that the less favourable or disadvantageous treatment would not have been encountered on non-discriminatory grounds.[261] In other words, this clause makes the intent of the respondent an aggravating circumstance in terms of sanctioning. As yet this provision has not been applied in practice. Nevertheless, prior to the adoption of the ARA, this factor seems to have been taken into account in the case law on the ADA. In the Murat case the judge of the summary-like procedure examined whether he could order the cessation of discrimination not only with respect to the particular applicant, but also pertaining to any persons on the grounds of nationality or ethnic origin.[262] In this respect it was remarkable that the respondent tried to prove the absence of the danger of recurrence by showing a text on their equal treatment policy which had been placed on their website. In other words, the respondent attempted to show the lack of his fault in order to avoid a specific sanction. The court established that a general text on equal treatment policy could not mitigate the sanction since it could, arguably, not curtail the respondent's liability or fault. According to the court

> the content of the internal mail and the reasoning pertaining to the objections of the clients point to a general reservation against employing persons of foreign origin and are not exclusively concerned with the person of the first applicant [i.e. Mr. Murat C. – M.A.].

Thus, the court correctly considered the respondent's fault in imposing this sanction.

In Hungary, the presence of this factor can be found in cases where the respondent failed to fulfil his positive obligations. In these cases the Authority demanded the elimination of the wrongful situation instead of prohibiting future discrimination. As yet, in only one case other than a complaint relating to reasonable accommodation has the Authority imposed this sanction. This case concerned the minority committee of a local government to which no Roma persons were elected. In the view of the AET this was contrary to the Minority Act and the Local Government Act which strongly suggests that the local governments elect minority members in the minority committee if possible. Thus, the sanction of eliminating discrimination meant that the local government should elect minority members to the minority committee. The question is, whether requiring the elimination of discrimination, positive

261 Art. 16(2) ARA.

262 *CGKR and C. Murat v. D. Yves and E-L. BVBA*, Gent Labour Court, summary proceedings, no. 176.893, 26 March 2007.

obligations would be forced upon the respondent even in the absence of prior legal duties to take action. As yet, the case law does not indicate that the Authority would go so far, which is quite regrettable in terms of effective enforcement and achieving substantive equality.

In addition to imposing the sanction of termination of the wrongful situation, the Authority has also taken this factor into consideration in fixing the amount of the fine. For instance, in a case against the Ministry of Agriculture the Authority imposed a fine because of its repeated discrimination on the grounds of motherhood.[263] It did not impose a fine when some measures were adopted following the initiation of the procedure and/or the discriminatory treatment.[264] Similarly, the Court of Appeal did not order the cessation of the wrongful situation in the Miskolc segregation case as the respondent had in the meantime taken appropriate steps in this regard.[265]

Finally, in the Netherlands the effect of the respondent's fault or own responsibility can also be discovered in some recommendations of the ETC. For example, when an insurance company was willing to take certain steps to provide an insurance policy for caravan dwellers under conditions comparable to others, the Commission's recommendation concentrated on further possible measures that could help the respondent to conduct business in harmony with the GETA.[266] Accordingly, the respondent's willingness could be interpreted as amounting to a decrease in the extent of the particular sanction. This is an effective preventive approach as it signals to the potential perpetrators that their good behaviour will also be considered.

7.10. Conclusions

The enforcement of the right to equal treatment can only be effective, if the breach of the prohibition of non-discrimination is appropriately addressed at the level of sanctions. The more properly the sanction reacts to the violation, the more effective enforcement becomes. Moreover, sanctions are special among the enforcement provisions as, not only in an indirect way, through guaranteeing or enhancing effective enforcement, but they can also directly aim to achieve substantive equality. Accordingly, the aim of redress should be to attain substantive equality, the first pillar of an adequate system of minority protection.

It is common knowledge that there is no right without appropriate redress, which is also explicitly recognised by Article 15 RED. This article makes

263 See inter alia EBH/142/3/2007.

264 See inter alia EBH/418/2007.

265 Miskolc, Debrecen Appeals Court, 26 June 2006. See also Supreme Court, Pvf. IV. 20 822/2001/4 (BH2003. 150), 3 April 2002.

266 Opinion 2006-5 ETC.

three requirements for sanctions in order to attain effective enforcement. Pursuant to this article and the steady line of jurisprudence of the ECJ, sanctions have to be effective, proportionate and dissuasive. These criteria can also be captured in the requirements to take into account the circumstances relating to both the victim and the respondent, and the nature of the violation when imposing a particular sanction. Admittedly, the assortment of sanctions is limited in a national legal system. Accordingly, the effect of the RED in this respect can mainly be explored in the case law. In this respect fact-finders have an important role to play as they decide on which sanction to impose in the particular case, and also, they convert the abstract rules into concrete obligations. More specifically, it can be examined in the case law whether fact-finders have considered these factors in their adjudication on sanctions. Arguably, the role of these factors also varies with the forms of sanctions. Based on their purpose the following forms of sanctions can be distinguished: reparative, punitive and preventive sanctions.

These forms of sanctions can be found in each country under review, though admittedly each country has created a preferred form of sanction. While in Belgium the emphasis has been placed on monetary compensation for the damage suffered, in Hungary the most often used equal treatment procedure generally aims to punish the perpetrator. In the Netherlands the Commission's non-binding opinions are the most often used way of enforcement which can be interpreted as preventive sanctions. Finally, from the Estonian equal treatment legislation it might be concluded that, as in the Netherlands, the focus is on preventing future violation through the non-binding opinions of the Commissioner.

The above mentioned varying emphasis also means that the countries' preferences are also discernible pertaining to the trio of victim-harm-respondent. While compensation is victim and harm oriented, similarly to preventive sanctions, punitive measures also centre around the perpetrator. In terms of the three requirements of the RED, in Belgium the focus is on effectiveness and proportionality, while in the other countries the stress has rather been placed on dissuasiveness. As argued, as soon as the victims of discrimination can effectively vindicate their right to equal treatment and are provided with effective and proportionate redress, it has a dissuasive effect on future perpetrators. However, the opposite is not true: a dissuasive procedure does not in itself guarantee effective and proportionate redress. In this light, the most often used procedures in Belgium can be regarded to fulfil the requirements of the RED. On the contrary, the presumedly most popular proceedings, in the other countries with their mainly dissuasive effects, do not entirely seem to comply with the criteria of effectiveness and proportionality. Importantly, however, the victims in these countries can also turn to civil courts, where the aim of the fact-finders is also to redress the victims. Nevertheless, the enforcement of the right to equal treatment would be more effective if the victim's perspective was also taken into account in the most frequently used procedures, which are at the same time fast-track and low-threshold proceedings.

Although all forms of sanction could theoretically very well be combined with positive action measures, fact-finders in general refrain from imposing positive obligations. Even monetary compensation is rarely awarded to interest organisations that could use it to promote substantive equality. As yet only Belgium is a positive exception in this respect. Accordingly, notwithstanding the potential for achieving substantive equality and enhancing minority protection the different forms of sanctions inherently include, neither the legislators nor the fact-finders in the countries under review have been creative or assertive enough in making the enforcement of the right to equal treatment as effective as possible.

Notwithstanding the fact that the palette of sanctions in the countries under review comply with the criteria of effectiveness, proportionality and dissuasiveness, they should also be observed in the individual cases. The practice shows that these requirements are not always or at least not explicitly taken into consideration endangering the effective enforcement of the right to equal treatment on the grounds of racial or ethnic origin, and subsequently failing to contribute to a developed level of minority protection.

Chapter 8

Specialised Bodies for the Promotion of Equal Treatment

Part A. Theoretical Framework

8.1. Introduction

It is generally accepted that national specialised bodies assigned for the promotion of equal treatment (hereafter referred to as national specialised bodies, specialised bodies or bodies) can play a significant role in the implementation and enforcement of anti-discrimination law.[1] This is also explicitly acknowledged in Recital (24) of the Directive, which states that "[*p*]*rotection* against discrimination based on racial or ethnic origin would itself be *strengthened* by the existence of a body or bodies in each Member State".[2]

The Race Directive was the first legislative document in the European Union to require the establishment of such bodies.[3] The requirement of establishing national specialised bodies was also required in later legislation

1 See also Cormack & Niessen (2005), at 23; Tyson (2001), at 216.

2 Recital (24) RED (emphasis added).

3 The same approach was not followed in the Framework Directive. Several explanations might be given for the refusal of the proposal for the establishment of specialised bodies within the context of the Framework Directive. One of the most plausible reasons seems to be that the FD covers a broad range of protected grounds, and it would be then too far-reaching to require the Member States to establish such bodies in relation to all these grounds.

on gender equality; more specifically in the 2002/73/EC[4] and the 2006/54/EC[5] Directives. At present, therefore, there is a general obligation on the Member States to designate bodies for the promotion of equal treatment on the grounds of racial or ethnic origin and gender. Importantly, several Member States have broadened the ambit of these bodies to all the protected grounds covered by EU equality law. Accordingly, the Member States seem convinced that these bodies can contribute to the effective enforcement of the right to equal treatment.

The theoretical part of this chapter is devoted to an analysis of the requirement of Article 13 RED on national specialised bodies and the possible implications of such law-enforcing agencies for minority protection. This part of the chapter is divided into two main sections. First of all, the competences and mandates of the national specialised bodies as required by the RED are discussed. Subsequently, the organisational and operational issues related to the independence of such bodies are examined. The most important implications for minority protection are addressed in each section. To start with, a short introduction is given on the evolution of the idea of creating national human rights bodies, in relation to which recommendations have been formulated, that could also be relevant for the national specialised bodies.

Article 13 RED reads as follows:

> Article 13
>
> (1) Member States shall designate a body or bodies for the promotion of equal treatment of all persons without discrimination on the grounds of racial or ethnic origin. These bodies may form part of agencies charged at national level with the defence of human rights or the safeguard of individuals' rights.
> (2) Member States shall ensure that the competences of these bodies include:
> - without prejudice to the right of victims and of associations, organisations or other legal entities referred to in Article 7(2), providing independent assistance to victims of discrimination in pursuing their complaints about discrimination,
> - conducting independent surveys concerning discrimination,
> - publishing independent reports and making recommendations on any issue relating to such discrimination.

[4] Directive 2002/73/EC of the European Parliament and of the Council of 23 September 2002 amending Council Directive 76/207/EEC on the implementation of the principle of equal treatment for men and women as regards access to employment, vocational training and promotion, and working conditions.

[5] Directive 2006/54/EC of the European Parliament and of the Council of 5 July 2006 on the implementation of the principle of equal opportunities and equal treatment of men and women in matters of employment and occupation (Recast Directive).

8.2. A Concise History of the Evolution of National (Human Rights/Specialised) Bodies

The history of national institutions for the promotion and protection of human rights (NHRIs) runs back over a long period.[6] As early as 1946, the idea of establishing national institutions came up during the second session of the Economic and Social Council of the UN. The Council invited its member states 'to consider the desirability of establishing information groups or local human rights committees within their respective countries to collaborate with them in furthering the work of the Commission of Human Rights.'[7] The next significant event took place in 1978 when the Commission of Human Rights convened a 'Seminar on National and Local Institutions for the Promotion and Protection of Human Rights', and a set of guidelines were proposed assigning two main functions to these national institutions: monitoring government compliance with international human rights norms and promoting these norms. In the meantime, several of these national institutions were established. In 1991, the first International Workshop on National Institutions for the Promotion and Protection of Human Rights was organised.[8] This workshop adopted the Paris Principles in 1993, endorsed by the Commission on Human Rights and the General Assembly.[9] McCrudden pointed out that "[t]hese Principles have been significant in influencing the approaches to national enforcement adopted by other international bodies and by national governments."[10] For instance, the Office of the UNHCHR uses these guidelines in its work to encourage the establishment or strengthening of national institutions.[11]

In Europe, meetings of the European Group of NHRIs were organised in 1994 and in 1997. In 1997 the Steering Committee for Human Rights of the

6 On the history of national human rights institutions see further Kjaerum (2003), at 6; De Beco (2007), at 337-338.

7 ECOSOC Res. 2/9, 21 June 1946. The Council adopted two more resolutions later on in which it, again, invited the governments to establish national human rights bodies. See ECOSOC Res. 772 B (XXX), 25 July 1960; ECOSOC Res. 888 F (XXXIV), 24 July 1962.

8 Seminar on National and Local Institutions for the Promotion and Protection of Human Rights, ST/HR/SER.A/2 (1978). On this seminar see Lindsnaes & Lindholt (2000), at 5-6.

9 Principles relating to the Status of National Institutions (The Paris Principles), Annex to National Institutions for the Promotion and Protection of Human rights, General Assembly, A/RES/48/134, 20 December 1993.

10 McCrudden (2001), at 284.

11 McCrudden (2001), at 282. See also General Recommendation No. 17: Establishment of National Institutions to Facilitate Implementation of the Convention, 25 March 1993.

Council of Europe drafted a recommendation[12] and a resolution[13] pertaining to these institutions. The recommendation suggests that the member states of the Council of Europe consider the establishment of such institutions, keeping in mind the Paris Principles.[14]

In the same year the ECRI made it clear that the ambit of such institutions does not need to be human rights in general, but can be confined to the principle of equal treatment. In its General Policy Recommendation Nr. 2 it proposed the establishment of specialised bodies to combat racism, xenophobia, anti-Semitism and intolerance at national level.[15] This recommendation was followed by the adoption of the Race Directive, Article 13 of which obliges the Member States to designate a body (or bodies) for the promotion of equal treatment on the grounds of racial or ethnic origin. Importantly, the requirement of the RED to establish such bodies has been directly linked to both the ECRI GR No. 2[16] and the Paris Principles.[17] Moreover, the European Parliament in its resolution on the RED explicitly recommends the use of the Paris Principles as reference points for monitoring the bodies designated for this task.[18] Taking into account the fact that references have been made

---

12 Recommendation on the Establishment of Independent National Institutions for the Promotion and Protection of Human Rights, Council of Europe Rec. No. R(97) 14, 30 September 1997.

13 Resolution on Cooperation Between National Human Rights Institutions of Member States and Between Them and the Council of Europe, Council of Europe Res. (97) 11, 30 September 1997.

14 See inter alia De Beco (2007), at 336-338.

15 ECRI General Policy Recommendation No. 2: Establishment of Specialised Bodies to Combat Racism, Xenophobia, Anti-Semitism and Intolerance at National Level, CRI(97) 36, 13 June 1997.

16 "This Article would bring the Directive into line with the recommendations of the European Commission against Racism and Intolerance on specialist bodies to combat racism and xenophobia at national level." Report on the proposal for a Council directive on implementing the principle of equal treatment between persons irrespective of racial or ethnic origin, COM(1999)566 – C5-0067/2000 – 1999/0253(CNS), A5-0136/2000, 16 May 2000, at 65.

17 "Taking into account Resolution 48/134 adopted by the General Assembly of the United Nations on 20 December 1993 on National Institutions for the Promotion and Protection of Human Rights." ECRI General Policy Recommendation Nr 2, Specialised bodies to combat racism, xenophobia, anti-Semitism and intolerance at national level, 13 June 1997. See also European Parliament resolution of 27 September on the application of Council Directive 2000/43/EC of 29 June 2000 implementing the principle of equal treatment between persons irrespective or racial or ethnic origin, 2007/2094(INI), para. 31.

18 "Recommends that the commission carefully monitor the independent functioning of equality bodies, for which purpose it can use as a reference the Principles relating to the Status of National Institutions ('the Paris Principles') as adopted by the UN General Assembly in its resolution 48./134 of 20 December 1993, which include principles on the adequate financing of such bodies" (European Parliament resolution of 27 September on the application of Council Directive 2000/43/EC, 2007/2094(INI), para. 31). Cormack and Niessen similarly argue that "[t]his provision complements General Policy Recommendation No. 2. […] This provision is also in line with resolutions and recommendations from the United Nations and the Council of

to these documents, they will be used as complementary documents in the assessment of the requirements of Article 13 RED.[19]

8.3. Competences and Mandates of National Specialised Bodies

When the discourse concerns the competences and mandates of the specialised equality bodies of the RED, it is generally their special tasks enumerated in Article 13(2) RED that are quoted, and no mention is made of their overarching competence/mandate to promote equal treatment under Article 13(1) RED.[20] This position is even more striking in the view of the fact that the special competences/mandates are solely exemplative since Article 13(2) RED begins with the word 'include'. Hence, this indicates that the special competences/ mandates that are enumerated in this article are regarded as the core content of the duty to promote.[21]

Pursuant to Article 13 RED, therefore, first of all an overarching competence to promote the right to equal treatment can be identified. In addition three special competences/mandates have also been enumerated in the RED. These are: providing independent assistance to victims of discrimination in pursuing their complaints about discrimination, conducting independent surveys concerning discrimination and publishing independent reports and making recommendations on any issue relating to such discrimination. These competences and/or mandates will be discussed below.

Europe according to which all States should establish an independent human rights commission and an ombudsman." Cormack & Niessen (2004), at 21.

19 As Holtmaat observed "[w]ith the inclusion of Article 13 in the Racial Equality Directive, the European Union acted in conformity with other international recommendations on the same topic." Holtmaat (2006a), at 14.

20 As Holtmaat observed "[t]he Directive gives three core competencies to the equality bodies" Holtmaat (2006a), at 25. In the wording of the Report from the Commission "[t]he Directive requires, as a minimum, that the body be able to give independent assistance to victims of discrimination, conduct independent surveys concerning discrimination, publish independent reports and make recommendations on discrimination issues" Report from the Commission to the Council and the European Parliament – The application of Directive 2000/43/EC, COM(2006) 643 final/2, 30 October 2006, para. 3.2.

21 See also the Report from the Commission on the RED according to which "[t]he Directive requires, as a minimum, that the body be able to give independent assistance to victims of discrimination, conduct independent surveys concerning discrimination, publish independent reports and make recommendations on discrimination issues." Report from the Commission to the Council and the European Parliament – The application of Directive 2000/43/EC, COM(2006) 643 final/2, 30 October 2006, para. 3.2.

8.3.1. Protection and Promotion of Equal Treatment

While in Article 13(1) RED the obligation to *promote* is enshrined, Recital (24) RED lays down that

> [*p*]*rotection* against discrimination based on racial or ethnic origin would itself be strengthened by the existence of a body or bodies in each Member State, with competence to analyse the problems involved, to study possible solutions and to provide concrete assistance for the victims.[22]

Strikingly, in the Paris Principles these obligations are formulated as two separate requirements. More specifically, it is stipulated that "[a] national institution shall be vested with competence to *promote* and *protect* human rights."[23] In the light of the Paris Principles and the formulations of the RED in Recital (24) and Article 13(1) it can be argued that both protection and promotion are necessary in order to ensure effective enforcement because of the respective obligations stemming from them.

Protection is generally interpreted to mean the duty "to prevent third parties from unduly interfering in the right-holder's enjoyment of a particular freedom or entitlement."[24] This duty often manifests in monitoring compliance or inspection and imposing sanctions.[25]

On the contrary, *promotion* seems to be a controversial notion. Some scholars have expressed their disappointment at the use of this term,[26] while others see it as demonstrating that the national bodies should be strong.[27] In the theory of both human rights law in general and anti-discrimination law in particular the term 'promotion' is generally regarded as soft and not neatly circumscribed.[28] The obligation to promote is considered open-textured[29] and policy-led, which is hard to enforce. In human rights law it is generally accepted that

---

22 Recital (24) RED (emphasis added).

23 Principles relating to the Status of National Institutions (The Paris Principles), adopted by General Assembly resolution 48/134, 20 December 1993, Competence and Responsibilities, 1 (emphasis added). Interestingly, the ECRI General Recommendation No. 2 talks about combating racism, and not about the promotion and/or protection of the principle of equal treatment.

24 Courtis (2008), at 45.

25 When the duty to protect is upon a state it is also required that there are regulations pertaining to the conduct of the parties. See also Courtis (2008), at 45.

26 See for instance Higgins (2003), at 401.

27 See for instance Bell (2001a), at 47-48.

28 See Fredman (2005a), at 374-375. Within the framework of equality Fredman distinguishes three types of proactive measures according to the precision of the duty. The most open-textured is mainstreaming, which is followed by the duty on public bodies to promote equality, and the most specific model is that which applies to employment and pay equity.

29 See Fredman (2005a), at 374-375.

> [h]uman rights impose three types or levels of obligations on States Parties: the obligation to respect, to protect and to fulfil. In turn, the obligation to fulfil incorporates both an obligation to facilitate and an obligation to provide.[30]

The obligation to facilitate is often referred to as the obligation to promote.[31] Importantly, the obligation to promote is in this context a positive obligation imposed on the states, compared with the obligation to respect which is considered to be a negative obligation.[32] Fredman also construes this duty within the framework of equal treatment, and labels promotion as an obligation to adopt positive action measures with a clear group aspect.[33] In the context of the right to housing, Leckie[34] translated the obligation to promote as the duty on states to

> place sufficient legal and policy emphasis on the full realization of [this right], through a series of active measures including national and/or local legislative and related policies, and the identification of discernable 'benchmarks' towards the full enjoyment of [this right] by all sectors of society.[35]

It is beyond doubt that it is much easier to define the content of negative obligations. For this reason promotional activities seem to include less straightforward duties than the duty to protect (and respect). Still, several concrete obligations can be brought under the notion of 'promotion' in relation to discrimination. Accordingly, depending on the willingness of the Member States specialised bodies can be vested with broad competences/mandates in order to promote the right to equal treatment and protect persons from discrimination.

---

30 Eide (2001), at 23. General Comment No. 12, Committee on Economic, Social and Cultural Rights (1999), para. 15.

31 See for example Henrard (2008c), at 32-34; Leckie (2001), at 155.

32 Henrard (2008c), at 32-34.

33 Fredman (2001a), at 27.

34 Leckie argued that "the obligation to promote compels government to recognize the multifaceted human rights dimensions of [the right] and to take steps to ensure that no measures are taken with the intention of deliberately eroding the legal and practical status of this right. Moreover, comprehensive legislative review should take place, with any existing legislation or policies negatively affecting the exercise of the right [...] subjected to repeal or alteration. [...] Accurately assessing the degree to which [this] right [...] remains unsatisfied or denied exists as a further element of the state's obligation to promote the norm. An identifiable effort must be made to identify where and to what extent the right is not in place, and consequently to target [...] policies and legal measures towards attaining the right for everyone in the shortest possible time." Leckie (2001), at 156-157.

35 Leckie (2001), at 156.

8.3.2. Providing Independent Assistance to Victims of Discrimination in Pursuing their Complaints about Discrimination

Pursuant to the present text of the first specific competence/mandate, national specialised bodies should provide "*independent assistance to victims* of discrimination in pursuing their complaints about discrimination".[36] The original proposal of this competence/mandate was somewhat different as it laid down that these bodies should *receive and pursue complaints from individuals*.[37]

This competence/mandate levied on the national specialised bodies raises a couple of questions. First of all, it is not evident what the term *assistance* means in this provision. In addition, it is not clear either how broad the *victim* requirement can be interpreted. What does the expression '*pursuing their complaints about discrimination*' mean? How should the phrase '*without prejudice to the right of victims and of associations, organisations or other legal entitites referred to in Article 7(2)*' be read in this context? As the answer to the first question is somewhat complicated and can be influenced by the interpretation of the other points, it seems to be reasonable to start with the latter questions.

In the wording of the RED and similarly to the ECRI GR No. 7, independent assistance should be provided to *victims* of discrimination. In the original proposal individuals were to be provided with assistance,[38] and the EP in its legislative proposal proposed to amend this term to "natural and legal persons and non-formalised groups of persons, associations or non-governmental organisations."[39] Similarly, the Paris Principles also recommended that "individuals, their representatives, third parties, non-governmental organizations, associations of trade unions or any other representative organizations" could turn to these bodies.[40] Arguably, the importance of the formulation is not irrelevant. While the term 'individuals' covers only natural persons, the

36 In the light of this amendment it is remarkable that the original version of the respective Recital of the RED already referred to providing "concrete assistance for victims of discrimination" instead of describing these bodies as entities that could receive and pursue complaints. Recital (19) RED.

37 Amended proposal for a Council Directive implementing the principle of equal treatment between persons irrespective of racial or ethnic origin, COM(2000)328 final – 1999/0253 (CNS), 31 May 2000, Article 12.

38 Significantly, the original proposal of Recital (19) RED already referred to victims. Report on the proposal for a Council directive on implementing the principle of equal treatment between persons irrespective of racial or ethnic origin, COM(1999)566 – C5-0067/2000 – 1999/0253(CNS), A5-0136/2000, 16 May 2000, at 14.

39 *Id.*, at 27.

40 Principles relating to the Status of National Institutions (The Paris Principles), adopted by General Assembly resolution 48/134, 20 December 1993, Additional principles concerning the status of commissions with quasi-jurisdictional competence.

term 'victims' seems to be broader and include legal or other persons as well. Accordingly, in addition to natural persons, interest organisations can also turn to these national bodies. This interpretation is also in accordance with Article 13(1) RED, which provides for the promotion of equal treatment for '*all persons*'.

This aspect also raises the question whether victims of *victimisation* could also be assisted by specialised bodies, since the provision talks about victims of *discrimination*. Irrespective of the fact whether victimisation is categorised as a form of discrimination or 'merely' as an enforcement provision in the national legislation, in an indirect way victims of victimisation have also been victims of discrimination, and for this reason they should also be given assistance.[41]

The RED requires that national specialised bodies be empowered with the competence to assist victims in *pursuing their complaints* of discrimination. This formulation clearly shows that victims should be assisted when they enforce their right to equal treatment, and does not specify at which phase of the enforcement the assistance can or should be provided. Accordingly, it might include giving legal advice even before starting a procedure as well as representation during the procedure before the fact-finding body.

Pursuant to the text of the RED, specialised bodies shall provide assistance in pursuing complaints about discrimination *on the grounds of racial or ethnic origin*. As many arguments can be and have been brought up in favour of a single equality body,[42] it is suggested that these bodies not only be concerned with this particular ground, but have competence with respect to other grounds as well.[43]

Article 13(2) RED also lays down that the competence of equality bodies to assist victims of discrimination in pursuing their claims must be "*without prejudice to the right of victims and of associations, organisations or other legal entities referred to in Article 7(2).*"[44] In this context this phrase has at least two important implications. As explained with respect to legal standing, it indicates that assistance can include legal representation. In other words, national specialised bodies can have legal standing before fact-finding bodies.[45] Secondly, reading this provision in conjunction with Article 7(2),

41 For a further elaboration on the importance of victimisation in the enforcement of discrimination law see Chapter 5 on victimisation.

42 See below on single equality bodies. See also Collins (2004); Cormack & Niessen (2004), at 27-28; O'Cinnéide (2002); Hepple, Coussey & Choudhury (2000), at 51-55; Schiek, Waddington & Bell (2007), at 875-879.

43 See also Recital (14) which lays down that "[i]n implementing the principle of equal treatment irrespective of racial or ethnic origin, the Community should, in accordance with Article 3(2) of the EC Treaty, aim to eliminate inequalities, and to promote equality between men and women, especially since women are often the victims of multiple discrimination."

44 See also Ch. 5 on legal standing.

45 See Ch. 5 on legal standing.

it also suggests that 'associations, organisations or other legal entities' can be given legal standing before a national specialised body,[46] if such body is a quasi-judicial organ and proceeds on the basis of (civil or) administrative procedural law.[47] From this latter observation it can also be inferred that a national specialised body should not necessarily provide the same victim with all types of assistance. It might only give, for instance, legal advice, or help find the best way of proceeding, and it may be an interest organisation that represents the victim in the procedure before the specialised body. In practice, if a specialised body acts as a representative, it is hard to imagine that, even if it has separate departments for legal assistance and decision-making, the body itself would represent the victim in its own procedure.[48] Accordingly, in order to ensure effective enforcement of anti-discrimination law, it is highly recommended that legal standing be given to 'associations, organisations or other legal entities' also in procedures before the national specialised bodies vested with quasi-judicial powers.[49]

Strikingly, while some observers welcome this provision of Article 13(2) RED, others criticise it. The optimism derives from the possible interpretation and the possible capacity the term '*assistance*' carries with it,[50] while the pessimism is attributed to the vagueness of this notion as it might give effect to an interpretation where practically no effective measures will or can be taken.[51] The vagueness of this term seems to have been a deliberate choice of the legislator, also taken into account the role of the Directive as such. As Tyson explained in relation to the drafting process of the RED, "[t]here was a good deal of concern' mainly because Member States found that 'the proposal overstepped the line between setting objectives and telling Member States how to achieve them."[52] As expected, a survey made by Holtmaat shows that there is no unequivocal interpretation of the term 'assistance' among the Member States either. According to some states investigating complaints is different from assistance, while others categorise quasi-judicial competences under

46 See also Ch. 5 on legal standing.

47 Art. 7(2) concerns 'any judicial and/or administrative procedure'.

48 Importantly, when quasi-judicial power is given to these bodies the aim is to establish an easily accessible fact-finding body which indicates that no representation should be required.

49 See also Ch. 5 on legal standing.

50 See, for example, Higgins (2003), at 401. "The requirement that Member States designate bodies with the capacity to provide assistance to victims of discrimination in pursuing their complaints is an important one. The bringing of a discrimination action by an individual is likely to prove stressful and expensive." Jacobsen & Rosenberg Khawaja (2006), at 10. "Assistance in discrimination cases is [...] a precondition for effective enforcement of anti-discrimination law and for ensuring that victims of discrimination are not provided with an effective remedy against discrimination in practice."

51 See for example Higgins (2003), at 402; Brown (2002), at 221. "The adopted version has been described as 'disappointing': 'assistance' may comprise only information on how to bring legal proceeding." Barry (2006), at 35.

52 Tyson (2001), at 216.

assistance.[53] In any event, it can be concluded that assistance does clearly include providing legal information and advice to persons turning to these bodies. This form of assistance will be referred to as 'concrete assistance'.

Concerning the further possible meanings of assistance[54] at least three main questions can be posed, bearing in mind both the original and the amended proposals of the RED. Does assistance include the legal standing of national specialised bodies before courts? Within the framework of assistance, can it be expected that a national specialised body decide on cases; that is that it acts as a quasi-judicial organ? Finally, and related to this latter question, how can such a body investigate cases?

8.3.2.1. Legal Standing in Court Proceedings

In addressing the matter of the legal standing of national specialised bodies before courts ECRI GRs No. 2 and No. 7 can serve as points of departure since they also include the competence of national specialised bodies to assist victims and provide some explanation on the possible interpretation of this term.[55] Pursuant to the Explanatory Memorandum of GR No. 7, "assistance

---

53 Holtmaat (2006a), at 24. "[S]ome experts were of the opinion that independent assistance to victims is something quite different from hearing and investigating complaints of discrimination. The latter term was reserved by these experts to institutions with a semi-judicial or quasi-judicial status that can give binding or non-binding judgments or opinions about cases. However, some experts did include these activities under the category of assistance to victims. It appeared that others included many other activities in this category, for instance providing information about the existence of anti-discrimination legislation and about the possibility of taking legal action against discrimination, referring the victim to an organisation/institution that could assist with formulating an official complaint, or helping the victim and the (alleged) perpetrator come to an amicable settlement (mediation)."

54 Assistance might also arguably refer to financial assistance. Admittedly, taken into consideration the general situation of national specialised bodies, it is hardly to be expected that they will provide victims of discrimination with financial assistance, since they are not equipped with an unlimited budget. What seems to be realistic in this context is that financial assistance is given in the form of free services. In this context, ECRI General Policy Recommendation No. 7 seems to be relevant, Art. 26 of which stipulates that "[t]he law should guarantee free legal aid and, where necessary, a court-appointed lawyer, for victims who wish to go before the courts as applicants or plaintiffs and who do not have the necessary means to do so" ECRI General Policy Recommendation No 7: National Legislation to Combat Racism and Racial Discrimination, CRI(2003) 8, 13 December 2002. Similarly, in the article on national specialised bodies, Art. 12(3) of the legislative proposal of the EP articulated that "[a]s a minimum, the Member States shall guarantee the treatment of complaints free of charge for those who are not in a position to make their own financial contribution." In summary, providing free of charge services would highly encourage victims to turn to a fact-finding organ with their complaints. By doing this, national specialised bodies would contribute to a great extent to a more effective access to justice, and so a more effective protection of the right to equal treatment.

55 ECRI General Policy Recommendation No. 2: Establishment of Specialised Bodies to Combat Racism, Xenophobia, Anti-Semitism and Intolerance at National Level, CRI(97) 36, 13 June 1997, Ch. C: Functions and responsibilities of specialised bodies, Principle 3. "Subject

to victims covers provision of *general advice* to victims and *legal assistance*, including *representation* in proceedings before the courts. It also covers *assistance in seeking friendly settlement* of complaints."[56] General advice still seems to be broad, but it might be interpreted as referring to all questions which cannot be regarded legal. Legal assistance, accordingly, is limited to legal questions, among which *representation* and mediation.

The original proposal of the relevant Recital referred to 'concrete assistance' and in this light the EP proposed to include 'providing concrete help'[57] in addition to 'receiving and pursuing complaints from individuals' among the competences/mandates of specialised bodies. Arguably, both concrete help and pursuing complaints could be interpreted as including the engagement of specialised bodies in court procedures. This view is also confirmed by the insertion of the phrase "without prejudice to the right of victims and of associations, organisations or other legal entities referred to in Article 7(2)."[58] Similarly, the Report from the Commission on the RED also seems to depart from the fact that such competence is included in the term 'assistance'. It diagnoses that

> [f]rom the information provided it is clear that the equality bodies give legal advice to individual victims of discrimination, *but* they *only support* a small number of cases before the courts.[59]

to national circumstances, law and practice, specialised bodies should possess as many as possible of the following functions and responsibilities: [...] d. to provide aid and assistance to victims, including legal aid, in order to secure their rights before institutions and the courts."

ECRI General Policy Recommendation No 7m *supra* note 54, Art. 24. "The law should provide for the establishment of an independent specialised body to combat racism and racial discrimination at national level. The law should include within the competence of such a body: assistance to victims; investigation powers; the right to initiate, and participate in, court proceedings; monitoring legislation and advice to legislative and executive authorities; awareness-raising of issues of racism and racial discrimination among society and promotion of policies and practices to ensure equal treatment."

56 ECRI General Policy Recommendation No 7, *supra* note 54, Explanatory Memorandum 54.

57 Report on the proposal for a Council directive on implementing the principle of equal treatment between persons irrespective of racial or ethnic origin, COM(1999)566 – C5-0067/2000 – 1999/0253(CNS), A5-0136/2000, 16 May 2000, at 27.

58 Art. 7 (2) RED "Member States shall ensure that associations, organisations or other legal entities, which have, in accordance with the criteria laid down by their national law, a legitimate interest in ensuring that the provisions of this Directive are complied with, may engage, either on behalf or in support of the complainant, with his or her approval, in any judicial and/or administrative procedure provided for the enforcement of obligations under this Directive."

59 Report on the proposal for a Council directive on implementing the principle of equal treatment between persons irrespective of racial or ethnic origin, COM(1999)566 – C5-0067/2000 – 1999/0253(CNS), A5-0136/2000, 16 May 2000 (emphasis added).

Finally, the EP resolution on the RED draws attention to the fact that

> in practice equality bodies *unfortunately* bring only a small number of cases before the courts, owing to the lack of financial and human resources; whereas it is often NGOs that provide victims of discrimination with *assistance* until the conclusion of the proceedings.[60]

Thus, the competence/mandate of legal standing before courts is included in the term 'assistance', and the European Parliament explicitly recommended

> that Member States make use of the best practices of other Member States, such as allowing equality bodies to initiate legal proceedings on behalf of victims or participate as amicus curiae in legal proceedings.[61]

From the perspective of the effective enforcement of the right to equality and enhancing minority protection, it could be argued that there is a general need for the engagement of the national specialised bodies in procedures before courts, provided some guarantees and some structural-organisational arrangements are available to safeguard their credibility and impartiality. The engagement of specialised bodies might give an extra, more society oriented dimension to the complaint. In this respect, the bodies would contribute to the general promotion of the principle of equal treatment instead of focusing on individual enforcement.[62]

8.3.2.2. Quasi-judicial competences

The original text of the relevant part of the article of the RED concerned read as follows: "receiving and pursuing complaints from individuals about discrimination on grounds of racial or ethnic origin, commencing investigations". The European Parliament was not satisfied with this version, and proposed to complement this provision with "giving an opinion on complaints from both natural and legal persons and non-formalised groups of persons, associations or non governmental organisations […], carrying out detailed investigations, providing concrete help for victims." According to the EP "[t]he independent bodies must have the power to investigate victims' complaints."[63] Moreover it has also been stated that such bodies "can also

60 European Parliament resolution of 27 September 2007 on the application of Council Directive 2000/43/EC of 29 June 2000 implementing the principle of equal treatment between persons irrespective of racial or ethnic origin, 2007/2094(INI), N (emphasis added).

61 *Id.*, para. 33.

62 However, the need for the engagement by the national specialised bodies depends largely on the national context: if the civil society in the given country is strong enough and has the capacity to engage in procedures, it is suggested that the national specialised bodies only engage in important cases, for instance strategic litigation.

63 Report on the proposal for a Council directive on implementing the principle of equal treatment between persons irrespective of racial or ethnic origin, COM(1999) 566 – C5-0067/2000 – 1999/0253(CNS), A5-0136/2000, 16 May 2000, at 28.

offer alternative approaches such as arbitration or delivering an opinion on cases before the courts."[64] Also, the Parliament proposed a third paragraph to this article stipulating that bodies must "have access to confidential documents such as pay and personnel data in order to be possibly able 'to give a *ruling*'."[65] These observations indicate that at least the original intent in the drafting process was to include quasi-judicial competences. Interestingly, the survey made by Holtmaat shows that some of the Member States also considered hearing and investigating complaints as falling under 'providing assistance', while others listed this competence separately.[66] For these reasons it can be argued that assistance can also cover quasi-judicial powers.[67]

It is commonly accepted that enforcement of the right to equal treatment can be regarded effective if the fact-finding body is accessible not only physically, but also financially and time-wise.[68] This is generally not the case with civil courts. The added value of specialised bodies would then be if they could function as easily accessible and low-threshold fact-finding bodies. It would save time, money and energy for the victims of discrimination if they could turn to these bodies for a decision and/or opinion. This is especially important for minorities, most of who are in a vulnerable position. Moreover, they are also socially disadvantaged, and often they cannot find their way through the labyrinth of court proceedings. A simplified procedure might therefore encourage them to vindicate their rights. The efficiency of such bodies in this context, and the specific arrangements in relation to this competence, naturally depend on many factors. In any event, the quasi-judicial powers of national specialised bodies would and could contribute to a more effective enforcement of the right to equal treatment. However, when the body is vested with such power, the other forms of assistance might be limited or extra guarantees should be built in in order to ensure their impartiality. More specifically, special divisions should be made within the body so that representing victims would be performed by a department separate from its decision-making section. The same can also be stated with respect to the advisory/reporting unit of the body: this should also be clearly separated from the other departments.[69]

The acting of the specialised bodies as quasi-judicial organs leads to the question whether the decisions of these bodies should have *legally binding force*. Courts are generally regarded as the ultimate providers of justice, where the case law also establishes precedents. Arguably, if a body issues

64 *Id.*, at 37.

65 *Id.*, at 28 (emphasis added).

66 Holtmaat (2006a), at 24.

67 Naturally, the quasi-judicial power of specialised bodies raises the question whether and how these bodies could then be given legal standing in court procedures. This matter will be addressed below within the framework of organisational and operational matters.

68 For more details see below on the publicity, accessibility and cooperation.

69 See for instance *Procola v. Luxembourg*, ECHR (1995) No. 27/1994/474/555, 31 August 1995.

legally binding decisions, it has the same advantage as court proceedings: their pronouncements have authoritative force. For this reason it is suggested that a body with quasi-judicial powers should also be empowered to issue legally binding decisions in order to facilitate effective enforcement of anti-discrimination law.

A legally binding decision also means that appeal against the decision has to be made available before regular courts. Reaching the court level is also important from a legitimacy perspective. These bodies concentrate on a very specific field: either human rights or anti-discrimination law, and their staff are trained in this field of law. On the contrary, courts focus not only on this specific field, but take into account the broader picture. For this reason their judgments might seem to be more balanced than those of the bodies. However, they do not usually have the same expertise in anti-discrimination law, thus the supposed balance might not exist in their decisions either. Still, in general, the judgment of a court might be more easily accepted by the public than the decision of a specialised organ with a much narrower focus. If the decision of the national specialised bodies is upheld by the court, their authenticity and legitimacy will in any event gain more acceptance.

The competence/mandate to be an intermediary or mediator in *alternative dispute resolutions* (ADRs) can also be linked to quasi-judicial powers. As argued in relation to ADRs, they can constitute a suitable alternative to the proceedings of courts or even specialised bodies for some victims. In order to guarantee appropriate legal knowledge and experience in such cases, it would be advisable that national specialised bodies act as third parties in the resolution process. This would ensure that the reached agreement would not be disproportionately disadvantageous for any of the parties.[70] The text of ECRI GR No. 7, cited above, highlights that assistance "also covers assistance in seeking friendly settlement of complaints."[71] Since the meaning of the term 'assistance' is very broad, nothing seems to hinder the Member States in vesting the national bodies with such a task, although no direct obligation to provide them with such a competence can be deduced from the RED.

8.3.2.3. Investigation

When a body is vested with quasi-judicial powers, it needs to investigate the case before it. The power of investigation was also emphasised during the legislative process of the RED, in which the original draft already included a reference to investigations.[72] Not only did the draft legislative proposal

70 See Ch. 4 on access to justice.

71 ECRI General Policy Recommendation No 7, *supra* note 54, Explanatory Memorandum, 54. See also Howard (2005), at 483.

72 "Member States shall ensure that the functions of these independent bodies include [...] commencing investigations or surveys concerning discrimination based on racial or ethnic origin". Report on the proposal for a Council Directive on implementing the principle of

emphasise its importance,[73] it even went further by adding a new paragraph to this article pursuant to which "[i]n so far as this is relevant to their operations, the independent bodies must be permitted to inspect confidential information, including pay and personnel administration data."[74] Similarly and importantly, the EP resolution on the RED recommends

> that the Member States provide their equality bodies with sufficient human and financial resources to enable them to perform their important role effectively, including the provision of appropriate assistance to victims of discrimination; considers that such bodies should also be given the necessary powers to investigate cases.[75]

However, even the EP does not consider, as the above quote indicates, that such power can unequivocally be deduced from the adopted text of the Directive – arguably, partly because of this vague formulation.

As the proposals show, investigation might mean investigation in individual cases or investigation at a general, society level. For an effective enforcement both aspects are arguably essential. Combating individual discrimination is fundamental for attaining equal treatment at society level as well. Giving the power of investigation to specialised bodies at both levels is important in terms of being able to carry out their other tasks too.

As explained above, Article 8 RED lays down special rules for the allocation of the burden of proof in discrimination cases. These rules are to be applied before courts or other competent authorities. The latter could also be a national specialised body with quasi-judicial powers. In this context it has also been argued that

> [o]ne of the main purposes of establishing specialised quasi-judicial bodies is to provide complainants in discrimination cases with a better alternative to the ordinary courts. It would not be in compliance with this objective for the complainant's legal position to be less favourable before the quasi-judicial bodies than before the ordinary courts.[76]

However, when a body is vested with full-scale investigative powers, such as criminal courts and administrative organs, there is arguably no need for the special allocation of the burden of proof as it is the fact-finding body itself that

---

equal treatment between persons irrespective of racial or ethnic origin, COM(1999) 566 – C5-0067/2000 – 1999/0253(CNS), A5-0136/2000 final, 16 May 2000, at 27.

[73] "[...] carrying out detailed investigations [...] commencing investigations or surveys concerning discrimination based on racial or ethnic origin". *Id.*, at 27.

[74] *Id.*, at 28. According to the justification given by the EP "[i]n order to be able to carry out detailed investigations into a complaint, and possibly to give a ruling, it is necessary for independent bodies to have access to confidential documents such as pay and personnel data."

[75] European Parliament resolution of 27 September 2007 on the application of Council Directive 2000/43/EC of 29 June 2000 implementing the principle of equal treatment between persons irrespective of racial or ethnic origin, 2007/2094(INI), para. 35.

[76] Jacobsen & Rosenberg Khawaja (2006), at 20-21.

has to find out all the relevant facts and circumstances of the case. This is also acknowledged in Article 8(3) RED, which states that the special allocation of the burden of proof need not apply "to proceedings in which it is for the court or competent body to investigate the facts of the case."[77] Consequently, a national specialised body not empowered with the competence of full-scale investigation, but acting as a quasi-judicial organ, has to apply the special rule when allocating the burden of proof between the two parties.

8.3.3. Conducting Independent Surveys Concerning Discrimination

The original proposal of the RED referred to 'commencing investigations or surveys concerning discrimination based on racial or ethnic origin'. Although this wording was left untouched by the European Parliament in its draft legislative proposal, as can be seen, in the final version the phrase 'commencing investigations' was dropped without further explanation, leaving 'conducting independent surveys concerning discrimination'. Interestingly, this formulation is still different from Recital (24) RED, which requires that national specialised bodies be vested 'with competence to analyse the problems involved, to study possible solutions'. Notwithstanding the omission of the phrase 'commencing investigations', it can hardly be envisaged that surveys could be conducted without any power to investigate.[78] This is similarly true with respect to the competence of 'publishing independent reports and making recommendations on any issue relating to such discrimination'. Surveys in general are considered to constitute a form of investigation, a way of examination, which means "to query in order to collect data for the analysis of some aspect of a group or area,"[79] and similarly "to view or consider comprehensively."[80] Bell's suggestion, that the competence to make independent reports and recommendations "should provide a legal foundation for insisting on an independent right of investigation for these bodies,"[81] can also be stated with respect to conducting independent surveys.

It has been argued that it is not at all clear what kind of surveys are meant in this provision.[82] As the survey on the tasks of these bodies prepared by Holtmaat showed

---

77 See also *Id.*, at 20-21. They argue that "[i]f the equality body has the competence to investigate the facts of the case before issuing a decision or opinion, the need to use the eased burden of proof is less compelling, hence the exception in these directives providing that the eased burden of proof need not apply in inquisitorial proceedings." See also McCrudden (2001), at 255.

78 See also Bell (2001a), at 48.

79 http://www.webster.com/cgi-bin/dictionary.

80 *Id.*

81 Bell (2001a), at 48.

82 See also Holtmaat (2006a), at 16.

> it was not clear whether this category of activity only covered surveys about the prevalence and forms of discrimination or whether surveys of the impact of anti-discrimination legislation or even surveys of the effects of the work of the equality body itself should also be included. Sometimes reports of cases that were heard and investigated and subsequently found to be discriminatory were included under this heading.[83]

Arguably, 'independent surveys' can include all these aspects depending on the other tasks of the body in the given Member State.

8.3.4. Publishing Independent Reports and Making Recommendations on any Issue Relating to Discrimination

The only provision in Article 13(2) RED that has not been amended during the drafting of the RED is the competence to publish independent reports and make recommendations on any issue relating to discrimination.[84] Still, it is not entirely clear what these terms exactly mean. It is not clear either, for instance, to whom these reports and recommendations should be addressed,[85] whether they are concerned with legislation only, or whether they can take the broader social context also into account, and so on. As Holtmaat's survey shows,

> [s]ome experts restricted this category of activities to reports about the prevalence and forms of discrimination as such, and to recommendations about the methods to be used to combat discrimination. Others included the evaluation of existing anti-discrimination legislation and comments on proposals for new legislation. Still others referred to reports on the investigation of individual complaints, or leaflets and brochures about the content and scope of anti-discrimination legislation under this heading.[86]

Nevertheless, it is obvious that similarly to independent surveys publishing reports and making recommendations definitely presuppose an investigation of some kind.

Arguably, the fact that the precise meaning of 'reports and recommendations' is not clear, should not be regarded as working to the detriment of the effectiveness of this provision, although there is a danger that Member

---

83 Holtmaat (2006a), at 24.

84 Art. 24 of ECRI General Policy Recommendation No. 7 also covers a comparable competence, which is to monitor legislation and advice to legislative and executive authorities. According to the Explanatory Memorandum "[t]he functions of the national specialised body should also include monitoring legislation against racism and racial discrimination and control of the conformity of legislation with equality principles. In this respect, the national specialised body should be entitled to formulate recommendations to the executive and legislative authorities on the way in which relevant legislation, regulations or practice may be improved." ECRI General Policy Recommendation No 7, *supra* note 54, Explanatory Memorandum, para. 53.

85 See also Holtmaat (2006a), at 16.

86 Holtmaat (2006a), at 24-25.

States interpret this competence/mandate too narrowly. Nevertheless, this competence can include, for instance, compiling reports to the legislator on the situation of equal treatment in a given year, to international organisations within the framework of the reporting obligations of the states, reporting on activities of the body, reporting on special current issues, and so on. Similarly, recommendations can also be interpreted broadly, as including both recommendations in relation to legislation to the legislator, but also recommendations to an employer on an equal treatment plan, or to respondents in a particular case, and so on.[87] From the perspective of effective enforcement, it is suggested that this competence be interpreted as broadly as possible, and be accommodated to the needs in a given country.

8.4. Independence

Not only does Article 13 RED stipulates the competences and mandates a national specialised body has to be vested with, it also requires that these competences and mandates be carried out in an independent fashion.[88] The fact that the requirement of independence was added to each competences, and it was used three times, clearly shows that

> the European legislator had in mind that independence is an important feature of the work of the equality bodies that it wanted to have established in each of the Member States.[89]

In the original proposal, and also in the proposed Recital, the term 'independent' characterised the competences/mandates of the bodies as well as the body itself.[90] Tyson reported that there was a great deal of concern and discussion on this proposal. It was especially questioned

[87] If a national specialised body can make recommendations on concrete cases, this can be, arguably, regarded as a quasi-judicial competence, as the body is empowered with issuing legally non-binding opinions.

[88] In this context Moon argued that "[t]he requirement in the Article is not for the body itself to be independent; it only has to have the capacity to perform each of the named functions independently. [...] It seems to assume that the body is only to be judged by results and not by looking at the structure. The structure under which such tasks are carried out is very likely to indicate the extent of the independence of the body. It need hardly be said that if the body itself is not independent, the credibility of its work is likely to be very considerably diminished." Schiek, Waddington & Bell (2007), at 888.

[89] Holtmaat (2006a), at 32. See also Cormack & Niessen (2005), at 23.

[90] "'Recital (19) Protection against discrimination based on racial or ethnic origin would itself be strengthened by the existence of an *independent body* in each Member State, with competence to analyse the problems involved, to study possible solutions and to provide concrete assistance for victims."

"Article 12(1) Member States shall provide for an *independent body* or bodies for the promotion of equal treatment of persons of different racial or ethnic origin. These bodies may

> 'what was meant by 'independence' and the potential impact on their national budgets. Long discussions followed about the impact on independence of financing from the Government or from Parliament, about the ability of the Government or an individual Minister to nominate members of a board or commission [...].[91]

As to the final text, Bell, for instance, finds it disappointing that this provision no longer requires the Member States to establish 'independent' bodies.[92] Nevertheless, independence is still required in executing the tasks, indicating that in order to be able to properly perform its task the body itself also has to be independent.[93] In other words, if a body is not independent, it cannot possibly carry out independent assistance, conduct independent surveys and compile independent reports.

The term 'independent' can be translated as being free from any influence. In this light, at least two separate meanings of the term 'independent' can arguably be distinguished as a point of departure in the context of national specialised bodies: being independent from politics in general and from the parties in particular cases. The previous aspect can be called independence *stricto sensu*, while the latter meaning of independence can be referred to as impartiality or neutrality. It has been argued that

> [i]ndependence calls for equality bodies to maintain complete neutrality and to ensure they are not overly influenced by any one interest group or be seen as the voice of one interest. Equality bodies must remain impartial in the face of demands from many sides, representing different parts of society [...] and representing different disadvantaged groups.[94]

The independence from any influence can arguably ensured by special arrangements related to the organisation and operation of the national

---

form part of *independent agencies* charged at national level with the defence of human rights or the safeguard of individuals' rights. Article 12(2) Member States shall ensure that the functions of these *independent bodies* include receiving and pursuing complaints from individuals about discrimination on grounds of racial or ethnic origin, commencing investigations or surveys concerning discrimination based on racial or ethnic origin and publishing reports and making recommendations on issues relating to discrimination based on racial or ethnic origin" (emphasis added).

91 Tyson (2001a), at 216-217.

92 Bell (2001a), at 48. See also Brown (2002), at 221.

93 Holtmaat, for instance, argues that "independent status is relevant to considering whether specific activities will be carried out in an independent fashion." Holtmaat (2006a), at 16. See also Schiek, Waddington & Bell (2007), at 888; European Parliament resolution of 27 September 2007 on the application of Council Directive 2000/43/EC of 29 June 2000 implementing the principle of equal treatment between persons irrespective of racial or ethnic origin, 2007/2094(INI), para. 31; Report on the proposal for a Council directive on implementing the principle of equal treatment between persons irrespective of racial or ethnic origin, COM(1999) 566 – C5-0067/2000 – 1999/0253(CNS), A5-0136/2000, 16 May 2000, at 27-28.

94 Cormack & Niessen (2005), at 26.

specialised bodies.[95] Organisation is meant to refer to the structure of the body, how it looks as an institution; and operation concerns the way in which it performs its activities.

An analysis will be made below of how independence from the government and the parties can be guaranteed in terms of the organisation and operation of the body. In analysing this, the Paris Principles will be used as guidelines, as suggested by the European Parliament itself.[96] Due to its special importance, the question of impartiality (independence from the parties) will also be addressed as a separate factor.

8.4.1. Independence through Organisational Matters

In order to appropriately carry out its competencies, a national specialised body has to function as an independent organisation, which means that it has to be vested with the capacity to act independently.[97] Adapting the model of Cormack and Niessen[98] to the present study, the following aspects of this capacity will be distinguished: power, structure and resources of the specialised bodies.

8.4.1.1. Power

Power is meant to describe *what kind of* competences and mandates a national specialised body is given and *how strong* they are. As a point of departure, it can be argued that the broader and stronger the competences of these bodies, the better protection can be provided against discrimination, and the better independence of the bodies can be guaranteed. This is also stipulated by the Paris Principles according to which "[a] national institution shall be given as broad a mandate as possible." Niessen and Cormack similarly argue that

---

95 On the organisational and operational matters concerning ombudsman institutions see inter alia Lloydd 2005.

96 European Parliament resolution of 27 September 2007 on the application of Council Directive 2000/43/EC of 29 June 2000 implementing the principle of equal treatment between persons irrespective of racial or ethnic origin, 2007/2094(INI). "31. Recommends that the Commission carefully monitor the independent functioning of equality bodies, for which purpose it can use as reference the Principles relating to the Status of National Institutions ('the Paris Principles') as adopted by the UN General Assembly in its resolution 48/134 of 20 December 1993, which include principles on the adequate financing of such bodies."

97 Cormack and Niessen, when discussing independence of the bodies, distinguished three criteria for the examination. These are the *authority to act*, *neutrality* and *capacity to act*. The analysis on organisational and operational matters is based on these criteria with the appropriate adaption and add-in to the matter concerned. See Cormack & Niessen (2005).

98 "The competences and capacity that a specialised equality body has at its disposal are of prime importance for securing its operational independence. Appropriate powers, composition and adequate financial and staffing resources, are key in this regard." *Id.*, at 26.

"[s]trong and multiple powers can considerably enhance the autonomy of an equality body's work, but caution must be exercised to avoid compromising the perceived independence of the body."[99] To explain why caution is necessary, they give the example, that a body might not be perceived to be independent if in addition to assisting victims it also receives and deliberates on complaints. In other words, the question is whether such a body is impartial and perceived to be so.[100] In fact, this dilemma can be solved by an appropriate structure within the body.[101] Accordingly, the more powers (in terms of types of powers and strength of powers) a specialised body has, the more its impartiality becomes essential.

8.4.1.2. Structure

Structure is meant to refer to how a specialised equality body is organised in terms of its *external* and *internal structure* and its *composition*.

External structure describes the form a specialised body takes in the national legal system. Article 13 RED describes a body from this perspective with just a few words. First of all, it stipulates that "Member States shall designate *a body* or *bodies*" for the given task.[102] Thus, it is up to the Member States whether they establish one or more bodies. As will be shown below establishing one single body seems to be the best solution in terms of independence.

This article, furthermore, specifies that "[t]hese bodies may form part of agencies charged at national level with the defence of human rights or the safeguard of individuals' rights."[103] Arguably, forming part of a human rights agency has both advantages and disadvantages. The most relevant disadvantage seems to be that the promotion of equal treatment might not get as much attention as it would be if it were allotted to a separate organisation. This 'problem', however, can easily be unmade through for instance effective awareness-raising campaigns, clear separation of functions in the bodies, and

---

99 *Id.*, at 27. See also European Parliament resolution of 27 September 2007 on the application of Council Directive 2000/43/EC of 29 June 2000 implementing the principle of equal treatment between persons irrespective of racial or ethnic origin, 2007/2094(INI), 35; General Comment No. 2: The Role of Independent National Human Rights Institutions in the Promotion and Protection of the Rights of the Child, Committee on the Rights of the Child, 15 November 2002, para. 9.

100 See also Lloydd (2005).

101 For more details see the elaboration below on the structure as well as the impartiality pertaining to these bodies.

102 Art. 13(1) RED (emphasis added).

103 Report on the proposal for a Council Directive on implementing the principle of equal treatment between persons irrespective of racial or ethnic origin, COM(1999)566 – C5-0067/2000 – 1999/0253(CNS), A5-0136/2000 final, 16 May 2000, at 27. See also Proposal for a Council Directive implementing the principle of equal treatment between persons irrespective of racial or ethnic origin, COM(1999)566 final – 1999/0253 (CNS), 25 November 1999, at 10; Holtmaat (2006a), at 21.

so on. Importantly, the advantages of forming part of a broader body might also help resolve this drawback. Forming part of a bigger agency seems to be advantageous in terms of personal, infrastructural and financial resources as well. In addition, such an agency seems to be more competent in finding the balance between conflicting human rights, which could also make the principle of equal treatment more acceptable in general. Furthermore, such an agency is more convenient for the public since it is easier for the customers to come to a 'one stop shop'.[104] And last but not least, in such a general agency protected grounds other than racial or ethnic origin can also be protected. This also confirms the view that a single equality body should be established.[105]

Several pros have been raised for setting up a single equality body. The main advantage of a single equality body is that it could provide protection in the case of intersectional discrimination. This form of discrimination is a widely spread phenomenon, but is very difficult to solve on the basis of the present national and international legislation.[106] No structural obstacles should therefore be created for examining such cases.[107] The main fear of having a single equality body is related to the fact that such a body would require the same approach to all the grounds, so that the important differences between the protected grounds will vanish, ending in reduced protection for certain grounds. However, guarantees can be inserted in order to ensure that the differences do not fade away in a single body. For instance subdivisions, inter-ground working groups can be created.[108] Naturally, a lot also depends on the national equal treatment legislation as the differences taken up there should also be followed by the national bodies.

A final important aspect of the external structure of these specialised bodies is whether local units are created and how they relate to the structure of the specialised bodies. As will be argued in relation to accessibility, it seems to be important that there are local bureaus which can give assistance to victims of discrimination. They do not necessarily have to be built in the structure

---

104 See also Collins (2004), at 9.

105 Much input was given to this discussion by the changes in the United Kingdom where a single Commission for Equality and Human Rights (CEHR) was established in 2006, taking over the roles of the previous equality commissions. See on this topic inter alia O'Cinnéide (2007); Choudhry (2006).

106 See also Bielefeldt (2007), at 22; O'Cinnéide (2002), at 31.

107 See also Collins (2004), at 9. "This approach allows us to mainstream equality and maximise opportunities, and allows us to learn lessons from one area to advantage other equality strands. We also have an easier engagement with multi-identity issues, in recognizing that all of us are defined in a multiplicity of ways, not just by our gender or race or other identity. In practical terms, as a much larger organization than any single strand body, we have much more influence and are much harder to ignore or sideline. It is also easier for our customers and stakeholder to come to a 'one stop shop' on equality advice and good practice, rather than go to several different agencies."

108 Jacobsen & Rosenberg Khawaja (2006), at 12. See also below concerning the impartiality of the bodies.

of the specialised bodies, but, arguably, they should have a good working relationship with the specialised bodies accessible in order to make a body accessible to all. This relationship should not impair the independence of the bodies.[109]

The *internal structure* refers to the internal or inner division of a specialised body.[110] Depending on whether a specialised body is a single equality body, a body competent 'only' in racial discrimination cases or forms part of a broader agency, several different divisions can be imagined and found appropriate for securing its independence.

Some important principles can be identified that should guide the internal division of specialised bodies. First of all, the inner division should prevent the duplication of either infrastructural or personal resources.[111] It should make it possible for experts of different grounds and/or fields of protection to share knowledge and experience.[112] Importantly, the internal structure of the bodies should prevent the protected grounds operating in isolation,[113] but at the same time it should ensure that the relevant differences between the different strands are upheld.[114] For instance, working groups can be established with the participation of experts of different protected grounds. Lastly, the internal structure should also provide guarantees concerning independence in operational matters. In other words, the clear separation of competences/mandates is required in order to be and be perceived as independent.[115] All in all, the inner division of each specialised body should build on cost-efficiency, dialogue, co-operation and separation of tasks.

As far as the *composition* of a specialised body is concerned,[116] it has been argued in several places that if it is a national human rights institute or a 'racial equality body', the body should reflect the composition of society;

[109] See also Proposal for a Council Directive implementing the principle of equal treatment between persons irrespective of racial or ethnic origin, COM(1999)566 final – 1999/0253 (CNS), 25 November 1999, 10. "A Member State may also decide that such bodies should be established on a regional or local level, on condition that the entire territory of the Member State is covered by such arrangements." See also Report from the Commission to the Council and the European Parliament – The application of Directive 2000/43/EC, COM(2006) 643 final/2, 30 October 2006, para. 3.2.

[110] See also O'Cinnéide (2002), at 35.

[111] See also *id.*, at 31; Collins (2004), at 7-9.

[112] See also O'Cinnéide (2002), at 31; Collins (2004), at 7-9.

[113] See also O'Cinnéide (2002), at 30-31; Collins (2004), at 7-9; Bielefeldt (2007), at 44.

[114] See also Jacobsen & Rosenberg Khawaja (2006), at 12.

[115] See also the judgment of the ECtHR in the case of *Procola v. Luxembourg* in which the Court established that "the mere fact that certain persons successively performed [advisory and judicial functions in the same case] is capable of casting doubt on the institution's structural impartiality. [...] That doubt in itself, however slight its justification, is sufficient to vitiate the impartiality of the tribunal in question." *Procola v. Luxembourg*, ECHR (1995) No. 27/1994/474/555, 31 August 1995.

[116] On the composition of the bodies see inter alia De Beco (2007), at 342-349; Kjaerum

accordingly, there should be space for the representation of persons belonging to racial or ethnic minorities, which would also ensure public legitimacy.[117] This seems to be indicated by the Paris Principles as well, which stipulate that

> [t]he composition of the national institution and the appointment of its members, whether by means of an election or otherwise, shall be established in accordance with a procedure which affords all necessary guarantees to ensure the *pluralist representation* of the social forces (of civilian society) involved in the protection and promotion of human rights.[118]

Similarly ECRI GR Nr. 2 also laid down that "[t]he composition of specialized bodies [...] should reflect society at large and its diversity."[119] It is not obvious what kind of representation these documents refer to. In any event, it can be argued that it is not so much the mirror representation of minorities that seems necessary, but rather the participation of each representative group in the work of the body that is fundamental.[120] An often stated argument in relation to minority representation is that "members of minorities are not necessarily the best representatives for minorities."[121] This argument seems to be true also in this context. To put it simply, it seems to be more important to focus on the participation of interested groups than to require strict mirror or descriptive representation in the body.[122] For instance, minorities can be involved in the nomination procedure of certain members of staff, or an expert or advisory

(2003), at 7-8; National Human Rights Institutions: Recommendations for Effective Protection and Promotion of Human Rights. Amnesty International (2001).

[117] See also De Beco (2007), at 343-344; O'Cinnéide (2002), at 35; Lindsnaes & Lindholt (2001), at 46; General Comment No. 2. Committee on the Rights of the Child (2002), at 12. See also the Paris Principles pursuant to which "[t]he composition of the national institution and the appointment of its members, whether by means of an election or otherwise, shall be established in accordance with a procedure which affords all necessary guarantees to ensure the pluralist representation of the social forces (of civilian society) involved in the protection and promotion of human rights, particularly by powers which will enable effective cooperation to be established with, or through the presence of, representative of: Non-governmental organizations responsible for human rights and efforts to combat racial discrimination, trade unions, concerned social and professional organizations, for example, associations of lawyers, doctors, journalists and eminent scientists; Trends in philosophical or religious thought; Universities and qualified experts; Parliament; Government departments (if these are included. Their representatives should participate in deliberations only in an advisory capacity)." Principles relating to the Status of National Institutions (The Paris Principles). Adopted by General Assembly resolution 48/134. 20 December 1993. Composition and guarantees of independence and pluralism.

[118] The Paris Principles (emphasis added).

[119] ECRI General Policy Recommendation No. 2: Establishment of Specialised Bodies to Combat Racism, Xenophobia, Anti-Semitism and Intolerance at National Level, CRI(97) 36, 13 June 1997, Principle 4.

[120] See also Model National Legislation for the Guidance of Governments in the Enactment of Further Legislation Against Racial Discrimination. Third Decade to Combat Racism and Racial Discrimination (1993-2003), 17-18.

[121] Henrard (2005), at 137. See also Pitkin (1967).

[122] See also Lloydd (2005), at 44.

group can be created from representatives. The involvement of minority groups would ensure the independence of the national specialised bodies in this respect.

8.4.1.3. Resources

Independence is usually associated with sufficient financial resources to enable the bodies to spend as they deem appropriate.[123] To be truly independent, a body should be equipped with sufficient financial, infrastructural and personal resources, and be able to manage these resources independently.[124] The accommodated resources cannot be political pawns, guarantees should be built into the regulations on the status of the bodies to secure regular sufficient resources.[125] The duty on the states to provide bodies with appropriate resources is also imposed by the Paris Principles stating that

> [t]he national institution shall have an infrastructure which is suited to the smooth conduct of its activities, in particular adequate funding. This funding should enable the body to have its own staff and premises, in order to be independent of the Government and not be subject to financial control which might affect its independence.

Similarly ECRI GR No. 2 proposes that "[s]pecialised bodies should function without interference from the State and with all guarantees necessary for their independence including [...] to manage their resources as they think fit."[126]

As hinted at supra, the word 'independence' in the proposal of Article 13 RED triggered much discussion during the drafting in terms of potential impact on the national budgets of the Member States, possible financing from the Government or from the Parliament and its effect on independence. It has been reported that

> [t]o avoid the question of what was meant by independence, the Commission proposed that, while the ideal situation was that the body should have its basis in law passed by Parliament with its financing guaranteed at a level which allowed it to perform its essential tasks, the key test was that it should be able

[123] See for instance Barry (2004), at 11; Higgins (2003), at 402; Barry (2003), at 418; O'Hare (2001), at 55; Report on Gender Equality Bodies. Network of Legal Experts on the application of Community law on equal treatment between women and men (2004), at 3-4.

[124] See also European Parliament resolution of 27 September 2007 on the application of Council Directive 2000/43/EC of 29 June 2000 implementing the principle of equal treatment between persons irrespective of racial or ethnic origin, 2007/2094(INI), 28, 32, 35, K; Report from the Commission to the Council and the European Parliament – The application of Directive 2000/43/EC, COM(2006) 643 final/2, 30 October 2006, para. 3.2; General Comment No. 2. Committee on the Rights of the Child (2002), at 10-11; Lloydd (2005), at 52-55.

[125] See also Kjaerum (2003), at 12; Tyson (2001), at 216-217.

[126] ECRI General Policy Recommendation No. 2: Establishment of Specialised Bodies to Combat Racism, Xenophobia, Anti-Semitism and Intolerance at National Level, CRI(97) 36, 13 June 1997, Principle 5.

> to organize its everyday work free from the interference of outside parties. [...] As a minimum the Member States must ensure that the body has sufficient resources to carry out the basic tasks allotted to it by the directive.[127]

The European Parliament also wanted to make clear that appropriate resources be allocated to these bodies, and for this purpose it prepared an amendment of the original proposal, in which it stipulates that "Member States shall ensure that sufficient financial resources are made available to the independent bodies."[128] However, no such provision can be found in the final text of the Directive. The absence of such a provision does not mean, though, that the requirement of independence would not put states under an obligation to provide appropriate resources. It is essential to independence to be provided with sufficient financial, infrastructural and human resources on the allocation of which the bodies are free to decide.

8.4.2. Independence through Operational Matters

Operational matters describe the authority of the specialised bodies to act independently. It is examined what the necessary conditions are for national specialised bodies to be independent in terms of operational matters and how their authority to act independently can be secured. Again, departing from the model of Cormack and Niessen,[129] the following aspects of operational matters are important in terms of ensuring independence: establishment and accountability, publicity, accessibility and cooperation and impartiality.

8.4.2.1. Establishment and Accountability

Establishment, first of all, refers to the legal framing of the body's founding statute. Arguably, the higher in the hierarchy of legal acts the statute of the body is, the better independence can be guaranteed.[130] This question was also discussed during the negotiations of the RED, arguably because it is

[127] Tyson (2001), at 216-217.

[128] Report on the proposal for a Council directive on implementing the principle of equal treatment between persons irrespective of racial or ethnic origin, COM(1999)566 – C5-0067/2000 – 1999/0253(CNS), A5-0136/2000, 16 May 2000, at 28.

[129] "Specialised equality bodies must have the authority to implement their mandate free from state interference. To this end, a robust legal basis laying down an independent mandate, independent legal status and careful positioning vis-à-vis governmental structures is crucial." Cormack & Niessen (2005), at 24.

[130] See Report on the proposal for a Council directive on implementing the principle of equal treatment between persons irrespective of racial or ethnic origin, COM(1999)566 – C5-0067/2000 – 1999/0253(CNS), A5-0136/2000, 16 May 2000, at 64; Amnesty International's recommendations for effective protection and promotion of human rights. National Human Rights Institutions Forum (2001); General Comment No. 2. Committee on the Rights of the Child (2002), para. 8; Lloydd (2005), at 40-42.

also mentioned in the Paris Principles. Tyson reported that according to the Commission the most ideal situation would be that "the body [...] have its basis in law passed by Parliament.'[131] The Paris Principles refer briefly but explicitly to the form of statute by specifying that this should be regulated in 'a constitutional or legislative text".[132] According to the UN Handbook on NHRIs

> [w]hatever their type, NHRIs should be established by law; preferably their existence should be entrenched in the Constitution, thus ensuring their long-term existence. This statutory basis is the most secure way to guarantee the institution's independence, as well as defend its legal powers if these are challenged.[133]

Consequently, to ensure independence the foundational statute of the body should take the form of a legislative act.

Establishment, secondly, also describes the way or procedure of establishment.[134] As, for instance, the Committee on the Rights of the Child stipulated

> [t]he establishment process should be consultative, inclusive and transparent, initiated and supported at the highest levels of Government and inclusive of all relevant elements of the State, the legislature and civil society.[135]

In this context, ensuring participation also from minority group either in the form of consultation or nomination or even both is essential.[136]

In relation to appointment, status and dismissal of members of national human rights institutions, the Paris Principles lay down that

> [i]n order to ensure a stable mandate for the members of the national institution, without which there can be no real independence, their appointment shall be effected by an official act which shall establish the specific duration of the mandate.[137]

The OHCHR NHRI Handbook defines some further principles that are to be followed concerning the composition of such bodies. It points out that

---

131 Tyson (2001), at 216-217.

132 The Paris Principles, Competence and responsibilities, at 2.

133 Assessing the Effectiveness of National Human Rights Institutions. Office of the United Nations High Commissioner for Human Rights (2005), at 13. See also Amnesty International's recommendations for effective protection and promotion of human rights. National Human Rights Institutions Forum (2001).

134 See above concerning the structure of the national specialised bodies.

135 General Comment No. 2. Committee on the Rights of the Child (2002), para. 10.

136 See also Henrard (2005), at 134-138.

137 The Paris Principles, at 3.

> [a]ppointment mechanisms are one of the most important ways to guarantee the independence, diversity and accessibility of NHRIs. Direct appointment by the executive branch of government is undesirable. Processes should be open and transparent.[138]

Nomination, furthermore, can take place through autonomous institutions, be it civil society organisations, the national Parliament or another institution, naturally depending on the given society. Criteria for appointment should be established in advance, and these criteria should be able to guarantee independence, pluralism and appropriate expertise.[139]

Most desirably, the legislative basis of the national institution should also lay down the lines of *accountability*.[140] Similarly to any public body, national bodies should also be held accountable most desirably by the national parliament. In order to ensure their independence, it is desirable that national bodies "should not answer to the government of the day, but to an authority other than the executive, most usually the legislature."[141] This accountability can be manifested, for instance, in the preparation of annual reports to the national parliaments or in answering enquiries from the parliament.

8.4.2.2. Publicity, Accessibility and Cooperation

Accountability is closely related to *publicity* because it also means that the way of operating should be made public.[142] However, publicity covers further aspects as well as it also includes the broader public. It therefore also refers to awareness-raising in general pertaining to the existence, competences/mandates and practice of the national specialised bodies and making their decisions, recommendations, opinions public to all interested parties.[143] Arguably, the more the body can reach the public or the broader the public the body can reach, the more its independence is guaranteed.

Publicity, furthermore, is closely correlated to accessibility since, arguably, publicity is a manner of being *accessible*.[144] Being accessible also means that interested persons, among them those exposed to violation of the principle

---

[138] Assessing the Effectiveness of National Human Rights Institutions. Office of the United Nations High Commissioner for Human Rights (2005), at 14.

[139] See inter alia Smith (2006), at 914; De Beco (2007), at 342-343.

[140] See also Assessing the Effectiveness of National Human Rights Institutions. Office of the United Nations High Commissioner for Human Rights (2005), at 12.

[141] *Id.*, at 12. See also Smith (2006), at 906.

[142] See also Amnesty International's recommendations for effective protection and promotion of human rights. National Human Rights Institutions Forum (2001).

[143] See Art. 10 RED which states that "Member States shall take care that the provisions adopted pursuant to this Directive, together with the relevant provisions already in force, are brought to the attention of the persons concerned by all appropriate means throughout their territory."

[144] See also Amnesty International's recommendations for effective protection and promotion of human rights. National Human Rights Institutions Forum (2001).

of equal treatment, should be able to have physical access to these bodies.[145] This can be guaranteed by setting up local offices, cooperating with other local organisations, building up a network etc.[146] Victims of discrimination are likely to be deterred if they have no access locally to an organisation competent either to deal substantially with their complaint or to transmit their case to the authorised body.[147] Other approaches than local offices are also worth considering in certain states, since from a cost-efficiency perspective it might be more effective to cooperate with specialised local NGOs, and so on. In this latter case, extra attention should be devoted to safeguarding impartiality as NGOs are hardly ever neutral. The role of NGOs in such cases should be made explicit, so that the decisions, recommendations, opinions of specialised bodies will be accepted as impartial and well-grounded.

In terms of accessibility, the *cooperation* of national specialised bodies with other organs, either governmental or non-governmental, is also an important matter. National specialised bodies are in a unique position, since they can be located somewhere in the middle in the continuum of governmental organs/civil society. This position requires that a good working relationship be upheld with both sides; however, this, again, should not impair the independence of these bodies.[148] Cooperation with both sides can enhance the effectiveness of the bodies' work.[149] They can benefit from the expertise of these entities without being obliged to follow their approach entirely. For instance, a case concerning employment is submitted to the national specialised body. The bodies, in most cases, only have general knowledge about particular labour law rules. To fill in this gap they might ask for the opinion of labour inspectorates. Although it might seem obvious, it is important to mention that cooperation is necessary between the local units of the national specialised bodies or the local organs to which victims can turn with their complaints. It has also been emphasised

[145] See also above concerning the structure of the national specialised bodies.

[146] See also Assessing the Effectiveness of National Human Rights Institutions. Office of the United Nations High Commissioner for Human Rights (2005), at 16; Comments and Discussion. In Discrimination in Working Life. Remedies and Enforcement. Towards the Uniform and Dynamic Implementation of EU Anti-Discrimination Legislation: The Role of Specialised Bodies. Report of the Fourth Experts' Meeting, 14-15 October 2003, at 41; Bielefeldt (2007), at 25.

[147] See also Comments and Discussion. In Discrimination in Working Life. Remedies and Enforcement. Towards the Uniform and Dynamic Implementation of EU Anti-Discrimination Legislation: The Role of Specialised Bodies. Report of the Fourth Experts' Meeting. 14-15 October 2003, at 41.

[148] See also Smith (2006), at 905.

[149] See also Report on the proposal for a Council directive on implementing the principle of equal treatment between persons irrespective of racial or ethnic origin, COM(1999)566 – C5-0067/2000 – 1999/0253(CNS), A5-0136/2000, 16 May 2000, at 64-65; Comments and Discussion. In Discrimination in Working Life. Remedies and Enforcement. Towards the Uniform and Dynamic Implementation of EU Anti-Discrimination Legislation: The Role of Specialised Bodies. Report of the Fourth Experts' Meeting, 14-15 October 2003, at 37.

that the national specialised bodies should also create international networks, which at the same time enhances the independence of these entities in relation to the government.[150]

8.4.2.3. Impartiality

The question of impartiality (neutrality) has also triggered much discussion because some specialised bodies believe that their task is to help victims of discrimination, while others operate as impartial quasi-judicial bodies. This aspect of impartiality can be translated in terms of achieving an appropriate balance concerning their different competences/mandates. Importantly, the RED itself also requires that bodies provide independent assistance to victims of discrimination. The question can relevantly be raised whether the requirement of assisting victims can be associated with independence and impartiality?

It can be argued that assistance might also be provided in an impartial manner. If assistance means giving information about the relevant legislative provisions, arguably, no issue challenging the impartiality of the body arises. However, if assistance refers to engagement in legal proceedings when the body is vested with quasi-judicial powers, the question of impartiality becomes highly relevant. In order to secure their impartiality, national specialised bodies should carry out thorough investigations before engaging in any procedure either on behalf or in support of the complainant. When engaging in a procedure bodies should prepare well-founded and thorough argumentation which would also make clear that their aim is to support the achievement of the principle of equal treatment and not only to assist the victim. The internal division of the bodies can help to solve this problem, and this internal allocation of competences/mandates should also be communicated to the public. It is advisable to create separate departments for assisting victims, conducting independent surveys, publishing reports and acting as a quasi-judicial organ.[151]

Neutrality should also be reflected in the composition of the bodies. As mentioned above, the composition of bodies should somehow mirror the pluralism of the given society, so that they cannot be accused of representing only certain segments of society.[152] Similarly, in allocating their resources to the different activities, the priorities should not reflect politics or the interests of a small section of society. [153]

---

[150] Kjaerum (2003), at 7.

[151] See also O'Cinnéide (2002), at 26. He argued that "[d]ue to concerns about the credibility of combining enforcement functions and ADR in the same organisation, some of the countries surveyed have placed mediation functions in the hands of an independent unit within the Commission, or in a separate body."

[152] See also O'Cinnéide (2002), at 35.

[153] See also Kjaerum (2003), at 12.

PART B. CASE STUDIES

8.5. Introduction

Mainly due to the vague formulation of Article 13 RED the specialised bodies in the examined countries can be regarded to comply with the minimum requirements in this provision as far as their competences/mandates are concerned. It is more challenging to examine whether and to what extent these bodies are independent from the parties involved in a discrimination complaint on the one hand and politics on the other.

The following organisations have been appointed or designated national specialised bodies by the particular states: the Centre for Equal Opportunities and Opposition to Racism (hereafter the Centre or CEOOR) in Belgium,[154] the Gender Equality and Equal Treatment Commissioner (hereafter the Commissioner) and the Legal Chancellor in Estonia,[155] the Authority on Equal Treatment (hereafter the Authority or AET) in Hungary[156] and the Equal Treatment Commission (hereafter Commission or ETC) in the Netherlands.[157] Three of these bodies already existed before the drafting of the RED: the Belgian Centre, the Estonian Legal Chancellor and the Dutch Commission. The two other bodies (the Estonian Commissioner and the Hungarian Authority) were established during the implementation of the RED.

The Belgian Centre, established in 1993, is an incorporated society and provides an autonomous federal public service.[158] The institution of the Estonian Legal Chancellor was established (or recreated) in 1992 in the Constitution.[159] In addition to its main function as ombudsman and the supervisor of the constitutionality and legality of legislation, as of 1 January 2004 it also conducts conciliation procedures involving discrimination between private persons in its function as national specialised body.[160] The Estonian Commissioner, first as Gender Equality Commissioner and as of 1 January 2009 as Gender Equality and Equal Treatment Commissioner, is an

[154] See inter alia De Schutter (2007), at 89-91; De Schutter (2004), at 58-61.

[155] See inter alia Poleshchuk (2007), at 59-64; Poleshchuk (2005), at 41-43; Explanatory Memorandum, Draft 262 SE I, 2008; The principle of equal treatment in jurisdiction and proceedings, Chancellor of Justice. Retrieved from http://www.oiguskantsler.ee/index.php?pageID=176.

[156] See inter alia Kádár (2007), at 72-76; Farkas & Kádár (2005), at 50-53.

[157] See inter alia Holtmaat (2007), at 64-65; Gijzen (2004), at 47-49.

[158] Art. 1 of the Act on the establishment of the Centre. See also http://www.diversiteit.be/?action=onderdeel&onderdeel=49&titel=About+the+Center.

[159] On the Legal Chancellor see inter alia Ernits (2003); Linguistic Minorities in Estonia: Discrimination must end, Amnesty International 2006. Retrieved from http://www.amnesty.org/en/library/info/EUR51/002/2006.

[160] For further information on the competences and mandates of the Legal Chancellor see http://www.oiguskantsler.ee/?menuID=52.

impartial, autonomous and independent expert who supervises the realisation of the principle of equal treatment. The Hungarian Authority, established in 2005, is an administrative organ supervising the realisation of the principle of equal treatment. Finally, the Dutch Commission, established in 1994, is an independent administrative body[161] created for the supervision of the realisation of the principle of equal treatment.

8.6. Competences and Mandates

The national specialised bodies carry out their activities in different ways. Nevertheless, most of their activities can be brought under the competences/mandates stipulated in the RED. It is striking that the bodies themselves recognise that they do not comply with all minimum requirements of the RED in this respect.

8.6.1. Providing Independent Assistance to Victims of Discrimination in Pursuing their Complaints about Discrimination

Concrete Assistance to Victims

The most elemental form of providing assistance to victims can be found in each country under review, with the exception of the Netherlands,[162] where it has been stated that due to the lack of competence of the ETC this country does not comply with this provision of the RED *strictu senso*.[163] However, it has been argued that this competence cannot be harmonised with the quasi-judicial powers of the Commission in terms of impartiality and this task is fulfilled by the local anti-discrimination bureaus with which the Commission has good relations.[164] As argued in the theoretical part, this apparent collision can be solved by creating different departments within the specialised body, and by emphasising that they aim to enforce the principle of equal treatment, which also means that they will decide in favour of the realisation of this principle and not necessarily in favour of the applicant. The Commission should therefore not refrain from giving legal aid for discrimination as it would be in the interest of victims to obtain assistance from the same forum.

As far as the other national bodies are concerned, giving advice, information and helping victims are clearly foreseen in the legal regulations

[161] See Jaarverslag 2006, CGB 2007, at 24.

[162] The Legal Chancellor is not given such competence either since it is believed that it would undermine its independence enshrined in the Constitution. See Poleshchuk (2007), at 5, 51. & 61.

[163] See inter alia Holtmaat (2007), at 65; Hamidi (2004), 7, 12, 20. & 45-46; Schriemer (2002), 3-5.

[164] See inter alia Schiek, Waddington & Bell (2007), at 873; Hamidi (2004), at 46.

of their competences.[165] In fact, it is only the Belgian Centre which considers providing concrete assistance to the victims as one of its prominent tasks as it is not a decision-making body.[166] On the basis of the practice of the Gender Equality Commissioner, who became the Commissioner[167] for all the other grounds, it can be concluded that, in addition to giving opinions, she also devotes much attention to consulting victims.[168] The Hungarian Authority, even though it is empowered to give advice, focuses on its quasi-judicial powers. It usually turns the attention of applicants to other entities that could provide them with assistance,[169] primarily the houses of equal chances, civil society organisations, ombudspersons or other institutions established by the state.[170]

Two of the bodies, the CEOOR[171] and the AET,[172] also provide a special form of assistance to victims, namely carrying out situation testing. This is a very significant task as victims could hardly carry out methodologically correct testing themselves. It is remarkable that the Authority, the only body among the countries that issues binding decisions, also carries out such testing. This competence of the Authority clearly emphasises that, in addition to issuing decisions, it also considers it important to help victims in submitting their claims. In fact, carrying out situation testing does harmonise with its investigatory tasks, and for this reason does not infringe its impartiality.

As explained in the theoretical part of this chapter, assistance can be interpreted in many ways. It is therefore very unlikely that a Member State would be found in violation of this provision. Moreover, it has also been argued that, in this evaluation, the role and tasks of other organs should also be taken into account as these bodies should live in symbiosis with the other organs empowered with some competences in the enforcement of the principle of equal treatment. In this light, both the Dutch and the Hungarian systems provide victims with sufficient local channels where they can look for advice and information, and for this reason cannot be regarded as not complying with the RED.

Legal Standing in Court Proceedings

Assistance in the form of engaging in court proceedings can also be explored in each country under review – with the clear exception of Estonia. In Estonia,

165 Arts. 2-3 of the Act on the establishment of the Centre; Art. 16 EETA; Art. 14 HETA; Arts. 12-15 GETA.

166 See inter alia Popelier (2003), at 283.

167 This competence is only given to the Commissioner, and not to the Legal Chancellor.

168 On the activities of the Commissioner see www.svv.ee.

169 See for instance EBH/141/2006.

170 Such an institution is the Roma Anti-Discrimination Service Network. See www.irm.gov.hu.

171 Specialised Bodies to Promote Equality and/or Combat Discrimination, Final Report, European Commission 2002, at 11.

172 Art. 13 of the governmental decree on the Authority on Equal Treatment.

neither the Commissioner nor the Legal Chancellor is given the competence to engage in the procedure on behalf of or in support of the victim and/or to initiate actio popularis claims.[173]

As hinted at supra, the prime competence (in addition to informing and advising victims) of the Centre is to initiate and/or intervene in procedures aiming to enforce the principle of equal treatment.[174] Importantly, courts also acknowledge that a case is given special meaning if the CEOOR engages in the procedure.[175] This competence of the Centre can clearly be harmonised with providing assistance, and does not impair its impartiality.

The Hungarian Authority on the other hand, as also mentioned before, has the power to engage in procedures either as a representative of the applicant, a third party or to initiate actio popularis claims, though as yet it has intervened in only a couple of cases.[176] The low intensity given to this competence can mainly be explained by its capacity and budgetary restraints. The only problem with this competence of the Authority is that the same personnel carry out investigations, engage in judicial procedures and fulfil the other tasks. It is suggested that a clear division be made on the basis of the tasks and competences of the Authority in order to ensure that it can carry out its tasks independently and impartially, and that it also be perceived as operating this way.

The Dutch Commission can also engage in procedures, but to a lesser extent than the Hungarian Authority. The Commission can initiate procedures before courts,[177] but cannot act as a representative. Similarly to the Authority, but due to theoretical concerns, it has not made use of this competence either. In the view of the Commission, it would work to the detriment of its impartiality as a quasi-judicial organ should it be engaged in court procedures. It has also been argued that this 'concern is understandable, especially when considering the extensive powers of the Commission to gather evidence when investigating a case brought before it.'[178] Nevertheless, similarly to Hungary, this problem can be solved with an appropriate distribution of the tasks between different departments.

---

173 See also Poleshchuk (2007), at 63.

174 Art. 31 ARA; Art. 3(5) of the Act on the establishment of the Centre. See also Vanheule (2003), at 395; Popelier (2003), at 283; Vrielink (2003a), at 223.

175 See for instance *CGKR and C. Murat v. D. Yves and E-L/ BVBA*, Ghent Labour Court, 26 March 2007.

176 Beszámoló az Egyenlő Bánásmód Hatóság tevékenységéről, valamint az egyenlő bánásmódról és az esélyegyenlőség előmozdításáról szóló 2003. évi CXXV. törvény alkalmazásának tapasztalatairól (2006. január 1 – december 31), Egyenlő Bánásmód Hatóság 2007. Retrieved from http://egyenlobanasmod.hu/index.php?g=EBH-jelentes07.htm.

177 Art. 15 GETA. See also Schiek, Waddington & Bell (2007), at 899; De Fey, Kellermann & Nieuwbroer (2004), at 134-136.

178 Blom (1995), at 87. See also Goldschmidt (2003), at 24.

Quasi-Judicial Competences

With the exception of the Belgian Centre,[179] the specialised bodies in the countries under review have quasi-judicial powers. While the Estonian Commissioner, the Legal Chancellor and the Dutch Commission issue non-binding rulings, the Hungarian Authority's decisions are binding on the parties. The Estonian Commissioner gives an opinion on the complaint of the applicant, and is entitled to receive information for investigating the alleged violation.[180] It is though yet to be seen how important this competence of the Commissioner will become. In the function of ombudsman, the Legal Chancellor's opinion is not binding either.[181] Nevertheless, the Chancellor has various means to push the particular organ in the direction of complying with its observations.[182] This function of the Legal Chancellor has been used several times.[183] The situation is quite similar to that in the Netherlands, where the Commission issues non-binding opinions,[184] but it also has some possibilities to enforce its opinions.[185] The Commission generally impels compliance with its opinions and recommendations in an informal manner. In the last couple of years the ETC has placed the emphasis on following up whether and to what extent measures have been taken for ensuring the realisation of the principle of equal treatment.[186] This approach has proved to be quite effective, and a survey showed that in 80% of the cases respondents adjusted their systems in accordance with the ETC's opinion and/or recommendation.

On the contrary, the Hungarian Authority on Equal Treatment can be located on the other side of the scale of the quasi-judicial powers:[187] its decisions are legally binding on the parties and it can also impose sanctions on the respondents should it find a violation has taken place.[188] As yet no survey has been made on the effective compliance with its decisions.

---

[179] See also Burri & Dorssemont (2005), at 547.

[180] Article 16(3) EETA. See also Muda (2002), at 115.

[181] Poleshchuk (2007), at 49; The principle of equal treatment in jurisdiction and proceedings, Chancellor of Justice. Retrieved from http://www.oiguskantsler.ee/index.php?pageID=176; Capacity Building of Civil Society dealing with Anti-Discrimination. A Training Manual. European Commission (2005), at 33-36; Chancellor of Justice of the Republic of Estonia (brochure).

[182] See for instance Article 31 of the Act on the Legal Chancellor.

[183] See the annual reports of the Legal Chancellor which are accessible at http://www.oiguskantsler.ee.

[184] See inter alia Rehbock & Van Dijk (2005), at 19; Loth (2004), at 224-226; Dierx & Rodrigues (2003); Goldschmidt (2003), at 23.

[185] Art. 13(3) GETA.

[186] See inter alia Havinga (2007), at 253; Third Report on the Netherlands, ECRI 2007, at 13; Schiek, Waddington & Bell (2007), at 896; Goldschmidt (2006), at 327; Gerards & Zoontjens (2009), at 14-15.

[187] Article 14(1) a) HETA. See also Kádár (2007), at 59. & 76; Gyulavári (2007), at 33-34; Schindlauer & Liegl (2007), at 14; Farkas & Kárpáti (2004), at 11; Farkas (2003).

[188] On the forms of sanctions the Authority can impose, see Ch. 7 on sanctions.

These quasi-judicial powers of the bodies have proved to be an important channel for the victims in enforcing their right to equal treatment. It is these bodies to which applicants first turn as they are easily accessible in all respects. Accordingly, it is advisable that the Belgian Centre be empowered with such a competence.

In addition to these quasi-judicial powers, almost every national specialised body is also empowered to act as mediator between the parties. Conciliation can be carried out by the Belgian Centre,[189] the Estonian Legal Chancellor,[190] the Hungarian Authority and the Dutch Commission. For both the Centre[191] and the Commission,[192] conciliation is a new experience, which they consider important. As yet, the conciliation procedure before the Legal Chancellor has not been successful:[193] the number of applicants has remained very low and respondents refuse to participate in the procedure.[194] It has been argued that the required consent of the respondent can be blamed for the failure of this procedure.[195] However, such procedures are generally dependent on the consent of parties in other countries as well. Thus, it seems that it is rather the absence of effective alternative procedures that makes the respondent abstain from participation.[196] To put it differently, it is generally the consequences

[189] Art. 3(4) of the Act on the establishment of the Centre. See also Jaarverslag 2006, CGKR 2007, at 46; Strategisch Driejarenplan 2008-2010, CGKR 2008, at 11. Retrieved from http://www.diversiteit.be/index.php?action=artikel_detail&artikel=39.

[190] The Gender Equality and Equal Treatment Commissioner is not given the competence to conduct conciliation.

[191] Jaarverslag 2006, CGKR 2007, at 46. See also Strategisch Driejarenplan 2008-2010, *supra* note 189, at 11.

[192] http://www.cgb.nl/cgb129.php; Pel (2003), at 109; Het verschil gemaakt. Evaluatie AWGB en werkzaamheden CGB 1999-2004, CGB 2005, at 69. & 91-92; Jaarverslag 2006, CGB 2007, at 8; Loth (2004), at 226-227; Gerards & Zoontjens (2009), at 14.

[193] In this respect the Committee on the Elimination of Racial Discrimination noted "with regret that the procedure before the Chancellor remains a limited instrument in terms of protection of the rights set out in the Convention." Committee on the Elimination of Racial Discrimination, Consideration of Reports Submitted by States Parties under Article 9 of the Convention, CERD/C/EST/CO/7, 22 August 2006.

[194] See inter alia Annual Report 2004 of the Chancellor of Justice, Tallinn 2005. Retrieved from www.oiguskantsler.ee/files/36.pdf; Examples of Good Practices. Specialised Bodies: Chancellor of Justice. Estonia. Retrieved from www.coe.int/t/e/human_rights/ecri/1-ecri/3-general_themes/2-examples_of_good_practices/1-Specialised_Bodies/SB_Estonia.asp#TopOfPage.

[195] See inter alia Annual Report 2007 of the Chancellor of Justice, Tallinn 2008, at 325-327. Retrieved from http://www.oiguskantsler.ee/public/resources/editor/File/Ylevaade_2007.pdf; Annual Report 2006 of the Chancellor of Justice, Tallinn 2007, at 392-394. Retrieved from http://www.oiguskantsler.ee/public/resources/editor/File/_levaade_2006_e_k_L_PLIK.pdf; Annual Report 2005 of the Chancellor of Justice, Tallinn 2006, at 150. Retrieved from http://www.oiguskantsler.ee/.files/130.pdf; Annual Report 2004 of the Chancellor of Justice, Tallinn 2005, at 105. Retrieved from www.oiguskantsler.ee/files/36.pdf.

[196] For a more elaborated analysis, see Ch. 4 on access to justice.

of other procedures that make the respondent agree with conciliation: an alternative dispute resolution procedure generally results in less demanding duties and legal consequences. Finally, the Authority may, as may each and every administrative organ in Hungary, conciliate between the parties, which has happened in a couple of cases.[197] It has been argued that the Authority might not be easily accepted as a party able to conduct conciliation procedures since a sanctioning administrative equality body would hardly be seen by the parties as an impartial and neutral third party.[198] A proper internal division would easily solve this problem.

8.6.2. Conducting Independent Surveys Concerning Discrimination

The competence to conduct independent surveys concerning discrimination can, though to varying extents, be found in each country subject to this analysis. Pursuant to the Act on the Establishment of the Centre, the Centre has the competence to carry out any studies and research necessary to realise its tasks,[199] and to collect statistical data and relevant jurisprudence.[200] Indeed, the Centre publishes different studies, and the relevant jurisprudence is also available on its website.[201] In this respect, the Centre can be regarded to act as a centre of expertise in the field of anti-discrimination law, which at the same time strengthens its position as an independent organ.

In Estonia both specialised bodies have some tasks in terms of this competence. Both the Commissioner[202] and the Legal Chancellor[203] have the competence to analyse the impact of equal treatment legislation on society.[204] As yet it is only the Commissioner who has conducted separate surveys pertaining to the principle of equal treatment.[205] The Legal Chancellor has only devoted attention to the principle of equal treatment as part of its broader research on the observation and realisation of fundamental rights and

197 See Kádár (2007), at 62.

198 See inter alia Farkas & Kárpáti (2004), at 33.

199 Art. 3(1) Act on the establishment of the Centre.

200 Art. 3(9) Act on the establishment of the Centre.

201 See inter alia Jaarverslag 'Discriminatie/Diversiteit' 2007, CGKR 2008; Jaarverslag Migratie 2007, CGKR 2008; Discriminatie van holebi's op de werkvloer, CGKR 2008. For more publications see http://www.diversiteit.be/?action=publicatie_list.

202 Article 16(4) EETA.

203 Article 3516(1) Legal Chancellor Act. See also Poleshchuk (2007), at 61.

204 For more information in this respect visit http://www.oiguskantsler.ee. The Gender Commissioner has also fulfilled this task, from which it can be concluded that she as a general Commissioner will also be willing to conduct surveys. For more information see www.svv.ee.

205 For instance the Commissioner participated in the project "In-country experiences in promoting gender mainstreaming in municipalities" of the EU and compiled a handbook on this subject. For further infomation see http://www.svv.ee.

freedoms.[206] Since the strongest weapon these bodies have is publicity, it is desirable that they carry out more investigations and publish more surveys in this respect, which simultaneously would also contribute to raising awareness and strengthen their position as independent organs.

The competence of the Authority to conduct independent surveys is 'not explicitly formulated, but the possibility to do so is implicitly included' in the HETA in the form of the competence/mandate to inform the public and the government, and assist in the preparation of governmental reports which is 'obviously only possible if the [Authority] possesses information about the nationwide situation concerning discrimination.'[207] This also shows that this competence cannot be regarded as one of its prominent tasks.[208] It is suggested that more emphasis be placed on this task and that the public is provided with more information in this respect. In this way, the decisions and reports of the AET would also gain more authority and acceptance.

The only explicit competence of the Commission enshrined in the GETA[209] in this respect is the competence to carry out *ex officio* investigations in order to establish whether systematic discrimination has taken place.[210] Although the Commission does not carry out many *ex officio* investigations, it takes this competence very seriously and conducts thorough examinations.[211] The number of such investigations is relatively low due to the enormous capacity such research requires. Still, this competence has been proved to be a good means to counterbalance the large amount of individual complaints coming before the Commission.[212] Moreover, these investigations also evince the

206 For more information see www.oiguskantsler.ee.

207 Kádár (2007), at 75.

208 No *ex officio* investigation has been carried out in 2007. See Tájékoztató az Egyenlő Bánásmód Hatóság 2007. évi tevékenységéről, valamint az egyenlő bánásmódról és az esélyegyenlőség előmozdításáról szóló 2003. évi CXXV. törvény alkalmazásának tapasztalatairól, at 19. In 2006 such investigation was conducted only in one case. See Beszámoló az Egyenlő Bánásmód Hatóság tevékenységéről, valamint az egyenlő bánásmódról és az esélyegyenlőség előmozdításáról szóló 2003. évi CXXV. törvény alkalmazásának tapasztalatairól (2006. január 1 – december 31.), Egyenlő Bánásmód Hatóság 2007. Retrieved from http://egyenlobanasmod.hu/index.php?g=EBH-jelentes07.htm.

209 Art. 15(5) HETA and Art. 12(1) GETA respectively.

210 Before the amendment of the GETA by the so called Implementation Act its investigation had to cover a whole sector. Thus, when there was a suspicion of systemic discrimination, the investigation should have covered the whole sector involved in this discrimination. Such an investigation required too much capacity from the Commission, that is the reason why this provision on the ex officio investigations have been amended. See inter alia Asscher-Vonk (1999), at 266; Third Report on the Netherlands, ECRI 2007, at 12; Het verschil gemaakt. Evaluatie AWGB en werkzaamheden CGB 1999-2004, CGB 2005, at 103; Dierx & Rodrigues (2003).

211 See inter alia http://www.cgb.nl/cgb254.php; Het verschil gemaakt. *id.*, at 104; Gerards & Zoontjens (2009), at 14.

212 Dierx & Rodrigues (2003).

Commission's expertise in the field of discrimination law and independence from the parties and politics.

8.6.3. Publishing Independent Reports and Making Recommendations on any Issue Relating to such Discrimination

The competence (and obligation) to publish reports is explicitly laid down with respect to each national body which, in this respect, complies with the requirements of the RED. Each year the Belgian Centre has to make a report on its activities.[213] Likewise, both the Hungarian Authority[214] and the Dutch Commission[215] have to compile annual reports on their activities. Moreover, the Commission also has to prepare a five-year evaluation report on its findings with respect to the application of the GETA.[216]

The Estonian Legal Chancellor also has to prepare annual reports, but not explicitly in its function as a national specialised body. Strikingly, the Commissioner is not obliged to make such a report, pursuant to Article 16(6) EETA she merely informs the Government and some other instances on matters related to the application of this Act. Formally speaking, the Commissioner does comply with the requirement of the RED concerned, but, in terms of independence in general and accountability in particular, it would be more advantageous if the Commissioner also compiled annual reports on its activities.

In addition to these reports, some of the bodies are also empowered to make or participate in the drafting of shadow reports within the framework of the supervision of international conventions. This power is given to the Centre[217] and the Authority,[218] which strengthens the view that they are independent and possess the necessary expertise in this field.

As far as recommendations are concerned, again, this competence is also given to each body. The Belgian Centre gives recommendations to the government in order to improve legislation,[219] or gives recommendations to the government, private persons and organisations on the basis of the

---

[213] Art. 6 Act on the establishment of the Centre. See also Popelier (2003), at 283.

[214] Art. 14(1) j) HETA. See also Art.14(1) e) HETA which lays down that the Authority has to inform both the governemnt and the public on the status of realisation of the principle of equal treatment. See also Indokolás az egyenlő bánásmódról és az esélyegyenlőség előmozdításáról szóló törvényjavaslathoz, at 6.

[215] Art. 20(1) GETA.

[216] Art. 20(2) GETA.

[217] Art. 3 on the establishment of the Centre.

[218] Art. 14(1) h) and j) HETA.

[219] Art. 3(2) Act on the establishment of the Centre.

results of its research.[220] The Estonian Commissioner,[221] together with the Legal Chancellor,[222] can also give recommendations to the government in relation to any necessary amendments to the Act or its realisation. Moreover, the Commissioner advises the government and other institutions on matters concerning the application and the enforcement of the EETA.[223] The Authority also drafts its recommendations on necessary amendments to the Act, and recommends the adoption of governmental decisions or laws in relation to equal treatment. Finally, although the GETA does not explicitly give the competence/mandate to the Commission to give advice to the legislator, it still formulates recommendations, mainly within the framework of its obligation to evaluate its activities and the effect of the equal treatment legislation.[224] The Commission also delivers its advice if it discovers a gap in the legislation or a problem with the application of the law.[225] It has planned to pay even more attention to this competence/mandate.[226] In addition, it also makes suggestions in the reports about its *ex officio* investigations into the existence of systematic discrimination.[227]

8.7. Independence through Organisational Matters

8.7.1. Power

As shown, almost all national specialised bodies comply with the requirements of the RED in terms of the competences they are vested with. However, it has also become apparent that the bodies do prioritise among these competences/mandates, so that the different competences and mandates are not carried out with the same intensity. As argued in the theoretical framework, the number

220 Art. 3(3) Act on the establishment of the Centre. See also Nota opgesteld ter attentie van Commissie Individuele Arbeidsverhoudingen met betrekking tot de herziening van de Collectieve Arbeidsovereenkomst nr. 38 (2008). Retrieved from http://www.diversiteit.be/diversiteit/files/File//Arbeid/20080208%20-%20aanbeveling%20aan%20NAR%20(NL).pdf; Opdrachten van het Centrum. Retrieved from http://www.diversiteit.be/?action=onderdeel&onderdeel =103&titel=Opdrachten+van+het+Centrum; Popelier (2003), at 283.

221 Art. 16(5) EETA.

222 Art. 3516(3) Legal Chancellor Act. See also Poleshchuk (2007), at 49-50.

223 Art. 16(6) EETA.

224 See also Schiek, Waddington & Bell (2007), at 931; Cremers-Hartman (2004), at 168.

225 http://www.cgb.nl/cgb64.php.

226 See Het verschil gemaakt. Evaluatie AWGB en werkzaamheden CGB 1999-2004, CGB 2005, at 103. During the adoption of the amendment to the GETA in order to bring it into line with the RED the government emphasised that the quasi-judicial power of the Commission can hardly be combined with giving advice on the legislation. On the contrary, in the view of the Commission the two competences in this combination strengthen each other. Het verschil gemaakt. Evaluatie AWGB en werkzaamheden CGB 1999-2004, CGB 2005, at 112.

227 Art. 12(1) GETA.

or extent of competences and the intensity with which these bodies execute or can execute the different competences/mandates has repercussions for their independence.

Remarkably, only the Belgian Centre does not have quasi-judicial powers (with the exception of conciliation in the broad sense of quasi-judicial powers), and it has the most and makes in the most extended way use of other assistance-related competences, conducting surveys and making reports and recommendations. In contrast, bodies in the other three countries with quasi-judicial powers pay much less attention to their other competences/mandates due to theoretical concerns or capacity and/or budgetary restraints. It is the Hungarian Authority that has the strongest power in terms of issuing binding judgments,[228] still it cannot be concluded that for this reason it should be regarded to be the most independent. Neither can this be concluded with respect to the Belgian Centre having the most compound competences/mandates: it is not more independent from either the parties or everyday political life than those with less competences/mandates. Admittedly, the extent of independence from this perspective is hard to define because the bodies differ only to a negligible extent from one other in this respect, and because also other factors influence their independence.

8.7.2. Structure

External structure

Neither of the national specialised bodies under review form part of a broader human rights institute, but have been particularly devoted to the promotion of the right to equal treatment. Interestingly, it is only the Belgian Centre where the competences/mandates do not extend to all protected grounds. All the other national specialised bodies are single bodies.

As indicated above, the Belgian Centre is not the only specialised body that has competence/mandate in the promotion of the principle of equal treatment as a specialised body.[229] An Institute for the Equality of Women and Men has also been established. As argued, the fact that the Centre is not a single equality body makes the enforcement of intersectional discrimination more difficult, the use of resources less effective, and the body less accessible to the public. Its accessibility is also hindered by the fact that the Centre is a federal organisation with the competence to carry out its tasks within the federal competence. For this reason, in its strategic plan the Centre proposed

[228] See inter alia Gyulavári (2007), at 33; Farkas, Kádár & Kárpáti (2003), at 126.

[229] See inter alia De Prins, Sottiaux & Vrielink (2003a), at 261; Bestrijding van discriminatie op de huisvestingsmarkt, CGKR 2008. Retrieved from http://www.diversiteit.be/diversiteit/files/File//Huisvesting/voorstel%2018%2001%2008.pdf.

its transformation into an interfederal organisation, so that it would become obvious to which organ to turn in each part of the country.[230]

In Estonia, both national specialised bodies have competences with respect to all protected grounds.[231] Importantly, during the drafting of the EETA (and the previous draft acts) particular attention was devoted to and extensive discussions addressed the question whether the Commissioner should be a single equality body or the already existing separate Commissioner for the ground of gender should be retained in addition to a Commissioner for the rest of the protected grounds.[232] In terms of effectiveness and accessibility it seems to be fortunate that the decision was made to establish a single body.

Similarly, both in Hungary and the Netherlands single equality bodies have been created without any particular discussion in this respect. Interestingly, in the Netherlands a debate is going on about the establishment of a national human rights institute which would include the specialised bodies involved in the protection and promotion of human rights.[233]

Internal structure

With the exception of the Estonian Commissioner,[234] each national specialised body has divided their tasks among different departments. Importantly, all bodies are empowered to act with respect to almost all the in the national equal treatment legislation stipulated protected grounds. This also has a clear affect on their internal division.

---

230 See inter alia De Schutter (2004), at 59; Jaarverslag 2006-2007, CGKR 2007, at 8; Strategisch Driejarenplan 2008-2010, CGKR 2008, at 8. Retrieved from http://www.diversiteit.be/index.php?action=artikel_detail&artikel=39; Aanbevelingen van het Centrum ter attentie van het Federale Parlement en de Federale Regering – Focus 2011, CGKR 2008, at 5; Antwoorden op de vraag van de Commissie over richtlijn 2000/43, para. 1.5; Fourth Report on the Netherlands, ECRI 2009, at 20.

231 Most of the discussions in the Parliament on the Estonian Equal Treatment Act centred on the position and competence of the Commissioner. Many of the members of the Parliament and organisations acting in the interest of women argued for the establishment of two separate commissioners: one for the protection of the principle of equal treatment on the grounds of gender and the other one for all the other grounds.

See also Explanatory Memorandum, Draft Equal Treatment Act 262 SE I, 2008; Draft Equal Treatment Act 67 SE, Rein Lang (Minister of Justice), 12 September 2007, http://www.riigikogu.ee/?op=steno&stcommand=stenogramm&pkpkaupa=1&toimetatud=1&toimetamata=0&date=1189600683&paevakord=592; Eelnõu 67 SE, Võrdse kohtlemise seadus – Draft Equal Treatment Act 67 SE, Urmas Reinsalu (member of the Constitutional Law Commission), 20 February 2008, http://www.riigikogu.ee/?op=steno&stcommand=stenogramm&pkpkaupa=1&toimetatud=1&toimetamata=0&date=1203510606&paevakord=1656.

232 See inter alia Poleshchuk (2007), at 52; discussions in the Parliament concerning Draft Equal Treatment Act 262 SE on 19 November 2008 and 21 October 2008. Retrieved from http://www.riigikogu.ee.

233 See inter alia Holtmaat (2007), at 69; Hendriks (2005); Goldschmidt (2005), at 291-294.

234 See Explanatory Memorandum, Draft 262 SE I, 2008. The Commissioner's office has not yet been established.

The Belgian Centre is composed of an Executive Board with a Directorate and has two main departments dealing with particular cases: one section has been appointed for taking up racial discrimination cases, one for the other grounds[235] and a separate institution has been established for combating discrimination on the grounds of gender.[236] Such a division and the lack of competence in gender discrimination cases significantly hamper the examination of intersectional discrimination. The advantage of such a division is that the differences between the protected grounds are definitely taken into account. However, in terms of the appropriate allocation of resources it cannot be regarded the most effective approach, as the experts in each ground should also have a sufficient knowledge of each field of law. Arguably, this division should be made permeable in order to ensure the sharing of expertise both in terms of the protected ground and the relevant field. In addition to these departments a legal advisor is appointed in a separate department. This is important in terms of impartiality as this advisor does not engage in the legal procedures; it only gives advice to the parties.

The internal division in the Office of the Estonian Legal Chancellor and the Hungarian Authority is made in accordance with the fields of law in relation to which the discrimination takes place. The Office of the Legal Chancellor[237] has four departments: three departments are created for different fields of law and the fourth department is a general one.[238] As it is the Chancellor who takes a position in a discrimination claim, and the parties can turn to the different departments for legal advice and not to the Chancellor himself, the impartiality of the Chancellor is not impaired.

In contrast to this, within the Hungarian Authority no departments or persons outside the decision-making section have been appointed to provide legal assistance to any of the parties. This clearly does not encourage the perception of an impartial organ, even though legal assistance is rarely given to the parties.[239] The internal structure within the Legal Department of the Authority is officially not regulated, but the work between the rapporteurs is divided on the basis of the field of law.[240] In addition, a separate Advisory Board is also appointed to the Authority in order to advise the AET in the interpretation

235 http://www.diversiteit.be/?action=onderdeel&onderdeel=102&titel=Organigram; Specialised Bodies to Promote Equality and/or Combat Discrimination, Final Report, European Commission 2002, at 64.

236 Institute for the equality of women and men. On this institute see http://igvm-iefh.belgium.be/en/index.jsp.

237 The Commissioner is supported by an office, but its establishment has not yet been finalised.

238 http://www.oiguskantsler.ee/?menuID=24. See also Examples of Good Practices. Specialised Bodies: Chancellor of Justice. Estonia. Retrieved from www.coe.int/t/e/human_rights/ecri/1-ecri/3-general_themes/2-examples_of_good_practices/1-Specialised_Bodies/SB_Estonia. asp#TopOfPage.

239 See also Farkas, Kádár & Kárpáti (2003), at 128.

240 See also Hodász & Scullion (2007), at 11.

of the law.[241] The existence of this Board contributes to the perception of independence. Arguably, in terms of impartiality and independence, it would have been better to give the quasi-judicial powers to the Board and the legal supporting work to the Authority, as is the case with the Dutch Commission.

The Dutch Treatment Commission has nine members who exercise the quasi-judicial powers of the body. The members work in chambers set up by them. The Commission is furthermore supported by an office that is empowered with the rest of the competences/mandates. Similarly to the Belgian Centre, a legal advisor is appointed in this office. This internal division of tasks clearly supports the perception of impartiality and independence as this structure resembles that of a court. Regrettably, none of the regulations on the Commission declare that the Commission executes its task in an independent way or that it functions independently. The only guarantee in this respect is that the members of the Commission are appointed in the same way as judges. It would be advisable to lay down explicitly the independent functioning of the Commission.

Composition

Admittedly, the general rules relating to the composition[242] of these national specialised bodies are not very strict which does not enhance their independence.

The members of the Executive Board of the Belgian Centre are appointed on the basis of their expertise, experience, impartiality and moral authority.[243] Moreover, the members should also represent the linguistic differences in the country: ten Dutch-, ten French- and one German-speaking members are to be appointed.[244] These requirements seem to ensure impartiality and independence, and also reflect the linguistic division of society and, in doing so, take care of social representation. The Centre also has a director, a deputy director and coordinators, for the appointment of whom no specific criteria are laid down, which again does not ensure the independence of the body. It is an open secret that some members of the Board are 'politically appointed'.[245] Strikingly, the political involvement of some members has been and could be presented as an advantage: it has been argued that they represent the general electorate, that they can ensure the better sharing of information, and that a 'greater degree of common understanding and respect for the work' of the

---

241 Art. 17/B(1)-(2) HETA.

242 Naturally, there are some overlaps between the composition and the establishment and accountability of these bodies, however, as far as possible the analysis concentrates on the relevant aspects for each factor.

243 Art. 1 Royal Decree on the organic statute of the Centre.

244 *Id.*

245 Specialised Bodies to Promote Equality and/or Combat Discrimination, Final Report, European Commission 2002, at 39; De Prins, Sottiaux & Vrielink (2005), at 410.

CEOOR can be achieved.[246] However, if the members are not proportionately appointed from each political party, they will not represent the general electorate; they will only represent the interests of the governing party which cannot be harmonised with the requirement of independence. Besides this, the quality of information sharing should not depend on any political orientation, because those organs that are competent in a certain field should be generally involved in the area of law or policy-making related to them. In a politicised society it is difficult not to be blamed for being politically influenced, but this should at least not be used as an advantage to obtain a better position. Importantly, in order to avoid that members of the Board are appointed on the basis of their political conviction, it has been proposed that this position should be incompatible with any political mandate.[247] The proposals have, however, not been adopted. Thus, no guarantees can yet be found in the ARA and the other relevant legislation which could ensure that, in terms of its composition, the Centre can be regarded as an independent organ.[248]

The Estonian Commissioner is appointed for five years,[249] but the EETA is silent on the necessary qualifications and requirements regarding the candidate. This Act only lays down that the already appointed Commissioner is an autonomous and impartial expert.[250] No special expertise and/or qualification are therefore required from the candidate to this position. In other words, although these requirements are implicitly indicated in the act, there are no guarantees that this will be the case. Accordingly, it would be desirable to introduce some rules guaranteeing that only a person independent of political influence and with sufficient knowledge in the field of anti-discrimination law and/or human rights is appointed.

The Hungarian Authority has a president and a vice-president who are appointed on the basis of their prominent knowledge[251] either in the field of equal treatment or in relation to the protection of human rights. Notwithstanding this apparent guarantee,

> [t]here have been a number of concerns expressed that its staff may not be competent or effective in handling discrimination complaints. Until recently, there have been concerns at the legal competence of the Body's staff. An

[246] Specialised Bodies, *id.*, at 39-40.

[247] Wetsontwerp tot wijziging van de wet van 30 juli 1981 tot bestraffing van bepaalde door racisme of xenofobie ingegeven daden, 3-2362/3, 24 April 2007, at 57.

[248] See also De Prins, Sottiaux & Vrielink (2003b), para. 94.

[249] Art. 15(1) EETA.

[250] Since the institution of the Legal Chancellor is an ombudsman-like institution, its independence and impartiality are guaranteed in the Legal Chancellor Act.

[251] While the vice-president was a well-known expert among human rights lawyers, this was clearly not the case concerning the president. Thus, it seems that, in contempt of these legal guarantees, the actual appointment of the members might not be based on these requirements.

> Advisory Committee, including prominent jurists, has [...] been established, but it is not yet clear whether this development can offset inexperience of the staff.[252]

Admittedly, more guarantees are built in for the appointment of the members of the Advisory Board. The particular members are nominated following a preliminary meeting with entities that are involved in the realisation of the principle of equality in this way ensuring the participation of the representative organisations. Furthermore, they have to have prominent experience (rather than knowledge, as required of the president and the vice-president) in the protection of human rights and the realisation of the principle of equal treatment;[253] and they must not have been involved in politics in two years preceding their nomination.[254] It has been argued that the legislator tried to strengthen the professional independence of the Authority by the formation of the Advisory Board.[255]

Although the legislator has not explicitly declared that the Commission is an independent body, certain guarantees are built in to ensure the independence of its members. Pursuant to the GETA, the members of the Commission are appointed in accordance with the rules applicable to the appointment of judicial civil servants.[256] The only disadvantage of this appointment procedure is that it does not incorporate any guarantees for including the voice of interest organisations.

8.7.3. Resources

The most problematic body in terms of resources is the Belgian Centre the budget of which forms part of the budget of the Prime Minister.[257] This gives the impression that the Centre is part of the office of the Prime Minister or a department of his office. The fact that, pursuant to the Royal Decree on the Centre, its Executive Board has all the authority that is necessary for the execution of the tasks of the Centre does not remove this deficiency concerning the allocation of resources. In other words, although the Board can decide on the allocation of the financial means, it seems to be the Prime Minister who decides on the total of the Centre's budget. This problem can, arguably, also be

[252] Submission to the European Commission concerning Implementation of the RED in the Czech Republic, Hungary, Romania and Slovakia, ERRC 2005. Retrieved from http://www.errc.org/cikk.php?cikk=2280.

[253] Art. 17/C(2) HETA. Interestingly, the requirements set out pertaining to the president and vice-president are less demanding: they have to have knowledge either in the protection of human rights *or* in the realisation of the principle of equal treatment.

[254] Art. 17/C(3) HETA.

[255] Bitskey & Gyulavári (2004).

[256] Art. 16(2) GETA.

[257] Art. 10 Royal Decree on the Centre.

explored in the symptom that the Centre's original tasks have been gradually extended without a respective increase in the necessary resources.[258] In any event, its financial independence does not seem to be fully guaranteed because of being placed under the Prime Minister.

A similar problem occurred in Hungary with respect to the Authority.[259] The Authority's budget formed a separate chapter in the state budget until May 2005, when the amendment of the HETA deprived the Authority of this authorisation, and placed its budget within the budgetary chapter of the supervising ministry. This meant that the minister was in fact able to modify the AET's budget at anytime during the year. This situation lasted until December 2006, when the Government Decree on the AET was amended. At present, Article 1(2) of this Decree declares that the Authority is a budgetary organ in charge of its own finances with "unrestricted competence to dispose over its own budgetary appropriations."[260] Accordingly, it is now for the president of the Authority to allocate the resources. At the same time "despite a clearly growing work load, the Authority's budget was substantially decreased."[261] Similarly to the Belgian Centre an insufficient budget endangers the effective operation of the Authority, even though its independence seems to be guaranteed.

The EETA is considerably succinct on the financing of the Commissioner; it only stipulates that its activities are financed from the state budget.[262] It seems that the Commissioner can decide on the allocation of its resources, but it is yet to be seen whether the government decree on the procedural rules of the Commissioner will provide further clarification in this respect.[263] As the Legal Chancellor is elected by the Parliament, it is also directly financed from the state budget, and its Office has a budget of its own.[264]

Finally, the budget of the Dutch Commission is dependent on the five constituent ministries, and its office and the personnel of the office are financed by the Ministry of Justice.[265] Thus, in this respect the Commission cannot be regarded as being financially independent.[266] Similarly to the Authority or the Commissioner, it would be advisable for the Commission to be directly endowed from the state budget.

[258] De Prins, Sottiaux & Vrielink (2003b), para. 94; Vrielink (2003a), at 224.

[259] Concerns have been formulated with respect to its financial independence. See inter alia Kádár (2007), at 73; Indokolás az egyenlő bánásmódról és az esélyegyenlőség előmozdításáról szóló törvényjavaslathoz, at 75; Fourth Report on Hungary, ECRI 2009, at 17.

[260] Kádár (2007), at 73.

[261] *Id.*, at 73.

[262] Art. 15(3) EETA.

[263] Due to its special position, that is an ombudsman-like institution, the financial independence of the Legal Chancellor is clearly guaranteed.

[264] Poleshchuk (2007), at 63.

[265] See Asscher-Vonk & Groenendijk (1999), at 246.

[266] See also Asscher-Vonk & Hendriks (2005), at 167; Havinga (2007), at 258.

8.8. Independence through Operational Matters

8.8.1. Establishment and Accountability

All the national specialised bodies under review are established through a legislative act, and 'only' some procedural aspects of their operation or existence are regulated in laws at a lower hierarchical level, either in a governmental or royal decree. The Centre has been established in an act, and its organic statute has been adopted in a Royal Decree. Pursuant to Article 3 of the Act, the Centre is entirely independent in exercising its competences and mandates.[267] The institute of the Estonian Commissioner has also been established in an act, the EETA, and its statute will be adopted by the government.[268] The EETA stipulates that the Commissioner is an autonomous and impartial expert who carries out its competences and mandates independently. As the Legal Chancellor is elected by the Parliament more safeguards have been enshrined for its independence, and its procedural rules are also regulated in a legislative act.[269] The Hungarian Authority and the Advisory Board[270] have been established in the HETA, and a governmental decree regulates its procedural rules. The HETA stipulates that the Authority is an administrative organ which cannot be instructed in the execution of its tasks.[271] And finally, the Commission has likewise been established in the equal treatment act, and its procedural rules were adopted in a Royal Decree. Conclusively, the existence and the main rules on these national bodies cannot be easily repealed, which constitutes a clear guarantee for their being independent from everyday political influence. It is quite remarkable that the independence of these bodies has been addressed in each country in the respective legislative acts, irrespective of the fact that the RED is not entirely clear in this regard.

Although the recommendations concerning national human rights or specialised bodies emphasise the importance of the members of these bodies being appointed by the legislature, the members of the national specialised bodies in the countries under review are appointed or nominated by the members of the government. In addition, the reports on their activities are also addressed to the ministers as opposed to the legislative branch.

The members of the Centre are appointed by the King on the proposal of the Prime Minister, for six years. The director of the Centre together with

[267] Art. 3 Act on the establishment of the Centre.
[268] Art. 15(6) EETA.
[269] Legal Chancellor Act.
[270] Before the amendment of the Act, the status of the Advisory Board was regulated in the governmental decree on the establishment of the Authority on Equal Treatment. See 2006. évi CIV. törvény indokolása az egyenlő bánásmódról és az esélyegyenlőség előmozdításáról szóló 2003. évi CXXV. törvény módosításáról.
[271] Art. 13(1) and (3) HETA.

the vice-director and four coordinators are also appointed by the King for six years, based on a motivated advice given by the council of ministers.[272] Notwithstanding this appointment procedure, the annual reports of the Centre are presented to the Prime Minister[273] who transmits them to the Parliament and ensures their publication.[274] Still, it has been argued that at present there is no such forum through which the representatives could be regularly informed of the publications of the Centre. It has been proposed that the absence of such a forum could be solved by establishing a commission with the Chamber which would follow up the materials compiled by the Centre.[275] In any event, the involvement of Parliament and the public in the process of reporting on its activities, even though this happens through the Prime Minister and only with respect to the Centre's annual reports, contributes to the independence of the Centre. At the same time, it would be highly desirable if both Parliament and representative organisations were to be involved in the nomination procedure.

The Estonian Commissioner is appointed by the minister of social affairs for five years.[276] The fact that she is appointed for a fixed period of time can balance to some extent the appointment by that particular minister. Strikingly, however, the Commissioner is not obliged to compile annual reports on her activities; she 'merely' informs the government, state organs and local governments on questions related to the enforcement of the equal treatment legislation.[277] In terms of independence, it would be highly preferable if the Commissioner were to submit annual reports to Parliament and in this way ensure some accountability towards the legislative branch.

The president of the Hungarian Authority is appointed by the Prime Minister on the recommendations of the Minister of Labour and Social Affairs and the Minister of Justice for an indefinite period of time in accordance with the Civil Servants Act. The Authority is supervised by the Minister of Labour and Social Affairs.[278] It has been observed that, pursuant to this Act, "the President's

[272] Art. 1ter.(1) Royal Decree on the organic statute of the Centre.

[273] See also De Prins, Sottiaux & Vrielink (2005), at 409.

[274] See also Popelier (2003), at 283.

[275] Aanbevelingen van het Centrum ter attentie van het Federale Parlement en de Federale Regering – Focus 2011, CGKR 2008, at 5.

[276] In previous proposals the Commissioner would have been appointed by the Prime Minister on the recommendation of the Minister of Social Affairs. In the view of the government the Commissioner could have been appointed by the Minister of Social Affairs had she not been given supervisory functions. Draft Equal Treatment Act 67 SE, Rein Lang (Minister of Justice), 12 September 2007. Retrieved from http://www.riigikogu.ee/?op=steno&stcommand=stenogramm&pkpkaupa=1&toimetatud=1&toimetamata=0&date=1189600683&paevakord=592.

[277] Again, due to its special position, the Legal Chancellor is elected by Parliament.

[278] Art. 1(1) Government Decree on the Authority. See also Kádár (2007), at 72; Tilk (2005), at 27. It has been argued that the Authority is "not independent, but is rather an appendage to a Ministry." Submission to the European Commission Concerning Implementation of the RED in the Czech Republic, Hungary, Romania and Slovakia, ERRC 2005. Retrieved from http://www.errc.org/cikk.php?cikk=2280; Farkas, Kádár & Kárpáti (2003), at 123.

appointment may be withdrawn at any time without any justification,"[279] which clearly works to the detriment of the independence of the Authority. Also, the annual reports on its activities have to be submitted to the government, as opposed to the Parliament.[280] Likewise, the members of the Advisory Board are appointed by the Prime Minister, but as mentioned supra, organisations active in the protection of the principle of equal treatment are also involved in the nomination procedure. Importantly, they are appointed for a fixed term of six years.[281] Again, more guarantees are built in for ensuring the independence of the Advisory Board, which is nevertheless not the decision-making unit of the Authority. From this perspective it would therefore be preferable for this Board to act as a fact-finding department of the Authority, while the office carried out the other competences/mandates and supported the work of the Board.

Likewise, the members of the Dutch Commission are also appointed by the Minister of Justice, in agreement with the ministers of Internal Affairs, Social Affairs and Employment, Education and Science and Welfare, Public Health and Culture, for a term of six years.[282] Again, in terms of appointment the independence of the Commission is guaranteed solely by the fixed period of appointment. The participation of representatives of the different segments of society is not ensured at all. Moreover, it is the Minister of Justice who appoints and dismisses the personnel of the office of the Commission, though on the proposal of the Commission.[283] The Commission makes its annual reports on its activities primarily available to and accessible to the public as opposed to the Parliament. The report is also submitted to the ministers and advisory bodies concerned.[284] Every five years the Commission also prepares a report on its findings with respect to the effects of the equal treatment legislation, which is passed on to the Minister of Internal Affairs.[285] The independence of the Commission would be better guaranteed if its reports were also addressed to Parliament because the Commission would be then accountable to the Parliament.

[279] Kádár (2007), at 74. See also Advisory Committee on the Framework Convention for the Protection of National Minorities, Second Opinion on Hungary adopted on 9 December 2004, ACFC/INF/OP/II(2004)003, 14 December 2004, at 13-14.

[280] See also Indokolás az egyenlő bánásmódról és az esélyegyenlőségről szóló törvényjavaslathoz, at 7.

[281] Art. 17/C(4) HETA.

[282] Art. 16(3) GETA.

[283] Art. 17(2) GETA.

[284] Art. 20(1) GETA.

[285] Art. 20(2) GETA.

8.8.2. Accessibility and Cooperation

As indicated in the theoretical part of this chapter, the publicity of the specialised bodies is closely related to their accountability in terms of their reporting activities. Since accountability has been addressed above, the analysis will here focus on the accessibility of these bodies. Importantly, most of the bodies have or work together with local centres in order to ensure their accessibility.

The Belgian Centre is a federal organ located in Brussels without any local units, which makes it less accessible to the public.[286] To counterbalance the lack of local branches there are, however, various complaint centres throughout the country to which the victims can turn and with which the Centre has good and effective working relationships.[287] Pursuant to Article 2 of the Act on the establishment of the Centre, the CEOOR carries out its tasks in a spirit of dialogue and cooperation with associations, institutions and so on which either entirely or partially perform the same tasks or are involved in the execution of these tasks.[288] For instance, the Centre works together with the Walloon housing association[289] and the Flemish Education Council,[290] it takes part in the project of establishing complaints offices in the Flemish and Walloon Regions/Communities,[291] and so on.[292] As the CEOOR is obliged to collect judicial decisions, it is, however, problematical that no legal duty is enshrined for cooperation with judicial organs.[293] Nevertheless, it does publish judicial decisions on its website.

In Estonia, no local complaint centres or anti-discrimination bureaus for can be found. This means that the Commissioner and the Legal Chancellor can only be accessed directly. For a short period of time the Legal Chancellor had

[286] See inter alia De Schutter (2007), at 91; De Schutter (2004), at 59; Jaarverslag 2006, CGKR 2007, at 8.

[287] See inter alia http://diversiteit.be/?action=onderdeel&onderdeel=50&titel=Links#A.%20 Meldpunten; Jaarverslag 2006, CGKR 2007, at 53-54; Wetsontwerp tot wijziging van de wet van 30 juli 1981 tot bestraffing van bepaalde door racisme en xenofobie ingegeven daden, 2720/009, 19 March 2007, at 141; Popelier (2003), at 282.

[288] See also De Prins, Sottiaux & Vrielink (2003b), para. 94; Strategisch Strategisch Driejarenplan 2008-2010, CGKR 2008, at 7. Retrieved from http://www.diversiteit.be/index.php?action=artikel_detail&artikel=39; Vrielink (2003a), at 224.

[289] De Centrum en de Waalse huisvestingsmaatschappij gaan samen optreden, CGKR 2008. Retrieved from http://www.diversiteit.be/index.php?action=artikel_detail&artikel=39.

[290] See inter alia Onderwijs. Retrieved from http://www.diversiteit.be/index.php?action=onder deel&onderdeel=110&titel=Onderwijs; Jaarverslag 2006, CGKR 2007, at 60; Opdrachten van het Centrum. Retrieved from http://www.diversiteit.be/?action=onderdeel&onderdeel=103& ti tel=Opdrachten+van+het+Centrum.

[291] Strategisch Driejarenplan 2008-2010, CGKR 2008, at 12. Retrieved from http://www.diversiteit.be/index.php?action=artikel_detail&artikel=39.

[292] See also Jaarverslag 2006, CGKR 2007, at 46, 52-54. & 66-67.

[293] Taelman (2004a), at 234.

an office in Narva, to ensure better accessibility.[294] Taking into consideration the facts that Estonia is quite a small country and that both institutions can be approached through Internet the lack of local information points might not narrow their accessibility to such a great extent as in other countries. In any event, it would be definitely desirable if some local bureaus, at least in the bigger cities, were established – keeping in mind the success of the office of the Legal Chancellor in Narva. In this respect, it is important that the Acts on the Commissioner and the Legal Chancellor dictate that these bodies cooperate with other persons or entities in promoting equal treatment.[295]

In Hungary, the Authority does not have local sub-offices,[296] but functions as a central organ. For this reason, it is of great importance that the HETA stipulates that the Authority cooperates with non-governmental organisations, interest representative organisations and the state entities concerned.[297] Related to this, in 2004 Houses of Equal Chances (HoEC) were established in each county.

> Hence, the HoEC are either set up within the local governments or are non-governmental organisations authorised by the local governments to fulfil the tasks assigned to the HoEC. These include the co-ordination of every aspect of equal opportunities in the country,[298]

such as providing victims of discrimination with legal support, information, and so on. In order to improve its accessibility the Authority finalised an agreement with these houses in 2006, under which the Authority provides HoEC staff with training.[299] The existence of these houses might also ease the Authority's workload as these houses could also filter out the inadmissible cases. In addition to these HoECs, the Authority also works together with other organisations.[300] Also, as another form of cooperation, the Act stipulates that the different competent administrative organs inform each other when they start a procedure based on the HETA.[301]

Although, like the Authority the Commission does not have local offices either, there are several local anti-discrimination bureaus (ADBs) throughout the country.[302] A new national association against discrimination was

---

[294] See inter alia Poleshchuk (2004), at 42; Poleshchuk (2007), at 60.

[295] Art. 16(8) EETA; Art. 3516(5) Legal Chancellor Act.

[296] See also Szajbély (2005a), at 332.

[297] Art. 14(1) f) HETA.

[298] Hodász & Scullion (2007), at 14.

[299] *Id.*, at 14.

[300] See also Az Egyenlő Bánásmód Hatóság jelentése az Európa Tanács 2000. június 29-én kelt 2000/43/EK irányelve a személyek közötti, faji vagy etnikai származásra való tekintet nélküli egyenlő bánásmód elve átültetéséről, 27 June 2005, at 3-4; Bischof & Samaluk (2007), at 12-13; Hodász & Scullion (2007), at 14.

[301] Art. 15(2) HETA. See also Iványi (2005).

[302] See also Third report on the Netherlands, ECRI 2007, at 14; Boog & Hamidi (2006), at 19 & 23; Makkonen (2007a), at 66; Het verschil gemaakt. Evaluatie AWGB en werkzaamheden

established in 2006 by local and regional ADBs and the then LBR[303] and started work in 2007, functioning as a national centre of expertise.[304] Importantly, the Commission is empowered to give its opinion with respect to all protected grounds. All things considered, it seems that its accessibility is ensured.

8.8.3. Impartiality

As argued in the theoretical part the impartiality or neutrality of the specialised bodies can be ensured by finding an appropriate balance between engaging in court procedures and issuing decisions or opinions.

The Belgian Centre is the only national specialised body examined which does not have quasi-judicial powers. For this reason no particular conflicts arise between its competences/mandates in terms of impartiality.

The national bodies in the other countries do have quasi-judicial powers: they issue either binding decisions or non-binding opinions. It is quite remarkable that almost all these bodies try to avoid being involved in representing victims in judicial procedures for one reason or another.

In addition to providing an opinion on whether discrimination has taken place the Estonian Commissioner also provides the victims with the necessary information on the complaints, but does not have the competence/mandate to engage in court proceedings. Arguably, due to the absence of this latter competence/mandate the balancing of its powers does not seem to cause any special problems. The same can be stated concerning the Legal Chancellor: he issues non-binding opinions and gives legal advice but does not represent the victim or initiate court proceedings.

Somewhat differently, the Dutch Commission can initiate court proceedings in addition to its quasi-judicial powers, while it is not vested with the competence/mandate to provide concrete assistance to victims or to represent them. Nevertheless, a balance should be found between its powers in order to be perceived as an impartial organ. As explained supra, the Commission is said to refuse giving advice and engaging in procedures because "[t]his role is seen to be conflicting with the role of investigating individual complaints and giving an opinion about them."[305] As yet, the Commission has not made use of its power to initiate court proceedings, also arguably because of the presumed conflict. However, as there are other organisations that could potentially engage in court procedures, it seems reasonable that the Commission waives this

CGB 1999-2004, CGB 2005, at 28 & 119; Dierx & Rodrigues (2003); Zwamborn (2002), at 30; Schiek, Waddington & Bell (2007), at 873; Opinion 2007-57 ETC; http://www.vrouwenrecht.nl/opinie/cwi/standpunt; Holtmaat (2007), at 69.

303 Landelijk Bureau ter bestrijding van Rassendiscriminatie (National Bureau for Combating Racial Discrimination).

304 Boog & Hamidi (2006), at 23.

305 Holtmaat (2007), at 65.

competence/mandate, and focuses on its quasi-judicial powers. Nevertheless, as argued, the balance of power can be ensured by the appropriate internal division.

In terms of neutrality, the Hungarian Authority is in the most delicate position in balancing its competences/mandates, due to the fact that not only can it provide concrete assistance to victims, but it can also engage in procedures and initiate actio popularis claims. As yet, it has not engaged in many procedures due to capacity restraints. Similarly to the Netherlands, however, there are several civil society organisations that can support the victims in court proceedings, so that the absence of the AETs engagement in this respect would not work to the detriment of the effective enforcement of the principle of equal treatment. In any event, as argued, different departments should definitely be appointed for the different competences/mandates.

8.9. Conclusions

The existence of national specialised bodies is essential for the victims who can be assisted by these bodies when enforcing their right to equal treatment. Due to their experience in discrimination law the more extended the participation of the bodies in the enforcement is, the more effective the enforcement of the right to equal treatment becomes. However, these bodies should also operate independently in order to be able to contribute to effective enforcement. Accordingly, the more independent a specialised body is, the more it can be conducive to effective enforcement of the right to equal treatment, through which to minority protection.

In the light of the significant effect a national specialised body can have on the enforcement of human rights, the RED requires the Member States to establish a body for promoting equal treatment and combating discrimination on the grounds of racial or ethnic origin. Article 13 RED enumerates a couple of minimum competences a body has to be vested with, the formulation of which, however, remains relatively vague. Nevertheless, the Directive is clear on the fact that these competences have to be carried out in an independent fashion, which arguably means that the body itself has to be independent. In other words, the effectiveness of the national specialised bodies is dependent on the extent of their independence in addition to fulfilling the competences the RED prescribes. This also means that in general the more independent the body is, the more effective the enforcement of the right to equal treatment becomes.

In order to ensure independence from the government and the parties some operational and organisational criteria can be drawn up which should be considered when establishing such a body. As far as the operation of these bodies is concerned it is important that power, structure and resource related matters are taken into account. With respect to the organisational set up the following aspects have to be kept in mind: the establishment and accountability, accessibility and impartiality of these bodies.

Due to the vague formulation of the RED pertaining to both their competences and independence, the national specialised bodies in the countries under review take several forms and are empowered with diverging competences. Importantly, none of the bodies form part of a broader human rights institution, but, with the partial exception of the Belgian Centre, they are single equality bodies ensuring an easily accessible one-stop-shop for victims of discrimination. Although each national specialised body can be regarded to carry out all the tasks that can be brought under the vaguely formulated competences of the RED, they do prioritise among their competences, and accomplish the tasks that are not given preference generally at a minimum level.

In terms of their competences two main types of bodies can be explored in the countries under review: bodies with and without quasi-judicial powers. This competence seems a decisive one concerning the other competences they have as well as their independence. Only the Belgian body is not entrusted with quasi-judicial powers. The main task of this body is to assist victims by engaging in procedures on behalf or in support of the applicant. On the contrary, in the other countries the main competence of these bodies is to issue opinions pertaining to the existence of discrimination in the particular case. Among these latter types of bodies only the Hungary Authority on Equal Treatment makes decisions that are legally binding on the parties. It is remarkable that in most of the cases the bodies with quasi-judicial competence do not engage in legal procedures, although they are given the competence to do so. This attitude of the bodies clearly contributes to being perceived as impartial, an important aspect of independence. The question of impartiality, however, can also be ensured with the help of an appropriate internal division which would allocate the conflicting tasks to separate departments within the body. Although the Dutch Commission has the most advantageous internal structure in this respect, it entirely refuses to engage in judicial procedures owing to impartiality related concerns. On the contrary, while the Hungarian Authority, which has the strongest power as it issues binding decisions, is not so reluctant to engage in judicial procedures, the internal division is far from being optimal for ensuring its impartiality.

In terms of the resources of these national specialised bodies, it is regrettable that they do not constitute separate and independent chapters in the state budget, but are generally brought under one or more ministries. Similarly, the members of the bodies are appointed by members of the government and their reports are also addressed to the executive rather than involving the national parliaments in these procedures. Little attention is paid to the voices of minority groups in the appointment procedure – with the clear exception of the Hungarian Advisory Board to the Authority. Notwithstanding these deficiencies a significant guarantee has been created for the independence of these bodies in terms of their establishment, which is that they are all established in a legislative act and only some procedural aspects of their operation are regulated in Royal or governmental decrees.

As the Estonian Equal Treatment Act has only recently been adopted, as yet it is difficult to say whether and how frequently the national specialised bodies will be asked to issue their opinions. The practice in Hungary and the Netherlands in this respect clearly shows that the existence of a low-threshold body with expertise in the field of anti-discrimination law is highly appreciated by the victims of discrimination, and in the first instance they turn to these bodies. In other words, it seems more important for the victims of racial discrimination that a (quasi-)decision-making body is available and accessible than that a body is able to assist them in a procedure. Accordingly, the competences of the Belgian national specialised body seem less effective than the arrangements in the other countries, though it is compensated by the fact that a low-threshold and fast-track civil law procedure has been created.

The case studies clearly illustrate the important role the national specialised bodies play in the enforcement of the right to equal treatment. Their existence contributes to a great extent to a more effective enforcement of the right to equal treatment, and therefore to enhancing minority protection.

Chapter 9

Final Conclusions

The Racial Equality Directive is a special piece of legislation as, unlike Community legislation in general, it includes several enforcement related rules in addition to the substantive provisions. This means that it has been regarded important to ensure real and effective enforcement of the right to non-discrimination on the grounds of racial or ethnic origin. Although the formulation of the rules on the burden of proof, access to justice, legal standing, victimisation, sanctions and national specialised bodies remained relatively vague, as the theoretical elaboration proved, they definitely carry the potential and render useful and suitable devices to guarantee the effective enforcement of the right to equal treatment on the grounds of racial or ethnic origin, thus enhancing minority protection. Some inconsistencies can at the same time be discovered between the scope of the substantive and procedural provisions working to the detriment of effective enforcement of the right to equal treatment. More specifically, the provision on legal standing does not make the enforcement of the protection against indirect and systemic discrimination entirely effective and/or possible.

Notwithstanding their potential for enhancing minority protection, the vague formulation of the (most important) enforcement provisions in the Racial Equality Directive and the relatively broad and general judgments of the ECJ in this respect do not assist in making appropriate use of them. Also, the Member States are left without helping hands in this regard. As a consequence, the potentially highest level of minority protection through the enforcement mechanisms of the RED has not yet been reached.

In order to compensate for the vague formulation and make the enforcement of the right to equal treatment effective and thus enhance minority protection, the enforcement provisions have to be interpreted in the light of the underlying objective of the concepts of discrimination enshrined in the RED, that is achieving substantive equality. In addition, the group aspect inherent in the minority protection phenomenon also has to be taken into consideration.

These two criteria also imply that the most important question of the effective enforcement of the right to equal treatment is whether and to what extent the victim's perspective is taken into account in the enforcement mechanisms. In other words, the procedural position of the victims needs to be facilitated, and ample attention should given to the victim's position, wishes and circumstances in order to make the enforcement of the right to equal treatment on the grounds of racial or ethnic origin effective.

The case studies showed the essential importance of and the vital need for clear lines of interpretation and the proper implementation and application of the enforcement mechanisms enshrined in the RED as several uncertainties and conceptual difficulties can be discovered pertaining to them in the countries under review.

In general it can be concluded that the RED strongly influenced the anti-discrimination legislation of the countries under review. In Belgium, Estonia and Hungary the implementation of the Racial Equality Directive resulted in the adoption of anti-discrimination codes with important enforcement provisions. In the Netherlands the implementation process necessitated some important amendments of, amongst others, the enforcement provisions of the GETA. As a general conclusion it can be established that the existence and enforcement of the anti-discrimination legislation can and does contribute to a great extent to the protection of the most vulnerable groups in each country. In Belgium and the Netherlands, given the lack of minority specific instruments, the equal treatment legislation is essential to immigrant groups. In Estonia, where the Act on the Cultural Autonomy for National Minorities cannot be regarded as effective, the Russian-speaking community can now make use of the means enshrined in the equal treatment legislation to achieve substantive equality. In Hungary, the Act on Ethnic and National Minorities mainly focuses on cultural rights and the right to self-government, which in fact cannot work effectively if substantive equality in other respects is not guaranteed. All in all, the obligation to implement the RED resulting in the adoption of the anti-discrimination codes with important enforcement provisions in general contributes to the protection of the most vulnerable groups in each country.

As explained in the introduction, the selection of the countries under review has been based on considerations related to the experience of the countries concerning the two pillars of minority protection and their demographic profile. The case studies demonstrate that the effective enforcement of the right to equal treatment seems to be primarily influenced by the experience a country has in this regard. The Belgian legislation and practice, for instance, is very telling in this respect. The present anti-discrimination Act is already the second piece of legislation that has been adopted within the framework of the implementation of the RED. It was the lessons learned from the 2003 Code that necessitated the amendments. Accordingly, a strong presumption is established that as soon as the Member States of the European Union accumulate ample experience and are willing to learn from their own mistakes and from each other, the effectiveness of the enforcement of the right to non-discrimination pertaining to racial or ethnic origin will be enhanced contributing to improved minority protection.

The close analysis of the enforcement mechanisms enshrined in the RED and implemented by the Member States under review revealed the potential and actual implications of the provisions at stake for minority protection. A concise overview of the particular enforcement mechanisms is given below pinpointing the difficulties with regard to effective enforcement both at European and national level and identifying the parameters that could influence the choice of the Member States concerning the particular measure.

Article 8 RED lays down special rules for the allocation of the burden of proof in order to facilitate the procedural position of the victim otherwise he would not be able to prove that he was discriminated against. In this way victims of racial discrimination would be encouraged and able to vindicate their right to equal treatment, the first pillar of minority protection. Pursuant to these special rules the assessment can be divided into two phases. Following a prima facie case of discrimination that has to be established by the applicant, in the second phase of the assessment the respondent can either negate any of the causal links (depending on the concept of discrimination) or can come up with an objective justification for the proven distinction. It is very important that the model of review based on these rules is adapted to the concept of discrimination at stake in order to prevent the evidentiary rules making the procedural position of either the applicant or the respondent heavier than it should be.

With the exception of Hungary, the countries under review have opted to insert the wording of Article 8 RED into their national legislations in the same way. Nevertheless, the application of these rules varies among these countries. As far as the first phase of the assessment is concerned, there are problems in Belgium and Hungary in the application of the presumption of discrimination which can arguably be attributed to the unfamiliarity with this concept and the different forms of discrimination. In Hungary the legislative provision does not require the establishment of a presumption of discrimination, but the presumption of two separate facts, which at first sight seems to be even more advantageous for the applicant than the standard in the RED. However, in addition to being conceptually incorrect, this regulation can also lead to a lenient scrutiny of the respondent's explanation, and finally result in the dismissal of the applicant's claim. Contrary to this approach, Belgian fact-finders have set too high requirements for a prima facie case of discrimination, and seemed to require the applicant to prove that discrimination has taken place.

With respect to the second phase of the assessment the same problem can be identified in Belgium, Hungary and the Netherlands. The existence of the stage of negation within the second phase of the assessment, prior to the stage of objective justification, is not explicitly acknowledged in these countries. While in Hungary the legislative provision does clearly provide for the possibility to consider these stages separately, fact-finders do not generally make a distinction between them. The situation is the same in Belgium, notwithstanding the difference in the legislative provision which is not so elaborate in this respect. Although the Dutch legislative provision is similar to the Belgian rule, the Equal Treatment Commission has found a creative solution for dealing with the stage of negation, which however cannot conceptually be regarded as entirely appropriate. The examination of the negation of the causal link takes place in the first phase of the assessment, though following the establishment of a prima facie discrimination. Notwithstanding this concern, it is the Netherlands which can be regarded as having the most appropriately implemented and applied the rules on the special allocation of the burden of proof, which can arguably be attributed to its long tradition in combating both direct and indirect discrimination. In Estonia as yet there is no practice in this respect, but by virtue of the same considerations made with regard to Belgium and Hungary, the proper allocation of the burden of proof will not presumably be without difficulties.

Concerning the forms of proof statistical evidence and situation testing have been regarded as particularly important in giving rise to a presumption of discrimination as by definition they include comparison which is also inherent in the concept of discrimination. In terms of the effective enforcement of the right to equal treatment, fact-finders cannot refuse or require these forms of proof. Concerning statistical evidence, the most sensitive questions are the lack of statistics and, where available, the appropriate choice of the pool of comparators. As far as situation testing is concerned, it is important that testing is carried out in a way that it can eliminate all possible reasons for the treatment but for the protected ground of the victims. This means that ample attention should be given to the neutralising variables in order to be able to carry out a methodologically correct testing that can be used as evidence. Both statistical evidence and situation testing are capable of giving rise to a presumption of discrimination.

The case studies have illustrated that the acceptance and methodologically correct application of statistical evidence and situation testing is generally also related to the familiarity with the different concepts of discrimination. Again, it is in the Netherlands where these forms are the most properly applied, while in the other countries without a long tradition in the enforcement of the right to equal treatment several problems and uncertainties occur in practice. In Belgium it is not clear whether situation testing will be accepted as appropriate evidence for giving rise to a presumption of discrimination due to concerns related to provocation. The acceptance of situation testing did no go smoothly in Hungary either. The complications here can arguably be tied to the unfamiliarity with the concept of presumption of direct discrimination. Proving with the help of statistical evidence in Hungary was not easy either mainly due to the absence of data broken down on the grounds of racial or ethnic origin. Fact-finders seem to expect statistical evidence even in cases where common knowledge obviously shows the disparate impact, and to set high requirements on the quality of data. These approaches do not improve the effectiveness of enforcing the right to equal treatment. All in all, it seems that the familiarity with the concepts of discrimination and the allocation of the burden of proof has influenced the approach to these forms of proof in the countries under review.

In order to enhance the effectiveness of the enforcement of the right to equal treatment, Article 7(1) RED requires the Member States to establish judicial review for complaints of discrimination. In addition and providing an alternative to judicial proceedings they are also expected to create low-threshold and fast-track procedures. The existence of both types of procedures guarantees that the victim's perspective is appropriately considered, which is clearly conducive to minority protection.

Concerning access to justice, all countries have introduced easily accessible and fast-track procedures in addition to the general civil law enforcement so that, strictly speaking, they comply with the RED in this respect. In Estonia, Hungary and the Netherlands the emphasis has been placed on the procedures of the national specialised bodies. In Belgium, summary-like civil procedures have been created. While in Estonia and the Netherlands the decisions of the specialised bodies are not binding, in Hungary the specialised body proceeds on the basis of administrative procedure law issuing binding decisions. The reason for introducing a binding procedure in Hungary might be related to the fact that the legislator might have wanted to avoid a duplication of institutions as non-binding ombudsman procedures for the enforcement of the principle of equal treatment already exist. It can be argued that, due to the long tradition of enforcing the right to equal treatment, in the Netherlands procedures with non-binding decisions can also be regarded as effective. Indeed, the Dutch equal treatment body has served as a good example for the other countries. In the light of the choice in Belgium and Hungary, where the equal treatment legislation is relatively recent, it is somewhat surprising that Estonia, which also adopted its anti-discrimination code only a short while ago, followed the example of the Netherlands. It is yet to be seen whether the procedures of the national specialised bodies in Estonia will provide an effective low-threshold alternative to civil law proceedings. In the light of the above observations, it can be concluded that the difference between the choices these countries have made as to the particular form of the procedure may mainly be linked to their enforcement traditions.

The second paragraph of Article 7 RED establishes rules for legal standing. This provision does not entirely take into consideration the group aspect of discrimination, thus the victim's perspective is not fully reflected in this provision. More concretely, it does not impose an obligation on the Member States to introduce actio popularis claims in their strict sense which would make the enforcement of the protection against indirect and systemic discrimination more effective and/or possible. This is a clear deficiency of the RED, and a missed opportunity to bring the enforcement mechanisms in accordance with the substantive provisions of the Directive. Notwithstanding this inconsistency between the substantive and procedural provisions, the effectiveness of the enforcement is enhanced, and thus a developed level of minority protection is ensured by the regulation that interest organisations can engage in procedures on behalf of or in support of the victims, with their consent.

In this respect, it is remarkable that all four countries have gone beyond the minimum requirements of the RED and to some extent allow actio popularis claims. In the Netherlands the possibility of initiating actio popularis claims is generally enshrined in the Civil Code and not specifically created for discrimination complaints. On the contrary, in the three other countries these procedures have been separately taken up in the equal treatment legislation. In Estonia this also means that the possibility of actio popularis claims has not been extended to judicial procedures, it is only possible in the procedures of the specialised bodies. This approach makes the judicial enforcement of the prohibition of systemic and/or indirect discrimination very difficult if not impossible. In any event, it is difficult to see what influenced the countries in their choice of introducing actio popularis complaints. Nevertheless, the group aspect present in certain forms of discrimination has been clearly addressed and taken into account with the establishment of actio popularis claims.

Article 9 RED imposes a duty on the Member States to provide protection against victimisation in order to encourage victims of discrimination to attempt to vindicate their right to equal treatment. From the perspective of achieving substantive equality the requirements of the RED cannot, however, be regarded as entirely effective. Although the concept of victimisation can, arguably, be regarded as a form of discrimination, the RED locates this prohibition among the enforcement provisions instead of defining it in the substantive part of the RED. The most important implications of this approach of the RED concern the uncertainty over whether the special rules on the allocation of the burden of proof have to be applied to this concept. Without the special allocation of the burden of proof in victimisation cases victims can hardly successfully vindicate their right to non-victimisation, also making the enforcement of the right to equal treatment less effective, with implications for the level of minority protection in this respect.

Contrary to the RED, the Estonian and Hungarian equal treatment legislations define victimisation as a form of discrimination. This also means that the enforcement of the prohibition of victimisation will also be facilitated due to the applicability of the special rules on the allocation of the burden of proof. The application of these rules to this concept is, however, not without difficulties in Hungary. This can, arguably, be linked to the difficulties with the burden of proof regulations. The position of the RED was followed in Belgium and the Netherlands, where the prohibition of victimisation is regarded as an enforcement provision. Accordingly, the concept is not taken as a form of discrimination, and the special rules pertaining to the allocation of the burden of proof are not applicable to a claim of victimisation. Although both countries have found ways to somewhat facilitate the procedural position of the victim, the enforcement of the prohibition of victimisation cannot be regarded as entirely effective. It is difficult to see what influenced this choice of the countries in this respect. Still, it is remarkable that, unlike the old ones, the two new Member States under review have gone beyond the minimum requirements of the RED.

Article 15 RED has remained fairly vague as it merely stipulates that sanctions have to be effective, proportionate and dissuasive. The case law of the ECJ seems to indicate that a sanction is *effective*, if it appropriately reacts to the wishes and circumstances of the *victim*. Moreover, the sanctions have to be *proportionate* to the *harm* caused. Finally, they have to have a *dissuasive* effect on the future *perpetrator*. From the perspective of effective enforcement of the right to equal treatment on the grounds of racial or ethnic origin and thus enhancing minority protection, of these criteria the most important is to attain effective and proportionate sanctions, as they do also have a dissuasive effect on the potential perpetrators. In contrast, an obviously dissuasive sanction does not necessarily comply with the requirements of effectiveness and proportionality as they might not reflect the harm or the circumstances related to the victim. In addition, the limits of individual enforcement can be eliminated or reduced with the help of using positive action measures as remedies.

Although a whole variety of sanctions can be found in each country under review, as there are procedures that are more often used, certain forms of sanctions are prioritised. Only in Hungary has the emphasis been placed on punitive measures which cannot be regarded as complying with all the requirements of the Directive. In Belgium, the most important sanction is monetary compensation in the form of forfaitair compensation that can be considered to meet the mentioned criteria. In Estonia and the Netherlands, the non-binding decisions of the national specialised bodies have been given preference, which might be classified as preventive measures. As indicated supra, while in the Netherlands this sanction might be regarded as appropriate, in Estonia it is not the case yet. Positive action measures as remedies are not explicitly mentioned in the legislation of the countries. It is only in the Netherlands where the Commission imposes positive obligations, which can be qualified as positive action measures, on the respondents even in the absence of discrimination. All in all, similarly to access to justice, the choice might have been influenced by the legal traditions of the country, but it also seems that the experience with enforcing the prohibition of discrimination might also have affected the choice of the sanction.

Finally, Article 13 RED imposes a duty on the Member States to establish specialised bodies for the promotion of equal treatment, the existence of which contributes to an effective enforcement of the right to equal treatment on the grounds of racial or ethnic origin, the first pillar of an adequate system of minority protection. Although the Directive is relatively silent on the concrete details, the competences enumerated in this article have to be carried out in an independent fashion. This can be accomplished only when the national specialised body itself is independent from any influence. The requirement of independence includes two main aspects: independence pertaining to organisational as well as operational matters. This also means that the effectiveness of the enforcement in this respect can be determined on the basis of the competences and the extent of the independence of these bodies.

National specialised bodies already existed in the old Member States, and were newly created in Estonia and Hungary. Of these bodies, the Netherlands has the longest tradition with its national specialised body, the good practice of which has also served as an example for the other countries. Nevertheless, the other national specialised bodies differ from the Dutch Equal Treatment Commission in many respects. A clear distinction can be made between the bodies as to whether they are quasi-judicial bodies or not. In this respect it is only the Belgian Centre that does not have any competence to issue decisions. As the practice of quasi-judicial bodies generally proved to be effective it would be important for the victims to be able to obtain opinions from the Belgian Centre. The national specialised bodies in the other countries can be classified as quasi-judicial bodies, while only the Hungarian Authority can deliver binding decisions. Of these bodies, the independence of the Dutch equal treatment body is the most satisfyingly guaranteed, which again can be attributed to its long-standing practice in the fight against discrimination. Due to concerns related to being perceived as an impartial body the Dutch Commission does not engage in court procedures. This approach of the Commission is regrettable as this body has the authority and expertise that could be very well used for achieving substantive equality through effective enforcement. Moreover, the structure of the body can very well guarantee its impartiality. In this light it is quite striking that the Hungarian Authority engages in judicial procedures, even though its internal structure does not ensure its impartiality. A means to guarantee impartiality would be to transform the Advisory Board into the decision-making unit of the Authority, and the present fact-finding department would be able to fulfil the other competences and mandates of the body. In addition, the financial independence of the specialised bodies in the four countries studied is not entirely ensured and stricter rules are generally desirable for their accountability and composition in order to guarantee their independence. The RED did not have significant influence on the competences/mandates and independence of the Belgian and the Dutch specialised bodies, as they had already existed at the time of its adoption. In contrast, the Estonian and Hungarian national specialised bodies have been founded on the basis of Article 13 RED. However, it is difficult to see what could inspire their choice of establishing a body with the competence to issue non-binding opinions on the one hand, and a body with binding decisions on the other.

As could be seen in this book, neither the ECJ nor the four Member States have fully realised the potential the enforcement mechanisms of the RED have for achieving effective enforcement of the right to equal treatment. Also the RED itself missed some opportunities to guarantee the effective enforcement of the right to equal treatment on the grounds of racial or ethnic origin. Nevertheless, important steps have been taken to make the enforcement of the right to equal treatment as effective as possible by taking the perspective of the victim into account, contributing to an enhanced level of minority protection. Effective protection of minorities through the prohibition of discrimination is essential as

> racism, racial discrimination, xenophobia and related intolerance, where they amount to racial discrimination, constitute serious violations of and obstacles to the full enjoyment of all human rights and deny the self-evident truth that all human beings are born free and equal in dignity and rights, are an obstacle to friendly and peaceful relations among peoples and nations, and are among the root causes of many internal and international conflicts, including armed conflicts, and the consequent forced displacement of populations.[1]

1 Durban Declaration and Programme of Action, Preamble, Durban, 31 August – 8 September 2001.

Bibliography

Selected Literature

Aasland, A., & Fløtten, T. (2001). Ethnicity and Social Exclusion in Estonia and Latvia. 53 Europe-Asia Studies 1023-1049.

Alen, A. (Ed.). (1992). Treatise on Belgian Constitutional Law, Deventer/Boston: Kluwer Law and Taxation Publishers.

Alen, A. (1995). Handboek van het Belgisch staatsrecht, Mechelen: Kluwer Rechtswetenschappen.

Alexy, R. (1985). Theorie der Grundrechte. Baden-Baden: Nomos Verlagsgesellschaft.

Andrews, N. (2001). Multi-Party Proceedings in England: Representative and Group Actions. 11 Duke Journal of Comparative and International Law 249-267.

Apollis, G. (1980). Le principe de l'égalité de traitement en droit économique communautaire. 1980 Revue du marché commun 72-84 & 140-159.

Aristotle (2000). Nicomachean Ethics. (R. Crisp, Trans). Cambridge: Cambridge University Press.

Arnardóttir, O.M. (2003). Equality and Non-Discrimination under the European Convention on Human Rights. The Hague/London/New York: Martinus Nijhoff Publishers.

Arnardóttir, O.M. (2007). Non-discrimination under Article 14 ECHR: The Burden of Proof. 51 Scandinavian Studies in Law 13-40.

Arnull, A.M., Dashwood, A.A., Ross, M.G., & Wyatt, D.A. (2000). Wyatt & Dashwood's European Union Law (4th ed.). London: Sweet & Maxwell 2000.

Asser, W.D.H. (1998). Rechtspraakoverzicht. Bewijslastverdeling. Deventer: Gouda Quint.

Asscher-Vonk, I.P. (1999). Towards One Concept of Objective Justification. In T. Loenen & P.R. Rodrigues (Eds.), Non-Discrimination Law: Comparative Perspectives (39-51). The Hague/London/Boston: Kluwer Law International.

Asscher-Vonk, I.P., & Groenendijk, C.A. (Eds.). (1999). Gelijke behandeling: Regels en realiteit. Een juridische en rechtssociologische analyse van de Gelijkebehandelingswetgeving. The Hague: SDU Publishers.

Asscher-Vonk, I.P., & Hendriks, A.C. (2005). Gelijke behandeling en onderscheid bij de arbeid. Deventer: Kluwer.

Bacik, I. (2003). Harassment. In C. Costello & E. Barry (Eds.), Equality in Diversity: The New Equality Directives (151-176). Dublin: ICEL.

Baker, A. (2004). Effective Deterrence v Accessible Remedies: What Not to Borrow from US Discrimination Law. 6 International Journal of Discrimination and the Law 109-139.

Bamforth, N. (1996). Limits of Anti-Discrimination Law: Legal and Social Concepts of Equality. In J. Dine & B. Watt (Eds.), Discrimination Law: Concepts, Limits and Justifications (49-62). London/New York: Longman.

Banton, M. (1999). Discrimination Entails Comparison. In T. Loenen & P.R. Rodrigues (Eds.), Non-Discrimination Law: Comparative Perspectives (107-117). The Hague/London/Boston: Kluwer Law International.

Barnard, C. (1996). Gender and Commercial Discrimination. In J. Dine & B. Watt (Eds.), Discrimination Law: Concepts, Limitations and Justifications (63-76). London/New York: Longman 1996.

Barnard, C., & Hepple, B. (1999). Indirect Discrimination: Interpreting Seymour-Smith. 58 Cambridge Law Journal 399-412.

Barnard, C, &. Hepple, B. (2000). Substantive Equality. 59 Cambridge Law Journal 562-585.

Barnard, C. (2001). The Changing Scope of the Fundamental Principle of Equality? 46 McGill Law Journal 955-977.

Barmes, L. (2003). Promoting Diversity and the Definition of Direct Discrimination. 32 Industrial Law Journal 200-213.

Barton, S. (2004). Ethnic Monitoring, Gypsies and Travellers. 2004 (Issue 2) Roma Rights Quarterly.

Barrett, G. (2003). The Concept and Principle of Equality in the European Community: Pouring New Wine into Old Bottles? In C. Costello & E. Barry (Eds.), Equality in Diversity: The New Equality Directives (99-134), Dublin: ICEL.

Barry, E. (2003). Different Hierarchies – Enforcing Equality Law. In C. Costello & E. Barry (Eds.), Equality in Diversity: The New Equality Directives (411-434). Dublin: ICEL.

Barry, E. (2004). Strategic Enforcement – From Concept to Practice. In Strategic Enforcement and the EC Equal Treatment Directives. Towards the Uniform and Dynamic Implementation of EU Anti-Discrimination Legislation: The Role of Specialised Bodies. Report of the Sixth Experts' Meeting (4-17).

Barry, E. (2006). Interventions and Amicus Curiae Applications. Making Individual Enforcement More Effective. In Strategic Enforcement. Powers and Competences of Equality Bodies. Report by Equinet Working Group 2 on Strategic Enforcement (31-42).

Bårdsen, A. (2007). Reflections on 'Fair Trial' in Civil Proceedings According to Article 6 § 1 of the European Convention on Human Rights. 51 Scandinavian Studies in Law 99-130.

Bayart, C., & Bosmans, I. (2008). De federale antidiscriminatiewetten en arbeidsbetrekkingen in de private sector: algemeen overzicht. In C. Bayart, S. Sottiaux, S. Van Drooghenbroeck (Eds.), De nieuwe federale antidiscriminatiewetten (537-596). Bruges: Die Keure.

Beaton, A.M., & Tougas, F. (2001). Reactions to Affirmative Action: Group Membership and Social Justice. 14 Social Justice Research 61-78.

Bell, M. (2000). Article 13 EC: the European Commission's Anti-Discrimination Proposals. 29 Industrial Law Journal 79-84.

Bell, M. (2001a). Meeting the Challenge? A Comparison between the EU Racial Equality Directive and the Starting Line. In I. Chopin & J. Niessen (Eds.), The Starting Line and the Incorporation of the Racial Equality Directive into the National Laws of the EU Member States and Accession States (22-54). Brussels: Commission for Racial Equality & MPG.

Bell, M. (2001b). Sexual Orientation Discrimination in Employment: An Evolving Role for the European Union. In R. Wintermute & M. Andenas (Eds.), Legal Recognition of Same-Sex Partnerships. A Study of National, European and International Law (653-676). Oxford/Portland: Hart Publishing.

Bell, M. (2002a). Combating Racism through European Laws: A Comparison of the Racial Equality Directive and Protocol 12. In I. Chopin & J. Niessen (Eds.), Combating Racial and Ethnic Discrimination: Taking the European Legislative Agenda further (7-34). Brussels: Commission for Racial Equality & MPG.

Bell, M. (2002b). Beyond European Labour Law? Reflections on the EU Racial Equality Directive. 8 European Law Journal 384-399.

Bell, M. (2002c). Anti-Discrimination Law and the European Union, Oxford: Oxford University Press.

Bell, M. (2004a). A Patchwork of Protection: The New Anti-discrimination Law Framework. 67 The Modern Law Review 465-477.

Bell, M. (2004b). Setting Standards in the fight against Racism: A Comparison of the European Union and the Council of Europe. In J. Niessen & I. Chopin (Eds.), The Development of Legal Instruments to Combat Racism in a Diverse Europe (213-233), Leiden/Boston: Martinus Nijhoff Publishers.

Bell, M. (2008). Extending EU Anti-Discrimination Law. Report of an ENAR Ad hoc Expert Group on Anti-Discrimination Law.

Bell, M., & Waddington, L. (2003). Reflecting on Inequalities in European Equality Law. 28 European Law Review 349-369.

Beloff, M.J. (2000). Who Whom? Issues in Locus Standi in Public Law. Liber Amicorum – Slynn – International Perspective. In M. Andenas & D. Fairgrieve (Eds.), Judicial Review in International Perspective: Liber Amicorum for Lord Slynn of Hadley Volume II (275-290). The Hague: Kluwer Law International.

Bernauw, K. (2004). De Wet Bestrijding Discriminatie en verzekeringen. In M. De Vos & E. Brems (Eds.), De Wet Bestrijding Discriminatie in de praktijk (277-308). Antwerp: Intersentia.

Bieback, K-J. (1997). Die mittelbare Diskriminierung wegen des Geschlechts. Ihre Grundlage im Recht der EU und ihre Auswirkungen auf das Sozialrecht der Mitgliedstaaten. Baden-Baden: Nomos.

Bielefeldt, H. (2007). Tackling Multiple Discrimination. Practices, Policies and Laws. Brussels: European Commission.

Bindman, G. (1992). Proof and Evidence of Discrimination. In B.A. Hepple & E.M. Szyszczak (Eds.), Discrimination: The Limits of Law (50-66). London: Mansell Publishing.

Bischof, K., & Samaluk, B. (2007). Report on the Communication Strategies for the Hungarian Equal Treatment Authority. Vienna: Ludwig Boltzmann Institute of Human Rights.

Bitskey, B., & Gyulavári, T. (2004). Az anti-diszkriminációs szabályozás reformja. 15 Acta Humana 13-40.

Bitskey, B. & Gyulavári, T. (2005). The Hungarian Equal Treatment Act: a new Member State's perspective. (In manuscript).

Blackstone, W.T. (1969). On the Meaning and Justification of Equality Principle. In W.T. Blackstone (Ed.), The Concept of Equality (117-133). Minneapolis: Burgess Publishing Company.

Blomeyer, C. (1994). Das Verbot der mittelbaren Discriminierung gemäss Art. 119 EGV. Seine Funktion im deutschen Arbeitsrecht. Baden-Baden: Nomos.

Blom, J. (1995). The Dutch Equal Treatment Commission. 24 Industrial Law Journal 84-89.

Boerefijn, I. et al. (Eds.). (2003). Temporary Special Measures – Accelerating de fact Equality of Women under Article 4(1) UN Convention on the Elimination of All Forms of Discrimination against Women. Antwerp: Intersentia.

Bodrogi, B., & Danka, A. (2006). Litigating Discrimination in Access to Employment in Hungary. 2006 (Issue 1) Roma Rights Quarterly.

Bodrogi, B. (2003). Testing for Discrimination. Identifying and Prosecuting Human Rights Abuses. Minneapolis: New Tactics Project of the Center for Victims of Torture.

Bodrogi, B. (2007). Legal Standing – The Practical Experience of a Hungarian Organisation. 2007 (Issue 5) European Anti-Discrimination Law Review 23-29.

Boog, I., & Hamidi, L. (2006). ENAR Shadow Report, Racism in the Netherlands. Brussels: ENAR.

Borghs, P. (2003). De ADW. Handleiding bij de wet ter bestrijding van discriminatie. Antwerp: Garant.

Bossuyt, M. (2002). Report of the Special Rapporteur: Prevention of discrimination. The concept and practice of affirmative action. E/CN.4/Sub.2/2002/21. Geneva: Economic and Social Council.

Bovenkerk, F. (1992). A Manual for International Comparative Research on Discrimination on the grounds of 'Race' and Ethnic Origin. Geneva: International Labour Organisation.

Bowers, J., & Moran, E. (2002). Justification in Direct Sex Discrimination Law: Breaking the Taboo. 31 Industrial Law Journal 307-312.

Bosse, C. (2003). Bewijslastverdeling in het Nederlands en Belgisch arbeidsrecht Deventer: Kluwer.

Brown, C. (2002). The Race Directive: Towards Equality for all the Peoples of Europe?, 21 Yearbook of European Law 195-227.

Brand, O. (2007). Conceptual Comparisons: Towards a Coherent Methodology of Comparative Legal Studies. 32 Brooklyn Journal of International Law 405-465.

Brennan, F. (2004). The Race Directive, Institutional Racism and Third Country Nationals. In T. Tridimas & P. Nebbia (Eds.), European Union Law for the Twenty-First Century. Rethinking the New Legal Order (371-386). Oxford/Portland Oregon: Hart Publishing.

Browne, K.R. (1999). The Use and Abuse of Statistical Evidence in Discrimination Cases. In T. Loenen & P.R. Rodrigues (Eds.), Non-Discrimination Law: Comparative Perspectives (411-423). The Hague/London/Boston: Kluwer Law International.

Burri, S.D., & Dorssemont, F. (2005). The Transposition of the Race Directive (2000/43/EC) and the Framework Directive on Equal Treatment in Employment (2000/78/EC) into Dutch and Belgian Law. 21 The International Journal of Comparative Labour Law and Industrial Relations 537-570.

Busstra, M.J. The Implications of the Racial Equality Directive for Minority Protection within the European Union. An Analysis of the Substantive Provisions of the Racial Equality Directive and their Implementation in Four Member States: Belgium, Estonia, Hungary and the Netherlands (PhD dissertation on file at the Erasmus University Rotterdam)

Busstra, M.J., & Henrard, K. (2006). Conflicting Rights: A Model. Presentation at the Conference on Conflicting rights. 15-16 December 2006, Ghent.

Cahn, C. (2004). Void at the Centre: (The Lack of) European Union Guidance on Ethnic Data. 2004 (Issue 2) Roma Rights Quarterly.

Cane, P. (2002). Responsibility in Law and Morality. Oregon: Hart Publishing.

Cardinale, G. (2007). The Challenges Ahead for European Anti-Discrimination Legislation: an ECRI perspective. 2007 (Issue 5) European Anti-Discrimination Law Review 31-40.

Caruso, D. (2003). Limits of the Classical Method: Positive Action in the European Union after the New Equality Directives. Boston University School of Law Working Paper Series 03-21. Retrieved from http://www.bu.edu/law/faculty/scholarship/workingpapers/abstracts/2003/pdf_files/CarusoD090903.pdf

Castermans, A.G. (2009). Rechtsvorderingen bij discriminatie. In J.H. Gerards & P.J.J. Zoontjens (Eds.), Gelijke behandeling: oordelen en commentaar 2008 (241-262). Nijmegen: Wolf Legal Publisher 2009.

Charpentier, L. (1998). The European Court of Justice and the Rhetoric of Affirmative Action. Working Paper RSC 98/30, European University Institute.

Choudhry, T. (2006). The Commission for Equality and Human Rights: Designing the Big Tent. 13 Maastricht Journal of European and Comparative Law 311-322.

Chopin, I., & Niessen, J. (Eds.). (2001). The Starting Line and the Incorporation of the Racial Equality Directive into the national Laws of the EU Member States and Accession States. Brussels: Commission for Racial Equality & Migration Policy Group.

Closset-Marchal, G., & Van Drooghenbroeck, S. (2008). L'Action en Cessation an Matière de Discriminations. In C. Bayart, S. Sottiaux & S. Van Drooghenbroeck (Eds.), De nieuwe federale antidiscriminatiewetten (361-418). Bruges: Die Keure.

Cohen, B. (2004). Remedies and Sanctions for Discrimination in Working Life under the EC Anti-Discrimination Directives. In Discrimination in Working Life:

Remedies and Enforcement. Towards the Uniform and Dynamic Implementation of EU Anti-Discrimination Legislation: The Role of Specialised Bodies. Report of the Fourth Experts' Meeting (17-25).

Cohn, Y. (2003). Affirmative Action for Women in the Workplace at Home Abroad: A Comparison of Johnson v. Transportation Agency and Abrahamsson v. Fogelqvist. 36 Columbia Journal of Law and Social Problems 277-328.

Collins, H. (2003). Discrimination, Equality and Social Inclusion. 66 The Modern Law Review 16- 43.

Collins, E. (2004). Challenges and Choices – Establishing a Single Equality Commission in Northern Ireland. In Considerations for Establishing Single Equality Bodies and Integrated Equality Legislation. Towards the Uniform and Dynamic Implementation of EU Anti-Discrimination Legislation: The Role of Specialised Bodies. Report of the Seventh Experts' Meeting (4-9).

Connolly, M. (2000). Discrimination Law: Victimisation. 29 Industrial Law Journal 304-311.

Connolly, M. (2002). Discrimination Law: Victimisation. 31 Industrial Law Journal 161-171.

Connolly, M. (2007). Discrimination Law and Victimisation: Reinterpreting Khan – Easy Case Makes Bad Law. 36 Industrial Law Journal 364-374.

Cooper, E.H. (2001). Class Action Advice in the Form of Questions. 11 Duke Journal Comparative and International Law 215-247.

Cormack, J., & Niessen, J. (2004). National Specialised Equality Bodies in the Wake of the EC Anti-Discrimination Directives. In Considerations for Establishing Single Equality Bodies and Integrated Equality Legislation. In Towards the Uniform and Dynamic Implementation of EU Anti-Discrimination Legislation: The Role of Specialised Bodies. Report of the Seventh Experts' Meeting (20-29).

Cormack, J., & Niessen, J. (2005). The Independence of Equality Bodies. 2005 (Issue 1) European Anti-Discrimination Law Review 23-30.

Costello, C. (2003). Positive Action. In C. Costello & E. Barry (Eds.), Equality in Diversity: The New Equality Directives (177-212). Dublin: ICEL.

Courtis, C. (2008). Courts and the Legal Enforcement of Economic, Social and Cultural Rights. Comparative experiences of justiciability. Geneva: International Commission of Jurists.

Craig, P. (2006). EU Administrative Law. Oxford: Oxford University Press.

Craig, R. (2007). Systemic Discrimination in Employment and the Promotion of Ethnic Equality. Leiden/Boston: Martinus Nijhoff Publishers.

Craig, P., & De Búrca, G. (2003). EU Law (3rd ed.). Oxford: Oxford University Press.

Cremers-Hartman, E. (2004). Gelijke behandeling bij de arbeid in zes wetten. Een actueel overzicht van hoofdlijnen, overeenkomsten en verschillen. Deventer: Kluwer.

Cuypers, D. (2003). There Will Never Be Equality in the Servant's Hall. Gelijkheid in het arbeidsrecht. In Vrijheid en gelijkheid. De horizontale werking van het gelijkheidsbeginsel en de nieuwe Antidiscriminatiewet (445-488). Antwerp: MAKLU.

De Beco, G. (2007). National Human Rights Institutions in Europe. 7 Human Rights Law Review 331-370.

De Boeck, A. (2003). Doorwerking van het gelijkheidsbeginsel in het contractenrecht. In Vrijheid en gelijkheid. De horizontale werking van het gelijkheidsbeginsel en de nieuwe Antidiscriminatiewet (413-444). Antwerp: MAKLU.

Dannemann, G. (2006). Comparative Law: Study of Similarities or Differences? In M. Reimann & R. Zimmermann (Eds.), The Oxford Handbook of Comparative Law (383-419). Oxford: Oxford University Press.

Davidović, M., & Van Walsum, S.K. (2009). Ras en nationaliteit. In J.H. Gerards & P.J.J. Zoontjens (Eds.), Gelijke behandeling: oordelen en commentaar 2008 (29-48). Nijmegen: Wolf Legal Publisher.

Davies, G., & Costello, C. (2006). The Jurisprudence of the Court of Justice in the Field of Sex Equality since 2000. 43 Common Market Law Review 1567-1616.

De Cruz, P. (1999). Comparative Law in a Changing World. Staffordshire University: Intl. Specialized Book Service Inc.

De Fey, C.C., Kellermann, A., & Nieuwbroer, J.W. (Eds.). (2004). Met recht discriminatie bestrijden. The Hague: Boom Juridische Uitgevers.

De Lange, R. (2009). Courts, Legislatures, and Fundamental Rights. The Hague: Boom Juridische Uitgevers.

Demeter, J. (2006). Az egyenlő bánásmódról és az esélyegyenlőség előmozdításáról szóló törvény – az Egyenlő Bánásmód Hatóság által lefolytatott eljárások tükrében. 17 Acta Humana 49-66.

De Prins, D. (2007). Geen praktijktest, geen discriminatiebescherming. Retrieved from http://www.kifkif.be/page?&orl=1&ssn=&lng=1&pge=22&searchlist=all&pge_old=9&zoek=de%20prins&are=1007.

De Prins, D., Sottiaux, S., & Vrielink, J. (2003a). De Antidiscriminatiewet: Een artikelsgewijze analyse (Deel 1). 2003 (Issue 23) Nieuw Juridisch Weekblad 258-275.

De Prins, D., Sottiaux S., & Vrielink, J. (2003b). De Antidiscriminatiewet: Een artikelsgewijze analyse (Deel 2). 2003 (Issue 24) Nieuw Juridisch Weekblad 294-302.

De Prins, D., Sottiaux, S., & Vrielink, J. (2005). Handboek discriminatierecht. Deventer: Kluwer.

De Schutter, O. (2001). Discriminations et marché du travail. Liberté et égalité dans les rapports d'emploi. Brussels: P.I.E.-Peter Lang.

De Schutter, O. (2003a). Proving Discrimination. Presentation at the Seminar The Fight Against Discrimination in the Daily Practice, Academy of European Law, Trier.

De Schutter, O. (2003b). Methods of Proof in the Context of Combating Discrimination. In Proving Discrimination. The Dynamic Implementation of EU Anti-Discrimination Law: The Role of Specialised Bodies. Report of the First Experts' Meeting (22-37).

De Schutter, O. (2004). Report on Measures to Combat Discrimination. Directives 2000/43/EC and 2000/78/EC. Country Report: Belgium. Brussels: European Commission.

De Schutter, O. (2005a). The Prohibition of Discrimination under European Human Rights Law. Relevance for EU Racial and Employment Equality Directives. European Network of Legal Experts in the Non-discrimination Field. Brussels: European Commission.

De Schutter, O. (2005b). Thematic Comment No. 3: The Protection of Minorities in the European Union. EU Network of Independent Experts on Fundamental Rights. Brussels: European Commission.

De Schutter, O. (2006). Three Models of Equality and European Anti-Discrimination Law. 57 Northern Ireland Legal Quarterly 1-56.

De Schutter, O. (2007). Report on Measures to Combat Discrimination. Directives 2000/43/EC and 2000/78/EC. Country Report: Belgium. Brussels: European Commission.

De Schutter, O., & Ringelheim, J. (2008). Ethnic Profiling: A Rising Challenge for European Human Rights Law. 71 The Modern Law Review 358-384.

De Vos, M. (2004). De bouwstenen van het discriminatierecht in de arbeidsverhoudingen na de wet bestrijding discriminatie. In M. De Vos & E. Brems (Eds.), De Wet Bestrijding Discriminatie in de praktijk (69-106). Antwerp: Intersentia.

De Vos, M. (2007). Beyond Formal Equality. Positive Action under Directives 2000/43/EC and 2000/78/EC. Brussels: European Commission.

De Varennes, F. (1996). Language, Minorities and Human Rights. The Hague: Kluwer.

De Witte, B. (2000). Politics Versus Law in the EU's Approach to Ethnic Minorities. 2000 (Issue 4) EUI Working Paper RSC.

De Witte, B., & Horváth, E. (2008). The Many Faces of Minority Policy in the European Union. In K. Henrard, & R. Dunbar (Eds.), Synergies in Minority Protection. European and International Law Perspectives (365-384).Cambridge: Cambrigde University Press.

Dhami, R.S., Squires, J., & Modood, T. (2006). Developing Positive Action Policies: Learning from the Experiences of Europe and North America. Research Report no. 406, Department for Work and Pensions.

Dierx, J., & Siegers, J. (1990). Indirecte discriminatie van deeltijdwerkers. Statistisch bewijs en objectieve rechtvaardiging. 1990 (Issue 15) NJB 554-560.

Dierx, J.R., & Rodrigues, P.R. (2003). The Dutch Equal Treatment Act in Theory and Practice. 2003 (Issue 1) Roma Rights Quarterly.

Dobrushi, A. (2007). Litigating Discrimination in Access to Social Services. 2007 (Issue 1) Roma Rights Quarterly.

Dougan, M. (1999). The Equal Treatment Directive: Retaliation, Remedies and Direct Effect. 24 European Law Review 664-673.

Driessen-Reilly, M., & Driessen, B. (2003). Don't Shoot the Messenger: A Look at Community Law relating to Harassment in the Workplace. 28 European Law Review 493-507.

Drijber, B.J., & Prechal, S. (1997). Gelijke behandeling van mannen en vrouwen in horizontaal perspectief. 45 SEW 122-167.

Edley, C. (1993). Implications of Empirical Studies on Race Discrimination. In M. Fix & R. Struyk (Eds.), Clear and Convincing Evidence: Measurement of Discrimination in America (377-391). Washington DC: The Urban Institute Press.

Eide, A. (2001). Economic, Social and Cultural Rights as Human Rights. In A. Eide, C. Krause & A. Rosas (Eds.), Economic, Social and Cultural Rights. A Textbook (299-318). The Hague: Martinus Nijhoff Publishers.
Ellis, E. (1994). The Definition of Discrimination in European Community Sex Equality Law. 19 European Law Review 563-580.
Ellis, L.G. (1996). Opportunities and Obstacles in Alternative Dispute Resolution Techniques. 1996 (February) CPA Journal 18-22.
Ellis, E. (1997). The Principle of Equality of Opportunity Irrespective of Sex: Some reflections on the present state of European Community law and its future development. In A. Dashwood & S. O'Leary (Eds.), The Principle of Equal Treatment in E.C. Law (172-188). London/Dublin/Hong Kong: Sweet & Maxwell.
Ellis, E. (1998) EC Sex Equality Law, Oxford: Oxford University Press.
Ellis, E. (2005). EU Anti-Discrimination Law, Oxford: Oxford University Press.
Erdal, U. (2001). Burden and Standard of Proof in Proceeding under the European Convention. 26 European Law Review 68-85.
Ernits, M. (2003). Õiguskantsler. 2003 (Issue 1) Juridica 14-17
Espín, E. (2005). Burden of Proof in Council Directives 2000/43/EC and 2000/78/EC on Equal Treatment. Presentation at the Seminar The Fight Against Discrimination in the Daily Practice, Academy of European Law, Trier.
Farkas, L. (2003). Will the Groom Adopt the Bride's Unwanted Child? The Race Equality Directive, Hungary and its Roma. 2003 (Issues 1-2) Roma Rights Quarterly.
Farkas, L. (2004a). The Monkey That Does Not See. 2004 (Issue 2) Roma Rights Quarterly.
Farkas, L. (2004b). Education, Education and More Education. Eumap 2004. Retrieved from http://www.eumap.org/journal/features/2004/minority_education/edmore/.
Farkas, L. (2005). A miskolci deszegregációs per első felvonása. 9 Fundamentum 157-164.
Farkas, L. (2006). A Good Way to Equality: Roma Seeking Judicial Protection against Discrimination in Europe. 2006 (Issue 3) European Anti-Discrimination Law Review 21-30.
Farkas, L. Kárpáti, J. (2004). Gyerekjáték összerakni? A magyar antidiszkriminációs testület modellje. TÁRKI: Budapest.
Farkas, L., & Kádár, A. (2005). Report on Measures to Combat Discrimination. Directives 2000/43/EC and 2000/78/EC. Country Report. Hungary. Brussels: European Commission.
Farkas, L., Kádár, A., & Kárpáti, J. (2003). Néhány megjegyzés az egyenlő bánásmódról szóló törvény koncepciójához. 7 Fundamentum 121-130.
Farkas, L., Kádár, A., & Kárpáti, J. (2006). Az egyenlő bánásmódról és az esélyegyenlőség előmozdításáról szóló 2003. évi CXXV. törvény magyarázata. Budapest: Másság Alapítvány 2006.
Faundez, J. (1994). Affirmative Action: International Perspectives. Geneva: International Labour Office.

Finlay, M. (2003). Indirect Discrimination and the Article 13 Directives. In C. Costello & E. Barry (Eds.), Equality in Diversity. The New Equality Directives (135-150). Dublin: ICEL.

Fitsum, A. (2000a). A tesztelés mint bizonyítási módszer a bírósági eljárásban. 4 Fundamentum 74-79.

Fitsum, A. (2000b). Testing to Prove Racial Discrimination: Methodology and Application in Hungary. 2000 (Issue 3) Roma Rights Quarterly.

Flynn, L. (1999). The Implications of Article 13 EC – After Amsterdam, Will Some Forms of Discrimination Be More Equal than Others? 36 Common Market Law Review 1127-1152.

Flynn, L. (2000). Whatever Happened to Emmott? The Perfecting of Community Rules on National Time-Limits. In C. Kilpatrick, P. Novitz & C. Skidmore (Eds.), The Future of Remedies in Europe (51-68). Oxford: Hart Publishing.

Foubert, P. (2004). Basisconcepten van de wet bestrijding discriminatie en haar verhouding tot andere antidiscriminatieregels. In M. De Vos & E. Brems (Eds.), De Wet Bestrijding Discriminatie in de praktijk (1-35). Antwerp: Intersentia.

Fredman, S. (2000). Affirmative Action and the European Court of Justice: a Critical Analysis. In J. Shaw (Ed.), Social Law and Policy in an Evolving European Union (171-195). Oxford: Hart Publishing.

Fredman, S. (2001a). Combating Racism with Human Rights: the Right to Equality. In S. Fredman (Ed.), Discrimination and Human Rights. The Case of Racism (9-44). Oxford: Oxford University Press.

Fredman, S. (2001b). Equality: A New Generation? 30 Industrial Law Journal 145-168.

Fredman, S. (2002). Discrimination Law. Oxford: Oxford University Press.

Fredman, S. (2005a). Changing the Norm: Positive Duties in Equal Treatment Legislation. 12 Maastricht Journal of Comparative and European Law 369-397.

Fredman, S. (2005b). Double Trouble: Multiple Discrimination and EU Law. 2005 (Issue 2) European Anti-discrimination Law Review 13-20.

Garrone, P. (1994). La discrimination indirecte en droit communautaire: vers une théorie générale. 11 RTDE 425-449.

Gerards, J.H. (2003). Het toetsingsmodel van de Commissie Gelijke Behandeling voor indirect onderscheid. In D.J.B. De Wolff (Ed.), Gelijke behandeling: oordelen en commentaar 2002 (77-95). Deventer: Kluwer.

Gerards, J.H. (2005a). Judicial Review in Equal Treatment Cases. The Hague: Martinus Hijhoff.

Gerards, J.H. (2005b). Noot. Hoogendijk v. the Netherlands, no. 58641/00, 6 January 2005. 24 EHRC.

Gerards, JH. (2006). Implementation of the Article 13 Directives in Dutch Equal Treatment Legislation. 13 Maastricht Journal of European and Comparative Law 291-308.

Gerards, J.H. (2007). Doorbreking gesloten systeem Awgb. In J.H. Gerards, B.P. Vermeulen & P.J.J. Zoontjens (Eds.), Gelijke behandeling: oordelen en commentaar 2006 (316-320). Nijmegen: Wolf Legal Publishers.

Gerards, J.H. & Heringa, A.W. (2003). Wetgeving gelijke behandeling. Deventer: Kluwer.

Gerards, J.H., & Zoontjens, P.J.J. (2009). Inleiding – algemene ontwikkelingen in the gelijkebehandelingsrecht. In J.H. Gerards & P.J.J. Zoontjens (Eds.), Gelijke behandeling: oordelen en commentaar 2008. (5-18). Nijmegen: Wolf Legal Publisher.

Gijzen, M.H.S. (2004). Report on Measures to Combat Discrimination. Directives 2000/43/EC and 2000/78 EC. Country Report: The Netherlands. Brussels: European Commission.

Gijzen, M.H.S. (2006). Selected Issues in Equal Treatment Law: a Multi-layered Comparison of European, English and Dutch law. Antwerp: Intersentia.

Gill, T., & Monaghan, K. (2003). Justification in Direct Sex Discrimination Law: Taboo Upheld. 32 Industrial Law Journal 117-121.

Goldschmidt, J. (2005). Gelijke behandeling in Europa: een grondrecht apart? Toezicht op gelijke behandeling. 30 NJCM-Bulletin 285-294.

Goldston, J.A. (2001). Race and Ethnic Data: A Missing Resource in the Fight against Discrimination. In A. Krizsán (Ed.), Ethnic Monitoring and Data Protection – The European Context (19-44). Budapest: Central European University Press.

Goldston, J.A. (2005). OAS Working Group to Prepare a Draft Inter-American Convention against Racism and All Forms of Discrimination and Intolerance. Presentation, Washington D.C.

Green, T.K. (1999). Making Sense of the McDonnell Douglas Framework: Circumstantial Evidence and Proof of Disparate Treatment under Title VII. 87 California Law Review 987-988.

Greenhouse, L. (2006). Supreme Court Gives Employees Broader Protection against Retaliation in Workplace, The New York Times, 23 June 2006.

Guild, E. (2000). The EC Directive on Race Discrimination: Surprises, Possibilities and Limitations. 29 Industrial Law Journal 416-423.

Gutteridge, H.K. (1949). Comparative Law: An Introduction to the Comparative Method of Legal Study and Research. Cambridge: Cambridge University Press.

Győrfi, T. (1996). A diszkrimináció tilalma: egy különleges státuszú jog. 51 Jogtudományi Közlöny 275-293.

Gyulavári, T. (2007). Három évvel az antidiszkriminációs szabályozás reformja után. 2007 (Issue3) Esély 29-61.

Halmai, G. (Ed.). (1998). A hátrányos megkülönböztetés tilalmától a pozitív diszkriminációig. A jog lehetőségei és korlátai. Budapest: AduPrint-INDOK.

Hamidi, L. (2004). ENAR Shadow Report. The Netherlands. Brussels: ENAR..

Happold, M. (2000). Fourteen against One: The EU Member States' Response to Freedom Party Participation in the Austrian Government. 49 International and Comparative Law Quarterly 953-963.

Hare, I. (2000). The Law of Standing in Public Interest Adjudication', Liber Amicorum – Slynn – International Perspectives. In M. Andenas & D. Fairgrieve (Eds.), Judicial Review in International Perspective: Liber Amicorum for Lord Slynn of Hadley Volume II (301-318). The Hague: Kluwer Law International.

Harlow, C., (2000). A Common European Law of Remedies', In C. Kilpatrick, T. Novitz & P. Skidmore (Eds.), The Future of Remedies in Europe (69-86). Oxford: Hart Publishing.

Harrington, J. (2001). Making Sense of Equality Law: A Review of the Hepple Report. 64 The Modern Law Review 757-766.

Haskovec, J. (2005). Note. A Beast of a Burden? The New EU Burden-of-Proof Arrangement in Cases of Employment Discrimination Compared to Existing U.S. Law. 14 Transnational Law and Contemporary Problems 1069-1106.

Havinga, T. (2007). Werkt de Algemeen wet gelijke behandeling? Twee Evaluatieonderzoeken besproken. In J.H. Gerards, B.P. Vermeulen & P.J.J. Zoontjens (Eds.), Gelijke behandeling: oordelen en commentaar 2006 (243-261). Nijmegen: Wolf Legal Publishers.

Hendriks, A. (2005). Mogelijkheid instelling van nationaal mensenrechteninstituut krijgt concrete vormen. 30 NJCM-Bulletin 1157-1165.

Henrard, K.A.M. (2000). Devising an Adequate System of Minority Protection. Individual Human Rights, Minority Rights and the Right to Self-Determination. The Hague/Boston/London: Martinus Nijhoff Publishers.

Henrard, K.A.M. (2002). The Impact of the Enlargement Process on the Development of a Minority Protection Policy within the EU: Another Aspect of Responsibility/ Burden-sharing? 9 Maastricht Journal of European and Comparative Law 357-392.

Henrard, K.A.M. (2003). New Minorities' and the Applicability of Minority Rights. In E. Bakker & J. Bomers (Eds.), 'New Minorities': Inclusion and Equality (19-23). The Hague: Netherlands Helsinki Committee.

Henrard, K.A.M. (2004). Ever-Increasing Synergy towards a Stronger Level of Minority Protection between Minority-Specific and Non-Minority-Specific Instruments. 3 European Yearbook of Minority Issues 15-41.

Henrard, K.A.M. (2005). 'Participation', 'Representation' and 'Autonomy' in the Lund Recommendations and their Reflections in the Supervision of the FCNM and Several Human Rights Conventions. 12 International Journal on Minority and Group Rights 133-168.

Henrard, K.A.M. (2006). The Impact of International Non-Discrimination Norms in Combination with General Human Rights for the Protection of National Minorities: The European Convention on Human Rights. Committee of Experts on Issues Relating to the Protection of National Minorities, (DH-MIN)(2006)020, 25 October 2006.

Henrard, K.A.M. (2007a). Equal Rights versus Special Rights? Minority Protection and the Prohibition of Discrimination. Brussels: European Commission.

Henrard, K.A.M. (2007b). Non-Discrimination and Full and Effective Equality. In M. Weller (Ed.), Universal Minority Rights. A Commentary on the Jurisprudence of International Courts and Treaty Bodies (75-148). Oxford: Oxford University Press.

Henrard, K.A.M. (2008a). Een zoektocht naar een beter inzicht van een adequaat toetsingsmodel voor indirecte discriminatie. Noot, D.H. and others v. Czech Republic, 13 November 2007. 33 NJCM-Bulletin 242-250.

Henrard, K.A.M. (2008b). A Patchwork of 'Successful' and 'Missed' Synergies in the Jurisprudence of the ECHR. In K. Henrard & Dunbar (Eds.), Synergies in

Minority Protection. European and International Law Perspectives (314-364). Cambridge: Cambridge University Press.
Henrard, K.A.M. (2008c). Mensenrechten vanuit internationaal en nationaal perspectief. The Hague: Boom Juridische Uitgevers.
Henrard K., & Dunbar, R. (Eds.), (2008). Synergies in Minority Protection. European and International Law Perspectives. Cambridge: Cambridge University Press.
Hensler, D.R. (2001). Revisiting the Monster: New Myths and Realities of Class Action and Other Large Scale Litigation. 11 Duke Journal of Comparative and International Law 179-213.
Hepple, B. (2004). Race and Law in Fortress Europe. 67 The Modern Law Review 1-15.
Hepple, B., Coussey, M., & Choudhury, T. (2000). Equality: A New Framework. Report of the Independent Review of the Enforcement of UK Anti-discrimination Legislation. Oxford: Hart Publishing.
Heringa, A.W. (1991). De AWGB: Is iets beter dan niets of is het zelfs iets al te veel? In A.W. Heringa, A.K. Koekkoek & L. Mulder (Eds.), Gelijk behandelen (1-28). Zwolle: W.E.J. Tjeenk Willink.
Hertogh, M.L.M., & Zoontjens, P.J.J. (Eds.). (2006). Gelijke behandeling: principes en praktijken Evaluatieonderzoek Algemene wet gelijke behandeling. Nijmegen: Wolf Legal Publishers.
Hidma, T.R. & Rutgers, G.R. (2004). Bewijs. The Hague: Kluwer.
Higgins, I. (2003). Enforcement and the New Equality Directives. In C. Costello & E. Barry (Eds.), Equality in Diversity. The New Equality Directives (391-409). Dublin: ICEL.
Hodász, M., & Scullion, G. (2007). Assessment Report into the Carrying out of the Hungarian Equal Treatment Authority's Statutory Mandate. Vienna: Ludwig Boltzmann Institute of Human Rights.
Hollo, L. (2006). Equality for Roma in Europe. A Roadmap for Action. Brussels: Open Society Institute. Retrieved from http://www.justiceinitiative.org/db/resource2/fs/?file_id=18173.
Holtmaat, R. (2003). Stop de inflatie van het discriminatiebegrip! Een pleidooi voor het maken van onderscheid tussen discriminatie en ongelijke behandeling. 2003 (Issue 25) NJB 1266-1276.
Holtmaat, R. (2006a). Catalysts for Change? Equality Bodies according to Directive 2000/43/EC – Existence, Independence and Effectiveness. European Network of Legal Experts in the non-discrimination field. Brussels: European Commission.
Holtmaat, R. (2006b). Discriminatie of onderscheid: the kleine verschil met grote gevolgen of the grote verschil met kleine gevolgen? In M.L.M. Hertogh & P.J.J. Zoontjens (Eds.), Gelijke behandeling: principes en praktijken. Evaluatieonderzoek Algemene wet gelijke behandeling (3-113). Nijmegen: Wolf Legal Publishers.
Holtmaat, R. (2007). Report on Measures to Combat Discrimination. Directives 2000/43/EC and 2000/78/EC. Country Report: The Netherlands. Brussels: European Commission 2007.

Holtmaat, R., & Tobler, C. (2005). CEDAW and the European Union's Policy in the Field of Combating Gender Discrimination. 12 Maastricht Journal of European and Comparative Law 399-425.

Houtzager, D., & Bochhah, N. (2004). Onderscheid op grond van ras bij de arbeid: nieuwe ontwikkelingen. 19 Sociaal Recht 272-278.

Houtzager, D. (2006). Changing Perspectives: Shifting the Burden of Proof in Racial Equality Cases. Brussels: ENAR.

Howard, E. (2004). The EU Race Directive: Its Symbolic Value – Its Only Value? 6 International Journal of Discrimination and the Law 141-163.

Howard, E. (2005). Anti Race Discrimination Measures in Europe: An Attack on Two Fronts. 11 European Law Journal 468-486.

Howard, E. (2008). Race and Racism – Why does European Law have Difficulties with Definitions? 24 The International Journal of Comparative Labour and Industrial Relations 5-29.

Hucker, J. (1999). Affirmative Action Canadian style: Reflections on Canada's Employment Equity Law. In T. Loenen & P.R. Rodrigues (Eds.), Non-Discrimination Law: Comparative Perspectives (265-277). The Hague/London/Boston: Kluwer Law International.

Humblet, P. (2003). Proving Sex Discrimination: Mission Impossible? In Proving Discrimination. The Dynamic Implementation of EU Anti-Discrimination Law: The Role of Specialised Bodies. Report of the First Experts' Meeting (4-10).

Hunyor, J. (2003). Skin-deep: Proof and Inferences of Racial Discrimination in Employment. 25 Sydney Law Review 535-554.

Iványi, K. (Ed.). (2004). Jogvédelem a gyakorlatban. Budapest: NEKI. Retrieved from http://www.neki.hu/kiadvanyok/jogvedelem_a_gyakorlatban.htm.

Iványi, K. (Ed.). (2005). Változások küszöbén. Új lehetőségek a jogvédelemben az esélyegyenlőségi törvény hatályba lépésével. Budapest: NEKI. Retrieved from http://www.neki.hu/kiadvanyok/valtozasok.htm.

Iványi, K., & Muhi, E. (2004). A tesztelés hazai és nemzetközi gyakorlata. Budapest: NEKI. Retrieved from http://www.neki.hu/kiadvanyok/teszteles/tartalomjegyzek.htm.

Jacobs, F. (1997). Enforcing Community Rights and Obligations in National Courts: Striking the Balance. In J. Lonbay & A. Biondi (Eds.), Remedies for Breach of EC Law (25-36). Chichester/NewYork/Weinheim/Brisbane/Singapore/Toronto: John Wiley & Sons.

Jacobs, C., & White, R. (2006). European Convention on Human Rights. Oxford: Oxford University Press.

Jacobsen, B.D., & Rosenberg-Khawaja, E.O. (2006). Legal Assistance to Individuals. Powers and Procedures for Effective and Strategic Individual Enforcement. In Strategic Enforcement. Powers and Competences of Equality Bodies (9-24). Brussels: Equinet.

Jackson, D.W. (1999). Affirmative Action in Comparative Perspective: India and the United States. In T. Loenen & P.R. Rodrigues (Eds.), Non-discrimination Law: Comparative Perspectives (249-264). The Hague/London/Boston: Kluwer Law International.

Jans, J.H. et al. (2007). Europeanisation of Public Law. Groningen: Europa Law Publishing.
Jaspers, A.P.C.M. (2001). Zetten we de tanden in de handhaving van de gelijke behandelingsnorm? In J.E. Goldschmidt, A.W. Heringa & L. Van Vliet, De zijkant van het gelijk. Het recht als instrument ter verbetering van de kansen op gelijke posities voor vrouwen (139-156). Zwolle: W.E.J. Tjeenk Willink.
Leader, S. (1996). Proportionality and the Justification of Discrimination. In J. Dine & B. Watt (Eds.), Discrimination Law. Concepts, Limitations and Justifications (110-120). London/New York: Longman.
Jennings, R., & A. Watts A. (Eds.). (1992). Oppenheim's International Law (9th ed.) Harlow: Longman.
Jones, T. (2003). The Race Directive: Redefining Protection from Discrimination in EU Law. 5 European Human Rights Law Review 515-526.
Jongbloed, A.W. (2002). Collectief actierecht, groepsacties en algemeen belangacties. In A.W. Jongbloed (Ed.), Samen sterk: over het optreden in rechte door groeperingen (1-26), The Hague: Boom Juridische Uitgevers.
Jõks, A. (2007). The Principle of Equal Treatment in Jurisdiction and Proceedings (Chancellor of Justice). Retrieved from http://www.oiguskantsler.ee/index.php?pageID=176.
Kádár, A. (2001). A magyar diszkrimináció-ellenes jogi szabályozás a faji megkülönböztetés tilalmáról szóló EU-irányelv tükrében. Presentation, 6-7 December 2001, Budapest.
Kádár, A. (2006). A bizonyítási teher megosztásának kérdései. 10 Fundamentum 115-124.
Kádár, A. (2007). Report on Measures to Combat Discrimination. Directives 2000/43/EC and 2000/78/EC. Country Report: Hungary. Brussels: European Commission.
Kaltenbach, J. (2001). From Paper to Practice in Hungary: The Protection and Involvement of Minorities in Governance. In A.-M. Biro & P. Kovacs (Eds.), Diversity in Action: Local Public Management of Multi-Ethnic Communities in Central and Eastern Europe (171-203). Budapest: LGI/OSI.
Kaltenbach, J. et al. (2007). Antidiszkriminációs kézikönyv, Budapest: Clone Design.
Kardos, G. (2007). Kisebbségek: Konfliktusok és garanciák. Budapest: Gondolat Kiadó.
Kárpáti, J. (2005). Az utolsó próbatétel. Ítélet a Háttér Társaság kontra Károli Egyetem ügyben. 9 Fundamentum 105-108.
Kárpáti, J. (2006). A közérdekű igényérvényesítés egyes kérdései. (Training Material).
Kerikmäe, T. (1997). European Convention on Nationality and States' Competence: The Issue of Human Rights. 2 Juridica International 25-29.
Kinsman, F. (2005). Fight against Discrimination – The Race and Framework Employment Directives. Presentation at the Seminar The Fight Against Discrimination in the Daily Practice, Academy of European Law, Trier.
Kirch, A. (1997). The Integration of Non-Estonians into Estonian Society: History, Problems and Trends. Tallinn: Estonian Academy Publishers.
Kitching, K. (Ed.). (2005). Non-Discrimination in International Law. A Handbook for Practitioners. London: Interights.

Kjaerum, M. (2003). National Human Rights Institutions Implementing Human Rights. København: Danish Institute for Human Rights.

Koch, H. (2001). Non-Class Group Litigation under EU and German Law. 11 Duke Journal Comparative and International Law 355-368.

Kokott, J. (1998). The Burden of Proof in Comparative and International Human Rights Law. Civil and Common Law Approaches with Special Reference to the American and German Legal Systems. The Hague/London/Boston: Kluwer Law International.

Kollonay-Lehoczky, Cs. (2006). Előnyben részesítés. 10 Fundamentum 71-78.

Kombos, C. (2006). Locus Standi of Representative Groups in the Shadow of Plaumann: Limitations and Possible Solutions. 47 Acta Juridica Hungarica 373-404.

Koukoulis-Spiliotopoulos, S. (2005). The Amended Equal Treatment Directive (2002/73): An Expression of Constitutional Principles/Fundamental Rights. 12 Maastricht Journal of European and Comparative Law 327-368.

Kovács, K. (2006). Az igazságos kvóta. 10 Fundamentum 5-16.

Krizsán, A. (2000). The Hungarian Minority Protection System: A Flexible Approach to the Adjudication of Ethnic Claims. 26 Journal of Ethnic and Migration Studies 247-262.

Krizsán, A. (2001). Diszkimináció-tilalom a kisebbségi biztos gyakorlatában. 5 Fundamentum 24-39.

Kusters, J. (2003). Discriminatie ten opzichte van allochtonen op de private huurmarkt. In Vrijheid en gelijkheid. De horizontale werking van het gelijkheidsbeginsel en de nieuwe antidiscriminatiewet (541-572). Antwerp: MAKLU.

Lacey, N. (1992). From individual to group? In B. Hepple & E. Szyszczak (Eds.), Discrimination: The Limits of Law (99-124). London: Mansell Publishing.

Lam, C. (2004). Positive Action in the Access to and Supply of Goods and Services. In Combating Discrimination in Goods and Services. Towards the Uniform and Dynamic Implementation of EU Anti-discrimination Legislation: The Role of Specialised Bodies. Report of the Fifth Experts' Meeting (15-21).

Latraverse, S. (2005). The Challenge of Evidence in Implementing EU Discrimination Law in Civil Law Countries – The Example of France. Presentation at the Seminar The Fight Against Discrimination in the Daily Practice, Academy of European Law, Trier.

Lauristin, M., & Heidmets, M. (2002). The Challenge of the Russian Minority. Emerging Multicultural Democracy in Estonia. Tartu: Tartu University Press.

Leckie, S. (2001). The Human Right to Adequate Housing. In A. Eide, C. Krause & A. Rosas (Eds.), Economic, Social and Cultural Rights. A Textbook (512-533). Nijmegen: Martinus Nijhoff Publishers.

Leenders, M.A.J. (1997). Bewijsrecht en discriminatie bij de arbeid. Zwolle: W.E.J. Tjeenk Willink.

Lerner, N. (2003). Group Rights and Discrimination in International Law. The Hague: Martinus Nijhoff.

Letsas, G. (2006). Two Concepts of the Margin of Appreciation. 26 Oxford Journal of Legal Studies 705-732.

Lewis, C. (1996). Remedies and Enforcement of European Community Law. London: Sweet & Maxwell ltd.
Lewis, C. (2004). Judicial Remedies in Public Law. London: Sweet & Maxwell Ltd.
Lindblom, P.H. (2007). The Growing Role of the Courts and the New Functions of Judicial Process – Facts or Flummery? 51 Scandinavian Studies in Law 281-310.
Lindell, B. (2007). Alternative Dispute Resolution and the Administration of Justice – Basic Principles. 51 Scandinavian Studies in Law 311-344.
Linderfalk, U. (2007). On the Interpretation of Treaties. The Modern International Law as Expressed in the 1969 Vienna Convention on the Law of Treaties. Dordrecht: Springer.
Lindsnaes, B., Lindholt, L. (2000). National Human Rights Institutions: Standard-Setting and Achievements. In B. Linsdnaes, L. Lindholt & Yigen (Eds), National Human Rights Institutions. Articles and Working Papers: Input into the Discussions on the Establishment and Development of the Functions of National (1-33). Human Rights Institutions, Copenhagen: The Danish Centre of Human Rights.
Lloyyd, M. (2005). Ombudsman Institutions and Minority Issues. A Guide to Good Practice. Flensburg: European Centre for Minority Issues.
Loenen, T. (1999). Indirect Discrimination: Oscillating between Containment and Revolution. In T. Loenen & P.R. Rodrigues (Eds.), Non-Discrimination Law: Comparative Perspectives (195-211). The Hague/London/Boston: Kluwer Law International 1999.
Loth, M. (2004). Synergie of rolvervanging. In R. Holtmaat (Ed.), Gelijkheid en (andere) grondrechten (221-237). Deventer: Kluwer.
Luxton, J. (1999). Equality and Sex Discrimination in the European Union – Is Shifting the Burden of Proof the Answer? Dickinson Journal of International Law 357-382.
Maduro, M.P. (2005). The European Court of Justice and Anti-Discrimination Law. 2005 (Issue 2) European Anti-Discrimination Law Review 21-28.
Maes, G. (2003). De afdwingbaarheid van sociale grondrechten. Bescherming van (aspecten van) sociale (grond)echten middels de toepassing van het gelijkheid- en non–discriminatiebeginsel. Antwerp: Intersentia.
Majtényi, B. (2001). A magyarországi kisebbbségi önkormányzati rendszer elvei és működése. 5 Fundamentum 34-42.
Majtényi, B. (2005). Mi lesz veled „bezzeggyerek"? Változóban a kisebbségi jogi szabályozás. 9 Fundamentum 109-120.
Majtényi, B., & Pap, A.L. (2006). Végtelen történet. A kisebbségi hovatartozásról. 10 Fundamentum 93-106.
Makkonen, T. (2002). Multiple, Compound and Intersectional Discrimination: Bringing the Experiences of the Most Marginalized to the Fore. Åbo/Turku: Åbo Akademi Institute for Human Rights Research. Retrieved from www.abo.fi/instut/imr/norfa/timo.pdf.
Makkonen, T. (2007a). European Handbook on Equality Data, Brussels: European Commission.

Makkonen, T. (2007b). Measuring Discrimination. Data Collection and EU Equality Law. European Network of Legal Experts in the Non-Discrimination Field. Brussels: European Commission.

Masselot, A. (2004). The New Equal Treatment Directive: Plus ça Change... . 12 Feminist Legal Studies 93-104.

Mälksoo, L. (2005). Report on the Situation of Fundamental Rights in Estonia in 2005. EU Network of Independent Experts on Fundamental Rights. Brussels: European Commission.

McColgan, A. (2005). Discrimination Law. London: Hart Publishing.

McCrudden, C. (1986). Rethinking Positive Action. 15 Industrial Law Journal 219-243.

McCrudden, C. (1999). Regulating Discrimination. In T. Loenen & P.R. Rodrigues (Eds.), Non-Discrimination Law: Comparative Perspectives (295-312). The Hague/London/Boston: Kluwer Law International.

McCrudden, C. (2001). International and European Norms Regarding National Legal Remedies for Racial Equality. In S. Fredman (Ed.), Discrimination and Human Rights. The Case of Racism (251-307). Oxford: Oxford University Press.

McCrudden, C. (2003). Theorising European Equality Law. In C. Costello & E. Barry (Eds.), Equality in Diversity. The New Equality Directives (1-38). Dublin: ICEL.

McInerney, S. (2000). Equal Treatment between Persons Irrespective of Racial or Ethnic Origin: A Comment. 25 European Law Review 317-323.

McInerney, S. (2002). Bases for Action against Race Discrimination. 27 European Law Review 72-79.

McInerney, S. (2003). Legal Protection against Discrimination Based on Racial or Ethnic Origin under European Union Law – Necessary But Not Sufficient? 6 International Journal of Discrimination and the Law 3-43.

Meenan, H. (2003). Age Equality after the Employment Directive. 10 Maastricht Journal of European and Comparative Law 39-82.

Meenan, H. (2007). (Ed.), Equality Law in an Enlarged European Union: Understanding the Article 13 Directives. Cambridge: Cambridge University Press.

Meijknecht, A.K. (2001). Towards International Personality: The Position of Minorities and Indigenous Peoples in International Law. Antwerp/Groningen: Intersentia/Hart.

Merrills, J.G. (1993). The Development of International Law by the European Court of Human Rights. Manchester University Press.

Micklitz, H. (2007). Collective Private Enforcement of Consumer Law: The Key Questions. In W. Van Boom & M. Loos (Eds.), Collective Enforcement of Consumer Law. Securing Compliance in Europe through Private Group Action and Public Authority Intervention (13-33). Groningen: Europa Law Publishing.

Michaels, R. (2006). The Functional Method of Comparative Law. In M. Reimann & R. Zimmermann (Eds.), The Oxford Handbook of Comparative Law (339-382). Oxford: Oxford University Press.

Monaghan, K. (2007). Equality Law. Oxford: Oxford University Press.

Momirov, A., & Naudé Fourie, A. (2009). Developing and Employing Vertical Comparative Legal Methodologies: Tools for Conceptualizing the International Rule of Law. 2 Erasmus Law Review 291-309.

Moon, G. (2004). Race and Employment Directives: Remedies. Presentation at the Seminar The Fight Against Discrimination in the Daily Practice, Academy of European Law, Trier.

Moon, G., & Allen, R. (2006). Dignity Discourse in Discrimination Law: A Better Route to Equality? Retrieved from www.justice.org.uk/images/pdfs/dignityfinal.pdf.

Moore, S. (1993). Compensation for Discrimination. 18 European Law Review 533-541.

Muda, M. (2002). Regulation of Gender Equality as a Fundamental Right in Estonia. 7 Juridica International 106-116.

Mulder, L. (1999). How Positive can Equality Measures be? In T. Loenen & P. Rodrigues (Eds.), Non-Discrimination Law: Comparative Perspectives (65-75). The Hague/London/Boston: Kluwer Law International.

Niessen, J. (2003). Making the Law Work. The Enforcement and Implementation of Anti-Discrimination Legislation. 5 European Journal of Migration and Law 249-257.

Nielsen, R. (2009). Is European Union Equality Law Capable of Addressing Multiple and Intersectional Discrimination yet? Precautions against Neglecting Intersectional Cases. In D. Schiek & V. Chege (Eds.), European Union Non-Discrimination Law. Comparative Perspectives on Multidimensional Equality Law (31-51). London/New York: Routlegde Cavendish.

O'Brien, C.C. (1984). What Rights Should Minorities Have? In B. Whitaker (Ed.), Minorities: A Question of Human Rights? (11-22). Oxford: Pergamon.

O'Cinnéide, C. (2002). A Single Equality Body: Lessons from abroad. Manchester: Equal Opportunities Commission.

O'Cinnéide, C. (2003). Taking Equal Opportunities Seriously: The Extension of Positive Duties to Promote Equality. London: Equality and Diversity Forum.

O'Cinnéide, C. (2004). The Racial Equality Directive as a Basis for Strategic Enforcement, Strategic Enforcement and the EC Equal Treatment Directives. Brussels: MPG 2004.

O'Cinnéide, C. (2006). Positive Action and the Limits of Existing Law. 13 Maastricht Journal of European and Comparative Law 351-364.

O'Cinnéide, C. (2007). The Commission for Equality and Human Rights: A New Institution for New and Uncertain Times. 36 Industrial Law Journal 141-162.

O'Donovan, K. (1985). Affirmative Action. In S. Guest & A. Milne (Eds.), Equality and Discrimination: Essays in Freedom and Justice (77-82). Stuttgart: Franz Steiner Verlag.

O'Hare, U. (2001). Enhancing European Equality Rights. 8 Maastricht Journal of European and Comparative Law 133-165.

Packer, J. (2000). The Origin and Nature of the Lund Recommendations on the Effective Participation of National Minorities in Public Life. 11 Helsinki Monitor 29-45

Pager, S. (2003). Strictness and Subsidiarity: An Institutional Perspective on Affirmative Action at the European Court of Justice. 26 Boston College International and Comparative Law Review 35-76.

Palmer, F. (2006). Re-dressing the Balance of Power in Discrimination Cases: The Shift in the Burden of Proof. 2006 (Issue 4) European Anti-Discrimination Law Review 23-30.

Parmar, S. (2004). The European Court of Justice and Anti-discrimination Law: Reflections on Gender Equality Jurisprudence for the Future Interpretation of the Race Directive. In J. Niessen & I. Chopin (Eds.), The Development of Legal Instruments to Combat Racism in a Diverse Europe (131-154). The Hague: Martinus Nijhoff.

Parrish, B.S. (2001). Walking an Evidentiary Tightrope: The Aftermath of Reeves v. Sanderson Plumbing Products Inc. 2001 (April) University of Memphis Law Review 667-697.

Pel, M. (2003). Mediation en gelijke behandeling in de arbeidsrelatie – dejuridisering en dequerulering? In D.J.B. De Wolff (Ed.), Gelijke behandeling: oordelen en commentaar 2002 (109-119). The Hague: Kluwer.

Peters, A., & Schwenke, H. (2000). Comparative Law beyond Post-Modernism. 49 International and Comparative Law Quarterly 800-834.

Petrova, D. (2004). Ethnic Statistics. 2004 (Issue 2) Roma Rights Quarterly.

Pettai, V. (2001). Estonia and Latvia: International Influences on Citizenship and Minority Integration. In J. Zielonka & A. Pravda (Eds.), Democratic Consolidation in Eastern Europe (257-280). Oxford: Oxford University Press.

Pitkin, H.F.(1967). The Concept of Representation. Berkeley: University of California Press.

Poleshchuk, V. (2005). Report on Measures to Combat Discrimination. Directives -2000/43/EC and 2000/78/EC. Country Report: Estonia. Brussels: European Commission.

Poleshchuk, V. (2007). Report on Measures to Combat Discrimination. Directives 2000/43/EC and 2000/78/EC. Country Report: Estonia. Brussels: European Commission.

Poleshchuk, V., & Helemäe, J. (2006). Estonia – In Quest of Minority Protection. In S. Spiliopoulou Åkermark (Ed.), International Obligations and National Debates: Minorities around the Baltic Sea (109-170). Mariehamm: The Åland Islands Peace Institute.

Poleshchuk, V., & Tsilevich, B. (2003). The Baltic States before EU Accession: Recent Developments in Minority Protection. 2 European Yearbook of Minority Issues 283-305.

Prechal, S. (1997). EC Requirements for an Effective Remedy. In J. Lonbay & A. Biondi (Eds), Remedies for Breach of EC Law (3-13). Chichester-New York-Weinheim-Brisbane-Singapore-Toronto: John Wiley and Sons.

Prechal, S. (2004). Equality of Treatment, Non-discrimination and Social Policy: Achievement in Three Themes. 41 Common Market Law Review 533-551.

Raïkka, J. (Ed.). (1996). Do We Need Minority Rights? Conceptual Issues. The Hague: Martinus Nijhoff.

Reimann, M. & Zimmermann, R. (2006). The Oxford Handbook of Comparative Law. Oxford: Oxford University Press.

Resnik, J. (1991). From 'Cases' to 'Litigation'. 54 Law and Contemporary Problems 5-68.

Reuter, N., Makkonen, T., & Oosi, O. (Eds.). (2004). Study on Data Collection to Measure the Extent and Impact of Discrimination in Europe. Brussels: European Commission.

Rodley, N.S. (1995). Conceptual Problems in the Protection of Minorities: International Legal Developments. 17 Human Rights Quarterly 48-71.

Riach, P.A., & Rich, J. (2004). Deceptive Field Experiments of Discrimination: Are They Ethical? 57 Kyklos 457-470.

Ringelheim, J. (2006). Processing Data on Racial or Ethnic Origin for Antidiscrimination Policies: How to Reconcile the Promotion of Equality with the Right to Privacy? 20006 (Issue 8) Jean Monnet Working Paper Series.

Rodrigues, P.R. (2002). Collectieve acties als structureel instrument tegen discriminatie. In A.W. Jongbloed (Ed.), Samen sterk: over het optreden in rechte door groeperingen (91-104). The Hague: Boom Juridische Uitgevers.

Rodrigues, P.R. (2004). Ras en nationaliteit. In S.D. Burri (Ed.), Gelijke behandeling: oordelen en commentaar 2003 (17-32). Nijmegen: Wolf Legal Publishers.

Rodrigues, P.R., & Van Walsum, S. (2008). Ras en nationaliteit. In J.H. Gerards (Ed.), Gelijke behandeling: oordelen en commentaar 2007 (21-57). Nijmegen: Wolf Legal Publishers.

Rombouts, H., Sardaro, P., & Vandeginste, S. (2006). The Right to Reparation for Victims of Gross and Systemic Violations of Human Rights. In K. de Feyter, S. Parmentier, M Bossuyt & P. Lemmens (Eds.), Out of the Ashes. Reparation for Victims of Gross and Systemic Human Rights Violations (345-503). Antwerp: Intersentia.

Rorive, I. (2006). Situation Tests in Europe: Myths and Realities. European 2006 (Issue 3) Anti-Discrimination Law Review 31-39.

Rorive, I. (2009). Proving Discrimination Cases – the Role of Situation Testing. London: MPG and Centre for Equal Rights.

Rorive, I., & Van der Plancke, V. (2008). Quels dispositions pour prouver la discrimination? In C. Bayart, S. Sottiaux & S. Van Drooghenbroeck, De nieuwe federale antidiscriminatiewetten (415-461). Bruges: Die Keure.

Russel, M., & O'Cinneide, C. (2003). Positive Action to Promote Women in Politics: Some European Comparisons. 52 International and Comparative Law Quarterly 587-614.

Schermers, H.G., & Waelbroeck, D.F. (2001). Judicial Protection in the European Union. The Hague: Kluwel Law International.

Schiek, D. (2000). Elements of a New Framework for the Principle of Equal Treatment of Persons in EC Law. Paper delivered to a conference on Discrimination and Affirmative Action on the Labour Market – Legal Perspectives, 6-7 November 2001, Brussels.

Schiek, D. (2002). New Framework on Equal Treatment of Persons in EC Law? Directives 2000/43/EC, 2000/78/EC and 2002/???/EC Changing Directive 76/207/ EEC in Context. 8 European Law Journal 290-314.

Schiek, D., Waddington, L., & Bell, M. (2007). Cases, Materials and Text on National, Supranational and International Non-Discrimination Law. Oxford/Portland/ Oregon: Hart Publishing.

Schindlauer, D., & Liegl, B. (2007). Consolidated Results of the Twinning Light Project HU2004/IB/SO01-TL "Enforcement of Equal Opportunity Policies and the Effective Implementation of the Anti-discrimination Law". Vienna: Ludwig Boltzmann Institute for Human Rights.

Shelton, D. (1999). Remedies in International Human Rights Law. Oxford: Oxford University Press.

Shelton, D. (2005). Remedies in International Human Rights Law (2nd ed.). Oxford: Oxford University Press.

Simon, P. (2004). Comparative Study on the Collection of Data to Measure the Extent and Impact of Discrimination within the United States, Canada, Australia, Great-Britain and the Netherlands. Medis Project, Measurement of Discrimination. INED – Economie & Humanisme.

Sjerps, I. (1999). Effects and Justifications, or How to Establish a Prima Facie Case of Indirect Discrimination. In T. Loenen & P. Rodrigues (Eds.), Non-Discrimination Law: Comparative Perspectives (237-248). The Hague/London/Boston: Kluwer Law International.

Smith, A. (2006). The Unique Position of National Human Rights Institutions: A Mixed Blessing? 28 Human Rights Quarterly 904-946.

Stratigaki, M. (2005). Gender Mainstreaming vs Positive Action. An Ongoing Conflict in EU Gender Equality Policy. 12 European Journal of Women's Studies 165-186.

Swennen, H., Demuynck, I., & Straetmans, G. (2002). Rechtshandhaving door de stakingsrechter. 2002 (Issue 40) RW 1237-1257..

Szajbély, K. (2005a). A magyar antidiszkriminációs szabályozás a 2000/43/EK Irányelv fényében. 5 Acta Universitatis Szegediensis Acta Juridica et Politica 309-346.

Szajbély, K. (2005b). A magyar antidiszkriminációs szabályozás fogalomrendszere. 3 Romániai Magyar Jogtudományi Közlöny 43-52.

Szajbély, K. (2005c). A magyar anti-diszkriminációs szabályozás szankciórendszere a közösségi követelmények fényében. 9 Európai Tükör 89-98.

Szente, Z. (2006). A pozitív megkülönböztetés problémái. 10 Fundamentum 17-44.

Szyszczak, E. (1996). Community Law on Pregnancy and Maternity. In T.K. Hervey & D.O. O'Keeffe (Eds.), Sex Equality Law in the European Union (51-62). Chichester: John Wiley.

Szyszczak, E. (1997). Remedies in Sex Discrimination Cases. In J. Lonbay & A. Biondi (Eds.), Remedies for Breach of EC Law (105-115). Chichester: John Wiley and Sons.

Taelman, P. (2004a). Het handhavingsrecht van de Wet Bestrijding Discriminatie. In M. De Vos & E. Brems (Eds.), De Wet Bestrijding Discriminatie in de praktijk (203-260). Antwerpen: Intersentia.

Taelman, P. (2004b). De stakingsvordering in de antidiscriminatiewet. Een maat voor niets? 2004 (Issue 8) Nieuw Juridisch Weekblad 506-519.

Taruffo, M. (2001). Some Remarks on Group Litigation in Comparative Perspective. 11 Duke Journal Comparative and International Law 405-421.

Tavits, G. (2004). Muudatused töölepinguliste suhete õiguslikus reguleerimises: kaitse otsingul Euroopa Liidu abiga. 2004 (Issue 8) Juridica 550-559.

Thiele, C. (1999). The Criterion of Citizenship for Minorities: The Example of Estonia. 1999 (Issue 5) ECMI Working Paper.

Thiery, Y. (2007). Gelijkheid, dienstverlening en verzekering: een herontdekkingstocht. 2007 (Issue 8) Tijdschrift voor Belgisch Handelsrecht 747-772.

Thornberry, P. (1980). Is there a Phoenix in the Ashes? – International Law and Minority Rights. 15 Texas International Law Journal 421-458.

Thornberry, P. (1991). International Law and the Rights of Minorities. Oxford: Clarendon Press.

Thornberry, P., & Estebanez, M.A.M. (2004). Minority Rights in Europe. Strasbourg: Council of Europe.

Thüsing, G. (2003). Following the U.S. Example: European Employment Discrimination Law and the Impact of Council Directives 2000/43/EC and 2000/78/EC. 19 The International Journal of Comparative Labour Law and Industrial Relations 187-218.

Tilk, P. (2005). Az egyenlőséghez való jog egyes garanciális szabályai Magyarországon. 16 Acta Humana 20-45.

Tobler, C. (2001). Rechtvaardiging van direct onderscheid in het EG-recht. 17 Nemesis 121-127.

Tobler, C. (2005a). Indirect Discrimination. A Case Study into the Development of the Legal Concept of Indirect Discrimination under EC Law. Antwerp: Intersentia.

Tobler, C. (2005b). Remedies and Sanctions in EU Non-Discrimination Law, Brussels: European Commission.

Tobler, C. (2006). Substantive Equality and Positive Action in EC Sex Equality Law. Paper presented at the ISL Workshop Equality as a social right: Towards a Concept of Substantive Equality in Comparative and International Law, 21 – 23 June 2006, Oñati.

Tobler, C. (2008). Limits and Potential of the Concept of Indirect Discrimination. Brussels: European Commission.

Toggenburg, G. (2002). The Race Directive: A New Dimension in the Fight against Ethnic Discrimination in Europe. 1 European Yearbook of Minority Issues 231-244.

Toms, N. (2008). Remedies and Sanctions for Unlawful Discrimination. Presentation at the Seminar The Fight Against Discrimination in the Daily Practice, Academy of European Law, Trier.

Townshend-Smith, R. (2000). Recent case. Seymour-Smith - the closing stages. Case C-167/97. R v Secretary of State for Employment ex parte Seymour-Smith and Perez. 29 Industrial Law Journal 296-304.

Tridimas, T. (1999). The General Principles of EC Law. Oxford: Oxford University Press.

Tyson, A. (2001). The Negotiation of the European Community Directive on Racial Discrimination. 3 European Journal of Migration and Law 199-229.
Tyson, A. (2004). The Negotiation of the European Community Directive on Racial Discrimination. In J. Niessen & I. Chopin (Eds.), The Development of Legal Instruments to Combat Racism in a Diverse Europe (111-130). The Hague: Martinus Nijhoff.
Valcke, C. (2004). Comparative Law as Comparative Jurisprudence – The Comparability of Legal Systems. 52 The American Journal of Comparative Law 713-740.
Van Boom, W., & Loos, M. (2007). Effective Enforcement of Consumer Law in Europe. Private, Public and Collective Mechanisms. In W. Van Boom & M. Loos (Eds.), Collective Enforcement of Consumer Law. Securing Compliance in Europe through Private Group Action and Public Authority Intervention (231-254). Groningen: Europa Law Publishing.
Vande Lanotte, J., & Haeck, Y. (Eds.). (2005). Handboek EVRM: Deel I: Algemene beginselen, Antwerpen: Intersentia.
Van Der Heijden, E.M. (2001). Punitive damages en de calculerende schadeveroorzaker. 2001 (Issue 36) NJB 1749-1756.
Van Gerven, W. (2000). Of Rights, Remedies and Procedures. 37 Common Market Law Review 501-536.
Vanheule, D. (2003). De Antidiscriminatiewet en de Antiracismewet. In Vrijheid en gelijkheid. De horizontale werking van het gelijkheidsbeginsel en de nieuwe antidiscriminatiewet (389-409). Antwerp: MAKLU.
Varju, M. (2005). The Right to Effective Judicial Protection in Community Law: Intervention before Community Courts. Acta Juridica Hungarica 51-72.
Vékás, L. (2006). Egyenlő bánásmód a polgári jogi jogviszonyokban? 61 Jogtudományi Közlöny 355-364.
Velaers, J. (2003). De horizontale werking van het discriminatieverbod in de antidiscriminatiewet. Enkele constitutionele beschouwingen. In Vrijheid en gelijkheid. De horizontale werking van het gelijkheidsbeginsel en de nieuwe antidiscriminatiewet (287-326). Antwerp: MAKLU 2003, p. 287-326.
Veldman, A. (1999). Preferential Treatment in European Community law: Current Legal Developments and the Impact on National Practices. In T. Loenen & P. Rodrigues (Eds.), Non-Discrimination Law: Comparative Perspectives (279-291). The Hague/London/Boston: Kluwer Law International.
Veldman, A. (2001). Ontslagrecht: de rol van opzeg- en discriminatieverboden bij beëindiging van de arbeidsovereenkomst. 16 Sociaal Recht 325-344.
Vick, D. (2001). Disparate Effects and Objective Justification in Sex Discrimination Law. 5 International Journal of Discrimination and the Law 3-38.
Vrielink, J. (2003a). De Belgische antidiscriminatiewet: een kritische bespreking. In Vrijheid en gelijkheid. De horizontale werking van het gelijkheidsbeginsel en de nieuwe antidiscriminatiewet (189-245). Antwerp: MAKLU 2003, p. 189-245.
Vrielink, J. (2003b). Discriminatie: van inflatie naar complicatie? Enkele bedenkingen bij R. Holtmaat's pleidooi voor het maken van onderscheid tussen discriminatie en ongelijke behandeling. 2003 (Issue 43) NJB 2252-2254.

Waaldijk, K., & Bonini-Baraldi, M. (Eds.). (2004). Combating Sexual Orientation Discrimination in Employment: Legislation in Fifteen EU Member States. Report of the European Group of Experts on Combating Sexual Orientation Discrimination about the implementation up to April 2004 of Directive 2000/78/EC establishing a general framework for equal treatment in employment and occupation. Leiden: University of Leiden.

Waaldijk, K., & Hendriks, A.C. (2000). Hetero- of homoseksuele gerichtheid en burgerlijke staat. In T. Loenen (Ed.), Gelijke behandeling: oordelen en commentaar 1999 (45-59). Deventer: Kluwer 2000.

Waddington, L. (2000). Article 13 EC: Setting Priorities in the Proposal for a Horizontal Employment Directive. 29 Industrial Law Journal 176-181.

Waddington, L. (2003). The New Equality Directives: Mixed Blessings. In C. Costello & E. Barry (Eds.), Equality in Diversity. The New Equality Directives (39-54). Dublin: ICEL.

Waddington, L. (2007). Protection for Family and Friends: Addressing Discrimination by Association. 2007 (Issue 5) European Anti-Discrimination Law Review 13-21.

Waddington, L., & Bell, M. (2001). More Equal than Others: Distinguishing European Union Directives. 38 Common Market Law Review 587-611.

Watson, P. (1995). Equality of Treatment: A Variable Concept? 36 International Law Journal 33-48.

Watson, G.D. (2001). Class Actions: The Canadian Experience. 11 Duke Journal of International and Comparative Law 269-287.

Weller, M., & Morawa, A.H.E. (Eds). (2004). Mechanisms for the Implementation of Minority Rights. Strasbourg: Council of Europe.

Weller, M. (Ed.). (2005). A Commentary for the European Framework Convention for the Protection of National Minorities. Oxford: Oxford University Press.

Weller, M. (2007). Universal Minority Rights. A Commentary on the Jurisprudence of International Courts and Treaty Bodies. Oxford: Oxford University Press.

Weinstein, J.B. (2001). Compensating Large Numbers of People for Inflicted Harms. 11 Duke Journal of Comparative and International Law 165-177.

Whittle, R. (2002). The Framework Directive for Equal Treatment in Employment and Occupation: An Analysis from a Disability Rights Perspective. 27 European Law Review 303-326.

Wintermute, W. (2000). From 'Sex' to 'Racial or Ethnic Origin': What Adjustments to EC Anti-Discrimination Law are Required? Paper delivered to the Conference on Discrimination and affirmative action on the labour market – legal perspectives, 6-7 November 2000. Brussels.

Wolcher, L.E. (2001). The Paradox of Remedies. In B. Leiser & T. Campbell (Eds.), Human Rights in Philosophy and Practice (549-586). Aldershot: Ashgate Dartmouth.

Woltjer, A.T. (2002). Ras en nationaliteit. In T. Loenen (Ed.) Gelijke behandeling: oordelen en commentaar 2001 (18-25). The Hague: Kluwer.

Yourow, H.C. (1996). The Margin of Appreciation Doctrine in the Dynamics of the European Court of Human Rights Jurisprudence. The Hague/Boston/London: Kluwer Law International.

Zakrzewski, R. (2005). Remedies Reclassified. Oxford: Oxford University Press.
Zlinszky, J. (2003). Gondolatok és aggályok egy koncepció kapcsán. 7 Fundamentum 131-136.
Zoontjens, P.J.J. (2006). De uitzondering inzake 'eenzijdig overheidshandelen'. In M.L.M. Hertogh & P.J.J. Zoontjens (Eds.), Gelijke behandeling: principes en praktijken. Evaluatieonderzoek Algemene wet gelijke behandeling (117-174). Nijmegen: Wolf Legal Publishers.
Zoontjens, P.J.J. (2007). Moet de CGB al het eenzijdige overheidshandelen toetsen? In J.H. Gerards, B.P. Vermeulen & P.J.J. Zoontjens (Eds.), Gelijke behandeling: oordelen en commentaar 2006 (291-307). Nijmegen: Wolf Legal Publishers.
Zwamborn, M. (2002). Anti-discrimination Legislation in EU Member States. A Comparison of National Anti-discrimination legislation on the grounds of racial or ethnic origin, religion or belief with the Council Directives: The Netherlands. Vienna: EUMC.
Zweigert, K., & Kötz, H. (1998). Introduction to Comparative Law. Oxford: Oxford University Press.

Selected Literature on the Countries under Review

Belgium

Alen, A. (Ed.). (1992). Treatise on Belgian Constitutional Law. Deventer/ Boston:Kluwer Law and Taxation Publishers.
Alen, A. (1995). Handboek van het Belgisch staatsrecht. Mechelen: Kluwer Rechtswetenschappen.
Bayart, C., & Bosmans, I. (2008). De federale antidiscriminatiewetten en arbeidsbetrekkingen in de private sector: algemeen overzicht. In C. Bayart, S. Sottiaux & S. Van Drooghenbroeck (Eds.), De nieuwe federale antidiscriminatie-wetten (537-596). Bruges: Die Keure.
Bernauw, K. (2004). De Wet Bestrijding Discriminatie en verzekeringen. In M. De Vos & E. Brems (Eds.), De Wet Bestrijding Discriminatie in de praktijk (277-308). Antwerpen: Intersentia.
Borghs, P. (2003). De ADW. Handleiding bij de wet ter bestrijding van discriminatie. Antwerpen: Garant.
Bosse, C. (2003). Bewijslastverdeling in het Nederlands en Belgisch arbeidsrecht. The Hague: Kluwer.
Burri, S.D., & Dorssemont, F. (2005). The Transposition of the Race Directive (2000/43/EC) and the Framework Directive on Equal Treatment in Employment (2000/78/EC) into Dutch and Belgian Law. 21 The International Journal of Comparative Labour Law and Industrial Relations 537-570.
Closset-Marchal, G., & Van Drooghenbroeck, S. (2008). L'Action en Cessation an Matière de Discriminations. In C. Bayart, S. Sottiaux & S. Van Drooghenbroeck (Eds.), De nieuwe federale antidiscriminatiewetten (361-413). Bruges: Die Keure.
Cuypers, D. (2003). There Will Never Be Equality in the Servant's Hall. Gelijkheid in het arbeidsrecht. In Vrijheid en gelijkheid. De horizontale werking van het gelijkheidsbeginsel en de nieuwe Antidiscriminatiewet (445-488). Antwerp: MAKLU.

De Boeck, A. (2003). Doorwerking van het gelijkheidsbeginsel in het contractenrecht. In Vrijheid en gelijkheid. De horizontale werking van het gelijkheidsbeginsel en de nieuwe Antidiscriminatiewet (413-444). Antwerp: MAKLU.

De Prins, D. (2007). Geen praktijktest, geen discriminatiebescherming. KifKif.

De Prins, D., Sottiaux, S., & Vrielink, J. (2003a). De Antidiscriminatiewet: Een artikelsgewijze analyse (Deel 1). Nieuw Juridisch Weekblad 258-275.

De Prins, D., Sottiaux, S., & Vrielink, J. (2003b). De Antidiscriminatiewet: Een artikelsgewijze analyse (Deel 2). Nieuw Juridisch Weekblad 294-302.

De Prins, D., Sottiaux, S., & Vrielink, J. (2005). Handboek discriminatierecht. Deventer: Kluwer.

De Schutter, O. (2004). Report on Measures to Combat Discrimination. Directives 2000/43/EC and 2000/78/EC. Country Report: Belgium. Brussels: European Commission.

De Schutter, O. (2007). Report on Measures to Combat Discrimination. Directives 2000/43/EC and 2000/78/EC. Country Report: Belgium. Brussels: European Commission.

De Vos, M. (2004). De bouwstenen van het discriminatierecht in de arbeidsverhoudingen na de wet bestrijding discriminatie. In M. De Vos & E. Brems (Eds.), De Wet Bestrijding Discriminatie in de praktijk (69-106). Antwerp: Intersentia.

Foubert, P. (2004). Basisconcepten van de wet bestrijding discriminatie en haar verhouding tot andere antidiscriminatieregels. In M. De Vos & E. Brems (Eds.), De Wet Bestrijding Discriminatie in de praktijk (1-35). Antwerp: Intersentia.

Kusters, J. (2003). Discriminatie ten opzichte van allochtonen op de private huurmarkt. In Vrijheid en gelijkheid. De horizontale werking van het gelijkheidsbeginsel en de nieuwe antidiscriminatiewet (541-572). Antwerp: MAKLU.

Maes, G. (2003). De afdwingbaarheid van sociale grondrechten. Bescherming van (aspecten van) sociale (grond)echten middels de toepassing van het gelijkheid- en non-discriminatiebeginsel. Antwerp: Intersentia.

Rorive, I., & Van der Plancke, V. (2008). Quels dispositions pour prouver la discrimination? In C. Bayart, S. Sottiaux & S. Van Drooghenbroeck, De nieuwe federale antidiscriminatiewetten (415-461). Bruges: Die Keure.

Taelman, P. (2004a). Het handhavingsrecht van de Wet Bestrijding Discriminatie. In M. De Vos & E. Brems (Eds.), De Wet Bestrijding Discriminatie in de praktijk (203-260). Antwerpen: Intersentia.

Taelman, P. (2004b). De stakingsvordering in de antidiscriminatiewet. Een maat voor niets? 2004 (Issue 8) Nieuw Juridisch Weekblad 506-519.

Thiery, Y. (2007). Gelijkheid, dienstverlening en verzekering: een herontdekkingstocht. 2007 (Issue 8) Tijdschrift voor Belgisch Handelsrecht 747-772.

Vanheule, D. (2003). De Antidiscriminatiewet en de Antiracismewet. In Vrijheid en gelijkheid. De horizontale werking van het gelijkheidsbeginsel en de nieuwe antidiscriminatiewet (389-409). Antwerp: MAKLU.

Velaers, J. (2003). De horizontale werking van het discriminatieverbod in de antidiscriminatiewet. Enkele constitutionele beschouwingen. In Vrijheid en gelijkheid. De horizontale werking van het gelijkheidsbeginsel en de nieuwe antidiscriminatiewet (287-326). Antwerp: MAKLU.

Vrielink, J. (2003a). De Belgische antidiscriminatiewet: een kritische bespreking. In Vrijheid en gelijkheid. De horizontale werking van het gelijkheidsbeginsel en de nieuwe antidiscriminatiewet (189-245). Antwerp: MAKLU.

Vrielink, J. (2003b). Discriminatie: van inflatie naar complicatie? Enkele bedenkingen bij R. Holtmaat's pleidooi voor het maken van onderscheid tussen discriminatie en ongelijke behandeling. 2003 (Issue 43) NJB 2252-2254.

Estonia

Ernits, M. (2003). Õiguskantsler. 2003 (Issue 1) Juridica 14-17.

Jõks, A. (2007). The Principle of Equal Treatment in Jurisdiction and Proceedings (Chancellor of Justice). Retrieved from http://www.oiguskantsler.ee/index.php?pageID=176.

Kerikmäe, T. (1997). European Convention on Nationality and States' Competence: The Issue of Human Rights. 2 Juridica International 25-29.

Kirch, A. (1997). The Integration of Non-Estonians into Estonian Society: History, Problems and Trends. Tallinn: Estonian Academy Publishers.

Lauristin, M., & Heidmets, M. (2002). The Challenge of the Russian Minority. Emerging Multicultural Democracy in Estonia. Tartu: Tartu University Press.

Mälksoo, L. (2005). Report on the Situation of Fundamental Rights in Estonia in 2005. EU Network of Independent Experts on Fundamental Rights. Brussels: European Commission.

Muda, M. (2002). Regulation of Gender Equality as a Fundamental Right in Estonia. 7 Juridica International 106-116.

Pettai, V. (2001). Estonia and Latvia: International Influences on Citizenship and Minority Integration. In J. Zielonka & A. Pravda (Eds.), Democratic Consolidation in Eastern Europe (257-280). Oxford: Oxford University Press.

Poleshchuk, V. (2005). Report on Measures to Combat Discrimination. Directives 2000/43/EC and 2000/78/EC. Country Report: Estonia. Brussels: European Commission.

Poleshchuk, V. (2007). Report on Measures to Combat Discrimination. Directives 2000/43/EC and 2000/78/EC. Country Report: Estonia. Brussels: European Commission.

Poleshchuk, V., & Helemäe, J. (2006). Estonia – In Quest of Minority Protection. In S. Spiliopoulou Åkermark (Ed.), International Obligations and National Debates: Minorities around the Baltic Sea (109-170). Mariehamm: The Åland Islands Peace Institute.

Poleshchuk, V., & Tsilevich, B. (2003). The Baltic States before EU Accession: Recent Developments in Minority Protection. 2 European Yearbook of Minority Issues 283-305.

Tavits, G. (2004). Muudatused töölepinguliste suhete õiguslikus reguleerimises: kaitse otsingul Euroopa Liidu abiga. 2004 (Issue 8) Juridica 550-559.

Thiele, C. (1999). The Criterion of Citizenship for Minorities: The Example of Estonia. 1999 (Issue 5) ECMI Working Paper.

Hungary

Bischof, K., & Samaluk, B. (2007). Report on the Communication Strategies for the Hungarian Equal Treatment Authority. Vienna: Ludwig Boltzmann Institute of Human Rights.

Bitskey, B., & Gyulavári, T. (2004). Az anti-diszkriminációs szabályozás reformja. 15 Acta Humana 13-40.

Bitskey, B. & Gyulavári, T. (2005). The Hungarian Equal Treatment Act: a new Member State's perspective. (In manuscript).

Bodrogi, B., & Danka, A. (2006). Litigating Discrimination in Access to Employment in Hungary. 2006 (Issue 1) Roma Rights Quarterly.

Bodrogi, B. (2007). Legal Standing – The Practical Experience of a Hungarian Organisation. 2007 (Issue 5) European Anti-Discrimination Law Review 23-29.

Demeter, J. (2006). Az egyenlő bánásmódról és az esélyegyenlőség előmozdításáról szóló törvény – az Egyenlő Bánásmód Hatóság által lefolytatott eljárások tükrében. 17 Acta Humana 49-66.

Farkas, L. (2003). Will the Groom Adopt the Bride's Unwanted Child? The Race Equality Directive. Hungary and its Roma. Roma Rights Quarterly 2003-1/2.

Farkas, L. (2004a). The Monkey That Does Not See. Roma Rights Quarterly 2004-2.

Farkas, L. (2004b). Education, Education and More Education. Eumap. Retrieved from http://www.eumap.org/journal/features/2004/minority_education/edmore/.

Farkas, L. (2005). A miskolci deszegregációs per első felvonása. 9 Fundamentum 157-164.

Farkas, L. (2006). A Good Way to Equality: Roma seeking Judicial Protection against Discrimination in Europe. 2006 (Issue 3) European Anti-Discrimination Law Review 21-30.

Farkas, L., & Kárpáti, J. (2004). Gyerekjáték összerakni? A magyar antidiszkriminációs testület modellje. TÁRKI: Budapest.

Farkas, L., & Kádár, A. (2005). Report on Measures to Combat Discrimination. Directives 2000/43/EC and 2000/78/EC. Country Report, Hungary. Brussels: European Commission.

Farkas, L., Kádár, A., &. Kárpáti, J. (2003). Néhány megjegyzés az egyenlő bánásmódról szóló törvény koncepciójához. 7 Fundamentum 121-130.

Farkas, L., Kádár, A., & Kárpáti, J. (2006). Az egyenlő bánásmódról és az esélyegyenlőség előmozdításáról szóló 2003. évi CXXV. törvény magyarázata. Budapest: Másság Alapítvány.

Fitsum, A. (2000a). A tesztelés mint bizonyítási módszer a bírósági eljárásban. 4 Fundamentum 74-79.

Fitsum, A. (2000b). Testing to Prove Racial Discrimination: Methodology and Application in Hungary. 2000 (Issue 3) Roma Rights Quarterly.

Győrfi, T. (1996). A diszkrimináció tilalma: egy különleges státuszú jog. 51 Jogtudományi Közlöny 275-293.

Gyulavári, T. (2007). Három évvel az antidiszkriminációs szabályozás reformja után. 2007 (Issue 3) Esély 29-61.

Halmai, G. (Ed.). (1998). A hátrányos megkülönböztetés tilalmától a pozitív diszkriminációig. A jog lehetőségei és korlátai. Budapest: AduPrint-INDOK.

Hodász, M., & Scullion, G. (2007). Assessment Report into the Carrying out of the Hungarian Equal Treatment Authority's Statutory Mandate. Vienna: Ludwig Boltzmann Institute of Human Rights.

Iványi, K. (Ed.). (2004). Jogvédelem a gyakorlatban. Budapest: NEKI. Retrieved from http://www.neki.hu/kiadvanyok/jogvedelem_a_gyakorlatban.htm.

Iványi, K. (Ed.). (2005). Változások küszöbén. Új lehetőségek a jogvédelemben az esélyegyenlőségi törvény hatályba lépésével. Budapest: NEKI. Retrieved from http://www.neki.hu/kiadvanyok/valtozasok.htm.

Iványi, K., & Muhi, E. (2004). A tesztelés hazai és nemzetközi gyakorlata, Budapest: NEKI. Retrieved from http://www.neki.hu/kiadvanyok/teszteles/tartalomjegyzek.htm.

Kádár, A. (2001). A magyar diszkrimináció-ellenes jogi szabályozás a faji megkülönböztetés tilalmáról szóló EU-irányelv tükrében. Presentation, 6-7 December 2001, Budapest.

Kádár, A. (2006). A bizonyítási teher megosztásának kérdései. 10 Fundamentum 115-124.

Kádár, A. (2007). Report on Measures to Combat Discrimination. Directives 2000/43/EC and 2000/78/EC. Country Report: Hungary. Brussels: European Commission.

Kaltenbach, J. (2001). From Paper to Practice in Hungary: The Protection and Involvement of Minorities in Governance. In A.-M. Biro & P. Kovacs (Eds.), Diversity in Action: Local Public Management of Multi-Ethnic Communities in Central and Eastern Europe (171-203). Budapest: LGI/OSI.

Kaltenbach, J. et al. (2007). Antidiszkriminációs kézikönyv. Budapest: Clone Design.

Kárpáti, J. (2005). Az utolsó próbatétel. Ítélet a Háttér Társaság kontra Károli Egyetem ügyben. 9 Fundamentum 105-108.

Kárpáti, J. (2006). A közérdekű igényérvényesítés egyes kérdései. (Training Material).

Kollonay-Lehoczky, Cs. (2006). Előnyben részesítés. 10 Fundamentum 71-78.

Kovács, K. (2006). Az igazságos kvóta. 10 Fundamentum 5-16.

Krizsán, A. (2000). The Hungarian Minority Protection System: A Flexible Approach to the Adjudication of Ethnic Claims. 26 Journal of Ethnic and Migration Studies 247-262.

Krizsán, A. (2001). Diszkiminráció-tilalom a kisebbségi biztos gyakorlatában. 5 Fundamentum 24-39.

Majtényi, B. (2001). A magyarországi kisebbbségi önkormányzati rendszer elvei és működése. 5 Fundamentum. 34-42.

Majtényi, B. (2005). Mi lesz veled „bezzeggyerek"? Változóban a kisebbségi jogi szabályozás. 9 Fundamentum 109-120.

Majtényi, B., & Pap, A.L. (2006). Végtelen történet. A kisebbségi hovatartozásról. 10 Fundamentum 93-106.

Schindlauer, D., & Liegl, B. (2007). Consolidated Results of the Twinning Light Project HU2004/IB/SO01-TL "Enforcement of Equal Opportunity Policies and the Effective Implementation of the Anti-discrimination Law". Vienna: Ludwig Boltzmann Institute for Human Rights.

Szajbély, K. (2005a). A magyar antidiszkriminációs szabályozás a 2000/43/EK Irányelv fényében. In Acta Universitatis Szegediensis Acta Juridica et Politica, Publ. Doct. Jur. Tomus 5, Fasc 12, Szeged. 309-346.

Szajbély, K. (2005b). A magyar antidiszkriminációs szabályozás fogalomrendszere. Romániai Magyar Jogtudományi Közlöny 43-52.

Szajbély, K. (2005c). A magyar anti-diszkriminációs szabályozás szankciórendszere a közösségi követelmények fényében. 9 Európai Tükör 89-98.

Szente, Z. (2006). A pozitív megkülönböztetés problémái. 10 Fundamentum 17-44.

Tilk, P. (2005). Az egyenlőséghez való jog egyes garanciális szabályai Magyarországon. 16 Acta Humana 20-45.

Vékás, L. (2006). Egyenlő bánásmód a polgári jogi jogviszonyokban? 61 Jogtudományi Közlöny 355-364.

Zlinszky, J. (2003). Gondolatok és aggályok egy koncepció kapcsán. 7 Fundamentum 131-136.

The Netherlands

Asser, W.D.H. (1998). Rechtspraakoverzicht. Bewijslastverdeling. Deventer: Gouda Quint.

Asscher-Vonk, I.P., & Groenendijk, C.A. (Eds.). (1999). Gelijke behandeling: Regels en realiteit. Een juridische en rechtssociologische analyse van de Gelijkebehandelingswetgeving. The Hague: SDU Publishers.

Asscher-Vonk, I.P., & Hendriks, A.C. (2005). Gelijke behandeling en onderscheid bij de arbeid. Deventer: Kluwer.

Blom, J. (1995). The Dutch Equal Treatment Commission. 24 Industrial Law Journal 84-89.

Boog, I., & Hamidi, L. (2006). ENAR Shadow Report, Racism in the Netherlands. Brussels: ENAR.

Bosse, C. (2003). Bewijslastverdeling in het Nederlands en Belgisch arbeidsrecht. The Hague: Kluwer.

Burri, S.D. & Dorssemont, F. (2005). The Transposition of the Race Directive (2000/43/EC) and the Framework Directive on Equal Treatment in Employment (2000/78/EC) into Dutch and Belgian Law. 21 The International Journal of Comparative Labour Law and Industrial Relations 537-570.

Castermans, A.G. (2009). Rechtsvorderingen bij discriminatie. In J.H. Gerards & P.J.J. Zoontjens (Eds.), Gelijke behandeling: oordelen en commentaar 2008 (241-262). Nijmegen: Wolf Legal Publisher.

Davidović, M., & Van Walsum, S.K. (2009). Ras en nationaliteit. In J.H. Gerards & P.J.J. Zoontjens (Eds.), Gelijke behandeling: oordelen en commentaar 2008 (29-48). Nijmegen: Wolf Legal Publisher.

De Fey, C.C., Kellermann A., & Nieuwbroer, J.W. (Eds.). (2004). Met recht discriminatie bestrijden. The Hague: Boom Juridische Uitgevers.

Dierx, J., & Siegers, J. (1990). Indirecte discriminatie van deeltijdwerkers. 1990 (Issue 15) NJB 554-560.

Dierx, J.R., & Rodrigues, P.R. (2003). The Dutch Equal Treatment Act in Theory and Practice. 2003 (Issue 1) Roma Rights Quarterly.

Gerards, J.H. (2003). Het toetsingsmodel van de Commissie Gelijke Behandeling voor indirect onderscheid. In D.J.B. De Wolff. (Eds.), Gelijke behandeling: oordelen en commentaar 2002 (77-95). Deventer: Kluwer.

Gerards, J.H. (2006). Implementation of the Article 13 Directives in Dutch Equal Treatment Legislation. 13 Maastricht Journal of European and Comparative Law 291-308.

Gerards, J.H. (2007). Doorbreking gesloten systeem Awgb. In J.H. Gerards & C. Waaldijk (Eds.), Gelijke behandeling: oordelen en commentaar 2006 (316-320). Nijmegen: Wolf Legal Publishers.

Gerards, J.H., & Heringa, A.W. (2003). Wetgeving gelijke behandeling. Deventer: Kluwer.

Gerards, J.H., & Zoontjens, P.J.J. (2009). Inleiding – algemene ontwikkelingen in the gelijkebehandelingsrecht. In J.H. Gerards & P.J.J. Zoontjens (Eds.), Gelijke behandeling: oordelen en commentaar 2008 (5-18). Nijmegen: Wolf Legal Publisher.

Gijzen, M. (2004). Report on Measures to Combat Discrimination. Directives 2000/43/EC and 2000/78 EC. Country Report: The Netherlands. Brussels: European Commission.

Hamidi, L. (2004). ENAR Shadow Report: The Netherlands. Brussels: ENAR.

Havinga, T. (2007). Werkt de Algemeen wet gelijke behandeling? Twee Evaluatieonderzoeken besproken. In J.H. Gerards, B.P. Vermeulen & P.J.J. Zoontjens (Eds.), Gelijke behandeling: oordelen en commentaar 2006 (243-261). Nijmegen: Wolf Legal Publishers.

Hendriks, A. (2005). Mogelijkheid instelling van nationaal mensenrechteninstituut krijgt concrete vormen. 30 NJCM-Bulletin 1157-1165.

Heringa, A.W. (1991). De AWGB: Is iets beter dan niets of is het zelfs iets al te veel? In A. W. Heringa, A. K. Koekkoek & L. Mulder (Eds.), Gelijk behandelen (1-28). Zwolle: W.E.J. Tjeenk Willink.

Hertogh, M.L.M., & Zoontjens, P.J.J. (Eds.). (2006). Gelijke behandeling: principes en praktijken Evaluatieonderzoek Algemene wet gelijke behandeling. Nijmegen: Wolf Legal Publishers.

Hidma, T.R., & Rutgers, G.R. (2004). Bewijs. The Hague: Kluwer.

Holtmaat, R. (2003). Stop de inflatie van het discriminatiebegrip! Een pleidooi voor het maken van onderscheid tussen discriminatie en ongelijke behandeling. 2003 (Issue 25) NJB 1266-1276.

Holtmaat, R. (2006b). Discriminatie of onderscheid: the kleine verschil met grote gevolgen of the grote verschil met kleine gevolgen? In M.L.M. Hertogh & P.J.J. Zoontjens (Eds.), Gelijke behandeling: principes en praktijken. Evaluatieonderzoek Algemene wet gelijke behandeling (3-113). Nijmegen: Wolf Legal Publishers.

Holtmaat, R. (2007). Report on Measures to Combat Discrimination. Directives 2000/43/EC and 2000/78/EC. Country Report: Belgium. Brussels: European Commission.

Jaspers, A.P.C.M. (2001). Zetten we de tanden in de handhaving van de gelijke behandelingsnorm? In J.E. Goldschmidt, A.W. Heringa & L. Van Vliet (Eds.),

De zij-kant van het gelijk. Het recht als instrument ter verbetering van de kansen op gelijke posities voor vrouwen (139-156). Zwolle: W.E.J. Tjeenk Willink.

Jongbloed, A.W. (2002). Collectief actierecht, groepsacties en algemeen belangacties. In A.W. Jongbloed (Ed.), Samen sterk: over het optreden in rechte door groeperingen (PPP). The Hague: Boom Juridische Uitgevers.

Leenders, M.A.J. (1997). Bewijsrecht en discriminatie bij de arbeid. Zwolle: W.E.J. Tjeenk Willink

Loth, M. (2004). Synergie of rolvervanging? In R. Holtmaat (Ed.), Gelijkheid en (andere) grondrechten (221-237). Deventer: Kluwer.

Pel, M. (2003). Mediation en gelijke behandeling in de arbeidsrelatie – dejuridisering en dequerulering? In D.J.B. De Wolff (Ed.), Gelijke behandeling: oordelen en commentaar 2002 (109-119). The Hague: Kluwer.

Rodrigues, P.R. (2002). Collectieve acties als structureel instrument tegen discriminatie. In A.W. Jongbloed (Ed.), Samen sterk: over het optreden in rechte door groeperingen (91-104). The Hague: Boom Juridische Uitgevers.

Rodrigues, P.R. (2004). Ras en nationaliteit. In S.D. Burri (Ed.), Gelijke behandeling: oordelen en commentaar 2003 (17-32). Nijmegen: Wolf Legal Publishers.

Rodrigues, P.R., & Van Walsum, S. (2008). Ras en nationaliteit. In J.H. Gerards (Ed.), Gelijke behandeling: oordelen en commentaar 2007 (21-57). Nijmegen: Wolf Legal Publishers.

Simon, P. (2004). Comparative Study on the Collection of Data to Measure the Extent and Impact of Discrimination within the United States, Canada, Australia, Great-Britain and the Netherlands. Medis Project. Measurement of Discrimination. INED – Economie & Humanisme.

Van Der Heijden, E.M. (2001). Punitive damages en de calculerende schadeveroorzaker. 2001 (Issue36) NJB 1749-1756.

Veldman, A. (2001). Ontslagrecht: de rol van opzeg- en discriminatieverboden bij beëindiging van de arbeidsovereenkomst. Sociaal Recht 325-344.

Waaldijk, K., & Hendriks, A.C. (2000). Hetero- of homoseksuele gerichtheid en burgerlijke staat. In T. Loenen (Ed.), Gelijke behandeling: oordelen en commentaar 1999 (45-59). Deventer: Kluwer 2000.

Woltjer, A.T. (2002). Ras en nationaliteit. In T. Loenen (Ed.) Gelijke behandeling: oordelen en commentaar 2001 (18-25). The Hague: Kluwer.

Zoontjens, P.J.J. (2006). De uitzondering inzake 'eenzijdig overheidshandelen'. In M.L.M. Hertogh & P.J.J. Zoontjens (Eds.), Gelijke behandeling: principes en praktijken. Evaluatieonderzoek Algemene wet gelijke behandeling (117-174). Nijmegen: Wolf Legal Publishers.

Zoontjens, P.J.J. (2007). Moet de CGB al het eenzijdige overheidshandelen toetsen? In J.H. Gerards, B.P. Vermeulen & P.J.J. Zoontjens (Eds.), Gelijke behandeling: oordelen en commentaar 2006 (291-307). Nijmegen: Wolf Legal Publishers.

Zwamborn, M. (2002). Anti-discrimination Legislation in EU Member States. A Comparison of National Anti-discrimination legislation on the grounds of racial or ethnic origin, religion or belief with the Council Directives: The Netherlands. Vienna: EUMC.

Selected European and International Documents

European and International Legal Texts

Convention for the Protection of Individuals with regard to Automatic Processing of Personal Data, 1981.

Convention on the Rights of Persons with Disabilities and its Optional Protocol, adopted on 13 December 2006 and entered into force on 3 May 2008.

Council Directive 2000/43/EC of 29 June 2000 implementing the principle of equal treatment between persons irrespective of racial or ethnic origin.

Council Directive 2000/778/EC of 27 November 2000 establishing a general framework for equal treatment in employment and occupation.

Council Directive 2001/23/EC of 12 March 2001 on the approximation of the laws of the Member States relating to the safeguarding of employees' rights in the event of transfers of undertakings, businesses or parts of undertakings or businesses.

Council Directive 2004/113/EC of 13 December 2004 implementing the principle of equal treatment between men and women in the access to and supply of goods and services.

Council Directive 76/207/EEC of 9 February 1976 on the implementation of the principle of equal treatment for men and women as regards access to employment, vocational training and promotion, and working conditions.

Council Directive 79/7/EEC of 19 December 1978 on the progressive implementation of the principle of equal treatment for men and women in matters of social security; Council Directive 91/533/EEC of 14 October 1991 on an employer's obligation to inform employees of the conditions applicable to the contract or employment relationship.

Council Directive 92/85/EEC of 19 October 1992 on the introduction of measures to encourage improvements in the safety and health at work of pregnant workers and workers who have recently given birth or are breastfeeding (tenth individual Directive within the meaning of Article 16 (1) of Directive 89/381/EEC).

Council Directive 97/80/EC of 15 December 1997 on the burden of proof in cases of discrimination based on sex.

Council Directive 98/49/EC of 29 June 1998 on safeguarding the supplementary pension rights of employed and self-employed persons moving within the Community.

Council Framework Decision 2008/913/JHA of 28 November 2008 on combating certain forms and expressions of racism and xenophobia by means of criminal law.

Directive 2002/21/EC of the European Parliament and of the Council of 7 March 2002 on a common regulatory framework for electronic communications networks and services (Framework Directive).

Directive 2002/73/EC of the European Parliament and of the Council of 23 September 2002 amending Council Directive 76/207/EEC on the implementation of the principle of equal treatment for men and women as regards access to employment, vocational training and promotion, and working conditions.

Directive 2004/113/EC of 13 December 2004 implementing the principle of equal treatment between men and women in the access to and supply of goods and services.

Directive 2006/54/EC of the European Parliament and of the Council of 5 July 2006 on the implementation of the principle of equal opportunities and equal treatment of men and women in matters of employment and occupation (the 'Recast Directive').

European Charter for Regional or Minority Languages, 5 November 1992.

European Parliament and Council Directive 95/46/EC of 24 October 1995 on the protection of individuals with regard to the processing of processing of personal data and on the free movement of such data.

Framework Convention for the Protection of National Minorities, 1 February 1995.

European and International Reports, Recommendations, Travaux Préparatoires

Advisory Committee on the Framework Convention for the Protection of National Minorities, Outline for reports to be submitted pursuant to Article 25 paragraph 1 of the Framework Convention for the protection of national minorities, 30 September 1998.

Amended proposal for a Council Directive implementing the principle of equal treatment between persons irrespective of racial or ethnic origin, COM(2000) 328 final – 1999/0253 (CNS), 31 May 2000.

Amnesty International's recommendations for effective protection and promotion of human rights, National Human Rights Institutions Forum 2001.

Assessing the Effectiveness of National Human Rights Institutions, Office of the United Nations High Commissioner for Human Rights 2005.

Capacity Building of Civil Society dealing with Anti-Discrimination. A Training Manual, European Commission 2005.

Commission on Human Rights resolution, E/CN.4/RES/1992/54, 3 March 1992.

Commission staff working document – Annex to the Communication for the Commission to the European Parliament, the Council, the European Economic and Social Committee and the Committee of the Regions – European electronic communications regulation and markets 2006 (12th Report) COM(2007) 155 final, SEC/2007/0403, 29 June 2006.

Communication from the Commission to the Council and the European Parliament – The application of Directive 2000/43/EC of 29 June 2000 implementing the principle of equal treatment between persons irrespective of racial or ethnic origin, COM(2006) 643 final, 30 October 2006.

Communication from the Commission to the European Parliament and the Council – Enhancing the patent system in Europe, COM(2007) 165 final, 3 April 2007.

Communication from the Commission to the European Parliament and the Council – Report on the implementation, functioning and effectiveness of the ".eu" TLD, COM(2007) 385 final, 6 July 2007.

Consideration of Report Submitted by States Parties under Article 9 of the Convention, Concluding Observations of the Committee on the Elimination of Racial Discrimination, CERD/C/EST/CO/7, 22 August 2006.

Consolidated guidelines for state reports, Human Rights Committee, CCPR/66/GUI/Rev.2, 26 February 2001.

Copenhagen Declaration on Social Development and Programme of Action of the world Summit for Social Development, A/CONF.166/9, 19 April 1995.

Durban Declaration and Programme of Action, Durban, 31 August – 8 September 2001.

ECOSOC Res. 2/9, 21 June 1946.

ECOSOC Res. 772 B (XXX), 25 July 1960.

ECOSOC Res. 888 F (XXXIV), 24 July 1962.

ECRI General Policy Recommendation No. 1: Combating Racism, Xenophobia, Anti-Semitism and Intolerance, CRI (96) 43 rev., 4 October 1996.

ECRI General Policy Recommendation No. 2: Establishment of Specialised Bodies to Combat Racism, Xenophobia, Anti-Semitism and Intolerance at National Level, CRI(97) 36, 13 June 1997.

ECRI General Policy Recommendation No. 4: National Surveys on the Experience and Perception of Discrimination and Racism from the Point of View of Potential Victims, CRI(98) 30, 6 March 1998.

ECRI General Policy Recommendation No 7: National Legislation to Combat Racism and Racial Discrimination, CRI(2003) 8, 13 December 2002.

European Parliament legislative resolution of 13 December 2005 on the proposal for a decision of the European Parliament and the Council on the European Year of Equal Opportunities for All (2007) – Towards a Just Society, COM(2005)0225 – C6-0178/2005 – 2005/0107(COD).

European Parliament resolution of 27 September 2007 on the application of Council Directive 2000/43/EC of 29 June 2000 implementing the principle of equal treatment between persons irrespective of racial or ethnic origin, 2007/2094(INI).

European Parliament resolution of 27 January 2005 on remembrance of the Holocaust, anti-Semitism and racism.

European Parliament resolution of 15 June 2006 on the increase in racist and homophobic violence in Europe.

European Parliament resolution of 14 June 2006 on non-discrimination and equal opportunities for all – a framework strategy, 2005/2191(INI).

European Parliament resolution of 8 June 2006 on the protection of minorities and anti-discrimination policies in an enlarged Europe, 2005/2008(INI).

From Principle to Practice. Evaluation of Legislation Dealing with Racial and Ethnic Discrimination in certain EU Member States, ENAR 2001.

General Comment Nr. 9: The Domestic Application of the Covenant, Committee on Economic, Social and Cultural Rights, 3 December 1998.

General Comment No. 12: The Right to Adequate Food, Committee on Economic, Social and Cultural Rights, 12 May 1999.

General Comment No. 2: The Role of Independent National Human Rights Institutions in the Promotion and Protection of the Rights of the Child, Committee on the Rights of the Child, 15 November 2002.

General Recommendation No. 4: Demographic Composition of the Population (Art. 9), Committee on the Elimination of Racial Discrimination, 25 August 1973.

General Recommendation No. 17: Establishment of National Institutions to Facilitate Implementation of the Convention, 25 March 1993.

General Recommendation No. 19: Racial Segregation and Apartheid (Art. 3), Committee on the Elimination of Racial Discrimination, 18 August 1995.

General Recommendation No. 27: Discrimination against Roma, Committee on the Elimination of Racial Discrimination, 16 August 2000.

Green Paper on a European order for payment procedure and on measures to simplify and speed up small claims litigation, COM/2002/0746 final, 20 December 2002.

Green paper on alternative dispute resolution in civil and commercial law, COM(2002) 196 final, 19 April 2002.

Model National Legislation for the Guidance of Governments in the Enactment of Further Legislation Against Racial Discrimination. Third Decade to Combat Racism and Racial Discrimination (1993-2003).

National Human Rights Institutions: Recommendations for Effective Protection and Promotion of Human Rights, Amnesty International 2001.

National Institutions for the Promotion and Protection of Human Rights, General Assembly, A/RES/48/134, 20 December 1993.

Opinion of the European Economic and Social Committee on the Proposal for a Directive of the European Parliament and of the Council amending Council Directives 89/665/EEC and 92/13/EEC with regard to improving the effectiveness of review procedures concerning the award of public contracts, COM(2006) 095 final/2 – COD 2006/0066, 18 January 2007.

Principles relating to the Status of National Institutions (The Paris Principles), Annex to National Institutions for the Promotion and Protection of Human rights, General Assembly, A/RES/48/134, 20 December 1993.

Proposal for a Council Directive establishing a general framework for equal treatment in employment and occupation, COM(1999) 565 final – 1999/0225 (CNS), 25 November 1999.

Proposal for a Council Directive implementing the principle of equal treatment between persons irrespective of racial or ethnic origin, COM(1999) 566 final – 1999/0253 (CNS), 25 November 1999.

Proposal for a Council Framework Decision on combating racism and xenophobia, COM(2001) 664 final – 2001/0270 (CS), 28 November 2001.

Proposal for a Directive of the European Parliament and of the Council amending Council Directive 76/207/EEC on the implementation of the principle of equal treatment for men and women as regards access to employment, vocational training and promotion, and working conditions, COM(2000) 334 final – COD 2000/0142, 7 June 2000.

Proposal for a Directive of the European Parliament and of the Council on the protection of consumers in respect of certain aspects of timeshare, long-term holiday products, resale and exchange, COM/2007/0303 final – COD 2007/0113, 7 June 2007.

Proposal for a Directive of the European Parliament and of the Council amending Council Directive 76/207/EEC on the implementation of the principle of equal treatment for men and women as regards access to employment, vocational training and promotion, and working conditions amending Council Directive 76/207/EEC on the implementation of the principle of equal treatment for men and women as regards access to employment, vocational training and promotion, and working conditions, COM(2000) 334 final – COD 2000/0142, 7 June 2006.

Putting Equality into Practice What role for positive action?, European Commission 2007.

Recommendation for second reading on the Council common position for adopting a European Parliament and Council directive on amending Council Directive 76/207/EEC on the implementation of the principle of equal treatment for men and women as regards access to employment, vocational training and promotion, and working conditions, 9848/1/2001 – C5-0387/2001 – COD 2000/0142, A5-0358/2001, 17 October 2001.

Recommendation on the Establishment of Independent National Institutions for the Promotion and Protection of Human Rights, Council of Europe Rec. No. R(97) 14, 30 September 1997.

Report from the Commission to the Council and the European Parliament – The application of Directive 2000/43/EC of 29 June 2000 implementing the principle of equal treatment between persons irrespective of racial or ethnic origin, COM(2006) 643 final/2, 15 December 2006.

Report on Gender Equality Bodies, Network of Legal Experts on the application of Community law on equal treatment between women and men 2004.

Report on the proposal for a Council directive on implementing the principle of equal treatment between persons irrespective of racial or ethnic origin, COM(1999) 566 – C5-0067/2000 – 1999/0253(CNS), A5-0136/2000, 16 May 2000.

Resolution on Cooperation Between National Human Rights Institutions of Member States and Between Them and the Council of Europe, Council of Europe Res. (97) 11, 30 September 1997.

Seminar on National and Local Institutions for the Promotion and Protection of Human Rights, ST/HR/SER.A/2 (1978).

Specialised Bodies to Promote Equality and/or Combat Discrimination, Final Report, European Commission 2002.

Standard Rules on the Equalization of Opportunities for Persons with Disabilities, Annex to the General Assembly, A/RES/48/96, 20 December 1993.

Submission to the European Commission Concerning Implementation of the RED in the Czech Republic, Hungary, Romania and Slovakia, ERRC 2005. Retrieved from http://www.errc.org/cikk.php?cikk=2280.

The Glass Box. Exclusion of Roma from employment, ERRC 2007.

Vienna Declaration and Programme of Action, A/CONF.157/23, 12 July 1993.

World Conference against Racism, Racial Discrimination, Xenophobia and Related Intolerance, Declaration, Durban, 31 August – 8 September 2001.

World Programme of Action concerning Disabled Persons, General Assembly, A/RES/37/52, 3 December 1982.

Written Comments in the case of Nachova and others v. Bulgaria, INTERIGHTS 2005. Retrieved from http://www.justiceinitiative.org/db/resource2/fs/?file_id=15404.

Selected National Documents

Selected National Legal Texts

Belgium

Act of 30 July 1981 on the punishment of certain acts motivated by racism or xenophobia (Anti-Racism Act)

Act of 25 February 2003 pertaining to the combat of discrimination and to the amendment of the Act of 15 February 1993 pertaining to the foundation of a centre for equal opportunities and opposition to racism (Anti-Discrimination Act)

Act of 15 February 1993 pertaining to the foundation of a Centre for Equal Opportunities and Opposition to Racism

Decree of the Flemish Parliament of 10 July 2008 pertaining to a framework for the Flemish policy of equal opportunities and equal treatment

Decree of the Flemish Community of 8 May 2002 pertaining to balanced participation on the labour market

Decree of the German Community of 17 May 2004 pertaining to guaranteeing equal treatment on the labour market

Decree of the Walloon Region of 27 May 2004 pertaining to equal treatment concerning employment and vocational training

Royal Decree of 28 February 1993 pertaining to the establishment of the organic statute of the Centre for Equal Opportunities and Opposition to Racism

Estonia

Employment Contract Act, RK, RT I 1992, 15/16, 241, 15 April 1992 (Repealed by Employment Contract Act, RK, RT I 2009, 5, 35, 17 December 2008)

Equal Treatment Act, RK, RT I 2008, 56, 315, 11 December 2008

Gender Equality Act, RK, RT I 2004, 27, 181, 7 April 2004.

Individual Labour Dispute Resolution Act, RK, RT I 1996, 3, 57, 20 December 1995

Legal Chancellor Act, RK, RT I 1999, 29, 406, 25 February 1999

Statute of the Gender Equality Commissioner, Decree Nr. 45 of the Government, 10 March 2005

Hungary

Act Nr. CXXV of 2003 on Equal Treatment and Promotion Equal Opportunities

Government Decree Nr. 362/2004 on the Authority of Equal Treatment and its Detailed Procedural Rules

The Netherlands

General Equal Treatment Act, 2 March 1994

Decision on the Procedure of the Equal Treatment Commission, 29 July 1994

National Reports, Recommendations, Travaux Préparatoires

Belgium

Advies geformuleerd door het Centrum voor gelijkheid van kansen en voor racismebestrijding en goedgekeurd door de Raad van Bestuur op 21 november 2006 inzake Het wetsontwerp ter bestrijding van bepaalde vormen van discriminatie en Het wetsontwerp tot wijziging van de wet van 30 juli 1981 tot bestraffing van bepaalde door racisme en xenofobie ingegeven daden, 22 November 2006.

Antwoorden op de vraag van de Commissie over richtlijn 2000/43.

Aanbevelingen van het Centrum ter attentie van het Federale Parlement en de Federale Regering – Focus 2011, CGKR 2008.

Aanpak discriminatie en racisme, CGKR 2004.

Bestrijding van discriminatie op de huisvestingsmarkt, CGKR 2008. Retrieved from http://www.diversiteit.be/diversiteit/files/File//Huisvesting/voorstel%2018%2001%2008.pdf.

De Centrum en de Waalse huisvestingsmaatschappij gaan samen optreden, CGKR 2008. Retrieved from http://www.diversiteit.be/index.php?action=artikel_detail&artikel=39.

Discriminatie van holebi's op de werkvloer, CGKR 2008.

Fourth Report on the Netherlands, ECRI 2009.

Jaarverslag 'Discriminatie/Diversiteit' 2007, CGKR 2008.

Jaarverslag 2006, CGKR 2007.

Jaarverslag Migratie 2007, CGKR 2008.

Strategisch Driejarenplan 2008-2010, CGKR 2008. Retrieved from http://www.diversiteit.be/index.php?action=artikel_detail&artikel=39.

Wetsontwerp tot wijziging van de wet van 30 juli 1981 tot bestraffing van bepaalde door racisme en xenofobie ingegeven daden, 2720/001, 26 October 2006.

Wetsontwerp tot wijziging van de wet van 30 juli 1981 tot bestraffing van bepaalde door racisme en xenofobie ingegeven daden, 2720/009, 19 March 2007.

Wetsontwerp tot wijziging van de wet van 30 juli 1981 tot bestraffing van bepaalde door racisme of xenofobie ingegeven daden, 3-2362/3, 24 April 2007.

Estonia

Advisory Committee on the Framework Convention for the Protection of National Minorities, Second Opinion on Estonia adopted on 24 February 2005, ACFC/INF/OP/II(2005)001, 22 July 2005.

Annual Report 2004 of the Chancellor of Justice, Tallinn 2005. Retrieved from www.oiguskantsler.ee/files/36.pdf.

Annual Report 2005 of the Chancellor of Justice, Tallinn 2006. Retrieved from http://www.oiguskantsler.ee/.files/130.pdf.

Annual Report 2006 of the Chancellor of Justice, Tallinn 2007. Retrieved from http://www.oiguskantsler.ee/public/resources/editor/File/_levaade_2006_e_k_L_PLIK.pdf.

Annual Report 2007 of the Chancellor of Justice, Tallinn 2008. Retrieved from http://www.oiguskantsler.ee/public/resources/editor/File/Ylevaade_2007.pdf.

Committee on the Elimination of Racial Discrimination, Consideration of Reports Submitted by States Parties under Article 9 of the Convention, CERD/C/EST/CO/7, 22 August 2006.

Examples of Good Practices. Specialised Bodies: Chancellor of Justice, Estonia. Retrieved from www.coe.int/t/e/human_rights/ecri/1-ecri/3-general_themes/2-examples_of_good_practices/1-Specialised_Bodies/SB_Estonia.asp#TopOfPage.

Linguistic Minorities in Estonia: Discrimination must end, Amnesty International 2006. Retrieved from http://www.amnesty.org/en/library/info/EUR51/002/2006.

Seisukoht võrdse kohtlemise põhimõtte rikkumise kohta, Nr. 7-5/070340/00705874, Õiguskantsler 2007.

Õiguskantsleri 2006. aasta tegevuse ülevaade, Tallinn 2007.

Õiguskantsleri 2007. aasta tegevuse ülevaade, Tallinn 2008.

The principle of equal treatment in jurisdiction and proceedings, Chancellor of Justice. Retrieved from http://www.oiguskantsler.ee/index.php?pageID=176.

Hungary

Advisory Committee on the Framework Convention for the Protection of National Minorities, Second Opinion on Hungary adopted on 9 December 2004, ACFC/INF/OP/II(2004)003, 14 December 2004.

A kisebbségi önkormányzatok kézikönyve, Nemzeti és Etnikai Kisebbségi Jogok Országgyűlési Biztosa 2006.

Beszámoló a Nemzeti és Etnikai Kisebbségi Jogok Országgyűlési Biztosának tevékenységéről, Nemzeti és Etnikai Kisebbségi Jogok Országgyűlési Biztosa 2005.

Beszámoló a Nemzeti és Etnikai Kisebbségi Jogok Országgyűlési Biztosának tevékenységéről, Nemzeti és Etnikai Kisebbségi Jogok Országgyűlési Biztosa 2006.

Beszámoló az Egyenlő Bánásmód Hatóság tevékenységéről, valamint az egyenlő bánásmódról és az esélyegyenlőség előmozdításáról szóló 2003. évi CXXV. törvény alkalmazásának tapasztalatairól (2006. január 1 – december 31.), Egyenlő Bánásmód Hatóság 2007. Retrieved from http://egyenlobanasmod.hu/index.php?g=EBH-jelentes07.htm.

Az Egyenlő Bánásmód Hatóság 2008. évi tevékenysége a számok tükrében, Egyenlő Bánásmód Hatóság 2009. Retrieved from http://www.egyenlobanasmod.hu/data/2008tevekenyseg_szamok_tukreben.pdf.

Az Egyenlő Bánásmód Hatóság jelentése az Európa Tanács 2000. június 29-én kelt 2000/43/EK irányelve a személyek közötti, faji vagy etnikai származásra való tekintet nélküli egyenlő bánásmód elve átültetéséről, 27 June 2005.

Indokolás az egyenlő bánásmódról és az esélyegyenlőségről szóló törvényjavaslathoz.

Fehér Füzet 2005. A Nemzeti és Etnikai Kisebbségi Jogvédő Iroda beszámolója, Másság Alapítvány 2006.

Fehér Füzet 2006. A Nemzeti és Etnikai Kisebbségi Jogvédő Iroda beszámolója, Másság Alapítvány 2007.

Fehér Füzet 2007. A Nemzeti és Etnikai Kisebbségi Jogvédő Iroda beszámolója, Másság Alapítvány 2008.

Fourt Report on Hungary, ECRI 2009.
Position No. 10.117/1/2006 TT of the Advisory Board of Equal Treatment on the division of the burden of proof, 13 January 2006.
Position No. 2/2007 (III.23) TT of the Advisory Board of Equal Treatment on segregation in public education, 23 March 2007.
Position No. 384/4/2008. (III.28.) TT of the Advisory Board of Equal Treatment on the division of the burden of proof, 28 March 2008.
Position No. 384/3/2008 (III.28) TT of the Advisory Board of Equal Treatment on victimization, 28 February 2008.

The Netherlands

Advies inzake de ingebrekestelling van Nederland door de Europese Commissie in verband met het niet correct omzetten van Richtlijn 2000/78/EG, CGB-Advies/2008/02, March 2008
Arbeidsmarktbeleid etnische minderheden 2000-2003, Brief van de Staatssecretaris van Sociale Zaken en Werkgelegenheid, 27 223, Nr. 73, 14 October 2005.
Commentaar van de CGB inzake implementatie van de gemeenschappelijke bepalingen van de EC-Kaderrichtlijn en de EC-anti-rassen-discriminatierichtlijn, CGB-advies/2001/03, 30 May 2001.
Commentary of the Netherlands' Equal Treatment Commission on the fifteenth and sixteenth Periodic Report of the Kingdom of the Netherlands on the implementation of the Convention on the Elimination of all forms of Racial Discrimination (CERD/C/452/Add.3), CGB-advies/2004/02, 26 February 2004.
Examples of Good Practices. Specialised Bodies: Equal Treatment Commission, The Netherlands. Retrieved from http://www.coe.int/t/e/human_rights/ecri/1-ecri/3-general_themes/2-examples_of_good_practices/1-Specialised_Bodies/SB_Netherlands.asp#TopOfPage.
Het verschil gemaakt. Evaluatie AWGB en werkzaamheden CGB 1999-2004, CGB 2005.
Implementatie van richtlijnen gelijke behandeling, 18 December 2001.
Implementatie van richtlijnen inzake gelijke behandeling, Brief van de Staatssecretaris van Sociale Zaken en Werkgelegenheid, 28 187, Nr. 2, 4 April 2002.
Implementatie van richtlijnen inzake gelijke behandeling, Brief van de Staatssecretaris van Sociale Zaken en Werkgelegenheid, 28 187, Nr. 1, 18 December 2001.
Implementatie van richtlijnen inzake gelijke behandeling, Brief van de Staatssecretaris van Sociale Zaken en Werkgelegenheid, 28 187, Nr. 1, 18 December 2001.
Jaarverslag 2006, CGB 2007.
Jaarverslag 2007, CGB 2008.
Mediation via de CGB. Retrieved from http://www.cgb.nl/brochure/mediation.
Nota opgesteld ter attentie van Commissie Individuele Arbeidsverhoudingen met betrekking tot de herziening van de Collectieve Arbeidsovereenkomst nr. 38, 2008. Retrieved from http://www.diversiteit.be/diversiteit/files/File//Arbeid/20080208%20-%20aanbeveling%20aan%20NAR%20(NL).pdf.
Third Report on the Netherlands, ECRI 2007.